Kenn Scribner

SAMS

Teach Yourself

ATL Programming

in 21 Days

SAMS

A Division of Macmillan USA
201 West 103rd St., Indianapolis, Indiana, 46290 USA

Sams Teach Yourself ATL Programming in 21 Days

Copyright © 2000 by Sams Publishing

International Standard Book Number: 0-672-31867-9

Library of Congress Catalog Card Number: 99-067340

Printed in the United States of America

First Printing: February, 2000

01 00 99   4 3 2 1

Trademarks

Warning and Disclaimer

ASSOCIATE PUBLISHER
Bradley L. Jones

ACQUISITIONS EDITOR
Chris Webb

DEVELOPMENT EDITOR
Thomas Cirtin

MANAGING EDITOR
Lisa Wilson

PROJECT EDITOR
Dawn Pearson

COPY EDITOR
Mary Lagu

INDEXER
Bill Meyers

PROOFREADERS
Jill Mazurczyk
Mona Brown

TECHNICAL EDITOR
Scott Roberts

TEAM COORDINATOR
Meggo Barthlow

MEDIA DEVELOPER
David Carson

INTERIOR DESIGNER
Gary Adair

COVER DESIGNER
Aren Howell

COPYWRITER
Eric Borgert

EDITORIAL ASSISTANT
Angela Boley

PRODUCTION
Dan Harris
Jeannette McKay

Contents at a Glance

Contents

About the Author

KENN SCRIBNER began his professional career managing a pizzeria. He soon realized fast food wasn't for him and turned to the United States Air Force for training and a career. Two degrees and a commission later, Kenn found himself retired from the Air Force and in need of work. This time, instead of managing a pizzeria, Kenn decided to pursue a second career as a Windows developer (a passionate hobby at the time).

As luck would have it, Kenn did find work programming Windows applications and does that to this day. He works for a leading legal information provider writing both client applications and server components. He also finds time to teach Windows programming from time to time.

Kenn also started The EnduraSoft Corporation (www.endurasoft.com), dedicated to writing and marketing ActiveX controls and eating pizzas from pizzerias someone else manages. Kenn doesn't sell a lot (he's a better programmer than marketer), but he does have fun running EnduraSoft and writing articles and books to keep his hobby juices flowing.

In his spare time, Kenn learns Tae Kwon Do from his awesome wife (a black-belt), reads to his children, and dreams of someday purchasing another Corvette to replace the beautiful machine he once had. Or maybe it will be a Ford Expedition. Dreams are cheap, even if the vehicles are not. If you have a chance, drop him an email at kenn@endura-soft.com to see what vehicle he's currently dreaming of. Questions are certainly welcome as well. He does his best to respond, but reading to the kids and spending time with his wife is still his first priority! He'll write back as soon as possible.

About the Technical Editor

SCOTT ROBERTS works as a software design engineer in the Internet Explorer group at Microsoft. He works on the HTML rendering engine (mshtml.dll) as well as the WebBrowser control. Scott has been a C and C++ developer for over nine years, during which time he has worked on many platforms, including various UNIX systems, Windows, and Windows NT. Scott co-authored *The Waite Group's C++ How-To* from Sams Publishing, and he is the author of *Programming Microsoft Internet Explorer 5* from Microsoft Press.

Dedication

I would like to dedicate this work to my loving wife, Judi, and my two wonderful children, Aaron and Katie, who put up with my red eyes and sunken face for the duration of my efforts and supported me throughout. You guys are terrific!

Acknowledgments

If you've never written a book before, I can only tell you that it's a monumental effort that usually drives you to the wee hours of the morning. Sleep is often optional, but invoking the option means something doesn't get done that night. You just can't do it alone.

So I'd like to take a moment of your time and thank all of those people who made this book possible. First and foremost, of course, is my wife Judi, and my children, Aaron and Katie. They put up with grumpy old daddy when he worked until 2:00 a.m., but still got up at 6:00 a.m. to hit the "day job."

Clearly, the folks at Macmillan USA stood by me all the way. I could almost hear the cheering from Indianapolis when I turned in the manuscript early! I owe a special thanks to Chris Webb who convinced me to submit the proposal and saw the project through many meetings and wickets. Tom Cirtin took the raw material I presented him and turned it into the fine, polished work you see. Being a frequent technical reviewer myself, I can't forget to thank my technical reviewer, Scott Roberts, for honing the material and correcting my otherwise poor technical descriptions. Any errors in technical material that remain are mine to live with and will forever haunt me. I would also like to thank the crew that stands in the background to bring books such as this to you: the layout technicians, the indexers, the artists, and all of the rest of the hardworking folks in the back office. My thanks extend to all of you.

I owe a special debt of gratitude to Jon Hill, who selflessly, and without question, made sure I had technical materials from which to draw my descriptions, especially those for IDL and OLE DB. (I really needed the help with OLE DB, thanks Jon!). I also would like to thank my colleague and ATL programmer extraordinaire Mark Stiver, who also knows a thing or two about Visual Basic (which is fortunate for you because I know relatively little!).

Finally, I would like to extend my thanks to you, the aspiring ATL programmer, for shelling out your hard-earned money to purchase this book. If anyone knows how hard you work for your paycheck, it's me. .I'm the guy in the next foxhole. I hope that you'll find the information I present well worth your dollar.More than that, I hope I keep the trust you placed in my experience, as well as in me, as I present this material to you. Thank you!

Tell Us What You Think!

As the reader of this book, *you* are our most important critic and commentator. We value your opinion and want to know what we're doing right, what we could do better, what areas you'd like to see us publish in, and any other words of wisdom you're willing to pass our way.

As an Associate Publisher for Sams, I welcome your comments. You can fax, email, or write me directly to let me know what you did or didn't like about this book—as well as what we can do to make our books stronger.

Please note that I cannot help you with technical problems related to the topic of this book, and that due to the high volume of mail I receive, I might not be able to reply to every message.

When you write, please be sure to include this book's title and author as well as your name and phone or fax number. I will carefully review your comments and share them with the author and editors who worked on the book.

Fax: 317-581-4770
Email: adv_prog@mcp.com
Mail: Bradley L. Jones
         Associate Publisher
         Sams Publishing
         201 West 103rd Street
         Indianapolis, IN 46290 USA

Introduction

When the idea to write a book about ATL programming popped into my head, the first thing I did was hit www.amazon.com to look for other books on the subject. Because there were relatively few, my book seemed possible. I saw two common failings in the books I did find. Either they were too general and merely described the Visual Studio wizards, or they were too technical, losing the reader somewhere along the way.

I decided I wasn't going to merely skim the wizards—I would provide a lot more detail than that. I also decided I had to start at the beginning and explain things step by step to make sure the reader kept up. Clearly, you're not a beginning programmer, or you wouldn't be reading this particular book (if you are, I'll lose you for sure). But that doesn't mean poor explanations on my part will enlighten you.

In this book, I intend to teach you ATL COM programming from the ground up. But I won't stop at merely describing ATL and COM. I touch on many topics, even if the topic is only indirectly related to ATL. I'll also lock horns with ActiveX, Distributed COM, OLE DB and database connectivity, and transactional processing (leading to COM+ and Windows 2000, which as I write this is scheduled to be delivered within a few months).

The book is broken into three parts (by week), with each part delivering more information than was presented in earlier weeks or building upon a given technology. Week 1 teaches fundamental concepts for creating basic ATL objects, where you become acquainted with ATL, COM, and IDL, including concepts and techniques you'll master in the remainder of the book. ATL is built upon COM, which lives and breathes interfaces. You'll explore these here. I'll then move on to describe basic C++ template programming, ATL's architecture, the ATL Visual Studio wizards, and how you add methods and properties to your COM objects. Many books drop you off here: I'll just be getting started.

Week 2 addresses intermediate ATL concepts and techniques, taking you deeper into the use of ATL to exploit the architecture to meet your particular COM programming needs. Here you'll see more about testing ATL COM servers, ATL helper classes to ease your programming workload, error handling, multithreading concepts, and the ubiquitous COM apartment. I'll also describe ATL's windowing classes and templates and explain the basics of COM automation to prepare you for developing ActiveX controls or other scriptable objects.

Finally, Week 3 covers practical ATL support for more advanced technologies, where you see how ATL meets and supports various COM-driven technologies. It's here you'll see how ATL handles custom and ActiveX controls, connection points, new and different class factory implementations, Distributed COM, OLE DB, and finally the Microsoft Transaction Server. I'll take you right to the doorstep of the new world of COM+ programming.

Who Should Read This Book

I don't want to fool you. This book is *not* a beginning programmer's book. Before you tackle ATL, you should be an intermediate-to-experienced C++ programmer with lots of Windows programming background. Although I dip down and try to describe all the basic concepts related to ATL programming, I'll move quickly through the material and assume you'll also review the sample code I'll present (which is the true authority on how things get done in the world of ATL).

I hope you have some experience with other Microsoft Windows programming technologies, such as MFC or Visual Basic. Experience there will help you develop associations between those technologies and ATL, which will help cement the ATL concepts I'll present here.

What You Will Need to Use This Book

All the ATL examples were developed using the Visual Studio Enterprise Edition, though the Professional Edition will easily suffice. I used a combination of Windows NT 4.0 (Service Pack 4), Windows 98, and Windows 95 (Service Release 2). For Day 19, "Distributed ATL: DCOM Around the Net," you'll require a network and a minimum of two computers that can communicate over the network (that list each other in the Network Neighborhood).

I also use the Microsoft Access ODBC driver for Day 20, "ATL and OLE DB: Storing More." You shouldn't require Access itself to run the examples, but you might want a copy handy to make changes and experiment. Finally, Day 21, "ATL and MTS: Coding with a Better COM," requires Windows NT 4.0 (Workstation or Server) with a minimum of Service Pack 4 installed, with MTS installed as an option. Although you can run a version of MTS from Windows 98 or 95, the Windows NT implementation is more robust and is what you'll find commonly used in enterprise installations.

WEEK 1

At a Glance

In this first week, you learn the fundamentals of ATL and the creation of ATL components. You start with a whirlwind session designed to take you through the entire Visual Studio ATL object-creation process. Later in the week, I'll break down the steps required to create the object and offer additional insight and guidance. This first week also provides you with some fundamental concepts upon which ATL is built, such as COM and the COM interface, as well as C++ template programming.

- Day 1: Create a new ATL COM object from the ground up.
- Day 2: Explore the Component Object Model.
- Day 3: Learn about interface-based programming, especially as it relates to COM.
- Day 4: Brush up your C++ template programming skills.
- Day 5: Break down ATL's architecture to see how the pieces fit together to implement COM objects.
- Day 6: Examine the two most fundamental Visual Studio ATL wizards, the ATL AppWizard and the ATL Object Wizard.
- Day 7: See how to add methods and properties to your COM interfaces using additional Visual Studio ATL wizards.

1

2

3

4

5

6

7

DAY **1**

Getting Started: Your First ATL COM Object

Welcome to ATL programming! I have a lot of material to present, so I'll get started right away. In this day, you will create an ATL-based COM object, as well as a program to test what you've written. Don't be too concerned at this point about why I'll do things or what they mean. After all, the rest of the book will address that, starting with Day 2, "Exploring COM: The Technology ATL Supports." I thought that, because this is a book about learning to write COM code using ATL, you should start by writing some ATL code. That way, you won't have to wade through five or six days before you can begin to do something really interesting.

When you create an ATL-based COM object, you begin by using the ATL AppWizard. You are no doubt familiar with using the Visual Studio AppWizards to create other types of projects. In this day, I'll also use other ATL wizards to add code to facilitate the implementation of the COM object. This day, then, provides a whirlwind tour of the wizards and how you access them. I'll discuss the wizards in much more detail in Day 6, "The ATL Wizards: Object Customization and Functionality." You'll certainly use them throughout the book.

Now, let's get started. In this lesson, you'll see

- How to create a basic ATL object framework
- How to add ATL objects to the framework
- How to add methods to an ATL COM interface
- How to compile an ATL project
- How to build a quick test application using MFC

Creating the Basic ATL Framework— the ATL AppWizard

You begin building an ATL COM object in much the same way you begin any other Visual C++ project. That is, you bring up the Visual Studio AppWizard selection dialog by clicking on File, New. Visual Studio whirrs for a moment, and then it presents you with a list of all known AppWizards present on your system. My system's list is shown in Figure 1.1. Select the ATL COM AppWizard item from the list, navigate to an appropriate project directory using the Browse button under Location, and then provide an overall project name under Project Name. Go ahead and make some selections here (mine are shown in Figure 1.1). When you are satisfied with the location and name of your new project, click the OK button.

FIGURE 1.1

The Visual Studio AppWizard selection dialog.

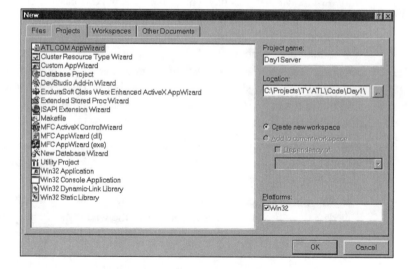

The ATL COM AppWizard has enough information to begin creating your project, but the wizard hasn't been told what kind of ATL COM object you want, so it presents another dialog, shown in Figure 1.2.

FIGURE 1.2

ATL object framework selection property sheet.

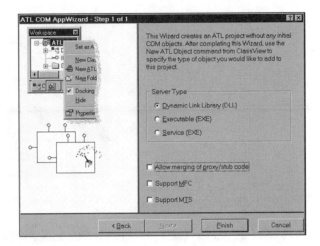

This property sheet's intent is to determine whether you want a DLL-based COM object, an EXE-based COM object, or an NT service-based COM object. For now, simply accept the default (DLL-based object) and click Finish. Don't worry about the check boxes at the bottom of the property page for now—leave them unchecked.

Visual Studio will now ask you if it has all the correct information in preparation for creating your new project. It summarizes the options you've selected and places them in a dialog box, shown in Figure 1.3. There isn't much to a basic ATL object framework project, as you can see; simply click OK.

At this point, the ATL COM AppWizard creates the source files you'll use to build your COM object. You also now have a Visual C++ project and several other files that have something to do with COM and DLL compilation. For example, you have a .DEF file, which you might recognize as a file used to define the exported DLL functions when compiling a dynamic link library. If you open the file *<project name>*.cpp (where *<project name>* is the name you previously supplied to the ATL COM AppWizard), you find several functions related to the mechanics of implementing a DLL, to include the declaration of DllMain() (the standard DLL entry point).

What you *don't* have is a functioning COM object, even if you compiled the source code at this time. The ATL COM AppWizard creates a framework into which you must place more ATL code to tailor the operation of your object. To add more functionality, you invoke the ATL Object Wizard, the topic of the next section.

FIGURE 1.3

*Summary of options
for your new project.*

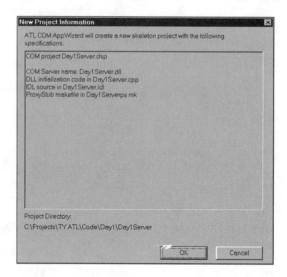

FIGURE 1.3

*Summary of options
for your new project.*

Adding an ATL Object—the ATL Object Wizard

You've already made a critical design decision. You've elected to create a DLL-based
COM object. It's time to make another critical decision—what type of COM object will
you code? Perhaps you want to build an ActiveX control. Or, you might need to write a
Visual Studio add-in component. Just as likely, you're out to create a run-of-the-mill,
simple COM object.

No matter which type of COM object you elect to build, you normally want to invoke the
ATL Object Wizard to generate more source code for you. After all, that's a wizard's job,
and it makes your coding task easier. To bring the Object Wizard to life, you first click
on the ClassView tab of the Workspace window, indicated in Figure 1.4. You access the
wizard by right-clicking on the tree control's root node (which generally says "*<project
name>* classes"). Doing so brings up the context menu you also see in Figure 1.4. At this
time, select the New ATL Object menu option.

After you select this menu option, you will be rewarded with the ATL Object Wizard
dialog box, as shown in Figure 1.5. When you select a category, the wizard presents you
with various object choices. It's here you see that you can create all manner of COM
object types, which I'll discuss a bit more in the next section. In this case, though, you
should select the Simple Object under the Objects category (this is the default selection).

FIGURE 1.4

The Visual Studio Workspace window's ClassView view.

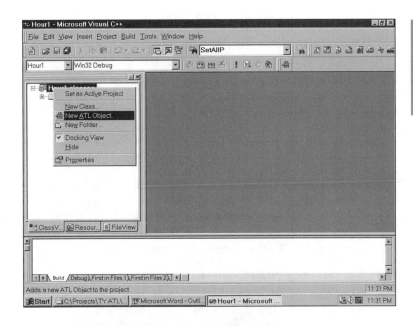

FIGURE 1.5

The ATL Object Wizard.

Before you click the Next button, however, I'll take a moment to introduce the basic ATL objects you have to select from. I'll describe some of these in more detail in Day 6.

Types of ATL Objects

You might be wondering about the object types available to you. What is an MMC snap-in, anyway? Why would you select a Simple Object over the snap-in?

I'll address those specific questions in more detail in Day 6. But for now, the answer is that you design the COM object and decide precisely what you want the object to do before you actually write any code. With your design in hand, you can intelligently select the type of object you want to insert using the ATL Object Wizard.

In any case, the Objects category provides you with a selection of traditional COM objects, from a basic one (Simple) to a more complex one designed to support Active Server Page scripts in Microsoft's Internet Information Server (ActiveX Server Component).

The Controls item under Categories presents you with various ActiveX control objects. These objects implement the code necessary to satisfy the ActiveX specification and are usually associated with user interface additions.

The Miscellaneous category has only a single option, and that is to build an application that supports a dialog box as its user interface. Yes, you can create a dialog-based application using ATL. In fact, you can do more than that, because ATL has support for Windows Win32 programming as you'll see in Day 13, "Creating ATL Applications: Where ATL Meets Win32." As you'll see there, you have to implement much of that code yourself. The Object Wizard doesn't support more than a basic dialog application.

The final category, Data Access, provides you with OLE DB support. In this case, the ATL Object Wizard uses OLE DB templates to provide you with (handy) OLE DB data access support, using data providers and consumers.

For this lesson, simply select the Simple Object under the Objects category and click Next. When you do, you'll be presented with a property sheet that will enable you to customize your COM object. I'll discuss customizing in the next section.

Customizing Your Object

When you select an object type (Simple, in this case) and click Next, you see a property sheet that will enable you to tailor your new object to some degree. The precise property pages you see will depend upon the type of object you select. In the case of a Simple Object, you see the property sheet shown in Figure 1.6.

FIGURE 1.6

The Simple Object property sheet's Names page.

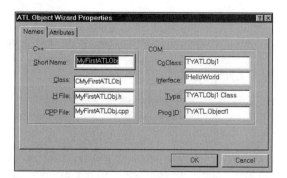

When the property sheet is initialized, the Names tab is active. On this sheet, you provide your COM object with a Short Name, variations of which will be used to name source files and create the COM-specific attributes that you'll see more of in Day 2. In Figure 1.6, you can see how I named my object. Note that when you type text into the Short Name edit control, the property page automatically creates text for the remaining edit fields. These are suggested values—feel free to modify them if you desire.

When you've completed all the edit fields in the Names tab, click on the Attributes tab, as shown in Figure 1.7.

FIGURE 1.7

The Simple Object property sheet's Attributes page.

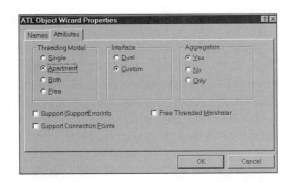

Choices you make here have far-reaching implications regarding the operation of your COM object, so choose wisely and carefully. For now, simply select the options I've shown in Figure 1.7. You'll learn much more about the attributes throughout the book, although I'll address them specifically in Day 6. Essentially, though, you're asking for an apartment-threaded COM object with a custom interface that doesn't support aggregation. In plain English, that means you want a COM object that can only be used by a single thread at a time, doesn't worry about being used in a scripted environment, and won't allow itself to directly expose its capabilities while consumed by another COM object.

After you have completed your selections (for both pages), click OK. The ATL Object Wizard will now modify your source files to add the code required to support the object type you selected with the customizations you specified. Now you can compile your ATL COM object and have a full-fledged COM object. But, there is a catch. It won't do anything interesting! For that, you must add methods to the interface you just created. Let's see how that's done.

Adding an Interface Method

If you watched closely, you might have seen the tree control in the Workspace window change slightly after the wizard completed modifying your files. Instead of the two nodes you had before you added an ATL object, you now find four. The added nodes are related to the object you just inserted. One node is targeted at the C++ aspects of your source code. Using this node, you can add C++ attributes and methods to the C++ class that implements the COM interface. The other node represents the COM interface aspects; for this example, this is the more interesting node.

Although you have a COM object that has an interface, the interface isn't very functional—it does nothing useful. It's time now to add methods to the interface, in much the same way you would add methods to a C++ class. (After all, a C++ class with just a constructor and destructor isn't very interesting, either.) As it happens, Visual Studio can again help you insert source code, and the mechanism is very similar to that for inserting the COM object itself. Simply invoke the context menu associated with the interface (the node with the icon that resembles a lollypop) by right-clicking the node. After the menu is available, select the Add Method item, as shown in Figure 1.8.

FIGURE 1.8

Invoking the inter-face's context menu.

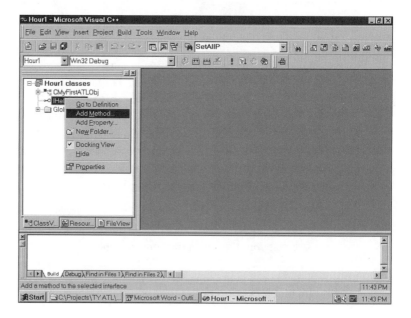

If you select this menu option, you should see the Add Method to Interface dialog box shown in Figure 1.9.

FIGURE 1.9

The ATL Add Method to Interface dialog box.

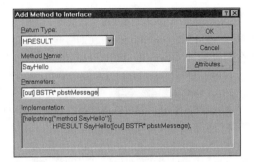

1

Don't be concerned about the method's return type at this time—simply accept the default. For this demonstration, I chose to add a method named SayHello(), which accepts as a parameter a pointer to something known as a BSTR. The parameter has an attribute, [out]. You'll learn precisely what a BSTR is when you reach Day 9, "Creating C++ Test Clients: You Can't Test What You Can't Execute." For now, just imagine it as a COM string. The [out] attribute is used by COM for memory management, and you'll see more of this in Day 3, "The COM Interface: COM's Foundation," when I discuss the Interface Definition Language (IDL). The attribute simply tells COM that a COM string will be returned from the SayHello() method, as opposed to being an input parameter. [out] parameters are always pointers, which is why the full SayHello() parameter list is shown as

```
[out] BSTR * pbstrMessage
```

When you have completed the method's parameter definition, click OK. (If you have more than one parameter, separate them by commas.) Visual Studio will now add the basic code necessary to support the new interface. It still won't do anything interesting, but until now you've not had to write a single line of code. That's not all bad!

So let's actually add some code. All I intend this interface to do is return a string with a simple message that the client application can display. The code in Listing 1.1 might, at first, appear a little odd, because the string type I'm dealing with is a BSTR instead of a typical C-style string. I've commented the code to explain what each line is doing.

I'm doing this the hard way—ATL provides helper classes, and one such class works with BSTRs, which you'll see in Day 9. If you're following along with the example that I've provided for this day, you'll find this code in the file MyFirstATLObj.cpp. The code I had to add in Listing 1.1 (versus what the wizard provided) is shown in italics.

LISTING 1.1   Implementation of the SayHello() Method

```
 1: // MyFirstATLObj.cpp : Implementation of CMyFirstATLObj
 2: #include "stdafx.h"
 3: #include "Day1Server.h"
 4: #include "MyFirstATLObj.h"
 5:
 6: /////////////////////////////////////////////////////////////////////
 7: // CMyFirstATLObj
 8:
 9:
10: STDMETHODIMP CMyFirstATLObj::SayHello(BSTR *pbstrMessage)
11: {
12:     // Check their pointer
13:     if ( pbstrMessage == NULL ) {
14:         // NULL pointer, so return an error code
15:         return E_POINTER;
16:     } // if
17:
18:     // Their return pointer was good, so create a BSTR
19:     // using their pointer.  We allocate the memory for
20:     // the string here.  The client application is
21:     // responsible for freeing the memory.
22:     *pbstrMessage = ::SysAllocString(L"Hello, ATL!");
23:
24:     return S_OK;
25: }
```

ANALYSIS   The code you see in Listing 1.1 checks the pointer that the client provided, and if it's NULL, the method returns an error code. (You'll read more about COM errors in Day 2.) If the pointer is nonNULL, I assume it's valid, allocate memory for the BSTR, and assign it the string "Hello, ATL!". The SysAllocString() API call, designed to work specifically with BSTRs, handles both tasks for me (allocation and assignment).

Now that you have the method's implementation, it's time to compile the project and produce a COM object. The next section explains the process.

Compiling the ATL Object

You're no doubt used to compiling traditional Windows applications, and initiating the compilation for this object is no different. You press F7 in Visual Studio or use the toolbar.

The difference is apparent if you watch the compilation output. Instead of a single compiler executing, you'll actually see output from two compilers in the output window. The first compiles some COM files the wizards created and modified on your behalf; these produce other files that COM and your client application require. Then, the traditional C++ compiler actually compiles the ATL code to produce the COM object itself. If the

1

compilation process was successful (to include linking), you'll see a message telling you that your COM object was successfully registered. This will become clearer as you progress though Days 2 and 3.

At this time, you have completed your first ATL COM object. Congratulations! Client applications can now use your object, assuming it works correctly. Does it work correctly? To determine that, you should build a test client and thoroughly test the COM object. I'll show you how to build such a test client in the next section.

A Quick Test Application

Building a test client can be a very complicated undertaking, or it can be very simple. It depends upon what your object does. In any case, you have four primary choices for the client application architecture:

- Traditional Win32 programming
- The Microsoft Foundation Classes (MFC)
- Visual Basic
- The Active Template Library

I chose to show you how to build a client application using MFC for several reasons. First, it uses C++. It would be easier to build a Visual Basic application, but I thought I'd stick with C++ for the purposes of this book. Developing an application with traditional Win32 programming methodologies takes too long, and you have to write far more code than you do in the other three methods.

It would be great to use ATL itself to write a test client, but clearly you haven't seen enough ATL to do so! So, MFC seemed to be the best alternative. If you're not that familiar with MFC, don't be too concerned. I'll provide you with explicit instructions that should get you through this example. If you're interested in learning more about MFC, you might pick up a copy of *MFC Unleashed Using Visual C++ 6.0*, ISBN 0-67-231557-2, from sams.net.

In any case, you begin creating the MFC test client in the same way you created the project for the ATL COM object. You invoke the Visual Studio AppWizard, as you'll see in the next section.

Creating the Project

If you have Visual Studio running, close any open project and click on File, New. You should see the same AppWizard selection list that you saw in Figure 1.1. This time, however, select the MFC AppWizard (exe) list item. As before, provide a project name and make sure the project directory is acceptable. If everything is fine, click OK.

This should bring up the MFC AppWizard—Step 1 dialog you see in Figure 1.10. The default MFC application is for a multiple-document application, which is more than you require here. Click the radio button for the dialog-based application and then click Next. The second wizard page provides you with several options. The default values are acceptable for all these, unless you'd like to change the initial dialog title. If you'd like to change the dialog's title, simply enter the new title text in the edit control provided.

FIGURE 1.10

The MFC AppWizard.

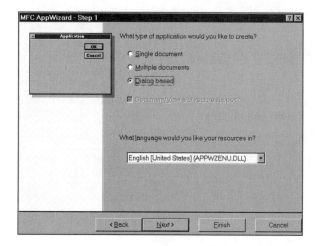

At this time, you've specified all the settings necessary to build the basic test application, so click Finish. You should see a dialog similar to that shown in Figure 1.11, which simply summarizes the settings the AppWizard will use when creating your new project. Just click OK, and the MFC AppWizard will generate your test application's project.

FIGURE 1.11

The MFC New Project Information dialog.

When the AppWizard has finished creating the source and project files and loaded the project into Visual Studio, you can begin editing the files to tailor the application to your needs. I'll show you what to do that next.

Modifications to a Basic MFC Dialog-Based Application

Luckily, the MFC AppWizard gave you pretty much everything you'll require, so the modifications you'll need to make are not terribly complicated. The project opens the dialog template in the resource editor, and you can modify it to appear as I've shown in Listing 1.12.

FIGURE 1.12

The MFC Test Client Application dialog template.

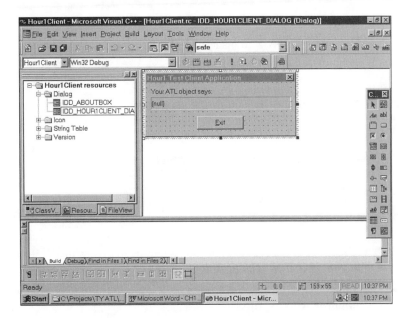

The two upper controls are simply text controls, although I gave the lower of the two a control ID so I could change its textual content later. I also changed its style to center the text vertically and show a sunken border. I chose to identify it using IDC_ATLMSG because it will contain the text returned from the ATL COM object. I deleted the OK button and renamed the Cancel button Exit. You're now done with the visual aspects of the application.

You'll need a mechanism to add the text to the text control, which MFC provides you. Simply press the Ctrl key and double-click on the lower text control (the one for which you provided an ID). That should bring up the MFC ClassWizard's Add Member Variable dialog box shown in Figure 1.13. The defaults are fine, although you do need to provide a name for the string variable MFC will associate with the Windows control. I chose m_strAtlMsg.

FIGURE 1.13

*The MFC
ClassWizard's Add
Member Variable
dialog box.*

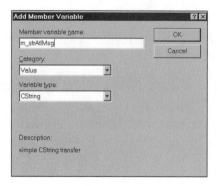

The MFC ClassWizard opens and modifies some of your project's files. When its job is done, open the source code for the dialog box (which, if you've been following my example, should be Hour1ClientDlg.cpp). It's now time to add some code.

At the top of the file, you should see the traditional C++ preprocessor `include` directives. On the line following the last directive, add the lines you see in Listing 1.2.

LISTING 1.2   Including the ATL COM Object's Information Files

```
// Add the ATL object's information
#include "..\Server\Day1Server.h"
#include "..\Server\Day1Server_i.c"
```

ANALYSIS   Note that I used a relative path to include files that I created when I compiled my object. As you might imagine, you must make sure the path and filenames are correct, or the preprocessor won't find them, and the client application compilation will terminate with an error.

The files you included specify some information that the compiler will require in order to actually create an instance of your COM object. The code you use to do that is provided in Listing 1.3. The code I added to the wizard-generated code is shown in italics.

LISTING 1.3   The Dialog's `OnInitDialog()` Method Implementation

```
BOOL CDay1ClientDlg::OnInitDialog()
{
    CDialog::OnInitDialog();

    // Add "About..." menu item to system menu.

    // IDM_ABOUTBOX must be in the system command range.
    ASSERT((IDM_ABOUTBOX & 0xFFF0) == IDM_ABOUTBOX);
    ASSERT(IDM_ABOUTBOX < 0xF000);
```

```
CMenu* pSysMenu = GetSystemMenu(FALSE);
if (pSysMenu != NULL)
{
    CString strAboutMenu;
    strAboutMenu.LoadString(IDS_ABOUTBOX);
    if (!strAboutMenu.IsEmpty())
    {
        pSysMenu->AppendMenu(MF_SEPARATOR);
        pSysMenu->AppendMenu(MF_STRING, IDM_ABOUTBOX,
                             strAboutMenu);
    }
}

// Set the icon for this dialog.  The framework does
// this automatically
//  when the application's main window is not a dialog
SetIcon(m_hIcon, TRUE);  // Set big icon
SetIcon(m_hIcon, FALSE); // Set small icon

// Start the COM runtime
CoInitialize(NULL);

// Create an instance of our ATL object
IHelloWorld* pIHelloWorld = NULL;
HRESULT hr = CoCreateInstance(CLSID_TYATLObj1,
                        NULL,
                        CLSCTX_INPROC_SERVER,
                        IID_IHelloWorld,
                        reinterpret_cast<void **>(&pIHelloWorld));
if ( FAILED(hr) ) {
    // We couldn't create the object...
    AfxMessageBox("Error creating the COM object!",
                MB_OK | MB_ICONERROR);
    CoUninitialize();
    EndDialog(IDCANCEL);
    return TRUE;
} // if

// Call the COM object
BSTR bstrMsg = NULL;
hr = pIHelloWorld->SayHello(&bstrMsg);
if ( FAILED(hr) ) {
    // We couldn't retrieve the message...
    m_strAtlMsg = "*Error retrieving the message*";
} // if
else {
    // Pull the message text
    m_strAtlMsg = bstrMsg;
```

continues

LISTING **1.3**   continued

```
            // Release the string memory
            ::SysFreeString(bstrMsg);
    } // else

    // Tell the COM object we no longer require its
    // services...
    pIHelloWorld->Release();

    // Put the string up on the dialog box
    UpdateData(FALSE);

    // Shut down COM
    CoUninitialize();

    return TRUE;  // return TRUE  unless you set the
                  // focus to a control
}
```

If you're familiar with MFC, you'll understand that I coded the test client in this manner simply to place all the code that supports the COM aspects of the application in a single method. MFC experts would likely do things a bit differently.

On the other hand, if some (or all) the code I've shown in Listing 1.3 appears to be so much gibberish, don't let that bother you at this point. After all, understanding this piece of code is what this entire book addresses. Just copy it verbatim into your source code or open the client project supplied on the book's CD.

When you have modified the dialog box code to create and call your ATL COM object, you should now be ready to compile your application and run it—to see what blows up. (Just kidding!) That's the next topic.

Running the Test

If you're courageous, you can simply press Ctrl+F5 to run the application. If you're more cautious, you can set a breakpoint in the client application and step into the code to watch it execute the first time. Assuming things run correctly, however, you should be rewarded with a dialog box much like the one you see in Figure 1.14.

The text you see in the sunken-bordered text control came from the ATL COM object, proving that, at least to this degree of testing, it works!

I'll be referring back to the code you've written in future days, partly to provide you with a better understanding of the code itself and partly because I'll simply need an available source file to discuss some given point or aspect of ATL COM programming. Throughout this book, you'll be exploring aspects of these source files or others like them, as well as ATL programming in general.

FIGURE 1.14

The ATL COM object's test application user interface.

Summary

In this lesson, you created your first ATL-based COM object and developed a quick test application that uses the object. You saw how to begin an ATL project and how to add code to tailor the basic ATL framework to become one of many ATL objects. You were able to take the basic object code, add new COM methods to perform specific tasks, and then compile the object for later use. After the object was successfully compiled, you saw how to create a quick-and-dirty MFC-based test application that can load your COM object and call a method.

If some of what you did made sense to you, that's terrific: You've already taken a step in the right direction. But if a lot of it made no sense whatsoever, don't despair. My goal in this lesson was to motivate you—to get you excited about developing ATL-based COM components. The best way to start is to actually *do* something. As you progress through the book, reflect back on what you did during this day, and things will quickly become clearer to you.

I'll make good on that promise with the next day when I take you through the basics of COM and introduce you to the many COM-related topics you should understand in order to develop robust ATL objects. What you see there forms the underpinnings of all you will do with ATL.

Q&A

Q I'm not terribly familiar with MFC. Will all of your test applications use MFC?

A The majority will, but they'll all follow the basic pattern you've seen today. Of course, there is more information coming in Day 9. I will provide many Visual Basic test applications as well, though most of them will be as solutions to specific examples. I'll also create ATL-based test applications later in the book. When you begin ActiveX control programming, I'll introduce yet another way to test your code when I show you how to use the ActiveX Control Test Container that ships with Visual Studio.

Q **When you inserted the ATL object into the basic ATL framework (using the ATL Object Wizard), you typed text into the ATL Object Wizard Properties Names tab's Short Name edit control that was propagated throughout the property page (refer to Figure 1.6). Must I accept what the wizard provides, such as for the object's filenames or ProgID?**

A No, these are just suggestions based upon the Short Name text you provided. I, myself, edited the CoClass, Type, and ProgID for each and every sample ATL object you'll see in this book (I did this to provide you with consistent object names and COM information). You'll often find yourself editing the Names information to suit your particular requirements…by all means feel free to do so.

Q **Do you generally rely upon the wizards for the majority of your ATL work?**

A I discuss this a bit in the Quiz section also, but I personally do (most of the professionals I work with also do). The reason is the wizards provide a tremendous productivity boost by inserting basic, framework-style code into the ATL project. This is code I don't have to write and debug, allowing me to concentrate on the task at hand, which is the implementation of the body of the method or interface, or even the entire object itself.

Workshop

The Workshop is designed to help you anticipate possible questions, review what you've learned, and get you thinking about how to put your knowledge into practice. The answers to the quiz are in Appendix A, "Answers."

Quiz

1. Why rely so heavily on the wizards to generate code?
2. Can you add additional objects to the ATL project (as you added the first)?
3. I see you can add methods and properties to your object—what are properties?

Exercises

1. Modify the ATL source code to return a different message.
2. Add a second method to the IHelloWorld interface to return an integer value instead of a string.
3. Create a Visual Basic test client for your ATL COM object.

DAY 2

Exploring COM: The Technology ATL Supports

Now that you have created a real, live ATL-based COM object, it's time to take a step back and look at the bigger picture. After all, if you don't understand what COM is about, using ATL to write COM code is just a faster way to write bad COM code.

If you are truly new to COM programming, you're in for a treat. COM programming is rewarding and even fun (at least when your code works properly). For you, this day should serve as a basic introduction to COM terms and concepts. Don't worry too much if some parts appear to be difficult—your grasp of the terms and concepts will solidify as you progress through the book. On the other hand, if you're somewhat experienced in the ways of COM, this day will serve as both a refresher and an introduction to the COM terms and concepts that are important for successful ATL COM programming.

In this day, you will learn

- The basics of COM
- How to invoke the COM runtime environment
- How COM objects are created
- How COM views threading issues
- How COM passes data from object to object
- How Windows knows a COM object exists on a system
- How to handle errors in COM

A Brief Introduction to COM

COM is many things, and it is even different things to different people. When I think of COM in the larger sense, I see COM as an interprocess data conduit and a mechanism for sharing reusable components.

If you've ever written code that needs to pass data from one process to another, you know your choices are somewhat limited. In my past programming experience, I've used each one of these mechanisms:

- A custom Windows message which is broadcast to another application
- Named pipes
- Shared memory

These mechanisms work, and for many applications, they work well. However, COM provides you with an alternative mechanism that is more robust, even to the point of enabling you to handle remote data access (that is, data that exists on remote computers) in the same manner as you access local data.

COM also provides for code reuse. When many programmers think of code reuse, they tend to think of source code reuse. COM takes a higher approach and reuses binary objects. Before you ever write a line of COM code, you design an interface that, after it is released for public use, is *immutable* (cannot be changed). I'll defer discussing data manipulation until later in the day, after you have a few concepts and terms under your belt. For now, let's explore the concept of object reuse.

Reusable Objects

What is an object? It seems everywhere you look in computing today you see the term *object*. Unfortunately, the term isn't used consistently in many cases. When I talk about a

COM object, for example, I'm talking about a very different beast than a C++ object. In this book, COM objects will certainly be comprised of C++ objects, but they are not the same.

Before I discuss reusing COM objects, let me first provide you with my definition of a *COM object*: a language-independent, self-contained, self-registering code module that adheres to the COM specification.

If I break this definition down, you see five constituent parts:

- Language-Independent: COM objects must be language-independent to work with clients written in any language. Therefore, the individual language's compiler must produce a binary image that meets the COM specification.

- Self-Contained: The COM object stands alone as a cohesive entity. It might require support from other objects; but, in and of itself, it is a complete entity.

- Self-Registering: This term refers to the object's capability to tell a given Windows system that the COM object exists and is ready to be reused. How the object does this differs among COM objects, but the result is the same: Information is written to the Windows Registry database.

- Code module: The COM code has been compiled (correctly) into either a dynamic link library (DLL) or an executable file (EXE). These are the only two forms of compiled object that the COM runtime infrastructure will recognize (although in some cases you could argue this point, given Visual Basic and Java).

- Adheres to the COM specification: The code implementing the COM object must be faithful to the COM specification if it is to live and work properly in the COM infrastructure. If the rules aren't followed, you can't expect the object to work properly.

Note

You'll find a plethora of COM information at the Microsoft Web site, `http://www.microsoft.com/com`. Of specific interest are the sample code files, the white papers, and the COM specification itself.

Contrast the COM object that I just described to a C++ object, which is really a C++ class. According to my previous description, the C++ object is ideally self-contained (if it is well designed). It is, however, clearly tied to the C++ language, has no concept of self-registration, is usually not a complete code module (again, by the description I gave earlier); but it certainly is *not* bound by the rules of COM.

Why the difference? The goal of COM object reuse is for compiled applications to share objects rather than be recompiled to share objects. A large part of the COM infrastructure is dedicated to making registered COM objects available dynamically to Windows applications written in any language and for managing the care and feeding of the COM object when it's in use. COM also provides you with facilities to make the COM objects location-independent, making them easier to reuse. If you know what object you want to use, COM will locate it for you (at least on a given machine).

COM objects are typically referred to as *servers*, whereas applications that make use of the object are known as *clients*. A COM object could serve clients and be a client of another COM object itself, although I've drawn the client as a Windows application in Figure 2.1. The client instantiates an instance of a particular COM object and uses its *interfaces* to process information or perform given tasks. The COM object will perform the work it was designed to do, then tell the client of the success or failure of the operation. I'll discuss interfaces in a moment, and they're the primary topic of Day 3, "The COM Interface: COM's Foundation."

A detail I'd like to point out to you regarding Figure 2.1 is the odd-looking figure that represents the COM object. This is typically how you'll see COM objects represented in figures. The rectangle represents the object, and the circles with attaching lines represent the object's interfaces. (These diagrams are sometimes referred to as *lollypop diagrams*.)

FIGURE 2.1

The relationship between COM client and server.

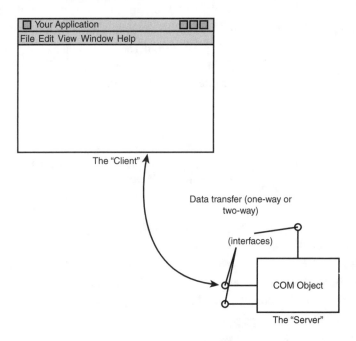

If you think about it, there must be some standard in place for this to be possible. This is the purpose of the COM Specification. The COM Specification tells us many things, one of which is that we must design our COM objects around interfaces, much in the same way electronic components are designed to functional and electrical interface standards. A *COM interface* is a collection of object methods and properties that together implement semantic functionality and that, after they are defined and released to the public, are immutable.

You can imagine that an interface is similar to a C++ class definition. There is more going on with an interface, but at some level they are synonymous. If you break this definition down, as I did with that of the COM object, you are left with three main parts:

- A collection of methods and properties: This part of the definition should be somewhat familiar to you as a C++ programmer. For each interface, you simply define methods and properties (similar in intent to the C++ attribute), to include their parameter lists and return values.

- Semantic functionality: The collection of methods and properties together implement a cohesive operation or set of operations. In a sense, your interface has a *syntactical* meaning, which is the declaration of the interface methods and properties, and a *semantical* meaning, which is the functionality the methods and properties are intended to implement (the defining reason the interface exists at all).

- Immutability: This term means an interface cannot change. In a nutshell, an interface is a binding contract between you, the developer, and your object's users, the public. If you change an interface, you have created a *new* interface. If you somehow try to reuse an old interface by adding methods or properties, or by changing the original semantical meaning, you will likely cause your user's applications to cease to function correctly.

Note

You are always free to create a new interface, but, in order to keep client applications in good working order, it is wise to also support the older interfaces. You can easily change an interface while you are developing it. After you release it, however, the rules of COM are in effect.

In COM, interfaces can derive from other interfaces, just as C++ classes can derive from C++ base classes. In fact, inheritance is the main mechanism for adding new interfaces, as you'll see in Day 8, "ATL Object Methods: Adding Functionality to Your Interface." You reuse the original interface as a base interface and add the functionality you require to the new interface—just as you would C++ classes. How COM and C++ each support inheritance is completely different, but the concept of the inheritance of a base-level functionality applies to both.

> Common COM coding practice dictates that the interface name begins with *I* and is followed by a meaningful descriptive name, such as IClassFactory (an interface you'll see later in the day). If the interface changes, a version number is commonly concatenated to the end of the original interface name, as in IClassFactory2.

Before I get too much further, I should note that some developers claim COM is not object-oriented. The three main tenets of object-oriented programming are encapsulation, polymorphism, and inheritance. Some argue COM supports encapsulation and polymorphism, but not inheritance. Clearly, interfaces not only provide for encapsulation but also enforce it vigorously. You only get what the interface provides. Given my previous discussion of interfaces inheriting from interfaces, you can see how an interface can be polymorphic. You realize different behavior depending upon which interface in the inheritance chain you obtain.

The stickler is the inheritance, primarily because COM objects don't inherit behavior in a source-code sense. Others argue COM is object-oriented because of the interface inheritance I just mentioned. I'll leave the argument to the purists—what's important to me is that I can use COM to solve object-oriented problems effectively. It works, and if it's applied correctly, it works very well.

To use a COM object and any interface it supports, you must have some way to create an instance of the object and ask it for the various interface pointers of interest. In the following section, I'll discuss how objects and interfaces are identified. Then, I'll show you how objects are created for use dynamically.

Naming Objects and Interfaces

The main issue when identifying an interface is that each interface is by definition unique (remember the immutability property). If this is so, how do I ensure that my interface is not named the same as any you have named? This is actually an old problem, solved many years ago when the Distributed Computing Environment (DCE) and the Remote Procedure Call (RPC) architectures were implemented. Those engineers faced the same problem, and they solved it by combining several pieces of information available on every computer. They elected to combine the current time, in 100 nanosecond intervals (since A.D. 1582), the network address of the computer (which is guaranteed to be unique by the vendor), and other ancillary information. If your computer has no network adapter, and hence no network address, the RPC architects provide an algorithm for otherwise identifying your computer in a unique manner.

The result of this algorithm is referred to as a *Universally Unique Identifier* (UUID), which is defined as a 128-bit data structure. Microsoft used this same algorithm to create unique 128-bit data structures for naming interfaces (and indeed even COM objects themselves). However, Microsoft elected to call this data structure a *Globally Unique Identifier*, or *GUID*. This definition of GUID came from BASETYPS.H, found in your global include directory:

```
typedef struct _GUID
{
    unsigned long Data1;
    unsigned short Data2;
    unsigned short Data3;
    unsigned char Data4[8];
}_GUID;
```

When a GUID is associated with a specific interface, it is usually referred to as an *Interface Identifier* (IID). Similarly, when a GUID is associated with the COM object itself, it is referred to as the object's *Class Identifier*, or CLSID. You'll find GUIDs used throughout COM, and there are even several useful COM runtime API methods available that deal specifically with this structure. For example, you can create a GUID, compare two GUIDs, and easily convert a GUID to a string representation and back again. (This is handy when working directly with the Registry.)

Even though GUIDs are used throughout COM, the most common use for them has to be when creating objects and asking those objects if they support various interfaces. Let's see how that is done, both for local and remote objects.

Creating Local Objects

To *instantiate* a COM object, that is, to create an instance of the object you can use, you commonly call the COM runtime API method CoCreateInstance(), as shown in Listing 2.1.

LISTING 2.1   CoCreateInstance() COM API Method Definition

```
1: STDAPI CoCreateInstance(
2:    REFCLSID rclsid,      //Class identifier (CLSID) of the object
3:    LPUNKNOWN pUnkOuter,  //Pointer to whether object is or isn't part
4:                          // of an aggregate
5:    DWORD dwClsContext,   //Context for running executable code
6:    REFIID riid,          //Reference to the identifier of the interface
7:    LPVOID * ppv          //Address of output variable that receives
8:                          // the interface pointer requested in riid
9: );
```

ANALYSIS When you use CoCreateInstance(), you pass in references to the CLSID of the COM object you're interested in using (line 2), as well as to the IID for the interface you desire (line 6). The pUnkOuter pointer, line 3, refers to something known as the controlling IUnknown. I will defer a definition of this term until Day 5, "ATL Architecture—How ATL Implements COM," when I discuss aggregation (often, this value is NULL).

The *ppv* parameter, line 7, is a pointer to a variable that receives the interface pointer, assuming CoCreateInstance() was successful. For example, consider Listing 2.2:

LISTING 2.2   Example Use of CoCreateInstance()

```
1: IMyInterface* pIMyItf = NULL;
2: HRESULT hr = CoCreateInstance(CLSID_MyCOMObject,
3:                               NULL,
4:                               CLSCTX_INPROC_SERVER,
5:                               IID_IMyInterface,
6:                               reinterpret_cast<void**>(&pIMyItf));
```

ANALYSIS In this case, I'm asking for MyCOMObject, line 2, to give me a pointer to its IMyInterface, line 5. If CoCreateInstance() is successful, the pIMyItf variable(line 6) will be nonNULL and contain a pointer to the interface that I can use to call methods and perform some task.

The context parameter, line 4, merits a bit more explanation. With this parameter, you tell COM whether you want an in-process server, a local server, or a remote server.

NEW TERM *In-process server:* a COM object that resides in the same process address space as the executable that created the object (for instance, a DLL).

NEW TERM *Local server:* a COM object that resides in another process address space (for example, an EXE).

NEW TERM *Remote server:* a COM object that resides on a remote computer. (The object itself can be either in-process or local on the remote machine.)

The actual value you pass into CoCreateInstance() comes from an enumeration defined in WTYPES.H in Listing 2.3.

LISTING 2.3   COM's Class Context Enumerated Values

```
1: typedef enum tagCLSCTX
2:     {CLSCTX_INPROC_SERVER    = 0x1,
3:      CLSCTX_INPROC_HANDLER   = 0x2,
4:      CLSCTX_LOCAL_SERVER     = 0x4,
```

```
 5:     CLSCTX_INPROC_SERVER16   = 0x8,
 6:     CLSCTX_REMOTE_SERVER     = 0x10,
 7:     CLSCTX_INPROC_HANDLER16  = 0x20,
 8:     CLSCTX_INPROC_SERVERX86  = 0x40,
 9:     CLSCTX_INPROC_HANDLERX86 = 0x80,
10:     CLSCTX_ESERVER_HANDLER   = 0x100
11:     } CLSCTX;
```

There are two more values you can use, CLSCTX_SERVER and CLSCTX_ALL, defined in
OBJBASE.H in Listing 2.4.

LISTING 2.4 Derived COM Class Context Values

```
 1: // With DCOM, CLSCTX_REMOTE_SERVER should be included
 2: #if (_WIN32_WINNT >= 0x0400 ) ¦¦ defined(_WIN32_DCOM) // DCOM
 3: #define CLSCTX_ALL            (CLSCTX_INPROC_SERVER¦ \
 4:                                CLSCTX_INPROC_HANDLER¦ \
 5:                                CLSCTX_LOCAL_SERVER¦ \
 6:                                CLSCTX_REMOTE_SERVER)
 7:
 8: #define CLSCTX_SERVER         (CLSCTX_INPROC_SERVER¦
 9:                                CLSCTX_LOCAL_SERVER¦
10:                                CLSCTX_REMOTE_SERVER)
11: #else
12: #define CLSCTX_ALL            (CLSCTX_INPROC_SERVER¦ \
13:                                CLSCTX_INPROC_HANDLER¦ \
14:                                CLSCTX_LOCAL_SERVER )
15:
16: #define CLSCTX_SERVER         (CLSCTX_INPROC_SERVER¦
17:                                CLSCTX_LOCAL_SERVER)
18: #endif
```

ANALYSIS   It's beyond the scope of this day to describe all the contexts in detail, but there
are three you will commonly use: CLSCTX_INPROC_SERVER (line 2, Listing 2.3);
CLSCTX_LOCAL_SERVER (line 4, Listing 2.3); CLSCTX_REMOTE_SERVER (line 6, Listing 2.3).
As you might imagine, they are directly related to the type of COM object you want to
instantiate. If you want an in-process server (a DLL) because you want fast data transfers
between your application and the COM object, you select CLSCTX_INPROC_SERVER. If, on
the other hand, you're more interested in separating your application from the COM
object (for process fault protection, perhaps), you might want a separate executable run
to serve your application's needs. For this, you select CLSCTX_LOCAL_SERVER. Of course,
CLSCTX_REMOTE_SERVER is used when you want to reach out and touch an object on a different machine on your network.

If CoCreateInstance() is successful, you will have a valid pointer returned to you that you can use to access the interface's methods. The beauty of this is that it's just another pointer, in no way different from the pointers you're used to using. If I have a pointer to a C++ class that I created using C++'s new operator, I access the class in this manner:

```
class CSomeClass;
CSomeClass* pSomeClass = new CSomeClass;
pSomeClass->SomeMethod();
```

If I have a COM interface pointer, I access it in this manner:

```
ISomeInterface* pSomeInterface;
CoCreateInstance(...);
pSomeInterface->SomeMethod();
```

Naturally, in real code you add the appropriate error checking, but the concepts are equivalent.

When dealing with remote interfaces, the issue of cost arises. When you think of instantiating remote objects, you should think *expensive*. It can easily take hundreds of times longer to bring up a remote object rather than a local object. For this reason, COM has a special extension to CoCreateInstance() for remote object instantiation. This reduces overall costs if you intend to create more than one object. Creating remote objects is the topic of the next section.

Creating Remote Objects

The special extension I mentioned is CoCreateInstanceEx(). The essential difference between CoCreateInstance() and its extended version is that you can pass in a list of IIDs for a given CLSID to be created on a specific remote machine, using CoCreateInstanceEx(), rather than be limited to creating just a single instance, which is the case with CoCreateInstance(). Listing 2.5 shows the method signature for CoCreateInstanceEx().

LISTING 2.5 CoCreateInstanceEx() COM API Method Definition

```
 1: HRESULT CoCreateInstanceEx(
 2:    REFCLSID rclsid,                //CLSID of the object to be created
 3:    IUnknown *punkOuter,            //If part of an aggregate, the
 4:                                    // controlling IUnknown
 5:    DWORD dwClsCtx,                 //CLSCTX values
 6:    COSERVERINFO *pServerInfo,      //Machine on which the object is to
 7:                                    // be instantiated
 8:    ULONG cmq,                      //Number of MULTI_QI structures in
 9:                                    // pResults
10:    MULTI_QI *pResults             //Array of MULTI_QI structures
11: );
```

ANALYSIS You specify the particular machine of interest by completing the COSERVERINFO structure, passed into CoCreateInstanceEx() on line 6. The IIDs of the interfaces you want to instantiate are spelled out in the MULTI_QI structure, an array of which is passed into CoCreateInstanceEx() on line 10.

For now, I'm not going to describe this method of accessing remote COM objects because that's the topic for Day 19, "Distributed ATL—DCOM Around the Net." If you leave this day understanding that you have this capability, that's all you need until Day 19. You certainly won't be working with remote objects until that time.

Throughout this book, you will explore interfaces and how they work in a COM environment. Although you are free to design your interfaces as you see fit, the COM specification tells us our objects *must* support a granddaddy interface, IUnknown.

The IUnknown Interface

Every COM object you ever write will support the IUnknown interface. The reason is simple—an object's client must have some mechanism for discovering what interfaces a given COM object implements and be able to control the COM object's lifespan. This is precisely what IUnknown enables you to do. Here are the methods IUnknown exposes:

- QueryInterface()
- AddRef()
- Release()

QueryInterface() is used to ask a COM object if it supports a given interface. If it does, great! You can use it. If it doesn't, at least your application can degrade gracefully and revert to an earlier interface or skip the functionality altogether. AddRef() and Release() are always used as a pair because they serve to increment and decrement a *reference count*. When the object's reference count reaches zero, COM unloads the object from memory. Because these are important concepts, I'll describe them in more detail, starting with QueryInterface().

Querying for Interfaces

Now that you know an interface is identified using an IID, which is simply a GUID, it's time to examine QueryInterface(). Here is the definition of QueryInterface():

```
HRESULT QueryInterface(
  REFIID iid,        //Identifier of the requested interface
  void ** ppvObject  //Address of output variable that receives the
                     //interface pointer requested in iid
);
```

The HRESULT return value is simply a long (32-bit integer) value that you'll see in more detail later in the day. The IID of the interface you want to query for is passed into QueryInterface() as the iid parameter. The REFIID data type refers to a reference to an IID, which makes sense from a parameter-passing perspective. You don't often want to copy 128-bit structures to the stack if you can avoid it.

QueryInterface() will compare the IID you supply against the set of interfaces the COM object supports. If there is a match, a pointer to the interface is placed in an object pointer variable, which you supply, and a successful HRESULT value is returned. If the COM object doesn't support the interface in question, QueryInterface() returns a NULL interface pointer and a failed HRESULT.

You should always check the returned HRESULT prior to using the interface pointer, just in case things failed. If you don't, you run the risk of calling methods using a NULL pointer! However, after you have this pointer, you use it just as if you had you called CoCreateInstance() and asked for the interface directly.

Now you've seen how to create COM objects and query them for the various interfaces they support. It's time to see how long the object is available for your use.

COM Reference Counting

Because every COM object supports IUnknown, every COM object supports *reference counting* through AddRef() and Release(). When you receive a COM interface, no matter how it was originally created (we've seen two methods already), the interface is given to you with a minimum reference count of one. When you are through with the interface, you will decrement the reference count. When the reference count reaches zero, the COM object will unload itself from memory until you instantiate it again. Not surprisingly, AddRef() increments the reference count, and Release() decrements it.

There are a few simple rules for COM object reference counting:

- Call AddRef() before you return an interface pointer.
- Call Release() when you are done with the object.
- Call AddRef() after assigning a new interface pointer.

The first rule applies to methods that return interface pointers (even QueryInterface() and CoCreateInstance()). Therefore, you need not call AddRef() if a COM method provides you with an interface pointer. The second rule should be apparent—when you're done using the object, release it. Essentially, the final rule tells you to increment the reference count whenever you create another reference to the same interface.

These rules sound simple, and they are; but, at times, they're very difficult to follow when writing actual COM code. You'll see in Day 5 and in Day 9, "Creating C++ Test Clients: You Can't Test What You Can't Execute," just how ATL makes your coding chores much simpler by handling the reference counting for you.

Managing a COM object's reference count is how you control the object's lifetime. I'm now going to introduce a completely different topic, although it's one I discussed earlier in the day. This topic is the dual interface, which is used in scripting architectures.

Dual Versus Custom Interfaces

I mentioned previously that interfaces can inherit from other interfaces. I also discussed the fact that all COM interfaces inherit from IUnknown. There is a special case of inheritance that you'll see from time to time, the *dual interface*.

Another interface you commonly see when scripting is discussed (scripting in the sense of Visual Basic, Visual Basic for Applications, and JScript) is the IDispatch interface, which I'll describe thoroughly in Day 13, "Creating ATL Applications: Where ATL Meets Win32." For now, I'll simply define a dual interface.

New Term　　*Dual interface:* an interface derived from IDispatch rather than from IUnknown.

It isn't important at this time to understand what IDispatch does for you. Simply note that there is a special interface, the dual interface, and it derives indirectly from IUnknown. You might think a dual interface that you create somehow skips derivation from IUnknown, but in reality, this isn't so. IDispatch derives from IUnknown, and because your interface derives from IDispatch, your interface also derives from IUnknown, albeit indirectly.

So far, I've discussed COM objects and their interfaces at length, and I've even discussed how you create the objects for use. But you can't simply start creating objects until you've told Windows you want to use COM. If the COM runtime isn't up and running when you begin calling COM API functions, such as CoCreateInstance(), your application fails very quickly. Now is a good time to take a look at how the COM runtime is invoked.

Invoking the COM Runtime

Asking Windows to start COM operations is actually a simple matter compared to implementing the COM principles you've seen so far. Formerly there were only two Win32 API calls you would have had to make. With the advent of distributed COM, a third was added to support multithreading.

To start COM processing, simply use the `CoInitialize()` API call:

```
HRESULT CoInitialize(
  LPVOID pvReserved  //Reserved; must be NULL
);
```

That's all there is to it. When you're finished with COM (for example, when your application shuts down, usually when processing WM_DESTROY), you call `CoUninitialize()`:

```
void CoUninitialize();
```

These two API calls must always be made in pairs. For each successful call to `CoInitialize()`, you must have a call to `CoUninitialize()`, although typically you'll call each only a single time from within your application.

The third, newer API call I mentioned is `CoInitializeEx()`. It's used primarily to create multithreaded COM objects. When using these, you take responsibility for the object's thread safety. You'll read more about this shortly, when I discuss apartments. For now, I'll simply introduce the API call:

```
HRESULT CoInitializeEx(
  void * pvReserved,  //Reserved, must be NULL
  DWORD dwCoInit      //COINIT value
);
```

The `COINIT` values come from `OBJBASE.H`, as shown in Listing 2.6.

LISTING 2.6 COM's `COINIT` Enumerated Values

```
 1: typedef enum tagCOINIT
 2: {
 3:   COINIT_APARTMENTTHREADED = 0x2, // Apartment model
 4:
 5: #if  (_WIN32_WINNT >= 0x0400 ) || defined(_WIN32_DCOM) // DCOM
 6:   // These constants are only valid on Windows NT 4.0
 7:   COINIT_MULTITHREADED     = 0x0, // OLE calls objects on any thread.
 8:   COINIT_DISABLE_OLE1DDE   = 0x4, // Don't use DDE for Ole1 support.
 9:   COINIT_SPEED_OVER_MEMORY = 0x8, // Trade memory for speed.
10: #endif // DCOM
11: } COINIT;
```

ANALYSIS In most cases, if you're using `CoInitializeEx()`, you'll use the `COINIT_MULTITHREADED` constant, line 7, to invoke the multithreaded COM runtime environment or the `COINIT_APARTMENTTHREADED` constant, line 3, to invoke the single-threaded COM runtime environment. The other values are rarely used in practice.

Now that you've learned how to request that the COM runtime be initiated and how you create COM objects, let's examine how COM actually creates the objects when you request them.

Creating COM Object Instances: The Class Object

COM objects have a special, additional object known as the class factory, or alternatively, the class object. When COM is notified that you want an instance of a specific COM object, COM searches for the object and executes its class factory.

You can imagine the class factory as providing a function similar to the C++ new operator. In fact, many C++ class factory implementations use the new operator to bring up a C++ class to handle the COM support. After you have a pointer to an object's class factory, you can create as many instances of the object as you want (unlike CoCreateInstance(), where you create a single instance of the object).

You obtain the class factory pointer using the CoGetClassObject() COM API call, as shown in Listing 2.7.

LISTING 2.7 CoGetClassObject() COM API Method Definition

```
 1: STDAPI CoGetClassObject(
 2:   REFCLSID rclsid,  //CLSID associated with the class object
 3:   DWORD dwClsContext,
 4:                      //Context for running executable code
 5:   COSERVERINFO * pServerInfo,
 6:                      //Pointer to machine on which the object is to
 7:                      // be instantiated
 8:   REFIID riid,       //Reference to the identifier of the interface
 9:   LPVOID * ppv       //Address of output variable that receives the
10:                      // interface pointer requested in riid
11: );
```

ANALYSIS And as you can see, it's very much like the other calls you've learned that create objects. The difference is that the riid value you pass, line 8, will be the IID for either the licensed or unlicensed class factory. (Typically, only one type of class factory is implemented, licensed or unlicensed, so CoGetClassObject() could fail if you request the wrong kind.) I'll now briefly discuss these two types of class factories.

Unlicensed Objects

Unlicensed COM objects support the IClassFactory interface, and to access this interface you pass in IID_IClassFactory to CoGetClassObject(). After you have a pointer to the object's IClassFactory interface, you can call the IClassFactory methods, CreateInstance() and LockServer(). CreateInstance() is used, well, to create objects. No surprise there. LockServer() is used to force the class object to remain in memory, providing for faster object instantiation if you need to create multiples of the particular COM object, even after no instances of active objects remain in memory.

Licensed Objects

Licensed objects support the IClassFactory2 interface, denoted by IID_IClassFactory2. In addition to supporting the IUnknown and IClassFactory methods, IClassFactory2 provides three new methods: CreateInstanceLic(); GetLicInfo(); and RequestLicKey().

The licensing mechanism is such that the COM object can actually be instantiated on machines with and without a license. GetLicInfo() will inform you if the object has determined it is to be created in a licensed or an unlicensed situation. If unlicensed, the license key must be embedded in the calling application (yours), or the class factory will refuse to create the COM object. If you, indeed, have the license information, call CreateInstanceLic(). If your license information is correct, you'll have a new COM object on your hands. If GetLicInfo() indicates you're about to create a COM object on a licensed machine, you can simply call RequestLicKey() to obtain the license key and pass that to CreateInstanceLic().

> **Note**
>
> You'll typically find licensed COM objects when dealing with ActiveX, which you'll read more about in Day 16, "ATL and ActiveX: Modern Control Packaging."

If all this seems confusing, don't be too concerned. I'll clear things up in Day 18, "ATL, Class Factories, and Licensed Objects: Creating Objects and Protecting Your Investment." For now, it's enough that you know you have the option to license your objects when they are instantiated. Time to press onward. Now that you've seen how COM creates the objects you request, it's time to examine threading implications.

COM Threading Models

If you reflect back to the days when Windows 3.1 was the latest version of Windows, COM was in its infancy. At that time, Windows was a *cooperative multitasking environment*, which means that when your application was done processing a Windows message, it would relinquish control to Windows. Windows would then activate another application. Eventually, your application would be allowed to process another message.

You probably remember, as I do, applications that hung while processing a message, which meant Windows itself hung. That was a bad thing, and Microsoft designed *preemptive multitasking* into Win32-based versions of the operating system. With preemptive multitasking, your application is given a portion of the CPU's processing time without respect to the completion of a particular Windows message. You're allowed so many milliseconds, and then it's off to another process until it's your turn again.

COM was born in the cooperative multitasking days, and because of this, it didn't truly have a concept of multitasking. The Windows message queue and your application's associated message pump provided all the synchronization you required. However, when preemptive multitasking was introduced, along with DCOM, the concept of a COM apartment was also introduced. Let's look briefly at apartments, saving the meat for Day 12, "ATL and Apartments: How Win32 Threads and COM Are Related."

Single-Threaded: The STA

The *single-thread apartment*, or STA, is the traditional COM environment in which all multithreading synchronization is accomplished via the Windows message pump. COM sends Windows messages to the COM object and forces synchronization in much the same way you would force only a single thread of execution using a critical section. (You'll see more about multithreading issues in Day 11, "Multithreading—How and When.") This relieves you, the programmer, from having to deal with multithreading issues (except for some specific cases, which I'll address in Day 12). COM will make sure any thread affinity is properly handled, so your COM object can assume only a single thread will ever access the object's internal state information.

Multithreaded: The MTA

Contrast the STA to the MTA, the *multithreaded apartment*. In this case, your COM object need not have a message pump. The implications of this are that you, the programmer, must provide for re-entrance, must worry about deadlocks, and must implement proper data synchronization. In this case, COM assumes you know what you are doing, and it will allow any thread, at any time, to access your COM object. (This could affect any internal state information, hence the warning to synchronize access to internal object data.)

Note Other apartments exist in addition to the STA and MTA, but these two are the most critical to understand at this time.

COM objects working in the MTA must certainly be concerned about passing data to and from other process address spaces. Objects in an STA must be concerned about this at various times. The process of passing data to and fro is known as *marshaling*, which is the topic of the next section.

COM Data Sharing: Marshaling

You can probably imagine why data manipulation is so critical to COM. After all, a pointer to an array of characters allocated in one address space is meaningless in another, yet you often will want to pass string data between COM objects or between a COM object (the server) and an application (the client). This is accomplished in one of two ways—universal marshaling and custom marshaling.

Universal Marshaling

When you use the *Universal Marshaler* (*UM*), what you're really doing is using data types that COM already understands. For example, COM knows how to pass integer data from address space to address space. The data types the UM handles are commonly referred to as the *automation data types* (you'll look more closely at automation beginning with Day 13. The automation data types include such things as short integers, long integers, interface pointers, strings (of a specific type), dates, currency, floats, and doubles.

The automation data types also provide for marshaling of pointers to these types, which is very handy. Remember that a pointer in one address space is meaningless in another. If you select data types from the automation data types list, COM will happily send the information from place to place with no additional work on your part. UM requires a type library, which I'll introduce shortly. It is often referred to as *type library marshaling*.

Custom Marshaling

There are times when the data you are working with can't be shoved into one of the automation data types. This calls for *custom marshaling*. Custom marshaling can be challenging to implement. Essentially, you must write code that COM will use to transfer data between address spaces. How you make this conversion is up to you, but the code you write will be compiled into what COM calls a proxy and a stub, which I discuss in the next section.

You can, if you want, build the proxy/stub DLL yourself. This is tricky, but the tradeoff is that you have total control over the marshaling. It is more common to use the proxy/stub DLL created when you compile your IDL file. You'll see how to do in Day 19.

You also have the option of using the *Free-Threaded Marshaler*, or *FTM*, which is commonly used in MTA situations. This is a fairly advanced technique, and one I won't describe in detail in this book. Essentially, though, the FTM implements the standard COM interfaces for marshaling parameter data. You incorporate it into your COM object and let it do the hard work for you. The trick is in the details, which I'll skip at this point.

Proxies and Stubs

When COM passes data from one address space to another, or when you're using custom marshaling, COM expects to use a *proxy* and a *stub*. Both the proxy and the stub are DLLs, and you can imagine them functioning almost like a pair of modems. They convert data in one form to data in an intermediate form. Later, they reverse the conversion. The components at either end have no clue that any conversion transpired and happily use the data.

A call to a COM object in one address space is passed to its proxy, which marshals the data. The data is passed to the stub DLL in another address space, which unmarshals the data and hands it to the client. Figure 2.2 shows this in a diagram.

FIGURE 2.2

The relationship between proxies, stubs, and the COM client and server.

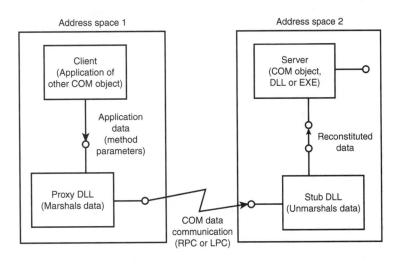

Note I mentioned the data is passed from address space to address space. This implies, then, that in-process COM servers (DLLs) don't require proxies and stubs. This is true, unless the in-process server is free-threaded (works in the MTA), in which case a proxy and a stub are required.

Type Libraries

When you compile a COM object, typically two compilers are brought into the picture. The first compiles the interface information you'll see in detail in Day 3. The second compiles your C++ code (and is the compiler with which you are most familiar). This first compiler is known as *MIDL*, for Microsoft IDL compiler. (*IDL* stands for Interface Definition Language, which you study in Day 3.) MIDL compiles the IDL that defines your COM object's interfaces, and it also builds what is known as a type library.

A *type library* is a tokenized form of the IDL used to define your interfaces (although, sadly, some information is lost during the compilation). It is the type library that most automation interfaces rely upon to discover, at runtime, precisely what the COM object is capable of doing—what functionality it supports. The type library is also used by the UM to determine how to marshal the interface parameter data, as well as by the Microsoft Transaction Server (MTS), which you'll come to know in Day 21, "ATL and MTS Concepts: Coding with a Better COM."

The type library is really nothing more than a blob (binary large object), and your compilation directives can either compile it to a separate file or compile it as a resource to incorporate it into your COM object's compiled image.

Memory Allocation

From time to time you'll need to be concerned about memory allocation. For example, if you want to pass a data structure between C++ classes, you typically use the C++ operator new to allocate the memory for the structure. In COM, if the structure is to be passed from object to client, you'll need to allocate memory on the client side of the operation from within your COM object. Since the client may be in a different process, or even on a different machine, you can't simply use the C++ operator new to allocate the memory. COM must perform the allocation for you. Similarly, COM must deallocate the memory on the client's end.

From your COM object you perform the memory allocation using CoTaskMemAlloc(), which takes as a parameter the total number of bytes to allocate. Like new or malloc(), you'll receive a pointer to the allocated memory, which you'll need to cast before use. After the structure has been marshaled (sent to the client), the client will ultimately need to release the memory using CoTaskMemFree(), passing in the pointer to the COM-allocated memory. There is also a CoTaskMemRealloc() function, should you want to change the size of the previously allocated memory block. I'll show you an example using the first two COM memory allocation API calls in Day 19.

Given that you designed an interface and compiled it into a COM object, let's see how Windows recognizes your COM object to enable client applications to use it effectively. This is known as registration, which I discuss next.

COM Object Registration

By their nature, contemporary COM objects are required to be self-registering. That is, Windows must be able to simply tap the COM object on the shoulder and say, "Register yourself." The COM object must comply. How an in-process server is registered differs from how a local server is registered, but the effect is the same. The pertinent CLSID is written into HKEY_CLASSES_ROOT, along with other important information, such as the threading type and filename. Figure 2.3 shows you this Registry information for a COM object registered on my system.

FIGURE 2.3

A COM Object example Registry entry.

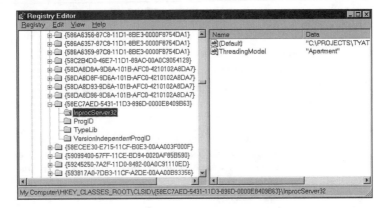

Note

To help you with registering and de-registering COM objects, I've provided a Registry script as this day's code sample that will allow you to right-click a given COM object's file (*.DLL or *.EXE) and either register or de-register it with a single mouse click. You'll find this extremely helpful in your COM development work. Double-click on the script's filename to install it. My thanks go to DevelopMentor for the idea.

You will also find that the COM object stores a Program Identifier, or ProgID. The ProgID is a more readable (to humans anyway) form of the CLSID. The ProgID is most commonly used with scripting languages to instantiate COM objects, but the problem with the ProgID is that it is not necessarily unique. You might conceivably have two COM objects register with the same ProgID.

ProgIDs have three sections, divided by a period:

```
<Program>.<Component>.<Version>
```

For example, the sample ATL program you created in the first day has a ProgID of
TYATL.Object1.1, if you followed my naming convention. You provided this when you
inserted the COM object and assigned its basic properties (refer back to Figure 1.6 in
Day 1, "Getting Started: Your First ATL COM Object.") When you create your COM
object, you decide how to name the ProgID.

Your best bet is to try to name it in a unique manner, such as with your company or
application name, followed by some string representing the function of the object. The
initial version should be version one, but this should be incremented as the associated
object's interface changes. COM objects also register a version-independent ProgID,
which is simply the ProgID with the version lopped off.

There are a number of COM API calls associated with converting CLSIDs to ProgIDs and
back again, should you need to do so—(CLSIDFromProgID() and ProgIDFromCLSID(),
respectively). In most cases, when using ATL, use the CLSID of the object and avoid
using the ProgID altogether, unless you are writing a scripting-based test application.

Note

> You might have heard of COM+, which is a new COM runtime available with
> Windows 2000. The registration I'm describing here applies to classic COM and
> not to COM+, which uses a completely different mechanism to register com-
> ponents. I'll discuss COM+ and the programmatical ramifications in Day 21.

Your introduction to COM is nearly complete. However, I haven't addressed the issue of
COM errors and error checking, which merits discussion in the next section.

COM Errors

When I described the technique you use to query for interfaces, I mentioned the HRESULT.
At that time, I simply claimed it was a 32-bit value that indicated the success or failure
of a COM method call (or API call). All COM method calls should return an HRESULT,
and Microsoft has defined many standard HRESULT values (although you can easily define
your own). You'll find them in WINERROR.H.

You'll also find in WINERROR.H that each bit of the HRESULT is important. The HRESULT
is really comprised of bit fields that serve to further identify the success or failure of the
COM method call. Listing 2.8 is the verbal definition of an HRESULT from WINERROR.H:

LISTING 2.8   HRESULT Bit Field Definitions

```
 1: // HRESULTs are 32 bit values layed out as follows:
 2: //
 3: //   3 3 2 2 2 2 2 2 2 2 2 2 1 1 1 1 1 1 1 1 1 1
 4: //   1 0 9 8 7 6 5 4 3 2 1 0 9 8 7 6 5 4 3 2 1 0 9 8 7 6 5 4 3 2 1 0
 5: //   +-+-+-+-+-+---------------------+-------------------------------+
 6: //   |S|R|C|N|r|    Facility         |            Code               |
 7: //   +-+-+-+-+-+---------------------+-------------------------------+
 8: //
 9: // where
10: //
11: //     S - Severity - indicates success/fail
12: //
13: //         0 - Success
14: //         1 - Fail (COERROR)
15: //
16: //     R - reserved portion of the facility code, corresponds to
17: //             NT's second severity bit.
18: //
19: //     C - reserved portion of the facility code, corresponds to
20: //             NT's C field.
21: //
22: //     N - reserved portion of the facility code. Used to indicate
23: //             a mapped NT status value.
24: //
25: //     r - reserved portion of the facility code. Reserved for
26: //             internal use. Used to indicate HRESULT values that
27: //             are not status values, but are instead message ids
28: //             for display strings.
29: //
30: //     Facility - is the facility code
31: //
32: //     Code - is the facility's status code
```

ANALYSIS   The fields of most interest are the severity field (line 11), the facility field (line 30), and the code field (line 32). The severity field contains either 0 or 1 (success or failure, respectively). The facility field tells you more precisely the type of error that occurred, such as a Win32 error or an RPC error. The code field is a facility-specific error number.

Feel free to examine the HRESULT bits if you desire, but common COM practice will tell you not to test the severity bit for success or failure (or even check the entire HRESULT against a standard value as defined in WINERROR.H). Instead, Microsoft has provided two macros you should use to test an HRESULT for a success or failure bit setting. The SUCCEEDED() macro returns TRUE if the severity bit is a success, whereas the FAILED() macro returns TRUE if the severity bit is a failure. After you've tested for success or failure, you can check for specific errors.

Summary

Now that you've completed this day, I'm sure you can appreciate the myriad of details associated with COM (and ATL) programming. Don't be discouraged, however, because after you have read this book and tried the examples, you should be well prepared to design and implement your own COM objects.

Just remember that COM provides a data conduit for object reuse. Using a pointer to a COM interface is no different than calling a C++ object, if you're given a pointer to the object. You don't instantiate objects in quite the same manner as in C++, but it isn't much more difficult. All COM methods will return an HRESULT. Typically, you use SUCCEEDED() or FAILED() to test for the success of the COM method invocation.

Q&A

Q Where can I go to learn more about COM?

A I would start with the Microsoft COM Web site I mentioned previously. There is a lot of information there, as well as links to other locations for more information. There are also a number of books available, as you might imagine. A classic you might find interesting is Dale Rogerson's *Inside COM* from Microsoft Press (1997, ISBN 1-57231-349-8). Dale's book teaches COM programming from a pure C++ perspective (no ATL). Another good reference is the *Waite Group's COM/DCOM Primer Plus* from Sams Publishing (1998, ISBN 0-672-31492-4). If you want to understand what COM is, purchase Don Box's masterpiece, *Essential COM,* from Addison-Wesley (1998, ISBN 0-210-63446-5). This is by no means a beginner's book, but it is well worth adding to your library in any case.

Q How do I know which object it is I want to use?

A The very first time I tried using a COM object, I wondered this. Did COM provide me with a menu from which I select a given object? You'll quickly see, however, that you don't ask COM for an object to perform "this" task or "that" function. Instead, you find (or write) the object yourself when you're developing your application and provide a means to be sure the object will reside on and be properly registered within a user's computer. That is, you'll need to install it yourself with your application or be sure it's a part of the standard operating system image that Microsoft installs for each platform. The remainder of this book is dedicated to writing just such COM objects yourself.

Q How does COM marshal data between the client and the server?

A That's an excellent question and one I can answer in a brief paragraph. However, COM will use one of two mechanisms, LPC or RPC. I mentioned RPC earlier in the day. LPC, or Local Procedure Call, is based upon RPC but optimized for data exchange within a single computer (between processes). COM will use the underlying mechanism most appropriate for the location of the client and COM object. Another aspect to the data transfer is determining what information is actually passed. When you write your COM object, you will tell COM which way to send the data (the data is really coded as parameters to your interface methods). From the COM object's perspective, the data can go from the client to the COM object only (incoming data), from the COM object to the client (outgoing data), or be bidirectional (in-out data). The COM marshaling code takes this into account to optimize things a bit. Finally, there is a COM interface designed to transfer the data, IMarshal. You can implement IMarshal yourself, but doing so is an advanced topic and beyond the scope of this book.

Workshop

The Workshop is designed to help you anticipate possible questions, review what you've learned, and get you thinking about how to put your knowledge into practice. The answers to the quiz are in Appendix A, "Answers."

Quiz

1. How do you instantiate a COM object?
2. Why are interface definitions immutable after they are publicly published?
3. What is a dual interface?
4. How do you invoke the COM runtime?
5. What interface does the COM runtime call to create an instance of a COM object?
6. What is the essential difference between the STA and the MTA?
7. How is data transmitted from address space to address space?
8. What macros do you use to test for the success or failure of a COM method call?

Exercises

1. Review the code you created for Day 1 and see if you can find references to CLSIDs, IIDs, and ProgIDs. Do you see any reference to IUnknown?
2. After you have compiled and registered the object from Day 1, open the Registry Editor (regedit.exe) and search for the value 58EC7AED, which represents the first eight characters of the object's CLSID. Is the information you find similar to what you see in Figure 2.3?

WEEK 1

DAY 3

The COM Interface: COM's Foundation

Now that you've learned a little about COM (in the previous lesson), you know COM objects expose interfaces. In fact, COM revolves around interfaces. You also know that, after you define an interface and release it to someone else, you have a binding contract not to change that interface's syntactical or semantical meaning. You know that interfaces can inherit from other interfaces and, indeed, all interfaces are derived from IUnknown.

In this lesson, I'll transform interfaces from an abstract concept to something you can actually begin to implement. You manage the interface definition separately from the interface implementation. In this lesson, you'll see the interface definition. In the remainder of the book, you'll see how to implement the interfaces using ATL.

In this lesson you'll cover

- Interfaces in more depth
- COM objects and their interfaces in more detail
- The language of interface definition, IDL

Taking a Closer Look at Interfaces

Up to this point, I've described an interface as similar to a C++ class. The interface has syntactical and semantical meaning and, after it is defined, it is immutable. And as far as it goes, that's a good definition. However, you don't code abstract definitions. There has to be a way to take the abstract concept and make it concrete.

In this section, I'll begin to cement the concept of an interface. You'll see how it is derived and how you use it in code. Later in the day, I'll introduce you to the language COM programmers use to define interfaces. For now, though, I'll return to the topic of identifying interfaces.

Interface Identification: The IID

Interfaces are immutable, which indirectly leads you to the conclusion that interfaces must be uniquely named. In COM, you use a GUID to identify an interface. When a GUID is associated with a particular interface, it is called an *interface identifier* or IID.

You might be wondering, "Where do GUIDs originate?" If you want to create an interface, you need a GUID, so who provides the GUID? The answer is the COM runtime provides you with GUIDs. When you need a new GUID, you simply use the COM API call CoCreateGUID():

```
HRESULT CoCreateGuid(
  GUID  *pguid  //Pointer to the GUID on return
);
```

Assuming you included BASETYPS.H in your source file (where the GUID definition exists), you simply obtain a GUID in this fashion:

```
GUID guidMyGUID;
HRESULT hr = CoCreateGUID(&guidMyGUID);
if ( FAILED(hr) )
{
    // Some error, so respond accordingly...
}
```

Assuming the call to CoCreateGUID() worked correctly, after it has completed its work you will have a new GUID that is unique in time and space.

This is terrific if you want to create GUIDs programmatically. Often, though, you'll be more interested in creating GUIDs you can copy into your source files. For this purpose, Microsoft has provided a utility program called GuidGen. (You'll find this program in C:\Program Files\Microsoft Visual Studio\Common\Tools. The source code is also shipped as an MFC sample application.) GuidGen enables you to create a new GUID and format it in one of several ways, depending upon the source file you're working with. Figure 3.1 shows you GuidGen in action.

After you decide upon the source code format, simply click the Copy button. The associated text will be copied to the clipboard, ready for you to paste into your source file.

FIGURE 3.1

The GuidGen user interface.

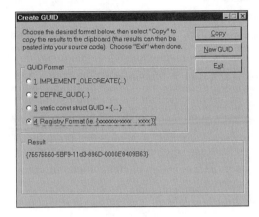

After you've created a new GUID, you can associate that GUID with an interface using IDL. You'll see how to do this later in the day. For now, let's turn to using the IID in a client application.

Because the IID is, in reality, a 128-bit data structure, in C++ there must be some way to declare the structure and allocate the memory it will require to store the data. This is the job of MIDL, which I mentioned in the previous lesson. MIDL will take your IDL source file and produce several files depending upon its compilation directives (the ATL AppWizard sets this up for you). Of interest to you here are the resulting .C and .H files that you can incorporate into your application's project. The .H file defines the IID, whereas the .C file declares the IID and provides for the memory allocation.

For example, the definition of the IHelloWorld interface (from the first lesson's sample ATL COM server) is shown in Listing 3.1

LISTING 3.1 IHelloWorld's IDL Definition

```
1: MIDL_INTERFACE("58EC7AEC-5431-11D3-896D-0000E8409B63")
2:     IHelloWorld : public IUnknown
3:     {
4:     public:
5:        virtual /* [helpstring] */ HRESULT STDMETHODCALLTYPE SayHello(
6:            /* [out] */ BSTR __RPC_FAR *pbstrMessage) = 0;
7:
8:     };
```

ANALYSIS   As you can see, the `IHelloWorld` interface derives from `IUnknown` (line 2)and has an additional method, `SayHello()`, which is pure virtual (lines 5 and 6). (It has the `virtual` keyword and is set equal to zero.) This establishes the function pointer table layout COM will use to access the `IHelloWorld` methods. The `MIDL_INTERFACE()` macro, line 1, is used as a convenience, because it really implements this code (from RPCNDR.H):

```
#define MIDL_INTERFACE(x)    struct __declspec(uuid(x)) __declspec(novtable)
```

Starting from the left, clearly the parameter x is being defined as a structure. The `__declspec()` operator is a Microsoft-specific addition to the C++ language that targets data storage. In this case, even though the structure is being defined, the compiler will allocate memory for the structure even before you declare an instance of the structure. When you use the `__declspec(uuid())` version, you're allocating memory for a GUID. The addition of the `__declspec(novtable)` qualifier simply tells the linker to remove any vtable associated with the structure. This often saves you memory. I'll discuss vtables in the next section.

You have seen what the macro says. Here is what it does for you. If you look at the first day's sample client application, you'll note I included two files MIDL generated:

```
// Add the ATL object's information
#include "..\Day1Server\Day1Server.h"
#include "..\Day1Server\Day1Server_i.c"
```

I didn't have to include both files. I could have ignored the legacy file Day1Server_i.c altogether. Had I done that, though, I would have to change the code I used to create the COM object. The original call to `CoCreateInstance()`, which looked like this

```
HRESULT hr = CoCreateInstance(CLSID_TYATLObj1,
                    NULL,
                    CLSCTX_INPROC_SERVER,
                    IID_IHelloWorld,
                    reinterpret_cast<void **>(&pIHelloWorld));
```

would then have to change to this:

```
HRESULT hr = CoCreateInstance(_uuidof(TYATLObj1),
                    NULL,
                    CLSCTX_INPROC_SERVER,
                    _uuidof(IHelloWorld),
                    reinterpret_cast<void **>(&pIHelloWorld));
```

Because the memory allocation for the IID (and CLSID) of the COM object had already been handled, the redeclaration of the IID in the Day1Server_i.c file is redundant, although in this case not in error. Presumably, Microsoft has done this to eliminate the need for the C-style declaration of GUIDs and to preclude the need for shipping two files (one to define a given GUID and another to declare it).

Both coding styles are correct, although eventually programmers will likely be using the second style exclusively. ATL, at least at this time, sticks with the legacy style and uses the _i.c file to declare the relevant GUIDs. I'll use that style throughout this book.

Having said all this, it's time I discussed the Day1Server_i.c file. Here is the relevant code from the first day's example, Day1Server_i.c:

```
const IID IID_IHelloWorld = {0x58EC7AEC,0x5431,0x11D3,
➥{0x89,0x6D,0x00,0x00,0xE8,0x40,0x9B,0x63}};

const IID LIBID_DAY1Lib = {0x58EC7AE0,0x5431,0x11D3,
➥{0x89,0x6D,0x00,0x00,0xE8,0x40,0x9B,0x63}};

const CLSID CLSID_TYATLObj1 = {0x58EC7AED,0x5431,0x11D3,
➥{0x89,0x6D,0x00,0x00,0xE8,0x40,0x9B,0x63}};
```

As you see, the object's IID, CLSID, and type library ID (which is also an IID) are declared as const values. The definition of IID is also provided in the file, slightly edited:

```
typedef struct _IID
{
    unsigned long x;
    unsigned short s1;
    unsigned short s2;
    unsigned char  c[8];
} IID;

typedef IID CLSID;
```

To avoid compilation errors, the Day1Server_i.c file should be included once, and only once, in your project. And you can see why—if it were included twice or more, you would be redeclaring the const values. Clearly, that's not syntactically legal. As a convenience, I often include this file (one for each COM object) in the stdafx.cpp file for my project.

To reiterate, MIDL compiles your object's IDL file into several other source files, at least one of which must be included in your client source code to compile (assuming you're not using the #import preprocessor directive). That's a topic for Day 9, "Creating C++ Test Clients: You Can't Test What You Can't Execute." Knowing this, it's time to see what Visual Studio actually compiles. To show you that, I'll begin with the topic of interface inheritance.

Interface Inheritance

When the designers of COM sat down and began to work their magic, they realized there had to be a mechanism for interface inheritance. At that time, C++ was still a relatively new language, but it was clear that C++ had solved inheritance issues by providing a table of pointers to the base and all derived classes. This table is known as the *vtable*, or *virtual function table*. Given a pointer to a C++ object, you obtain a pointer to the base or any derived class by casting the pointer to the desired class.

I'll talk more about casting pointers in COM later in the day, when I discuss COM objects themselves. The vtable, however, is of interest here. When implementing COM using C++, and ATL is nothing more than C++ with template support, you define your interfaces in a special C++ base class that contains nothing but pure virtual functions. (Actually, MIDL does this for you). That is, the methods that the interface supports are defined to be pure virtual functions. If I typedef the C++ keyword class to interface, an interface definition looks something like this:

```
interface IFooBar : public IUnknown
{
    virtual HRESULT Foo() = 0;
    virtual HRESULT Bar() = 0;

};
```

What this tells the compiler is that a vtable must be established for IFooBar, which derives from IUnknown. (A pointer to IUnknown will then also be stored in the vtable.) The C++ compiler will provide for the vtable's memory allocation, but it will be up to you to implement the interface's methods. That is, a pure virtual base class cannot stand on its own because the function pointers are all initialized to zero (NULL). Your C++ implementation will be derived from IFooBar, and it must provide an implementation for all the interface's pure virtual functions. If you fail to implement all the methods, the compiler will quit compiling with an error.

Caution

On several occasions I have been unlucky enough to choose an interface name (that's a name, not an IID) that matches a name found somewhere in one of the Visual Studio header files. Microsoft has identified hundreds (if not thousands) of interfaces, so the likelihood of this is great and increasing. If you choose a name for your interface that Microsoft has already defined (for example, IClassFactory), odds are you won't be using the same methods as the Microsoft-defined interface unless you specifically intend to reimplement this interface.

If you unknowingly select an interface name that matches a predefined Microsoft interface name, your code won't compile for the reason I mentioned—the methods you're implementing, in all probability, don't match those Microsoft implemented. You'll receive many compiler errors informing you that you didn't provide an implementation for this or that virtual method. When this happens, simply rename your interface in IDL and in your C++ source files and recompile.

I'll show you how to establish interface inheritance when I discuss IDL later in the lesson. Now, let's see how you change an interface after it has been established.

Changing an Interface

Actually changing an interface that you created isn't much more difficult than creating a new interface. Simply create a new IID, inherit your new interface from your old interface, and provide the new methods to the derived interface. Remember, though, to leave the existing interface unchanged because your clients depend upon the stability of that interface. When they upgrade their code, they'll likely incorporate your new interface at that time. I'll provide an example of this in Day 8, "ATL Object Methods: Adding Functionality to Your Interface."

Note

> If you're trying to replace an existing interface that a third party designed and implemented, COM has a mechanism to accomplish that task, also. It is more involved than a mere recompilation. However, I'll leave that topic for you to research in the online documentation or in a COM-specific text. If you ever need to do this, at least you'll know there is such a capability.

Now that you've seen a bit more about interfaces, it's time to roll them into objects.

Objects and Their Interfaces

Although an interface is the basis for COM implementations, it is a COM object that exposes the interfaces. A given COM object could expose a single interface, or it could expose a collection of interfaces. The choice of architecture is really up to you. There are good arguments for implementing objects both ways. As always, review all your options and select the one that best meets your development needs.

For this discussion, I'll concentrate on how interfaces are collected into an object. I'll revisit this shortly when I introduce the IDL necessary to do the job. For now, let's take a closer look at how objects are identified and their interfaces obtained.

Object Identification: The CLSID

As I've mentioned, COM objects are identified by a GUID, called a class identifier or CLSID. An object with a given CLSID might (or might not) expose an interface with a given IID. Several objects with different CLSIDs could expose interfaces with the same IID! (This is often the case when developers re-implement standard interfaces, such as when using custom marshaling.)

In theory, given a CLSID, you instantiate the object and query for interfaces of interest. In reality, you know the CLSID and the interfaces it exposes, so the process isn't as dire as guessing a CLSID and seeking an interface to use. You instantiate the object and go right for the interface you need.

If you're using objects you've developed, you have access to the files MIDL creates (discussed later in this lesson), which identify the object and its interfaces. On the other hand, if you're using a predefined object, such as Microsoft COM objects, you'll often be given a header file to define the interfaces. You will need to link to a library file to obtain the actual object and interface declarations (DirectX, for example). In some cases, you're given none of these things and have to hope the COM object in question has a type library incorporated into its code (such as ActiveX controls). If it does, Visual Studio has a mechanism for reading the type library and building the files that you'll require to compile and use the COM object (I'll discuss this in Day 18, "ATL, Class Factories, and Licensed Objects: Creating Objects and Protecting Your Investment").

As I mentioned, in most cases, you can simply obtain the interface pointer you need by calling CoCreateInstance(). In some cases, though, you'll want access to a different interface in the inheritance chain. Unlike C++, where you would simply cast the class's pointer, COM has a specific mechanism for obtaining base or other inherited interface pointers. Let's take a closer look at this process to see a little more about what it does and why.

QueryInterface() Revisited

Now that you understand interface inheritance, I can paint QueryInterface() in a slightly different light. There are two things to remember about QueryInterface():

- You can imagine QueryInterface() as COM's pointer casting operator
- Even though an object exposes multiple interfaces, be sure you're querying the correct interface

The first point tells you that you use QueryInterface() to access interfaces in the inheritance chain. You do this in the same manner as you would use C++'s dynamic_cast<>() operator to return pointers to objects in the C++ inheritance chain. For example, you might have the situation shown in Listing 3.2.

LISTING 3.2 Using C++ dynamic_cast<>() to Obtain a Base Class Pointer

```
1: class A { ... };
2:
3: class B : public A { ... };
4:
5: void f()
6: {
```

```
 7:    A* pa1 = new A;
 8:    B* pb = new B;
 9:    A* pa2 = dynamic_cast<A*>(pb);
10:    // pa2 now points to an object of type A
11: }
```

ANALYSIS In this case, class B inherits publicly from class A (line 3). Given a pointer to an object of type B (line 8), you obtain a base class pointer (to A) using dynamic_cast<>() (line 9). You pass into dynamic_cast<>() the base class type you're looking for, as well as an actual object pointer. If the cast is successful, the result is a pointer to the base class object.

QueryInterface() is very much the same, as the next example shows. This example is really pseudocode, however, because interfaces aren't declared as I've shown here. The example in Listing 3.3 is for illustration (and comparison) only.

LISTING 3.3   Using IUnknown's QueryInterface() to Obtain a Base Interface Pointer

```
 1: interface IA;
 2:
 3: interface IB : public IA;
 4:
 5: void f()
 6: {
 7:    IA* pa1 = CoCreateInstance(...); // create an instance of IA
 8:    IB* pb= CoCreateInstance(...); // create an instance of IB
 9:    IA* pa2 = NULL;
10:    pb->QueryInterface(IID_IA,&pa2); // "cast" pb to IA*
11:    // pa2 now points to an interface of type IA
12:    // pa1 and pa2 should be the same pointer value
13: }
```

ANALYSIS As you see, the structure of the code is the same as you saw in Listing 3.2, as is the result. Interface IB inherits publicly from interface IA (line 3). Given a pointer to interface IB (line 8), you obtain a pointer to its base IA interface using QueryInterface() (line 10). You have now obtained a pointer to an interface in the interface inheritance chain.

Because you're using C++, you might be tempted to simply cast an interface pointer and forgo QueryInterface(). Don't do it. For one thing, you might be dealing with a proxy DLL rather than the true COM object, in which case the cast has no meaning. You might also cause the marshaling to fail. Always obtain related COM pointers using QueryInterface().

The second point, which I mentioned previously, is meant to remind you that QueryInterface() is used to access interfaces in an inheritance chain. If you are using an object that exposes two (unrelated) interfaces, you have to call CoCreateInstance() twice to obtain pointers to the interfaces. You can't use QueryInterface() given one pointer to obtain a pointer to the other interface, even though the same COM object exposes both interfaces. The interfaces are unrelated and, therefore, know nothing of each other. QueryInterface() will fail in this case.

I've talked a lot about interfaces and objects in general terms. Now it's time to see how you actually create COM interfaces and objects. To do this, you use the Interface Definition Language and a special IDL compiler, MIDL.

The Language of Interfaces: IDL

I've sprinkled references to IDL throughout this and the previous lesson, but I've elected to defer a discussion of IDL until now. Actually, this situation is one of those "chicken and egg" scenarios. To truly understand an interface, you have to know IDL. But introducing IDL before interface concepts might be confusing. I took the second route. Now, you have enough of an understanding of interfaces and COM objects to understand IDL and what it provides.

Ideally, when you design a COM object and its interfaces, you design the interfaces first. After the interface definitions are complete, *then* you implement the interfaces. I say *ideally* because often you'll use some Visual Studio wizard to help you create code, which often masks the steps you would normally take when developing COM objects. Instantly, code exists where before there was none.

You now have an understanding of an interface. Computers, however, execute code. For the computer to understand an interface, you must codify it somehow. When you code, you compile (or interpret) the code to be sure it is correct, at least from a syntactical point of view. The code (language) you use to create an interface is IDL, and the compiler you use to compile the IDL is the *Microsoft IDL Compiler*, or MIDL (pronounced *middle*). In fact, if you used the ATL AppWizard to create a basic ATL framework, the wizard creates a basic IDL file and inserts a custom build step to run MIDL prior to the basic Microsoft Visual C++ compiler. Assuming MIDL compiled your IDL code without error, IDL will produce several output files that you'll need to correctly compile your basic COM object. I've discussed some of these files in this lesson.

At first glance, you might be surprised how closely the IDL language resembles C++. In fact, the two are very similar; so learning IDL usually isn't too challenging for seasoned C++ programmers. To prove that, let's take a look at an IDL file and see what it contains.

Layout of an IDL File

If you were to open the IDL file you generated for the first day's sample ATL COM object, you would see the code shown in Listing 3.4.

LISTING 3.4   Day1Server.idl file Contents

```
// Day1Server.idl : IDL source for Day1Server.dll
//

// This file will be processed by the MIDL tool to
// produce the type library (Day1Server.tlb) and marshalling code.

import "oaidl.idl";
import "ocidl.idl";
    [
        object,
        uuid(58EC7AEC-5431-11D3-896D-0000E8409B63),

        helpstring("IHelloWorld Interface"),
        pointer_default(unique)
    ]
    interface IHelloWorld : IUnknown
    {
        [helpstring("method SayHello")] HRESULT SayHello([out] BSTR*
pbstrMessage);
    };

[
    uuid(58EC7AE0-5431-11D3-896D-0000E8409B63),
    version(1.0),
    helpstring("Day1Server 1.0 Type Library")
]
library DAY1Lib
{
    importlib("stdole32.tlb");
    importlib("stdole2.tlb");

    [
        uuid(58EC7AED-5431-11D3-896D-0000E8409B63),
        helpstring("TYATLObj1 Class")
    ]
    coclass TYATLObj1
    {
        [default] interface IHelloWorld;
    };
};
```

3

With the exception of the parameter list for the SayHello() method, all the code in Listing 3.4 was generated automatically for you. You specified the parameters to SayHello() when you added the method to the interface, but even then the wizard added this information to the IDL file for you. So, let's see what the wizards have given to you.

The first thing you see, aside from the introductory comments, is the inclusion of two standard IDL files:

```
import "oaidl.idl";
import "ocidl.idl";
```

IDL doesn't use the same keyword as C++ for file inclusion, but the result is the same—the files are included into your file when the file is compiled. OAIDL.IDL defines the automation-based information you require to deal with COM automation and scripting. OCIDL.IDL defines the information you need to work with ActiveX specifically, although there are other important definitions in there, such as that for IClassFactory2.

The next sections are delineated by square brackets ([and]). Keywords enclosed in square brackets denote attributes to be applied to the following item (in this case the object's definition). I'm sure you've noticed that the first section identifies a COM object and its interfaces. If you have more than one interface, you see multiple interface definitions. In this example, though, the IDL file simply defines a single COM object with a single interface.

The general syntax for object definition is this:

```
[ object, uuid(string-uuid)[ , interface-attribute-list] ]
    interface interface-name : base-interface
    {
        (definition of interface methods)
    };
```

The interface definition and the definition of the interface methods clearly resemble C++ class definitions, though the keyword interface is used instead of class. The information within the square brackets provides the attributes (meta-information) about the interface. This meta-information typically provides for marshaling optimization, but that is not all you can specify.

Following the COM object definition is the definition of the object's type library, which is syntactically similar to the definition of the COM object. The keyword object is not used, and the keyword library replaces the keyword interface. As you recall, the type library is a tokenized (compiled) form of the IDL file. Unlike a COM object definition, where multiple objects can be defined, there should only be a single type library definition. The type library describes what the COM server provides, which is what the DLL or EXE provides. Clients will query the type library associated with a given DLL or EXE to see precisely what the file can do.

That's the general layout. You include some basic IDL information, define your COM objects and their interfaces, and then finally define the type library if you intend to provide one. I glossed over some details, so let's go back and take a look at how you define interfaces in IDL.

Defining Objects and Interfaces

If you refer back to Listing 3.4, you see the definition of the COM object that you created in the first lesson:

```
[
    object,
    uuid(58EC7AEC-5431-11D3-896D-0000E8409B63),

    helpstring("IHelloWorld Interface"),
    pointer_default(unique)
]
interface IHelloWorld : IUnknown
{
    [helpstring("method SayHello")]
➥HRESULT SayHello([out] BSTR* pbstrMessage);
};
```

Ignoring the object attributes for now, the interface keyword tells MIDL you're defining an interface named IHelloWorld, which derives from IUnknown. Had this been a dual interface, IHelloWorld would have derived from IDispatch. IHelloWorld has but a single method, SayHello(), which like the interface itself, has bracketed attributes. The method returns an HRESULT and accepts as a parameter a BSTR pointer named pbstrMessage.

The first interesting thing to note is the [out] attribute associated with the BSTR pointer parameter in SayHello(). As I mentioned, IDL will always enclose attributes in square brackets, and as you see, you can have attributes in many places. The [out] attribute tells MIDL the parameter will be outgoing only, so no information, other than the pointer variable itself, needs to be marshaled from the client to the server.

Some information will require marshaling from the server to the client, though. In this case, a new string will be created within the COM object and passed to the client. Knowing this level of detail enables MIDL to optimize the marshaling for you. Other parameter attributes, such as [in] and [in, out] perform other, similar optimizations. [in] parameters can be passed by value, but [out] and [in, out] parameters must be passed by reference (as pointers to the data).

You might be interested in other IDL parameter attributes as you become more proficient with COM programming, such as those aimed at passing array data back and forth from client to server. You might want to simulate the return of a value other than an HRESULT (typically for Visual Basic). For now, though, the attributes I've discussed here will be most useful to you. For a complete discussion of IDL, I would recommend Wrox Press's *COM IDL and Interface Design*, ISBN 1-86-100225-4. I'll return to IDL attributes in Day 8, when I discuss adding methods and parameters to your interface.

Moving to the SayHello() method itself, only one attribute is shown, helpstring(). This attribute isn't terribly interesting to a C++ programmer, but to a Visual Basic programmer it's very useful. When a Visual Basic programmer adds your object to his project, the help string provides him with a little more information regarding the method. Visual Basic displays the help string as programmers rummage through the list of methods your interface exports.

Other interesting method attributes include hidden, propget, propput, and propputref. The hidden attribute hides the method from type library viewers, such as Visual Basic, to preclude those programmers from using the method. In a sense, it's like marking the method as private to the interface. Actually, it's a suggestion, and the viewers are free to display the method if they wish. Typically, they don't violate your design, so hidden methods are not usually displayed.

The propXXXX attributes are all related to properties. Logically, a COM object could have properties just as a C++ class has member attributes. Unlike a C++ class, a COM object's properties are simulated—they're really values returned by interface methods. Some programming environments, such as Visual Basic, make the parameters *appear* to be simple attributes (in the C++ sense), but this is a convenience to the Visual Basic programmer.

Generally, each property will have two methods: an accessor method and a mutator method. In English, that means there is a method to get the property value and a method to set the property value. (If a property is read-only, the mutator method is not present.) The IDL method attribute propget simply indicates, to Visual Basic anyway, that the method is used to retrieve a property value. propput works in a similar manner with regard to the property mutator. The propputref attribute is used like popput, except that a reference to the property, rather than the property value itself, is provided.

The method attributes I've discussed here aren't the only attributes you can apply to an interface method, but they are the most common. You'll see a few additional attributes that you'll want to use to tailor ActiveX methods when you reach Day 16, "ATL and ActiveX: Modern Control Packaging." In any case, if you would like to see the complete list, I would again refer you to *COM IDL and Interface Design*.

Having seen both the parameter method attributes, it's time to move to the object's attributes. If you refer back to Listing 3.4, you should see this IDL code just prior to the interface keyword:

```
[
object,
uuid(58EC7AEC-5431-11D3-896D-0000E8409B63),

helpstring("IHelloWorld Interface"),
pointer_default(unique)
]
```

Here you see four attributes: `object`, `uuid()`, `helpstring()`, and `pointer_default()`. The first attribute, `object`, is required when compiling COM objects. It is required because IDL was originally designed to define interfaces for DCE RPC. If you omit the `object` attribute, MIDL will generate a DCE RPC interface rather than a COM interface. If you use the `object` attribute, you must also use the `uuid()` attribute to identify your interface by GUID.

The `helpstring()` attribute is similar to the help string that you provided for the interface's methods. It simply adds value for environments that deal primarily with type libraries.

The `pointer_default()` attribute merits some discussion. The `pointer_default()` attribute tells MIDL how to deal with all pointers except pointers that appear in parameter lists. This includes embedded pointers (such as pointers that appear in structures, unions, and arrays), as well as to pointers returned by functions. `pointer_default()` accepts one of three values: `ptr`, `ref`, and `unique`.

`ptr` pointers are *full* pointers (in IDL terms) and act just like C pointers. They can be NULL, and during a method invocation, they can change from NULL to nonNULL, just as normal C-style pointers do. Full (and unique) pointers cannot be used to describe the size of an array or union when marshaling because these pointers can have the value NULL. MIDL restricts the use of this pointer type to prevent an error that can result when a NULL value is used as the data size.

`ref` pointers are *references*. Unlike `ptr` and `unique` pointers, a `ref` pointer cannot be NULL. It must be referencing something. A reference pointer's value never changes during a method invocation, and it can't be used to allocate memory on the client. The memory must have already been allocated.

3

Note

> Pointers used in interface methods don't use the value indicated by the `pointer_default()` attribute. Instead, they are assumed to be `ref` pointers, unless individually marked with `ptr` or `unique`.

Given my previous note, you might wonder why the server example from the Day 1 worked at all, given the BSTR pointer was a `ref` pointer. After all, didn't `SysAllocString()` allocate memory on the client to store the returned BSTR? Yes, it did, but it didn't allocate memory for the pointer passed into `SayHello()`, and that's the difference. The client allocated the four bytes used to store the returned pointer, not the COM method. The COM method allocated memory for the returned data and filled the existing four bytes with a pointer to that data.

The final pointer type, `unique`, is like the `ptr` pointer type in that it can be `NULL` and can change from `NULL` to nonNULL during a method invocation. The difference is that, if a `unique` pointer changes from `NULL` to nonNULL (through allocation on the client), it is assumed the pointer will be pointing to a data object of the same type on both client and server. The data can also be *orphaned*, which is to say, if the `unique` pointer is later set to `NULL`, the client must have some other mechanism for releasing the memory. This enables the server to allocate memory on the client, but absolve itself from all responsibility for the later release of the memory (on the client). That is the client's responsibility.

Returning now to object attributes, other object attributes you will commonly see in use are `version()` and `local`. `version()` simply applies a version number (as a string) to the object. It cannot be used in combination with the `uuid()` attribute, however. If you think about it, that stands to reason. The GUID already uniquely identifies the interface, so a version number is irrelevant. A different interface version must have a different GUID. The `local` attribute is used to mark an object as nonremotable. That is, the object should not be used over a network. You might mark an object in this manner, for example, if it somehow deals with window handles or device contexts. A window handle or device context on one system is completely meaningless to a remote system.

Now that the object, or objects, have been defined, it's time to roll their information into a type library.

Defining Type Libraries

If you again refer back to Listing 3.4, you should see this code toward the end of the listing:

```
[
    uuid(58EC7AE0-5431-11D3-896D-0000E8409B63),
    version(1.0),
```

```
    helpstring("Day1Server 1.0 Type Library")
]
library DAY1Lib
{
    importlib("stdole32.tlb");
    importlib("stdole2.tlb");

    [
        uuid(58EC7AED-5431-11D3-896D-0000E8409B63),
        helpstring("TYATLObj1 Class")
    ]
    coclass TYATLObj1
    {
        [default] interface IHelloWorld;
    };
};
```

By now, a lot of this should look familiar. For example, the library has attributes of uuid(), version(), and helpstring(). Note that because the library isn't an object (there is no object attribute), the uuid() and version() attributes can both be present. You've seen what these attributes do for you, so I won't reiterate their definitions here.

The library is defined by the library keyword and is assigned the name that follows (DAY1Lib, in this case). This is immediately followed by the actual definition of the library, which begins with the importation (importlib())of two standard type libraries, STDOLE32.TLB and STDOLE2.TLB. These libraries simply provide for the base functionality that all derived type libraries should implement.

Following that, you see the definition of a single coclass, with attributes. You could imagine a *coclass* as a COM Class. Each object you've previously defined in the IDL file will have a corresponding coclass definition in the IDL file. Note that the single coclass defined here is named TYATLObj1, which happens to match the CLSID textual name. The attributes associated with the coclass are simply uuid() and helpstring(), both of which you've seen before. It's no coincidence the GUID here matches the GUID in the object definition.

The coclass definition encapsulates all the interfaces the COM object exposes, which in this case is the single interface IHelloWorld. Even though there is but a single interface for this coclass, the wizard added the default attribute. This is really more useful when a single coclass implements multiple interfaces. The default interface is the main programmable interface that the object will expose, and it is usually targeted towards scripting environments. (That makes sense, because the type library itself is similarly targeted.) I should mention it is possible to have two default interfaces. In that case, you would have a default outgoing (source) interface and a default incoming (sink) interface. You'll see this in more detail in Day 17, "ATL and Connection Points: Supporting COM's Event Model," when you learn about COM events and connection points.

That completes your tour through the IDL file. There is very much more you can do with IDL, such as define enumerations and structures, and even pass C++ code unmolested through to the resulting header file (for comments or other purposes). I'll be using some of the more advanced features IDL provides throughout the book. As I use them, I'll describe what they do for you. Given the basic background you now have, understanding more advanced features should be a simple matter.

Summary

To COM, interfaces define your objects. Without interfaces, you have no COM objects. To create interfaces the computer understands, you use the Interface Definition Language and MIDL.

In this lesson, you took a closer look at interfaces and how COM objects themselves incorporate interfaces. You examined some of the source files MIDL generated for you when your IDL file was compiled. You now know why those files are included into your client's source code (they define and declare the IIDs and CLSIDs of the COM objects your client intends to use).

You also studied the format of a real COM object's IDL file. You saw how COM objects, their interfaces, and the server's type library are defined. You also had the chance to explore some of the attributes you can apply to various pieces of the definitions to tailor the output MIDL will produce.

In the next lesson, I'll switch gears a bit and discuss C++ rather than COM. You'll work with C++ templates. So far, this book has been devoted to COM and the way you implement and use COM objects. But the *T* in ATL stands for templates, and those are C++ constructs. To be a successful ATL programmer, you must understand templates. Read on!

Q&A

Q It seems odd to me that GUIDs could possibly be unique, given so many computers. How does this work?

A The key lies with the manufacturers of network adapter cards, Ethernet. Every Ethernet card ever manufactured has a unique number assigned when it is created. After all, this is how Ethernet packets ultimately are routed to a specific Ethernet card. It's somewhat like your own postal address. It's also unique, although the postal service isn't necessarily as accurate as TCP/IP.

Knowing that, you now know how to obtain a unique value for a GUID. GUIDs also incorporate a time factor, which is primarily directed at making sure GUIDs from the same machine are unique. The combination of these two data items leads to astronomical odds against duplicate GUIDs.

Q Tell me more about this "binding contract" between the interface and the clients of the interface.

A The goal, or at least one goal, of COM is to create reusable binary objects. If clients are written to use an interface that they expect works in a certain manner, but later they connect to a different COM object exposing the same interface that actually works differently, the clients' behavior is undefined.

That's a nice way to say the client code might work just fine, but it's more likely the client application will die a horrible death. It's the "undefined behavior" you want to avoid. So, it's taboo to modify an interface after other people have had access to that interface. Rather, you should create a new interface and advertise that fact. Soon, the world will use your new interface.

Workshop

The Workshop is designed to help you anticipate possible questions, review what you've learned, and get you thinking about how to put your knowledge into practice. The answers to the quiz are in Appendix A, "Answers."

Quiz

1. How do you create a GUID?
2. How would you create a GUID as text to be pasted into your source code?
3. What two server source files should be included in your client's source code? Do you need both?
4. What is a vtable?
5. Can a single COM server (DLL or EXE) support more than one COM object?
6. Can several COM objects support the same interface (IID)?
7. How do you cast COM pointers?
8. What is the general layout of an IDL file?
9. What are the required attributes for a COM object in IDL?
10. How are a COM object's properties and methods different?
11. Do you have to implement a type library?

Exercises

1. MIDL creates files in addition to the .h and the _i.c files I mentioned. Can you spot which ones?

2. Read the MSDN article, "Designing COM Interfaces," by Charlie Kindel (included with the MSDN CDs or online at
   `http://msdn.microsoft.com/library/techart/msdn_design.htm`).

DAY 4

C++ Templates: You Can't Code What You Don't Understand

I have to be honest. The first time I saw ATL was also the first time I saw C++ templates in use commercially. Frankly, the syntax was new to me—and bizarre. I fought more with the template syntax than I fought to understand what the pieces of COM ATL were meant to implement. When I finally took a step back and learned how templates were formed, ATL made more sense as well.

Even though I didn't fully understand templates at first, I could use ATL. Now I can do more than just use ATL: I understand what ATL is doing, which is more important. Therefore, in this lesson, I'll explain pure C++ templates. No COM. No ATL. Just templates. The goal is to demystify templates themselves so that when you look at a given ATL template, you won't get hung up on the syntax of templates.

In this lesson you will learn about

- C++ templates in general
- Templates that implement classes
- Templates that implement functions

What Is a Template?

When I look at templates now, I realize they're nothing more than a way to implement an algorithm with a generic data type. Imagine you have a stack algorithm. In many cases, when you implement your algorithm, you implement it for specific data types. That is, you might implement a stack to keep track of integer IDs of some kind. Later, you might find you need a stack for string information. Often, I see the developer literally copy the integer stack source code into a new file and change all of the data type references from integer to string. While reusing source code is a good thing to do, this style of programming (cut, paste, then edit) often introduces bugs and requires nearly as much time to implement as a completely new implementation from scratch. With C++ templates, there is a better way.

The goal of the template is to capture the algorithm, leaving the insertion of the data type until compilation time. The data type is passed into the template as a parameter, and the compiler manages the rest for you. You can pass in multiple data types, and you can even pass in nontype arguments (which pass through as their data type rather than a generic data type).

You can, where you need to, explicitly tell the compiler what data type to use. This is called *explicit specialization*. This is especially useful when you actually want to handle some data types differently than others, for example when sorting integers versus strings. If you have provided an explicit specialization of the sorting template, the compiler will use the specialized version in lieu of the generalized version, depending upon the data type you've passed to the template when you invoke it. I won't mention this technique again in this lesson, but you should be aware that it exists.

There are two basic types of C++ templates. The first implements an entire C++ class, while the second simply implements a specific function. Let's first look at the generic class, then the generic function.

Class Templates

When you specify a C++ class, you use this general syntax:

```
class class-name
{
```

```
...
};
```

The keyword `class` tells the compiler you're about to define a class with the name `class-name`. In much the same way, you specify a C++ class template using this syntax:

```
template <class Ttype> class class-name
{
...
}
```

Using the `template` keyword with the generic type `Ttype` (a C++ class, in this case) identifies the template. Following that, you'll note that you use the standard syntax for class definition, as in the previous example.

When you use a C++ class, you simply declare a variable of the class type, in this manner:

```
class CFoo {...}; // define the CFoo behavior
CFoo ob; // create an instance of CFoo
```

Happily, using a template is not much more difficult, as shown in Listing 4.1.

LISTING 4.1   Example Template Definition and Specialization

```
1: class CFoo {...}; // define the CFoo behavior
2: template <class T> CBar {...}; // use a generic class when defining
3:                                // the behavior of CBar. The letter
4:                                // 'T' is commonly used, though the
5:                                // actual name doesn't matter...
6: CBar<CFoo> ob; // create an instance of CBar using CFoo as the
7:                // specialization
```

ANALYSIS   In the case of the template, note you don't have to create an instance of `CFoo` prior to passing it into `CBar` (line 6). The compiler will handle that for you. In this case, `CFoo` represents the data type that `CBar` will deal with (note `CFoo` was defined in line 1). Therefore, you're really creating an object of type `CBar` that might create `CFoo`s as required (that depends upon the implementation of `CBar`).

Now that you've seen the general form of template syntax, let's see a more concrete example of a template class definition.

Defining Template Class Behavior

Defining a templated class isn't really much different than defining any other C++ class, so it is not too surprising to find they're commonly defined in a header file. Using the `CBar` example I began above, you might find code such as this in `CBar`'s header file:

```
template <class T> class CBar
{
    CBar();
    virtual ~CBar;
    void FnOne(T t);
    int FnTwo(int i, T t);
    T FnThree();
};
```

I'll present a real-world example shortly. For now, though, notice the class and its member functions are defined pretty much as you'd expect. There's no outrageous syntax to worry about, except for the template keyword before the class definition. In this case, aside from the constructor and destructor, CBar has three methods, FnOne(), FnTwo(), and FnThree().

FnOne() has as a parameter an object of type T, which is the template specialization parameter. If you created a CBar object with an integer as the specialization parameter, you can imagine all references to T will be replaced with int. FnTwo() has two parameters. The first is nothing more than an integer, and the second is the specialization parameter. FnThree() is interesting because it returns an object of type T.

That's all there is to defining a template. Note that there is nothing that says you can't have these situations, however:

```
template <class T, class S> class C1 {...};
template <class T = char, int i> class C2 {...};
template <class T> class C3 : public C2 {...};
```

The first template uses two specialization parameters instead of just one. The second template uses a specialization parameter and an integer. Note the specialization parameter has a default type of char. And the final template simply shows templates can inherit from base classes (which might have been templates themselves).

Now that you've learned more about defining a template, it's time you looked at the syntax for implementing the templated class. Although the syntax isn't quite as straightforward, armed with what you've learned, you'll see it isn't too complicated.

Implementing Template Class Behavior

The template's methods can be implemented in either a header (.H) or an implementation (.CPP) file. In many cases, the template's methods are implemented immediately following the definition of the class (this is how ATL does it). No matter which method you use, the template file(s) still must be included into your source file. As with any C++ class, for the linker to be able to link the resulting executable image, you must bring the class definition into the source file in which you use the class. I'll revisit this when I discuss the example in the next section.

The template's methods are implemented using syntax similar to the implementation of normal C++ methods. The difference is that the template keyword and the specialization parameter precede each method. For the CBar example I've been using, I implement five methods: the constructor and destructor; FnOne(); FnTwo(); and FnThree(). Listing 4.2 shows how I would do this.

LISTING 4.2 Example CBar Template Implementation

```
 1: template <class T> CBar<T>::CBar()
 2: {
 3: }
 4: template <class T> CBar<T>::~CBar()
 5: {
 6: }
 7: template <class T> void CBar<T>::FnOne(T t)
 8: {
 9:     // Work with the specialization parameter, t
10:     ...
11:     return;
12: }
13: template <class T> int CBar<T>::FnTwo(int i, T t)
14: {
15:     // Work with the two parameters, i and t
16:     ...
17:     return i;
18: }
19: template <class T> T CBar<T>::FnThree()
20: {
21:     // Create an instance of the specialization
22:     // parameter.
23:     T t;
24:
25:     // Work with the specialization parameter t
26:     ...
27:     return t; // presumably uses copy constructor!
28: }
```

ANALYSIS The syntax certainly looks bizarre, at least to me, but it's clear what's going on. The template keyword, lines 1, 4, 7, 13, and 19, tells the compiler that something related to a template is coming up. The template keyword is followed by a declaration of the specialization class (<class T>). From there it's normal C++ syntax, with the exception of the specialization parameter concatenated to the end of the class name, just prior to the scoping operator (CBar<T>). This simply ties the specialization parameter to the class and enables it to be used within the class method.

I've waved my hands long enough. It's time to show you a real example instead of these conjured classes that I've been using. In the next section, then, I'll build a templated stack class.

An Example

A stack is a well-known algorithm. You push things onto the stack, and then you pop them off again. The items are accessed in a *LIFO* fashion, which stands for last-in, first-out. Essentially, the items are popped off of the stack in the reverse order in which you pushed them. Stacks are typically used for temporary storage.

My generic stack class, therefore, has two methods in addition to the constructor and destructor—push() and pop(). Listing 4.3 shows you how I defined my stack template, which you'll find in this day's example, ClsTemplate.h.

LISTING 4.3 Class Definition for a Generic Stack

```
 1: // ClsTemplate.h : Defines the stack template.
 2: //
 3:
 4: #if !defined(__CLSTEMPLATEHDR)
 5: #define __CLSTEMPLATEHDR
 6:
 7: // Define the stack template. Note we pass in the
 8: // specialization parameter as well as the preferred
 9: // stack size (which defaults to 5 items).
10: template <class T, int iStackSize = 5> class CStack
11: {
12:     public:
13:         // Construction and destruction
14:         CStack();
15:         virtual ~CStack();
16:
17:         // Stack operations
18:         void push(T t); // 'T' is type, 't' is parameter
19:         T pop();
20:
21:     protected:
22:         int m_iTop;
23:         T m_tStack[iStackSize];
24: };
25:
26: #endif // __CLSTEMPLATEHDR
```

ANALYSIS In addition to the public methods push() and pop() (lines 18 and 19), you see I have protected attributes m_iTop and m_tStack (lines 22 and 23). m_iTop are used to point to the next available stack location, which is implemented in the array m_tStack. A more robust stack might use some storage mechanism other than an array, but for demonstration purposes, this should do nicely. (I'll ask you to implement the stack using a linked list as an exercise.)

Note that I chose to pass two arguments to the template—the specialization type and a value used to size the stack, which is in reality an array. One of the handy things about a template is the capability to size things, such as arrays, when you specialize the template (that is, when you use it). Normally, you can't simply change the size of an array, but in this case, I set the default to five stack positions. When I actually use the stack template, I'm free to pass in any array value I want, within reason, of course.

I chose to implement the template functions in a separate file, ClsTemplate.cpp. This is a matter of style, and I could have just as easily implemented them in the header file ClsTemplate.h. I have to provide implementations for four methods—the constructor, the destructor, push(), and pop(). Listing 4.4 shows you how I implemented these methods.

LISTING 4.4 Method Implementation for a Generic Stack

```
 1: // ClsTemplate.cpp : Implements the stack template.
 2: //
 3:
 4: #include "stdafx.h"
 5: #include "ClsTemplate.h"
 6:
 7: #include <iostream>
 8: using namespace std;
 9:
10: // Construction and destruction
11: template <class T, int iStackSize> CStack<T, iStackSize>::CStack() :
12:     m_iTop(0)
13: {
14: }
15:
16: template <class T, int iStackSize> CStack<T, iStackSize>::~CStack()
17: {
18: }
19:
20: // Push items onto the stack
21: template <class T, int iStackSize> void CStack<T, iStackSize>::push(T t)
22: {
23:     // Check to see if we're full
24:     if ( m_iTop == iStackSize ) {
25:         // We're full...
26:         cout << "Stack is full!" << endl;
27:     } // if
28:     else {
```

continues

4

LISTING 4.4 continued

```
29:        // Push the item...
30:        m_tStack[m_iTop++] = t;
31:     } // else
32: }
33:
34: // Pop items from the stack
35: template <class T, int iStackSize> T CStack<T, iStackSize>::pop()
36: {
37:     // Check to see if we're empty
38:     if ( !m_iTop ) {
39:         // We're empty...
40:         cout << "Stack is empty!" << endl;
41:         return 0; // NULL on empty stack...
42:     } // if
43:
44:     // Pop the item...
45:     return m_tStack[ —m_iTop];
46: }
```

ANALYSIS   As you can see, there are no surprises. Items are simply added to the array (lines 21 through 32) and removed again (lines 35 through 46), as you would expect. Remember, though, this is a template. Nothing really is done here unless you *use* the template. Therefore, I had to create a file that uses a stack.

I chose to create a console-based application simply to test the stack. You'll find this in Listing 4.5.

LISTING 4.5 Using the Generic Stack

```
 1: // main.cpp : Defines the entry point for the console application.
 2: //
 3:
 4: #include "stdafx.h"
 5: #include "ClsTemplate.h" // definition of the template
 6: #include "ClsTemplate.cpp" // implementation of the template
 7:
 8: #include <iostream>
 9: using namespace std;
10:
11: int main(int argc, char* argv[])
12: {
13:     // Declare an integer stack
14:     CStack<int,10> s1;
15:
16:     // Declare a double stack
```

```
17:     CStack<double,10> s2;
18:
19:     // Push some items...
20:     s1.push(2);
21:     s1.push(4);
22:     s1.push(6);
23:     s1.push(8);
24:     s2.push(2.2);
25:     s2.push(4.4);
26:     s2.push(6.6);
27:     s2.push(8.8);
28:
29:     // Now display the items
30:     for ( int i = 0; i < 4; i++ ) {
31:         // Display the integer at this stack position
32:         cout << "Stack position (integer) " << i;
33:         cout << ", value " << s1.pop() << endl;
34:     } // for
35:
36:     for ( i = 0; i < 4; i++ ) {
37:         // Display the double at this stack position
38:         cout << "Stack position (double) " << i;
39:         cout << ", value " << s2.pop() << endl;
40:     } // for
41:
42:     // For fun, try to pop another item...
43:     s1.pop();
44:
45:     return 0;
46: }
```

If you compile and execute this, the output you see is shown in Figure 4.1.

FIGURE 4.1

ClsTemplate *generic stack screen output.*

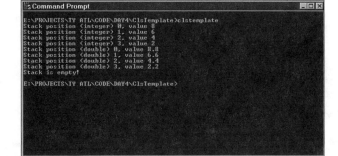

You've now seen how to create generic C++ classes. As it happens, C++ also supports adding templated C++ methods. ATL doesn't do this, to my knowledge, but I mention them for completeness, in case you run across them in the future.

Function Templates

As the name implies, function templates are used to build generic functions rather than entire C++ classes, as you did previously. Perhaps the function stands alone, or just as likely, the generic function is a method of a C++ class (which can also be templated). Just as you use a templated class to deal with arbitrary data types when creating an instance of the class, you use a templated function to deal with arbitrary parameter data types.

The syntax for defining a generic function is actually quite similar to the definition of a normal C++ function. Of course, you must add the `template` keyword and the specification class, but other than that this should look familiar:

```
template <class Ttype> return-type function-name(parameter list)
{
    ...
}
```

The specialization parameter is often used as part of the parameter list or as a return value. Note the function returns a value (`return-type`), has a name (`function-name`), and has a parameter list, just as you would expect.

In the next section, I'll show you how generic functions are defined. Then, in the following sections, I'll describe how they're implemented and show a real-world example.

Defining and Implementing a Generic Function

Because you're dealing with a function rather than a class, you really don't need a separate definition and implementation for your generic function. Instead, you can do everything at once.

For example, let's say you have a generic function called `DoSomething()`, defined in this manner:

```
template <class T> int DoSomething(T t, int i)
{
    // Do something!
    ...
    return 0;
}
```

Everything the compiler requires to compile this function is present. In this case, the specialization parameter T is passed to the function, as is an integer value, and DoSomething() returns an integer value.

To make this a bit clearer, let's move to a real example. Many developers have had to swap variable contents, and before templates, this was typically done with a preprocessor macro. Let's see how this is done with a generic function.

An Example

The generic function I'm going to show you is intended to replace this macro, one many programmers have probably written:

```
#define SWAPVARS(i,j) { int x = i; i = j; j = x; }
```

This macro works fine, except it's designed for integer values alone. If you wanted to swap double values, you'd have to define another macro. There is a better way—use the generic function.

Listing 4.6 shows you the better way. The template swapvars<>() accepts any data type when you specialize the function template (you'll find this implemented in the FnTemplate example application). In this case, I use it to swap integers, doubles, and characters. Granted, I had to type a bit more than I typed for the macro I showed earlier, but then, I only had to type the template once instead of creating three different macros (one for each data type I mentioned). If you consider that, I actually saved myself some code! (Note you may need to implement a copy constructor and operator=() in more complicated data types to be able to correctly swap them using this template.)

LISTING 4.6 Using a Generic Swap Function

```
 1: // FnTemplate.cpp : Defines the entry point for the console application.
 2: //
 3:
 4: #include "stdafx.h"
 5:
 6: #include <iostream>
 7: using namespace std;
 8:
 9: // Define our generic function to swap two values
10: template <class T> void swapvars(T &a, T &b)
11: {
12:     // Declare a temporary holder
13:     T t;
14:
15:     // Swap the values
16:     t = a;
```

continues

LISTING 4.6   continued

```
17:        a = b;
18:        b = t;
19: }
20:
21: int main(int argc, char* argv[])
22: {
23:        // Declare some variables and fill them with values
24:        int i = 2, j = 4;
25:        double x = 10.4, y = 20.8;
26:        char a = 'A', b = 'B';
27:
28:        // Display the original values
29:        cout << "Original integer values: " << i << ", " << j << endl;
30:        cout << "Original double values: " << x << ", " << y << endl;
31:        cout << "Original char values: " << a << ", " << b << endl;
32:        cout << endl;
33:
34:        // Swap the values
35:        swapvars(i,j);
36:        swapvars(x,y);
37:        swapvars(a,b);
38:
39:        // Display the swapped values
40:        cout << "Swapped integer values: " << i << ", " << j << endl;
41:        cout << "Swapped double values: " << x << ", " << y << endl;
42:        cout << "Swapped char values: " << a << ", " << b << endl;
43:
44:        return 0;
45: }
```

The screen output from this program is shown in Figure 4.2.

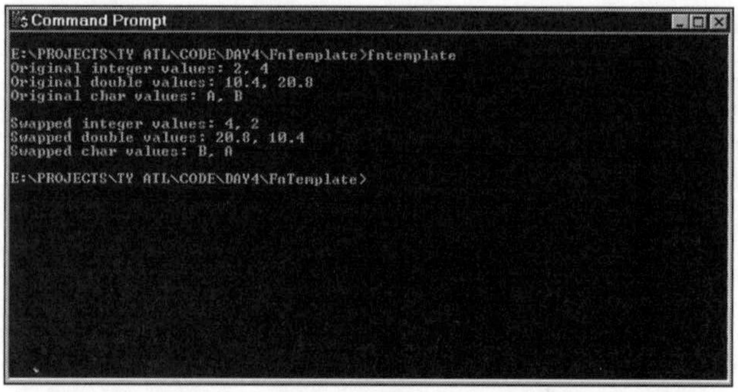

FIGURE 4.2

FnTemplate *generic function screen output.*

I've shown you a generic function that stands on its own. It is possible to create generic functions within C++ classes, and even those classes can be templates. Things can get complicated quickly. However, the time you save and the reuse benefits you gain are generally well worth the effort.

> **Caution**
>
> The Visual C++ compiler has a bug, or a feature (if you'd rather look at it that way), that forces generic functions within generic classes to be inline. Furthermore, the function body (or bodies) must reside in the .H file, or the code will not compile.

Summary

In this lesson, I introduced you to the C++ template and discussed how you can produce generic C++ classes and functions. I tried to demystify the template syntax, which at first glance can be intimidating. Given what you've seen in this lesson, you should be able to look at the ATL class definitions, either in the online help or in their respective source files, and understand what they're doing and how they're doing it. In the next lesson, Day 5, "ATL Architecture: How ATL Implements COM," you'll begin your trek into the workings of ATL.

Q&A

Q Will I really need to completely understand templates before I use ATL?

A No. I certainly didn't when I started using ATL. In my case, though, I often refer to the source code Microsoft kindly provided with Visual Studio (in fact, at times I'd be lost without the source code). If you also tend to dive into the source code to see how thing are implemented, or to understand why something isn't working as you believe it should, you would be wise to familiarize yourself with templates. That's what the *T* in A*T*L stands for, after all.

Workshop

The Workshop is designed to help you anticipate possible questions, review what you've learned, and get you thinking about how to put your knowledge into practice. The answers to the quiz are in Appendix A, "Answers."

4

Quiz

1. Why are templates beneficial?
2. What is a specialization parameter?
3. Can a generic class be derived from other classes? From other templates?
4. Do the template and the implementation have to be in the same source file?
5. Can a generic function reside in a class? In a generic class?

Exercises

1. Modify the generic stack to become a generic queue.
2. Modify the generic stack to use a linked list rather than an array.

DAY 5

ATL Architecture: How ATL Implements COM

You've been introduced to quite a few concepts thus far. You learned how to create an ATL-based COM object and a test client; you learned a bit about COM itself; you studied interfaces, objects, and IDL; and you looked at C++ templates and their syntax. The pieces are all in place to begin your study of ATL.

If you start by looking at the architecture of ATL and understand the overriding philosophy behind it, much of what you run across when you're on your own will make more sense to you. Without a big picture, it's all too possible to get lost in the weeds.

That's the intent of this lesson. I'll roll ATL into a neat package and present it to you as a single technology. Subsequently, the remainder of the book will deal with ATL's constituent parts as I target specific ATL constructs and implementations.

In this lesson, you will see

- The philosophy of ATL
- How ATL implements IUnknown
- How ATL implements other aspects of COM
- How ATL objects are registered

The Philosophy of ATL

The overriding goal of the ATL development team was to provide you with the leanest, tightest COM programming template library possible. If they found any fat in their work, they cut it out. They want ATL to produce the smallest, fastest COM objects possible.

Everything in ATL is geared towards this goal. For example, if you are compiling a standard Windows application, or even a console application, the compiler loads and initializes the C runtime library for you. This isn't so with ATL. If you use C library functions from within your ATL COM object, you'll find you can compile and execute a debug version of your object. However, when you build a release version, you'll get this link error you see in Figure 5.1.

FIGURE 5.1

Missing C runtime link error.

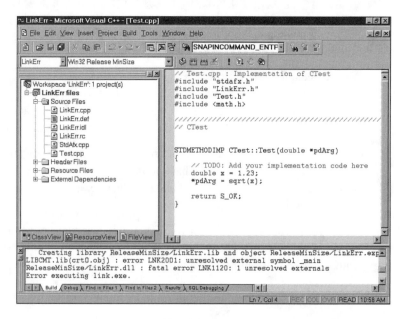

You receive this error because, although ATL excludes the C runtime library from the release version of the object, you're trying to use the C runtime library. Does this mean you can't use the C runtime library? Not at all, feel free. On the other hand, if you don't use the C runtime library, you don't have to sustain the overhead of loading and initializing the C runtime environment. The default, which produces the fastest, tightest code, excludes using the C runtime library. If you want different behavior, simply change the way ATL handles things.

> **Tip**
>
> To use the C runtime library in release builds, you must remove the preprocessor definition for _ATL_MIN_CRT. Access the project's settings by clicking the Project, Settings menu in Visual Studio. Then select the C/C++ property page. Select Preprocessor from the Categories drop-down list control. You'll find the _ATL_MIN_CRT as the last definition under the Preprocessor Definitions edit control. Delete the text and the preceding comma and click OK. Now you should be able to compile your project.

Another area where you'll find ATL's code frugality in effect is when registering an ATL-based COM component. All COM components must be registered in the Registry (with the exception of COM+ components, but that topic will wait for Day 21, "ATL and MTS: Coding with a Better COM"). It won't be surprising to find many COM objects re-implementing the same code to self-register.

ATL takes a different approach—ATL uses the ATL Registrar object, which is a COM object implemented in ATL.DLL. All of the basic registration code is in the Registrar rather than in your ATL COM object. All that your object requires is a tiny Registry script, which you'll find in the wizard-generated .RGS file associated with your ATL project. This script is simply placed into your ATL object's resources. When called upon to register itself, your object will send the script to the Registrar to actually be recorded into the Registry. The script is far smaller than the equivalent registration code. You'll see this in more detail later in the lesson.

But just as when you use the C runtime library, you don't have to register your ATL COM object in this fashion. You can define the preprocessor value _ATL_STATIC_REGISTRY and have the registration coded added to your compiled object. It adds about 5K, and although that might not seem like much, remember the goal of the ATL team was to shave every byte and CPU cycle they could. To them, I'll bet saving 5K per object is a major victory. Note, if you compile a release version of your object using the minimum dependency setting, this value is defined for you, so you need not redefine it.

The final detail I'll mention is that you'll find ATL uses C++'s *multiple inheritance capability*. That means the C++ implementation of your COM object, which uses ATL templates, will inherit from more than a single base class. Contrast this to, for example, MFC's implementation that uses nested interface classes. With ATL, your interfaces display an *is-a* relationship because of the multiple inheritance. For example,

5

IMyInterface *is-a* IUnknown interface. With MFC, the nested class becomes an attribute of a parent class, effecting a *has-a* relationship. That's not quite as natural. IMyInterface doesn't really *have-a* IUnknown interface, it *is-a* IUnknown interface. To correct for this, MFC provides the plumbing and overhead necessary to present the nested interface to the COM runtime with the proper interface inheritance chain intact. It's that plumbing and overhead that ATL seeks to avoid, and the ATL team shaves some fat by using multiple inheritance. ATL simply maps things right into the vtable, which is far more efficient.

The bottom line is that if you want more features and functions added to your ATL object, you must take some action to force that to happen, depending upon what it is you're trying to do. As a rule, ATL objects are very Spartan by nature. Knowing this, it's time to look at how ATL implements the various pieces of COM.

IUnknown

As you know, all COM interfaces must be derived from and implement IUnknown. IUnknown is used to query for derived interfaces and maintain the object's reference count. But if you refer back to the ATL-based COM object (MyFirstATLObj.cpp) that you developed on the first day, "Getting Started: Your First ATL COM Object," you won't see a reference to IUnknown in the definition of the C++ class that implements the IHelloWorld interface:

```
class ATL_NO_VTABLE CMyFirstATLObj :
    public CComObjectRootEx<CComSingleThreadModel>,
    public CComCoClass<CMyFirstATLObj, &CLSID_TYATLObj1>,
    public IHelloWorld
{...};
```

If the C++ class derives from the classes I've shown, from where does the class CMyFirstATLObj inherit the IUnknown behavior? The answer lies with these two templates: CComObjectRootEx<> and CComCoClass<>.

IUnknown, as implemented by ATL, is actually split into several templates, all of which work together to provide the capability your object requires to properly support IUnknown. ATL doesn't do things this way to make life more complicated, because implementing IUnknown isn't terribly difficult. Instead, ATL does things in this manner to allow you more flexibility while maintaining a smaller resulting code base.

For example, take the class CMyFirstATLObj you just saw. Figure 5.2 shows you the bigger picture.

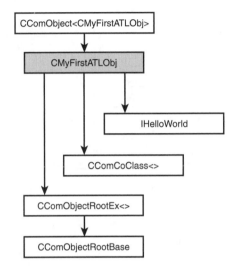

FIGURE 5.2

ATL's object hierarchy for the CMyFirstATLObj *class.*

Starting from the bottom box in Figure 5.2, the CComObjectRootBase class provides the counter variable used for reference counting, as well as a base implementation of QueryInterface(). CComOjbectRootEx<>, the template, uses another template as a specialization parameter. This specialization template depends upon the threading model you have selected for your object, CComSingleThreadModel<> or CComMultiThreadModel<>. (The difference is the multithreaded version implements thread-safe increments and decrements.) Here, then, you have the basis for IUnknown.

The CComCoClass<> template manages your class factory's default implementation and your object's aggregation model. I discussed class factories in Day 2, "Exploring COM: The Technology ATL Supports." but I deferred discussing aggregation until this point. *Aggregation* refers to one of the three ways in which your COM object might use another COM object.

Your COM object might simply be a client of another COM object, in which case the relationship between your object and the client is no different from any you've seen thus far in this book. Perhaps, though, you want to give a capability that another object provides to your own clients without re-implementing the other object's code. In this case, you have two choices. You can completely hide the fact that another object is actually in use. This ensures that all interface method calls are directly deferred to the other object (referred to as *containment*). You can also aggregate the other COM object, which means your COM object provides clients with the other object's interface pointer directly. These last two situations are shown in Figure 5.3.

5

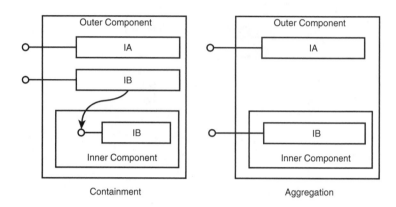

FIGURE 5.3

Containment versus aggregation.

You'll use containment when another object's interface provides nearly all of the functionality you want, but not all. This way, you can provide the added functionality while hiding the fact that another object is used for some of the work. You'll use aggregation, on the other hand, when another object exposes an interface *exactly* as you want it to be implemented. You can pass the other object's interface directly to a client (who believes the interface is your own).

But this presents a problem. A client of the other COM object will expect to be able to obtain an IUnknown pointer to an interface you've implemented. It expects the same pointer value as an IUnknown pointer to the aggregated interface. This is how the COM Specification tells you to check whether two interface pointers point to the same object—you compare their IUnknown pointer values. Yet there is no way your interface's IUnknown pointer and the aggregated interface's IUnknown pointer can possibly have the same value!

The solution to this is to write COM objects with aggregation in mind. If a COM object determines it is to be aggregated, it defers its own IUnknown pointer (called the *inner*–IUnknown) to the controlling object's IUnknown (called the *outer*–IUnknown). A COM object knows it is to be aggregated when it is created with a nonNULL controlling (outer) IUnknown pointer value.

I'm sure all of this aggregation stuff doesn't sound very easy to use, but in reality it isn't terribly difficult. It mostly involves a bit of bookkeeping. However, you use ATL to implement COM objects because ATL manages the details for you.

Perhaps you also see why a template such as CComCoClass<> exists. You're free to tailor the aggregation model you desire for a given COM object without changing other base implementations, such as for reference counting. Your object must still supply code to maintain a reference count no matter if it's aggregated or not.

If you now refer back to Figure 5.2, CMyFirstATLObj has three base classes:
CComObjectRootEx<>, CComCoClass<>, and IHelloWorld. You've just seen what functionality CComObjectRootEx<> and CComCoClass<> provide. Of course, you implement
IHelloWorld, although you'll learn more about that shortly when I discuss the various
ATL maps. Note CMyFirstATLObj can't be instantiated directly, although that might not
be terribly obvious. (A clue is given with the ATL_NO_VTABLE macro, which tells the compiler not to generate a vtable. A vtable is not required for a base class that can't be
instantiated directly.) CMyFirstATLObj is a pure virtual base class.

That's why you see CMyFirstATLObj as a base class for CComObject<>, which provides
users of your COM object a way to actually instantiate a CMyFirstATLObj object with an
IHelloWorld COM interface. CComObject<> also provides the final details required to
support IUnknown, as everything ATL requires to create an instance of your object is now
specified.

To summarize, IUnknown is implemented by several ATL templates and base classes:
CComObjectRootEx<>, CComCoClass<>, and CComObject<>. The reason is simple, even if
the implementation is not. ATL provides you with maximum flexibility to tailor the operation of your COM object. The next piece of the ATL puzzle involves the ATL Module,
which is what ATL uses to perform much of the work required to keep your object up
and running.

Note

> Although not related to ATL's implementation of IUnknown, CComObjectRootEx<>
> provides two helpful methods of which you should be aware: FinalConstruct()
> and FinalRelease(). FinalConstruct() enables you to complete any initial-
> ization prior to your COM object's use by a client, and FinalRelease()
> enables you to perform any cleanup actions required as your COM object is
> destroyed. To be sure your COM object isn't inadvertently released during
> FinalConstruct(), you can use the DECLARE_PROTECT_FINAL_CONSTRUCT macro
> (this is especially useful when aggregating other objects). The online docu-
> mentation has more details.

5

The ATL Module

Every ATL COM object has an instance of an ATL module, which is an instance of
CComModule (or a derived class, such as CExeModule for local servers). It is the module
that manages some of the other COM details for you, such as for locking your server into
memory, providing for thread-specific heaps, and for registering your server and type
library when required to do so.

If you go back to the example you created in Day 1 and open the Day1Server.cpp file, you should see this line of code near the top of the file:

```
CComModule _Module;
```

This line of code declares an instance of CComModule called _Module.

 Caution

> Although you are free to create classes derived from CComModule and use them in place of CComModule, you cannot change the instance from _Module to something else. ATL uses the variable name _Module within its header files (especially ATLCOM.H). If you rename the instance of the module, your project will not compile.

Let's take a closer look at what the ATL Module provides. I'll start with the basic functionality you can expect, and then I'll move to different types of modules for different situations.

Keeping the COM House

The ATL Module is a critical ATL component because it is here your COM object's thread information is kept. For example, the CComModule class derives from _ATL_MODULE, which is defined in ATLBASE.H as shown in Listing 5.1.

LISTING 5.1   _ATL_MODULE Structure Definition

```
 1: struct _ATL_MODULE
 2: {
 3: // Attributes
 4: public:
 5:     UINT cbSize;
 6:     HINSTANCE m_hInst;
 7:     HINSTANCE m_hInstResource;
 8:     HINSTANCE m_hInstTypeLib;
 9:     _ATL_OBJMAP_ENTRY* m_pObjMap;
10:     LONG m_nLockCnt;
11:     HANDLE m_hHeap;
12:     union
13:     {
14:         CRITICAL_SECTION m_csTypeInfoHolder;
15:         CRITICAL_SECTION m_csStaticDataInit;
16:     };
17:     CRITICAL_SECTION m_csWindowCreate;
18:     CRITICAL_SECTION m_csObjMap;
19: // Original Size = 100
20: // Stuff added in ATL 3.0
21:     DWORD dwAtlBuildVer;
```

```
22:      _AtlCreateWndData* m_pCreateWndList;
23:      bool m_bDestroyHeap;
24:      GUID* pguidVer;
25:      DWORD m_dwHeaps;      // Number of heaps we have (-1)
26:      HANDLE* m_phHeaps;
27:      int m_nHeap;          // Which heap to choose from
28:      _ATL_TERMFUNC_ELEM* m_pTermFuncs;
29: };
```

ANALYSIS   Of particular interest here is the fact that CComModule is storing such things as an instance handle (lines 6 and 7), an instance to the type library (line 8), and the lock counter (line 10). (This is used to lock the COM object's server into memory. It is separate from the object's reference count. The server lock keeps the DLL or EXE in memory rather than releasing an object's interface.) The CComModule also stores a handle to a heap (line 11) and an important pointer to an object map (line 9), which I'll discuss shortly.

Clearly there is some important stuff being cached here, and a surprising amount of this information is available to you through the _Module variable. For example, you can access the server's instance handle, m_hInst, by using CComModule::GetModuleInstance().

CComModule itself provides additional capabilities (such as the mechanism you use to register your COM object and its type library), manages the lifetime of the object's class factory, and provides handy wrapper methods for accessing module-specific data, as you've seen earlier.

In general, you'll use either CComModule (for DLLs) or CExeModule (for EXEs), but you do have an interesting alternative. CComModule clearly is tied to a specific thread. If you want to manage access to more than one thread, you can use CComAutoThreadModule instead, which is the topic of the next section.

Different Module Classes for Different Needs

If you've written Windows NT services, you know you often require multiple threads to handle various situations. ATL provides you with another module class, CComAutoThreadModule, designed to provide you with a thread pool you can use to create your objects. Generically, a *thread pool* is a collection of threads you have at your disposal to perform various, required tasks. In this case, the threads will be used to run instances of your object. CComModule, of course, is designed to work with a single thread.

The ATL AppWizard, however, will assume you want CComModule functionality. To gain access to CComAutoThreadModule, you must derive a new module class (typically in STDAFX.H), such as that shown in Listing 5.2.

LISTING 5.2 Example CThrdPoolModule Class Definition

```
1: class CThrdPoolModule :
2: public CComAutoThreadModule<CComSimpleThreadAllocator>
3: {
4: public:
5:     LONG Unlock()
6:     {
7:         LONG l = CComAutoThreadModule<CComSimpleThreadAllocator>::Unlock();
8:         if (l == 0)
9:             PostThreadMessage(dwThreadID,WM_QUIT,0,0);
10:        return l;
11:    }
12:
13:    DWORD dwThreadID;
14: };
```

Note

If you use this module, you'll need to remove the _ATL_MIN_CRT preprocessor definition from any release build to allow you access to the C runtime library.

ANALYSIS CComAutoThreadModule has two methods of particular interest, CreateInstance() and GetDefaultThreads(). CreateInstance() selects a thread and creates an instance of the object in the selected apartment. You use this to create the multiple objects CComAutoThreadModule provides. GetDefaultThreads() simply returns to you the default number of threads available to you, which is hard-coded to be four times the number of processors installed on the particular computer that happens to be running your object. Should you want more than four threads per processor in your thread pool, you'll have to build your own module class. (Use CComAutoThreadModule as a guide. You'll find the source code for CComAutoThreadModule in ATLBASE.H.)

I've mentioned that the module and the classes that implement IUnknown use maps. Let's now look at ATL maps to see both what they are and how they are used.

ATL Maps

ATL can't know beforehand precisely what methods your interface will support. In fact, ATL can't know precisely how many objects a given ATL COM server will support. For ATL to know these things, the objects you implement and the interfaces they expose must be supplied in maps ATL can read at runtime.

ATL COM Map

The first type of map to which I referred is called the *ATL COM Map*, and its job is to tell ATL which interfaces are supported by a given COM object. Returning to the code you'll find in MyFirstATLObj.h, you should see the COM map specified as such:

```
BEGIN_COM_MAP(CMyFirstATLObj)
    COM_INTERFACE_ENTRY(IHelloWorld)
END_COM_MAP()
```

The macros BEGIN_COM_MAP(), COM_INTERFACE_ENTRY(), and END_COM_MAP() simplify the source code a bit and make it a lot easier to read. BEGIN_COM_MAP() expands to that shown in Listing 5.3.

LISTING 5.3 BEGIN_COM_MAP() Macro Definition

```
 1: #define BEGIN_COM_MAP(x) public: \
 2:     typedef x _ComMapClass; \
 3:     static HRESULT WINAPI _Cache(void* pv, REFIID iid,
 4: ➥void** ppvObject, DWORD dw)\
 5:     {\
 6:         _ComMapClass* p = (_ComMapClass*)pv;\
 7:         p->Lock();\
 8:         HRESULT hRes = CComObjectRootBase::_Cache(pv, iid,
 9: ➥ppvObject, dw);\
10:         p->Unlock();\
11:         return hRes;\
12:     }\
13:     IUnknown* _GetRawUnknown() \
14:     { ATLASSERT(_GetEntries()[0].pFunc == _ATL_SIMPLEMAPENTRY);
15: ➥return (IUnknown*)((int)this+_GetEntries()->dw); } \
16:     _ATL_DECLARE_GET_UNKNOWN(x)\
17:     HRESULT _InternalQueryInterface(REFIID iid, void** ppvObject) \
18:     { return InternalQueryInterface(this, _GetEntries(), iid,
19: ➥ppvObject); } \
20:     const static _ATL_INTMAP_ENTRY* WINAPI _GetEntries() { \
21:     static const _ATL_INTMAP_ENTRY _entries[] = { DEBUG_QI_ENTRY(x)
```

5

ANALYSIS Now you can see why there is a macro for this! It looks quite complicated, but essentially all that's happening here is BEGIN_COM_MAP() provides a few additional C++ class methods and declares an array of function pointers. In the macro you see these methods:

- _Cache() (line 3)
- GetRawUnknown() (line 13)
- _InternalQueryInterface() (line 17)
- _GetEntries() (line 15)

_Cache() is used for more advanced ATL features such as aggregation and *tear-off interfaces* (which are simply interfaces that defer their initialization until the last minute, typically, to conserve resources such as database connections). GetRawUnknown() returns the IUnknown pointer for the object (which is quite efficient if you, yourself, require your object's IUnknown pointer). _InternalQueryInterface() isn't the object's QueryInterface() function itself, but it is used by ATL to query for an interface. The fact that an interface pointer can be returned by a global function increases the efficiency of the code, especially considering each interface (C++) class must duplicate the code. Finally, _GetEntries() returns an entry into the function pointer array _entries[]. At this point, you see other macros destined to fill the array. I'll discuss those macros in a moment.

END_COM_MAP() expands to this and is used to terminate the list and provide for the pure definitions of the IUnknown methods, as shown in Listing 5.4.

LISTING 5.4 END_COM_MAP() Macro Definition

```
 1: #ifdef _ATL_DEBUG
 2: #define END_COM_MAP() {NULL, 0, 0}}; return &_entries[1];} \
 3:     virtual ULONG STDMETHODCALLTYPE AddRef( void) = 0; \
 4:     virtual ULONG STDMETHODCALLTYPE Release( void) = 0; \
 5:     STDMETHOD(QueryInterface)(REFIID, void**) = 0;
 6: #else
 7: #define END_COM_MAP() {NULL, 0, 0}}; return _entries;} \
 8:     virtual ULONG STDMETHODCALLTYPE AddRef( void) = 0; \
 9:     virtual ULONG STDMETHODCALLTYPE Release( void) = 0; \
10:     STDMETHOD(QueryInterface)(REFIID, void**) = 0;
11: #endif // _ATL_DEBUG
```

ANALYSIS The macro defines a terminating array member, {NULL, 0, 0}, and returns a pointer to the (interface pointer) array (lines 2 or 7, depending upon the compiler settings).

> **Tip**
>
> _ATL_DEBUG is used in conjunction with _ATL_DEBUG_QI and _ATL_DEBUG_INTERFACES to instruct ATL to display, in the debugger's output window, the IID of each interface queried for by the client (and in the case of _ATL_DEBUG_INTERFACES, you'll also see the reference count). It's often helpful, even instructive, to see what interfaces are queried for and when. Oftentimes things don't work precisely as you might imagine.

In between BEGIN_COM_MAP() and END_COM_MAP(), you see the COM_INTERFACE_ENTRY() macro, which expands to this:

```
#define COM_INTERFACE_ENTRY(x)\
    {&_ATL_IIDOF(x), \
    offsetofclass(x, _ComMapClass), \
    _ATL_SIMPLEMAPENTRY},
```

COM_INTERFACE_ENTRY() is simply adding another member to the _entries[] array defined in BEGIN_COM_MAP(). The entry itself consists of the IID of the interface, the offset of the derived (C++) class from its base class, and a pointer to a function used to create an instance of the class (conveniently hidden behind the macro _ATL_SIMPLEMAPENTRY).

But COM_INTERFACE_ENTRY() isn't the only macro available for interface mapping. Others are available that tailor aspects of the interface or its creation. Here are all of the macros available to you:

- COM_INTERFACE_ENTRY()
- COM_INTERFACE_ENTRY_BREAK()
- COM_INTERFACE_ENTRY_NOINTERFACE()
- COM_INTERFACE_ENTRY_IID()
- COM_INTERFACE_ENTRY2()
- COM_INTERFACE_ENTRY2_IID()
- COM_INTERFACE_ENTRY_FUNC()
- COM_INTERFACE_ENTRY_FUNC_BLIND()
- COM_INTERFACE_ENTRY_TEAR_OFF()
- COM_INTERFACE_ENTRY_CACHED_TEAR_OFF()
- COM_INTERFACE_ENTRY_AGGREGATE()
- COM_INTERFACE_ENTRY_AGGREGATE_BLIND()
- COM_INTERFACE_ENTRY_AUTOAGGREGATE()

5

- COM_INTERFACE_ENTRY_AUTOAGGREGATE_BLIND()
- COM_INTERFACE_ENTRY_CHAIN()

As you can see, there are a great many macros you can use. Which one you use depends upon many things, and I'd encourage you to research these macros in the online help as space constraints preclude me from describing each in detail. There are a couple I would like to mention further, in addition to the important COM_INTERFACE_ENTRY() macro I've already discussed (which simply adds an entry to the array).

The COM_INTERFACE_ENTRY_IID() macro enables you to pass in the IID of the interface at hand. You'll find this useful if the textual interface identifier doesn't have the form IID_*name*. COM_INTERFACE_ENTRY2() is useful when you have a single interface supported by two C++ base classes. This macro tells ATL to turn to two C++ classes for the interface implementation instead of the typical single C++ class.

That's how the interface (COM) map is established. When your object is instantiated and a particular interface is requested, ATL will search the COM map for the interface in question. If the interface is there, ATL returns it. If not, the client will receive an error HRESULT (E_NOINTERFACE, 0x80004002).

Tip

ATL searches the _entries[] array from beginning to end for a specified interface IID. To increase ATL's efficiency, be sure to put commonly used interfaces at the beginning of the COM map. ATL will find the interfaces more quickly if you do so. Don't be concerned about editing the COM map, even though the wizard generated the code for you. Simply move the frequently used interface macro(s) toward the beginning of the COM map and recompile your object.

Now you know how ATL handles interfaces for a given object. Although this technique might seem convoluted, it is actually quite efficient, especially when your object supports many interfaces. You probably won't be surprised, then, to find ATL uses a similar mechanism to determine what objects a given DLL or EXE supports. This map is called the ATL *Object Map*, and is the topic of the next section.

ATL Object Map

Returning to the ATL source code you created in the first lesson, open the Day1Server.cpp file and look for this code:

```
BEGIN_OBJECT_MAP(ObjectMap)
OBJECT_ENTRY(CLSID_TYATLObj1, CMyFirstATLObj)
END_OBJECT_MAP()
```

These lines specify your object map, and it's no coincidence they're global (static) in scope and are declared in the same file as the exported DLL support functions. ATL will search the object map in the same way it searched the COM map to find an individual object's supported interface.

And just like the COM map, the object map uses several macros to make reading the code a bit easier on the eyes. Happily, they're not as complicated as those you saw associated with the COM map! The three macros you should see are BEGIN_OBJECT_MAP(), OBJECT_ENTRY(), and END_OBJECT_MAP(). Let's look at each to see what they're doing under the covers.

If you open ATLCOM.H, you should find the definition of BEGIN_OBJECT_MAP():

```
#define BEGIN_OBJECT_MAP(x) static _ATL_OBJMAP_ENTRY x[] = {
```

This macro merely declares a static array of _ATL_OBJMAP_ENTRY values. _ATL_OBJMAP_ENTRY is a structure containing information about each of the COM objects the server file supports. Its definition looks like Listing 5.5 (from ATLBASE.H).

LISTING 5.5   _ATL_OBJMAP_ENTRY Macro Definition

```
 1: struct _ATL_OBJMAP_ENTRY
 2: {
 3:     const CLSID* pclsid;
 4:     HRESULT (WINAPI *pfnUpdateRegistry)(BOOL bRegister);
 5:     _ATL_CREATORFUNC* pfnGetClassObject;
 6:     _ATL_CREATORFUNC* pfnCreateInstance;
 7:     IUnknown* pCF;
 8:     DWORD dwRegister;
 9:     _ATL_DESCRIPTIONFUNC* pfnGetObjectDescription;
10:     _ATL_CATMAPFUNC* pfnGetCategoryMap;
11:     HRESULT WINAPI RevokeClassObject()
12:     {
13:         return CoRevokeClassObject(dwRegister);
14:     }
15:     HRESULT WINAPI RegisterClassObject(DWORD dwClsContext,
16: ➡DWORD dwFlags)
17:     {
18:         IUnknown* p = NULL;
19:         if (pfnGetClassObject == NULL)
20:             return S_OK;
21:         HRESULT hRes = pfnGetClassObject(pfnCreateInstance,
22: ➡IID_IUnknown, (LPVOID*) &p);
23:         if (SUCCEEDED(hRes))
24:             hRes = CoRegisterClassObject(*pclsid, p, dwClsContext,
25: ➡dwFlags, &dwRegister);
26:         if (p != NULL)
```

continues

LISTING 5.5 continued

```
27:                p->Release();
28:          return hRes;
29:    }
30: // Added in ATL 3.0
31:    void (WINAPI *pfnObjectMain)(bool bStarting);
32: };
```

ANALYSIS I won't go through this in great detail, but you can see it contains things ATL would be interested in accessing quickly, such as the object's CLSID (line 3) and pointers to the object's class factory and creation function (lines 5 and 6 respectively). It's simply a handy container for information ATL will want to access quickly and often.

The object map items themselves can be either OBJECT_ENTRY() or OBJECT_ENTRY_NON_CREATEABLE(). The essential difference between these map entries is that an OBJECT_ENTRY() object can be created using CoCreateInstance() by an external client, whereas OBJECT_ENTRY_NON_CREATEABLE() objects are registered, but cannot be externally created. You might use OBJECT_ENTRY_NON_CREATEABLE() when creating server-private objects.

You can see this difference when you expand the macros. Here is the macro for OBJECT_ENTRY():

```
#define OBJECT_ENTRY(clsid, class) {&clsid, class::UpdateRegistry,
➥class::_ClassFactoryCreatorClass::CreateInstance,
➥class::_CreatorClass::CreateInstance, NULL, 0,
➥class::GetObjectDescription, class::GetCategoryMap,
➥class::ObjectMain },
```

As you can see, the OBJECT_ENTRY() macro completes the _ATL_OBJMAP_ENTRY structure with the object's (known) information. ATL now can access this information quickly when searching for and instantiating a given object.

The OBJECT_ENTRY_NON_CREATEABLE() macro is very similar to the OBJECT_ENTRY() macro except that certain _ATL_OBJMAP_ENTRY values are set to NULL:

```
#define OBJECT_ENTRY_NON_CREATEABLE(class) {&CLSID_NULL,
➥class::UpdateRegistry, NULL, NULL, NULL, 0, NULL,
➥class::GetCategoryMap, class::ObjectMain },
```

An OBJECT_ENTRY_NON_CREATEABLE() object is assigned a CLSID of CLSID_NULL and has no functions to register or revoke a class object. Note this means ATL won't present this object to an external client. That does not mean the object itself can't be created. Other objects contained within the same server DLL (or EXE) can create an instance of an OBJECT_ENTRY_NON_CREATEABLE() object because they have knowledge of the specific object in question (you provide this when you write the code). This mechanism simply makes the given object private to the server file.

After all the objects are inserted into the map, the map must be terminated. In the usual ATL fashion, the map is terminated using an ending macro, END_OBJECT_MAP(), which expands to this:

```
#define END_OBJECT_MAP()   {NULL, NULL, NULL, NULL,
➥NULL, NULL, NULL, NULL}};
```

The map ends with a NULL-filled entry and has the (required) closing brace and semicolon.

You've now seen how ATL knows what objects a given server file supports. If ATL finds the object in the object map, it can look to the COM map for the particular object to see if a given interface is supported. That's ATL, however, not COM. It's now time to see how ATL supports object registration, which is how COM itself knows an object exists on a given system. That's next!

The ATL Registrar Object

As you read in Day 2, all COM objects must be registered. True, the registration mechanism will change with the advent of COM+, but there is still some sort of registration. Prior to ATL, you implemented registration yourself, but if you've written much Registry-access code, you know that writing that code isn't much fun. Moreover, it's all boilerplate code, which is to say, very little of the code changes from COM object to COM object.

ATL comes to your rescue by providing for COM object registration. And better yet, ATL has the capability to support registration using another COM object, which means your object doesn't need to contain the redundant, boilerplate code. As a result, you spend less time writing and debugging registration code, and your object's resulting footprint is much smaller.

ATL does this using the ATL Registrar, which is a COM object with the CLSID CLSID_Registrar ({44EC053A-400F-11D0-9DCD-00A0C90391D3}) that supports the IRegistrar interface ({44EC053B-400F-11D0-9DCD-00A0C90391D3}). You can find the methods that IRegistrar exposes by examining ATLIFACE.H. The ATL.DLL server file implements the Registrar object.

You shouldn't need to conjure up the Registrar yourself. Instead, ATL handles that for you. You will have to provide a registry script that the Registrar will understand. I'll explain more about registry scripts shortly.

5

When I addressed registration in Day 2, I skipped some detail, preferring to address the finer points in this section. Before I explain the Registrar and registry scripting in more detail, let me go back and more fully explain the registration process in general, at least as it applies to legacy COM objects. I'll discuss COM+ registration issues in Day 21.

COM Registration Revisited

As you know, COM servers come in two forms—in-process (DLLs) and local (EXEs). Both servers can be remote objects. In both cases, the COM servers must provide a mechanism for their constituent COM objects to register some important information into the given computer's Registry database.

This information includes such things as the COM object's CLSID and associated server's file path, the CLSID's related ProgID, and the IID of the object's type library, if any. If the server is a DLL, you'll find its threading model specified. There is additional information available in many cases, but what I've mentioned here is most important, at least for this discussion.

This information finds its way into the Registry when each object the server supports registers itself. The underlying code to perform the actual registration is often similar, but the mechanism to kick off this registration differs between DLLs and EXEs.

Executable servers are told to register and de-register their objects by using a command line argument (/RegServer and /UnregServer respectively). When the EXE is provided these command line arguments, it should perform any required registration (or deregistration) and terminate the application.

Dynamic link library servers, on the other hand, must export four functions (according to the COM Specification), although only two of those functions are actually responsible for registration. The functions are

- DllCanUnloadNow()
- DllGetClassObject()
- DllRegisterServer()
- DllUnregisterServer()

DllCanUnloadNow() provides for DLL memory locking, so that COM can determine if the DLL can be removed from memory. If COM wants to remove the DLL from memory, but the DLL is supporting COM objects with valid reference counts outstanding, DllCanUnloadNow() will return FALSE. If the DLL can be unloaded from memory, DllCanUnloadNow() will return TRUE.

`DllGetClassObject()` is available for COM to easily obtain a class factory for a given CLSID. When a new object is created, COM will grab a pointer to its class factory using `DllGetClassObject()` and hang onto it while the DLL is resident in memory. When the DLL is unloaded, COM will revoke the class factory for the object that the DLL supported.

For registration purposes, the DLL must export `DllRegisterServer()` and `DllUnregisterServer()`. Not surprisingly, each function does as it claims— `DllRegisterServer()` registers the COM objects, and `DllUnregisterServer()` de-registers them.

The information that is written to the Registry is placed in the `HKEY_CLASSES_ROOT` *hive* under the `CLSID` key. The Registry information for the COM object that you developed is partially shown in Figure 5.4.

FIGURE 5.4

Registry information for the `CLSID_TYATLObj1` *object.*

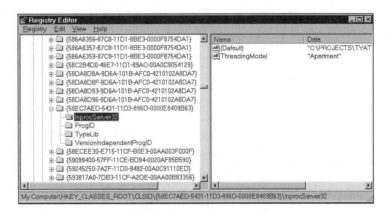

Figure 5.4 is a screen-shot of the Registry Editor on my computer. It shows some of the information recorded into the Registry when the COM object from Day 1 was registered. Note you can see the server's file path and the DLLs threading model (apartment). The information you see in Figure 5.4 is the minimum COM requires to locate the COM object's server, to activate it, and to pass back to you a pointer to a new COM object of your choice. Because I used ATL to develop the COM object, let's now see how ATL implements COM object registration.

ATL Registry Scripting

I let the cat out of the bag earlier when I mentioned that ATL uses the ATL `Registrar`. You now know *what* ATL uses to register COM objects. The question remaining is *how* does ATL know what to register?

The answer is that you, or the ATL AppWizard or Object Wizard, must create a registry script the Registrar will use to extract the Registry information to be placed into the Registry. You can see a registry script in action if you open the first day's .RGS file. You should see something similar to Listing 5.6.

LISTING 5.6   Day1Server's Registry Script

```
 1: HKCR
 2: {
 3:     TYATL.Object1.1 = s 'TYATLObj1 Class'
 4:     {
 5:         CLSID = s '{58EC7AED-5431-11D3-896D-0000E8409B63}'
 6:     }
 7:     TYATL.Object1 = s 'TYATLObj1 Class'
 8:     {
 9:         CLSID = s '{58EC7AED-5431-11D3-896D-0000E8409B63}'
10:         CurVer = s 'TYATL.Object1.1'
11:     }
12:     NoRemove CLSID
13:     {
14:         ForceRemove {58EC7AED-5431-11D3-896D-0000E8409B63} =
15: ➥s 'TYATLObj1 Class'
16:         {
17:             ProgID = s 'TYATL.Object1.1'
18:             VersionIndependentProgID = s 'TYATL.Object1'
19:             InprocServer32 = s '%MODULE%'
20:             {
21:                 val ThreadingModel = s 'Apartment'
22:             }
23:             'TypeLib' = s '{58EC7AE0-5431-11D3-896D-0000E8409B63}'
24:         }
25:     }
26: }
```

ANALYSIS   Let's pick this script apart to see what makes it tick. To begin, in line 1 you see the keyword HKCR, which tells the Registrar the data to follow (in the brackets) goes into HKEY_CLASSES_ROOT. That makes sense given what you know about COM object registration.

The next block of code you see is this (lines 3 through 6):

```
TYATL.Object1.1 = s 'TYATLObj1 Class'
    {
        CLSID = s '{58EC7AED-5431-11D3-896D-0000E8409B63}'
    }
```

This tells the Registrar to create a key (under HKEY_CLASSES_ROOT) called TYATL.Object1.1 and assign it a string value of "TYATLObj1 Class". Under that key, add a new value CLSID (of type string) that contains the string "{58EC7AED-5431-11D3-896D-0000E8409B63}". What you've done is to write the versioned ProgID to the Registry and to add the associated CLSID. Given this ProgID (such as when using Visual Basic to create a client application), COM will come here to determine which CLSID to use to actually instantiate the object. Note the ProgID sports version one.

Following the versioned ProgID, you see the version-less ProgID (lines 7 through 11):

```
TYATL.Object1 = s 'TYATLObj1 Class'
    {
        CLSID = s '{58EC7AED-5431-11D3-896D-0000E8409B63}'
        CurVer = s 'TYATL.Object1.1'
    }
```

This is similar to the previous code block, but note the difference. This code writes the ProgID to the Registry without a version. The CurVer key (again set to version one) indicates the current version.

The next block is even more interesting, as it modifies the CLSID key (starting with line 12):

```
NoRemove CLSID
{
    ...
}
```

Note the keyword NoRemove. This tells the Registrar *not* to remove the CLSID key when the COM object de-registers itself. This is *critical*! The Registrar is a powerful tool, and it will happily clean the system's Registry of *all* values if you let it. In this case, you don't want to remove the CLSID key if the Registrar is told to de-register the COM object using this script.

However, the next code block not only allows the Registrar to remove the keys and values, it *requires* it, as shown in Listing 5.7.

LISTING 5.7 Day1Server's CLSID Registration Code Block

```
 1: ForceRemove {58EC7AED-5431-11D3-896D-0000E8409B63} = s 'TYATLObj1 Class'
 2: {
 3:     ProgID = s 'TYATL.Object1.1'
 4:     VersionIndependentProgID = s 'TYATL.Object1'
 5:     InprocServer32 = s '%MODULE%'
 6:     {
 7:         val ThreadingModel = s 'Apartment'
 8:     }
 9:     'TypeLib' = s '{58EC7AE0-5431-11D3-896D-0000E8409B63}'
10: }
```

5

ANALYSIS When registering, the `Registrar` will create a key named {58EC7AED-5431-11D3-896D-0000E8409B63} under `HKEY_CLASSES_ROOT\CLSID` (line 1). When de-registering, the `Registrar` will *completely* remove the {58EC7AED-5431-11D3-896D-0000E8409B63} key and all subkeys and data. In this code block you see the same key/value pairs you saw in Figure 5.4. Note the script expanded the replaceable parameter %MODULE% to the actual path to the server's file (line 5).

Having seen a real script, you can now see the basic form emerge:

    Key = Value

In this case, `Key` is written to the Registry with a default value of `Value`. If you prefaced `Value` with the keyword `val`, the value will be added to the Registry as a named value. Values can be strings (keyword `s`), decimal (keyword `d`), or binary (keyword `b`). The values themselves are enclosed in single quotes.

Any given key can be prefaced with `NoRemove`, `ForceRemove`, or `Delete`. `NoRemove` forces the key to remain even after deregistration (the default action is to remove the key/value pair). `ForceRemove` causes the key/value to first be removed, then be re-written upon registration. This is useful when underlying key/value pairs are changing between registrations. `Delete` is used to force deletion when de-registering (usually not specified because this is the default action). The braces indicate key levels. `CurVer` is under `TYATL.Object1`, which is, in turn, under `HKEY_CLASSES_ROOT`, and so on.

You're not limited to modifying Registry data under `HKEY_CLASSES_ROOT`, either. If you added this code to the first day's .RGS file, recompiled, and re-registered, then opened the `HKEY_CURRENT_USER/Software/TYATL` key using the Registry editor, you should see the key `Message` with the string value `"Hello, World!"` (see Listing 5.8).

LISTING 5.8   Example `HKEY_CURRENT_USER` Registry Script Code Block

```
 1: HKCU
 2: {
 3:     NoRemove Software
 4:     {
 5:         ForceRemove TYATL = s 'Teach Yourself ATL Test Registry Entry'
 6:         {
 7:             val Message = s 'Hello, World!'
 8:         }
 9:     }
10: }
```

The valid Registry hives you can access are

- HKCR (HKEY_CLASSES_ROOT)
- HKCU (HKEY_CURRENT_USER)
- HKLM (HKEY_LOCAL_MACHINE)
- HKPD (HKEY_PERFORMANCE_DATA)
- HKDD (HKEY_DYN_DATA)
- HKCC (HKEY_CURRENT_CONFIG)

The final thought I'll leave you with is you do not have to use the COM-based ATL Registrar. You can, if you want, compile the Registrar code into your COM server, which you might want to do to preclude having to ship ATL.DLL. To do this, simply define the preprocessor value _ATL_STATIC_REGISTRY in your project's settings (use the C/C++ tab, Preprocessor category). This will add approximately 5K to your compiled module, but the added size might be well worth it to preclude shipping another DLL simply to register your COM object. Note this is done for you if you compile using the release version, minimum dependency setting.

 Note

> Note the ATL Registrar (ATL.DLL) comes in both ANSI and Unicode varieties. Should you need to ship ATL.DLL to other systems, be sure you install the correct version (Win9x will use the ANSI version, whereas WinNT will use the Unicode version). You'll find the redistributable versions on the first of the Visual Studio CDs. The Unicode version will be in the OS\System directory whereas the ANSI version will be in the OS\System\ANSI directory.

5

And that completes ATL and COM registration, at least for legacy COM objects. I'll leave you with this warning: The Registrar is powerful, and as I mentioned, it will happily remove all sorts of Registry keys you definitely don't want removed (such as HKEY_CLASSES_ROOT/CLSID). If you make a mistake here, you'll be reloading Windows, so *be careful*.

Summary

In this lesson, I provided a deeper discussion of ATL and how ATL implements COM. I began with a dissertation of the ATL philosophy, which is to produce the tightest, fastest code possible. I then addressed how ATL manages IUnknown, the granddaddy interface all COM interfaces must support. Then I went into the COM and object maps and described how the macros you see there actually implement the maps. I talked about how

ATL uses the maps to determine what objects are supported on a given server and what interfaces are supported by a given object.

Finally I addressed COM and COM object registration, as well as ATL's high-performance implementation, the ATL `Registrar`. I also described the syntax and use of registry scripts. In the next lesson, I'll revisit the ATL AppWizard and more fully explore the code the wizard provides when you select the various AppWizard options.

Q&A

Q **You mentioned ATL is lean and mean, but it requires several base classes and templates to support something as simple as `IUnknown`. Why is this?**

A The answer is simply that, although there appears to be a lot of code to wade through, it's very efficient and easily customizable (a good feature to support if you're a template). It's not that ATL uses the minimum amount of code required for a specific case, but rather that ATL uses the minimum code necessary to support the widest variety of cases, yet still be quite efficient.

Q **In most cases do I need to mess with changing the ATL object's C++ class's base classes by hand?**

A Often you don't, and certainly, for the more common object implementations, you can use what the wizards have provided to you. There are special cases, though, and I'd be remiss if I didn't at least mention there are other ATL base templates available to you to manage those cases. (An example of a special case is `ISupportsErrorInfoImpl`, which you will meet in Day 10, "ATL and Errors: What to Do When Things Break.")

Workshop

The Workshop is designed to help you anticipate possible questions, review what you've learned, and get you thinking about how to put your knowledge into practice. The answers to the quiz are in Appendix A, "Answers."

Quiz

1. What is the overriding goal of ATL?
2. What ATL classes and templates are used to implement `IUnknown`?
3. How does C++ multiple inheritance (versus nested classes) better support the COM object model?

4. Of what purpose are the ATL COM map and object maps?

5. How does ATL support self-registration, and why must I use it judiciously?

Exercises

1. Open atlbase.h and atlcom.h and peruse the source code you find there. (You'll find most of the mysterious macros ATL uses defined in these two files.)

2. Modify the registry script from Day 1 to write a value to
HKEY_LOCAL_MACHINE\Software\TYATL. Does this value disappear when you de-register the COM server? (You can de-register the COM server by right-clicking on the DLL in the Windows Explorer and selecting the context menu option Unregister COM Server.) Please heed my warnings!

5

DAY 6

The ATL Wizards:
Back to Basics

If you think back to what you learned in the first lesson, creating an ATL-based COM object is a two-step process. First, you create some framework code using the ATL AppWizard, and then you customize the framework using the ATL Object Wizard. Now that you have had some exposure to ATL and COM, it's time to revisit these wizards to understand exactly what the code they provide does for you. After all, it's tough to modify (and enhance) code you don't understand.

In this lesson, I will deal first with the ATL AppWizard. Initially, it appears there isn't much to the wizard. But as you'll see, it will generate very different frameworks depending upon which options you select.

Then, given the basic ATL server framework you created, I'll go on to describe the ATL Object Wizard, which you'll use to help you add COM objects to the server framework. I'll give you some details regarding several of the objects the wizard will insert for you as well. When you're through, I'm sure you'll be amazed by how much code the Visual Studio wizards will create for you with very little effort on your part.

So let's get started. In this lesson, you'll learn about

- The ATL AppWizard basic options
- The basic DLL server framework
- The basic EXE server framework
- The basic NT service framework
- Invoking the ATL Object Wizard
- Some of the objects the wizard produces and what they can do for you
- The basic options for those objects and what they mean

The ATL AppWizard

You might recall the ATL AppWizard from the first day, but to reiterate, I've placed its screen image into Figure 6.1.

FIGURE 6.1

The ATL AppWizard.

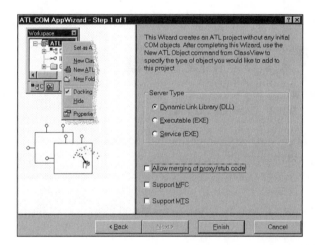

As you can see from Figure 6.1, there really isn't much to the AppWizard, as far as Visual Studio AppWizards go. Compare the ATL AppWizard to the MFC AppWizard you used in Day 1 "Getting Started: Your First ATL COM Object," for example. The selections you make here have very far-reaching implications. Clearly, the selection of server type—DLL, EXE, or NT service—makes for very different implementations after the AppWizard has generated your framework code.

The remaining options also greatly affect your code, although only if you select an in-process (DLL) server framework (the option controls themselves are disabled if you select a server type other than DLL). They affect performance, object size, and even the environment in which the object will live and breathe.

I'll begin by discussing the types of servers you can implement and list some of the files the wizard produces and their basic contents. Then, in later sections, I'll talk about the options you have when using an in-process server. Later in the day, I'll examine the code the wizard produces. First, though, let's talk about the types of servers the wizard produces.

Server Type

As I've mentioned, there are three types of servers the wizard can produce:

- Dynamic Link Library (in-process server)
- Executable (local server)
- NT Service (service-based local server)

You've read quite a bit so far about DLL-based servers, but I haven't addressed EXE-based servers to any great degree. I certainly haven't discussed NT services, a complete discussion of which is beyond the scope of this book. Therefore, I'll discuss the files related to each type of server, and then I'll address some of the details surrounding the local COM server.

When you create a basic ATL framework project, the AppWizard will provide you with several source files. These files are common to all the types of ATL frameworks you can create (where *<project>* is the project name you provided when you created the project):

- RESOURCE.H
- *<project>*.CPP and *<project>*.H
- *<project>*.IDL
- *<project>*.RGS
- *<project>*ps.MK and *<project>*ps.DEF
- *<project>*.DSP and *<project>*.DSW

RESOURCE.H is typically used to define symbols commonly used in your project, such as for string table entries and control identifiers. *<project>*.CPP and *<project>*.H will contain the basic code required to establish your server, whether it's a DLL or an EXE. If it's an EXE, you'll find the traditional local server is a bare-bones, Windows-based application (it implements a message pump). The service-based local server, however, is a console application (it has no message pump). Note the local server code doesn't bring up a window—it handles its COM requirements and, thereafter, just pumps messages. If you want a user interface, you'll need to add that code yourself.

Of course, because you're creating COM components, you have a *<project>*.IDL file. Because you're using ATL, you'll find your registry script in the *<project>*.RGS file. You automatically get two files used to create your proxy/stub DLL, *<project>*ps.MK,

6

the DLL's makefile, and *<project>*ps.DEF, the DLL's exported function definition file. Naturally, to even compile your project, you must have a project and workspace file, *<project>*.DSP and *<project>*.DSW, respectively.

If you've elected to create an NT service-based server, these are all the files you will begin with. However, if you are creating a traditional local or in-process server, you will find two additional files, STDAFX.CPP and STDAFX.H. These files are used to create your precompiled header file, as well as to define and declare items that might be global to your project. An in-process server has one additional file, the *<project>*.DEF file, which declares the functions the DLL exports. I'll open the files and examine the code they contain shortly.

At this time, however, I'll talk a bit about your selection of server type from a user perspective. If you elect to create an in-process server, the resulting code module, a DLL, will be loaded into the client's address space either into an STA or the single process MTA. (Review Day 2 "Exploring COM: The Technology ATL Supports" if your memory of STAs and MTAs is a bit foggy.) If the DLL is poorly implemented or goes astray for some other reason, the DLL can (and probably will) take the client's process down with it.

Note

> Note if your object runs in an STA, you won't (normally) require marshaling. If your object is destined for the MTA, however, you'll need to marshal your interface method's parameters. (Doing so, typically, involves Universal Marshaling or the creation of a proxy/stub DLL, as you saw in Day 2.)

To protect yourself from this potential disaster, you can produce a local server. This EXE-based COM server, when instantiated, runs in its own process address space. You lose some performance because your interface method's parameters must be marshaled, but you gain significant benefit from knowing a rogue COM server won't have access to your process's private information. In addition, it is unlikely your client application will go down if there is a significant COM server error. As always, you can marshal your parameters using Universal Marshaling, a proxy/stub DLL created by MIDL, or you can even implement your own custom marshaling scheme.

The NT service, being an EXE, is similar to the local server. The difference between the two is that a service is a program Windows NT loads when it boots and executes from that moment onward, if the service is so configured. (Some services are configured to be started manually). Although local servers require some users to be logged in to run the server, an NT service is executed by the operating system and has no requirement to be executed in a user's session. It also will remain in memory even if it has no outstanding active COM objects. If you're working with Windows NT, and you want to save yourself the time involved with creating new processes (local servers), the NT service approach might be quite useful to you.

That concludes your basic introduction to the files the ATL AppWizard will produce and to the reasons why you might select one framework over another. I'll discuss the code the wizard produces a bit later in the day. In the next few sections, I will address the additional options the wizard provides to you if you have selected an in-process COM server.

Merging the Proxy and the Stub

In many situations, you will require a proxy/stub DLL to effect marshaling. If you're shipping a COM server that requires a proxy/stub DLL, you have the additional headache of installing the proxy/stub DLL and registering it. But if your COM server already is a DLL, wouldn't it be nice to add the code required to manage the marshaling right into the COM server? In that case, you ship and register a single DLL instead of two.

You can do exactly this if you select the ATL AppWizard option to merge the proxy/stub DLL code into your main DLL's source code stream. If you select this option, you'll find further instruction in your *<project>*.CPP file (see the comments at the top of the file). Note the only instruction that pertains to Visual C++ 6.0 is the first one, which tells you to add the preprocessor value _MERGE_PROXYSTUB and to turn off the precompiled header option for one of the additional source files the wizard provides, DLLDATAX.C. The remaining instructions are targeted for earlier versions of Visual C++ and, probably, remain solely as legacy code (that is, Microsoft didn't update the wizard's code template for Visual C++ 6.0!).

Supporting MFC

If you're interested in using the Microsoft Foundation Classes (MFC) with your ATL object, check this ATL AppWizard option. If you do, the AppWizard will modify your basic project to link in the MFC libraries at runtime and will add several lines of code to your STDAFX.H and *<project>*.CPP files.

The additions to the STDAFX.H file are simply to include two MFC header files: AFXWIN.H and AFXDISP.H. AFXWIN.H defines the MFC Win32 support, such as that for for CWnd, the GDI, and various other support classes, such as CString. AFXDISP.H defines the MFC OLE support, meaning the support MFC provides for COM.

The changes to *<project>*.CPP are more dramatic, as the ATL AppWizard has to add code to create a CWinApp-based class to kick off MFC processing, as shown in Listing 6.1. Note the ATL module is initialized in CWinApp::InitInstance() and terminated in

6

`CWinApp::ExitInstance()`, as you would expect if you were writing an MFC-based application. (All your significant application initialization and termination actions should take place in these two methods.)

LISTING 6.1   ATL AppWizard MFC Support

```
 1: class CYourProjectApp : public CWinApp
 2: {
 3: public:
 4:
 5: // Overrides
 6:     // ClassWizard generated virtual function overrides
 7:     //{{AFX_VIRTUAL(CYourProjectApp)
 8:     public:
 9:     virtual BOOL InitInstance();
10:     virtual int ExitInstance();
11:     //}}AFX_VIRTUAL
12:
13:     //{{AFX_MSG(CYourProjectApp)
14:         // NOTE - the ClassWizard will add and remove member functions here.
15:         //    DO NOT EDIT what you see in these blocks of generated code !
16:     //}}AFX_MSG
17:     DECLARE_MESSAGE_MAP()
18: };
19:
20: BEGIN_MESSAGE_MAP(CYourProjectApp, CWinApp)
21:     //{{AFX_MSG_MAP(CYourProjectApp)
22:         // NOTE - the ClassWizard will add and remove mapping macros here.
23:         //    DO NOT EDIT what you see in these blocks of generated code!
24:     //}}AFX_MSG_MAP
25: END_MESSAGE_MAP()
26:
27: CYourProjectApp theApp;
28:
29: BOOL CYourProjectApp::InitInstance()
30: {
31:     _Module.Init(ObjectMap, m_hInstance, &LIBID_YOURPROJECTLib);
32:     return CWinApp::InitInstance();
33: }
34:
35: int CYourProjectApp::ExitInstance()
36: {
37:     _Module.Term();
38:     return CWinApp::ExitInstance();
39: }
40:
41: ////////////////////////////////////////////////////////////////////////
42: // Used to determine whether the DLL can be unloaded by OLE
43:
```

```
44: STDAPI DllCanUnloadNow(void)
45: {
46:     AFX_MANAGE_STATE(AfxGetStaticModuleState());
47:     return (AfxDllCanUnloadNow()==S_OK &&
➡ _Module.GetLockCount()==0) ? S_OK : S_FALSE;
48: }
```

ANALYSIS Note the AppWizard also added MFC support code to the DllCanUnloadNow() function (line 46). Although I haven't addressed DllCanUnloadNow() yet, you can compare this to the code you'll find in Listing 6.4 to see the differences.

I won't describe the MFC additions extensively, because I assume you're familiar with MFC if you're interested in this ATL AppWizard option. If you aren't terribly familiar with MFC and want to learn more, I would recommend the Sam's Net publication *MFC Unleashed Using Visual C++ 6.0*, ISBN 0-672-31557-2.

I will tell you this much, however. MFC requires a CWinApp-derived class to implement a message pump, which you'll require if you're linking in the MFC library. That's why you see the CWinApp-derived class in Listing 6.1. The majority of the code that the wizard added is simply to create the CWinApp-derived class and to get it going. For example, you must provide an implementation for CWinApp:InitInstance(), and this is a good place to initialize your ATL module.

The other significant line of code I'd like to point out is the AFX_MANAGE_STATE(AfxGetStaticModuleState()) in DllCanUnloadNow(). Although a complete discussion of MFC and its state data is beyond the scope of this book, be aware that MFC maintains state information. One type of state information MFC maintains is module state information.

The other two types are process and thread state information. Applications and DLLs that use MFC each has its own module state information, which is why the module state must be switched when DllCanUnloadNow() is executed. The process calling DllCanUnloadNow() might use MFC, or it might not, but if it does, its module state must be preserved prior to swapping in the DLL's module state. This is the function of the MFC macro AFX_MANAGE_STATE(). In fact, any DLL function you implement in your in-process server should switch the module state as you see in DllCanUnloadNow(). If you fail to protect MFC's module state, for either your DLL or the client, any number of problems can arise, and none of them are pleasant.

6

Supporting MTS

If your in-process server is destined to run under the Microsoft Transaction Server (MTS) runtime environment, the ATL AppWizard will add basic MTS support to your project. Specifically, MTX.LIB (MTS API) and MTXGUID.LIB (MTS GUIDs) are added to the link step, and MTXEX.DLL is delay-loaded when your object is instantiated. (Delay-loading allows the linker to statically link the MTXEX library yet allow MTXEX.DLL to be brought into memory and activated only after your object makes its first call into MTXEX.DLL, reducing the memory requirements and increasing scalability.)

Note you'll need to add MTX.H to your source files to define the various MTS COM objects you'll be using. The AppWizard doesn't do this for you, oddly enough. (It could have easily added this task to STDAFX.H.) I'll discuss implementing ATL-based COM objects for use within MTS in Day 21, "ATL and MTS: Coding with a Better COM."

This completes my discussion of the ATL AppWizard itself. Now I'll turn to the source code the wizard provides. It's time to crack open some files to see what's inside.

DLL Implementation

Imagine I have created a project using the ATL AppWizard entitled DLLSrvr, and I left the additional options alone (no MFC or MTS support, and I want a separate proxy/stub DLL). The truly interesting code, at least at this point, is contained in STDAFX.H, DLLSrvr.idl and DLLSrvr.cpp, so I'll limit my discussion to those files.

STDAFX.H contains several interesting things, as you see in Listing 6.2.

LISTING 6.2   ATL DLL COM Server STDAFX.H

```
 1: // stdafx.h : include file for standard system include files,
 2: //      or project specific include files that are used frequently,
 3: //      but are changed infrequently
 4:
 5: #if !defined(
 6: ➥AFX_STDAFX_H__679C37E4_5431_11D3_896D_0000E8409B63__INCLUDED_)
 7: #define
 8: ➥AFX_STDAFX_H__679C37E4_5431_11D3_896D_0000E8409B63__INCLUDED_
 9:
10: #if _MSC_VER > 1000
11: #pragma once
12: #endif // _MSC_VER > 1000
13:
14: #define STRICT
```

```
15: #ifndef _WIN32_WINNT
16: #define _WIN32_WINNT 0x0400
17: #endif
18: #define _ATL_APARTMENT_THREADED
19:
20: #include <atlbase.h>
21: //You may derive a class from CComModule and use it if you want to
22: ➥override
23: //something, but do not change the name of _Module
24: extern CComModule _Module;
25: #include <atlcom.h>
26:
27: //{{AFX_INSERT_LOCATION}}
28: // Microsoft Visual C++ will insert additional declarations
29: ➥immediately before the previous line.
30:
31: #endif // !defined
32: ➥(AFX_STDAFX_H__679C37E4_5431_11D3_896D_0000E8409B63__INCLUDED_)
```

ANALYSIS There are a couple of things you should note in Listing 6.2. First, note the value STRICT is defined (line 14). This enforces safe type checking when compiling C and C++ code and is especially useful when dealing with WINDOWS.H. In WINDOWS.H, for example, the compiler enforces type checking of handle types to make sure you're not mixing and matching different handles. See Visual C++ Technical Note 12 for more information.

I'm sure you'll also note _WIN32_WINNT is defined to be 0x0400 (Windows NT, version 4.0), even though you might be compiling and using your COM server on Win9x machines. Why? The Visual C++ header files contain many references to this preprocessor value, but the code to which you have most apparent access, in a COM sense anyway, is Distributed COM, or DCOM. You'll look at DCOM in Day 19, "Distributed ATL: DCOM Around the Net."

Note Be sure to remove the _WIN32_WINNT definition, if you intend your COM object to run on Win9x systems without DCOM installed. Remember, Windows 95 shipped prior to the introduction to DCOM, so if you require DCOM support on Windows 95, you'll have to install it yourself. There is also an upgrade for Windows 98. See Microsoft Knowledge Base article Q198600 for more information.

6

The next interesting thing you'll note is that the value _ATL_APARTMENT_THREADED is defined. This provides the default threading model for your COM server. What makes this so interesting is that, at this point, you haven't added an ATL COM object, so you've not been given the chance to specify a threading model to use. If you intend for your object to run in the MTA, meaning your object is to be free threaded, you should remove this preprocessor definition and specify instead _ATL_FREE_THREADED. The other available default threading model is _ATL_SINGLE_THREADED, which should not be used when coding for 32-bit Windows operating systems.

Following this, you see the inclusion of two ATL header files and the external declaration of your ATL module. If you intend to create a derived CComModule class, this is a good place to do it (you'll see examples of this with the local and service-based servers shortly). ATLBASE.H brings in many of the Windows header files and defines the basic ATL functionality and API. ATLCOM.H defines much of the ATL COM-specific behavior.

That's it for STDAFX.H, so let's turn now to the IDL file the AppWizard provides, which you'll see in Listing 6.3. As you can see, there isn't much here yet. If you were to compile the DLL code you have at this point, all the IDL file provides is an empty type library. After all, you have no objects defined, so at this point your COM server isn't very functional. You'll find the ATL Object Wizard will add significantly more code to your IDL file as you add objects.

LISTING 6.3 Initial ATL DLL COM Server IDL

```
 1: // DLLSrvr.idl : IDL source for DLLSrvr.dll
 2: //
 3:
 4: // This file will be processed by the MIDL tool to
 5: // produce the type library (DLLSrvr.tlb) and marshalling code.
 6:
 7: import "oaidl.idl";
 8: import "ocidl.idl";
 9:
10: [
11:     uuid(679C37E1-5431-11D3-896D-0000E8409B63),
12:     version(1.0),
13:     helpstring("DLLSrvr 1.0 Type Library")
14: ]
15: library DLLSRVRLib
16: {
17:     importlib("stdole32.tlb");
18:     importlib("stdole2.tlb");
19:
20: };
```

The final DLL server file I'll discuss is the DLL implementation file, DLLSrvr.cpp. It's here that the basic DLL functions are coded and your ATL module is declared and managed.

Exported DLL Functions

If you refer to Listing 6.4, you'll see that the DLL functions Win32 and COM require you to support and implement a COM in-process server. This is also a good place to declare the ATL module, as the module can handle the basic DLL COM-oriented functionality for you.

LISTING 6.4   ATL DLL COM Server DLL Implementation

```
 1: // DLLSrvr.cpp : Implementation of DLL Exports.
 2:
 3:
 4: // Note: Proxy/Stub Information
 5: //       To build a separate proxy/stub DLL,
 6: //       run nmake -f DLLSrvrps.mk in the project directory.
 7:
 8: #include "stdafx.h"
 9: #include "resource.h"
10: #include <initguid.h>
11: #include "DLLSrvr.h"
12:
13: #include "DLLSrvr_i.c"
14:
15:
16: CComModule _Module;
17:
18: BEGIN_OBJECT_MAP(ObjectMap)
19: END_OBJECT_MAP()
20:
21: /////////////////////////////////////////////////////////////////////
22: // DLL Entry Point
23:
24: extern "C"
25: BOOL WINAPI DllMain(HINSTANCE hInstance, DWORD dwReason,
26: ➡LPVOID /*lpReserved*/)
27: {
28:     if (dwReason == DLL_PROCESS_ATTACH)
29:     {
30:         _Module.Init(ObjectMap, hInstance, &LIBID_DLLSRVRLib);
31:         DisableThreadLibraryCalls(hInstance);
32:     }
33:     else if (dwReason == DLL_PROCESS_DETACH)
34:         _Module.Term();
35:     return TRUE;    // ok
36: }
```

6

continues

LISTING **6.4**   continued

```
37:
38: //////////////////////////////////////////////////////////////////////
39: // Used to determine whether the DLL can be unloaded by OLE
40:
41: STDAPI DllCanUnloadNow(void)
42: {
43:     return (_Module.GetLockCount()==0) ? S_OK : S_FALSE;
44: }
45:
46: //////////////////////////////////////////////////////////////////////
47: // Returns a class factory to create an object of the requested type
48:
49: STDAPI DllGetClassObject(REFCLSID rclsid, REFIID riid, LPVOID* ppv)
50: {
51:     return _Module.GetClassObject(rclsid, riid, ppv);
52: }
53:
54: //////////////////////////////////////////////////////////////////////
55: // DllRegisterServer - Adds entries to the system registry
56:
57: STDAPI DllRegisterServer(void)
58: {
59:     // registers object, typelib and all interfaces in typelib
60:     return _Module.RegisterServer(TRUE);
61: }
62:
63: //////////////////////////////////////////////////////////////////////
64: // DllUnregisterServer - Removes entries from the system registry
65:
66: STDAPI DllUnregisterServer(void)
67: {
68:     return _Module.UnregisterServer(TRUE);
69: }
```

ANALYSIS   The first thing you should note is the inclusion of DllSrvr_i.c in line 13, which (as you remember) declares the GUIDs for your objects and interfaces. At this time, you have no DLLSrvr_i.c file, but after you compile your project, MIDL will generate this file for you.

Your instances of the ATL module and object map come next, in lines 16 and 18 respectively. When you run the ATL Object Wizard, the object map will be updated to reflect which objects this server will expose. At this time, the map is empty (no entries between the begin and end macros).

Following the object map, you'll find the functions the DLL must export to satisfy Win32 and COM requirements. For example, you must have a main entry point, which in this case is the commonly-used `DllMain()`. You also see the DLL exported functions COM dictates you provide (as you saw in Day 5, "ATL Architecture: How ATL Implements COM").

`DllMain()`, line 25, manages the lifetime of your ATL module. When a process attaches to the DLL, the module is initialized. The `DisableThreadLibraryCalls()` function disables the `DLL_THREAD_ATTACH` and `DLL_THREAD_DETACH` notifications Win32 would normally provide. In keeping with the goal of ATL, this usually reduces the size of the working code set for your server. These notifications aren't required for module management, so unless you require them otherwise, you can safely ignore the thread-based notifications.

The other DLL functions simply defer their implementation to the ATL module. For example, if COM tells the server to register itself by calling `DllRegisterServer()` (line 55), `_Module.RegisterServer(TRUE)` actually does the job. Be sure to compare the implementation of `DllMain()` and `DllCanUnloadNow()` (line 41) in Listing 6.4 to the implementations in Listing 6.1, where MFC managed the module's and server's lifetimes for you. The mechanisms are very different.

That's it for the interesting in-process server code the ATL AppWizard provides you. Now let's move on to the local server case to see what the AppWizard does for you.

EXE Implementation

In many ways, the code the AppWizard generates for a local server is similar to the code it generates for an in-process server. Clearly, the implementation of the server is different, but many of the other files are nearly identical, such as the IDL file. Other files have minor changes, such as STDAFX.H. To see a sample local server, assume I created an ATL-based local server project named EXESrvr.

Having completed the basic AppWizard work, Listing 6.5 shows you the local server version of STDAFX.H generated by the wizard. I've highlighted the difference between the local and in-process server versions. Essentially, `CComModule` has been used as a base class for a new local server module class, `CExeModule`.

6

LISTING 6.5   ATL EXE COM Server STDAFX.H

```
1: // stdafx.h : include file for standard system include files,
2: //      or project specific include files that are used frequently,
3: //      but are changed infrequently
4:
5: #if !defined
```

continues

LISTING 6.5   continued

```
 6: ➥(AFX_STDAFX_H__679C37F0_5431_11D3_896D_0000E8409B63__INCLUDED_)
 7: #define
 8: ➥AFX_STDAFX_H__679C37F0_5431_11D3_896D_0000E8409B63__INCLUDED_
 9:
10: #if _MSC_VER > 1000
11: #pragma once
12: #endif // _MSC_VER > 1000
13:
14: #define STRICT
15: #ifndef _WIN32_WINNT
16: #define _WIN32_WINNT 0x0400
17: #endif
18: #define _ATL_APARTMENT_THREADED
19:
20: #include <atlbase.h>
21: //You may derive a class from CComModule and use it if you want to
22: ➥override
23: //something, but do not change the name of _Module
24: class CExeModule : public CComModule
25: {
26: public:
27:     LONG Unlock();
28:     DWORD dwThreadID;
29:     HANDLE hEventShutdown;
30:     void MonitorShutdown();
31:     bool StartMonitor();
32:     bool bActivity;
33: };
34: extern CExeModule _Module;
35: #include <atlcom.h>
36:
37: //{{AFX_INSERT_LOCATION}}
38: // Microsoft Visual C++ will insert additional declarations
39: ➥immediately before the previous line.
40:
41: #endif // !defined
42: ➥(AFX_STDAFX_H__679C37F0_5431_11D3_896D_0000E8409B63__INCLUDED_)
```

The reason ATL creates a new module class is to add startup and shutdown capability to your executable file. As you might remember, I mentioned earlier in the day that the EXE server has a message pump, but it does not implement a user interface. If that's the case, there has to be some mechanism in place, other than user input, to shut down the application. This is precisely the capability CExeModule provides, as you can see from Listing 6.6.

LISTING 6.6   ATL EXE COM Server EXE Implementation

```
 1: // ExeSrvr.cpp : Implementation of WinMain
 2:
 3:
 4: // Note: Proxy/Stub Information
 5: //       To build a separate proxy/stub DLL,
 6: //       run nmake -f ExeSrvrps.mk in the project directory.
 7:
 8: #include "stdafx.h"
 9: #include "resource.h"
10: #include <initguid.h>
11: #include "ExeSrvr.h"
12:
13: #include "ExeSrvr_i.c"
14:
15:
16: const DWORD dwTimeOut = 5000; // time for EXE to be idle before
17: ➥shutting down
18: const DWORD dwPause = 1000; // time to wait for threads to finish up
19:
20: // Passed to CreateThread to monitor the shutdown event
21: static DWORD WINAPI MonitorProc(void* pv)
22: {
23:     CExeModule* p = (CExeModule*)pv;
24:     p->MonitorShutdown();
25:     return 0;
26: }
27:
28: LONG CExeModule::Unlock()
29: {
30:     LONG l = CComModule::Unlock();
31:     if (l == 0)
32:     {
33:         bActivity = true;
34:         SetEvent(hEventShutdown); // tell monitor that we
35: ➥transitioned to zero
36:     }
37:     return l;
38: }
39:
40: //Monitors the shutdown event
41: void CExeModule::MonitorShutdown()
42: {
43:     while (1)
44:     {
45:         WaitForSingleObject(hEventShutdown, INFINITE);
46:         DWORD dwWait=0;
47:         do
48:         {
```

6

continues

LISTING 6.6 continued

```
49:                     bActivity = false;
50:                     dwWait = WaitForSingleObject(hEventShutdown, dwTimeOut);
51:             } while (dwWait == WAIT_OBJECT_0);
52:             // timed out
53:             if (!bActivity && m_nLockCnt == 0) // if no activity let's
54: ➡really bail
55:                 {
56: #if _WIN32_WINNT >= 0x0400 & defined(_ATL_FREE_THREADED)
57:                     CoSuspendClassObjects();
58:                     if (!bActivity && m_nLockCnt == 0)
59: #endif
60:                         break;
61:                 }
62:         }
63:         CloseHandle(hEventShutdown);
64:         PostThreadMessage(dwThreadID, WM_QUIT, 0, 0);
65: }
66:
67: bool CExeModule::StartMonitor()
68: {
69:     hEventShutdown = CreateEvent(NULL, false, false, NULL);
70:     if (hEventShutdown == NULL)
71:         return false;
72:     DWORD dwThreadID;
73:     HANDLE h = CreateThread(NULL, 0, MonitorProc, this, 0,
74: ➡&dwThreadID);
75:     return (h != NULL);
76: }
77:
78: CExeModule _Module;
79:
80: BEGIN_OBJECT_MAP(ObjectMap)
81: END_OBJECT_MAP()
82:
83:
84: LPCTSTR FindOneOf(LPCTSTR p1, LPCTSTR p2)
85: {
86:     while (p1 != NULL && *p1 != NULL)
87:     {
88:         LPCTSTR p = p2;
89:         while (p != NULL && *p != NULL)
90:         {
91:             if (*p1 == *p)
92:                 return CharNext(p1);
93:             p = CharNext(p);
94:         }
95:         p1 = CharNext(p1);
96:     }
97:     return NULL;
```

```
 98: }
 99:
100: ////////////////////////////////////////////////////////////////
101: //
102: extern "C" int WINAPI _tWinMain(HINSTANCE hInstance,
103:     HINSTANCE /*hPrevInstance*/, LPTSTR lpCmdLine, int /*nShowCmd*/)
104: {
105:     lpCmdLine = GetCommandLine(); //this line necessary for
106: ➥_ATL_MIN_CRT
107:
108: #if _WIN32_WINNT >= 0x0400 & defined(_ATL_FREE_THREADED)
109:     HRESULT hRes = CoInitializeEx(NULL, COINIT_MULTITHREADED);
110: #else
111:     HRESULT hRes = CoInitialize(NULL);
112: #endif
113:     _ASSERTE(SUCCEEDED(hRes));
114:     _Module.Init(ObjectMap, hInstance, &LIBID_EXESRVRLib);
115:     _Module.dwThreadID = GetCurrentThreadId();
116:     TCHAR szTokens[] = _T("-/");
117:
118:     int nRet = 0;
119:     BOOL bRun = TRUE;
120:     LPCTSTR lpszToken = FindOneOf(lpCmdLine, szTokens);
121:     while (lpszToken != NULL)
122:     {
123:         if (lstrcmpi(lpszToken, _T("UnregServer"))==0)
124:         {
125:             _Module.UpdateRegistryFromResource(IDR_ExeSrvr, FALSE);
126:             nRet = _Module.UnregisterServer(TRUE);
127:             bRun = FALSE;
128:             break;
129:         }
130:         if (lstrcmpi(lpszToken, _T("RegServer"))==0)
131:         {
132:             _Module.UpdateRegistryFromResource(IDR_ExeSrvr, TRUE);
133:             nRet = _Module.RegisterServer(TRUE);
134:             bRun = FALSE;
135:             break;
136:         }
137:         lpszToken = FindOneOf(lpszToken, szTokens);
138:     }
139:
140:     if (bRun)
141:     {
142:         _Module.StartMonitor();
143: #if _WIN32_WINNT >= 0x0400 & defined(_ATL_FREE_THREADED)
144:         hRes = _Module.RegisterClassObjects(CLSCTX_LOCAL_SERVER,
145:             REGCLS_MULTIPLEUSE | REGCLS_SUSPENDED);
```

6

continues

LISTING 6.6   continued

```
146:            _ASSERTE(SUCCEEDED(hRes));
147:            hRes = CoResumeClassObjects();
148: #else
149:            hRes = _Module.RegisterClassObjects(CLSCTX_LOCAL_SERVER,
150:                REGCLS_MULTIPLEUSE);
151: #endif
152:            _ASSERTE(SUCCEEDED(hRes));
153:
154:            MSG msg;
155:            while (GetMessage(&msg, 0, 0, 0))
156:                DispatchMessage(&msg);
157:
158:            _Module.RevokeClassObjects();
159:            Sleep(dwPause); //wait for any threads to finish
160:        }
161:
162:        _Module.Term();
163:        CoUninitialize();
164:        return nRet;
165: }
```

ANALYSIS   To really understand what's happening in Listing 6.6, look first to the Win32 entry point _tWinMain(), line 102. When the executable begins processing, the first thing it does is retrieve its command line to check for COM registration instructions later. Note it uses GetCommandLine() instead of argc, and argv. GetCommandLine() is a Win32 function, which precludes the use of the C runtime library.

After your local server has the command line tucked away, it initializes the COM runtime environment. Note it will use either CoInitialize() or CoInitializeEx()(lines 109 or 111), depending upon the default threading model you have defined in STDAFX.H.

Assuming no problems to this point, the server then initializes the ATL module and provides its thread ID to the module for later use, lines 114 and 115. After the ATL module has been initialized, the server can examine the command line for registration directives, lines 121 through 138.

It does that using the FindOneOf() helper function, which is defined earlier in the source file. If the server is being directed to register or deregister, it defers the registration action to the ATL module and sets a value (bRun) that will cause the application to terminate when the registration is complete (lines 127 and 134).

However, if the server finds no registration directive on the command line, it skips the registration code and begins its normal COM operations. There is a lot going on at this point, so I'll break the code down a few lines at a time.

In the case where bRun is TRUE, the first thing the server does is execute this line of code (line 142):

```
_Module.StartMonitor();
```

If you recall, this method was added as part of CExeModule.
CExeModule::StartMonitor() looks like this:

```
bool CExeModule::StartMonitor()
{
    hEventShutdown = CreateEvent(NULL, false, false, NULL);
    if (hEventShutdown == NULL)
        return false;
    DWORD dwThreadID;
    HANDLE h = CreateThread(NULL, 0, MonitorProc, this, 0, &dwThreadID);
    return (h != NULL);
}
```

StartMonitor() begins by assigning CExeModule::hEventShutdown a new auto-reset event handle value. If the handle is valid (nonNULL), StartMonitor() creates a new thread whose task is to check the status of the event handle just created:

```
// Passed to CreateThread to monitor the shutdown event
static DWORD WINAPI MonitorProc(void* pv)
{
    CExeModule* p = (CExeModule*)pv;
    p->MonitorShutdown();
    return 0;
}
```

The thread's MonitorProc() function casts the incoming 32-bit value as a CExeModule pointer (passed into the thread function as CExeModule's this pointer when the thread is created) and calls CExeModule::MonitorShutdown(), as shown in Listing 6.7.

LISTING 6.7 CExeModule::MonitorShutdown() Implementation

```
 1: //Monitors the shutdown event
 2: void CExeModule::MonitorShutdown()
 3: {
 4:     while (1)
 5:     {
 6:         WaitForSingleObject(hEventShutdown, INFINITE);
 7:         DWORD dwWait=0;
 8:         do
 9:         {
10:             bActivity = false;
11:             dwWait = WaitForSingleObject(hEventShutdown, dwTimeOut);
12:         } while (dwWait == WAIT_OBJECT_0);
```

continues

6

LISTING 6.7 continued

```
13:          // timed out
14:          if (!bActivity && m_nLockCnt == 0) // if no activity let's really
bail
15:          {
16: #if _WIN32_WINNT >= 0x0400 & defined(_ATL_FREE_THREADED)
17:              CoSuspendClassObjects();
18:              if (!bActivity && m_nLockCnt == 0)
19: #endif
20:                  break;
21:          }
22:      }
23:      CloseHandle(hEventShutdown);
24:      PostThreadMessage(dwThreadID, WM_QUIT, 0, 0);
25: }
```

ANALYSIS The first thing `MonitorShutdown()` does is wait (forever) for the event handle to be signaled (line 6). At this point, the monitoring thread is blocked on the event handle, and the server is ready to manage the next task. I'll come back to this suspended thread shortly.

For now, let's return to `_tWinMain()`, where the server is now ready to register the class factories for all the objects it exposes (see Listing 6.8).

LISTING 6.8

```
 1: #if _WIN32_WINNT >= 0x0400 & defined(_ATL_FREE_THREADED)
 2:     hRes = _Module.RegisterClassObjects(CLSCTX_LOCAL_SERVER,
 3:             REGCLS_MULTIPLEUSE | REGCLS_SUSPENDED);
 4:     _ASSERTE(SUCCEEDED(hRes));
 5:     hRes = CoResumeClassObjects();
 6: #else
 7:     hRes = _Module.RegisterClassObjects(CLSCTX_LOCAL_SERVER,
 8:             REGCLS_MULTIPLEUSE);
 9: #endif
10: _ASSERTE(SUCCEEDED(hRes));
```

ANALYSIS If the server is free threaded, it registers the class factories in a suspended state (lines 2 and 3). After all have registered, it resumes the class factories, allowing them to begin creating objects as required (line 5). If the server is apartment or single threaded, it simply registers the class factories and moves on (line 7).

The server now enters its message pump, where it remains until it receives a WM_QUIT message:

```
MSG msg;
while (GetMessage(&msg, 0, 0, 0))
    DispatchMessage(&msg);
```

Now the server is processing Windows messages and serving COM clients as required. As clients come and go, the server's lock count is incremented and decremented. When clients release the server's active COM objects, CExeModule::Unlock() will be executed (see Listing 6.9).

LISTING 6.9 CExeModule::Unlock() Implementation

```
 1: LONG CExeModule::Unlock()
 2: {
 3:     LONG l = CComModule::Unlock();
 4:     if (l == 0)
 5:     {
 6:         bActivity = true;
 7:         SetEvent(hEventShutdown); // tell monitor that we
 8: ➥transitioned to zero
 9:     }
10:     return l;
11: }
```

ANALYSIS Each call to CExeModule::Unlock() is passed to the base class's method by the same name, CComModule::Unlock()(line 3). When the lock count finally reaches zero, things get interesting again. CExeModule::bActivity is set to true (line 6), and the shutdown event is signaled (line 7).

As you recall, there is a monitor thread sitting out there blocked on CExeModule::hEventShutdown. At this point, the block clears, and the thread is released, which brings the monitoring thread to this loop in MonitorShutdown():

```
do
{
    bActivity = false;
    dwWait = WaitForSingleObject(hEventShutdown, dwTimeOut);
} while (dwWait == WAIT_OBJECT_0);
```

This loop is a delay mechanism, presumably to allow time for threads to clean up prior to the termination of the process. This time, WaitForSingleObject() doesn't wait an infinite time; it waits for a dwTimeOut period (initially set to 5000 milliseconds, or five seconds, which you see on line 16 of Listing 6.6). As long as the event handle remains signaled, it will remain in this loop. (Note, though, the event handle was created as an

6

auto-reset event. The SetEvent() call triggered the event, but then the event handle was immediately reset.) If the event was again triggered, WaitForSingleObject() returns WAIT_OBJECT_0, and the loop continues processing. If instead the timeout period expired, WaitForSingleObject() returns WAIT_TIMEOUT, and the loop terminates.

When the loop terminates, the monitor thread makes a quick check to see if processing is complete (see Listing 6.10).

LISTING 6.10 CExeModule::MonitorShutdown() Class Object Suspension Implementation

```
1: // if no activity let's really bail
2: if (!bActivity && m_nLockCnt == 0)
3: {
4: #if _WIN32_WINNT >= 0x0400 & defined(_ATL_FREE_THREADED)
5:     CoSuspendClassObjects();
6:     if (!bActivity && m_nLockCnt == 0)
7: #endif
8:     break;
9: }
```

If no more processing is active, the entire monitor processing loop is exited (after suspending the class factories—if the server is free threaded, line 5 in Listing 6.10). Before the thread exits entirely, it cleans up after itself by releasing the event handle and sending the requisite WM_QUIT message to the main thread:

```
CloseHandle(hEventShutdown);
PostThreadMessage(dwThreadID, WM_QUIT, 0, 0);
```

At this point, the local server's message pump sees the WM_QUIT message, and GetMessage() returns zero to terminate the message pump. The server then revokes the class factories and delays a while (default of 1 second) for any threads to finish their termination:

```
_Module.RevokeClassObjects();
Sleep(dwPause); //wait for any threads to finish
```

After the sleep period has expired, the server terminates the module, closes down the COM runtime, and returns from _tWinMain():

```
_Module.Term();
CoUninitialize();
return nRet;
```

Whew! There is a lot of interesting code there, and you haven't yet added a single object. But the code does properly manage the lifetime of the server itself, and you have a robust framework into which you can now place objects for the server to expose. Two down, and one more to go. Next up, the NT service server.

Service Implementation

Because NT services are a beast unto themselves (and are well beyond the scope of this book), I'm going to do a lot of hand-waving instead of a downright thorough code review. The reason is simple—if you already are familiar with NT services, I wouldn't be telling you anything new. If you're not familiar with NT services, I couldn't possibly address all the issues in this small space adequately enough to explain the code to you. So, I'm going to take the easiest way out and gloss over just about all the details. If you are interested in NT services, I would recommend reading Wrox Press's *Professional NT Services*, ISBN 1-86-100130-4.

I can also compare some aspects of the service COM server to the local server that I just described in some detail. For example, the local server derived `CExeModule` from `CComModule`. As it happens, the service server does the same thing—it derives `CServiceModule` from `CComModule`. `CServiceModule` and `CExeModule` are vastly different classes, to be sure, but the reasoning behind the classes is very much the same. The wizard added functionality to the module class to make the module's care and feeding a bit easier.

Like the local server, the service server has a number of additional helper functions and `CServiceModule` methods that manage both the COM aspects and service aspects of the server. For example, the service server also must read and parse the command line in `_tWinMain()` to check for registration requirements, and it uses the same `FindOneOf()` helper function as the local server to do so.

The operation of the service server, however, is vastly different from that of the local server, and this is where I bid the service server a fond *adieu*. NT services are very compelling, but they're also very complex if you're looking at service code for the first time. Okay, they're complex if you're looking at service code for the tenth time. But the underlying ATL principles are the same. You have an ATL module. The ATL module manages the COM aspects of your server using an object map and COM map(s). When the service server is tagged to create an exposed COM object, it will do so until all COM objects have been released. Unlike the local server, the service server remains in memory until the operating system is shut down. This feature is of significant value when you consider the time savings involved in just starting and stopping local servers.

6

Note

> If you do write NT services and wish to export COM objects from within your service, you should be aware of the Microsoft Knowledge Base article Q175653, "Err Msg: At Least One Service or Driver Failed...". Essentially, you will receive an access denied error if your service has a module name with spaces (making it a long file name no matter the actual length). The solution to this is to enclose your module name with quotes before you call CreateService():
>
> ```
> ...
>     ::GetModuleFileName(NULL, szTmpFilePath, _MAX_PATH - 2);
>
>     // To fix Access Denied (0005) problem in registry entry
>     // Surround path with quotes
>     _tcscpy(szFilePath, "\"");
>     _tcscat(szFilePath, szTmpFilePath);
>     _tcscat(szFilePath, "\"");
>
>     SC_HANDLE hService = ::CreateService(
>     ...
> ```

The ATL Object Wizard

Now that you have an understanding of the basic framework the ATL AppWizard will provide, it's time to add the code you require to implement COM objects. The framework, as you remember, is really meant to support the server itself. To actually do anything useful, you must add COM objects to the server. After you've done this, client applications can instantiate one of your objects, which activates the server so that COM, ATL, and your own code can get down to business.

When you're using ATL, the easiest way to add a COM object is to use the ATL Object Wizard. The reason is simple and practical: To correctly add a COM object, you must add quite a bit of code to several of the server's source files. If there is an automated way to do this, it makes sense (to me anyway) to use the automated tool. This increases your productivity and decreases the likelihood of coding errors.

This section, then, is devoted to the ATL Object Wizard. You'll look at the wizard itself; and for several of the objects you can insert, you'll look at some of the specific options available to you. The options, as with nearly any wizard, simply tailor the code the wizard will inject. If you understand the options available to you, you can make better selections, alleviate mistakes, and reduce recoding efforts later.

Invoking the Wizard

Before I tackled ATL, I taught myself MFC. I began coding MFC applications by hand, completely avoiding any wizard except for the MFC AppWizard itself. Over time, though, I realized the MFC ClassWizard was extremely helpful. More than that, I could whip out complex MFC classes in relatively little time, simply by understanding what the wizard could do for me.

When I did come to learn ATL, therefore, I was prepared to make good use of the ATL Object Wizard. I assumed I would see the productivity gain I mentioned. I also knew the wizard would add correct ATL code. Because I was just beginning to use ATL, this was important to me. I could learn from the wizard rather than learn the hard way as I did with MFC.

This isn't so with the ATL Object Wizard. There are two ways to access the wizard, and one is a bit less than obvious. To invoke the wizard, the more obvious way is to use the Visual Studio Insert menu and select the New ATL Object item. To activate the wizard in the less obvious way, you must first activate the ClassView tab in the Workspace window, as I've shown in Figure 6.2. When you do, you will see a tree control whose root node is the name of your server's project. If you expand the node, you should see global information, such as the exported DLL files (if your server is in-process).

FIGURE 6.2

The Visual Studio ClassView tab within the Workspace window.

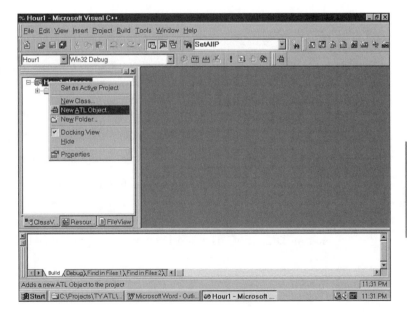

6

Place the cursor over the project's name (the root node) and right-click. You should see a context menu similar to that shown in Figure 6.2. The menu item you should select is New ATL Object. If you click this menu item, you should be rewarded with the ATL Object Wizard, whose user interface is shown in Figure 6.3.

FIGURE 6.3

The Visual Studio ATL Object Wizard.

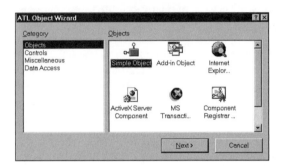

As you see from Figure 6.3, the Object Wizard consists of a dialog box with two list controls. The first list control, Category, controls the content of the second list control, Objects. Clicking on an item in the Category list causes the items in the Object list to change, thus providing you with several alternative object selections, as you'll see in the next section.

ATL Objects

In Day 1, I briefly described the objects that the Object Wizard supported. I'll review them here, as well as provide a bit more detail. One important thing to remember is that some of the objects are designed for use from an in-process server (DLL) only, while others can be implemented in either an in-process server or local server (EXE). I'll annotate each object with the server types it supports (DLL only or both).

The Objects category should present you with these object types:

- *Simple* (both): The Simple object merely implements a basic COM object with no additional ATL support (such as for ActiveX). This is a traditional COM object, suitable for most business logic applications.
- *Add-In* (DLL only): The Add-In object is designed to add functionality to Visual Studio.
- *Internet Explorer* (DLL only): The Internet Explorer object adds interfaces that you need to support Internet Explorer, but omits the user-interface code.
- *ActiveX Server* (both): The Microsoft Internet Information Server (IIS) uses the ActiveX Server object to support Active Server Page (ASP) scripting.

- *MMC SnapIn* (DLL only): The MMC SnapIn object provides the code you'll need to create a module intended for use with the Microsoft Management Console.

- *MS Transaction Server* (DLL only): The MS Transaction Server object contains some basic code to execute in the MTS environment.

- *Component Registrar* (DLL only): The Component Registrar object has the code necessary to register individual objects in a single DLL server, if you implement more than one.

As I mentioned, some objects can be used in either an in-process or local server, whereas some objects must be implemented in a DLL. The wizard will happily enable you to insert objects into any ATL project, which means you can mismatch an object type (place a DLL-only object into an EXE server). This won't cause your server to break, but neither will you be able to instantiate the incompatible object.

If you select the Controls item under Category, you should see several types of COM controls:

- *ActiveX control with a lite version* (DLL only): The ActiveX control implements the full suite of ActiveX interfaces, which you'll see more of in Day 16, "ATL and ActiveX: Modern Control Packaging."

- *Composite control with a lite version* (DLL only): The Composite control acts as a container for other controls.

- *HTML control with a lite version* (DLL only): The HTML control adds support for Dynamic HTML and displays a Web page in its user-interface.

- *Property Page* (DLL only): The Property Page control implements a property page, commonly used when configuring ActiveX controls.

The difference between the *lite* and *full* versions of these objects lies in the interfaces the wizard implements for you. The lite versions offer fewer interfaces, but they are typically the most commonly used interfaces. Choosing the full version ensures that your control works with the widest range of control containers, but at the cost of additional code (and a larger file, resulting in potentially longer download times).

The Miscellaneous category has only a single option: Dialog Box (both). Although ATL provides support for much more than mere dialogs, this is all the Object Wizard provides you. I'll discuss other ATL windowing alternatives in Day 13, "Creating ATL Applications: Where ATL Meets Win32." In this case, the dialog object isn't a COM object. It merely inserts the ATL wrappers to support dialog box creation and management.

The final category, Data Access, provides you with OLE DB support:

- *Provider* (both)

- *Consumer* (both)

6

In this case, the ATL Object Wizard inserts OLE DB templates to provide you with OLE DB data access support, using data provider and consumer templates. You'll see more of this in Day 20, "ATL and OLE DB: Storing More." These objects aren't truly COM objects. Their purpose is to allow you easier access to the OLE DB data support templates.

I'll now discuss several of the Object Wizard objects in more detail. I will specifically show you the additional options that each object supports and give you some direction for completing those options to your benefit. I'll start with the Simple object.

The Simple Object

If you select the Simple object under the Objects category, you see the property sheet shown in Figure 6.4 (which is a reproduction of Figure 1.6). The property sheet supports two pages, one for naming the object and one for specifying the specific COM attributes you want in place when the object is executing.

FIGURE 6.4

The Simple object property sheet's Names page.

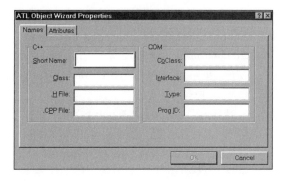

Note

The information you provide here is directly translated to C++ and IDL source code and is sprinkled throughout several files. Before you click OK, be sure the options are established precisely as you'd like to see them. It's a more difficult task to go through all your source files to change this information at a later time.

In the first lesson, I glossed over this information pretty quickly. I did that because, if you hadn't been exposed to COM before, I didn't want to cloud the issue at hand. I wanted you to create a COM object quickly. Now that you've progressed to this point in the book, the meanings of the strings in the Names page should be more apparent.

You begin by entering some text in the Short Name edit field. This text is used as a model, and it's propagated throughout the remaining edit fields as suggested string values.

The edit fields are split into two categories: C++ information and COM information. The relationship between the C++ information and the short name is relatively simple to deduce. The short name is prefixed with a capital C to produce a C++ class name. The source code for this will be stored in the .H and .CPP files, named as shown in the file name edit fields. Feel free to rename things here as you see fit. These are suggested names only. You might find that you must edit the C++ file names simply because they have the same names as files that already exist in your project. The ATL Object Wizard will let you know if there is a file name collision, and if there is, you can simply change the file name text as required.

Turning now to the COM information, the short name you provide turns into the COM CoClass and Interface names. That is, your COM object will have a CLSID of CLSID_ShortName and an IID of IID_ShortName, unless you change the text in these fields at this time. The string in the Type field will be inserted into your type library's IDL source as the library's help string. And finally, the ProgID will be assigned the value <project>.<shortname>.1 unless you change the ProgID string here. As always, these strings are suggestions only, so don't hesitate to change any or all of them if you feel the urge.

When you've completed all the name information, click the Attributes tab to view the COM attributes you can assign to this object. This page is shown in Figure 6.5. Now, perhaps, these options make a bit more sense after reading the basic COM information in Day 2.

FIGURE 6.5

The Simple object property sheet's Attributes page.

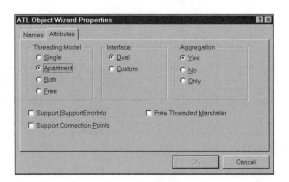

The first thing you do is to select the appropriate threading model your object will implement. Then, select the basic interface from which your object should derive, IUnknown (*Custom*) or IDispatch (*Dual*). If you want your object to be aggregatable, leave the Aggregation model alone (Yes). If not, you can specify that your object never be aggregated (No) or always be aggregated (Only).

Note If you decide to implement a free-threaded object (Free or Both), be sure to change the default threading model in STDAFX.H. The ATL AppWizard initialized this to _ATL_APARTMENT_THREADED, but you'll want to change this to _ATL_FREE_THREADED.

The remaining options provide further object specialization options. *ISupportErrorInfo* is an interface commonly used in scripted environments (typically using a dual interface) to return richer error information than a simple HRESULT. *Connection points* are typically used to provide a callback mechanism between objects. You'll also find these commonly used with scriptable objects with a dual interface. I'll discuss connection points in detail in Day 17, "ATL and Connection Points: Supporting COM's Event Model."

The final option, used to select the Free-Threaded Marshaler, or FTM, is quite advanced and well beyond this book. The FTM implements the basic COM marshaling interfaces, and if you aggregate it into your COM object, you can use it to marshal your data rather than a proxy/stub DLL or the UM. I recommend that, until you're very familiar with COM, ATL, and the MTA, you forgo this option and use proxies and stubs or even the UM.

Note Some other ATL objects use the Names and Attributes pages. If they do, I'll simply mention the fact and move on to the additional pages the objects provide.

As I'm sure you now see, the Simple ATL object provides the minimum code necessary to implement a COM object. The other objects I'll discuss add more functionality because they're designed to work in very specific environments rather than as general-purpose COM objects. A good example is the ActiveX control, which you'll see in the next section.

ActiveX Control

I'll defer a full discussion of ActiveX until Day 16, so if the options I describe here aren't clear to you now, that day will elaborate. If you select the Controls category list item, then select Full Control from the object list, you will be generating the basic code you need to implement an ActiveX control. The ActiveX control uses the Names and Attributes property pages, just as the Simple object did. The ActiveX control, however, adds two new pages, Miscellaneous and Stock Properties.

The Miscellaneous page is shown in Figure 6.6. Here, you can tailor the behavior of your ActiveX control, which is usually (but not always) a control designed to enhance a given user interface. You can see many of the options are related to how the control is viewed and drawn.

FIGURE 6.6

The ActiveX object property sheet's Miscellaneous page.

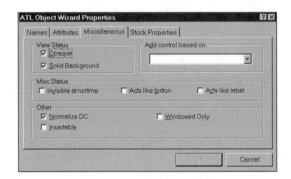

The *Opaque* option, and the related *Solid Background* option, are used to specify whether the container's background will show through your ActiveX control. If your control draws itself entirely, select the Opaque option. If your control is opaque, you can speed things up by using a solid background versus a patterned background. If this is your intention, select Solid Background.

If you intend to write an ActiveX control that is based upon an existing Windows control, you can *superclass* the existing control and simply tailor the specific behavior you desire. Remember, though, that superclassing a control does more than affect a single instance of a control. It affects *all* controls of that type. If you superclass the edit control, for example, you will be modifying the behavior of all edit controls on the given user's system. Be careful.

You can select various miscellaneous status options, such as Invisible at Runtime, Acts like Button, and Acts like Label. ActiveX controls that are invisible at runtime are typically used to fire events, generally at timed intervals. They tend to remain behind the scenes, and they don't implement a user interface. If your control acts like a button, it means your control will be capable of acting as the default button, which is a button to which the container has given the BS_DEFPUSHBUTTON button style. The effect of this is more visual than anything—your control should draw a thicker border to visually indicate it is the default button. To the user that means your button will be activated if they press the Enter key. Finally, if your control acts like a label, your control's text will replace the label that the container assigned to your control.

6

The final collection of options comes from the Other group, and it includes *Normalize DC*, *Insertable*, and *Windowed Only*. ActiveX controls should not make assumptions about the state of a device context they are given when they are asked to paint themselves. Anything, even everything, could have been modified. This includes the current color selections, brush, palette, pen, line style, mapping mode, and so forth. You can, if you wish, request a normalized device context from the container, which assures you the device context is in a known state. But there is, of course, a performance penalty because the container must create the device context for you. If the control is insertable, it means the control will appear under the Insert, Object menu and can be inserted into an OLE document. And, finally, if the control is marked as Windowed Only, it means your control will have a window, even in containers that support windowless controls. If you don't select this option, your control will be windowless in containers that support this, but will have a window in containers that don't support the windowless control. You'll see more of these particular options in Day 16, "ATL and ActiveX: Modern Control Packaging."

The final property page is shown in Figure 6.7. ActiveX controls support a set of *stock properties*, which are settings that establish the behavior of the control. You'll look more closely at properties in Day 8, "ATL Object Methods: Adding Functionality to Your Interface," as well as in Day 16.

When you develop an ActiveX control, you're free to implement any property that fits your control. Not surprisingly, though, Microsoft has implemented a set of basic properties that ActiveX controls should strive to implement, if it makes sense to use that property given your control's intended purpose. For example, there is a property each for background and foreground color, for the control's caption or text, and to set or reset the control's enabled state. These stock properties, as they are called, are shown in the Not Supported list control in Figure 6.7. If you see a stock property you would like to support in that list, you shift it to the Supported list using the buttons between the list controls.

The ActiveX control I've just been discussing is a client-side control. That is, it is a control designed to be loaded into a client container and executed, such as within Internet Explorer. There is another type of ActiveX control, called a server component, which is used with ASP scripts under IIS. That's the control I'll address in the next section.

ActiveX ASP Server

When you select ActiveX Server Component from the Object Wizard's Objects list, the first two property pages are the same as for the Simple object. That is, you'll have the standard Names and Attributes pages. There is one additional page, however, as shown in Figure 6.8. This is the ASP page, and its goal is to tailor the operation of the server component in the IIS environment.

FIGURE 6.7

The ActiveX object property sheet's Stock Properties page.

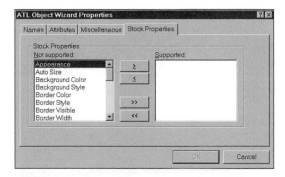

FIGURE 6.8

The ActiveX Server object property sheet's ASP page.

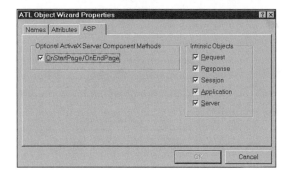

Although I'll address the client-side ActiveX control in Day 16, I won't discuss the ActiveX Server Component in detail in this book. For a complete discussion, I would recommend *Developing ASP Components* by Shelley Powers from O'Reilly and Associates, ISBN 1-56-592446-0; *Beginning ASP Components* by Richard Anderson, et al., from Wrox Press, ISBN 1-86-100288-2; and *Creating Lightweight Components with ATL* by Jonathan Bates, from Sams, ISBN 0-672-31535-1.

To generalize, though, you can imagine an ActiveX Server Component fulfilling the same task as a module called from within the old Common Gateway Interface (CGI). Both mechanisms are simply there to provide for server-based code to manage requests for data or action from the client's Web browser.

In any case, there are several options available to you on the ASP property page. The first requests whether you wish to support the additional ActiveX Server Component methods `OnStartPage()` and `OnEndPage()`. These are *callback functions* that IIS will call when a client begins and finishes viewing a Web page supported by your component. They allow you to tailor the component's operation by finalizing some processing or releasing some resources. These methods are required if you want to support ASP's intrinsic objects,

6

which are shown to the right in Figure 6.8. From a scripting perspective, your component can support one or several *intrinsic objects*, which are objects the ASP script can access to retrieve information from your ActiveX Server Component.

I won't detail the objects themselves, as that would exceed the scope of this book; the books I mentioned previously will give you the details you need to properly code for the IIS environment.

As you now know, ActiveX Server Components run within IIS and provide support for ASP scripts. If you have some experience administering IIS or MTS, you are familiar with the Microsoft Management Console, or MMC. The MMC is a new administration utility Microsoft provides with their more recent technologies. The interesting thing about MMC is that it's merely a container. All the interesting work is performed by *snapin components*, which is my next topic.

MMC Snapin

As with the ActiveX Server Component, writing an MMC snapin component is well beyond my intentions for this book. If you're interested in coding MMC snapins, I'd recommend Richard Grimes' *Professional ATL COM Programming* from Wrox Press, ISBN 1-861001-4-01. However, I will provide you with a general description of the options available to you to get you started.

If you select the MMC snapin object from the Object Wizard's Objects list, you are presented with two property pages. The first is the standard Names page you're now familiar with. The second, though, targets the snapin itself and is shown in Figure 6.9.

FIGURE 6.9

The MMC snapin object property sheet's MMC Snapin page.

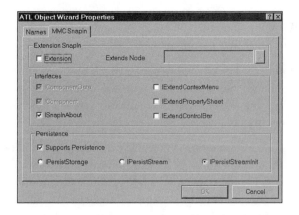

This page tailors the snapin code. For example, you can choose to extend an existing snapin node, or you can create one from scratch. Simply check the Extension check box. If you extend an existing snapin, you select the particular snapin using the Extends Node drop-down list.

You then decide precisely which interfaces related to snapins you would like to support. The first two, IComponentData and IComponent, are enabled only if you're writing an extension snapin. These two interfaces are used to provide the MMC container with data the user needs to see. The ISnapInAbout interface gives the MMC container a way to obtain the snapin's version and copyright information. The IExtendXXXX interfaces all tailor the look and feel and the operation, of context menus, property sheets, and tool bars the MMC container already provides. They simply provide a mechanism for you to integrate your snapin's user interaction requirements with the existing MMC user interface.

Note

The IExtendXXXX name in the preceding paragraph isn't a typo, even though the figure has no such interface. It's common practice in COM to collect interfaces together and X-out the non-common portions of the name. For example, there are tons of IEnumXXXX interfaces. All I did here was use some shorthand notation.

The final three interfaces are for persistence, which is how the MMC ultimately stores the settings and similar things your object provides to the user. You can elect to support persistence by checking the Supports Persistence check box. If you wish to support persistence, you select the specific persistence interface you desire, IPersistStorage, IPersistStream, and IPersistStreamInit. Because of space limitations here, I'll leave it to you to research these interfaces and select the one most appropriate for your MMC snapin object.

I mentioned the MMC is used to administer MTS, and one of the things you can administer is the installation and operation of *MTS packages*, which I'll review in Day 21. Packages consist of MTS objects, which I discuss next.

MTS Object

An MTS object is a COM in-process server designed to run within the bounds of MTS. It doesn't necessarily have to support transaction processing, nor be transactional itself, but such objects are commonly created to participate in transactional processing at some level. I'll show you MTS coding basics in Day 21. If you're interested in writing MTS components, adding an ATL MTS object here is a great way to start.

If you select MS Transaction Server Component from the Object Wizard's Objects list, you should see two property pages. The first page is the Names page you've become accustomed to. The second page, MTS, tailors the MTS settings the wizard will use to generate code for your component. This is the page you see in Figure 6.10.

6

FIGURE 6.10

The MTS object property sheet's MTS page.

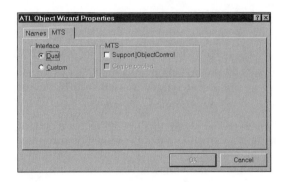

On the MTS page, you can elect to support either a dual or a custom interface. Remember the dual interface derives from IDispatch rather than from IUnknown directly and is used primarily for scripting. You can also choose to support the IObjectControl interface, which you use to control context-specific initialization and cleanup, as well as for object recycling. You'll see this interface in more detail in Day 21. If you do support IObjectControl, you can also decide to pool your object. This enables MTS to keep several of your objects around to speed creation and use. Currently, MTS doesn't support pooling, but Windows 2000 and COM+ do.

Including the MTS object, I've described the option property pages ATL provides you for the most frequently used ATL objects. There are other objects you can insert, however. Some I'll cover later in the book, such as the OLE DB templates and ActiveX property pages. As for the remaining objects, because they're far less common (add-ins and so forth), I'll skip entirely for space reasons. You'll find more information included in the online help, should you be interested in researching them further.

Summary

It's amazing that such a simple AppWizard could provide such different code depending upon which radio button you selected. But as you've seen, this is indeed the case. However, no matter which server type you elect to use and what additional options you choose, the AppWizard provides you with a starting point. It's up to you to take this basic framework and add COM object code and functionality, as you require.

You had the opportunity to see some of this basic code, and I described a fair amount of it to make sure you had a good idea what the wizard-generated code can do. If you have a good understanding of the wizard code, you can confidently make changes to your source files and know precisely what those changes will do to the overall workings of your COM server.

I described what files were generally provided, as well as their basic content (and intent). I then discussed some of the additional options you have if you select an in-process server, as well as what changes to the basic code you should expect. I then went on to describe the three types of servers and provided a detailed tour through the code you find when you create in-process and local COM servers.

But after all this, you still have only a basic framework. None of the servers actually do anything interesting by themselves.

To perform the truly interesting tasks, you must add the COM objects your server is destined to support. To help you with this, I introduced you to several of the objects you can insert using the ATL Object Wizard in some detail. For the more commonly used objects, I described all of the wizard options available. For some lesser-used objects, I gave you an idea as to where they might be useful.

You should now see a pattern emerging:

1. Create the ATL-based server project.
2. Add ATL COM objects.
3. Tailor the workings of the COM objects to meet your particular requirements.

You're moving from very general to very specific, and the wizards are there to help you with each step.

Q&A

Q I've decided I need a local server, and I'll use custom marshaling with the proxy/stub DLL the MIDL compiler produces for me. How do I compile this?

A I provide an alternative to this answer in Appendix C. But I can also suggest using the command line compiler, nmake, directly. After you compile your object, you'll need to register the proxy/stub DLL using REGSVR32.EXE. To do this, use these two command lines:

```
nmake -f <project>ps.mk
regsvr32 <project>ps.dll
```

Q You mentioned the Object Wizard modifies files within my project, but you didn't mention which ones. Why?

A I omitted this information partly because the files differ depending upon which object you introduce. Also, I'll go into detail about the more common objects in later lessons. Having said that, the wizard always changes the IDL file and adds implementation files (.H and .CPP) for the object you add. In some cases, the

6

wizard modifies your project settings (beyond adding the object's implementation files). I thought it better to simply describe the objects and their settings here and leave these details to the days in which I discuss the objects themselves.

Q If I did happen to dismiss the object's property sheet and later decide I had not selected options I wanted or had included options I didn't want, how do I recover?

A This also depends upon the object and the specific options you did or did not select. If you misnamed the object, the coclass, the interface name, or the ProgID, turn to the IDL file and change what you see there. Be sure to search for the misnamed text throughout your project and change the text as you find it.

If you're dealing with an object-specific option, and you don't have the luxury of starting all over again (too much code already completed), you might try creating a dummy project with the settings you desire and determine how that code differs from what you currently have. Take care, though. At times option settings involve seemingly minor code changes. Search with a keen eye or use the Visual Studio tool WinDiff.exe to see differences in the source file text.

Workshop

The Workshop is designed to help you anticipate possible questions, review what you've learned, and get you thinking about how to put your knowledge into practice. The answers to the quiz are in Appendix A, "Answers."

Quiz

1. In general, what are the three most interesting files the wizard creates for you, at least at this time?

2. To which server type are the three additional ATL AppWizard options directed (integrating the proxy/stub code, MFC support, and MTS support)?

3. What ATL object supports server locking and registration, and what is its C++ base class?

4. What mechanism does the ATL local server use to manage its lifetime?

5. What is one benefit of using a service-based server over a local server?

6. How do you access the ATL Object Wizard?

7. If I provide information in the Names property page I later regret, can I correct the values?

8. If I accidentally add an in-process only object to my local server code, will that adversely affect my project?

9. I just want to create a common COM object—which object should I insert into my ATL project?

10. Are the objects I see as provided by the Object Wizard all I can insert?

Exercises

1. Modify the local server source code to bring up a user interface. Do you still require the monitor thread?

2. Create an in-process server and request that the proxy/stub code be incorporated into the server. How do the DLL exported functions differ?

3. Create a service-based server and examine the source code the wizard provides. Does it make sense, or is it magic?

4. Add a second, or even a third object to your server. What files change?

5. Create two ATL in-process projects, inserting a simple object into one and an ActiveX (client) control into the other. What differences in the various source files do you see?

6. Rummage through the online documentation to see if you can find further descriptive references to the types of ATL objects you can insert using the Object Wizard.

6

DAY 7

The ATL Object Wizard: Customizing the Basic ATL Framework

With the notable exception of the first day, you've not written much ATL code. Even then, the wizards did most of the work for you. In a sense, this day will prove to be little different: You're still using the wizards to generate some basic code. However, after you've had a chance to create a few ATL COM servers, you'll find you're pretty good with the wizards. You will have more time to write interesting code. That means you'll spend more time writing method implementations than you will writing code to wire up the methods to ATL.

Using the ATL AppWizard, you've created an ATL-based COM server that you'll use as a framework. You then used the ATL Object Wizard to insert some type of COM object. But even at this point, you don't have a very interesting COM object because the interface it supports does little more than support IUnknown. We'll correct that deficiency in this lesson.

Let's get to work. In this day you'll see

- More about adding methods to your ATL-based COM object
- What changes the wizard makes to your source files
- How to add new interfaces with additional functionality
- More IDL attributes you can use to tailor your method calls
- How to add properties to your ATL-based object
- How properties differ from methods
- How an object's properties appear to Visual C++ and to Visual Basic
- IDL attributes associated with properties
- Helpful IDL property constructs

Adding Methods

If you've been working with ATL for some time, you're probably quite happy adding methods to interfaces by hand. It isn't difficult, although you do need to keep track of the source files you've changed to be sure you've added the new method everywhere. A quick compilation will tell you if you added everything correctly.

But even grizzled veterans often use the automated wizard (if you can promote it to a wizard level) that Visual Studio provides for adding new interface methods. The reason is simple: You don't have to worry about each and every source file that requires modification just to add an interface method. Visual Studio does that for you. You can, instead, concentrate on the method signature, which is the most important step when adding methods.

As is common when using ATL, you access the method wizard through the Visual Studio Workspace window. How you call the wizard into action and what you do with it after it's ready to go is precisely what I'll cover next.

Calling Mr. Wizard

It's now time to write another ATL object. Fire up Visual Studio and create a new ATL project (I called mine *Day7Server1*). Next you add a new, simple ATL object with a custom interface called IAddMethodDemo supported by the C++ class CMySecondATLObj. This is the first interface you'll work with in this lesson.

At this time, you should see in your Visual Studio Workspace window something similar to what you see in Figure 7.1. The ATL Object Wizard adds two nodes to the tree—one for the C++ class you added and one for the interface you added. In this case, you see the CMySecondATLObj C++ class and the IAddMethodDemo interface.

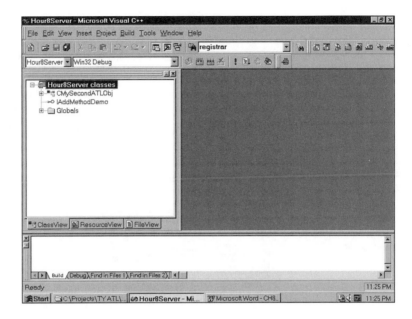

To add a method to the IAddMethodDemo interface, you right click on the interface node and select the Add Method menu item from the resulting context menu. You can see this in action in Figure 7.2.

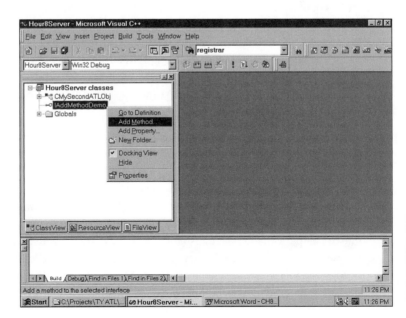

7

If things work as they should, you will be rewarded with the Add Method to Interface dialog box you see in Figure 7.3. Here, you specify the method signature, beginning with the return value. Because this is a COM method, you should always return an HRESULT. (You'll note this is the default value in the Return Type drop-down list control.) Next, you specify a method name, just as you would if you were adding a method to a C++ class. I strive to make method names somewhat descriptive, so I call this first method SquareArg, as you see in Figure 7.3. The method is simply going to take an input argument, square it, and return it to the client. You might want to review some of the IDL attributes I presented in Day 3, "The COM Interface: COM's Foundation." You'll be seeing many of them again here.

FIGURE 7.3

The Visual Studio Add Method wizard.

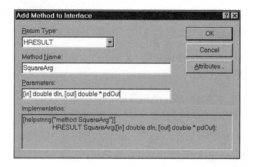

At this point, you decide what arguments to pass into and out of the method. As you insert parameters, you also specify the IDL method parameter attributes associated with the parameters. In this case, I decided I required two parameters. The first parameter is an incoming double parameter ([in], in IDL attribute terms), which will be passed in by value. That is, the [in] attribute will cause the marshaling code to pass the actual double value between the client and the COM server (if marshaling is required at all). This is the value I'll eventually square.

Because the method SquareArg() returns an HRESULT, I can't simply return the squared value. Instead, I add a second parameter whose value I can modify. This means I need a pointer to an output variable. For that, I use the IDL method parameter attribute [out]. This attribute causes the marshaling code to allocate memory for a double value in the COM server's address space and to pass the COM server's method a pointer to that memory (again, if marshaling is in effect). After I square the input argument and shove it into the output variable, the marshaling code will take the actual value placed into the memory it just allocated, ship that value to the client, and shove the value into the client's variable for me. Remember that marshaling provides a data conduit, and you're giving the marshaling code a hint by using the correct IDL attributes.

Something else to remember is that COM knows what a double data type is and can automatically allocate memory for the returned [out] value on the client's end. Had I been returning a structure or array instead, I would need to allocate the memory myself (using CoTaskMemAlloc(), or SysStringAlloc() for a BSTR).

My final parameter list, which I type into the wizard's Parameters edit control, looks like this:

```
[in] double dIn, [out] double * pdOut
```

Before you click OK to actually create the method, take a moment and click the Attributes button. This brings up the Edit Attributes dialog box, which is designed to add method IDL attributes. One has already been added, as you see in Figure 7.4. This is the commonly used helpstring attribute that many type library browsers use to further describe your interface's method.

If you want to change the help string text, you can do so by clicking within the text in the Attributes list control. If you drop the list in the Name combo box, you will see a list of the germane IDL method attributes you can use to further tailor this method. For example, if you don't want this method to be used by remote clients, you select the local attribute. I elect to go with just the helpstring attribute, so I click Cancel to return to the method wizard.

FIGURE 7.4

The Visual Studio Add Method wizard's Attributes dialog.

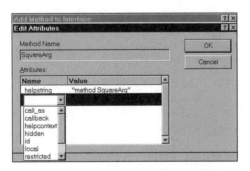

If you've completed both the method name and parameter edits, you can click OK to have the wizard actually modify your source files. Before I discuss the source files themselves, I'd like to add another method to IAddMethodDemo. This new method, CubeArg, is added in the same way you added SquareArg. This method, though, will have a single parameter instead of two.

This single parameter will have the IDL attribute [in, out]. Because it's an [out] parameter, you expect it to be a pointer variable. But because it's also an input parameter, CubeArg expects to find the value to cube indicated by the pointer variable. The marshaling, in this case, combines the two forms of marshaling I mentioned previously. That

7

is, the input value is copied from client to server where the memory is allocated to store this value. Then, a pointer to that memory is passed to the COM server. The server does some work and writes a new value to the allocated memory (via the pointer). The value is then sent back to the client and inserted into the client's variable.

I added this parameter to CubeArg:

```
[in, out] double * pdArg
```

When everything appears to be in order, I click OK and add the interface's second method.

Assuming things didn't go too far astray, IAddMethodDemo should have two new methods, SquareArg() and CubeArg(). Let's see what the wizard has done to the source files to implement these methods.

Changes to Your Files

In Day 3, I described some of the code you generated in Day 1, "Getting Started: Your First ATL COM Object." I'm going to do the same thing here with the sample ATL code you just created. However, you've been exposed to a bit more COM and ATL since the third day, so I can emphasize a few more interesting points of which you should be aware.

The project I just created, to which I added the simple ATL COM object and the two methods, is called Day7Server1. The C++ class I added when I inserted the simple object is called CMySecondATLObj. Therefore, if you open this day's example, or if you've been working along with me, you should find these files contained within the Day7Server1 project:

- Day7Server1.idl
- MySecondATLObj.h
- MySecondATLObj.cpp

There are certainly additional files to be found in the project, but these are the files the method wizard changed.

Let's start by examining the IDL file for Day7Server1. As a rule, this is a good place to start exploring any COM object if you happen to have the IDL file to peruse. The Day7Server1.idl file is similar to what you see in Listing 7.1.

LISTING 7.1   Day7Server1.idl File Contents

```
 1: // This file will be processed by the MIDL tool to
 2: // produce the type library (Day7Server1.tlb) and marshaling code.
 3:
 4: import "oaidl.idl";
 5: import "ocidl.idl";
 6:     [
 7:         object,
 8:         uuid(39606340-663E-11D3-896D-0000E8409B63),
 9:
10:         helpstring("IAddMethodDemo Interface"),
11:         pointer_default(unique)
12:     ]
13:     interface IAddMethodDemo : IUnknown
14:     {
15:         [helpstring("method SquareArg")]
16: ➥HRESULT SquareArg([in] double dIn, [out] double * pdOut);
17:         [helpstring("method CubeArg")]
18: ➥HRESULT CubeArg([in, out] double * pdArg);
19:     };
20:
21: [
22:     uuid(39606334-663E-11D3-896D-0000E8409B63),
23:     version(1.0),
24:     helpstring("Day7Server1 1.0 Type Library")
25: ]
26: library DAY7SERVER1Lib
27: {
28:     importlib("stdole32.tlb");
29:     importlib("stdole2.tlb");
30:
31:     [
32:         uuid(39606341-663E-11D3-896D-0000E8409B63),
33:         helpstring("TYATLObj2 Class")
34:     ]
35:     coclass TYATLObj2
36:     {
37:         [default] interface IAddMethodDemo;
38:     };
39: };
```

ANALYSIS   Much of what you see in Listing 7.1 should be familiar, so I won't reiterate a description of the code. You can find that in Day 3, if you need a refresher. In this listing, though, I've italicized several areas to examine more closely. The first is simply the declaration of the IAddMethodDemo interface (line 13):

```
interface IAddMethodDemo : IUnknown
```

In this case, the IDL file tells you the interface is a custom interface rather than a dual interface. You know this because IAddMethodDemo derives directly from IUnknown rather than from IDispatch. I'll discuss dual interfaces in more detail in Day 14, "ATL and Automation: Creating RoboObjects."

Returning to the IAddMethodDemo interface, you can see the two methods the wizard added to the source code (lines 15 through 18):

```
[helpstring("method SquareArg")]
➥HRESULT SquareArg([in] double dIn, [out] double * pdOut);
[helpstring("method CubeArg")]
➥HRESULT CubeArg([in, out] double * pdArg);
```

The wizard took the information I provided and inserted it directly into the IDL file. That's one reason why I added the method attribute tags [in], [out], and [in, out] when I specified the parameter list. The wizard won't add those for you, so you have to know enough IDL to add the attributes when you add the method parameters. Of course, if you later decide to modify the IDL attributes, feel free to edit the IDL file yourself.

Now let's turn to the C++ class's header file. This is where ATL will implement the COM object. The IDL file defines the interfaces the object exposes. The C++ files actually provide the functionality as defined by the IDL file.

If you open MySecondATLObj.h, you should see something similar to the code in Listing 7.2.

LISTING 7.2   MySecondATLObj.h File Contents

```
 1: // MySecondATLObj.h : Declaration of the CMySecondATLObj
 2:
 3: #ifndef __MYSECONDATLOBJ_H_
 4: #define __MYSECONDATLOBJ_H_
 5:
 6: #include "resource.h"        // main symbols
 7:
 8: /////////////////////////////////////////////////////////////////////////
 9: // CMySecondATLObj
10: class ATL_NO_VTABLE CMySecondATLObj :
11:     public CComObjectRootEx<CComSingleThreadModel>,
12:     public CComCoClass<CMySecondATLObj, &CLSID_TYATLObj2>,
13:     public IAddMethodDemo
14: {
15: public:
16:     CMySecondATLObj()
17:     {
18:     }
19:
```

```
20: DECLARE_REGISTRY_RESOURCEID(IDR_MYSECONDATLOBJ)
21:
22: DECLARE_PROTECT_FINAL_CONSTRUCT()
23:
24: BEGIN_COM_MAP(CMySecondATLObj)
25:     COM_INTERFACE_ENTRY(IAddMethodDemo)
26: END_COM_MAP()
27:
28: // IAddMethodDemo
29: public:
30:     STDMETHOD(CubeArg)(/*[in, out]*/ double * pdArg);
31:     STDMETHOD(SquareArg)(/*[in]*/ double dIn, /*[out]*/ double * pdOut);
32: };
33:
34: #endif //__MYSECONDATLOBJ_H_
```

ANALYSIS I've again highlighted a couple of interesting things in Listing 7.2. First, note that CMySecondATLObj inherits multiply from several base classes, including IAddMethodDemo (line 13).Also note that the wizard added the two methods as public members of CMySecondATLObj (lines 30 and 31). One nice thing the wizard did was to place the IDL attributes as comments. I often find this helpful.

So far, the wizard has done everything for you. However, when you open MySecondATLObj.cpp, you'll find the method stubs waiting for your creative inputs. MySecondATLObj.cpp, as the wizard left it, is shown in Listing 7.3.

LISTING 7.3 MySecondATLObj.cpp File Contents

```
1: // MySecondATLObj.cpp : Implementation of CMySecondATLObj
2: #include "stdafx.h"
3: #include "Day7Server1.h"
4: #include "MySecondATLObj.h"
5:
6: /////////////////////////////////////////////////////////////////////
7: // CMySecondATLObj
8:
9:
10: STDMETHODIMP CMySecondATLObj::SquareArg(double dIn, double *piOut)
11: {
12:     // TODO: Add your implementation code here
13:
14:     return S_OK;
15: }
16:
```

7

continues

LISTING 7.3   continued

```
17: STDMETHODIMP CMySecondATLObj::CubeArg(double *pdArg)
18: {
19:     // TODO: Add your implementation code here
20:
21:     return S_OK;
22: }
```

Now you can write some code! Let's change the method stubs to actually do something.
Clearly, their intent is to square and cube an incoming value, so feel free to implement
the code yourself before you review Listing 7.4, which shows you how I implemented
them.

LISTING 7.4   Revised MySecondATLObj.cpp File Contents

```
 1: // MySecondATLObj.cpp : Implementation of CMySecondATLObj
 2: #include "stdafx.h"
 3: #include "Day7Server1.h"
 4: #include "MySecondATLObj.h"
 5:
 6: /////////////////////////////////////////////////////////////////////
 7: // CMySecondATLObj
 8:
 9:
10: STDMETHODIMP CMySecondATLObj::SquareArg(double dIn, double *pdOut)
11: {
12:     // Check their pointer
13:     CHECKPTR2(pdOut,0.0)
14:
15:     // Check the input value's range.  We'll allow
16:     // numbers greater than -32767.0 but less than
17:     // 32767.0.  This just prevents overflow (and the
18:     // resulting error) for demo purposes.
19:     if ((dIn < -32767.0) || (dIn > 32767.0)) {
20:         // The value is out of range...
21:         return E_INVALIDARG;
22:     } // if
23:
24:     // The value passed, so do the multiplication
25:     // and store the result.
26:     *pdOut = dIn * dIn;
27:
28:     return S_OK;
29: }
30:
31: STDMETHODIMP CMySecondATLObj::CubeArg(double *pdArg)
32: {
```

```
33:     // Check their pointer
34:     CHECKPTR(pdArg)
35:
36:     // Check the input value's range.  We'll allow
37:     // numbers greater than -32767.0 but less than
38:     // 32767.0.  This just prevents overflow (and the
39:     // resulting error) for demo purposes.
40:     if ((*pdArg < -32767.0) || (*pdArg > 32767.0)) {
41:         // The value is out of range...
42:         return E_INVALIDARG;
43:     } // if
44:
45:     // The value passed, so do the multiplication
46:     // and store the result.
47:     *pdArg = *pdArg * *pdArg * *pdArg;
48:
49:     return S_OK;
50: }
```

ANALYSIS As for my implementation, both methods are nearly the same. In each case, I check the pointer-based parameters to see if they're NULL using one of two macros I wrote (lines 12 and 13)

```
// Check their pointer
CHECKPTR2(pdOut,0.0)
```

and (lines 33 and 34)

```
// Check their pointer
CHECKPTR(pdArg)
```

Both macros are designed to return an error HRESULT, E_POINTER, if the pointer is NULL (remember you can find the standard HRESULT values in WINERROR.H). I use the first macro, CHECKPTR(), for [in, out] parameters:

```
#define CHECKPTR(p) if ( p == NULL ) { return E_POINTER; }
```

In this case, I do nothing more than check the pointer. True, the parameter shouldn't be NULL because the client had to pass a value into the CubeArg() method, but it's safer to protect your code by checking just in case.

The more interesting situation arises with [out] parameters. In this case, the client passes your interface method a pointer variable into which you will place the outgoing data (which may be a value or another pointer). As a general rule of thumb, you should

7

always initialize [out] parameters, if they are pointers, to NULL at the beginning of your interface method (such as a pointer to BSTR data, or an array or structure you'll create). That way, if you later return an error HRESULT for some reason, the client (who may not have checked the HRESULT) won't have a bogus pointer to act upon.

I typically take this a step further. I choose to initialize any outgoing data before I work through the interface method. To do this, I use the CHECKPTR2() macro:

```
#define CHECKPTR2(p,val) if ( p == NULL ) { return E_POINTER; } \
                         else { *p = val; }
```

If the pointer the client passes to my interface method is NULL, I return E_POINTER. If not, I fill the variable with a default return value. For pointers, I would pass into CHECKPTR2() NULL as the val. In this case, for SquareArg(), I pass in 0.0 (line 13 in Listing 7.4). So, if anything goes wrong in SquareArg(), the client will be left with the value 0.0 in their variable.

If the pointer parameters successfully pass through my pointer checking macros, I then place an artificial limit on the value I will handle (lines 19 and 40):

```
if ((*pdArg < -32767.0) || (*pdArg > 32767.0)) {
    // The value is out of range...
    return E_INVALIDARG;
} // if
```

I placed a range restriction on the incoming argument because I haven't yet covered exception handling and other error topics. I'll get to those issues in Day 10, "ATL and Errors: What to Do When Things Break." If the incoming parameter is out of the bounds I decided to handle, I return another error HRESULT, E_INVALIDARG. If I didn't limit the range, the client could pass in any value, possibly causing a mathematical overflow.

Assuming the incoming value passed these tests, I then actually do the math (line 26)

```
*pdOut = dIn * dIn;
```

and (line 47)

```
*pdArg = *pdArg * *pdArg * *pdArg;
```

You can see I avoided the C runtime library by simply multiplying the values. I could also have used pow(). If I can avoid using the C runtime library, I do. This keeps the resulting module smaller, as you know; but it also reduces my need to ship a copy of the pertinent C runtime library every time I distribute new software. You won't always be able to do this; but if you can, it's a wise idea.

The COM object is now complete, so simply compile and register the resulting DLL. For this example, I also created another MFC-based test client, which you'll find with the sample code for this day. I won't discuss the client code here because it's not that different from what you saw in Day 1. You'll see a lot more MFC and client programming in Day 9, "Creating C++ Test Clients: You Can't Test What You Can't Execute."

I'd like to turn now to a topic that doesn't often receive much coverage, at least in the books I personally have purchased. Now that you've defined IAddMethodDemo and, presumably, you've shipped software using this COM object, what do you do if you find you want to add an additional method? You can't change IAddMethodDemo, because that interface is now immutable. There is a way to handle this situation, though, and that's up next.

Extending an Existing Interface

If you later wish you had added more functionality to IAddMethodDemo, but it has already been released to the public, you must create a new interface with the added method. (Remember, interfaces are immutable after you release them.) For example, I want to add a method to take the square root of the argument, but I left this out of the original interface definition. To add this method, I would have to edit the IDL file, by hand, and add a new interface and method, as shown in Listing 7.5.

LISTING 7.5   Revised Day7Server1.idl File Contents

```
 1: [
 2:         object,
 3:         uuid(39606350-663E-11D3-896D-0000E8409B63),
 4:
 5:         helpstring("IAddMethodDemo2 Interface"),
 6:         pointer_default(unique)
 7:     ]
 8:     interface IAddMethodDemo2 : IAddMethodDemo
 9:     {
10:         [helpstring("method SqrtArg")]
11: ➥HRESULT SqrtArg([in, out] double * pdArg);
12:     };
```

ANALYSIS   This definition follows the original definition for IAddMethodDemo. See the italicized section (lines 8 through 12). IAddMethodDemo2 derives from IAddMethodDemo, so IAddMethodDemo2 provides the two methods of IAddMethodDemo in addition to the new method to take the square root.

7

As you see, I had to create a new GUID to identify the interface. Note I also add the new interface IAddMethodDemo2 to the type library definition that you'll find towards the end of the IDL file. (I also promoted IAddMethodDemo2 to be the default interface the object exposes.)

```
coclass TYATLObj2
{
    [default] interface IAddMethodDemo2;
    interface IAddMethodDemo;
};
```

Note This technique works for custom interfaces only. Dual interfaces offer other problems, as I discuss in Day 14.

Note To instantiate this object, using CoCreateInstance() and the IID for IAddMethodDemo2, you can use the methods of IAddMethodDemo directly, or you can use QueryInterface() (and IID_IAddMethodDemo) to obtain a pointer to IAddMethodDemo and use its methods that way.

After I add the new interface to the IDL file, I change the MySecondATLObj.h header file. First, I add the new interface to the class's inheritance hierarchy:

```
class ATL NO VTABLE CMySecondATLObj :
    public CComObjectRootEx<CComSingleThreadModel>,
    public CComCoClass<CMySecondATLObj, &CLSID_TYATLObj2>,
    public IAddMethodDemo2
{
```

It is interesting that you no longer need to derive CMySecondATLObj from IAddMethodDemo because IAddMethodDemo2 is already derived from IAddMethodDemo. If you leave IAddMethodDemo in the inheritance chain, you generate a compilation error (after you recompiled the IDL file, that is).

```
c:\projects\ty atl\code\day7\day7server1\mysecondatlobj.h(15) :
        ➡error C2584: 'CMySecondATLObj' : direct base 'IAddMethodDemo'
        ➡is inaccessible; already a base of 'IAddMethodDemo2'
c:\projects\ty atl\code\day7\day7server1\day7server1.h(83) :
➡see declaration of 'IAddMethodDemo'
```

After I change the class's inheritance list, I then add a member to the COM map:

```
BEGIN_COM_MAP(CMySecondATLObj)
    COM_INTERFACE_ENTRY(IAddMethodDemo2)
    COM_INTERFACE_ENTRY(IAddMethodDemo)
END_COM_MAP()
```

In this case, both interfaces are listed because I want clients to have access to both from this server. Because I made the `IAddMethodDemo2` interface the default interface in the IDL file, I placed it before `IAddMethodDemo` in the COM map. I expect `IAddMethodDemo2` to be used more often, so I'm helping ATL (and my object's clients) by placing it at the beginning of the COM map so that ATL can return the interface pointer more quickly.

Finally, I would add the definition of the `SqrtArg()` method to the class definition:

```
// IAddMethodDemo
public:
    STDMETHOD(CubeArg)(/*[in, out]*/ double * piArg);
    STDMETHOD(SquareArg)(/*[in]*/ double iIn, /*[out]*/ double * piOut);

// IAddMethodDemo2
public:
    STDMETHOD(SqrtArg)(/*[in, out]*/ double * pdArg);
```

Because the IDL file tells me there will be a `SqrtArg()` method, as does the definition of `CMySecondATLObj`, I'd also have to add the implementation of the method to MySecondATLObj.cpp. I'd place the implementation after the existing implementations, as shown in Listing 7.6.:

LISTING 7.6 Further Revised MySecondATLObj.cpp File Contents

```
 1: STDMETHODIMP CMySecondATLObj::SqrtArg(double *pdArg)
 2: {
 3:     // Check their pointer
 4:     CHECKPTR(pdArg)
 5:
 6:     // Their return pointer was good, so check the value's
 7:     // sign.  If it's negative, return an error.
 8:     if ( *pdArg < 0.0 ) {
 9:         // Negative...
10:         return E_INVALIDARG;
11:     } // if
12:
13:     // It's not negative, so take the square root
14:     *pdArg = sqrt(*pdArg);
15:
16:     return S_OK;
17: }
```

Of course, to access the `sqrt()` method, I had to include the MATH.H file:

```
#include "stdafx.h"
#include "Day7Server1.h"
#include "MySecondATLObj.h"
#include <math.h>
```

7

Be aware that I resorted to using the C runtime call sqrt() to actually perform the square root calculation. Because I now have a dependency on the C runtime, I must remember to remove the _ATL_MIN_CRT preprocessor value from the release compilation project settings, or they will not link properly. I also have to ship the C runtime library with my components, if I want the correct version available on the target computer (they're different for Win9x and WinNT). Otherwise, I have to link it statically.

> **Note**
>
> As I'm sure you noted, I didn't use a wizard to add the new interface. That's because none is available. The technique I've shown you here, revising an existing interface, is also used to add one or more independent interfaces to an ATL COM object. The ATL Object Wizard helps you create the first interface, and that's it. If your COM object needs to provide more interfaces, you're on your own. As you have seen, it isn't difficult to do.

That completes my discussion of adding ATL COM object methods. But before I finish discussing interface methods and move on to properties, I want to give you a bit more detail regarding some of the IDL parameter attributes available to tailor your COM object's methods and marshaling.

IDL Method Attributes Revisited

You're probably now comfortable with the IDL parameter attributes [in], [out], and [in, out]. You should be familiar with a few more IDL parameter attributes, however. You won't need them often, at least in most cases; but when you do require them, it'll be helpful to have seen them at least once. The Universal Marshaler uses none of these, so keep that in mind. You'll need to provide proxy/stub DLLs with your objects if you marshal data using these attributes.

The first is string. If one of your parameters is a string value, either char, byte, or wchar_t, you should use the string attribute to help MIDL with marshaling. For example, if you have this method defined in your IDL file

```
HRESULT Method1([in, string] char * szString);
```

MIDL is able to write the proxy/stub code required to check the length of the string when the data is marshaled and can pass the correct data to your COM object. Otherwise, you have to pass character data as an array of chars (or bytes, or wchar_ts).

There are times when you do want to pass arrays as parameters, and this is where the size_is() or max_is() IDL attributes come in handy. In general, MIDL won't have any idea how much memory to allocate and how many bytes of data to transfer if you pass array data back and forth from client to server (the exception is string data, as you've seen). For example, I might have an array of integer values I want to pass into a COM object. My client code was written to allocate a specific amount of memory to store the integer data, perhaps on the stack like this:

```
int iData[32];
```

COM, though, has no knowledge regarding the size of the iData array. Without this knowledge, COM cannot marshal the array from client to server.

Therefore, the COM method should apply the size_is() or max_is() IDL parameter attributes:

```
HRESULT Method2([in] iSize, [in, size_is(iSize)] int * piDataArray);
```

or

```
HRESULT Method3([in] iNumElements, [in, max_is(iNumElements)] int *
piDataArray);
```

As you see, you pass the array data along with an additional value, either the total size of the array or the maximum number of elements to transfer. You can't use both size_is() and max_is() within the same parameter list, but either will work. They are related in that specifying size_is(x) is the same as specifying max_is(x-1). Which you use is a matter of choice and optimization given your particular needs.

The final IDL attribute I'll describe here involves passing pointers to other COM objects. MIDL is capable of generating marshaling code to pass COM objects via their IUnknown pointers. But if all you received on the other end was an IUnknown pointer, you have to QueryInterface() for the correct interface pointer. Instead, IDL provides the iid_is() attribute that's used in a similar manner to size_is() or max_is(). Instead of simply passing in the interface pointer alone, you also pass in a discriminator, which for iid_is() is the IID of the interface. In this case, you can use the interface pointer that you receive directly instead of its IUnknown base interface pointer.

For example, assume you have this method defined in your IDL file:

```
HRESULT Method4([in] REFIID riid, [out, iid_is(riid)] IUnknown ** ppvObject);
```

When you use this method, the supporting COM object will produce and return to you an interface pointer of type riid rather than IUnknown, which will be returned to you in the ppvObject variable you pass into the method.

There are a great many more things you can do with IDL method attributes, but as a rule, the ones I've presented are, by far, the most common. As I mentioned in Day 3, Wrox Press's *COM IDL and Interface Design*, ISBN 1-86-100225-4, is an excellent guide to high-performance interface design and IDL coding.

7

Adding Properties

Now that you've seen how to create an ATL-based COM object and add methods to your interfaces, it's time to learn about properties. I've mentioned properties throughout the book, and in a nutshell, I described a property as a method that appears to be an attribute (in the C++ sense) of the interface (or object) to certain containers, such as Visual Basic. Why is this, and how does it work?

Properties Versus Methods

As you've seen, interface methods simply implement the functionality the interface provides. A method, to a COM interface, is no different than a method to a C++ class. For example, this interface has a method Foo(), shown in IDL:

```
[
    // (IDL object attributes here)
]
interface IBar : public IUnknown
{
    [helpstring("method Foo")] HRESULT Foo();
};
```

Compare this to this C++ class that also has a method Foo():

```
class CBar
{
public:
    unsigned long Foo();
};
```

Both the C++ class CBar and the interface IBar have the public method Foo(), and you use Foo() similarly for both.

I can add a public attribute to CBar that clients of my C++ class could easily change:

```
class CBar
{
public:
    unsigned long Foo();
    unsigned long iFooBar;
};
```

As a C++ programmer, you're quite familiar with this situation. For example, consider this code:

```
CBar* pBar = new CBar;
unsigned long iBarAttribute = pBar->iFooBar; // accessor
iBarAttribute += (pBar->Foo() + 1); // call method
pBar->iFooBar = iBarAttribute; // mutator
```

The goal of the COM interface property is the same, which is to enable the client programmer to deal with an object attribute in the same way I did with the C++ object CBar I just presented. Instead of having to call a function to retrieve a specific value from the object (an *accessor* method call), change it, and then write it back to the object using another function (a *mutator* method call), the programmer simply writes something like this:

```
object.attribute = value
```

or this

```
variable = object.attribute
```

Interface properties, then, are a simplification, at least for some development environments. Visual Basic is one such environment, but there are others, such as Microsoft Access or any of the Office suite of products. Interface properties are not a simplification for C++, however, as you'll see shortly. As a C++ programmer, you'll deal with properties as separate accessor and mutator methods.

The development environments that provide the property simplification I mentioned do so because they honor the IDL attributes applied to the interface's property methods. That is, you must provide accessor and mutator methods to your interface (either or both). You then anoint them with the proper IDL attributes to make them appear as a single entity to type library viewers, such as Visual Basic. You'll see the details of this a bit later in the day.

For now, let's build a new COM object and add some methods and properties. You'll use this object to compare the differences between methods and properties in two development environments, Visual C++ and Visual Basic.

Inserting Properties into Your Interface

As it happens, the mechanics of adding a property are very much the same as those for adding a method, at least until you have the wizard up and running. At that point, you begin to see the difference between properties and methods.

Let's begin by creating a new ATL-based COM object. I created a new object, Day7Server2, as an in-process (DLL) server, and to that I added an ActiveX control called MyThirdATLObj. To add an ActiveX control object, you select Controls from the Object Wizard, and from there you select Full Control. I've shown the Names property page in Figure 7.5 to help you with the object's naming. This will be important when you load the control into the various development environments, at least if you want to follow my example.

7

FIGURE 7.5

The MyThirdATLObj's Names property page.

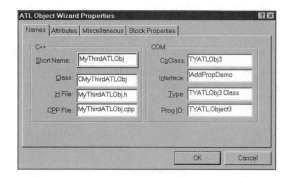

For this example, you needn't be concerned about changing any of the other object settings on the remaining property pages. You won't actually use the control you develop here to do anything. I merely want to show you how properties differ from methods in the development environments, not the control as it appears when it is executing. That's for Day 16, "ATL and ActiveX: Modern Control Packaging."

After you've created the basic ActiveX control, you should add a method called SomeMethod(). The method should return an HRESULT, and it isn't necessary for the method to accept any parameters. The information I used is shown in Figure 7.6. This is very similar to the work you did earlier in the day, so refer back to that part of the lesson if you have any questions about adding a method to your object.

FIGURE 7.6

MyThirdATLObj's SomeMethod() *wizard settings.*

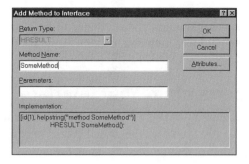

This will provide you with a method you can use for comparison to the property you'll insert in the next section. Just as you used a wizard to add the method, you'll use a wizard to add a property.

Mr. Wizard Revisited

Because you just added an interface method, you probably already have the Visual Studio Workspace window handy—with the tree control showing the interface you just created. As when adding a method, right-click on the interface tree node and select Add Property from the context menu, as you see in Figure 7.7.

FIGURE 7.7

Invoking the Visual Studio Add Property wizard.

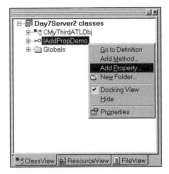

If you do this, the ATL property wizard should pop up, as shown in Figure 7.8.

FIGURE 7.8

The Visual Studio Add Property wizard.

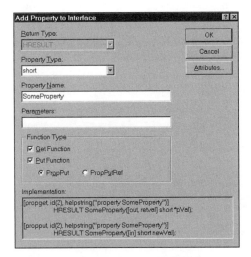

The first thing you should note is that the property's return type is an HRESULT, and you can't change this! Not only does the property have a return type, (indicating the property is implemented as a method), but the property value itself isn't returned directly from the method itself.

What you can change, however, is the property type, the property name, the parameters, and the function type. The property type is simply the data type of the property, be it a short integer, long integer, IDispatch pointer, or any number of other types you can select from the Property Type drop-down list. The property I added uses short integers (you'll see why I chose this data type when I discuss property enumerations). The property name is simply the name of the property, and in most cases, you don't want to add any parameters in the Parameters edit control. Additional parameters within property

7

method calls are difficult for some languages to easily express, so I recommend you avoid adding parameters to your properties altogether. The Function Type controls are used to specify the access to the property.

For example, if you want clients of your object to have property read and write capability, leave the function type `GetFunction` and `PutFunction` controls checked. For a read-only property, uncheck the `PutFunction` control. If, for some reason, you want a write-only property, uncheck the `GetFunction` control. If you allow property writes, you can specify that the property be passed out of your property method as either a value (`PropPut`) or by reference (`PropPutRef`), which indicates the parameter value is to be exported via a pointer (similar to using the `[out]` IDL method attribute).

After you've made your choices, you can click OK and have the wizard process your source files. Before you do, however, click the Attributes button. The Attributes dialog you see, shown in Figure 7.9, is very similar to the same dialog you saw for methods (Figure 7.4). There is an additional attribute, the `ID`, and the attributes drop-down list contains more and different IDL attributes than were available for mere methods. I won't cover all the attributes in this list, but a few merit closer inspection. I'll cover these when I cover the IDL attributes for properties.

FIGURE 7.9

The Visual Studio Add Property Wizard's Attributes Dialog Box.

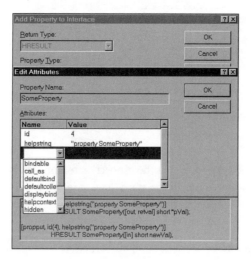

Feel free to add attributes and change their values. When you're finished with the attributes dialog, click OK if you made changes or click Cancel if you followed my request and were just looking. Assuming the property settings look good, click OK to close the ATL property wizard.

The wizard will now open your source files and insert some code. Just what files are changed and what code is added is the topic of the next section.

Changes to Your Files

You probably won't be surprised to learn the files modified by the ATL Property wizard are the same files modified by the ATL Method wizard. After all, properties *are* methods to your COM object. If you followed my naming convention, these are the files that were changed after you added the property:

- Day7Server2.idl
- MyThirdATLObj.h
- MyThirdATLObj.cpp

Of course, the interface changed, so it makes sense that the IDL file is modified. Because there has to be some code involved with managing the property, it makes sense that the C++ declaration (.H) and implementation (.CPP) files also be modified to support the new property. Let's look at each in more detail.

The IDL file, after the insertion of the property, is shown in Listing 7.7. By now I'm sure you're getting more comfortable with looking at IDL code, so I'll skip right to the good part, which I've highlighted in Listing 7.7.

LISTING 7.7   Day7Server2.idl File Contents

```
 1: // Day7Server2.idl : IDL source for Hour9Server.dll
 2: //
 3:
 4: // This file will be processed by the MIDL tool to
 5: // produce the type library (Day7Server2.tlb) and marshaling code.
 6:
 7: import "oaidl.idl";
 8: import "ocidl.idl";
 9: #include "olectl.h"
10:
11:     [
12:         object,
13:         uuid(49E7910C-5431-11D3-896D-0000E8409B63),
14:         dual,
15:         helpstring("IAddPropDemo Interface"),
16:         pointer_default(unique)
17:     ]
18:     interface IAddPropDemo : IDispatch
19:     {
20:         [id(1), helpstring("method SomeMethod")]HRESULT SomeMethod();
21:         [propget, id(2), helpstring("property SomeProperty")]
            ➥HRESULT SomeProperty([out, retval] short *pVal);
```

continues

7

LISTING 7.7   continued

```
22:          [propput, id(2), helpstring("property SomeProperty")]
             ➥HRESULT SomeProperty([in] short newVal);
23:      };
24:
25: [
26:      uuid(49E79100-5431-11D3-896D-0000E8409B63),
28:      version(1.0),
29:      helpstring("Day7Server2 1.0 Type Library")
30: ]
31: library DAY7SERVER2Lib
32: {
33:      importlib("stdole32.tlb");
34:      importlib("stdole2.tlb");
35:
36:      [
37:          uuid(49E7910D-5431-11D3-896D-0000E8409B63),
38:          helpstring("TYATLObj3 Class")
39:      ]
40:      coclass TYATLObj3
41:      {
42:          [default] interface IAddPropDemo;
43:      };
44: };
```

ANALYSIS   The property actually consists of two methods, one to access the property value and one to set it (lines 20 through 23):

```
[propget, id(2), helpstring("property SomeProperty")]
➥HRESULT SomeProperty([out, retval] short *pVal);
[propput, id(2), helpstring("property SomeProperty")]
➥HRESULT SomeProperty([in] short newVal);
```

The accessor function is indicated first, as you see by the propget IDL method attribute. The mutator is similarly marked using the propput attribute. The id(2) value indicates this property is the second method in the dispatch interface (ActiveX controls require a dual interface, which implements IDispatch). Note both the accessor and mutator methods use the same dispatch ID. The retval parameter attribute shown with the accessor function is used to make the indicated value appear to be returned from the method. The method actually returns an HRESULT, but the data stored in pVal appears to be returned from the method in the client's code. This is part of the simplification that takes place in the client's development environment.

The MyThirdATLObj.h file is pretty ugly at this point, but that's because I haven't introduced ActiveX yet. This is another one of those "which goes first" situations. ActiveX exploits properties, but it makes sense to understand properties before tackling the complex topic of ActiveX in general. So when you look at the code in Listing 7.8, don't let it scare you. Believe me, it'll make a lot more sense in Day 16, "ATL and ActiveX: Modern Control Packaging."

That said, MyThirdATLObj.h is shown in Listing 7.8. I've again highlighted the interesting sections, at least for this discussion.

LISTING 7.8   MyThirdATLObj.h File Contents

```
 1: // MyThirdATLObj.h : Declaration of the CMyThirdATLObj
 2:
 3: #ifndef __MYTHIRDATLOBJ_H_
 4: #define __MYTHIRDATLOBJ_H_
 5:
 6: #include "resource.h"       // main symbols
 7: #include <atlctl.h>
 8:
 9:
10: //////////////////////////////////////////////////////////////////////
11: // CMyThirdATLObj
12: class ATL_NO_VTABLE CMyThirdATLObj :
13:     public CComObjectRootEx<CComSingleThreadModel>,
14:     public IDispatchImpl<IAddPropDemo, &IID_IAddPropDemo,
15: ➥&LIBID_DAY7SERVER2Lib>,
16:     public CComControl<CMyThirdATLObj>,
17:     public IPersistStreamInitImpl<CMyThirdATLObj>,
18:     public IOleControlImpl<CMyThirdATLObj>,
19:     public IOleObjectImpl<CMyThirdATLObj>,
20:     public IOleInPlaceActiveObjectImpl<CMyThirdATLObj>,
21:     public IViewObjectExImpl<CMyThirdATLObj>,
22:     public IOleInPlaceObjectWindowlessImpl<CMyThirdATLObj>,
23:     public IPersistStorageImpl<CMyThirdATLObj>,
24:     public ISpecifyPropertyPagesImpl<CMyThirdATLObj>,
25:     public IQuickActivateImpl<CMyThirdATLObj>,
26:     public IDataObjectImpl<CMyThirdATLObj>,
27:     public IProvideClassInfo2Impl<&CLSID_TYATLObj3, NULL,
28: ➥&LIBID_DAY7SERVER2Lib>,
29:     public CComCoClass<CMyThirdATLObj, &CLSID_TYATLObj3>
30: {
31: public:
32:     CMyThirdATLObj()
33:     {
34:     }
35:
36: DECLARE_REGISTRY_RESOURCEID(IDR_MYTHIRDATLOBJ)
37:
38: DECLARE_PROTECT_FINAL_CONSTRUCT()
```

7

continues

LISTING 7.8 continued

```
39:
40: BEGIN_COM_MAP(CMyThirdATLObj)
41:     COM_INTERFACE_ENTRY(IAddPropDemo)
42:     COM_INTERFACE_ENTRY(IDispatch)
43:     COM_INTERFACE_ENTRY(IViewObjectEx)
44:     COM_INTERFACE_ENTRY(IViewObject2)
45:     COM_INTERFACE_ENTRY(IViewObject)
46:     COM_INTERFACE_ENTRY(IOleInPlaceObjectWindowless)
47:     COM_INTERFACE_ENTRY(IOleInPlaceObject)
48:     COM_INTERFACE_ENTRY2(IOleWindow, IOleInPlaceObjectWindowless)
49:     COM_INTERFACE_ENTRY(IOleInPlaceActiveObject)
50:     COM_INTERFACE_ENTRY(IOleControl)
51:     COM_INTERFACE_ENTRY(IOleObject)
52:     COM_INTERFACE_ENTRY(IPersistStreamInit)
53:     COM_INTERFACE_ENTRY2(IPersist, IPersistStreamInit)
54:     COM_INTERFACE_ENTRY(ISpecifyPropertyPages)
55:     COM_INTERFACE_ENTRY(IQuickActivate)
56:     COM_INTERFACE_ENTRY(IPersistStorage)
57:     COM_INTERFACE_ENTRY(IDataObject)
58:     COM_INTERFACE_ENTRY(IProvideClassInfo)
59:     COM_INTERFACE_ENTRY(IProvideClassInfo2)
60: END_COM_MAP()
61:
62: BEGIN_PROP_MAP(CMyThirdATLObj)
63:     PROP_DATA_ENTRY("_cx", m_sizeExtent.cx, VT_UI4)
64:     PROP_DATA_ENTRY("_cy", m_sizeExtent.cy, VT_UI4)
65:     // Example entries
66:     // PROP_ENTRY("Property Description", dispid, clsid)
67:     // PROP_PAGE(CLSID_StockColorPage)
68: END_PROP_MAP()
69:
70: BEGIN_MSG_MAP(CMyThirdATLObj)
71:     CHAIN_MSG_MAP(CComControl<CMyThirdATLObj>)
72:     DEFAULT_REFLECTION_HANDLER()
73: END_MSG_MAP()
74: // Handler prototypes:
75: //  LRESULT MessageHandler(UINT uMsg, WPARAM wParam, LPARAM lParam,
    ➥BOOL& bHandled);
76: //  LRESULT CommandHandler(WORD wNotifyCode, WORD wID, HWND hWndCtl,
    ➥BOOL& bHandled);
77: //  LRESULT NotifyHandler(int idCtrl, LPNMHDR pnmh, BOOL& bHandled);
78:
79:
80:
81: // IViewObjectEx
82:     DECLARE_VIEW_STATUS(VIEWSTATUS_SOLIDBKGND | VIEWSTATUS_OPAQUE)
83:
84: // IAddPropDemo
85: public:
```

```
86:     STDMETHOD(get_SomeProperty)(/*[out, retval]*/ short *pVal);
87:     STDMETHOD(put_SomeProperty)(/*[in]*/ short newVal);
88:     STDMETHOD(SomeMethod)();
89:
90:     HRESULT OnDraw(ATL_DRAWINFO& di)
91:     {
92:         RECT& rc = *(RECT*)di.prcBounds;
93:         Rectangle(di.hdcDraw, rc.left, rc.top, rc.right, rc.bottom);
94:
95:         SetTextAlign(di.hdcDraw, TA_CENTER|TA_BASELINE);
96:         LPCTSTR pszText = _T("ATL 3.0 : MyThirdATLObj");
97:         TextOut(di.hdcDraw,
98:             (rc.left + rc.right) / 2,
99:             (rc.top + rc.bottom) / 2,
100:             pszText,
101:             lstrlen(pszText));
102:
103:        return S_OK;
104:     }
105: };
106:
107: #endif //__MYTHIRDATLOBJ_H_
```

ANALYSIS Whew! There is a lot here. Luckily, you didn't have to type it. The wizards really do a nice job. This header file is a typical ActiveX header file, and although it looks complex, it really is just a COM object that manages a number of interfaces (the interfaces required to support ActiveX). Because of this, the inheritance list is long, and the number of COM map entries is greater than in any COM map you've seen so far. The basic ATL principles hold—this object exposes interfaces, and the interfaces are listed in both the inheritance list (as ATL templates) and the COM map (as interfaces the object exposes).

If you look closely, you'll see how ATL supports dual interfaces. All the ATL-based COM objects you've examined in this book have had custom interfaces, so the interface implementation is a part of the C++ class's inheritance chain. This is not directly so with the dual interface. Instead, your interface is a part of the dual interface, as shown here (from lines 14 and 15 of Listing 7.8):

```
public IDispatchImpl<IAddPropDemo, &IID_IAddPropDemo,
➡&LIBID_DAY7SERVER2Lib>,
```

The IDispatchImpl<> template uses your C++ interface implementation, your interface's IID, and your interface's type library IID to fully implement IDispatch for you. Because there is still the custom nature of the dual interface (your interface derives from

7

IDispatch, but it provides its own implementation), you'll see your interface in the COM map (line 41):

```
COM_INTERFACE_ENTRY(IAddPropDemo)
```

A lot of other supporting ActiveX code follows the COM map, such as the property map (BEGIN_PROP_MAP(), line 62), which allows the ActiveX control to store properties. You'll often add entries to the property map that correspond to properties you add to the control (as you're doing in this day). I'll discuss the ActiveX property map further in Day 16.

Following the property map, you see the message map (BEGIN_MSG_MAP(), line 70). ActiveX controls process Windows messages, and the message map tells ATL which Windows messages this control is interested in processing. Although I'll revisit this map in Day 16, you'll really see more detail in Day 13, "Creating ATL Applications: Where ATL Meets Win32," in which I address using ATL as a Windows API wrapper.

If you look a little further, you see some familiar things. Here you find the (C++) definition of the method and parameter you just added to the ActiveX control (lines 86 through 88):

```
STDMETHOD(get_SomeProperty)(/*[out, retval]*/ short *pVal);
STDMETHOD(put_SomeProperty)(/*[in]*/ short newVal);
STDMETHOD(SomeMethod)();
```

As you can see, the wizard took the property name you provided and concatenated it to get_ and put_ to create the true C++ implementations. These methods have now been defined, and you'll find their (initial) implementations in MyThirdATLObj.cpp, which I've included in Listing 7.9.

LISTING 7.9　MyThirdATLObj.cpp File Contents

```
 1: // MyThirdATLObj.cpp : Implementation of CMyThirdATLObj
 2:
 3: #include "stdafx.h"
 4: #include "Day7Server2.h"
 5: #include "MyThirdATLObj.h"
 6:
 7: /////////////////////////////////////////////////////////////////////////
 8: // CMyThirdATLObj
 9:
10:
11: STDMETHODIMP CMyThirdATLObj::SomeMethod()
12: {
13:     // TODO: Add your implementation code here
14:
15:     return S_OK;
16: }
```

```
17:
18: STDMETHODIMP CMyThirdATLObj::get_SomeProperty(short *pVal)
19: {
20:     // TODO: Add your implementation code here
21:
22:     return S_OK;
23: }
24:
25: STDMETHODIMP CMyThirdATLObj::put_SomeProperty(short newVal)
26: {
27:     // TODO: Add your implementation code here
28:
29:     return S_OK;
30: }
```

As usual, there isn't much to the wizard's implementations but it's a good starting point. Properties, in general, are actually C++ attributes when implemented in C++. This isn't a universal rule, but you'll find it is often true. So let's add an attribute to CMyThirdATLObj that the property methods can change.

In this case, I added a public attribute m_iProperty to MyThirdATLObj.h:

```
// IAddPropDemo
protected:
    short m_iProperty;
```

I also changed the class's constructor to initialize the property value to zero:

```
CMyThirdATLObj() : m_iProperty(0)
{
}
```

Now that I have a variable in which I can store the property, I can finalize the implementation of the property methods:

```
STDMETHODIMP CMyThirdATLObj::get_SomeProperty(short *pVal)
{
    // Check their pointer
    CHECKPTR2(pVal,NULL)

    // Simply return their value
    *pVal = m_iProperty;

    return S_OK;
}

STDMETHODIMP CMyThirdATLObj::put_SomeProperty(short newVal)
{
```

7

```
    // Simply accept their value
    m_iProperty = newVal;

    return S_OK;
}
```

With this code in place, compile and register the object as you normally would. Next, you will see how two different development environments look at the property you just added.

Object Properties in Visual C++

To see how Visual C++ handles properties, create a new MFC (EXE) project. It won't matter what type of MFC application it is, although I usually select the dialog-based application for testing purposes. I say that it won't matter because you won't actually compile the application today. The goal here is to simply insert the control into the MFC project and examine some source code. I'll really get into the details in Day 9, "Creating C++ Test Clients: You Can't Test What You Can't Execute," where I show you more about creating MFC test applications.

You begin by creating a dialog-based test application project named *Day7Client2* (accept all the defaults for the project to speed things up). After Visual Studio creates the source code and loads the project, add the ATL COM object you just created. You do this by using the Components and Controls Gallery, which you access through Project, Add To Project, Components and Controls. This is shown in Figure 7.10. To see all the registered ActiveX controls, double-click on the Registered ActiveX Controls folder.

FIGURE 7.10

The Visual Studio Components and Controls Gallery.

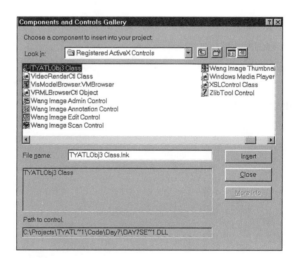

To insert the control, scroll the list of ActiveX controls over until you see the control named TYATLObj3 Class (clearly, I need remedial object naming help!). Double-click on this list item and click OK on the resulting confirmation dialog. Visual Studio then asks you to provide some information about how to name the source files it is about to create, as you see in Figure 7.11.

FIGURE 7.11

The Visual Studio Confirm Classes dialog.

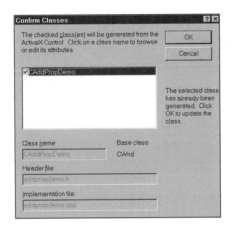

In this case, just click OK to accept the defaults. This dialog will disappear, leaving you at the Components and Controls Gallery dialog, at which time you should click Close.

Visual Studio will then read the control's type library and create two new source files, which it includes in your project. If you accepted the default filenames, you should find ADDPROPDEMO.CPP and ADDPROPDEMO.H added to your project, and it's these files I want you to examine.

First, open the ADDPROPDEMO.H file and look towards the bottom for this code:

```
class CAddPropDemo : public CWnd
{

    (edited for brevity)


// Operations
public:
    void SomeMethod();
    short GetSomeProperty();
    void SetSomeProperty(short nNewValue);
};
```

I edited the code above to remove the MFC-specific stuff not of interest to this topic (most of it is MFC wrapper code related to creating an instance of the control). It's here you see that Visual C++ implements the property as two methods, GetSomeProperty()

7

and `SetSomeProperty()`. If you were to create an instance of `CAddPropDemo`, you could change the property using these two methods.

You'll find the implementation of the property methods in the ADDPROPDEMO.CPP file:

```
short CAddPropDemo::GetSomeProperty()
{
    short result;
    InvokeHelper(0x2, DISPATCH_PROPERTYGET, VT_I2, (void*)&result, NULL);
    return result;
}

void CAddPropDemo::SetSomeProperty(short nNewValue)
{
    static BYTE parms[] =
        VTS_I2;
    InvokeHelper(0x2, DISPATCH_PROPERTYPUT, VT_EMPTY, NULL, parms,
        nNewValue);
}
```

The implementation uses the MFC `CWnd::InvokeHelper()` method, named after the `IDispatch::Invoke()` function. Here you see that the dispatch ID (`0x2`), which was the same as that specified in the IDL file. You also see the data consists of `VT_I2` (get) or `VTS_I2` (put), each of which indicates that a short integer is to be used (the 2 in `VT_I2` and `VTS_I2` indicates 2 bytes, which is a short integer in 32-bit Windows platforms).

You'll see very much more of this in Day 9 and Day 16, so I won't fully describe this MFC test application. Here is the code that reads and writes the ActiveX control's property:

```
void CDay7Client2Dlg::OnChange()
{
    // Take the value from the edit control and provide it
    // to the ActiveX control.
    UpdateData(TRUE);
    m_CTYATLObj3.SetSomeProperty(atoi(m_strPropValEdit));

    // Then, read the ActiveX control's property
    // and place that value in the text control.
    m_strPropValText.Format("%d",m_CTYATLObj3.GetSomeProperty());
    UpdateData(FALSE);
}
```

At this time, it's enough to see that Visual C++ reads the ActiveX control's type library and creates wrapper source code for you. This wrapper code implements property methods as true accessor and mutator methods, rather than as attributes of a C++ class. You see this in the code I just presented. This is very different from what you'll see in Visual Basic, which I'll show you in the next section.

Object Properties in Visual Basic

To create a test application in Visual Basic, activate Visual Basic and select the Standard EXE list item. This creates a blank form onto which you can add controls and glue logic. To see what effect your control has within Visual Basic, load the ActiveX control into the Visual Basic control palette. You do this by selecting your control from the controls list you activate by selecting Tools, Components. The dialog box on my system is shown in Figure 7.12. To select your control, simply check the box next to Day7Server2 1.0 Type Library and click OK.

FIGURE 7.12

The Visual Basic Components dialog box.

After you've selected the control, Visual Basic will place its icon on the component toolbar, as you see in Figure 7.13. Unless you changed the icon (I didn't), you'll see the standard ATL control icon on the toolbar. Click and release this button, then click and drag the mouse over the Visual Basic form (Form1) to size the control. If you size the control rectangle to be large enough, you should see the text `ATL 3.0 : MyThirdATLObj` within the rectangle.

At this point, you've successfully inserted the control into your Visual Basic form. If you glance at the Properties window, you should see `SomeProperty` in the left-hand column. If you click inside the associated right-hand column, you can provide the property with a default value (I used zero). This is shown in Figure 7.14. Feel free to change this property value. (Be sure to try a value larger than 32767 to see what happens if you provide a value too large for a short integer to contain.)

7

FIGURE 7.13

*The Visual Basic
Component Toolbar.*

FIGURE 7.14

*The Visual Basic
Properties window.*

I added a few controls to the form, as well as some glue logic, to allow for interactive
property changes. The form appears as you see it in Figure 7.15.

FIGURE 7.15

*The Visual Basic con-
trol test form.*

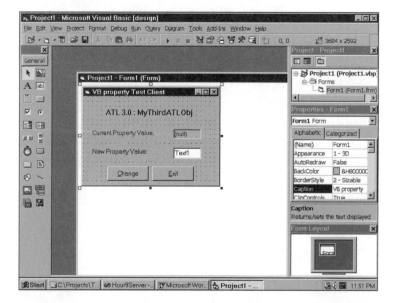

If you provide a value in the edit control and then click Change, the value is taken from the edit control and provided to the ActiveX control for use. I then request the value back from the ActiveX control and display the result in the upper (label control) value. The code I use to do this is quite simple, as you can see:

```
Private Sub cmdChange_Click()
    'Read the value from the edit control,
    'then assign it to the ActiveX control.
    'If successful, fill the text control
    'with the ActiveX control property.
    TYATLObj31.SomeProperty = edtPropVal
    lblPropVal = TYATLObj31.SomeProperty
End Sub
```

Visual Basic makes things quite easy, as I'm sure you'll agree. I added the control to my palette, dragged it to my form, added some other controls, and wired things up. No muss, no fuss. But, you should also realize that Visual Basic hid from you the true nature of the property, so you lost a bit of control over the system as things were abstracted. I see this as neither good nor bad, as long as you know this has happened and are happy to let Visual Basic mask this type of thing to provide for speedier application development.

I'm sure you now have the idea—methods are methods and properties are methods. Some development environments, though, hide this fact from you to make it appear the property is really some sort of control attribute. The key is in the IDL you define, which I'll turn to next.

IDL Property Attributes

I quickly glossed over the IDL property attributes available to you when you added the property to your ActiveX control. It's time I provided a quick overview of the more commonly used attributes you can apply to your object's properties.

For example, `bindable` indicates the property supports data binding, which allows for container (client) notifications whenever the data changes. `bindable` works with `displaybind`, in that the development environment shows the `bindable` parameter as actually `bindable`. `defaultbind` indicates that this property is the single property that best represents this control, and there should be only one `defaultbind` property associated with the control. `requestedit` indicates that this property supports edit request notification, which is a type of handshaking or negotiation, which the control and the container can perform to make sure the property can indeed be changed.

As with methods, there is a local attribute and a hidden attribute. `local`, of course, indicates that the parameter is nonremotable. `hidden` indicates that the property should not be made available to type library browsers. The Visual Basic programmer, for example,

7

won't see this property if you mark it as `hidden`. `nonbrowsable` indicates that the property will appear in an object browser (such as the OleView tool that ships with Visual Studio), but it won't appear in the property list of type library (property) browsers, such as Visual Basic. This makes the property hidden to the Visual Basic developer from within Visual Basic, but not to the general browsing public. Speaking of Visual Basic, you'll find `retval` used often with properties to simulate the return value of the accessor method. Instead of showing the client the true return value, which is an `HRESULT`, the development environment instead indicates that the return value is the property value itself (if you specify [`out`, `retval`] as the property method's attribute).

Finally, `restricted` indicates that the property cannot be arbitrarily used. What this actually means is that the property can't be used in a scripted environment, but it can be used from a compiled environment. You can't manage this property from Microsoft Access, but you can do so from Visual C++.

These are the more useful attributes you can use with property methods. One more IDL topic you might find useful is enumeration. If you want to restrict the client's selections for a given property, you can have the property accept an enumerated parameter. That's explained next.

Property Enumerations

In C++, you commonly find enumerated variables instead of simple numerical variables, especially where attributes are concerned. Consider the following C++ class:

```
class CFooBar
{
public:
    enum Colors { Black = 0, Red, Green, Blue, White };
    Colors m_clr;
...
};
```

The attribute `CFooBar::m_clr` is of `Color` type, so it might contain the values `Black` through `White`, not 0 through 4 or anything else— just `Black` through `White`. The enumeration limits you to your selection of values `m_clr` can take.

You can do much the same thing with properties, and the secret again is the IDL definition. There is a catch, though. First, I'll show you how to properly define a property enumeration, and then I'll show you how they're used.

Enumerations in IDL are very much like those in C++. For example, the Color enumeration I used in the previous C++ class looks like this in IDL:

```
enum Colors { Black = 0, Red, Green, Blue, White };
```

Here's the catch. If you used this enumeration, because IDL is based on C and not C++, you must define every variable parameter as enum Colors. Because you're probably more interested in defining the parameter as being of type Colors instead (no enum), you probably typedef the enumeration, as shown here:

```
typedef enum { Black = 0, Red, Green, Blue, White } Colors;
```

This is called an *anonymous enum*, and it still won't work. The reason is that MIDL will assign all anonymous enums a name that is a concatenation of the IDL file name and an internal counter. If you compiled this enumeration into your ActiveX control, the resulting .H file would show the enumeration defined like this:

```
enum __MIDL___MIDL_itf_Day7Server2_0000_0001
    { Black = 0,
      Red   = 1,
      Green = 2,
      Blue = 3,
      White = 4
    } Colors;
```

Now, instead of referring to enumerated parameters as enum Colors, you would have to refer to them as enum __MIDL___MIDL_itf_Day7Server2_0000_0001! That's clearly worse than the first situation.

The final answer is simply not to define anonymous enumerations. If you change the IDL to make the enumeration look like the following, you will finally be able to refer to enumerated parameters as being of type Colors:

```
typedef enum Colors { Black = 0, Red, Green, Blue, White } Colors;
```

To show this in action, I added the Colors enumeration to the IDL for this day's ActiveX server. I added the helpstring attribute, not just because I can, but because it helps the object's clients further identify the values the property can assume. Here is the final Colors enumeration:

```
typedef enum Colors
{
    [helpstring("Black")] Black = 0,
    [helpstring("Red")] Red = 1,
    [helpstring("Green")] Green = 2,
    [helpstring("Blue")] Blue = 3,
    [helpstring("White")] White = 4,
} Colors;
```

This is placed just prior to the definition of the object itself. This must be so because I intend to use the enumeration as part of a property definition. In fact, I did just this by adding a new property, SomeProperty2, which is defined in this way:

7

```
[propget, id(3), helpstring("property SomeProperty2")]
➥HRESULT SomeProperty2([out, retval] Colors *pVal);
[propput, id(3), helpstring("property SomeProperty2")]
➥HRESULT SomeProperty2([in] Colors newVal);
```

I then had to add two new methods to the C++ class, *CMyThirdATLObj*. I first added the method definitions to the MyThirdATLObj.h file:

```
STDMETHOD(get_SomeProperty2)(/*[out, retval]*/ Colors *pVal);
STDMETHOD(put_SomeProperty2)(/*[in]*/ Colors newVal);
```

I added a public attribute m_clrProperty2:

```
Colors m_clrProperty2;
```

And I initialized it to Black in the class's constructor:

```
CMyThirdATLObj() : m_iProperty(0), m_clrProperty2(Black)
{
}
```

Finally, I added the implementations for the property methods to MyThirdATLObj.cpp:

```
STDMETHODIMP CMyThirdATLObj::get_SomeProperty2(Colors *pVal)
{
    CHECKPTR2(pVal,Black)

    // Simply return their value
    *pVal = m_clrProperty2;

    return S_OK;
}

STDMETHODIMP CMyThirdATLObj::put_SomeProperty2(Colors newVal)
{
    // Simply accept their value
    m_ clrProperty2= newVal;

    return S_OK;
}
```

The best way to see the effect of this change is to load the Visual Basic test client you created that uses the ActiveX control you created. If you examine the properties for the control, you should see SomeProperty2 set to Black. If you drop the property values list, you'll see the remaining enumerated values. I've done this in Figure 7.16.

FIGURE 7.16

The Visual Basic Properties window revisited.

Tip	IDL enumeration values, by default, are short integers (hence my data type choice when I added the property methods). If you find that you would rather use the full 32 bits rather than the default 16, you should use the [v1_enum] attribute to the enumeration definition:

```
typedef [v1_enum] enum MyEnum {...} MyEnum;
```

Summary

At this point, you know enough to begin writing general purpose ATL COM objects, and in my experience, most of the COM programmers I know operate at this level. You know how to create an ATL project, how to add an ATL object (at least a simple one), and you can add methods to the object's interface that enable the object's clients to actually do some work.

In this day, you took a more in-depth look at adding methods to interfaces. You reviewed how to invoke the ATL method wizard and how to specify the method signature within the wizard. After you have completed your work there, you examined the files the wizard modified to see what code was added and where you would add your own code to provide the functionality the method would ultimately support. I showed you how to create a new interface from an existing interface. This is commonly done to add methods to an existing interface. And finally, you saw a few more useful IDL parameter attributes for special situations, such as when passing strings, arrays, and interface pointers.

Today I also introduced you to COM object properties and how they are implemented in ATL-based COM objects. To demonstrate properties in use, you created a basic ActiveX

7

control you could use from both Visual C++ and from Visual Basic. After your control was created, compiled, and registered, you saw how these two development environments viewed the same property as very different entities.

To demonstrate this, I showed you how to invoke and use the ATL property wizard, as well as the specific changes the wizard makes to your project files as you add properties. I took you through the steps necessary to load the ActiveX control into both Visual C++, using the Components and Controls Gallery, and Visual Basic, using the Components dialog box. Finally, I created two test applications to demonstrate property usage dynamically.

This day concludes your basic introduction to ATL. Congratulations! The remainder of the book will take you through various aspects of using ATL, as well as other features of ATL you can use to implement better and faster COM objects. Before you get too far, it's time to take a closer look at some of the ways ATL helps you write better, faster COM objects. You will look at the helper classes and functions ATL provides you. You'll use some of these classes with nearly every COM object you write with ATL, so it pays to understand what the classes are and how they can help.

Q&A

Q If I add a method using the ATL method wizard, and then I later change my mind, can the wizard help me modify the method's signature? Delete the method?

A Sadly, no. The wizard can only add new methods. Any changes to be made will be made by hand, to include method deletion.

Q Are new interfaces really created from existing interfaces in practice? Isn't this theory only?

A Oh, no, it isn't theory. It's done in practice. In fact, look at some of the interfaces used for DirectDraw, which is Microsoft's high performance graphics drawing interface. The current version, Version 7.0, sports IDirectDraw7, which is based upon IDirectDraw4 (from Version 4.0), which is based upon...you see my point. The good thing about this mechanism is if you create a client application that uses IDirectDraw4, but the given target system has the latest version of DirectDraw, the application you created will still work. Your application doesn't know about the IDirectDraw7 methods, but because the DirectDraw object supports IDirectDraw4 through IDirectDraw7 (by interface inheritance), things still work—at least most of the time.

Q If I were to build an ATL-based COM object that implemented custom interfaces (versus dual interfaces and ActiveX), would I be interested in using properties?

A No, not normally, although there is nothing that precludes you from doing so. The concept of a *property* is really specific to the ActiveX paradigm. I have added property methods in previous custom-interface projects, but that was because I knew I required accessor and mutator methods (yes, I took the easy way out!).

Q I tried to add an enumerated property. When I compiled my project, I received a lot of `pure virtual function was not defined` errors. Why?

A If you're seeing this error, and I assume everything compiled correctly before you added this property, the most likely cause is a difference between your IDL method definitions and the C++ implementation. MIDL takes the IDL file and compiles it into a .H file, which your C++ implementation uses to define the pure virtual base class on which your derived class is based. If your implementation doesn't faithfully implement the methods in the virtual base class, you get this error.

If you change the IDL file so that your interface uses the enumeration as a property method parameter, and MIDL correctly compiles that IDL file, you should check the C++ files to make sure they are also using the enumeration as a property method parameter. If you remember, I told the ATL property wizard to use short integers initially. Later, I changed the short integer to an IDL enumeration. That meant I also had to modify the C++ property methods to use the enumeration. Had I failed to do that, I would have received the compilation error you described.

Workshop

The Workshop is designed to help you anticipate possible questions, review what you've learned, and get you thinking about how to put your knowledge into practice. The answers to the quiz are in Appendix A, "Answers."

Quiz

1. How do I invoke the ATL method wizard?
2. What source files does the wizard modify?
3. What do the `[in]`, `[out]`, and `[in, out]` attributes do for me?
4. How do I add a new interface based upon an existing one?
5. With respect to IDL, what is the difference between using the `string` attribute versus passing in an array of `chars` and using `size_is()`?

7

6. How do COM object methods and properties differ?

7. Why did this day use an ActiveX control to demonstrate properties rather than a simple COM object?

8. What IDL attributes signify a method as a property accessor or mutator method?

9. How do you create a read-only property?

10. Can a given property be tied to a data source (such as a database)?

11. What is the ATL property map used for?

12. Why would I use an enumerated property?

Exercises

1. Add a method to `IAddMethodDemo` that halves the incoming value. Is any special error checking necessary?

2. Modify the example MFC client application to incorporate the method you created in Exercise 1.

3. Add a third interface to the object, called `IAddMethodDemo3`, which has a new method that doubles the incoming value. Should this new interface derive from `IAddMethodDemo` or `IAddMethodDemo2`?

4. The MFC property test application used an earlier version of the ActiveX control (without SomeProperty2). Modify the MFC test application to incorporate the new version and test SomeProperty2. What happens when you try to reload the control using the Components and Controls Gallery? (Hint: You might need to delete some files and other things before you reload the ActiveX control.)

5. Add a third property to the ActiveX control and test it using Visual Basic. For extra credit, use an enumeration.

WEEK 1

In Review

This week you were introduced to some of the most fundamental concepts of ATL (and COM) programming. With this information in mind, you'll be able to move on to more indepth ATL work, which you'll find in store for you in the next week's reading.

My goal for Day 1 was to take you through the creation of a basic, though fully functional, ATL COM object. I intended to give you a feeling for what is in store for you in later days and weeks. You created the basic ATL framework project and then added a simple ATL object and interface. To that object, you added a single method and implemented its functionality. With the basic object coding complete, you then created a quick MFC-based dialog application to instantiate the object and test its basic capabilities.

In Day 2, you took a step back and looked at the Component Object Model, which is the model ATL strives to implement. You saw how to invoke the COM runtime environment, how COM objects are created, and how Windows knows a COM object exists on a given system. You were also given an overview regarding how COM views threading issues and how it handles errors. You also learned about COM's data manipulation capabilities (marshaling). You then took a brief look at how objects are created locally and remotely.

Day 3 was directed toward introducing the COM interface and interface-based programming using the Interface Definition Language. You learned about CLSIDs and IIDs, which uniquely identify the COM object itself and the interfaces it supports. I also discussed two of the more important aspects of interface programming—interface inheritance. You then saw how to modify an interface after it has been published.

Day 4 transitioned from Microsoft technology in general to C++ syntax specifically when you reviewed (or learned) C++ template programming. Because the *T* in ATL stands for *template*, it only made sense to examine the C++ template syntax to better understand how ATL implements the COM model via C++ templates. You saw two forms of templates, the generic class and the generic function. (ATL heavily uses the former.)

With Day 5 you left fundamental COM architectural and C++ programmatical concepts to begin working with ATL directly. You broke down the ATL architecture to study how ATL implements COM. You saw how ATL implements IUnknown, the basic COM interface, as well as how other higher-level interfaces are supported from within ATL. You also learned how ATL registers your COM objects on a given Windows system using the ATL Registrar object.

Day 6 took you back to the first day to see more about using the two most important Visual Studio ATL wizards, the ATL AppWizard and the ATL Object Wizard. Through these wizards you learned how to create in-process and local COM servers and how to add objects of various kinds to each server type. You'll use these wizards each time you create an ATL-based COM object, so understanding their use is important.

Day 7 further described Visual Studio's ATL wizardry when it discussed interface methods and properties (and their similarities and differences) and how you can add either or both to your particular interface. You saw which files the wizards modified and what code they provided, as well as more basic IDL programming information.

Preview

You now have the basic skills you need to create simple ATL-based COM objects, so it's time to move to a more intermediate level. The next week targets, in particular, ATL support for Win32 programming, COM programming helper classes and functions, and ATL debugging assistance. It also looks at ATL, COM, and threading in more detail, especially where multithreading is concerned. To help with object testing, a day is dedicated to creating MFC-based test applications. The week ends with details regarding ATL and COM automation technology, which leads you to the more advanced work you'll find in the last week.

WEEK 2

At a Glance

Given the basic understanding you gained from the past week's efforts, it's time to cement those concepts and skills by moving to more intermediate-level topics. You'll begin by examining some ATL helper classes and functions that make COM programming quite a bit easier. You'll then take a more detailed look at creating test applications and learn what to do about errors that occur when your ATL objects are running. The week advances further when you learn about ATL, COM, and threading issues, especially when using multiple threads. You'll wrap up the week by studying COM automation and how ATL supports the dual interface, the foundational scripting interface.

- Day 8: Look at ATL helper functions and classes to learn how ATL simplifies COM programming tasks.
- Day 9: Learn more about testing ATL COM objects and how to create MFC-based test applications.
- Day 10: See how to incorporate C++ exception handling into your object and how to return standard and custom HRESULT values.
- Day 11: Take your first detailed look at multithreading in general.
- Day 12: Apply multiple threads in a COM environment.
- Day 13: Sidestep COM for the moment and see how to create basic Win32 applications using ATL windowing classes.
- Day 14: Study the basic automation concepts you must understand to move to more advanced COM (and ATL) programming topics.

DAY **8**

ATL Object Methods: Adding Functionality to Your Interface

As you've seen throughout the book, ATL exists to help you with the COM programming details so you can concentrate on working through the central issue, which is to provide the code your object uses to do the real work. But even ATL needs a little help from time to time, so Microsoft built many support classes into ATL. Everyone can use as these classes as the need arises.

For example, ATL provides you with a smart pointer class that manages the object's reference counting details. Being COM-oriented, ATL wraps the variant and BSTR data types. Because ATL can work in a multithreaded environment, ATL can manage a critical section for you. Because everyone has to deal with the Registry at some time or another, ATL has a helper class just to access Registry data.

In this lesson, you'll look at these ideas:

- ATL and smart pointers
- How ATL manages the BSTR
- How ATL deals with the variant
- How to manage a critical section with ATL
- ATL and Registry access
- Other useful ATL helper functions

Smart Pointers

If you look back to Day 2, "Exploring COM: The Technology ATL Supports," I mentioned the three rules governing COM object lifetime management:

- Call `AddRef()` before you return an interface pointer.
- Call `Release()` when you are done with the object.
- Call `AddRef()` after assigning a new interface pointer.

These rules seem simple enough, but the experienced COM programmer has likely spent hours debugging her application looking for reasons why a particular COM server wasn't unloading from memory when she expected it to do so. The issue is, generally, that the rules *seem* simple. In practice, life can be very different from theory. The same experienced COM programmer probably typed `Release()` as soon as she typed `CoCreateInstance()`—in the same way that the experienced C and C++ programmer types the closing brace to preclude brace mismatches.

Because you're using C++, you can harness the power of C++ and build a new class that manages the COM interface pointer. It could overload all sorts of operators, and you'd wisely build into the class support for proper `AddRef()` and `Release()` processing. ATL provides exactly this, and it comes in two forms. The first form, `CComPtr<>`, contains an interface pointer you provide. `CComQIPtr<>`, the second form, contains an interface pointer the class obtains using `QueryInterface()`. Let's look at each of these smart pointer classes.

ATL and the Smart Pointer: `CComPtr`

`CComPtr` is a templated class that accepts as its specialization parameter an interface type:

```
template< class T > class CComPtr
```

In practice, you'd use `CComPtr` as shown in Listing 8.1.

8

LISTING 8.1   An Example Using `CComPtr`

```
 1: // Create the COM object
 2: CComPtr<IMyInterface> spIMyInterface;
 3: HRESULT hr = spIMyInterface.CoCreateInstance(CLSID_MyObject,
 4:                                              NULL,
 5:                                              CLSCTX_INPROC_SERVER);
 6: if ( SUCCEEDED(hr) ) {
 7:     // Use the COM object
 8:     spIMyInterface->SomeMethod();
 9:     ...
10: } // if
```

ANALYSIS   The true interface pointer is stored in `spIMyInterface`'s `p` attribute, so if you need to access the raw interface pointer, you use `spIMyInterface.p` (line 2). Note I use the `CComPtr::CoCreateInstance()` to instantiate the object. `CComPtr` provides this method as a type-safe way to create an object, although I personally find it handy because I have to provide fewer parameters.

The beauty of `CComPtr` is it will automatically release the interface pointer for you when the variable goes out of scope or when you set the variable to `NULL`:

```
spIMyInterface = NULL;
```

Tip

> Smart pointers, such as `CComPtr`, are very useful when combined with C++ exception handling. If you declare the smart pointer within the `try` block and an exception is thrown, the COM object will automatically be released for you.

Typically, you work with `CComPtr` using its overloaded operators, as shown in Table 8.1. For example, the overloaded `->` operator returns the raw interface pointer you need to call an interface method. You can tell if an interface pointer is `NULL` by using `CComPtr`'s `!` operator.

Table 8.1   `CComPtr` Operators

Operator	Description
`T*`	Converts the `CComPtr` object to `T*`
`*`	Returns the dereferenced value of the member pointer `p`
`&`	Returns the address of the member pointer `p`
`->`	Returns the member pointer `p`
`=`	Assigns a pointer value to the member pointer `p`
`!`	Returns `TRUE` if `p` is nonNULL and `FALSE` if `p` is `NULL`

CComPtr also has several methods you can call to perform certain tasks. I won't list them all here, but you'll see some of them in action in later parts of the book. Table 8.2 gives you a few of the more commonly used functions.

Table 8.2   CComPtr Commonly Used Methods

Method	Description
CoCreateInstance()	Ensures type-safe object instantiation
QueryInterface()	Ensures type-safe QueryInterface()
CopyTo()	Copies the internal pointer p to a target and AddRef()s, the target pointer
IsEqualObject()	Compares two objects for equivalence
Attach()	Attaches a pointer that has already been AddRef()d
Detach()	Detaches the internal pointer

ATL provides you with another smart pointer class, CComQIPtr. CComQIPtr is a handy smart pointer class for those situations when you receive an interface pointer via QueryInterface(), as you'll see next.

A Smarter QueryInterface(): CComQIPtr

CComQIPtr is similar to CComPtr, except the constructor accepts an interface as an input parameter in order to query for the interface you desire. If the query is successful, the internal pointer p will be nonNULL. If the query fails, p remains NULL and the failed HRESULT is returned. CComQIPtr has the same operators and methods as CComPtr, so glance back to Tables 8.1 and 8.2 for the details.

CComQIPtr is defined in this way:

```
template< class T, const IID* piid > class CComQIPtr
```

When using CComQIPtr in practice, you pass into the constructor two specialization parameters—the interface type of the internal pointer and a reference IID of the interface to query for. The constructor then accepts an input parameter, typically a COM pointer, which will be queried. For example, you have a base interface, IMyBaseInterface, from which another interface, IMyDerivedInterface, is derived. Given the derived interface, you can query for the base interface and assign it to the ATL smart pointer in one line of code:

```
CComQIPtr<IMyBaseInterface, IID_IMyBaseInterface>
➥spIMyBaseInterface(pIMyDerivedInterface);
```

If the `QueryInterface()` is successful, the internal pointer p will be nonNULL and the method will return S_OK. You can then use spMyBaseInterface just as you would any COM pointer.

> **Note**
>
> Don't use `CComQIPtr` with `IUnknown` as the specialization parameter (that is, `CComQIPtr<IUnknown, IID_IUnknown> ptr(...)`). Instead use `CComPtr<IUnknown>(ptr)`. The reason for this is `CComQIPtr` is already specialized for `IUnknown` in ATLBASE.H. Creating the same specialization in your code will override the specialization in ATLBASE.H, potentially breaking `CComQIPtr`.

A Better BSTR: CComBSTR

COM is based upon a standard, the COM Specification. The COM Specification tells us that character data as manipulated by the COM runtime will be Unicode character data, which is another standard for character representation. This is true even on Windows 95 and 98 systems. Character data coming into the COM runtime is converted to Unicode, so there is a penalty for not using Unicode in the first place.

Unicode (*wide-character*) strings are essentially just strings that require more than a single byte to encode their constituent character data. That mean that when you deal with the ANSI character set, all characters, printable or not, range from 0–127 or, in some cases, from 0–255. The ANSI character set is based upon a single byte.

Some languages, especially those with more idiomatic character sets, require more than 256 characters to depict their alphabets (for example, *Kanji*, a Japanese alphabet). Clearly, in such an alphabet, one byte can't adequately describe a single character. Unicode solves this by using two bytes for encoding characters instead of one. (There is more to it than that, but what's important here is to understand the basic data-storage requirements.)

The BSTR is a special COM data type developed primarily to support automation. BSTRs contain wide-character (Unicode) string data terminated by a NULL character (`'\0'`), but they have an unusual two-byte character count prefixed to the string data (see Figure 8.1). This facilitates marshaling and eases script engine data handling requirements. I say this because the BSTR can contain embedded NULL characters; therefore, you can't simply look for the terminating NULL character. The character count is the only reliable way to determine how many characters are contained within the BSTR. If this is so, the scripting engines don't need to concern themselves with the details and implement character counting code.

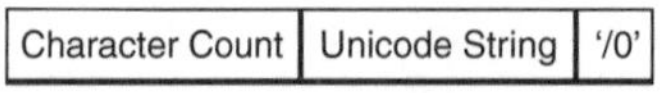

FIGURE **8.1**

The layout of the BSTR.

| Character Count | Unicode String | '/0' |

BSTR variables themselves are pointers to the Unicode string. Oddly enough, they're *not* pointers to the character count, as you might expect. In that sense, BSTRs can be treated as any wide-character data type, such as the OLECHAR.

Working with wide characters is difficult enough, but working with BSTRs can be more challenging because you have a plethora of API calls that deal with the allocation and manipulation of BSTRs. (See Appendix D, "ATL String Conversion Macros," for help with general-purpose character conversions.) You can see why, given the odd data pointer arrangement. The character count must stay with the BSTR, yet the pointer you're given doesn't include the character count. You saw this in Day 1, "Getting Started: Your First ATL COM Object," when I passed a raw BSTR to the IHelloWorld::SayHello() method. I had to use SysAllocString() to create the BSTR and SysFreeString() to discard it.

ATL really helps when it comes to BSTRs. The CComBSTR class rolls all the BSTR API calls into a nice package, so you don't have to worry about allocating memory for the BSTR or even remember to deallocate the memory. CComBSTR handles all that for you.

CComBSTR stores the BSTR data in its m_str member, and most of the operators and methods work with m_str, as you see from Tables 8.3 and 8.4. Table 8.3 shows you the operators CComBSTR overrides, whereas Table 8.4 provides a few of the more commonly used CComBSTR methods. Although I didn't show them in Table 8.4, CComBSTR provides methods to persist the BSTR, which can be useful at times. See the online documentation for all the details.

Table 8.3 CComBSTR Operators

Operator	Description
=	Assigns a value to m_str
+=	Appends another CComBSTR
&	Returns the address of m_str
!	Returns TRUE if m_str is nonNULL and FALSE if m_str is NULL
BSTR	Converts the CComBSTR object to a BSTR

Table 8.4 CComBSTR Commonly Used Methods

Method	Description
Copy()	Returns a copy of m_str
Empty()	Frees m_str
Length()	Returns the m_str character count
LoadString()	Loads m_str from resources

If you do a lot of ActiveX work or you are writing dual interface objects destined to be used in a scripted environment, you'll undoubtedly use CComBSTR to manage your string data. Just as ATL wraps the BSTR, so ATL wraps another automation data type, the variant.

ATL Scripting Assistance: CComVariant

The variant is a discriminated union that contains an integer (the discriminator) denoting the data type of the variant and a union containing all the possible data types. You assign the integer an enumerated value that indicates what data is stored in the union, and then you assign the data itself.

COM uses the variant in automation to simplify the job of the scripting engine and to provide a standardized marshaling mechanism when automation is employed. The Universal Marshaler knows how to marshal any of the variant data types, such as long integers, boolean values, BSTRs, and so forth. It also knows the variant will be precisely 16 bytes in size, so it never has to marshal any more or any less.

You'll find the variant structure defined in OAIDL.H (see Listing 8.2).

LISTING 8.2 Variant Structure Definition

```
1: struct  tagVARIANT
2:     {
3:     union
4:         {
5:         struct  __tagVARIANT
6:             {
7:             VARTYPE vt;
8:             WORD wReserved1;
9:             WORD wReserved2;
10:            WORD wReserved3;
11:            union
12:                {
13:                LONG lVal;
```

continues

```
14:              BYTE bVal;
15:              SHORT iVal;
16:              FLOAT fltVal;
17:              DOUBLE dblVal;
18:              (edited for brevity)
19:              } __VARIANT_NAME_3;
20:          } __VARIANT_NAME_2;
21:      DECIMAL decVal;
22:      } __VARIANT_NAME_1;
23:   };
```

The VARTYPE is ultimately an enumeration defined in WTYPES.H (see Listing 8.3).

LISTING 8.3   VARTYPE Definition and VARENUM Enumeration

```
 1: typedef unsigned short VARTYPE;
 2: enum VARENUM
 3:    {   VT_EMPTY = 0,
 4:        VT_NULL = 1,
 5:        VT_I2 = 2,
 6:        VT_I4 = 3,
 7:        VT_R4 = 4,
 8:        VT_R8 = 5,
 9:        (edited for brevity)
10:    };
```

Clearly, working directly with variants involves a lot of pointer and structure work! That's why there are many API calls available to create, fill, and manipulate variants (just as there are for BSTRs). To simplify things, ATL provides the CComVariant class:

```
class CComVariant : public tagVARIANT
```

You'll also find this class handy when working with automation. CComVariant has several useful operators and methods, as you see in Tables 8.5 and 8.6.

Table 8.5   CComVariant Operators

Operator	Description
=	Assigns a value to the variant
==	Indicates the CComVariant is equal to the specified variant
!=	Indicates the CComVariant is not equal to the specified variant

Table 8.6 CComVariant Commonly Used Methods

Method	Description
ChangeType()	Converts the variant to a new variant type
Clear()	Clears the CComVariant
Copy()	Copies the variant to the CComVariant
Attach()	Attaches an existing variant to the CComVariant
Detach()	Detaches the variant from the CComVariant

As I did with CComBSTR, I mentioned the most commonly used CComVariant methods. Also like CComBSTR, CComVariant has a mechanism to persist the variant should you need to do so.

ATL doesn't just support data types, however. ATL also provides help when you're programming in a multithreaded environment, as you'll see in the next section.

ATL Multithreading Support: CComCriticalSection

If you're programming in a multithreaded environment, you're going to need a mechanism for data synchronization. You'll see why in Day 11, "Multithreading: How and When." One tool for data synchronization is the *critical section.*

Critical sections act as gates, or doors, to specific portions of code. After you create and initialize the critical section, you use it to monitor access to code in much the same way a flagger will monitor traffic when road construction reduces a two-lane road to one lane. Clearly cars can't travel in both directions at the same time, and the flagger's job is to make sure traffic flows in only one direction at a given time.

Critical sections don't dictate a direction (my analogy breaks down there), but they do limit thread access to the code wrapped by the critical section. If one thread is accessing the code, other threads will *block* until the first thread is through the code section. That is, they wait, just as you wait when the flagger is allowing traffic from the other direction to pass.

Windows provides for critical sections using the CRITICAL_SECTION, and there are API calls to initialize, enter, leave, and destroy critical sections. As you've seen with BSTRs and variants, whenever there are many API calls involved, ATL probably wrapped it. In this case, ATL provides the CComCriticalSection and the related CComAutoCriticalSection.

These classes were really created to support CComMultiThreadModule, but there is no reason you can't use them yourself. When you use them, you can also use them in their typedef'd forms:

```
typedef CComAutoCriticalSection AutoCriticalSection;
typedef CComCriticalSection CriticalSection;
```

In your code, you see CComMultiThreadModule::CriticalSection and CComMulti-ThreadModule::AutoCriticalSection. Although the single-threaded module class CComSingleThreadModule also has these typedefs, they refer to the *fake critical section*, CComFakeCriticalSection. After all, you normally don't need a critical section when dealing with single-threaded code. CComFakeCriticalSection has the same methods as CComCriticalSection, but they're empty.

The difference between the two true critical section classes is the initialization and destruction of the internal CRITICAL_SECTION (m_sec) contained within the two classes. CComAutoCriticalSection manages the lifetime of m_sec via the constructor and destructor, whereas CComCriticalSection allows you to decide when to initialize and destroy m_sec.

Both classes offer two methods used to control the critical section, Lock() and Unlock(). You call Lock() when you enter the critical section and Unlock() when you leave. CComCriticalSection also provides the methods you need to initialize and destroy the critical section—Init() and Term(), respectively.

The critical section is the only data synchronization mechanism ATL wraps. It doesn't wrap the mutex or sempahore, for example. These data synchronization mechanisms are, at least, relatively lightweight. One area that ATL does wrap (that is always painful to deal with) is the Registry database, which I discuss next.

Registry Access Made Easy: CRegKey

If you've ever had to access the Registry programmatically using the Win32 API Registry calls, you clearly understand why wrapping Registry access in a C++ class makes a lot of sense. There are a lot of API calls that deal with the Registry, and most of them accept quite a few parameters. Keeping the API calls straight and the parameters correct is often a lot of work. That equates to a lot of code. Worse, you have to deal with Registry keys. If an exception is thrown, will your code close any open Registry key handles?

ATL neatly wraps the Registry API calls in its CRegKey class. Instead of dealing with Registry keys directly, you call CRegKey methods to open, read, write, delete, and close the specific Registry information you're dealing with.

CRegKey's constructor sets the member m_hKey to NULL, and if m_hKey is nonNULL when the destructor is executed, the Registry key is closed for you automatically using CRegKey::Close().

CRegKey has a single operator, HKEY, which turns the CRegKey object into a true Registry key handle. But CRegKey has several useful methods, as you see from Table 8.7.

Table 8.7 CRegKey Methods

Method	Description
Open()	Opens the specified key
Close()	Closes and releases m_hKey
Attach()	Attaches an existing HKEY to the CRegKey object
Detach()	Detaches m_hKey
Create()	Creates or opens the specified key
QueryValue()	Retrieves the specified value field data indicated by m_hKey
SetKeyValue()	Sets the specified value field of a specified key
SetValue()	Sets the specified value field indicated by m_hKey
DeleteValue()	Deletes the value field indicated by m_hKey
DeleteSubKey()	Deletes a subkey
RecurseDeleteKey()	Recursively deletes subkeys, then the key itself

As you can see, CRegKey makes your Registry access chores a lot easier. The RecurseDeleteKey() method is especially welcome, as you normally must delete any subkeys individually before you can delete a specified key using the Win32 API.

With CRegKey, I've discussed the major ATL helper classes. However, ATL provides other helper functions and macros you'll find useful. I'll show these to you next.

Other Useful ATL Helper Functions

ATL provides several single functions designed for a specific task. They're not class-based, which is why they're in this section. They stand alone. I see them as forming two categories—general helpers and debugging aids. I'll start with the general helper category.

General ATL Helper Functions

If you open ATLBASE.H and skim to the end of the file, you'll find definitions for several undocumented helper functions that you can use in your own ATL-based code. Table 8.8 shows you the functions and provides a brief description. There are quite a few more functions available in ATLBASE.H, but they are a bit more advanced. For example, you can register and deregister your COM object using some of these functions. I've taken the more basic functions and placed them into Table 8.8. Don't let that fool you, though. These functions are quite powerful.

Table 8.8 Undocumented ATL Helper Functions

ATL Function	Description
AtlGetVersion()	Returns the version of ATL in use
AtlGetDllVersion()	Returns the version of the specified DLL
AtlGetCommCtrlVersion()	Returns the version of the installed Common Controls DLL
AtlGetShellVersion()	Returns the version of the shell

AtlGetVersion() returns the current version of ATL you're currently using:

```
DWORD AtlGetVersion(void* pReserved);
```

With the current version of ATL (3.0), this function returns the dwAtlBuildVer attribute of the ATL module structure. The pReserved parameter isn't currently used (or checked), but it's wise to pass in NULL. If you use this function with the current version of ATL, it will return the value 0x00000300.

There are two versions of AtlGetDllVersion(). The first accepts an HINSTANCE to a DLL already loaded using LoadLibrary():

```
HRESULT AtlGetDllVersion(HINSTANCE hInstDLL,
                     DLLVERSIONINFO* pDllVersionInfo);
```

The second takes the DLL's name as a parameter and performs the LoadLibrary() for you:

```
HRESULT AtlGetDllVersion(LPCTSTR lpstrDllName,
                     DLLVERSIONINFO* pDllVersionInfo);
```

If the DLL exists, the pDllVersionInfo structure will be completed, and the function will return the result of the DLL's GetDllVersion() call. If the DLL doesn't support version query using GetDllVersion(), the function will return E_NOTIMPL.

A task that continuously confounds applications programmers is how to correctly determine the version of the Common Controls DLL installed on the target computer. ATL helps by providing the AtlGetCommCtrlVersion() function:

```
HRESULT AtlGetCommCtrlVersion(LPDWORD pdwMajor, LPDWORD pdwMinor);
```

The return HRESULT is the value AtlGetDllVersion() returns.

`AtlGetCommCtrlVersion()` helps by extracting the major and minor version numbers from the `DLLVERSIONINFO` data structure. The current (pre-Windows 2000) versions are shown in Table 8.9.

Table 8.9   Common Control DLL Major and Minor Versions

Shell	Major	Minor
Win95/WinNT 4.0	4	0
Win98	4	72
IE 3.x	4	70
IE 4.x	4	71
IE 5.x	5	80

Finally, you can check the shell version number using `AtlGetShellVersion()`:

```
HRESULT AtlGetShellVersion(LPDWORD pdwMajor, LPDWORD pdwMinor);
```

The current shell versions (pre-Windows 2000) are shown in Table 8.10. The Web column indicates the shell has Web integration (also known as the *active desktop*).

Table 8.10   Shell Major and Minor Versions

Shell	Web	Major	Minor
Win95/WinNT 4.0	N	4	0
Win98	N	4	72
Win98	Y	4	72
IE 3.x/IE 4.0	N	4	0
IE 4.0	Y	4	71
IE 4.01	Y	4	72
IE 5.0	N	4	0
IE 5.x	Y	4	72

All these functions help you tailor your object to the target system's environment. ATL also helps you, however, when you're writing and debugging your code. I'll show you some of these functions in the next section.

ATL Debugging Macros and Functions

ATL also provides several invaluable debugging functions and macros. The three major ATL global debugging functions are `AtlReportError()`, `AtlTrace()`, and `AtlTrace2()`. The three major ATL debugging macros are `ATLTRACE()`, `ATLTRACE2()`, and

ATLASSERT(). There is also ATLTRACENOTIMPL() for use when you are developing your interface and haven't fully implemented its methods.

AtlReportError() creates and initializes an IErrorInfo interface to provide error information to your object's clients. You provide, as input, a string to be used as the text description of the error. When the client receives the HRESULT that you specify when you call AtlReportError(), the client can access the IErrorInfo structure for details regarding the error. You'll learn more about IErrorInfo in Day 10, "ATL and Errors: What to Do When Things Break."

AtlTrace() formats debugging text to be sent to the dump device (usually Visual Studio's debugger window). Although you can use AtlTrace() in release builds, you should carefully consider before doing this. The trace output will still be sent to the debug stream, which will likely impact your object's performance. Instead, consider using the ATLTRACE() macro which uses AtlTrace(). ATLTRACE() wraps AtlTrace() with conditional compilation code so that AtlTrace() will not be called in a release build. Note a limitation of AtlTrace() and ATLTRACE() is that you must limit the text to 511 characters after formatting.

If you use AtlTrace() (or ATLTRACE()), everything going to the debugger will be displayed in the debug stream. This can amount to quite a bit of text. If you'd like to be more selective with your debugging information, AtlTrace2() (and the corresponding ATLTRACE2() macro) provides you the capability to tailor the messages ATL sends. ATLTRACE2() uses a category and level to determine which messages are to be output. The macro looks like this:

```
ATLTRACE2(DWORD category, UINT level, LPCSTR lpszFormat, ... )
```

The lpszFormat parameter is simply the message formatting string, followed by the input arguments for the string. This is no different than ATLTRACE() (or printf()). The first two parameters, however, give ATLTRACE2() its capability.

The category parameter enables you to choose more precisely which debugging message categories to pass. The default is defined within ATLBASE.H:

```
#ifndef ATL_TRACE_CATEGORY
#define ATL_TRACE_CATEGORY 0xFFFFFFFF
#endif
```

This essentially passes all message categories. If you'd like to be more specific, you can select the type of message category from this enumeration, also defined in ATLBASE.H (see Listing 8.4).

LISTING 8.4 ATL's atlTraceFlags Enumeration

```
 1: enum atlTraceFlags
 2: {
 3:     // Application defined categories
 4:     atlTraceUser      = 0x00000001,
 5:     atlTraceUser2     = 0x00000002,
 6:     atlTraceUser3     = 0x00000004,
 7:     atlTraceUser4     = 0x00000008,
 8:     // ATL defined categories
 9:     atlTraceGeneral   = 0x00000020,
10:     atlTraceCOM       = 0x00000040,
11:     atlTraceQI        = 0x00000080,
12:     atlTraceRegistrar = 0x00000100,
13:     atlTraceRefcount  = 0x00000200,
14:     atlTraceWindowing = 0x00000400,
15:     atlTraceControls  = 0x00000800,
16:     atlTraceHosting   = 0x00001000,
17:     atlTraceDBClient  = 0x00002000,
18:     atlTraceDBProvider = 0x00004000,
19:     atlTraceSnapin    = 0x00008000,
20:     atlTraceNotImpl   = 0x00010000,
21: };
```

If you'd rather not pass all message categories, you can combine the particular message categories you do want to pass (logical or) and use that as a parameter to ATLTRACE2(). You can also define ATL_TRACE_CATEGORY (using the selected categories before including ATLBASE.H) and use that instead.

Note
An earlier version of ATLBASE.H ignores your definition of ATL_TRACE_CATEGORY and defines it again rather than checking whether it is already defined. If you're not seeing the debug messages you expect, it's probably because ATL has ignored your definition and blindly overridden ATL_TRACE_CATEGORY. To cure this, first open ATLBASE.H to see how ATL_TRACE_CATEGORY is defined. You might need to define ATL_TRACE_CATEGORY in STDAFX.H *after* including ATLBASE.H.

The level parameter to ATLTRACE2() enables you to select the severity of message to be output. A level of zero indicates only the most severe of messages make it to the debug stream. ATLTRACE2() compares the level you provide against the global trace level indicated by ATL_TRACE_LEVEL. If the level is greater than or equal to the global ATL_TRACE_LEVEL, the message is sent to the debug stream. If not, the message is discarded. The default value of ATL_TRACE_LEVEL comes from ATLBASE.H:

```
#ifndef ATL_TRACE_LEVEL
#define ATL_TRACE_LEVEL 0
#endif
```

If you want less severe messages to be output, define ATL_TRACE_LEVEL prior to including ATLBASE.H.

The next macro, ATLASSERT(), is a macro that simply wraps _ASSERTE() (from ATLDEF.H):

```
#ifndef ATLASSERT
#define ATLASSERT(expr) _ASSERTE(expr)
#endif
```

To use ALTASSERT(), the global preprocessor value _DEBUG must be defined. If you are debugging and _DEBUG is defined, ATLASSERT() will evaluate expr. If expr evaluates to TRUE, your object continues processing. On the other hand, if expr is FALSE, your code will force a debug break, and you will have the option of running Visual Studio to see the problem (if you're not already running under Visual Studio).

 Tip

> If you've never used Assertions, you'll find out that they are very handy debugging aids. The goal is to pass in an expr that you expect to be true. If for some reason your logic or data is faulty or other than you expected, the assertion will fire, and you'll be able to see the cause of the assertion. A few well-placed assertions can save you hours of debugging time later.

The final helpful macro I'll describe is ATLTRACENOTIMPL. Whenever you're developing interfaces, and especially if you're replacing interfaces, any method you don't support should return E_NOTIMPL (not implemented). To your developer friends, this means you haven't had the time to add the functional code. To your object's clients, it means the method is available for use, but the object doesn't support the functionality at this time. The client can then do as it pleases, usually tossing up an error dialog of some kind.

ATLTRACENOTIMPL looks something like Listing 8.5.

LISTING 8.5   ATLTRACENOTIMPL Implementation (Edited)

```
1: #ifdef _DEBUG
2: #define ATLTRACENOTIMPL(funcname)   ATLTRACE2(atlTraceNotImpl, 2,
3: ➡_T("ATL: %s not implemented.\n"), funcname); return E_NOTIMPL
4: #else // !DEBUG
5: #define ATLTRACENOTIMPL(funcname)   return E_NOTIMPL
6: #endif // !DEBUG
```

ANALYSIS   I edited the code from ATLBASE.H to make it easier to see the dual definition of the macro. If you're debugging, ATLTRACENOTIMPL will send a trace message to the debug stream and then return E_NOTIMPL (lines 2 and 3). If _DEBUG is not defined (a release build of some kind), ATLTRACENOTIMPL just returns E_NOTIMPL (line 5).

You often see these helper functions and macros described in other books and magazines, and I'll make heavy use of them from this point onward. In fact, it's been hard for me *not* to use them to this point! Note that I saved the discussion of the debugging macros until the end of the day. I wanted you to leave with these macros on your mind. They're defined in ATL for one reason, and that's to help you write better defect-free code. Use them liberally! They won't affect you when you build a release version of your object. At least, they won't if you use the macro versions.

Summary

In this lesson, I discussed some of the support ATL provides to wrap common or complex topics. ATL implements classes, functions, and macros that help you write more code faster with fewer defects. ATL itself uses all these tools to achieve its effective and efficient COM implementation.

I began by discussing ATL's smart pointer classes CComPtr() and CComQIPtr(). They manage the stored object's lifetime for you, so you needn't be concerned about AddRef() and Release(). I then talked about the BSTR and ATL's CComBSTR class. It wraps the large number of BSTR API calls you typically must make when using a BSTR, which you'll often do when supporting automation. I then discussed the CComVariant class, which, similar to CComBSTR and the BSTR, wraps automation's variant data type.

I moved from data types to multithreading topics when I addressed CComCriticialSection. That ATL class and the related CComAutoCriticalSection wrap the CRITICAL_SECTION data type and handling API to effect critical sections. Of course, I mentioned ATL provides support to Registry access using the CRegKey class. This class relieves you from worrying about Registry keys: You just go for the data and let the class manage the details.

Finally, I discussed some of the remaining ATL helper functions and macros. I mentioned several of the ATL-version helper functions that assist you with determining various system component versions, including the Common Controls DLL and the shell. The last group of helpers I mentioned included all ATL's debugging support, especially ATLTRACE2() and ATLASSERT().

I'll use these classes and macros heavily in the remainder of the book, and I heartily recommend you use them where appropriate in your own code. They've already been developed and debugged, and they definitely help you write and debug code.

Q&A

Q At times, I'm happy to let a smart pointer manage my COM object's lifetime, and at other times, I want to have manual control. Is there a good way to do this?

A Let me first say this: Don't be tempted to retrieve the object's actual pointer `CComPtr::p` or `CComQIPtr::p` and use that to call `AddRef()` or `Release()`. That interferes with the smart pointer's own internal state. Instead, you should either call the smart pointer's `Release()` method or call its `Detach()` method and deal with the pointer yourself from that point onward. If you later want the smart pointer to take control, you can always `Attach()` it again.

Q I (or my company) has created an internal debugging facility. Can I use this in conjunction with the ATL macros?

A Sure, I would assume so. At least, I would try it and see how things work. You can also redefine `ATLTRACE()` and `ATRTRACE2()` to call your custom debugging logic and then use the default ATL logic. In this case, your code is more portable. Be sure to redefine these methods after you include ATLBASE.H in STDAFX.H.

Workshop

The Workshop is designed to help you anticipate possible questions, review what you've learned, and get you thinking about how to put your knowledge into practice. The answers to the quiz are in Appendix A, "Answers."

Quiz

1. What are the two ATL smart COM interface pointer classes and how do they differ?
2. What is a BSTR and why manage it with `CComBSTR`?
3. What is a variant and why manage it with `CComVariant`?
4. How are the category and level used to control debug stream message output? Which ATL debugging macro uses these?
5. What is an assertion and why do you use it?

Exercise

1. Add debugging support to the `IHelloWorld` interface you developed in Day 1. Where would you most likely place an `ATLASSERT()` and why?

DAY 9

Creating C++ Test Clients: You Can't Test What You Can't Execute

I have always found that writing ATL-based COM objects is a ton of fun. ATL manages the grungy details for me, enabling me to concentrate on the true nature of the COM object. I design my interfaces and then piece the puzzle together as I weave functionality into the object. It's not enough to write the COM code itself. In order for me to exercise the code, *something* has to use the COM component as a client. It's gratifying to see the object come to life and actually do whatever I intended it to do (assuming it can!).

Today, you have a wide range of possibilities for developing test containers to exercise your components. Depending upon the object you are using, you can load it from a Web site, use it in Microsoft Word or Access, or write it into an application using Visual Basic or Visual C++. Deciding which test paradigm to use for this book was tough simply because of the plethora of choices. However, I decided to go with MFC and Visual C++ because this is a book about ATL, and ATL is also based upon C++. Many ATL programmers have a background in application development for the Microsoft Foundation Classes (MFC) or are, at least, somewhat conversant in MFC.

I hope you have seen (maybe even used) the MFC. If so, today will be a refresher, and I might even show you a trick or two. If you've never used MFC, this lesson should teach you enough so that you are able to test your COM components from within Visual C++.

Therefore, today I'll detail

- How to create a simple MFC dialog-based application
- How MFC and COM work together
- How to incorporate ATL into your MFC application to use the various ATL helper classes and templates
- How to add and use other Windows controls to assist you with your testing
- How to add your component to the MFC project and use it there

MFC and the Dialog-Based Application

Testing your COM object is a necessity. But if you think about it, you don't generally earn your pay by writing test code—you earn it by writing the COM object itself. Customers purchase the actual software, not the testing code. However, the more quickly and effectively you can test your software, the faster you can ship higher quality products. Software quality and testing is a huge arena that I won't enter here. I hope that I can help you to create applications designed to test your components more quickly. One way to do that, if you're using C++, is to use MFC, and the fastest way to obtain an MFC-based test application is to create one based upon a dialog box.

MFC is to Windows application programming as ATL is to COM object programming. As in ATL, you can create an application program with a surprisingly high level of functionality in moments using the Visual Studio wizards. I see ATL and MFC as complementary. Although ATL will provide you some support for creating Windows application programs, its primary use is for COM object creation. (You'll see some of this in Day 13, "Creating ATL Applications: Where ATL Meets Win32.") Conversely, you can code COM objects using MFC, but it is really geared toward enabling you to create Windows applications in minimal time. I believe the analogy is valid, however.

Don't be confused. ATL and MFC are very different when it comes to implementation. Unlike ATL, MFC is not template based, although there are a few MFC templates in the library. Rather, MFC provides you with a suite of C++ base classes. MFC also eschews multiple inheritance. You tailor your particular application's functionality by deriving a new class from a single base class. When you do implement COM using MFC, you use specialized MFC macros and nested classes. Nonetheless, MFC is a terrific choice for application development—if you're using C++.

MFC dialog-based applications won't suit every component, nor will they encompass every conceivable test. Sometimes a simple console application will do. By and large, the majority of COM objects I've seen can be tested from an MFC application, especially those that implement a dialog as the user interface.

Actually, you've already taken this step. This is precisely what you did in Day 1, "Getting Started: Your First ATL COM Object," and Day 8, "ATL Object Methods: Adding Functionality to Your Interface." Because you did this to exercise your component, you're already somewhat familiar with the process.

What I'd like to do in this section is fine-tune your understanding a bit. I'll give you a brief tour of the relevant MFC classes, and I'll show you some of the MFC-isms you should understand to really use the tool. I'll start by describing the application creation process.

Creating the Application

As you've seen, you use the MFC AppWizard to create MFC applications. Unlike the ATL AppWizard, which has a single property page, the MFC AppWizard has several. They differ depending upon options you select when you create the application. To invoke the MFC AppWizard, click File, New from the Visual Studio menu. I've redrawn Figure 1.10 here as Figure 9.1. In it, I show you the AppWizard's initial property page. To create a dialog-based application, click the Dialog Based radio button.

FIGURE 9.1

The MFC AppWizard.

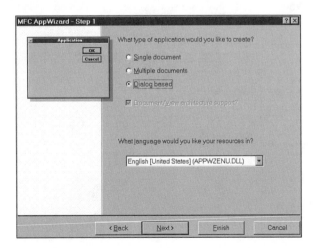

Generally, if you're simply after a quick test application, you won't need to change any other AppWizard setting. Just click Finish and start coding. However, let's go through the AppWizard pages one by one to see what each provides.

The second AppWizard page, shown in Figure 9.2, provides you with the useful option to type in the dialog's title. The remaining options on the second page are fairly self-explanatory and should be left defaulted in most cases.

FIGURE 9.2

The MFC AppWizard's Step 2 property page.

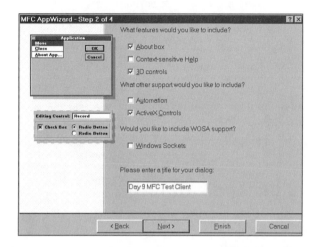

The third AppWizard page, Figure 9.3, does little except to remove source comments, if for some reason you don't want them. You do have the option of changing the MFC DLL's link step (static versus dynamic), but unless you're sending the application to a coworker who might not have the same version of MFC installed, I'd recommend leaving the DLL dynamically linked. That creates a smaller disk (executable) file.

FIGURE 9.3

The MFC AppWizard's Step 3 property page.

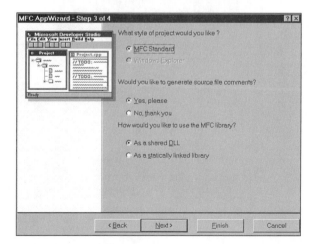

The final AppWizard property page, Figure 9.4, is more functional if you select the traditional single- or multiple-document user interfaces. In the case of a dialog-based application, all you can do is change the class name for your MFC WinApp–derived and CDialog–derived C++ classes and their filenames.

FIGURE 9.4

The MFC AppWizard's Step 4 property page.

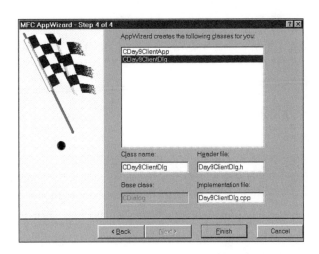

If all the options are acceptable, click Finish to review the options you selected, as shown in Figure 9.5. This dialog summarizes the options, and if you see something you missed or would like to change, you can click Cancel and return to the wizard to select (or change) the option once again.

FIGURE 9.5

The MFC New Project Information dialog.

On the other hand, if everything looks good, click OK to instruct Visual Studio to create your new test application's project. After Visual Studio has completed its work, you should find the project opened for you and the dialog editor active, ready for you to modify the dialog template according to your requirements.

A Little MFC Goes a Long Way

Visual Studio will create several files, but four are of most interest:

- *<project>*.rc
- *<project>*.cpp
- *<project>*Dlg.cpp
- *<project>*Dlg.h

The *<project>*.rc file is your resource file, which is where the dialog template, as well as other resource data, is stored. You don't normally edit this file directly. Rather, you use Visual Studio's resource editor to visually make changes to your application's resources. You do this using the ResourceView tab of the Workspace window.

<project>.cpp contains the implementation of your `CWinApp`-derived application class. To use MFC for programming applications, you must have a class derived from `CWinApp`. Perhaps Figure 9.6 can shed some light on this concept. `CWinApp` derives from `CWinThread`, which in turn derives from `CCmdTarget`, which is itself derived from `CObject`. The key is that all these MFC classes provide the basic Windows programming support for handling Windows messages (`CWinApp`'s message pump handles messages `CCmdTarget` routes). `CWinThread` manages the main process thread for `CWinApp`. `CObject` supports runtime type checking that all classes use to make sure things are running as expected. I'll revisit this `CWinApp`-derived class shortly when I discuss initializing the COM runtime.

FIGURE 9.6

CWinApp's MFC class inheritance chain.

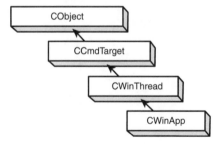

The *<project>*Dlg.cpp and *<project>*Dlg.h files contain the code that encapsulates the Windows dialog box. CWnd encapsulates generic Windows, but dialogs, being a specialization of a window, use the additional functionality captured in CDialog. CDialog's lineage is shown in Figure 9.7. As you can see, CDialog derives from CCmdTarget, so it, too, can process Windows messages, just as CWinApp can.

FIGURE 9.7

CDialog's MFC class inheritance chain.

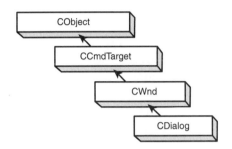

You add capability to the MFC classes by using them as base classes (hence, the requirement to have an application class derived from CWinApp). For the dialog-based application, you'll probably modify your *<project>*.cpp code infrequently, but you'll be accessing your dialog window's code quite often as you add controls to the dialog box and generally wire things up.

MFC and COM

One modification you'll almost certainly make to your CWinApp-based class will be to the CWinApp::InitInstance() method. This is an ideal place to initialize the COM runtime. I didn't mention this in Day 1 because I wanted to demonstrate the use of CoInitialize() and CoUninitialize(). I chose to defer the discussion of CWinApp until now.

As you know, the COM runtime must be activated for you to use COM. At times, MFC will do this for you, although at other times it won't. If you are using an ActiveX control you have inserted into your project using the Components and Controls Gallery, you need do nothing special (see Day 7's MFC test application). But if you're using your object in any other manner, you'll need to explicitly start COM processing before you attempt to load and use your object. I'll describe the error that you'll see (if you neglect to do this) in the section "Including the MIDL-Generated Files." The behavior is different for different techniques.

MFC provides a handy API function to start COM for you, AfxOleInit(). AfxOleInit() manages both CoInitialize() and CoUninitialize(), so you needn't be concerned with terminating COM operations. MFC will handle that for you. AfxOleInit() returns a boolean value, which you can test to be sure COM initialized correctly. Typically, you do this as the first action within InitInstance(), as shown in Listing 9.1.

Note

> Actually, AfxOleInit() manages the calls to OleInitialize() and OleUninitialize(), which add functionality over and above that provided by CoInitialize() and CoUninitialize(). For the purposes of this book, however, you can consider the sets of API calls functionally equivalent.

LISTING 9.1 An Example Using AfxOleInit()

```
 1: BOOL CMyProjectApp::InitInstance()
 2: {
 3:     // This MFC API call encapsulates CoInitialize()
 4:     // and CoUninitialize():
 5:     if ( !AfxOleInit() ) {
 6:         // Error loading COM runtime environment...
 7:         return FALSE;
 8:     } // if
 9:
10:     ... // (more code)
11: }
```

With AfxOleInit() in place, you can begin integrating your COM object into your MFC test application. You can do this by using the built-in Visual C++ support for COM or by integrating a little ATL into your MFC application to utilize some of the ATL support classes and templates you saw in detail yesterday.

MFC and ATL

Although I discussed using the ATL helper classes and templates from within ATL in Day 8, there isn't any reason you can't use them from within your MFC application. For example, I use the CComPtr<>, CComQIPtr<>, and CComBSTR() templates and classes frequently from within MFC applications.

If you would like to use some of the ATL support templates and classes, you'll need to incorporate ATL into your MFC source code. To do this, include ATLBASE.H to your STDAFX.H file:

```
#include <atlbase.h>
```

Everything you'll need to use ATL from within MFC is defined within ATLBASE.H, and by placing it in STDAFX.H, you incorporate ATL into your precompiled headers and make ATL available to all your source files.

Now that you've initialized COM from InitInstance() and incorporated ATL support into your application (if you intend to use it), it's time to actually add controls to your dialog. I'll show you how in the next section.

Adding Dialog Controls

I mentioned previously you don't edit your *<project>*.rc file directly. Instead, you use the resource editor, which you access via the ResourceView of the Workspace window. I've expanded the resources for today's first MFC sample application and drawn it in Figure 9.8.

FIGURE 9.8

Visual Studio's ResourceView.

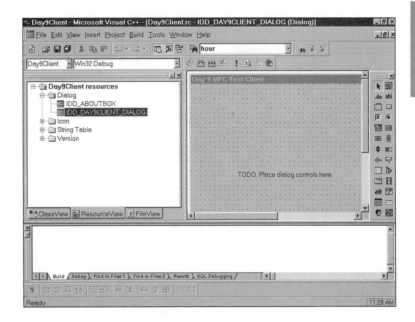

To edit any of the resources you see, expand the tree to access the particular resource and double-click on it. In Figure 9.8, you can see I'm about to edit the main dialog box template for the Day9Client application. After I double-click on the IDD_DAY9CLIENT_ DIALOG tree node, Visual Studio displays the dialog template and provides me with a control palette, as you see in Figure 9.9.

From here, you can resize the dialog box, change its title and style, and add dialog controls using the control palette. To resize, simply grab the resize bars at the sides of the dialog (or the corner) and drag the dialog to the appropriate size. If you want to change the dialog's title or its style settings, click the dialog template (to give it the input focus) and press Enter to activate the Dialog Properties property sheet you see in Figure 9.10.

FIGURE 9.9

Visual Studio's dialog template editor and control palette.

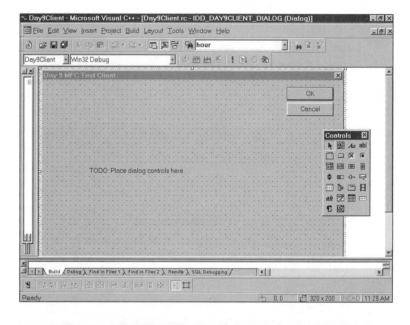

FIGURE 9.10

The Dialog Properties property sheet.

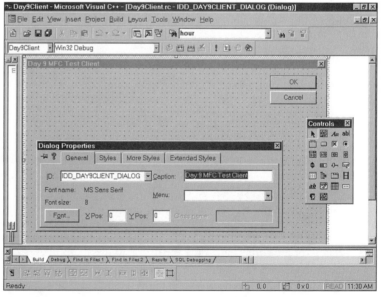

You can use the Dialog Properties pages to change all manner of dialog style settings. Typically, though, I just enter a dialog title using the Caption control if I forgot to do this when I created the project using the MFC AppWizard.

After you have the dialog styles established, it's time to add controls. To do this, you select the control from the control palette and either drag it to the dialog template or click within the dialog template to initially place the control. The control will be displayed with resizing handles, so feel free to stretch it as necessary.

When you have the control placed, click the control and press Enter to view its properties, as I've shown in Figure 9.11. Which set of property pages you see will depend entirely upon the control you select. Edit controls, for example, have a different set of properties than buttons do.

FIGURE 9.11

The Push Button Properties property sheet.

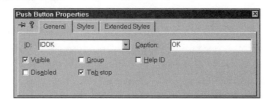

At least one property all controls have in common, though, is the ID setting. Visual Studio will assign a default control ID to your control, but you'll often want to change the default ID to something more appropriate. By the way, if you're interested in working directly with any of the static controls, such as static text or group boxes, you'll need to change the default control ID of IDC_STATIC to something else. Windows won't allow you to access dialog controls with an ID of IDC_STATIC.

After you've placed and sized your controls, as well as established their respective settings, you should make sure the tab order is correct. The tab order is the order in which the controls will receive the input focus as the user presses the Tab key while the dialog is active. To do this, select Layout, Tab Order from the Visual Studio menu. Each control will display a number, which is its place in tab order. To change the tab order, start with the first control and click. You'll see the tab order numbers change dynamically. Then proceed to the second and subsequent controls, in order, until the order you see is the order you want. Click outside the dialog template (or press Esc) to quit tab-order editing.

In many cases, the tab order won't matter to you. You're probably not shipping this application to customers, so the Human Factors people won't have the opportunity to complain about your user interface design. I mention tab order because, if you use radio button controls, the tab order matters.

If your dialog box uses radio buttons, it's important to establish the proper tab order because MFC will read the tab order and manage the group of radio buttons for you. If the tab order is incorrect, your dialog will likely behave radically as you click the buttons. For example, you might be able to click some buttons but not others. Or, one button might remain selected no matter which other radio button you click on.

Each grouping of radio buttons must be established as a *control group*. If you glance back at Figure 9.11, you'll see on the first control property page the Group checkbox. The first radio button in each radio button collection should have this property checked. In addition, be sure to check this option for the controls that follow the final radio buttons in your groupings. This tells MFC precisely which radio buttons are collected into which grouping.

The radio button groupings and control IDs are important because MFC will manage the control windows for you. One of the most powerful features of MFC is its capability to map Windows controls to C++ variables. Edit controls can map to strings, if you wish (or integers, if the edit control is set up to be numerical input only). Radio buttons map to integers—the first button is 0, the second button is 1, and so on. This is why it's important to establish the tab order and groupings correctly. I show you how to control this mapping next.

Wiring Things Up

To help you map your dialog controls to their respective C++ variables, MFC provides you with the ClassWizard. There are many ways to invoke the ClassWizard and many ways to use it, a few of which I'll discuss here. You can read much more about MFC and the ClassWizard in *MFC Unleashed Using Visual C++ 6.0*, ISBN 0-672-31557-2.

If you're an experienced MFC programmer, feel free to work with the ClassWizard as you've become accustomed to. If you're new to MFC programming, the easiest way to invoke the ClassWizard is to select it from the Visual Studio menu using View, ClassWizard. If you invoke the ClassWizard, you see the property sheet I've shown in Figure 9.12.

FIGURE 9.12

The MFC Class-Wizard's Message Maps page.

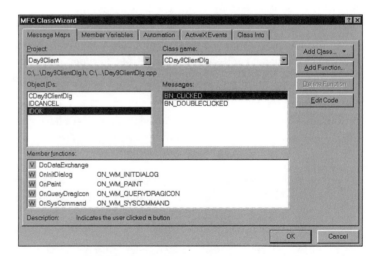

The ClassWizard will normally show you the Message Maps tab first. If you have any button controls on your dialog, for example, you'll want to know when the user clicked the button. To do this, you must handle the BN_CLICKED notification, which is incorporated within the WM_COMMAND message that the button, when it is clicked, sends your dialog.

MFC Event Notification

MFC will add the necessary code to your files if you select the specific button from the Object IDs list and then select BN_CLICKED from the Messages list. After you've selected the control and the notification, click Add Function to add the command handler. MFC will ask you how to name the function, so modify the function name if you desire and click OK. MFC will then modify your *<project>*Dlg.h and *<project>*Dlg.cpp files to add the new function and the appropriate code to intercept the appropriate Windows message. All you need to do after this is add the code to manage the event from within the function you just added.

MFC Window-Variable Mapping

That's all there is to event notifications from button controls or edit controls. Other controls contain data, and for these you'll want to add C++ variables to reflect the data the Windows controls contain. To do this, you again use the ClassWizard, but this time, select the Member Variables page as you see in Figure 9.13.

FIGURE 9.13

The MFC ClassWizard's Member Variables page.

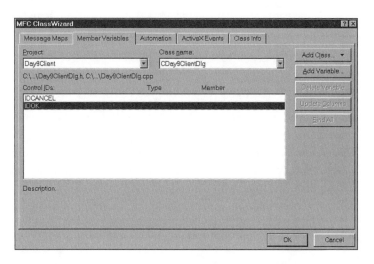

To associate a C++ variable with a control on your dialog, first find the control ID of the desired control in the left-hand column of the list control. This is why you cannot affect controls with the IDC_STATIC identifier—they don't show up in this list.

With the control ID highlighted, click the Add Variable button to bring up a dialog in which you name the variable and select its data type. Different controls will allow you to select different data types, such as MFC CStrings and integers or MFC control C++ classes, such as CEdit or CProgressCtrl. Name the variable as you desire, select the data type, and then click OK.

You should now see the middle and right-hand columns completed. They show you the data type (Type) and variable name (Member) you selected. If you later decide to change the name or data type, you must delete the variable using Delete Variable button and re-enter the information using Add Variable once again.

MFC Window-Variable Data Exchange

At this point, you have a Windows dialog control—for example, an edit control. You also have a C++ variable that is an attribute of your CDialog-based class. How does the data get transferred from the Windows control to the C++ variable and back again?

The answer is MFC's Dialog Data Exchange (DDX). I'll leave the details of DDX to other references (such as *MFC Unleashed Using Visual C++ 6.0*). The mechanics of using DDX are an important concept in the following quick look at MFC.

The ClassWizard did more than just add a member variable to your C++ class. It also added code to facilitate DDX—code to manage both the C++ and Windows aspects of your application. You control when the data is exchanged by using CWnd::UpdateData() (CWnd is the base class that supports UpdateData(), even though you access it through CDialog).

If you want to transfer information from the Windows control to your C++ variable, you use UpdateData(TRUE). If you want the reverse, that is to pass information from your C++ variable to the Windows control, you use UpdateData(FALSE).

Perhaps an example would shed some additional light. Imagine your dialog box has a button, GO!, a checkbox, and an edit control. Depending upon whether the checkbox is checked, you either read the data from the edit control and do something with it (such as pass it to your COM object), or you pull data from your COM object and put it into the edit control. The trigger for this is the GO! Button. (In fact, this is the premise for today's sample programs.) You're interested in making sure you can ship text to your object and have it correctly manipulate the text to be returned for further processing.

You used ClassWizard to insert a BN_CLICKED message handler into your CDialog class, so you can now react to the user's button click. The method you added is called OnGO(). You then added a boolean variable m_bDataIn that represents the check box, as well as a CString variable m_strData that represents the edit control.

When the user clicks GO! you read the state of the check box and then transfer data to or from the edit control based upon that state. The check box controls the user's selection of the direction of the transfer. This pseudocode shows you what will happen:

```
void CMyPseudoDlg::OnGO()
{
    // Transfer data from the Windows controls
    // to the MFC C++ variables.
    UpdateData(TRUE);

    // Determine which way the data should go
    if ( data goes to control ) {
        // Data goes to control
        /* magic COM stuff */;
    } // if
    else {
        // Data comes from control
        /* more magic COM stuff */;
    } // else

    // Update Windows controls from the MFC C++ variables
    UpdateData(FALSE);

    // Set focus to the edit control if data came from control

    return
}
```

The magic COM stuff in the preceding sample pseudocode depends upon the mechanism you used to add your COM object to your MFC application. So far in this book, you've seen two ways to do this. I'll reiterate those, as well as introduce a third mechanism, in the sections that follow.

Adding Your COM Object

After your basic MFC application is up and running, it's time to integrate your COM object and begin testing. How you do this is usually a matter of choice, depending upon the COM object.

If you're using a COM object with a custom interface, you can include the files MIDL generated for you or you can use the Visual C++ #import directive (I used the former in Day 1). If you're using an ActiveX control, on the other hand, you'll insert it into the dialog editor's control palette using the Components and Controls Gallery. The COM object I'll use is a simple ActiveX control that I developed. It displays text you provide (if you use it as an ActiveX control). Because this lesson targets MFC, I won't detail how

I created the ActiveX control. For the curious, though, I created it in the same way I created the ActiveX control in Day 7, except I added a property that accepts a BSTR instead of a short integer. The control will concatenate a numerical value to the string to prove it did something. I then paint the string's content in OnDraw(), if the control is allotted a user interface.

> **Note**
>
> The control modifies the string property when the client provides it, which is unusual. Normally, you don't change or modify properties when clients pass them to your COM objects. I did this merely for demonstration purposes.
>
> Also, ActiveX controls utilize a dual interface, so you are free to use either the IDispatch interface or the custom interface. I use both for the sample client applications, which is also a bit unusual. Most ActiveX clients load the control, not as a custom-interfaced COM object, but as an ActiveX control using IDispatch. I use today's control both ways to demonstrate not only that you can do this (if you like), but also to use a single COM object for all the client application demonstrations. This makes for a better comparison between the MFC client programming techniques I demonstrate.

Including the MIDL-Generated Files

As you know, MIDL creates several files that you typically use from within your COM server and also from within your COM client application. These files, as you know from Day 3, "The COM Interface: COM's Foundation," contain the definitions and declarations of your object's various GUIDs. After you include these files in your client source code, you can use CoCreateInstance() to instantiate the server object. It makes no difference whether you use the full CLSID and IID or you use _uuidof() to create the object.

In fact, because this is the classic COM client programming technique, I've been using it through most of the book. You create the object, call its methods (and check for bad HRESULTs), and then release the object when you're finished with it. I won't belabor this client programming technique here. I simply included Day9Server.h and Day9Server_i.c in the projects and compiled the client application.

> **Note**
>
> If you receive the HRESULT CO_E_NOTINITIALIZED (0x800401F0), be sure to add the call to AfxOleInit() or manage the calls to CoInitialize() and CoUninitialize() yourself.

The first two of today's client examples use this technique to allow you to compare this programming style with the others I'll mention in this lesson. The first example, Day9Client1a, doesn't utilize ATL support for smart pointers and BSTRs, although the second example, Day9Client1b, does. As you know from Day 8, ATL frees you from worries about releasing the COM object or freeing the BSTR, so I personally prefer the code you see in Day9Client1b.

Listings 9.2 and 9.3 show you the OnGO() method implementation that matches the pseudocode I presented earlier. Although you don't see the differences in the use of the COM pointer, you do see differences in how I deal with the BSTR data (I've highlighted this to make it more apparent). Listing 9.2 shows you how to use a plain BSTR. Note you have to free the BSTR using SysFreeString().

LISTING 9.2   The OnGO() Method Using a Simple BSTR Data Type

```
 1: void CDay9Client1aDlg::OnGo()
 2: {
 3:      // Transfer data from the Windows controls
 4:      // to the MFC C++ variables.
 5:      UpdateData(TRUE);
 6:
 7:      // Determine which way the data should go
 8:      if ( m_bPutData ) {
 9:          // I have the data I need in m_strData, so
10:          // ship it to the COM object here...
11:          HRESULT hr = m_pIDemoMFCClient->put_Data(m_strData.AllocSysString());
12:          if ( FAILED(hr) ) {
13:              // I couldn't send the data...
14:              m_strData = _T("*Error putting data*");
15:          } // if
16:
17:          // Toggle the checkbox
18:          m_bPutData = FALSE;
19:      } // if
20:      else {
21:          // Pull the data from the COM object and stuff
22:          // it into m_strData.
23:          BSTR bstrData = NULL;
24:          HRESULT hr = m_pIDemoMFCClient->get_Data(&bstrData);
25:          if ( FAILED(hr) ) {
26:              // I couldn't retrieve the data...
27:              m_strData = _T("*Error getting data*");
28:          } // if
29:          else {
30:              // Pull the message text
31:              m_strData = bstrData;
```

continues

LISTING 9.2   continued

```
32:
33:                  // Release the string memory
34:                  ::SysFreeString(bstrData);
35:
36:                  // Toggle the checkbox
37:                  m_bPutData = TRUE;
38:              } // else
39:          } // else
40:
41:      // m_strData and/or m_bPutData have now changed,
42:      // so I want to make the controls reflect the
43:      // new states...
44:      UpdateData(FALSE);
45:
46:      // If the checkbox is now checked, give the edit
47:      // control the input focus and select all of
48:      // the text.
49:      if ( m_bPutData ) {
50:          // Set focus and select text
51:          CEdit* pEdit = (CEdit*)GetDlgItem(IDC_DATA);
52:          ASSERT_VALID(pEdit);
53:          pEdit->SetFocus();
54:          pEdit->SetSel(0,-1);
55:      } // if
56: }
```

Listing 9.3, on the other hand, uses CComBSTR to manipulate the BSTR data. Note how
the BSTR handling is greatly simplified. In this example you see only a single BSTR,
but CComBSTR really helps when you're dealing with many BSTRs because it's too easy
to forget to free the string.

LISTING 9.3   The OnGo() Method Using CComBSTR ATL Support

```
 1: void CDay9Client1bDlg::OnGo()
 2: {
 3:     // (Edited for brevity...same as in Listing 9.2)
 4:
 5:     // Determine which way the data should go
 6:     if ( m_bPutData ) {
 7:         // I have the data I need in m_strData, so
 8:         // ship it to the COM object here...
 9:         HRESULT hr = m_spIDemoMFCClient-
>put_Data(m_strData.AllocSysString());
10:         if ( FAILED(hr) ) {
11:             // We couldn't send the data...
12:             m_strData = _T("*Error putting data*");
```

LISTING 9.3   continued

```
13:              } // if
14:
15:              // Toggle the checkbox
16:              m_bPutData = FALSE;
17:          } // if
18:          else {
19:              // Pull the data from the COM object and stuff
20:              // it into m_strData.
21:              CComBSTR bstrData;
22:              HRESULT hr = m_spIDemoMFCClient->get_Data(&bstrData);
23:              if ( FAILED(hr) ) {
24:                  // We couldn't retrieve the data...
25:                  m_strData = _T("*Error getting data*");
26:              } // if
27:              else {
28:                  // Pull the message text
29:                  m_strData = bstrData.m_str;
30:
31:                  // Toggle the checkbox
32:                  m_bPutData = TRUE;
33:              } // else
34:          } // else
35:
36:      // (Edited for brevity...same as in Listing 9.2)
37: }
```

For both of these sample applications, I used the custom interface IDemoMFCClient. In the next section, you'll revisit adding a COM object to your project as an ActiveX control. This time, you'll use the object's IDispatch interface through the MFC ActiveX wrapper classes.

Using the Components and Controls Gallery

The first two sample client applications are very traditional in their approach to using a COM object. This section reinforces a more modern approach, which is to use the COM object as an ActiveX control (if the object is indeed an ActiveX control!). The beauty of this client programming technique is in its simplicity. It's very easy to access and use the ActiveX object from your client application.

Although I briefly discussed adding ActiveX controls to your project in Day 7, I'll quickly go over the process again. Then, I'll show you how OnGO() changed to support ActiveX.

Instead of modifying your source code to include MIDL-generated files, as you did in
the last section, you add ActiveX controls visually. To do this, select the dialog box to
which you will add the control from the ResourceView tab of the Workspace window.
After it has been loaded into the resource editor, activate the Components and Controls
Gallery from the main Visual Studio menu by choosing Project, Add To Project,
Components and Controls.

Figure 9.14 shows you the installed ActiveX controls on my computer from Components
and Controls Gallery. I've highlighted today's sample server, shown as TYATLObject4
Class in the list control. If you double-click this (or any) ActiveX control, and affirm
Visual Studio's request to add the control, you see the dialog box shown in Figure 9.15.

FIGURE 9.14

*The ActiveX folder of
the Components and
Controls Gallery.*

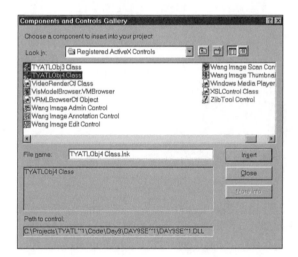

This dialog enables you to modify the C++ class name and implementation filenames
Visual Studio will create as the control is loaded. After you make any changes and click
OK, Visual Studio will generate some source files and add them to your project. At the
same time, Visual Studio will pull the icon from the control and place it on the Resource
Editor's controls palette, ready for you to insert into your dialog box. At this time, you
can add another ActiveX control or click Close to dismiss the Component and Controls
Gallery.

Now that the control is available to you from the controls palette, you can drag an
instance into your dialog just as you would any other control. Feel free to resize it, relo-
cate it, and change any properties the control exposes. You change the properties as you
would any control—activate the control with a single-click and press Enter. Today's
ActiveX control has two property pages, which are shown in Figures 9.16 and 9.17. You
establish the basic control information using the General page, to include the object's

control ID. If the control exposes any properties, you'll see additional property pages. In this case, today's control has only a single additional property page, All, and on that page you can specify the default text the control should display when it is activated. Because I didn't implement property persistence (I'll leave that for Day 16, "ATL and ActiveX: Modern Control Packaging"), the control will always initially display the text unused at present that I coded into the control as its default textual message.

FIGURE 9.15

The Components and Controls Gallery Confirm Classes dialog.

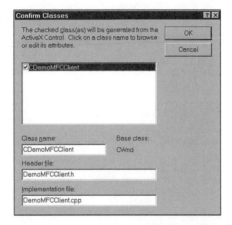

FIGURE 9.16

Day9Server's General property page.

FIGURE 9.17

Day9Server's All property page.

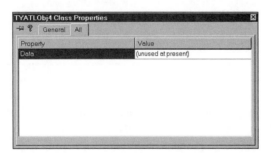

With the control's sizing and properties established, you can now invoke the ClassWizard to assign the control a C++ variable in the usual fashion. Note the control has only a single category—Control. You can't deal with the ActiveX control as a string, for example. In this case, the control's C++ class will be named CDemoMFCClient. For this example, I called the C++ variable m_CDemoCtrl.

This sample client is now a little more interesting than the first two (or the next) because the ActiveX control has a user interface. When you provide new text data and update the user interface, the control will display the new information. You had to retrieve that information yourself in the previous examples. The manipulation of the data is the same for all the examples, but it's interesting to see the control itself display the data.

In any case, Listing 9.4 shows you the OnGO() method for the ActiveX control. It's very different than the first two implementations because the C++ variable wraps the ActiveX COM aspects nicely.

LISTING 9.4 OnGO() Method Using MFC ActiveX Support

```
 1: void CDay9Client2Dlg::OnGo()
 2: {
 3:     // (Edited for brevity...same as in Listing 9.2)
 4:
 5:     // Determine which way the data should go
 6:     if ( m_bPutData ) {
 7:         // I have the data I need in m_strData, so
 8:         // ship it to the COM object here...
 9:         m_CDemoCtrl.SetData(m_strData);
10:
11:         // Toggle the checkbox
12:         m_bPutData = FALSE;
13:     } // if
14:     else {
15:         // Pull the data from the COM object and stuff
16:         // it into m_strData.
17:         m_strData = m_CDemoCtrl.GetData();
18:
19:         // Toggle the checkbox
20:         m_bPutData = TRUE;
21:     } // else
22:
23:     // (Edited for brevity...same as in Listing 9.2)
24: }
```

ANALYSIS
I've again highlighted the relevant portions of OnGO(). Note there is no BSTR! MFC wrapped that aspect of the data property, so you deal directly with CStrings and LPTSTR values (lines 9 and 17). That's handy. There is also no need to be concerned about creating an instance of the ActiveX control or releasing it when you're through with it. MFC handles all this for you. Note if there is a problem accessing the ActiveX control, or if the invocation results in a failed HRESULT, MFC throws a COleException or a COleDispatchException. In a real application you would want to handle these situations.

I've used this and the previous two techniques before in this book when I wrote test clients to demonstrate the ATL-based COM object I was discussing. I hope you're a bit more comfortable working with COM objects using MFC-based clients. There is one more technique I'll show you. That technique uses COM classes built into the Visual C++ compiler itself.

Importing the Type Library

Microsoft added a new feature to the Visual C++ 5.0 compiler, and it carries over to the current version. That is the `#import` directive and built-in COM support. It makes sense, to me anyway, that Visual C++ should support COM with or without MFC or ATL. This is exactly what the `#import` directive and the template classes that you'll find in COMDEF.H are designed to do.

The `#import` directive accepts a path to a type library, whether it's a .TLB file or it's contained within a DLL. The compiler loads the type library and examines the information it finds there. This information is written to two files, a .TLH file and a .TLI file. Both are just text files, so feel free to open and examine them. Don't make changes, however. They're created automatically, so any changes you make will later be destroyed.

The *type library header* file (*.TLH* file) defines your COM interface to be a `struct`, defines the interface's IID in another structure, and creates a smart pointer (similar to CComPtr). The smart pointer is created using the `_COM_SMARTPTR_TYPEDEF()` macro you find in COMDEF.H., and this is important to you because of the highlighted portion of the macro as I have expanded it:

```
typedef _COM_SMARTPTR<_COM_SMARTPTR_LEVEL2<Interface, &IID> > \
        Interface ## Ptr
```

If you're interested in all the details, I'd highly recommend Richard Grimes' *Professional ATL COM Programming* from Wrox Press, ISBN 1-861001-4-01. In fact, Richard's book is an excellent reference for everything I'll address in this section. In any case, the result of this macro is that a new smart pointer variable is defined that you can use from within your source code. The variable is named `<interface>Ptr`, and it gets this name from the code I italicized (the `##` preprocessor directive concatenates text). I've been using the interface `IDemoMFCClient` for my examples today. The equivalent smart pointer created by `_COM_SMARTPTR_TYPEDEF()` is called `IDemoMFCClientPtr`.

The *type library implementation* or *inline* file (TLI file) is analogous to a .CPP file. You'll find each method the interface supports implemented here, and the .TLH file happens to include this file.

Returning to the `#import` directive itself, you can concatenate attributes after the type library path that tailor the creation of the .TLH and .TLI files. You can apply several attributes, but to keep things somewhat brief (this will be a quick test application, after all!), I'll mention the two I commonly use. The remaining available attributes are documented in the online help files.

The attributes I find most useful are `no_namespace` and `named_guids`. `no_namespace` tells the preprocessor not to create a new namespace for the interface(s) contained in the .TLH and .TLI files. Normally, the compiler creates a new namespace based upon the library directive contained in the IDL file. For example, the IDL file for today's sample COM object contains this code:

```
library DAY9SERVERLib
{
    ...
}
```

This translates to the following namespace definition in the .TLH file:

```
namespace DAY9SERVERLib {
  ...
} // namespace DAY9SERVERLib
```

Because I'm just whipping out a quick test application, I'm not too concerned about name collisions (which the C++ `namespace` keyword is designed to do). I'm probably not using so many COM objects that I need to worry. Omitting the namespace simply enables me to access the smart pointer in the global namespace and skip all the extra typing (the namespace identifier and the C++ scoping operator, `::`).

The `named_guids` attribute provides me with the traditional CLSID and IID variables I've always used, such as `IID_IDemoMFCClient`. I'm used to using these versus `__uuidof()`, and with `named_guids` I can continue to use these old-style variables.

Today's fourth demo, then, has this line of code in the Day9Client3Dlg.h file:

```
// Add the ATL object's information
#import "..\Day9Server\Day9Server.tlb" no_namespace named_guids
```

With the type library imported, I can define the COM object's pointer like this:

```
// The COM object
IDemoMFCClientPtr m_spIDemoMFCClient;
```

The COM object itself is instantiated in `CDay9Client3Dlg::OnInitDialog()`:

```
// Create an instance of the ATL object
m_spIDemoMFCClient.CreateInstance(CLSID_TYATLObj4);
if ( m_spIDemoMFCClient == NULL ) {
    // Couldn't create the object...
```

```
AfxMessageBox("Error creating the COM object!", MB_OK | MB_ICONERROR);
EndDialog(IDCANCEL);
return TRUE;
} // if
```

And the resulting OnGO() handler is shown in Listing 9.5.

LISTING 9.5   The OnGO() Method Using Visual C++ COM Support

```
 1: void CDay9Client3Dlg::OnGo()
 2: {
 3:     // (Edited for brevity...same as in Listing 9.2)
 4:
 5:     // Determine which way the data should go
 6:     if ( m_bPutData ) {
 7:         // I have the data I need in m_strData, so
 8:         // ship it to the COM object here...
 9:         m_spIDemoMFCClient->PutData(m_strData.AllocSysString());
10:
11:         // Toggle the checkbox
12:         m_bPutData = FALSE;
13:     } // if
14:     else {
15:         // Pull the data from the COM object and stuff
16:         // it into m_strData.
17:         _bstr_t bstrData = m_spIDemoMFCClient->GetData();
18:         if ( !bstrData ) {
19:             // We couldn't retrieve the data...
20:             m_strData = _T("*Error getting data*");
21:         } // if
22:         else {
23:             // Pull the message text
24:             m_strData = (char*)bstrData;
25:
26:             // Toggle the checkbox
27:             m_bPutData = TRUE;
28:         } // else
29:     } // else
30:
31:     // (Edited for brevity...same as in Listing 9.2)
32: }
```

ANALYSIS   As you can see, the Visual C++ COM support uses the smart _bstr_t class rather than a raw BSTR or a CComBSTR (line 17). I check to see if the BSTR is empty using the classes overloaded ! operator (line 18), and I extract the character data from the BSTR variable using its overloaded (char*) operator (line 24).

9

I'd like to point out two things to note about using the Visual C++ COM compiler support classes. First, they will throw exceptions if there is a problem with the COM method invocation. If for some reason the method returned a failed HRESULT, your application will die a horrible death unless you're handling exceptions. Second, unless the COM object's type library changes, you don't need to re-import the type library each time you compile. Many developers I know will remove (comment) the #import and instead use #include to incorporate the .TLH file.

Summary

You covered a lot of ground today, but then, the MFC wizards (as with ATL) do a lot of the work, so things aren't as difficult as they might have seemed at first. You must have a test client if you expect to test your COM object. If you need more than a simple console application and you want to stick with C++, MFC is the way to go.

Today you saw how to create a basic MFC dialog-based application and how to insert the MFC code to invoke the COM runtime. You then had a quick tour of the important MFC files and classes the wizard produced for you. I then showed you how to bring ATL support into your MFC application (if you wanted this support). I closed the first major section by describing how to add controls to your dialog box and add the glue code you need to handle events, such as button clicks and data transfer (C++ variable to Windows control) using DDX.

I then discussed the three main ways you can incorporate your COM object into your MFC test application. The traditional way includes the files MIDL generates when the object's IDL file is compiled. To demonstrate this, I've provided two sample client applications—one that uses straight COM pointers and one that uses ATL support. Then you saw (again) how to add an ActiveX control to your project. Finally, I described the #import directive and how Visual C++ supports COM programming with or without MFC and ATL.

Two of the three methods, as you remember, involve exceptions. I cover these and error handling, in general, in Day 10, "ATL and Errors: What to Do When Things Break."

Q&A

Q You've been doing this for a long time. Which COM object insertion mechanism do you use?

A Unless I'm adding an ActiveX control, in which case I use the Components and Controls Gallery, I tend to include the MIDL files and use ATL smart pointers and classes. I like examining HRESULTs myself to see if there is a problem, rather than having to decide what to do when I find myself in an exception handler. Often, a failed HRESULT doesn't necessarily indicate there is truly a problem—that decision is interface specific, and often I want to tune how I deal with error conditions. If I later decide the HRESULT is bad enough to merit an exception, I tend to throw the exception with additional information, as I'll show you in Day 10.

Q MFC programming is completely new to me. I'm concerned about having to learn another class library in addition to ATL. Would you still recommend MFC for me?

A That depends. I hope this chapter provided enough overview of MFC to get you started. But the real question is do you want to stick with C++ or not? If you do, without some class library help, many people find developing Windows applications to be very time consuming and bug prone. If you forgo the user interface, you could always use a console application. If you skip C++ altogether, you could use Visual Basic, HTML, or VBA (such as within Microsoft Access), or even use the ActiveX Test Container that ships with Visual C++. You'll probably find many professionals using Visual Basic because implementing applications takes so little time. I tend to stick with C++ because I'm comfortable with MFC and C++, and I like the added control I get by using C++ instead of Visual Basic. I'd recommend, however, you use what you are most comfortable with. You don't want to spend all your time writing test code if your job is to write the COM objects themselves.

Workshop

The Workshop is designed to help you anticipate possible questions, review what you've learned, and get you thinking about how to put your knowledge into practice. The answers to the quiz are in Appendix A, "Answers."

Quiz

1. How do I create an MFC application?
2. Which two MFC classes will your main application classes derive from?
3. What MFC API function do I use to invoke the COM runtime?
4. How do I add an event handler to my application (a button click, for example)?
5. How do I add a C++ variable to manage the Windows control information? How is the information transferred?
6. What three mechanisms can I use to integrate my COM object into my application?

Exercise

1. Create a Visual Basic test application that mimics the behavior of the MFC applications I've shown you here. Which was easier for you to create? How would you change the Visual Basic code if the object under test did not have a dual interface?

DAY 10

ATL and Errors: What to Do When Things Break

Things go wrong. They just do. Code that's run for thousands of hours breaks for no apparent reason. A server locks up, causing major enterprise shutdown. Usually things *do* break for a reason. The reason usually involves an unanticipated condition that throws a kink in the system. How you handle error conditions in your code speaks volumes about your level of coding experience. The more experience you have, the more likely you are to manage exceptional conditions.

In this respect, programming COM objects is no different from coding any other type of application. Runtime errors will creep in, and you must prepare your code for the worst. COM imposes an additional requirement, however. Your COM object *must* handle the exceptional conditions. You can't simply pass the problem on to the client application. You can notify the client the error has occurred, but your COM object can't just croak. You can croak, but you must croak in a predictable fashion.

I believe this is a critical topic to study and understand. You can't know too much. Therefore, in this day you will

- Revisit the HRESULT
- Learn why you should not allow exceptional conditions to cross the interface boundary
- Learn how C++ handles exceptions
- Understand how you can better handle exceptions
- Learn about COM's rich error-handling capability using ISupportErrorInfo

The HRESULT

You've seen HRESULTs throughout the book. After all, you can't program in a COM environment and not see an HRESULT, especially when you're just beginning. Ideally, all COM methods, except AddRef() and Release(), return HRESULTs to indicate the success or failure of the method.

An HRESULT, as defined in WINERROR.H, is an unsigned long integer that consists of several bit fields (you saw this in Day 2, "Exploring COM: The Technology ATL Supports"). The most important bit is the *severity* bit, because it indicates the success or failure of the method. But the other fields are important, too. The *facility* field tells you what major subsystem failed, such as FACILITY_RPC and FACILITY_WIN32. Of course, each facility has a set of error codes, and you'll find this in the code field.

As you remember, you test for the success or failure of an HRESULT using SUCCEEDED() and FAILED(). If you later want to check for specific information, feel free to do so.

But that's how you use the HRESULT on the client side of the interface. As the interface's author, it's up to you to return an appropriate HRESULT. Often, that can be a challenge. For example, if a client passes you a NULL pointer, do you return E_POINTER or E_INVALIDARG? The answer is that you, as the designer, must decide. When you do, you also should provide some documentation to the client's author so he knows what the object will do under normal conditions.

I often find myself reading through WINERROR.H to find some HRESULT that meets my requirements. Just about as often, no predefined HRESULT appears to suit the task, and I have to turn to custom HRESULTs.

Tip   Error results from calling Win32 functions won't require a custom HRESULT even though you won't find them (as HRESULTs) in WINERROR.H. Instead, you use GetLastError() to retrieve the error code, then convert that to an HRESULT using HRESULT_FROM_WIN32(err), where err is the error code returned from GetLastError(). The HRESULT_FROM_WIN32() macro is defined in WINERROR.H.

If you elect to create custom HRESULTs, you first decide what facility-specific codes to use and what they indicate. The HRESULT code field contains 16 bits, so you have 65,535 different custom HRESULTs your interface can return. You might at first believe you would have 65,535 codes available per facility code, but Microsoft reserves all but one of the HRESULT facility codes and their respective HRESULT bits for themselves. The only facility your custom HRESULT can use is FACILITY_ITF (0x4), so you truly are limited to 65,535 different custom HRESULTs per interface. By the way, FACILITY_ITF represents the *interface-specific facility*.

I'll show you a handy trick for defining your custom HRESULTs shortly. First I will describe how you generate custom HRESULTs from within your COM object.

Assuming you have a list of custom error codes ranging from 0x0000 to 0xFFFF, you select the code you desire and pass that to the MAKE_HRESULT() macro (from WINERROR.H):

```
#define MAKE_HRESULT(sev,fac,code) \
    ((HRESULT) (((unsigned long)(sev)<<31) |
➡((unsigned long)(fac)<<16) | ((unsigned long)(code))) )
```

In this case, the sev parameter is SEVERITY_SUCCESS (0x0) or SEVERITY_ERROR (0x1), and the fac is (must be) FACILITY_ITF. The code parameter is the particular error code you defined. For example, you might use code similar to Listing 10.1 to send to your object's client some predefined checksum error.

LISTING 10.1   An Example of Using of a Custom HRESULT

```
 1: // The error code:
 2: #define E_CHECKSUM 0x0100
 3:
 4: HRESULT hr = S_OK;
 5: if ( !bCheckSumOK ) {
 6:     // Error with checksum
 7:     hr = MAKE_HRESULT(SEVERITY_ERROR, FACILITY_ITF, E_CHECKSUM);
 8: } // if
 9:
10: return hr;
```

You won't find E_CHECKSUM in WINERROR.H (although there is an ERROR_CRC Win32 error defined there). I made it up, presumably because my interface can calculate a checksum and might find the checksum didn't match a given key value. The point is you, too, can create your own HRESULTs to better suit your interface's needs.

Now that you know how to send a custom HRESULT back to your client, how would you best define the custom HRESULTs? If you place them in some header file, you'll have to send the header file around with your object so the client application programmers can use them. Perhaps you can put them into the type library.

As it happens, both methods are often used. To insert codes into the type library, you would most likely place the custom error codes in an IDL enumeration, just as you saw in Day 8, "ATL Object Methods: Adding Functionality to Your Interface." Your object's client can first test the success or failure of a method call, then test the facility code of the error HRESULT for FACILITY_ITF. If the HRESULT had the FACILITY_ITF bit set, the client can check the code field against the enumerated error values. If you're using the #import directive, Visual C++ will take the IDL enumerations and convert them to #define values you can use.

If, on the other hand, you are #include-ing the object's header file, you can use the IDL enumeration also. To be different, however, you might choose to use the cpp_quote() IDL command. cpp_quote() takes a string as an argument, and while MIDL compiles the IDL file and creates the .H file, the argument to cpp_quote() is inserted verbatim. For example, you can put these lines of code into your object's IDL file:

```
cpp_quote("// Custom HRESULT code values");
cpp_quote("// (Be sure to test for FACILITY_ITF");
cpp_quote("// before testing against these values.)");
cpp_quote("#define E_CHECKSUM 0x0100");
```

The choice is yours, but consider this. Placing the codes in the type library as an enumeration makes the codes available to a wider audience. Only C++ cares about .H files.

There is something else only C++ cares about, and that's the C++ exception. Let's see why exception handling is so important to COM.

Exceptions and COM

Exceptions are going to happen. In many cases, the error is a total surprise to your object, such as when the user pulls the network cable from the wall outlet and disconnects your object from its remote data source. Sometimes, though, you throw the exception (you'll see why and how shortly). You detect an error and want to exercise your error logic. In any case, no matter how the exception was thrown, never allow the exception to cross the interface boundary.

What I mean by *interface boundary* is that your object's client expects an HRESULT, not an exception. For example, C++ can handle C++ exceptions, but Visual Basic can't, nor can a script. The main objection to passing exceptions on to clients is that, typically, the clients are holding system resources, and the exception might cause them to crash. The resources might not be released properly, or they might not be released at all until the next time the system is booted.

The best way to prevent a client from eating your object's exception is to wrap all your interface methods in C++ try/catch blocks. I'll show you what I mean by this in the next section.

C++ Exception Handling

ATL, by default, deactivates C++ exception handling. It does this because the compiler must add code to manage exceptions, which means more code and added CPU cycles. This opposes ATL's philosophy, which is to create the smallest, fastest objects possible. If you're sure you'll never see the down side of an exception, by all means forgo exception handling and create the tiniest possible COM objects.

However, I would contend that most COM objects should sustain the overhead associated with handling exceptions. The system penalties for not doing so are great, and, frankly, it's just good programming style to code defensively.

You enable C++ exception handling by accessing your project's settings. If you don't explicitly enable exception handling, but your code handles exceptions (the next section), the Visual C++ compiler will complain with this warning:

```
warning C4530: C++ exception handler used, but unwind semantics are not enabled.
➥Specify -GX
```

The compiler inserts exception-handling code for you, but it also warns you that it isn't specifically authorized to do so. To correct the warning condition, access your project's settings. If you look at the C/C++ tab of your project's settings, you see something like the dialog I show in Figure 10.1. Notice I selected C++ Language from the Category drop-down list to access the exception check box. Simply check this option and click OK. Note you'll need to do this for every build type you intend to use—Debug, Release MinDependency, and so forth.

The compiler knows you're using exception handling because you inserted a try/catch *block*. Let's see how try and catch() work together to handle C++ exceptions.

10

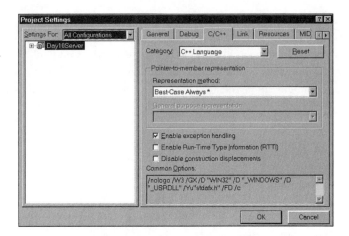

FIGURE 10.1

The Project Settings C/C++ tab with exceptions enabled.

Try/Catch

Because exceptions happen, the C++ language incorporates a mechanism for cleanly handling them. C++ provides you with the try/catch block, which is a combination of the C++ keyword try and one or more catch() statements. Any code that you believe might generate an exception should be placed within the try statement. If an exception is generated, the catch() statements have a chance to process the exception. By the way, most programmers refer to exceptions as being *thrown* because you can create one yourself using the C++ throw() function. You might also see exception generation referred to as *raising* an exception.

For example, the code in Listing 10.2 will throw an exception and then catch it.

LISTING 10.2 ExceptTest.cpp File Contents (Slightly Edited)

```
 1: #include <iostream>
 2: using namespace std;
 3:
 4: int main(int argc, char* argv[])
 5: {
 6:     // Forced exception
 7:     try {
 8:         // Divide by zero (I declare these variables
 9:         // as volatile to prevent their optimization
10:         // from the code in a release build).
11:         volatile int iBadValue = 1;
12:         volatile int iZero = 0;
13:         iBadValue /= iZero;
14:
15:         // Print a message
```

LISTING 10.2 continued

```
16:         cout << "You won't see this!" << endl;
17:     } // try
18:     catch(...) {
19:         // Exception caught
20:         cout << "Caught an exception" << endl;
21:     } // catch
22:
23:     return 0;
24: }
```

> **Note**
>
> You'll find this code in the ExceptTest sample program included on the Web site for this book.

10

ANALYSIS Any code that I'm concerned might throw an exception should be included within the braces (a *compound statement*) following the try keyword, such as you see in line 7. The catch block, lines 18 through 21, uses a special version of catch() that catches any unprocessed exception. It isn't unusual at all to catch specific things, such as a particular C++ class (the next section), integers, pointers, and so on. For example, when programming COM you might see code such as that in Listing 10.3.

LISTING 10.3 Example COM Interface Method Exception Processing

```
 1: try {
 2:     HRESULT hr = pSomeInterface->SomeMethod();
 3:     if ( FAILED(hr) ) throw(hr);
 4:     // Continue processing...
 5: } // try
 6: catch(HRESULT hrErr) {
 7:     // Do something with a COM-specific failed
 8:     // HRESULT
 9:     return hrErr;
10: } // catch
11: catch(...) {
12:     // Some other exception
13:     return E_UNEXPECTED;
14: } // catch
15:
16: return S_OK;
```

ANALYSIS In this case, the catch block that handles HRESULTs has the first opportunity to handle the exception, lines 6 through 10. If the exception parameter data type is

unsigned long (an HRESULT), this catch block will be executed. If the exception parameter data type is something else, the generic handler—catch(...)—will manage that
and return the ubiquitous E_UNEXPECTED, as you see starting with line 11.

I see two additional benefits from exception handling, aside from the obvious program
crash prevention and cleaner error handling. The first is that I no longer have to nest
if/then statements for HRESULT checking. For example, consider Listing 10.4.

LISTING 10.4   Example Nested Function Return Code Processing

```
 1: HRESULT hr = pSomeInterface->SomeMethod();
 2: if ( SUCCEEDED(hr) ) {
 3:     // Succeeded
 4:     hr = pSomeInterface->SomeMethod2();
 5:     if ( SUCCEEDED(hr) ) {
 6:         // Succeeded
 7:         hr = pSomeInterface->SomeMethod3();
 8:         if ( SUCCEEDED(hr) ) {
 9:             // Succeeded
10:             hr = pSomeInterface->SomeMethod4();
11:             // And so on...
12:         } // if
13:         else {
14:             // Failed...
15:             return hr;
16:         } // else
17:     } // if
18:     else {
19:         // Failed...
20:         return hr;
21:     } // else
22: } // if
23: else {
24:     // Failed...
25:     return hr;
26: } // else
27:
28: return S_OK;
```

This gnarly mess can easily be replaced by the code in Listing 10.5.

LISTING 10.5   Example Exceptional Return Code Processing

```
 1: try {
 2:     HRESULT hr = pSomeInterface->SomeMethod();
 3:     if ( FAILED(hr) ) throw hr;
 4:
```

LISTING 10.5 continued

```
 5:     hr = pSomeInterface->SomeMethod2();
 6:     if ( FAILED(hr) ) throw hr;
 7:
 8:     hr = pSomeInterface->SomeMethod3();
 9:     if ( FAILED(hr) ) throw hr;
10:
11:     hr = pSomeInterface->SomeMethod4();
12:     if ( FAILED(hr) ) throw hr;
13: } // try
14: catch(HRESULT hrErr) {
15:     // Return the failed HRESULT
16:     return hrErr;
17: } // catch
18: catch(...) {
19:     // Unexpected error
20:     return E_UNEXPECTED;
21: } // catch
22:
23: return S_OK;
```

10

ANALYSIS The second alternative is much cleaner. If you're a real purist, you can even remove the additional `return` statements (inside the catch blocks, lines 16 and 20) and have a single exit point at the end of the code.

The second benefit I see from exception handling is that I gain the ability to throw any data type I desire. If that's true, I should be able to create an exception C++ class to better manage exception processing. In fact, that's my next topic.

Custom Exception Classes

It would be hard for me to anticipate each and every possible error condition for any application you might write. But I can easily see creating a C++ class to contain error information that would be flexible enough to manage many situations. You can be as fancy or as simple as you like, and the class is yours to modify to your liking. I'll get quite a bit fancier in the next section on rich error handling.

I often find it useful to know not only the failed HRESULT, but also the particular line of code that received the bad result. For this, I use the compiler's predefined __LINE__ macro. It's also helpful to combine that with the __FILE__ macro to specifically state which file caused the error. Given this, I can send this information to the debug stream or otherwise log the error. For COM exception-handling classes, I'll also provide a descriptive string or even rich error information—such as you'll see in the final section of this day.

I created a sample program to demonstrate the use of a C++ class as the exception parameter. You'll find the example ClassExceptTest's contents in Listing 10.6.

LISTING 10.6   ClassExceptTest.cpp File Contents (Slightly Edited)

```
 1: #include <iostream>
 2: using namespace std;
 3:
 4: class CException
 5: {
 6: public:
 7:     CException() : m_iLine(0)
 8:     {
 9:         // Copy in bogus file name
10:         strcpy(m_szFile,"(no file specified)");
11:     }
12:
13:     CException(int iLine) : m_iLine(iLine)
14:     {
15:         // Copy in bogus file name
16:         strcpy(m_szFile,"(no file specified)");
17:     }
18:
19:     CException(int iLine, char* pszFile) : m_iLine(iLine)
20:     {
21:         // Copy in file name
22:         strcpy(m_szFile,pszFile);
23:     }
24:
25:     virtual ~CException()
26:     {
27:     }
28:
29:     int GetLine()
30:     {
31:         // Return line number
32:         return m_iLine;
33:     }
34:
35:     char* GetFile()
36:     {
37:         // Return pointer to file path text
38:         return m_szFile;
39:     }
40:
41: protected:
42:     int m_iLine;
43:     char m_szFile[_MAX_PATH];
44: };
45:
46: int main(int argc, char* argv[])
47: {
48:     // Thrown exception
49:     try {
```

LISTING 10.6 continued

```
50:          // Print a message
51:          cout << "About to throw an exception" << endl;
52:
53:          // Throw the exception
54:          throw new CException(__LINE__,__FILE__);
55:
56:          // Print another message
57:          cout << "You won't see this!" << endl;
58:       } // try
59:       catch(CException* e) {
60:          // CException caught
61:          cout << "Caught my own exception, line " << e->GetLine();
62:          cout << ", file \"" << e->GetFile() << "\"" << endl;
63:
64:          // Don't forget to delete it...
65:          delete e;
66:       } // catch
67:       catch(...) {
68:          // Exception caught
69:          cout << "Caught generic exception" << endl;
70:       } // catch
71:
72:       return 0;
73: }
```

10

ANALYSIS I've highlighted where I throw the exception in Listing 10.6 (line 54), as well as where I catch it (line 59). Because I create an instance of the CException class using the C++ new operator, I must also delete that instance when I handle the exception to prevent the memory leak. I set the __LINE__ value when the exception is thrown because I want that line number. I can't set the line number in the exception handler because that gives me the line in the handler, and that information isn't as valuable to me. I'd rather know what line of code brought me to the handler.

Clearly the CException class I've used is relatively simple-minded. However, it shows you the power of using a C++ class with C++ exception handling. You can store any information known at the time of the exception into the class and use it in the handler without declaring variables of higher scope. This makes for cleaner programming.

The exception class can also perform some generic processing for you. For example, I'll combine the C++ exception class with the rich error information you'll see in the next section to create a very powerful exception-handling ally.

Rich Error Handling

Rich error handling is COM's answer to the C++ exception class I just discussed, and you'll find it commonly used in a scripted environment (dual interfaced components). No requirement exists stating that rich error handling be used only in those environments, however, or only by a dual interface. The goal is to pass additional error information back to the client.

It probably isn't too surprising to find COM has defined interfaces for just this purpose. The COM server uses the ICreateErrorInfo interface, whereas the client uses the IErrorInfo interface. Several COM API calls are designed to help you with these interfaces. For example, the COM server calls CreateErrorInfo() to create an instance of ICreateErrorInfo. After setting the error information, using ICreateErrorInfo methods, the COM server calls SetErrorInfo(). SetErrorInfo() establishes this error information object as the current object for this thread (other threads will have other error objects). By the way, IErrorInfo is a base interface for ICreateErrorInfo, so given ICreateErrorInfo you retrieve the IErrorInfo interface using QueryInterface(). You'll find this necessary when creating the error information record, as you'll see shortly.

Note

You might remember from Day 8 that the AtlReportError() function handles these details for you. I recommend using it, instead of coding all this yourself. My intention here, however, is to discuss rich error handling itself so that you gain some understanding of the process, rather than just asking ATL to manage it.

The client uses GetErrorInfo() to retrieve the error information stored by the COM server. After retrieving the error-information object, the client accesses the various data items to display them to the user or otherwise process the data on the user's behalf.

The ICreateErrorInfo and IErrorInfo interfaces mirror each other. That is, ICreateErrorInfo enables you to establish error information, whereas the IErrorInfo interface enables you to access it. Perhaps this will be clearer if you examine Tables 10.1 and 10.2. Table 10.1 provides you the methods ICreateErrorInfo implements, whereas Table 10.2 shows you what information IErrorInfo allows you to access.

Table 10.1 `ICreateErrorInfo` Methods

Method	Purpose
SetDescription()	Establishes a descriptive error information string
SetGUID()	Establishes the interface from which the error originated (IID)
SetSource()	Establishes the interface from which the error originated (ProgID)
SetHelpContext()	Establishes a help context for more information
SetHelpFile()	Establishes a help file (used in association with the help context) for more information

Table 10.2 `IErrorInfo` Methods

Method	Purpose
GetDescription()	Retrieves the descriptive error information string
GetGUID()	Retrieves the interface from which the error originated (IID)
GetSource()	Retrieves the interface from which the error originated (ProgID)
GetHelpContext()	Retrieves the help context
GetHelpFile()	Retrieves the help file

10

So if you step back a moment and reflect, this is exactly the sort of thing ATL typically wraps for you. In fact, ATL does it with the `AtlReportError()` helper function. To show you how this mechanism works, I'll provide a useful, but minimal implementation a bit later in this section. (One of this lesson's examples will ask you to provide a more robust implementation.)

Before I actually implement a C++ class that wraps rich error handling, I should mention your interface must support the `ISupportErrorInfo` interface. This is an easy requirement to fulfill with ATL because, as you recall, the ATL Object Wizard asks you if you want to support this interface when you access the *Attributes* property page (see Figure 6.5 in Day 6). If you check the Support `ISupportErrorInfo` option, the wizard will insert this into your C++ class's inheritance list:

```
class ATL_NO_VTABLE CMyATLObj :
    public CComObjectRootEx<CComSingleThreadModel>,
    public CComCoClass<CMyATLObj, &CLSID_MyObj>,
    public ISupportErrorInfo,
    public ISomeInterface
{
    ...
};
```

It will insert code similar to the following into your class's implementation:

```
STDMETHODIMP CMyATLObj::InterfaceSupportsErrorInfo(REFIID riid)
{
    static const IID* arr[] =
    {
        &IID_ISomeInterface
    };
    for (int i=0; i < sizeof(arr) / sizeof(arr[0]); i++)
    {
        if (InlineIsEqualGUID(*arr[i],riid))
            return S_OK;
    }
    return S_FALSE;
}
```

Clients interested in determining whether your object supports rich error information query your custom interface for ISupportErrorInfo. If the interface is found, they pass an IID to ISupportErrorInfo::ISupportErrorInfo(). If that interface supports error information, the client will receive an S_OK. If the interface does not support error information, the client will receive S_FALSE.

ATL does provide an implementation of the code I just presented with the ISupportErrorInfoImpl<> template. The limitation is that the ATL template supports only a single interface, whereas the code the Object Wizard inserts is more flexible. You can manage as many interfaces as you like by simply adding their IIDs to the arr[] array. In any case, to use ISupportErrorInfoImpl, replace the ISupportErrorInfo interface in your class's inheritance list:

```
class ATL_NO_VTABLE CMyATLObj :
    public CComObjectRootEx<CComSingleThreadModel>,
    public CComCoClass<CMyATLObj, &CLSID_MyObj>,
    public ISupportErrorInfoImpl<&IID_ISomeInterface>,
    public ISomeInterface
{
    ...
};
```

Now, the implementation code that the Object Wizard inserted is no longer necessary and can be removed.

It would be nice to wrap all the rich error handling into a C++ class, perhaps even adding some of the other information I presented earlier, such as the line and filename of the offending code. I've created a basic implementation that I call CAtlException, which you'll find in both the Day10Server example and in Listing 10.7.

LISTING 10.7   CAtlException

```
 1: // AtlException.h : Declaration of the CAtlException
 2:
 3: #ifndef __ATLEXCEPTION_H_
 4: #define __ATLEXCEPTION_H_
 5:
 6: /////////////////////////////////////////////////////////////////////
 7: // Maximum exception string length
 8: #define MAXEXSTRLEN 255
 9:
10: // _T macro definition
11: #include <TCHAR.H>
12:
13: /////////////////////////////////////////////////////////////////////
14: // CAtlException
15: class CAtlException
16: {
17: public:
18:     CAtlException(HRESULT hrErr, int iLine,
19:                   LPCTSTR strFile, LPCTSTR strDesc)
20:       : m_hrError(hrErr),
21:         m_iLine(iLine)
22:     {
23:         // Store the filename string, if any
24:         if ( strFile ) {
25:             _tcsncpy(m_strFile,strFile,_MAX_PATH);
26:         } // if
27:         else {
28:             _tcscpy(m_strFile,_T("(No file information provided.)"));
29:         } // else
30:
31:         // Store the message string, if any
32:         if ( strDesc ) {
33:             _tcsncpy (m_strMsg,strDesc,MAXEXSTRLEN);
34:         } // if
35:         else {
36:             _tcscpy(m_strMsg,_T("(No error information provided.)"));
37:         } // else
38:
39:         // Fill in the error information
40:         CComBSTR bstrDesc(m_strMsg);
41:         CompleteErrorInfo(bstrDesc);
42:     }
43:
44:     CAtlException(HRESULT hrErr, int iLine,
45:                   LPCTSTR strFile, UINT uiDescID)
46:       : m_hrError(hrErr),
47:         m_iLine(iLine)
48:     {
```

continues

10

LISTING 10.7 continued

```
49:            // Store the filename string, if any
50:            if ( strFile ) {
51:                _tcsncpy(m_strFile,strFile,_MAX_PATH);
52:            } // if
53:            else {
54:                _tcscpy(m_strFile,_T("(No file information provided.)"));
55:            } // else
56:
57:            // Fill in the error information
58:            CompleteErrorInfo(uiDescID,m_strMsg);
59:        }
60:
61:        HRESULT GetHRESULT()
62:        {
63:            // Simply return the HRESULT
64:            return m_hrError;
65:        }
66:
67:        int GetLine()
68:        {
69:            // Simply return the line
70:            return m_iLine;
71:        }
72:
73:        LPCTSTR GetFile()
74:        {
75:            // Return the pointer
76:            return m_strFile;
77:        }
78:
79:        LPCTSTR GetMsg()
80:        {
81:            // Return the pointer
82:            return m_strMsg;
83:        }
84:
85: // Protected methods
86: protected:
87:        HRESULT CompleteErrorInfo(int iResID, LPTSTR strMsg = NULL)
88:        {
89:            // Load the resource into a BSTR
90:            CComBSTR bstrDesc;
91:            bstrDesc.LoadString(iResID);
92:
93:            // Fill in the message, if asked
94:            if ( strMsg ) {
95:                USES_CONVERSION;
96:                LPTSTR pszData = OLE2T(bstrDesc);
97:                _tcsncpy(strMsg,pszData,MAXEXSTRLEN);
```

LISTING 10.7   continued

```
 98:           } // if
 99:
100:           // Fill the error record
101:           return CompleteErrorInfo(bstrDesc);
102:       }
103:
104:       HRESULT CompleteErrorInfo(BSTR bstrDesc)
105:       {
106:           HRESULT hr = S_OK;
107:           try {
108:               // Create the error information record
109:               m_pICreateErrInfo = NULL; // release any existing record
110:               HRESULT hr = CreateErrorInfo(&m_pICreateErrInfo);
111:               if ( FAILED(hr) ) throw hr;
112:
113:               // Set the error information
114:               hr = m_pICreateErrInfo->SetDescription(bstrDesc);
115:               if ( FAILED(hr) ) throw hr;
116:               hr = m_pICreateErrInfo->SetGUID(IID_IErrorDemo);
117:               if ( FAILED(hr) ) throw hr;
118:               hr = m_pICreateErrInfo->
119: ➥SetSource(CComBSTR("TYATL.Object5"));
120:               if ( FAILED(hr) ) throw hr;
121:               hr = m_pICreateErrInfo->SetHelpContext(0xFFFFFFFF); // -1
122:               if ( FAILED(hr) ) throw hr;
123:               hr = pICreateErrInfo->SetHelpFile(CComBSTR());
124: ➥// NULL string
125:               if ( FAILED(hr) ) throw hr;
126:
127:               CComQIPtr<IErrorInfo,&IID_IErrorInfo>
128: ➥pIErrInfo(m_pICreateErrInfo);
129:               if ( pIErrInfo.p == NULL ) throw E_NOINTERFACE;
130:               hr = SetErrorInfo(0,pIErrInfo.p);
131:               if ( FAILED(hr) ) throw hr;
132:           } // try
133:           catch(...) {
134:               // Do nothing, as the return HRESULT will
135:               // already have been set
136:               /* nothing */;
137:           } // catch
138:
139:           return hr;
140:       }
141:
142: // Protected attributes
143: protected:
144:       TCHAR m_strMsg[MAXEXSTRLEN];
145:       TCHAR m_strFile[_MAX_PATH];
```

continues

LISTING 10.7 continued

```
146:    HRESULT m_hrError;
147:    int m_iLine;
148:    CComPtr<ICreateErrorInfo> m_pICreateErrInfo;
149: };
150:
151: #endif // __ATLEXCEPTION_H_
```

ANALYSIS CAtlException might at first appear daunting, but there isn't that much to it after you break it down. The class has two constructors, lines 18 and 44, into which you pass the failed HRESULT, the offending line, filename, and a descriptive error-message string. The difference between the constructors is solely in the descriptive string, which can either be a string value or a resource ID. Notice I resort to some trickery to obtain the error message if I'm passed a resource ID. I use the CComBSTR::LoadString() method to load the BSTR, and then I convert that to a form I can better deal with (line 91 and lines 95 through 97). USES_CONVERSION and OLE2T() are covered in Appendix D, "ATL String Conversion Macros." I did this to show the conversion macro in action. You can instead use LoadString(), using the resource handle you obtain using CComModule::GetResourceInstance() and the string ID, if you'd rather (this would be more efficient but wouldn't be as interesting to demonstrate).

The constructors copy in the file and error message strings and then call one of the class's two CompleteErrorInfo() methods. One accepts a string, line 104, and the other accepts a resource ID, line 87. This method manages the creation of the error-information object and its submission. Assuming things work as they should, after CompleteErrorInfo() has finished establishing the error information, the constructors are done, and the exception will be thrown.

I also added several accessor methods to the class to facilitate retrieval of the basic exception information. I did this primarily to enable the information to be displayed in the debug stream, preferably using ATLTRACE2().

The example calculates a checksum and verifies the checksum it calculates against a value you provide. By the way, a checksum is simply the arithmetical addition of the bytes that compose the input data, which in this case is a string. Some checksums also take the modulus of the sum with a specified value, but this is more often done to stuff the resulting sum into a small data area, such as a byte or two. In any case, if the values match, the VerifyCheckSum() method returns S_OK. However, if the values aren't the same, VerifyCheckSum() throws and catches an exception that includes the custom HRESULT E_CHECKSUM:

```
hr = MAKE_HRESULT(SEVERITY_ERROR,
                  FACILITY_ITF,
                  E_CHECKSUM);
throw new CAtlException(hr,__LINE__,__FILE__,IDS_E_NOVERIFY);
```

The catch block that handles this exception looks like Listing 10.8.

LISTING 10.8   Day10Server Exception Processing

```
 1: catch (CAtlException* e) { // CAtlException*
 2:     // Debug output
 3:     ATLTRACE2(atlTraceNoVerify,
 4:               TRACE_EXCEPTION_LEVEL,
 5:               "***Exception: \n\tHRESULT %#08x,\n\tline %d,\n\tfile
                  ➥\"%s\",\n\tmsg \"%s\"\n",
 6:               e->GetHRESULT(),
 7:               e->GetLine(),
 8:               e->GetFile(),
 9:               e->GetMsg());
10:
11:     // Set the return HRESULT, just to be sure
12:     hr = e->GetHRESULT();
13:
14:     // Note the error record has already been built...now
15:     // I just delete the exception object
16:     delete e;
17: } // catch
```

ANALYSIS   The AtlTraceNoVerify and TRACE_EXCEPTION_LEVEL values, which you see passed to ATLTRACE2() in lines 3 and 4, are defined in STDAFX.H to be AtlTraceUser and 0 (zero), respectively. I did this primarily for readability.

The client application you find in *Day10Client* instantiates the *Day10Server* object and calls the IDemoError::VerifyCheckSum() method. The client's user interface is shown in Figure 10.2. As you type text into the String to Verify edit control, the checksum is automatically calculated and inserted into the Checksum edit control. If you don't change the checksum value prior to clicking Verify, the checksum will match, and no error will result. On the other hand, if you force an error by changing the checksum value, VerifyCheckSum() will calculate a mismatch in the checksum and exercise the error logic I just described.

10

FIGURE 10.2

*The Day10Client
sample user interface.*

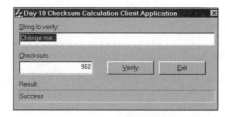

VerifyCheckSum() will return the E_CHECKSUM error in this case. The client application looks for failed HRESULTs and reads the descriptive string contained within the thread's IErrorInfo object, as you see in Listing 10.9.

LISTING 10.9   CDay10ClientDlg's OnVerify Handler

```
 1: void CDay10ClientDlg::OnVerify()
 2: {
 3:     // Call the COM object to verify the checksum
 4:     UpdateData(TRUE);
 5:     long iCheckSum = atoi(m_strCheckSum);
 6:     HRESULT hr = m_pIErrorDemo->VerifyCheckSum(iCheckSum,
        ➥m_strData.AllocSysString());
 7:     if ( FAILED(hr) ) {
 8:         // Show error information.  Note you would normally query
.9:         // IErrorDemo for ISupportErrorInfo and ask that interface
10:         // if IErrorInfo is supported.  I took the lazy approach
11:         // and simply requested the IErrorInfo interface because
12:         // I knew IErrorDemo supported rich error information.
13:         CComPtr<IErrorInfo> pIErrInfo;
14:         hr = GetErrorInfo(0,&pIErrInfo);
15:         if ( FAILED(hr) ) {
16:             // Error creating error record!
17:             m_strResult = _T("Error, but no error information");
18:         } // if
19:         else {
20:             // Pull the error information
21:             CComBSTR bstrDesc;
22:             pIErrInfo->GetDescription(&bstrDesc);
23:             m_strResult = bstrDesc.m_str;
24:         } // else
25:     } // if
26:     else {
27:         // No error
28:         m_strResult = _T("Success");
29:     } // else
30:
31:     // Display result
32:     UpdateData(FALSE);
33: }
```

ANALYSIS Because I knew the IDemoError interface supported rich error information, I saved a few CPU cycles and bypassed the normal query for ISupportErrorInfo and all the rich error discovery protocol (lines 8 through 24). Arguably, I don't consider this an error, but the purist would ask that I implement the full protocol. If I had used a third-party object instead, I would have joined the purists and implemented the protocol. In that case, I have no absolute knowledge that the rich error information is available.

Summary

How you handle error conditions directly affects how well your COM object will perform in the field. Anyone who has written and shipped software to customers knows problems will happen in the customer's environment. Your best defense against this is to proactively fight bugs and exceptions by adding good error-handling code.

To help you with this task, I described several compelling techniques for handling errors. I first described how you can create custom HRESULT codes and offered some suggestions for how a client might automatically get the custom HRESULT information without an additional .H file. I then went on to describe why you should never allow an unhandled exception to cross the interface boundary to be handled by your object's client.

To prevent unhandled exceptions, I showed you how to use C++ exception-handling using try, catch, and throw. I further discussed the merits of using a specialized C++ exception class to contain exception information that might be extracted and used in the catch block. I concluded the day by talking about COM's rich error-information object and how you create and initialize its data. I also rolled rich error information into a custom C++ exception class and demonstrated it with a sample application.

The next day, "Multithreading: How and When," begins to address multithreaded programming issues in preparation for writing objects that work in the MTA. You're half way done!

Q&A

Q Are custom HRESULTs often necessary?

A I believe that's a matter of style and taste, although in my experience, custom HRESULTs are necessary. Some programmers I know always use E_FAIL, but I find this to be a disservice to the client. As the author of the COM object, you have specific knowledge about the cause of the error, so why not pass this information on to the client? True, it forces you to write more interface documentation. If you've ever been on the client end of the interface and had to figure out why a particular method failed with so little information, you'll know why I feel the way I do (you DirectX programmers know what I mean). Adding custom return codes isn't hard to do, and it makes the client's job that much easier.

Q Doesn't C++ exception handling add to my code base and decrease overall performance?

A Yes, and yes. But I would also add that broken components will likely lead to a decrease in sales and profits, too. The overall growth in compiled code and reduction in performance isn't significant for a vast variety of objects. If your object is the exception (no pun intended), by all means skip handling exceptions. If you have the choice, though, I recommend you wrap everything in try/catch blocks and make sure exceptions don't travel to the client.

Workshop

The Workshop is designed to help you anticipate possible questions, review what you've learned, and get you thinking about how to put your knowledge into practice. The answers to the quiz are in Appendix A, "Answers."

Quiz

1. What are the three main components (bit fields) of an HRESULT?

2. Which facility code is the only code you can use for custom HRESULT implementation?

3. What C++ keywords facilitate C++ exception handling? Does ATL support this automatically?

4. What data types can be thrown?

5. What is the sequence of events for completing the rich error object?

Exercises

1. Add a new method to IDemoError that incorporates the forced exception code from ExceptDemo, except omit the try/catch blocks to allow the exception to trickle to the client. What happens when the client receives the exception?

2. I fibbed. I am a purist. Modify the OnVerify() handler in CDay10ClientDlg to implement the full rich error protocol.

DAY 11

Multithreading: How and When

Multithreading is a wonderfully complex topic, rich with spectacular victories and failures—and that's just in my own experience. Before I address multithreading in a COM world, I'm going to address multithreading concepts in general. I want to be sure you've been introduced to the issues that will confront you when you write multithreaded COM code. Today, then, is devoted to the basics of multithreading.

The fact is, sometimes multithreading is a grand idea and sometimes it isn't. I've even seen cases where an application at first appeared perfectly suited for multithreading, but later turned out to perform so poorly it had to be rewritten to be (primarily) single threaded. The overhead associated with multithreading was greater than the gains multithreading provided.

Here is what you'll see today:

- Multithreading concepts
- Reasons why you might (or might not) want to introduce multiple threads to your application

- Data integrity issues and ways to synchronize data access
- How to create threads on a Windows platform
- Suggestions for testing multithreaded applications

 Note Although I'll be writing multithreaded code on a Win32 platform, the concepts you'll see here apply to computing in general, except where I specifically indicate a Windows dependency.

The Multithreading Concepts

Multithreading! What a fascinating concept! Imagine a spider weaving a web and then imagine 10 spiders weaving the same web. The single spider weaves from start to finish and is busy until the work is completed. With many spiders, each is freed from its tasks more quickly because each has a bit less to weave. So why don't you ever see 10 spiders weaving the same web?

I'll leave the issues of spider sociology to those who love to study arachnids and look at the problem in a more pragmatic way. First, the work has to be divided into logical groupings. Then, the work must be somehow coordinated. There is also the issue of spiders meeting on the same strand—what happens if they collide or refuse to share space on the strand? Finally, given the overhead I mentioned, it's entirely possible the web won't be completed in less total time with 10 spiders than with one!

I submit one possible answer to the question "Why don't you see 10 spiders weaving the same web?" is that the spiders haven't overcome these issues (I refuse to say they haven't learned to multithread!). Besides, they'd then have to share the catch, but that's back to spider sociology. Spiders have determined it's more effective for spiderdom as a whole to have each individual spin its own web.

You will run into these same issues if you elect to break your application into multiple threads. For example, breaking an application into logical groupings, or work units, can sometimes be difficult. Even for those applications where the division of work units is obvious, there are still issues with coordinating the threads, thread-to-thread communication, threads working with the same data pool, and threads that require the same resources to complete their tasks

In this lesson, I can't help you break your application into logical work units because each application (and COM object) has its own unique issues. But if you do decide to try to apply multiple threads to solve your problems, I can at least help you understand the concepts involved and show you some tips and tools to prevent catastrophic error. I'll begin with the concept of a thread and talk about processes in general.

Threads and Processes

Earlier in the book I reflected back to the Windows 3.1 days. Compared to earlier versions of Windows and other then-contemporary graphical user interfaces, Windows 3.1 was a marvel. You could actually run several applications on a single personal computer at the same time. In reality, most background applications didn't do much more than wait to be activated. At least, you could have several programs active at the same time and switch between them on the fly. This was very unlike the days of DOS.

Windows 3.1 employed *cooperative multitasking*. Each application processed a Windows message, and then it relinquished control to Windows. Windows then allowed another application to process a message. If a given application hung while processing its latest message, Windows itself hung because Windows had no way to break the application's control loop and seize control again.

Windows 95 forged yet another breakthrough when it arrived with *preemptive multitasking*. Instead of a Windows message being the unit of work, the CPU provides its resources to all the active applications (including the operating system) for a limited time. This time period is known as a *time slice*, or *time quantum*. When your application's time slice has expired, the CPU ruthlessly places your application in the background and allows the next application in line to process for the duration of its time slice.

You can control how often you receive the time slice by adjusting your application's *priority*. Higher priority applications receive CPU time more often than those having a lower priority. If you have more than a single CPU, and you're using Windows NT, you also have the option of specifying the *CPU affinity*, which identifies the CPU your application will gravitate to most often.

Preemptive multitasking comes at a cost. The overhead of deactivating one application to run another is called *context switching*. It takes time to stuff one application into the background and pull another into the CPU for execution. If too many applications are vying for CPU time, the context-switching overhead becomes more significant in terms of overall CPU use.

In the preceding paragraphs, I used the word *application*, but I would have been more correct to use the term *thread*, which is a single executable block of code.

Your computer's CPU cares little about entire applications. It cares about threads. A single Windows application, or COM object, might be made up of many threads. For example, I'm using Word 97 to write this text. If I misspell a word, Word 97 marks the misspelled word with a red underline. Word 97 has one thread available to receive the characters I type, and it provides another thread to check the spelling as I go. If I were to print this document, it would create a third thread (or possibly more, I don't know) to paginate the document and send it to the printer.

11

Word 97 itself runs as a *process*: a collection of one or more threads designed to work together within the same address space.

An operating system that manages applications by process uses the process to manage the collection of threads that make up the overall application. The individual threads themselves will share the same address space, which is to say they can all access the same data without the penalty of changing address spaces (this penalty can be significant).

When you start an application, such as Word 97, Windows loads and executes the code that implements WinMain(). This code is run as your process's *main thread*. After WinMain() is running, you're free to create as many other secondary (*child*) threads as you like. Each of them will be scheduled by the operating system to receive its share of CPU time according to its individual priority.

This architecture enables you to create Windows applications that appear to do many things simultaneously. In reality, unless you have more than one CPU, only one thread is executing at any given time, so nothing is truly simultaneous. It's just that the time quantum is smaller than humans can perceive, so the application *appears* to do things simultaneously.

Before you go off on your own and create thousands of threads designed to accept characters and check spelling, I should tell you that multithreading isn't a silver bullet—a tool destined to solve all your programming problems. Multithreading makes good sense in some cases, such as when polling or doing background processing to make the user interface more responsive. But multithreading also brings with it a lot of baggage, and poorly implemented multithreaded applications almost certainly perform poorly. You must examine the problem at hand and your proposed architectural solution, and if both appear to be well-suited to multithreading, by all means use it. If not, don't. The extra code you must write and the additional testing burden probably won't justify the expense.

An example of the expense I mentioned is the effort needed to get around the issue of thread affinity and manage thread state. Let's see what those are all about in the next section.

Thread Affinity and State

The word *affinity* normally means *attraction*. I have an affinity for Diet Mountain Dew, and given a choice, I'll most often select Diet Mountain Dew over other beverages. I don't always choose this way, but in most cases I do. This concept also applies to threads, but it is even more stringent. (I understand most threads also prefer Diet Mountain Dew, but that's just a rumor.)

Thread affinity refers to the reuse of a given thread for a particular action, such as a method invocation. In a C++ sense, you can assign a given thread to execute a polling method, and when there is a hit, reuse that same thread to run the polling method again. This is the same in a COM sense—the same thread will always execute your object's method(s). This enables COM to store *state data* associated with your object in *thread local storage*, or *TLS*. COM typically stores an execution context here. Win32 stores locks that cross method invocations within the TLS to coordinate their efforts (such as data synchronization mechanisms that I'll address shortly). Of course, different threads have different TLS blocks.

And now, perhaps, you begin to see the problem. If you store information in the TLS, you obviously expect it to be there for you the next time that you execute your C++ or COM method. Unfortunately, if you make this assumption in a multithreaded environment, your method will likely not execute as you intend (I'm being kind). Any time you store thread state information, you have created a thread-affinity situation. These situations must be avoided in a multithreaded environment.

Data Integrity

I mentioned that threads execute in the process's address space. Because of this, all the threads can access process-global data. If the threads are all accessing and modifying global data, there are often issues involving data integrity. You ensure data integrity by using the data synchronization mechanisms that I'll present later in the day.

Threads synchronize themselves by *blocking* or *sleeping*. If Thread B wants to access Datum X, but Thread A is already doing so, Thread B will inform the operating system that it is waiting for Thread A to finish with Datum X. The operating system will no longer schedule CPU quantums for Thread B until Thread A indicates it is done with Datum X. Thread B is said to be blocked. You decide if Thread B blocks forever or for a given time period.

This synchronization is designed to prevent two or more threads from changing important global (or shared) information while both require the data. If Thread A uses the value in Datum X to schedule cans of Diet Mountain Dew to be filled and Thread B fills the cans, the number of cans in the line had better be correct. Otherwise, some cans will go unfilled, or Diet Mountain Dew will spill over and erode the concrete floor of the processing facility (it will, too).

Imagine Thread A increments the can count in Datum X and Thread B decrements it (see Listing 11.1). Thread A uses a `while` loop to send 12 cans at a time into the filling station.

11

LISTING 11.1 A Sample Thread Procedure Implementation

```
 1: // Can counter
 2: g_iCanCount = 12; // "Datum X"
 3:
 4: // Thread A:
 5: DWORD WINAPI ThreadA(LPVOID lpThreadParm)
 6: {
 7:     while ( g_iCanCount >= 1 ) {
 8:         ReleaseCanToFillStation();
 9:         --g_iCanCount;
10:     } // while
11:
12:     return 0;
13: }
```

Now imagine Thread B fills cans and increments the can count as they fill (see Listing 11.2). Because it can't handle more than 12 cans before it has to get more Diet Mountain Dew, it has a loop that terminates when it has filled 12 cans:

LISTING 11.2 A Second Sample Thread Procedure Implementation

```
 1: // Thread B:
 2: DWORD WINAPI ThreadB(LPVOID lpThreadParm)
 3: {
 4:     while ( g_iCanCount < 12 ) {
 5:         ++g_iCanCount;
 6:         FillCurrentCan();
 7: } // while
 8:
 9:     // Need more soda
10:     GetMoreDew();
11:
12:     return 0;
13: }
```

ANALYSIS What will happen when these threads execute? If you can imagine Larry, Curly, and Moe filling cans of Diet Mountain Dew, you're on the right track. Thread A will execute for a period of time, and the can count will be left in some state (from line 9 of Listing 11.1). Then Thread B will execute and modify the can count (line 5 of Listing 11.2), completely throwing Thread A's loop off the next time Thread A executes. You'll wind up with a random number of filled cans, empty cans, and a mess on the floor. You can see these very threads run if you try the CanDemo1 sample application. Clearly, though, some variable must contain the current count of cans.

This is a colorful example of data integrity, or the lack of it. Yes, I took some artistic license. But the problem I'm describing is a very serious issue in more problem spaces than just assembly line and process coordination. I'll show you how to solve this later in the day.

Deadlock

Another situation that appears in multithreaded applications is *deadlock*. If you remember, I mentioned that a thread will block as it waits for a resource. Take this a step further and imagine two threads and two resources. The programmer was conscientious and synchronized the access to the resources, but he also wrote the two threads so that each one had to acquire both resources to execute.

It often happens Thread A will acquire Resource X while Thread B acquires Resource Y. Thread A blocks waiting for Resource Y to become available. Likewise, Thread B blocks to wait for Resource X. At this point you have deadlock. Neither thread will ever be activated because neither will ever acquire the second resource. Both threads will sleep forever unless they're terminated by user or operating system intervention. Win32 itself has no deadlock detection mechanism, so your application's user will be the one to break the deadlock by terminating the application. He'll probably lose any unsaved work in the process.

All the problems I've mentioned here have revolved around global data and access to that data. You can't control precisely when a thread is scheduled for execution, but you *can* specify how threads access your data. This is called *thread synchronization*, and it is the topic of the next section "Protecting Data." First, however, let's see how to properly create multiple threads in Win32.

Protecting Data

If accessing global or shared data causes so many problems, you might be inclined to avoid using global data. If you can do so, you should. But often global or shared data is a necessity because the threads are somehow related by the data. An example is a process-wide state variable, such as the can counter I mentioned earlier in the lesson. That example wasn't as contrived as you might imagine.

Win32 provides the tools you need to control a thread's access to your data. Although Win32 won't help you with deadlock conditions, other tools (including COM and MTS) will detect deadlocks and allow for user intervention to break the deadlock. For this reason, as well as for efficiency, always use the operating system to synchronize your data. That is, don't formulate a mechanism yourself such as that in Listing 11.3.

LISTING 11.3 Synchronization the Wrong Way

```
1: // Thread A: wait...  Note g_bMySynch is a global
2: // boolean variable
3: while ( !g_bMySynch ) /*wait*/;
4: // Continue processing
5:
6: // Thread B
7: DoSomething();
8: g_bMySynch = TRUE;
9: // Continue processing
```

ANALYSIS In this case, Thread A spins through a while loop (line 3) waiting for Thread B to signal that it's fine for Thread A to continue by setting g_bMySynch to TRUE (line 8).

This is bad for several reasons. For one thing, the blocking mechanism Win32 employs is highly efficient, while Thread A's loop is definitely wasteful of precious CPU cycles. Also, if for some reason g_bMySych is never set to TRUE (Thread B threw an unhandled exception in DoSomething(), for example), Thread A spins forever. If Thread A has a high priority, the entire system will appear more sluggish. If Thread A has the highest priority, the entire system grinds to a halt and becomes completely unresponsive to the user's inputs (even to the three-fingered reboot). Finally, this process bypasses any dead-lock detection that might otherwise be employed.

The first data synchronization mechanism I'll address is the critical section, which you saw initially in Day 8, "ATL Object Methods: Adding Functionality to Your Interface," where I discussed ATL's CComCriticalSection. Let's take a closer look at critical sections themselves to see how they can help you with data integrity issues.

Critical Sections

The *critical section* is a small block of code that requires exclusive access to global (or shared) data before it can execute. Of all the mechanisms I'll discuss, the critical section is the easiest to use.

 Note

Unlike the other data synchronization mechanisms, the critical section can only be used by threads within the same process. The other data synchronization mechanisms are *kernel objects*. Therefore, they can span all processes and synchronize data access system-wide, rather than just process-wide.

You can imagine a critical section as a hallway with two doors. When you come to the first door, you press a button to signal you're waiting to enter the hallway. If nobody is already in the hallway, the door will open, and you can enter. If someone is already in the hallway, you must wait for them to leave. After you enter the hallway, you walk to the second door and press another button to signal you are leaving. After the second door closes behind you, another individual, waiting to enter the hallway, can do so.

This example demonstrates what happens to your code. After you've created and initialized a critical section, threads wanting access to global data must *enter* the critical section. If another thread is already using the critical section (which wraps the global data access in that thread), the second thread blocks until the first *leaves* the critical section.

A critical section is defined by the Win32 `CRITICAL_SECTION` data type, and a critical section variable must be accessible by any thread that uses the critical section. After you declare the critical section, you must call `InitializeCriticalSection()` to initialize it for use.

Within your threads, you use `EnterCriticalSection()` and `LeaveCriticalSection()` to wrap the code segment accessing the global data:

```
// g_cs is a global CRITICAL_SECTION variable
// previously initialized...
EnterCriticalSection(&g_cs);
DoSomethingWithGlobalData();
LeaveCriticalSection(&g_cs);
```

You can see a critical section in action if you examine the code I provided in the *CanDemo2* example application for this day. The critical section itself is created as follows:

```
CRITICAL_SECTION g_cs;
...
// Initialize the critical section
InitializeCriticalSection(&g_cs);
```

Listing 11.4 shows you the changes I made to the individual threads to support critical sectioning.

LISTING 11.4 CanDemo2 Threads with Critical Section Support

```
1: // Thread A:
2: DWORD WINAPI ThreadA(LPVOID lpThreadParm)
3: {
4:     // Protect this thread's access to g_iCanCount
```

continues

LISTING 11.4 continued

```
5:      EnterCriticalSection(&g_cs);
6:
7:      // Release cans
8:      while ( g_iCanCount >= 1 ) {
9:          ReleaseCanToFillStation();
10:          --g_iCanCount;
11:      } // while
12:
13:      // Need more cans
14:      GetMoreCans();
15:
16:      // Done releasing cans
17:      LeaveCriticalSection(&g_cs);
18:
19:      return 0;
20: }
21:
22: // Thread B:
23: DWORD WINAPI ThreadB(LPVOID lpThreadParm)
24: {
25:      // Protect this thread's access to g_iCanCount
26:      EnterCriticalSection(&g_cs);
27:
28:      // Fill cans
29:      while ( g_iCanCount < 12 ) {
30:          ++g_iCanCount;
31:          FillCurrentCan();
32:      } // while
33:
34:      // Need more soda
35:      GetMoreDew();
36:
37:      // Done filling cans
38:      LeaveCriticalSection(&g_cs);
39:
40:      return 0;
41: }
```

ANALYSIS In this case, Thread A enters the critical section first because I created it first (line 5). It processes 12 cans (lines 8–14), then leaves the critical section (line 17). Thread B now takes over and fills the 12 cans Thread A released. It also enters the critical section (line 26), does its work (lines 29–35), and then terminates (line 38).

Another synchronization tool at your disposal is the *mutex*. As you'll see, the mutex acts like a critical section—not only for threads in a single process, but also for several processes.

Mutexes

Critical sections are fast, but they are limited to a single address space (process). The mutex, on the other hand, is useful to synchronize interprocess data access as well as intraprocess data access. (The name stems from *mutual exclusion*.) In practice, you use the mutex much as you would use the critical section. Before I discuss mutexes specifically, let me back up a step and discuss kernel objects in general. You'll be seeing them throughout the remainder of the lesson.

A *kernel object* is an object created by and manipulated by the operating system. Whenever you create one, all you ever get from the operating system is a *handle*. A handle is simply a 32-bit value, and its meaning is specific to the kernel object. It rarely has meaning to you, other than it identifies the object you created.

Because the kernel object is owned and manipulated by the operating system, you never access it yourself. Instead, you typically use API calls to create and manipulate the object, usually by passing in the handle. When you're through with the object, you close its handle and the operating system releases the associated kernel object's resources. For this, you always use the `CloseHandle()` API call.

Data synchronization revolves around the kernel object and its state. The object can be *signaled* or *reset*. Your synchronized code typically uses the `WaitForSingleObject()` or `WaitForMultipleObjects()` functions to block and wait for the kernel object or objects (in this case, a mutex) to become signaled. This will be true of all kernel objects you'll see this day. `WaitForSingleObject()` takes a kernel object handle and a timeout period, in milliseconds (or the value `INFINITE`) and waits for the handle to become signaled within the timeout period. `WaitForMultipleObjects()` takes an object count, an array of kernel object handles (the number of which should match the count), a flag to indicate whether it should wait for all the objects or just for the first one to signal, and the timeout period in milliseconds.

11

> **Caution**
>
> Although this lesson is concentrating on multithreading concepts in general, when you mix COM and multithreading, you must *never* call `WaitForSingleObject()` or `WaitForMultipleObjects()` from a COM object running in an STA. The shallow reason is the thread will deadlock. The deeper reason is COM sends messages to your STA thread through your thread's window message pump. If you block on a kernel object, you don't process Windows messages and can't recover from the blocking call. `WaitForSingleObject()` and `WaitForMultipleObjects()` are meant for worker threads in the MTA *only*.

If the handle is signaled within the timeout period, `WaitForSingleObject()` and `WaitForMultipleObjects()` return the value `WAIT_OBJECT_0` or `WAIT_OBJECT_0`, plus an object number in the multiple object case. On the other hand, if the object isn't signaled within the timeout period, both functions will return `WAIT_TIMEOUT`. You might recall seeing `WaitForSingleObject()` in Day 6, "The ATL App Wizard: Back to Basics," when I discussed the ATL EXE COM server's implementation as created by the ATL AppWizard.

The mutex is a kernel object you create using `CreateMutex()`:

```
HANDLE CreateMutex(
  LPSECURITY_ATTRIBUTES lpMutexAttributes,
                        // pointer to security attributes
  BOOL bInitialOwner,   // flag for initial ownership
  LPCTSTR lpName        // pointer to mutex-object name
);
```

`CreateMutex()` requires three parameters, the first of which is common among all Win32 API functions that return a kernel object's handle. It's a pointer to a completed `SECURITY_ATTRIBUTES` structure. It is `NULL` for the default security descriptor. It's used primarily in Windows NT to determine if child processes can use the handle. For Windows 95 and 98, you typically pass in `NULL`. The `bInitialOwner` flag controls assignment of the mutex. If you pass in `TRUE`, the thread calling `CreateMutex()` owns the mutex initially, whereas `FALSE` allows the first thread to request the mutex to gain ownership. The final parameter is a string denoting the name of the mutex, and you can pass in `NULL` to create an unnamed mutex. Named mutexes are useful for interprocess synchronization because each process can create a mutex with the same name. The operating system then creates only a single mutex to be shared by all processes. Unnamed mutexes are commonly used between threads in a single process. This naming capability is also common among the synchronization kernel objects.

In the CanDemo3 sample, I create a mutex in this fashion:

```
HANDLE g_hMutex = NULL;
...
// Create the mutex
g_hMutex = CreateMutex(NULL,FALSE,NULL);
```

In this case the mutex has no special security considerations, is initially not owned, and is unnamed.

`CreateMutex()` returns the handle of the new mutex or `NULL` if the mutex could not be created. This handle is used by the rest of the mutex-related Win32 functions to control the mutex state.

For example, only a single thread can use the mutex at any one time. Threads wanting to use the mutex will block using WaitForSingleObject(). If the mutex is available, WaitForSingleObject() will return WAIT_OBJECT_0, and your thread will continue processing. After your thread has completed its tasks and no longer requires the mutex, it should call ReleaseMutex() and pass in the mutex handle. At this time, the next thread waiting for the mutex will fall through WaitForSingleObject() and begin its processing.

When all your threads have completed their work and the mutex is no longer required, you must close the mutex handle using CloseHandle(). This informs the operating system you are finished with the mutex, and it will release the associated system resources.

I use the mutex to synchronize the can-filling demonstration in the CanDemo3 sample application. I begin by creating the mutex and starting the threads. Because I start Thread A before I start Thread B, Thread A obtains the mutex first and begins sending cans down the line. After 12 cans have been sent, it releases the mutex, and Thread B begins to fill the cans. You can see the code for this in Listing 11.5.

LISTING 11.5 CanDemo3 Threads with Mutex Support

```
 1: // Thread A:
 2: DWORD WINAPI ThreadA(LPVOID lpThreadParm)
 3: {
 4:     // Protect this thread's access to g_iCanCount
 5:     if ( WaitForSingleObject(g_hMutex,INFINITE) == WAIT_OBJECT_0 ) {
 6:         // Release cans
 7:         while ( g_iCanCount >= 1 ) {
 8:             ReleaseCanToFillStation();
 9:             --g_iCanCount;
10:         } // while
11:
12:         // Need more cans
13:         GetMoreCans();
14:
15:         // Done releasing cans
16:         ReleaseMutex(g_hMutex);
17:     } // if
18:     else {
19:         // Unable to get the mutex!
20:         cout << " !Thread A: Unable to get mutex!" << endl;
21:     } // else
22:
23:     return 0;
24: }
```

continues

LISTING **11.5**   continued

```
25:
26: // Thread B:
27: DWORD WINAPI ThreadB(LPVOID lpThreadParm)
28: {
29:     // Protect this thread's access to g_iCanCount
30:     if ( WaitForSingleObject(g_hMutex,INFINITE) == WAIT_OBJECT_0 ) {
31:         // Fill cans
32:         while ( g_iCanCount < 12 ) {
33:             ++g_iCanCount;
34:             FillCurrentCan();
35:         } // while
36:
37:         // Need more soda
38:         GetMoreDew();
39:
40:         // Done filling cans
41:         ReleaseMutex(g_hMutex);
42:     } // if
43:     else {
44:         // Unable to get the mutex!
45:         cout << " !Thread B: Unable to get mutex!" << endl;
46:     } // else
47:
48:     return 0;
49: }
```

ANALYSIS The effect is all 12 cans go down the line (lines 2–23), and then all 12 cans are filled (lines 27–48). Each time you run this simulation, you'll always end up with 12 perfectly filled cans, which indicates the synchronization is working properly.

Mutexes aren't the only kernel object synchronization mechanism. For example, you could use an event, which I describe in the next section.

Events

Many people consider the *event* the most primitive kernel synchronization object, but I also see it as one of the most frequently used objects. You can use an event to protect data, but you can also use an event to indicate that an action has completed and another waiting thread can now take further action.

An event simply indicates a signaled or reset state, and you can create events that reset automatically after being signaled or events that require you to reset them manually. Autoreset events allow only a single waiting thread to be signaled, so if five threads are waiting, only the first will proceed past WaitForSingleObject(). Manually reset events allow all five threads to proceed.

You create an event object by using the Win32 function CreateEvent(), which returns a handle to the event object or NULL if one could not be created:

```
HANDLE CreateEvent(
  LPSECURITY_ATTRIBUTES lpEventAttributes,
                       // pointer to security attributes
  BOOL bManualReset,  // flag for manual-reset event
  BOOL bInitialState, // flag for initial state
  LPCTSTR lpName      // pointer to event-object name
);
```

Here you again see the SECURITY_ATTRIBUTES and name parameters you saw with CreateMutex(). This event, however, has two other parameters. The first, bManualReset, determines whether the event is manually (TRUE) or automatically reset (FALSE). The second, bInitialState, indicates whether the event is initially signaled (TRUE) or reset (FALSE).

I've demonstrated the event in the CanDemo4 sample, where I created one using this code:

```
HANDLE g_hReleaseEvent = NULL;
...
// Create the event handle
g_hReleaseEvent = CreateEvent(NULL,FALSE,TRUE,NULL);
```

As with the mutex, I've applied no special security attributes to the object and the object is unnamed. I've requested the event object be automatically reset after I've signaled it, and it begins life in the signaled state.

Assuming you successfully created an event object and have its handle, you use one of several Win32 functions to control the event. SetEvent(), for example, signals the event. After the event is signaled, one or more threads can proceed, depending upon the type of event (manually or automatically reset). ResetEvent() returns the event to a reset state in the case of a manually reset event object. You can also use PulseEvent() to combine the SetEvent() and ResetEvent() calls, although this is only useful for manually reset events. Automatically reset events don't require the ResetEvent() call, so the reset performed by PulseEvent() has little function.

Threads are waiting on the event object to signal block when they call WaitForSingleObject(). The threads will be released in the order they executed WaitForSingleObject(), and you determine how many threads will go at one time by choosing the manually or automatically reset event, as I described earlier.

When your threads are through with their tasks and you no longer require the event, you use CloseHandle() to release the event object. As with the mutex, the event resources will be released to the system for later use.

11

Listing 11.6 shows you how I changed the thread code for the CanDemo4 example application. In this case, 12 cans are again sent to the filling station. After the last can has
been released, I signal an event and the can-filling operation begins.

LISTING 11.6   CanDemo4 Threads with Event Support

```
 1: // Thread A:
 2: DWORD WINAPI ThreadA(LPVOID lpThreadParm)
 3: {
 4:     // Protect this thread's access to g_iCanCount
 5:     if ( WaitForSingleObject(g_hReleaseEvent,INFINITE) == WAIT_OBJECT_0 ) {
 6:         // Release cans
 7:         while ( g_iCanCount >= 1 ) {
 8:             ReleaseCanToFillStation();
 9:             --g_iCanCount;
10:         } // while
11:
12:         // Need more cans
13:         GetMoreCans();
14:
15:         // Signal the event (cans will be filled)
16:         SetEvent(g_hReleaseEvent);
17:     } // if
18:     else {
19:         // Event never signaled!
20:         cout << " !Thread A: Event never signaled!" << endl;
21:     } // else
22:
23:     return 0;
24: }
25:
26: // Thread B:
27: DWORD WINAPI ThreadB(LPVOID lpThreadParm)
28: {
29:     // Protect this thread's access to g_iCanCount
30:     if ( WaitForSingleObject(g_hReleaseEvent,INFINITE) == WAIT_OBJECT_0 ) {
31:         // Fill cans
32:         while ( g_iCanCount < 12 ) {
33:         ++g_iCanCount;
34:         FillCurrentCan();
35:         } // while
36:
37:         // Need more soda
38:         GetMoreDew();
39:     } // if
40:     else {
41:         // Event never signaled!
42:         cout << " !Thread B: Event never signaled!" << endl;
```

LISTING 11.6 continued

```
43:     } // else
44:
45:     return 0;
46: }
```

The last synchronization mechanism I'll describe is the semaphore. It's a bit different from the previous mechanisms, as you'll see.

Semaphores synchronize threads and data by acting as resource counters. That is, they maintain a count of available resources, whatever those resources might be. They can be database connections, active network sockets, or (in the case of my example for this section) available cans to be filled.

As resources become available, you tell the semaphore to increment its resource count. As resources are removed from the semaphore, the count decreases. The semaphore itself guarantees you the resource count will not be corrupted by multiple-thread access.

By now, you've probably guessed you create a semaphore using the Win32 function CreateSemaphore():

```
HANDLE CreateSemaphore(
  LPSECURITY_ATTRIBUTES lpSemaphoreAttributes,
                        // pointer to security attributes
  LONG lInitialCount,   // initial count
  LONG lMaximumCount,   // maximum count
  LPCTSTR lpName        // pointer to semaphore-object name
);
```

As with the mutex and event objects, you have the option of specifying both security and naming parameters. The semaphore, however, has two count-related parameters. The first, lInitialCount, tells the semaphore object how many resources it has initially. The second parameter, lMaximumCount, tells the semaphore the maximum number of resources it can manage.

And as with the previous objects, I've provided a sample program using the semaphore called CanDemo5. In the sample, I create a semaphore like this:

```
int g_iCanCount = 12; // starting with 12 empty cans
HANDLE g_hCansAvailable = NULL;
...
// Create the semaphore handle
g_hCansAvailable = CreateSemaphore(NULL,0,g_iCanCount,NULL);
```

Once again, the security attributes parameter is NULL, so no special security arrangements are necessary. I also didn't name the object because I knew it wouldn't be shared across process boundaries. The other parameters tell the semaphore object how many resources it has to deal with, from 0 to 12 (in this case indicated by g_iCanCount).

You increment the number of available resources by calling ReleaseSemaphore() using the semaphore handle you obtained when you created the object. If the name of the call and the action it effects seem incongruous, I agree. Nonetheless, you *release* the semaphore to *increment* its resource count. You can think of *release,* in this case, as releasing a resource for use, which is the same as adding to your count of available resources.

Threads waiting on resources block using, once again, WaitForSingleObject(). As resources become available and the threads pass through WaitForSingleObject(), the semaphore's resource count is decremented. If no resources are available, the thread blocks indefinitely or until the time period specified in WaitForSingleObject() expires.

When your threads are done and you no longer require the semaphore, you close its handle using CloseHandle() just as you did for the other kernel objects. The operating system then knows to release the semaphore's system resources.

The final example application for this day, CanDemo5, uses a semaphore to send Mountain Dew cans down the line to be filled. I show the changes to the thread code in Listing 11.7.

LISTING 11.7   CanDemo5 Threads with Semaphore Support

```
 1: // Thread A:
 2: DWORD WINAPI ThreadA(LPVOID lpThreadParm)
 3: {
 4:     // Release cans
 5:     while ( g_iCanCount >= 1 ) {
 6:         ReleaseCanToFillStation();
 7:         --g_iCanCount;
 8:         ReleaseSemaphore(g_hCansAvailable,1,NULL);
 9:     } // while
10:
11:     // Need more cans
12:     GetMoreCans();
13:
14:     return 0;
15: }
16:
17: // Thread B:
18: DWORD WINAPI ThreadB(LPVOID lpThreadParm)
19: {
20:     // Fill cans
21:     while ( TRUE ) {
22:         // Wait for a can to become available.  If after 500ms
```

LISTING 11.7   continued

```
23:          // there is no can, exit the loop and get more soda
24:          if ( WaitForSingleObject(g_hCansAvailable,500) == WAIT_OBJECT_0 ) {
25:              FillCurrentCan();
26:          } // if
27:          else {
28:              // Must be out of cans...
29:              break;
30:          } // else
31:      } // while
32:
33:      // Need more soda
34:      GetMoreDew();
35:
36:      return 0;
37: }
```

ANALYSIS   I changed the flavor of the threads slightly in Listing 11.7. The filling thread, Thread B, waits on individual cans (the semaphore's resource) instead of waiting for all 12 cans to come down the line, as you can see in line 24. If no cans are available within 500 milliseconds, the thread begins to terminate itself as it executes line 29. Thread A, on the other hand, releases cans one at a time (line 8), and for each can it releases the semaphore. The semaphore is maintaining a can count rather than a 12-pack count, so the fill thread blocks for a shorter time between can fills than it does in the previous examples.

That completes the data synchronization mechanisms that I wanted to present in this lesson. If you intend to write multithreaded code, you'll use one or many of the mechanisms I've shown you here. Given that you're thinking about writing multithreaded code, especially multithreaded COM objects, there are other things to consider as you begin the design and implementation phases of your object's development. I'll cover some of those in the next section.

 Note

Returning to a COM flavor for the moment, you'll find these synchronization methods necessary when dealing with COM rather than COM+. With COM+, you can simply set the synchronization required flag when installing your component and COM+ will manage the thread synchronization for you.

11

Testing Threaded Code

It would be great if I had all the answers for you, but I don't. The truth is multithreading introduces *nondeterministic behavior* to your application. That means nobody can determine, prior to your application's execution, precisely what will happen. The operating system schedules the threads for execution, and you can't be sure in what order or how often threads will run. Other threads running currently impact those parameters.

Testing multithreaded applications is somewhat of an art form, but there are some guidelines I can provide:

- Test early, test often.
- Use assertions liberally within your code to test your assumptions.
- Test your application with both debug and release builds.
- Test the code in a variety of platforms, from single to multiple CPUs, Intel (Pentium-class CPUs, for example) to Digital (Alpha-class CPUs), and definitely test your application under Windows 95, Windows 98, and Windows NT 4.0 or 5.0.

Test Early, Test Often

You should test early and often to check for two things. First, you want to make sure your multithreaded architecture is sound before you waste too much time writing code supporting a bad architecture. Second, seemingly minor changes in code can have major impacts upon other threads in your process. You want to catch this type of logical error as soon as it creeps in.

In a practical sense, this means you must take the time to design your architecture and check the soundness of your design often as you progress through your development. You would not be the first to find that a multithreaded solution, which at first appears to be the ideal answer, adds more headaches than it solves during implementation. The sooner you know this, the sooner you can abandon the poor architecture in favor of a sounder one.

Also, as you add function to your threads, test each one, even after a minor change. If you follow the big-bang theory of multithreaded software development, it becomes much harder to pinpoint true sources of error. Be sure to create specific test code to exercise portions of your application and run each test regressively as you add functionality. This sounds like it takes a lot of your time—and it does. But it takes far less time than you will spend searching for deeply buried bugs later—when you have much more code (and many more function points) to wade through.

Assert Liberally

Adding assertions costs you little and gives you tremendous advantages. If you believe a given situation should be in effect at a given point in your code, make an assertion.

The problem with multithreaded code is that it is no longer sequential. You can't depend upon State A being established prior to State B, as you can with single-threaded code. This is especially true given multiple CPUs. You might be surprised how many of your assertions fail because you are thinking sequentially, yet the code is running through multiple threads in parallel.

Assertions are also helpful when placing synchronization logic and for detecting deadlock. If variables are being changed somehow and your assertions are failing, you should add some data synchronization. I also add timeout periods to `WaitForSingleObject()` in debug builds. If a thread waits for an excessive period, I forcibly fail an assertion and break into the debugger to try to determine why the thread blocked for so long.

Test with Debug and Release Builds

Debug and release code is different. Period. Just because code works in a debug build doesn't necessarily mean it will work in a release build. Be sure to compile and test both versions from time to time to make sure the differences in the generated code don't adversely affect your application.

For example, debug code runs more slowly and is less efficient. It might take a few microseconds longer to complete a loop in a debug build than it does in a release build, and that brief time might have a horrible impact on the timing of other threads. If you have such timing dependencies, it's best to determine what they are earlier in your application's development than later.

Test with a Variety of Platforms

Clearly, most developers test their code on the various Windows platforms, but few test their code with different manufacturers' CPUs or on multiple CPU systems. If you're writing multithreaded code, you're wise to be one of the few.

Multithreaded code runs differently on different manufacturers' CPUs and on multiple CPU systems. The difference in CPUs changes the way the individual opcodes are scheduled for execution within the CPU and how they're pipelined. Code that runs well on an Intel platform, for example, could die horribly on an Alpha. Even if you're not interested in shipping code to Alpha-based platforms, this problem might indicate a logical error in your code.

11

Using a multiple CPU system is a little more obvious because threads can now be truly concurrent. On a single CPU system, threads actually run sequentially. Only one thread is executing at a time. However, on multiple CPU systems, several threads can execute at the same time, and this often exposes logical errors and data integrity problems.

The bottom line is test, test, and test again. Even the best veteran multithreaded programmer makes mistakes, and even seemingly error-free code can be subject to logical and design errors. The guidelines I've outlined should help you write more error-free code at far less cost than otherwise.

Summary

This day provided the groundwork you'll need to successfully write multithreaded COM objects. Although I discussed the concepts and API calls in terms of applications, they are equally valid with respect to ATL COM object programming.

I began by discussing some basic multithreading concepts, starting with threads and processes and how they differ. I then went on to describe thread affinity and state, data integrity issues, and deadlock. Given the problems with data integrity, I outlined several techniques for protecting shared and global data including the use of critical sections, mutexes, events, and semaphores.

Given your understanding of the basic concepts involved with multithreading, the problems associated with having multiple threads access data, and the ways to prevent these problems, I described two functions you can use to create threads and the limitations and uses of both. Finally, I discussed testing multithreaded applications and provided several suggestions for more effective testing.

The next day returns you to the COM apartment, where you'll see how the STA and MTA differ and why such things as apartments exist in the first place. I cover the critical design decisions regarding how your COM object is threaded and in which apartment it resides.

Q&A

Q You've made multithreaded programming sound quite difficult. Is it really?

A Yes and no. The most common use of additional threads I've seen is to replace polling loops. Rather than have their main application spin in a tight loop looking for some polled value, the programmers create a separate thread to do so. This makes their main application more responsive to the user. This form of multithreaded programming is not terribly difficult to achieve nor test adequately, though the data integrity issues remain. However, if you get much more complex than that, be prepared to accept the additional burden of testing your application to make sure it responds as expected under all your test conditions. I've seen incredibly complex multithreaded applications, and some of them still exhibit anomalies even after years in the field.

Q Does multithreading in a COM environment significantly change the basic multithreading concepts you described?

A In general no, but there are additional concerns you should be aware of when you deal with multithreaded COM objects. I'll discuss these in the next lesson.

Workshop

The Workshop is designed to help you anticipate possible questions, review what you've learned, and get you thinking about how to put your knowledge into practice. The answers to the quiz are in Appendix A, "Answers."

Quiz

1. What is a critical section? What is a mutex? How do they differ?
2. Why is `PulseEvent()` not useful given an auto-reset event object?
3. How does a semaphore differ from the other synchronization objects?
4. What are the two thread creation functions you can use, and which is better?
5. If, in your process, you create two additional child threads, how many threads are running in your process?
6. What are some testing techniques you can use to help better test your multi-threaded applications?

Exercise

1. Modify the CanDemo4 example to set the event whenever a single can is released instead of when all 12 cans have been released.

DAY 12

ATL and Apartments: How Win32 Threads and COM Are Related

The multithreading concepts I presented in the previous day didn't play a role in the development of COM objects when COM was invented. But as the operating systems Microsoft produces have grown in capability and complexity, so has the COM environment grown and become more complex. COM is no longer just the shared data technology it was in its early years, when it was known as Object Linking and Embedding (OLE).

Microsoft had to employ a new paradigm for COM that incorporated the threading issues I mentioned, as well as others COM itself introduced. This new paradigm is called the *apartment*. A COM object always runs in only one apartment. What type of apartment it runs in is primarily determined by the mechanism that the thread uses to invoke the COM runtime and what apartment preference the object identifies. The COM object might share the same apartment as its client, or it might find itself in a completely different apartment.

COM+ takes the concept of an apartment further by subdividing the apartment into contexts. Although I'll direct my discussion primarily to COM as it existed prior to Windows 2000, where there are significant differences, I'll note them and describe the differences. I'll provide an apartment selection cookbook that will help you choose the proper apartment type for either COM or COM+.

In this lesson, you'll explore the COM apartment to see what it's all about, as well as what being in certain apartments means to you (what you can and can't do). For example, you'll see

- What an apartment is and how COM manages your object
- Single-threaded objects in the main process apartment
- Single-threaded objects in their own single-threaded apartment
- Multithreaded objects in the multithreaded apartment
- Objects that are happy in any apartment
- Objects in a COM+ thread-neutral apartment
- An apartment selection cookbook

COM and Apartments

I've briefly mentioned why Microsoft introduced the concept of an apartment (it addresses the technical limitations COM originally didn't have to overcome), but I've not provided a concrete definition of an apartment. So here is my definition of an apartment.

The *COM apartment* is the union of a Win32 thread, a COM object, and the COM runtime environment. This definition may sound simplistic, and to some it might be obvious. Most of the descriptions I've read of the COM apartment are more complicated than my definition. I believe that's because many of the authors I've read try to explain COM apartments using deeply technical terms instead of telling you the simple truth—a COM object *must* be given a Windows thread to execute. When a thread invokes the COM runtime and starts an object, the thread and COM object are considered to be in an apartment.

There are currently two types of apartments, although Windows 2000 and COM+ will introduce a third. I'll address this new apartment type at the end of the lesson, when I explain the thread-neutral apartment. In any case, just as you can create threads with different attributes, such as priority or security, you can create apartments with differing attributes. The two basic types of apartments are the single-threaded apartment (STA) and the multithreaded apartment (MTA). You might recall that I introduced the terms in Day 2, "Exploring COM: The Technology ATL Supports."

The apartment attributes I referred to determine how COM manages, or doesn't manage, multithreading issues (such as data integrity) and how information is passed between COM objects (marshaling or not).

It's important to understand how Windows and COM work together to provide you with the relatively seamless integration of COM objects and Windows applications. The most apparent way to describe this interrelationship is to think of processes and threads, but keep in mind that the process itself is (most likely) driving a Windows application. The Windows application might have created multiple threads, and on any of those threads it might have invoked the COM runtime to use COM objects. I'll start with the wider view, looking at COM apartments and the Windows process. I'll then move on to apartments and threads.

Processes and Apartments

As you remember from the last lesson, when a Windows application is initially executed, the operating system creates a main process thread. At some point, imagine that there is an application called `CoInitialize()`, which invoked the COM runtime environment. At this point the process, from COM's perspective, creates its first apartment. This apartment is called the *main* or *primary STA* (the marriage here is COM and the *main* process thread). Before this, the process had *no* STA. If the application creates child threads and those threads are called `CoInitialize()`, the objects that those threads instantiate exist in secondary STAs. A process can then have zero or more STAs, one of which is considered the main STA.

`CoInitialize()`, as you remember from Day 2, is a shorthand form of `CoInitializeEx()` with a COINIT value of `COINIT_APARTMENTTHREADED`. `CoInitialize()` and `CoInitializeEx()` invoke the COM runtime. At that time, you nail down what type of apartment you want. That apartment is in effect for the duration of the thread's lifetime, or until the thread calls `CoUninitialize()` and restarts the COM runtime with different settings. After you have an apartment, you're stuck with it until COM shuts down on that thread.

With COM, rather than COM+, when any thread uses `CoInitializeEx()` with `COINIT_APARTMENTTHREADED`, a brand new STA is created for that thread. The objects that thread instantiates will run within that apartment. Clearly, the thread can create more than one COM object. The COM objects are free to pass data back and forth between themselves and the thread without worrying about marshaling. Pointer values, as an example, are valid between the objects and between an object and the owning thread. This is because all the objects are within the *same* apartment.

12

> **Note**
>
> COM+ introduces the notion of *context*. Two or more COM+ objects within the same apartment and context can deal with each other as I just described. If the objects happen to reside in the same apartment but differ by context, they must marshal transferred data. What is a context? It boils down to the additional information you specify in the COM+ Catalog that further describes the object, such as security, transactional nature, synchronization, and so on. Clearly, even if two COM+ objects share an apartment but have different security requirements, for example, they are logically separated and must marshal data.

If two child threads each call `CoInitializeEx()` with a `COINIT` value of `COINIT_APARTMENTTHREADED`, COM will create two new STAs. If the code in one apartment wants to access an object in the other apartment, the interface pointer of the COM object *must* be marshaled. The apartments are not related, and marshaling is required. This is also true for COM+.

If, on the other hand, any process thread called `CoInitializeEx()` with a `COINIT` value of `COINIT_MULTITHREADED`, COM would create an MTA. The *only* way you can create an MTA is by using `CoInitializeEx()`. If subsequent process threads also initialized the COM runtime by calling `CoInitializeEx()` using `COINIT_MULTITHREADED`, COM does not create multiple MTAs. Instead, COM provides each thread with the first MTA created, and the thread is said to *join* the MTA (like joining a party). A process can have *zero or one* MTA. Note you can still have zero or more STAs working in your process with or without an MTA.

I mentioned that objects working within a single STA can freely share pointers and data among themselves (at least with COM as it exists prior to Windows 2000). The MTA becomes a little more restrictive. Objects created in the MTA by a single thread can access each other freely. However, objects created in the MTA by different threads not only require data to be marshaled, but also require some or all the data synchronization techniques I mentioned in the last lesson. That's why it's wise to always protect multi-threaded code when your object exists in the MTA—you don't know which thread will drop in and execute your object's methods. It might be the thread that created the object, or it might be a completely different thread.

Regarding COM+, if there is a COM+ contextual difference among objects created by the same thread in the MTA, the objects could all wind up in the MTA, but still be logically separated by context.

This mixing and matching of STAs and the MTA lead to four types of Windows processes as far as COM is concerned (the trivial case where COM is not used is omitted).

A *single-threaded process* is a process with a single STA. An *apartment model process* is one with no MTA and two or more STAs. *A free-threaded process* is a process with an MTA but no STAs. A *mixed-model process* is a process with an MTA and one or more STAs. I mention these because you will likely see these terms used in COM literature. I've provided an illustration of these terms in Figure 12.1.

FIGURE 12.1

COM process models.

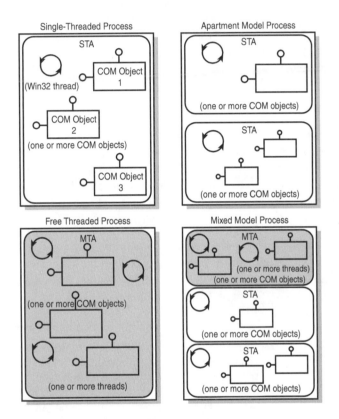

You now have some idea how processes, threads, and apartments relate. A Win32 process contains one or more threads. That same process can contain one or more COM STAs and zero or one MTA. Any combination will work.

Threads and Apartments

A thread can only ever be tied to a single apartment, whether it's an STA or the single process-wide MTA. If it initializes COM using CoInitialize() or CoInitializeEx() with COINIT_APARTMENTTHREADED, COM will create a new STA that only this thread can use. On the other hand, if the thread calls CoInitializeEx() with COINIT_MULTITHREADED, COM joins this thread with the threads already using the MTA (if the MTA already exists). COM will create the MTA if this is the first attempt to use it.

Threads using the MTA have no special requirements, although the COM objects they're running should be written to be thread-safe. However, threads that create an STA do have a rather large requirement imposed by COM—they must implement a Windows message loop or must otherwise handle Windows messages (such as by using `MsgWaitForMultipleObjects()`). A typical message loop (for a child thread) looks like this:

```
// Main message loop:
MSG msg;
while (GetMessage(&msg, NULL, 0, 0)) {
    DispatchMessage(&msg);
} // while

return msg.wParam;
```

COM will send Windows messages to your thread as the COM object is used. Because Windows saves messages in a queue, which is a first-in, first-out data structure, all Windows messages are serialized. That is, they are processed in the order they arrive, one at a time. This sounds a lot like synchronization, and that's exactly what COM is doing. It's synchronizing access to your COM object by using the thread's message queue.

Therefore, your STA thread must *have* a message queue. Actually, all Windows threads have a message queue, but not all Windows threads process Windows messages. So you must take the additional step of providing code to flush the message queue, and that's precisely what `GetMessage()` and `DispatchMessage()` do in the code snippet I just presented.

 Note

I mentioned in the last lesson that you should never call `WaitForSingleObject()` or `WaitForMultipleObjects()` from your STA-based COM objects. This might have seemed like a curious statement, because you certainly have no such restriction when programming (non-COM) Win32 applications. The reason for this is that COM will actually create a second thread it will use to process the out-of-apartment COM method call.

Your original STA thread will continue processing Windows messages. The thread COM created will then wait for the COM method to complete, but this thread is the one that will block using `WaitForSingleObject()` and `WaitForMultipleObjects()`. The communications link between the COM-generated thread and your apartment's thread will now be forever blocked because the COM thread is not the thread that will receive notification that the particular synchronization object has signaled. For this reason, you should, instead, use `MsgWaitForMultipleObjects()`.

At this point, you've looked at apartments from the Windows point of view, that is, by process and thread. Now let's turn to the COM viewpoint, which is the view from a COM object.

Single-Threaded Objects

The truly single-threaded COM object is essentially the COM object of yore, and this threading model is almost universally avoided today in favor of the apartment-threaded object. There are two reasons for this. For one thing, objects marked as single-threaded (versus apartment-threaded), will be instantiated *only* with the main thread. Once there, the object and the application share the main application's message loop. The second reason why single-threaded objects aren't used is that single-threaded objects execute sequentially with each other and the main application—just as they would in the days of Windows 3.1. Your application's performance can suffer.

One advantage the single-threaded object has, however, is that it can access the main application's data. Because it runs in the main process thread, any data the application exposes is visible to the single-threaded object. But this advantage is very slight, and the single-threaded object is typically not implemented today.

Because the object shares the main thread's message loop, single-threaded objects can only be in-process servers (DLLs). EXE servers can't be single-threaded in this sense. Also, you can tell that an object is single threaded by looking in the Registry under the object's CLSID. If you examine the InprocServer32 key, you will find no ThreadingModel value.

Single-Threaded Apartment Objects

Instead of creating single-threaded COM objects that run *only* in the main STA, you can now create modern COM objects to run in *any* STA, one of which can be the main STA. Though these COM objects are single threaded, they are referred to as being *apartment threaded*. In reality, if the COM object is using the main STA, it's no different (from your perspective) than a single-threaded object. There is a big difference, however, from the COM object's perspective. The COM object has no requirement to work in the main STA. It can easily work in a secondary STA with no adverse effects. You tell COM your ATL-based COM object is single-apartment threaded by selecting the Apartment radio button from the ATL Object Wizard, as you saw in Figure 1.7.

The COM object uses the message loop of the given thread (main process thread or otherwise) to manage the data synchronization that the COM object requires. COM makes sure only the thread that created the object uses the instance of the object it created. But note how I phrased that last sentence.

12

COM makes sure only the thread that created the object uses *the instance* of the object it created. That says nothing about the COM server *itself*. If your COM object is exposed by a local server, (an EXE), you need not be concerned with what I'm about to tell you. However, if your COM server is a DLL, there is something else you need to know.

With respect to DLLs in general, Windows fools you into believing different applications that access the same DLL actually access different copies of the same DLL. That is, if I start one copy of an application that uses MYDLL.DLL and then I start a second copy of the same application, Windows will create two new processes, each with its own address space. Because the address spaces are not the same, MYDLL.DLL is loaded into memory differently in each process (or at least it can be loaded differently). Windows manages the memory location adjustments as the DLL is slid around in different process address spaces.

So I have two copies of my application running with two copies of MYDLL.DLL, right? Actually, that's incorrect. You *do* have two copies of the application running, but Windows is frugal with memory and actually loads a *single* copy of the DLL to service both applications. Windows itself shields you from this and manages the plumbing necessary to make this sleight of hand work.

Now take the DLL and make it an in-process COM server and have two threads within the same process create an instance of a COM object it supports. Then add to that DLL some global or static variables that the COM objects can later access. Do you see where I am leading? Even though the COM server exists in two different STAs, the COM objects share data from two different threads. You have a potential data synchronization problem in this case!

Caution

> This behavior is by design, so be aware you could have significant data synchronization problems if you use global or static data in your apartment-threaded objects.

The solution is to either avoid global and static data in the first place or, barring that, protect it by using any of the synchronization mechanisms I discussed in the last lesson, even if your object is destined to be single threaded. Alternatively, you can take the plunge and create a free-threaded object.

Multithreaded Apartment Objects

You indicate your COM object is free threaded by selecting the Free radio button from the ATL Object Wizard's Attributes property page (see Figure 1.7 for a refresher). The free-threaded COM object is always instantiated in the MTA, and like objects existing within a given STA, this free-threaded object can share unmarshaled interface pointers with other objects in the same MTA. After all, the objects all belong to the same overall process, so they share the same address space. Pointer values have meaning in this case.

Because COM assumes the object protects its data, all free-threaded objects should synchronize access to their data accordingly. This makes sense because any thread that joined the MTA can access any object existing in the MTA (and in the same COM+ context, if using COM+), even if the object was created by another thread. This is very much the classic multithreading situation I described in the previous day, and all the benefits and problems associated with multithreading apply in this case.

However, if an object in an STA wants to access an object in the MTA, or vice versa, the interface pointers (and data) *must* be marshaled, even if the two threads belong to the same process. This also makes sense if you consider how the STA synchronizes data access. *Something* has to be responsible for sending Windows messages to the STA, yet the thread that creates the free-threaded object has no requirement to generate such messages. That's the job of the marshaling layer, which you implement using either the proxy/stub DLL the ATL wizards create for you, by using the Universal Marshaler, or by aggregating the Free-Threaded Marshaler. I won't reiterate the UM here, but I will briefly further describe the proxy/stub DLL and the FTM.

Proxies and Stubs Revisited

Now you see the two main uses of the proxy/stub DLL. The proxy and the stub convert data into a form that can be transmitted from process to process, and they indirectly manage the creation of Windows messages as they convert COM interface pointers (COM itself will issue the messages).

The proxy/stub DLL is itself a COM object that is used by the marshaling layer. To the client, the proxy looks like the object. To the object, the stub looks like the client. The proxy manages the data conversion across apartment boundaries. The stub makes sure the call stack is correctly reassembled in the object's apartment and actually calls the object's method on behalf of the client. In between, COM handles the Windows messaging details.

12

Proxy/stub DLLs are associated with interfaces, not the server. That is, the proxy/stub DLL doesn't coincide with the server DLL or EXE. Rather, the proxy/stub DLL coincides with the interfaces the server exposes. COM can tell if a given interface has an associated proxy/stub DLL by looking into the Registry. When the proxy/stub DLL is registered, the interface's IID is registered in the Interface key of HKEY_CLASSES_ROOT. Under the IID key, there should be a value called ProxyStubClsid32 that contains the CLSID of the proxy/stub DLL. The InprocServer32 key of the proxy/stub's CLSID key will contain the path to the proxy/stub DLL.

Tip

> If you call an object's interface method and receive the failed HRESULT
> REGDB_E_IIDNOTREG (0x80040155), it means you have not registered your
> proxy/stub DLL, but COM believes one is required.

If you don't provide a proxy/stub DLL, you have to use another method of marshaling. Perhaps you're using the Universal Marshaler, which you invoke by using either the dual or oleautomation interface attributes in your interface's IDL description (oleautomation is for custom interfaces). Or perhaps you've written a custom proxy/stub DLL. If you have a free-threaded object, however, you can use the Free-Threaded Marshaler, which I discuss in the next section.

Free-Threaded Marshaling

Before I describe the FTM to any great degree, let me warn you that using the FTM solves many sticky problems, but it is also an advanced topic. My intention here is to describe the situation in which the FTM is useful and why it helps solve problems. I will not show you how to use it. Keep the FTM in mind, in case you meet the situation I'll describe.

I mentioned there is a problem with global or static data in COM in-process DLLs, and that the problem manifests itself when the same DLL is used in two STAs in the same process. The FTM was created to solve another issue that is similarly related to using COM objects in the same process versus different processes.

Threads in a single process all use the same virtual address space. Threads in different processes exist in different address spaces. Pointer values passed between threads of the same process access the same address space. Pointers passed between processes have no meaning, as the virtual memory blocks are completely different.

But COM imposes the requirement that interface pointers to COM objects must be marshaled between apartments, even if the apartments are created by threads in the same address space. In reality, there is no reason to convert the interface pointer to some intermediate form just to send it to another apartment in the same process. If you're interested in this sort of efficiency, you implement custom marshaling and provide an implementation of IMarshal as one of your object's base interfaces. Your custom marshaling code then simply passes the raw pointer between the apartments.

But how can you know that the request for the interface pointer, and hence the use of the COM object, didn't come from an apartment in another process? In this case, your custom marshaling code blindly passes the raw pointer to the other apartment in the other address space. Clearly, the other process is unable to use the pointer it receives, and it will probably throw an exception and crash.

What you need here is *smart* custom marshaling code that can distinguish between apartments in the same address space versus apartments in another address space. Although you could write this yourself, Microsoft has provided just such an object in the form of the FTM. The FTM is smart enough to properly marshal the interface pointer, whether the pointer is destined for the same process (pointer is untouched) or another process (pointer is marshaled). In a sense, when you use the FTM, you're telling the system to forget using the standard COM plumbing, so use it wisely.

To use the FTM, you aggregate it. When COM comes looking for the IMarshal interface, your object passes the IMarshal interface of the FTM to COM, and the FTM takes over. ATL helps you with this when you create your object using the ATL Object Wizard. It gives you a Free-Threaded Marshaler check box (see Figure 1.7). If you check this, the wizard adds several lines of code to your interface's C++ .H file to manage this aggregation for you.

The FTM is really designed to speed things up when marshaling interface pointers and, therefore, the use of interapartment COM objects within the same process. If the interface pointer is passed to another process, the FTM marshals the pointer in the standard fashion and isn't any better or worse than any other method of marshaling.

I hope that at this point you understand both apartment-threaded and free-threaded COM objects. There is another type of object. It is an object that is perfectly comfortable being used in both traditional COM apartments as well as the COM+ thread-neutral apartment. That object is the topic of the next section.

Objects That Go Both Ways

If you specify a threading model of Both, versus Free or Apartment, when you choose your object's attributes (refer back to Figure 1.7), you're about to implement an object that can exist in either an STA or the MTA. Because it can exist in the MTA, it has the proper synchronization code, but this same code will probably slow its performance if it finds itself in an STA. You've gained flexibility, however.

Because the both-threaded object can happily exist in the MTA, how is it different than a free-threaded object? In practice, there is absolutely no difference, if the COM server is an EXE. For the DLL-based COM server, it comes down to your decision to create threads from within your COM object and how closely you want the COM object tied to its parent (the code that invoked the object).

Your COM object's child threads will need access to the parent COM object, and you'll get the best performance if the object is created in the MTA (pointers must be marshaled between STAs, remember). In this case, you will likely want to mark your object as free-threaded. If you don't intend to create child threads from within your COM object, both-threaded is the better threading model choice because the object will be created in your apartment. Because this threading model is often confusing, I'll address it again when I discuss the apartment model cookbook.

Objects That Don't Care

COM+ has introduced a new type of apartment that is called the *thread-neutral apartment*, or *TNA*. You'll sometimes see this apartment referred to as the *rental apartment*. The goal of the TNA is to allow quick access to COM objects that don't reside in your particular apartment. The drawback is that you can use the objects, but your thread can't maintain their state (they have none, by design). In fact, they're not tied to any particular thread, so all threads in the process can use their services.

You tell COM+ your object is destined for the TNA by setting a flag in the COM+ Catalog and by marking your object as neutral-threaded in the `InprocServer32` Registry key's `ThreadingModel` value.

A good question to ask at this point is how to determine what apartment is right for a given object? There are some basic guidelines, as I'll show you next.

Apartment Threading Model Selection Cookbook

Although the apartment types and threading models might seem confusing, there is a reasonable way to approach the selection of the proper apartment and threading model type. I'll first present a table that summarizes what I've presented so far, and then I'll provide you with a decision tree you can use to select the appropriate apartment type.

Table 12.1 shows you into which apartment your object will go if marked with certain apartment types. It also shows you if data synchronization is necessary, as well as how to mark the synchronization if using COM+.

TABLE 12.1   Object Apartment Creation Guide

Threading Model Synchronization	Apartment	Synchronize?	COM+
None	Main STA	No	(empty)
Apartment	Note 1	Note 2	None or Supported
Free	MTA Only	Yes	Required
Both	Creator's Apt	Yes	Required or Supported
Neutral	TNA Only	Yes	Requires New

Note

The object can be created in any STA if created from an STA-based thread. If an MTA thread creates the object, COM will create a ghost STA apartment called the *host STA* and execute the object there. All such MTA-created objects will reside in the single, process-wide host STA.

Note

You'll need to synchronize access to global or static data only.

12

To assist you in your apartment type selection, follow this pseudocode decision tree:

```
IF coding with HWNDs or Win32 user interface APIs
    THEN object must be apartment-threaded
ELSE IF calling WaitForSingleObject() or other kernel synchronization
    THEN object must be free-threaded
ELSE IF object could be shared by applications but will be accessed privately
        when instantiated
    THEN object should be both-threaded
ELSE IF objects could be shared by applications and can be shared by other
        objects when instantiated
    THEN object should be neutral-threaded
ELSE
    Try to synchronize your object's data and make free-threaded. If that's
    not possible, make apartment-threaded.
```

You can read more about this in the May 1999 issue of the "Microsoft System's Journal."

ATL and Thread Models Revisited

Before I close this chapter, I want to tie the thread models you've seen back to ATL so you can how ATL helps you implement the thread models. As you've seen, the threading model that you select when you choose your object's attributes from the Object Wizard has a significant effect upon how COM will instantiate your object and what clients of your object will expect it to do or not do.

The easiest support to see is the ThreadingModel Registry value the wizard placed into your object's .RGS file. If the ThreadingModel is blank, the object is single threaded. If the ThreadingModel has a value of Apartment, Free, or Both, the COM object is assumed to support that particular threading model (note that the tool doesn't support COM+ at this time). I say *assumed* because there is one case that I know of where an external application will change this value, but that's a topic for the last day of the book.

You'll also see other apparently minor changes. For example, your object's C++ implementation class might inherit from either CComSingleThreadModel or CComMultiThreadModel, depending upon your threading model choice. If you reflect back to Day 5, "ATL Architecture: How ATL Implements COM," you might recall the CComSingleThreadModel ATL class simply increments and decrements the reference count. But the CComMultiThreadModel ATL class protects the reference count with one of two special Win32 API calls: InterlockedIncrement() and InterlockedDecrement(). You're seeing thread synchronization in action.

Finally, I mentioned in Day 8 that ATL provides some measure of thread synchronization support through the CComCriticalSection and CComAutoCriticalSection classes. True, if you want mutex, event, or semaphore support, you're on your own; but at least ATL does help to some degree.

An ATL Apartment and Thread Model Example

I've provided a sample application that uses an ATL-based COM server. I created the in-process Day12Server project and added two ATL Objects, MySixthATLObj and MySeventhATLObj. The former object is a single-threaded object with no special data synchronization. It implements two methods on its ISingleThrdDemo interface: SquareVal() and GetSignature(). SquareVal() takes a double [in, out] value and simply squares it. GetSignature() returns a BSTR with the text Single to prove the single-threaded object is active. MySeventhATLObj exposes the IMultiThrdDemo interface with the same two methods. Its signature, however, is Multi.

I then created a test application called Day12Client that uses these two objects. The goal is to test whether it's possible to create single-threaded objects given only the MTA, or vice versa. You can see Day12Client's user interface in Figure 12.2.

FIGURE 12.2

Day12Client's user interface.

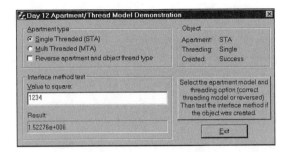

The goal of the application and COM object is to show you how COM apartments are created and destroyed, but a side benefit is that you can also see similar methods coded to be single versus multithreaded. The interfaces that the two objects expose have the same methods. Be sure to look at MySixthATLObj.cpp and MySeventhATLObj.cpp for the implementations.

Under the covers, Day12Client has a CreateObject() helper function designed to read the state of the user interface controls and create both an apartment type and an object that implements a given threading model. I showed this in Listing 12.1. Normally, if you create an STA, you want a single-threaded object. What happens if you, instead, instantiate a multithreaded (free) object? This example enables you to explore this type of scenario.

LISTING 12.1   Implementation of the CreateObject() Method

```
 1: void CDay12ClientDlg::CreateObject(BOOL bSingleThrd /*=TRUE*/)
 2: {
 3:     // Clear any input
 4:     UpdateData(TRUE);
 5:     m_strValue.Empty();
 6:     m_strResult.Empty();
 7:     UpdateData(FALSE);
 8:
 9:     // Set the focus to the edit control
10:     CWnd* pEdit = GetDlgItem(IDC_VALUE);
11:     ASSERT_VALID(pEdit);
12:     pEdit->SetFocus();
13:
14:     // Clear any COM objects
15:     m_spISingleThrdDemo = NULL;
16:     m_spIMultiThrdDemo = NULL;
17:
18:     // Shut down COM
19:     CoUninitialize();
20:
21:     if ( !m_iAptType ) {
```

12

continues

Listing 12.1 continued

```
22:         // Bring up COM in an STA
23:         InitCOM(TRUE);
24:
25:         // Create an instance of the COM object
26:         if ( !m_bCreateReverse ) {
27:             // Single threaded...
28:             CreateSingleThrdObject();
29:         } // if
30:         else {
31:             // Multithreaded...
32:             CreateMultiThrdObject();
33:         } // else
34:     } // if
35:     else {
36:         // Bring up COM in an MTA
37:         InitCOM(FALSE);
38:
39:         // Create an instance of the COM object
40:         if ( !m_bCreateReverse ) {
41:             // Multithreaded...
42:             CreateMultiThrdObject();
43:         } // if
44:         else {
45:             // Single threaded...
46:             CreateSingleThrdObject();
47:         } // else
48:     } // else
49:
50:     // Transfer data from the MFC C++ variables
51:     // to the Windows controls.
52:     UpdateData(FALSE);
53: }
```

The InitCOM() method brings up the COM runtime with either an STA or the MTA, depending upon the Boolean input parameter. I show you this in Listing 12.2.

Listing 12.2 Implementation of the InitCOM() Method

```
1: HRESULT CDay12ClientDlg::InitCOM(BOOL bSingleThrd /*=TRUE*/)
2: {
3:     // Bring up COM...
4:     HRESULT hr = S_OK;
5:     if ( bSingleThrd ) {
6:         // ...in an STA
7:         hr = CoInitializeEx(NULL,COINIT_APARTMENTTHREADED);
8:         m_strAptType.LoadString(IDS_APTSTA);
```

LISTING 12.2   continued

```
 9:     } // if
10:     else {
11:         // ...in an MTA
12:         hr = CoInitializeEx(NULL,COINIT_MULTITHREADED);
13:         m_strAptType.LoadString(IDS_APTMTA);
14:     } // else
15:
16:     return hr;
17: }
```

ANALYSIS The CreateSingleThrdObject() (lines 28 and 46 of Listing 12.1) and CreateSingleThrdObject() (lines 32 and 42 of Listing 12.1) methods simply perform the relevant CComPtr::CoCreateInstance() and complete some of the user interface feedback strings, such as an indication that the creation was successful and the display of the signature string from the COM object itself (to prove the particular object was indeed instantiated). As the two methods are very similar, I only show the CreateSingleThrdObject() method in Listing 12.3.

LISTING 12.3   Implementation of the CreateSingleThrdObject() Method

```
 1: HRESULT CDay12ClientDlg::CreateSingleThrdObject()
 2: {
 3:     // Create a single threaded COM object
 4:     m_strThreadType.LoadString(IDS_SINGLE);
 5:     HRESULT hr = m_pISingleThrdDemo.CoCreateInstance(CLSID_TYATLObj6,
 6:                                     NULL,
 7:                                     CLSCTX_INPROC_SERVER);
 8:     if ( FAILED(hr) ) {
 9:         // Some error
10:         m_strCreated.LoadString(IDS_ERROR);
11:         AfxMessageBox("Error creating single threaded COM " \
12:                     "object!",MB_OK | MB_ICONERROR);
13:     } // if
14:     else {
15:         // No error
16:         m_strCreated.LoadString(IDS_SUCCESS);
17:
18:         // Obtain signature from the object itself
19:         // for proof
20:         CComBSTR bstrSig;
21:         hr = m_pISingleThrdDemo->GetSignature(&bstrSig);
22:         if ( FAILED(hr) ) {
23:             // Some error...
24:             m_strThreadType.LoadString(IDS_ERROR);
```

continues

12

LISTING 12.3   continued

```
25:          } // if
26:          else {
27:              // Load signature
28:              m_strThreadType = bstrSig.m_str;
29:          } // else
30:      } // else
31:
32:      return hr;
33: }
```

After you click on an apartment-type radio button (STA or MTA), the application creates an apartment of the selected type and instantiates an object to match the type. That is, if you create the MTA, the application also instantiates the free-threaded COM object. However, you can check the Reverse Apartment and Object Thread Type check box and reverse the apartment/threading model if you wish. For the situation I just mentioned, the application creates the MTA, and it also instantiates the apartment-threaded object.

If you mismatch the apartment type and threading model of the COM object you want to instantiate, COM is forced to create an apartment of the correct type for your object. This automatically forces your process from either a single-threaded or free-threaded process to a mixed-model process. I suggest a couple of interesting twists to this application in the exercises. One thing to note, however, is that you'll require the proxy/stub DLL for things to work correctly. I modified the project settings to automatically compile and register the proxy/stub DLL for you.

Summary

As you progress through the ATL Object Wizard's property pages, probably one of the most critical design decisions you make is the selection of the threading model. Objects designed to run in the STA, the MTA, or both each have individual strengths and weaknesses. I hope that I've shed enough light on this typically confusing topic to help you make the correct decision for your objects.

I began by paring down the definition of the COM apartment as the marriage between a Win32 thread and an instance of a COM object working with the COM runtime environment. Your Win32 thread selects the apartment type by calling CoInitializeEx() with either COINIT_MULTITHREADED or COINIT_APARTMENTTHREADED, or by calling the old COM CoInitialize() API function, which forces the creation of an STA. I described how COM apartments fit into Win32 processes, and I talked about what requirement COM imposes upon threads that desire STA COM access (they must have a Windows message loop).

I went on to describe the various types of COM threading models, from single threaded to multithreaded, and discussed some of the marshaling implications you face as you send object pointers from apartment to apartment and process to process:

- Single-threaded objects must exist in the main thread's STA, whereas single apartment-threaded objects can work in any STA.

- Free-threaded objects will find themselves in the MTA, whereas objects with the threading model can work in either the MTA or an STA.

- Neutral-threaded objects will be created in the TNA, but can be accessed by either STA or MTA threads.

Whenever object pointers are sent across apartment bounds, the pointers must be marshaled.

I believe this lesson is one of the more important in this entire book, even though it's not specifically related to ATL. ATL does help you implement objects that support these threading models, for example, CComSingleThreadModel versus CComMultiThreadModel.

Day 13, next, is devoted to another often overlooked aspect of ATL: ATL's capability to provide wrappers for the Win32 Windows API calls, and how you can use these wrappers in your applications.

Q&A

Q I tried to compile an application that used CoInitializeEx(), but it wouldn't compile. Why?

A That depends on whether you have other syntax or project errors, but barring that, you're probably compiling on Windows 95 and haven't defined a preprocessor value necessary to allow the multithreaded COM API method call. In your project settings, after the currently defined preprocessor values, insert this (the comma should be included):

```
, _WIN32_DCOM
```

Q The COM Specification mentions COM objects using an *execution context*. What is this?

A It's just another name for *apartment*. If you turn the two words execution context into a sentence, perhaps it makes more sense: "A COM object requires the context of an existing thread of execution." The full name for a thread is a *thread of execution*, and each thread carries with it context, or state information. This is just a more formal way to say you have to have an existing Win32 thread before you can execute your COM object.

12

Workshop

The Workshop is designed to help you anticipate possible questions, review what you've learned, and get you thinking about how to put your knowledge into practice. The answers to the quiz are in Appendix A, "Answers."

Quiz

1. What are the four types of COM process models and how do they differ?

2. What requirement does COM impose on a thread that creates an STA and why?

3. Why are single-threaded objects avoided in favor of apartment-threaded objects, which are also single threaded?

4. When would you select the free-threading model over the both-threading model?

5. How does ATL support your choice of threading model?

Exercises

1. Find the Day12Server's proxy/stub DLL (Day12Serverps.dll) and right-click on its filename (you should be able to deregister the COM server at the corresponding context menu, assuming you ran the Registry script from Day 2). Now try the Day12Client application again using mixed mode. What happens now?

2. Change `MySeventhATLObj`'s threading model from free to both and recompile. After de-registering the Day12Serverps.dll server (as in the previous example), run the Day12Client application. Which object's signature appears when you select a mixed-mode environment?

DAY **13**

Creating ATL Applications: Where ATL Meets Win32

I think it might be time for a brief respite, especially given the deep topics you've studied in the past two days. Today will prove to be a little bit different!

In this lesson, I'm going to discuss how the current version of ATL supports traditional Win32 programming. You know from your earlier reading that ATL supports the dialog box. In fact, it's an object you can insert into your COM server using the ATL Object Wizard. (See Day 6, "The ATL App Wizard: Back to Basics," for a quick review.) ATL 3.0, however, provides support for more than the simple dialog box. It also provides general Win32 windowing support, which you'll explore in this lesson. If you haven't dusted off your classic copy of *Programming Windows* by Charles Petzold (Microsoft Press, ISBN 1-57231-995-X) in some time, you'll have the chance here. If you don't have a copy of *Programming Windows*, you should consider picking it up; it's a classic reference.

Here is a more precise list of what's in store for you this day:

- ATL's philosophy regarding Win32 programming support
- How to create windows using ATL
- A look at several types of Windows messages and how ATL supports them
- Subclassing windows using ATL

ATL's Windowing Philosophy

I've mentioned ATL's philosophy towards implementing COM, and I'm sure you've noticed how frugal ATL is with sheer lines of code. You don't have to write much to implement high-powered ATL COM objects, and when the compiler has finished its work, you're left with a very small file for redistribution. In other words, ATL doesn't add layer upon layer of fat to get the job done.

ATL didn't originally provide classes to support traditional Win32 application development. Starting with ATL 2.0, however, there was a modicum of support (such as for the dialog box). However, with ATL 3.0 there is a tremendous amount of Win32 programming support built into the library. The trouble is, not many people seem to know it's there.

When the ATL developers decided to implement traditional Win32 classes, I imagine they approached the topic with the same philosophy as they used in their COM implementation—be lean and mean. Unlike MFC, ATL doesn't require a fat support DLL or add hundreds of kilobytes to your executable if it is linked statically. Unlike bare-bones Win32 programming, ATL does provide superior C++ class support for many of the programming tasks you must perform to manage Win32 Windows applications.

When doing these things, ATL doesn't necessarily provide all the support MFC provides. For example, ATL doesn't have built-in support for ISAPI or splitter windows. In some cases, you'll want to use the Standard Template Library to gain some of the functionality MFC provides, such as that for the container classes and strings. ATL also doesn't wrap every aspect of Win32 application functionality, as MFC does—such as `WinMain()`. You still have to be familiar with traditional Windows programming (hence, my reference to *Programming Windows* in the introduction). But what you give up in integrated feature support and functionality, you gain in performance and size.

Creating a Window with ATL

ATL provides several C++ templates designed to give you control over specific Windows functionality. Table 13.1 lists the ATL window classes and their functions.

Table 13.1   ATL's C++ Window Classes

Class	Use
CWindow	Wraps basic Win32 windowing API
CWindowImpl	Creates a new window or subclasses an existing window class
CContainedWindow	Implements a child window that uses the message map of the parent or subclasses/superclasses an existing window class
CSimpleDialog	Creates simple dialog boxes based on a dialog template
CDialogImpl	Provides additional dialog box functionality (such as modeless operation)
CAxWindow	Creates a window that is capable of containing ActiveX controls
CAxDialogImpl	Creates a dialog box that is capable of containing ActiveX controls

ATL also provides other lower-level window base classes, but you'll typically not use these on a regular basis. Instead, you'll nearly always use the higher-level classes I've shown here. Each of these classes is a typedef of the templated name. For example, CContainedWindow comes from CContainedWindowT. This will be important later in the day.

How you will use the classes depends upon what you are doing; but, in general, you create a derived class using one of these classes as a base class. Some classes provide more capability than do others. For example, CAxWindow provides more functionality than CWindowImpl, because CAxWindow adds the code you need to host an ActiveX control. CWindowImpl, in turn, provides more capability than CWindow (although CWindowImpl uses CWindow as a base class). I'll illustrate this with a quick example.

13

> **Note**
>
> If you are interested in using ATL to create Windows applications, you should know Microsoft released a full-strength ATL template library to do just this as a sample with the Platform SDK for Windows 2000 RC3. This library has support for MDI, splitter windows, views, toolbars, and more. The information I'll present here applies only to ATL 3.0 and not to the enhanced ATL Windows Template Library included with the Platform SDK sample.

A Basic Window

Because no ATL AppWizard is designed to create a Win32 program, you can use the Win32 Application AppWizard for this example. The wizard will create the basic project, and then you'll modify the files. Although you can select any of the Win32 Application wizard application types, I'd use the simple application type in this case. The empty project will require you to add too much, and the "Hello World" application will force you to delete too much.

After you've created your new Win32 project (I named mine ATLWindow1), in addition to the Visual Studio project files you should find three source files: STDAFX.H, STDAFX.CPP, and *<project>*.CPP (AtlWindow1.cpp in this case).

The first change you'll make is to STDAFX.H, where you'll change these lines

```
#include <windows.h>


// TODO: reference additional headers your program requires here
```

to these

```
// ATL support
#include <atlbase.h>
extern CComModule _Module;
#include <atlwin.h>
#include <atlcom.h>
```

WINDOWS.H will be included for you by the ATL header files, so don't be concerned about omitting it from STDAFX.H directly.

The bigger change will be made to the *<project>*.CPP file. The initial source file is completely useless:

```
int APIENTRY WinMain(HINSTANCE hInstance,
                     HINSTANCE hPrevInstance,
                     LPSTR     lpCmdLine,
                     int       nCmdShow)
{
    // TODO: Place code here.

    return 0;
}
```

This does nothing more than declare the main executable entry point WinMain(). To make the application functional, you must add code from Listing 13.1 to create a window, display it, and operate its message pump. You also must add the support ATL requires to maintain your application's state. To do this, you must declare an instance of CComModule named _Module and initialize it using its CComModule::Init() method.

LISTING 13.1   `WinMain()` with Basic ATL Window Support

```
 1: CComModule _Module;
 2:
 3: int APIENTRY WinMain(HINSTANCE hInstance,
 4:                      HINSTANCE hPrevInstance,
 5:                      LPSTR     lpCmdLine,
 6:                      int       nCmdShow)
 7: {
 8:     // Initialize the ATL module
 9:     _Module.Init(NULL,hInstance);
10:
11:     // Create an ATL window
12:     CWindow win;
13:     win.Create(_T("EDIT"),                  // window class
14:                NULL,                        // no parent
15:                NULL,                        // default rectangle
16:                _T("My first ATL window!"),// window caption
17:                WS_VISIBLE);                 // creation style
18:
19:     // Show the window
20:     win.ShowWindow(nCmdShow);
21:
22:     // Process Windows messages...note that since this demo
23:     // has no mechanism for sending the WM_QUIT message, this
24:     // application will run forever unless you terminate it
25:     // using the Task Manager or the Visual Studio debugger.
26:     MSG msg;
27:     while ( GetMessage(&msg,0,0,0) ) {
28:         TranslateMessage(&msg);
29:         DispatchMessage(&msg);
30:     } // while
31:
32:     return 0;
33: }
```

ANALYSIS Because I created a window based upon the EDIT window class and CWindow, rather than a derived class using a window class I registered (line 13), I have no way to intercept and handle Windows messages. In fact, you'll need to terminate this application in the debugger or press Alt+F4 if you're using a release version. I can't add any message handlers because I used a predefined window class.

Window classes are types of windows registered with the operating system. You've undoubtedly used each of the standard Windows controls, such as the edit control, the list control, the button, and so forth. Each of these has a defined window class that tells Windows what sorts of things the window requires, such as the main window menu, the default mouse cursor, and scroll bar notifications. There is much more to it, but this is

13

more of a Win32 programming issue than an ATL programming issue. If you're unclear about window classes versus C++ classes, grab Petzold.

The underlying point I want to make is that one of the items you register when you create a window class is the main window procedure. The main window procedure is the function Windows calls when it has messages to be processed. In this example, the EDIT window class has its own window procedure which is used in lieu of the message pump I provided (GetMessage() and the trailing while loop). Any input to the sample's window is handled directly by the edit control (and not by my code) after the edit control has been initialized and is accepting messages.

Although it's gratifying to see a window pop up on the screen in reaction to your code, the window isn't terribly interesting. Even though you can insert text (it implements a lot of functionality, all from the EDIT window class), you can't do much more than that with it. You can't even save the text to a file.

To do more, you have to register your own window class. After you do, you can handle Windows messages yourself and respond to user and system input. That's exactly what CWindowImpl provides and what I'll cover in the next section.

A Window You Can Use

To show you CWindowImpl in action, I created a new Win32 Application project, just as I did the first project. (I called it ATLWindows2). I added the same code as before to STDAFX.H to incorporate ATL into my project. The changes to ATLWindows2.cpp were slightly different, however, as you'll see. Before I get to those, note that I had to create (by hand) a new source file, MyAtlWindow.h.

MyAtlWindow.h is simply a file that defines the CMyAtlWindow class, which derives from CWindowImpl. You see this in Listing 13.2.

LISTING 13.2   MyAtlWindow.h

```
 1: // MyAtlWindow.h : Declaration of the CMyAtlWindow
 2:
 3: #ifndef __MYATLWINDOW_H_
 4: #define __MYATLWINDOW_H_
 5:
 6: #include <atlhost.h>          // window class definitions
 7:
 8: ////////////////////////////////////////////////////////////////////////
 9: // CMyAtlWindow
10:
11: class CMyAtlWindow :
12:     public CWindowImpl< CMyAtlWindow, CWindow,
         ➥CWinTraits<WS_OVERLAPPEDWINDOW | WS_VISIBLE, 0> >
```

```
13: {
14: // Construction
15: public:
16:     CMyAtlWindow()
17:     {
18:     }
19:
20:     ~CMyAtlWindow()
21:     {
22:         if ( ::IsWindow(m_hWnd) ) {
23:             // If the window handle is still valid, destroy it
24:             DestroyWindow();
25:         } // if
26:     }
27:
28: // ATL Message Map
29: BEGIN_MSG_MAP(CMyAtlWindow)
30:     MESSAGE_HANDLER(WM_PAINT, OnPaint)
31:     MESSAGE_HANDLER(WM_CLOSE, OnClose)
32: END_MSG_MAP()
33:
34: // Message handlers
35:     LRESULT OnPaint(UINT uMsg, WPARAM wParam, LPARAM lParam,
        ➥BOOL& bHandled)
36:     {
37:         // Set up for painting
38:         PAINTSTRUCT ps;
39:         HDC hDC = BeginPaint(&ps);
40:         if ( hDC == NULL ) {
41:             // Some error...
42:             return 0;
43:         } // if
44:
45:         // Determine client area
46:         RECT rcClient;
47:         GetClientRect(&rcClient);
48:
49:         // Draw a message
50:         DrawText(hDC,_T("Hello from ATL!"),-1,&rcClient,
51:                 DT_SINGLELINE | DT_CENTER | DT_VCENTER);
52:
53:         // Done painting
54:         EndPaint(&ps);
55:
56:         return 0;
57:     }
58:
```

13

continues

LISTING 13.2   continued

```
59:      LRESULT OnClose(UINT uMsg, WPARAM wParam, LPARAM lParam,
         ➡BOOL& bHandled)
60:      {
61:          // Quit the application
62:          PostQuitMessage(0);
63:          return 0;
64:      }
65:
66: // Implementation
67: protected:
68:
69: };
70:
71: #endif // __MYATLWINDOW_H_
```

ANALYSIS   I created the CMyAtlWindow class to access the functionality of CWindowImpl
while providing my own customizations. There are a couple of things to note
from Listing 13.2. For example, this is the basic class definition starting with line 11:

```
class CMyAtlWindow :
    public CWindowImpl< CMyAtlWindow, CWindow,
 ➡CWinTraits<WS_OVERLAPPEDWINDOW | WS_VISIBLE, 0> >
{
    (stuff)
};
```

As you can see, CMyAtlWindow inherits publicly from CWindowImpl, which is itself a template. The specialization parameter is my class, CMyAtlWindow, but it also requires two other parameters. CWindowImpl itself requires a base class, and in this case I used CWindow (I've not seen anyone use anything different, but that doesn't mean you can't). The last parameter, CWinTraits, provides the window style bits that will be used to create the window.

There are many window style bits, and over time, even more were required, so Microsoft introduced the extended window style bits. The two parameters you see given to CWinTraits specify the traditional window style bits and the extended window style bits, respectively. For a complete list of the style bits, you should refer to the online documentation (look for ::CreateWindow()) or look them up in Petzold. In this case, I specify no special extended style bits, but I do want a window that is initially visible (WS_VISIBLE) and one that provides all the usual Windows user interface paraphernalia, such as sizeable edges, minimize and maximize boxes, close box, and a caption (WS_OVERLAPPEDWINDOW).

CMyAtlWindow's constructor is pretty basic, but the destructor is somewhat interesting (lines 20 through 26):

```
~CMyAtlWindow()
{
    if ( ::IsWindow(m_hWnd) ) {
        // If the window handle is still valid, destroy it
        DestroyWindow();
    } // if
}
```

Every window in Windows has a window handle, which is used to reference a structure Windows maintains in memory containing information pertinent to that window. Most of the information you'll find there is directly related to the information you provide when you register the window class, by the way. In this case, the window handle is stored in CWindow::m_hWnd. When the destructor for CMyAtlWindow is executed, if the window handle is still valid, the destructor makes sure the window is properly closed and all the associated system resources are released—CWindow::DestroyWindow().

The next portion of the class definition shows you how to define ATL message maps (lines 28 to 32). I'll cover message maps in more detail in the next section; but for now, this code implements the basic message-handling customizations CMyAtlWindow provides for:

```
// ATL Message Map
BEGIN_MSG_MAP(CMyAtlWindow)
    MESSAGE_HANDLER(WM_PAINT, OnPaint)
    MESSAGE_HANDLER(WM_CLOSE, OnClose)
END_MSG_MAP()
```

I had to add the beginning and ending macros I've highlighted, but I added the message handlers themselves using the Add Windows Message Handler menu item available from the context menu of the CMyAtlWindow ClassView tree node (accessed in the typical ATL manner by right clicking the tree node). The menu you see is shown in Figure 13.1. The resulting wizard is shown in Figure 13.2.

Note

The beginning and ending macros must appear as I've shown them or the menu option to invoke the message handler wizard will be disabled. The BEGIN_MSG_MAP(classname) takes the class name as a parameter, followed by the END_MSG_MAP() macro. They should be placed somewhere within your class definition and be publicly accessible.

13

Figure 13.1

Invoking the ATL Add Message Handler wizard.

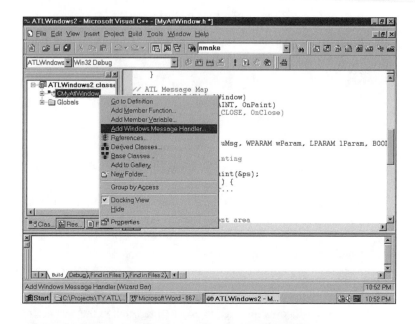

Figure 13.2

The ATL Add Message Handler wizard.

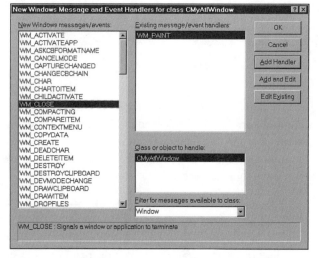

To insert the message handler, simply select the Windows message you want to handle from the New Windows Messages/Events list and click either Add Handler (if you want to add more handlers at this time) or Add and Exit to insert the particular handler and exit the wizard.

The wizard will add a message-handling macro to the message map and then insert some stub code for you to modify. For example, the wizard will add this handler for the WM_PAINT message:

```
LRESULT OnPaint(UINT uMsg, WPARAM wParam, LPARAM lParam,
➥BOOL& bHandled)
{
    // TODO : Add Code for message handler. Call DefWindowProc
➥if necessary.
    return 0;
}
```

Clearly this won't do for painting purposes! So I modified the stub code to actually paint something:

```
 1: LRESULT OnPaint(UINT uMsg, WPARAM wParam, LPARAM lParam, BOOL& bHandled)
 2: {
 3:     // Set up for painting
 4:     PAINTSTRUCT ps;
 5:     HDC hDC = BeginPaint(&ps);
 6:     if ( hDC == NULL ) {
 7:         // Some error...
 8:         return 0;
 9:     } // if
10:
11:     // Determine client area
12:     RECT rcClient;
13:     GetClientRect(&rcClient);
14:
15:     // Draw a message
16:     DrawText(hDC,_T("Hello from ATL!"),-1,&rcClient,
17:             DT_SINGLELINE | DT_CENTER | DT_VCENTER);
18:
19:     // Done painting
20:     EndPaint(&ps);
21:
22:     return 0;
23: }
```

This is pretty standard painting code, and I'll leave it to Petzold to describe the details, if they're not clear by inspection. I added a handler for the WM_CLOSE message in the same manner.

13

At this point I have a window that derives from CWindowImpl. CWindowImpl will register this window with Windows and enable me to process Windows messages. The two messages I elected to process at this time are WM_PAINT and WM_CLOSE. What I have not done is to actually create this window when the application initializes.

To do that, I have to modify the ATLWindows2.cpp file to add the window definition, the creation code, and the message pump. The code I use is shown in Listing 13.3.

LISTING 13.3 ATLWindows2.cpp

```
 1: // ATLWindows2.cpp : Defines the entry point for the application.
 2: //
 3:
 4: #include "stdafx.h"
 5: #include "MyAtlWindow.h"
 6:
 7: CComModule _Module;
 8:
 9: int APIENTRY WinMain(HINSTANCE hInstance,
10:                      HINSTANCE hPrevInstance,
11:                      LPSTR     lpCmdLine,
12:                      int       nCmdShow)
13: {
14:     // Initialize the ATL module
15:     _Module.Init(NULL,hInstance);
16:
17:     // Calculate a default height and width
18:     // (1/4 of screen each way)
19:     SIZE sWin = {GetSystemMetrics(SM_CXFULLSCREEN) / 3,
20:                  GetSystemMetrics(SM_CYFULLSCREEN) / 4};
21:
22:     // Calculate the initial left/top coordinate
23:     int iX = (GetSystemMetrics(SM_CXFULLSCREEN) / 2) - (sWin.cx / 2);
24:     int iY = (GetSystemMetrics(SM_CYFULLSCREEN) / 2) - (sWin.cy / 2);
25:
26:     // Provide a default screen location with
27:     // new windows centered on screen
28:     RECT rcPos = {iX,iY,(iX + sWin.cx),(iX + sWin.cy)};
29:
30:     // Create an ATL window
31:     CMyAtlWindow win;
32:     win.Create(NULL,rcPos,_T("A Real ATL Window!"));
33:     win.ShowWindow(nCmdShow);
34:
35:     // Process Windows messages...
36:     MSG msg;
37:     while ( GetMessage(&msg,0,0,0) ) {
38:         TranslateMessage(&msg);
39:         DispatchMessage(&msg);
```

```
40:    } // while
41:
42:    return 0;
43: }
```

 This code is very much like the first example, except I get a bit fancier and specify a window starting position rather than allowing Windows to place my window for me (lines 17 through 28). The code merely centers the window on the screen and makes its width and height one-third by one-fourth of the screen width. If you compile the project and execute the resulting file, you should see a window something like the one in Figure 13.3.

FIGURE 13.3

The ATLWindows2 window.

The capability to process Windows messages is crucial to any Win32 application. ATL takes much of the dirty work out of your hands by implementing a message map, which is the perfect topic to discuss next.

Windows Message Mapping

The key to managing windows is to manage the messages the window receives. Traditional Win32 programming requires you to provide a window procedure that somehow manages to process the Windows messages coming to your window. Typically, the window procedure resembles what you see in Listing 13.4 (which I extracted from what the Win32 Application that the AppWizard provides you if you select a `Hello, World` application).

13

LISTING 13.4   Traditional Win32-Style Window Procedure

```
1: LRESULT CALLBACK WndProc(HWND hWnd, UINT message, WPARAM wParam,
   ➥LPARAM lParam)
2: {
3:     int wmId, wmEvent;
4:     PAINTSTRUCT ps;
```

continues

LISTING 13.4 continued

```
 5:      HDC hdc;
 6:      TCHAR szHello[MAX_LOADSTRING];
 7:      LoadString(hInst, IDS_HELLO, szHello, MAX_LOADSTRING);
 8:
 9:      switch (message)
10:      {
11:          case WM_COMMAND:
12:              wmId    = LOWORD(wParam);
13:              wmEvent = HIWORD(wParam);
14:              // Parse the menu selections:
15:              switch (wmId)
16:              {
17:                  case IDM_ABOUT:
18:                      DialogBox(hInst, (LPCTSTR)IDD_ABOUTBOX, hWnd,
                          ➥(DLGPROC)About);
19:                      break;
20:                  case IDM_EXIT:
21:                      DestroyWindow(hWnd);
22:                      break;
23:                  default:
24:                      return DefWindowProc(hWnd, message, wParam, lParam);
25:              }
26:              break;
27:          case WM_PAINT:
28:              hdc = BeginPaint(hWnd, &ps);
29:              // TODO: Add any drawing code here...
30:              RECT rt;
31:              GetClientRect(hWnd, &rt);
32:              DrawText(hdc, szHello, strlen(szHello), &rt, DT_CENTER);
33:              EndPaint(hWnd, &ps);
34:              break;
35:          case WM_DESTROY:
36:              PostQuitMessage(0);
37:              break;
38:          default:
39:              return DefWindowProc(hWnd, message, wParam, lParam);
40:      }
41:      return 0;
42: }
```

ANALYSIS To expand the messages you want to process, you add a case to the (rather large) switch statement for each message you want to process (starting with line 9). If a message doesn't match any you want to handle, you pass it to ::DefWindowProc() for disposition, as you see in lines 24 and 39.

ATL provides you with the `CMessageMap` class, and this class is used as a base class for all ATL classes that maintain a window. The class itself is quite simple (see Listing 13.5).

LISTING 13.5   ATL's `CMessageMap` Implementation

```
1: ///////////////////////////////////////////////////////////////
2: // CMessageMap - abstract class that provides an interface for message maps
3:
4: class ATL_NO_VTABLE CMessageMap
5: {
6: public:
7:     virtual BOOL ProcessWindowMessage(HWND hWnd, UINT uMsg,
       ➥WPARAM wParam, LPARAM lParam,
8:         LRESULT& lResult, DWORD dwMsgMapID) = 0;
9: };
```

ANALYSIS   As you can see, `CMessageMap` is a pure virtual base class (line 8), which means somewhere in the code you provide you must implement the `ProcessWindowMessage()` method. This task is managed by the various message-mapping macros ATL provides, as you'll see in the next section.

Main Message Map

On the surface, ATL appears to take a different approach to message manipulation than a traditional Win32 window procedure by providing a *message map*. Messages you're interested in manipulating should be added to the map. In reality, though, the message map isn't that different from the mega-`switch` statement you see in Listing 13.4. Let's break the message mapping macros apart to see what I mean.

Starting with the `BEGIN_MSG_MAP(theClass)` macro, ATLWIN.H provides the implementation shown in Listing 13.6.

LISTING 13.6   ATL's `BEGIN_MSG_MAP()` Macro Implementation

13

```
1: ///////////////////////////////////////////////////////////////
2: // Message map
3:
4: #define BEGIN_MSG_MAP(theClass) \
5: public: \
6:     BOOL ProcessWindowMessage(HWND hWnd, UINT uMsg,
       ➥WPARAM wParam, LPARAM lParam, LRESULT& lResult,
       ➥DWORD dwMsgMapID = 0) \
7:     { \
8:         BOOL bHandled = TRUE; \
```

continues

LISTING 13.6   continued

```
 9:           hWnd; \
10:           uMsg; \
11:           wParam; \
12:           lParam; \
13:           lResult; \
14:           bHandled; \
15:           switch(dwMsgMapID) \
16:           { \
17:           case 0:
```

ANALYSIS   I've italicized the switch statement that ATL implements (line 15), which is not really that different from what you saw in Listing 13.4. Note, however, that ProcessWindowMessage() is actually implemented here, starting with line 6.

The message map is terminated by the END_MSG_MAP() macro, also found in ATLWIN.H (see Listing 13.7).

LISTING 13.7   ATL's END_MSG_MAP() Macro Implementation

```
1: #define END_MSG_MAP() \
2:           break; \
3:           default: \
4:             ATLTRACE2(atlTraceWindowing, 0, T("Invalid message map ID
              ➥(%i)\n"), dwMsgMapID); \
5:             ATLASSERT(FALSE); \
6:             break; \
7:           } \
8:           return FALSE; \
9:       }
```

ANALYSIS   This macro provides the default case of the switch statement, line 3, which merely asserts and then sets up the return value for the ProcessWindowMessage() method defined in BEGIN_MSG_MAP(theClass).

Individual message handlers are added in between the begin and end message map macros, and there is a variety of macros for this purpose. The most commonly used is MESSAGE_HANDLER(), as shown in Listing 13.8.

LISTING 13.8 ATL's MESSAGE_HANDLER() Macro Implementation

```
1: #define MESSAGE_HANDLER(msg, func) \
2:     if(uMsg == msg) \
3:     { \
4:         bHandled = TRUE; \
5:         lResult = func(uMsg, wParam, lParam, bHandled); \
6:         if(bHandled) \
7:             return TRUE; \
8:     }
```

ANALYSIS If the message coming into the window matches the msg parameter of ProcessWindowMessage(), the message is sent to the handler procedure (line 5). If the message isn't destined for processing via the map, ProcessWindowMessage() returns FALSE (line 8 from Listing 13.7).

If I clean this up a bit after expanding the macros (and I edit the code for brevity), the message map looks something like Listing 13.9.

LISTING 13.9 ATL's ProcessWindowMessage() Method (Edited)

```
 1: BOOL ProcessWindowMessage(HWND hWnd, UINT uMsg,
    ➥WPARAM wParam, LPARAM lParam, LRESULT& lResult,
    ➥DWORD dwMsgMapID = 0) \
 2:     { \\
 3:     (stuff edited)
 4:     switch(dwMsgMapID) \
 5:         { \
 6:         case 0:
 7:             if(uMsg == msg) \
 8:             { \
 9:                 bHandled = TRUE; \
10:                 lResult = func(uMsg, wParam, lParam, bHandled); \
11:                 if(bHandled) \
12:                     return TRUE; \
13:             }
14:             {more message handlers)
15:         break; \
16:         (other message maps)
17:         default: \
18:             ATLTRACE2(atlTraceWindowing, 0,
                ➥_T("Invalid message map ID (%i)\n"), dwMsgMapID); \
19:             ATLASSERT(FALSE); \
20:             break; \
21:         } \
22:     return FALSE; \
23:     }
```

13

ANALYSIS The switch statement, as you see starting with line 4, doesn't check for the actual Windows message as it would in the traditional Win32 window procedure (as it did in Listing 13.4). Rather, it checks for the message map number, the first of which is map number zero (line 6). This is your *main message map* number. You can add secondary message maps, which I'll discuss a bit further in this section. The assertion in the default case, line 18, is telling you that you're using an invalid message map number.

The messages themselves are handled within the switch's case statements as a chain of if statements. You see an example of this on line 7. When you add message handlers, you're really adding additional if statements. As messages come into your window, they're checked again and again for processing by sending them through this gauntlet of if statements. Assuming the message is accepted by one of the if statements, its handler is invoked and the message is processed accordingly, as on line 10.

The MESSAGE_HANDLER() macro is probably the most commonly used macro for mapping messages, but there are others. Some, like MESSAGE_RANGE_HANDLER(msgFirst, msgLast, func), map a range of messages to a single handler. Others are designed to manage a specific Windows message, as WM_COMMAND is by the COMMAND_HANDLER(id, code, func) macro or WM_NOTIFY is by the NOTIFY_HANDLER(id, cd, func) macro. The remaining message mapping macros are used for more specialized cases, so I won't describe them here. The online documentation has a complete list of the macros and their uses.

The handler procedures themselves are declared in this way:

```
LRESULT MessageHandler(UINT uMsg, WPARAM wParam,
                       LPARAM lParam, BOOL& bHandled);
LRESULT CommandHandler(WORD wNotifyCode, WORD wID,
                       HWND hWndCtl, BOOL& bHandled);
LRESULT NotifyHandler(int idCtrl, LPNMHDR pnmh, BOOL& bHandled);
```

The name of the individual handler is usually related to the Windows message it manages, such as OnPaint(...) for the WM_PAINT message.

Returning to the message map itself, the switch statement implements a zero case and a default case. This clearly assumes that there is a mechanism for adding additional message map case statements. In fact, there is. ATL calls these alternate message maps, which I'll discuss next.

Alternate Message Maps

The additional, or *alternate*, message maps are added using the ALT_MSG_MAP(msgMapID) macro:

```
#define ALT_MSG_MAP(msgMapID) \
        break; \
        case msgMapID:
```

The most common use of the alternate message map is to process messages on behalf of child (subclassed) controls. The macro simply adds another case to the message map switch statement. Unlike the main message map, which always uses the map number of zero, the alternate message maps can use any value you wish, although they traditionally start with one and increment the map number from there.

Chained Message Maps

Instead of using an alternate map, you might find that your particular ATL (C++) window class is derived from a base ATL class that also implements a message map. The macros I've shown don't provide a mechanism for passing messages to your C++ base class(es). For this, you use the CHAIN_MSG_MAP(theChainClass) macro of one of the related variations you'll find in the online documentation (such as for an alternate map or individual message). The CHAIN_MSG_MAP(theChainClass) macro is placed at the end of your message map to forward all messages to the base class's map.

Reflected Messages

If your window is destined to contain an ActiveX control, it's possible for the ActiveX control to send your window messages, which you actually want the ActiveX control to manage for you. These are called *reflected messages*, because your window receives the message, and then ships it right back to the ActiveX control for processing (as light is reflected from a mirror). Your window will use the REFLECT_NOTIFICATIONS() macro to ship off the messages whereas the ActiveX's message map will typically use the DEFAULT_REFLECTION_HANDLER() macro to process them.

13

Subclassing Windows with ATL

I've mentioned subclassing previously in this lesson, and in the book, but now it's time to actually see how to subclass a window using ATL. As you may remember, *subclassing* a window refers to establishing a new window procedure to handle specific Windows messages on behalf of the subclassed window, which already has its own window procedure. This really means you're going to intercept and process a few selected Windows messages to tailor the behavior of the other window. This happens most often when you want to paint a given control differently, but there are other situations you might want to manage as well.

ATL provides a class designed just for containing windows and subclassing, CContainedWindow. For example, CContainedWindow::SubclassWindow() enables you to specify the window handle of the window to subclass, as well as the alternate message map number to use for processing the messages you want to tailor.

To show you subclassing in action, I created an example application that uses a sub-classed edit control. I'll save the fun painting work for Day 15, "Custom Controls: Basic Control Development Techniques," when you'll develop a new custom control. For this example, I'll handle the WM_PASTE message instead. Whenever text is pasted into the edit control, the edit control will reverse the string. (If I tied a date to the new control, it would make an excellent April Fool's Day joke!) The example will also provide a platform for demonstrating the use of CDialogImpl, because I'll create a dialog-based application using just ATL.

Creating a Dialog-Based ATL Application

Unfortunately, as I mentioned previously, there is no wizard available to create ATL applications. However, you can add a dialog object to your ATL COM server. This gives you a choice—either you create a dialog-based application from scratch or you create an EXE ATL server, add a dialog object, and remove the code you don't require. I've done it both ways. To be honest, neither way is better than the other. For this example, however, I chose to implement the application from scratch as I did in the previous two sample applications this lesson.

I began by creating a basic Win32 application, as before. I edited the STDAFX.H file to include ATL support, but I added a twist I'll discuss momentarily. I then edited the main application's procedure to invoke a dialog box that I created from CDialogImpl. All of this wasn't necessarily difficult, but there are a lot of in-between steps.

I'll begin with STDAFX.H. I again removed the inclusion of WINDOWS.H and the TODO comment, replacing it with this code:

```
// ATL support
#include <atlbase.h>
extern CComModule _Module;
#include <atlwin.h>
#include <atlcom.h>
#include <atlcontrols.h>
```

The change from the two previous examples is the addition of the ATLCONTROLS.H file. If you did nothing more than compile the project at this time, however, it would fail.

That's because there is no ATLCONTROLS.H file included with the standard release of ATL. And yet, I can't imagine writing a Win32 application without this file!

The file actually comes from the ATLCON sample program that ships with Visual Studio. Someone on the Visual Studio development team took the time to wrap each and every standard and common Windows control with an ATL C++ class, and then they shipped their work with this sample. If you write Win32 applications with ATL, you'll be glad they did, for now you don't have to do the same yourself. Open the sample and copy the file to your local drive, or use the copy I've provided with this day's sample applications.

Tip

I personally took this a step further and copied the file to my Visual Studio directory, under the ATL header subdirectory. The compiler will automatically find it there when I reuse it.

Take the edit control as an example. ATLCONTROLS.H provides the CEdit classes that wrap the additional functionality of the edit control window over and above whatever a standard window provides. For example, CEdit provides a SetSel() method to set the selected text within the edit control. It manages sending the EM_SETSEL command to the control window for you.

Space won't permit me to describe every class and every method in the ATLCON-TROLS.H file. However, each templated class is defined at the beginning of the file, so I do recommend you take a quick peek to see what's there. Another thing you'll notice is that the file creates a new namespace, ATLControls. The edit control wrapper class is then really ATLControls::CEdit, unless you use the namespace keyword in your source files:

```
namespace ATLControls;
```

Now you can use the simple CEdit class name when defining your own edit control variables. I'll return to ATLCONTROLS.H and CEdit shortly.

After I modified STDAFX.H, I modified the main application loop, which you'll find in ATLWindows3.cpp. I've placed the code you'll find there in Listing 13.10.

13

LISTING 13.10   ATLWindows3.cpp

```
 1: // ATLWindows3.cpp : Defines the entry point for the application.
 2: //
 3:
 4: #include "stdafx.h"
 5: #include "MainDlg.h"
 6:
 7: CComModule _Module;
 8:
 9: int APIENTRY WinMain(HINSTANCE hInstance,
10:                      HINSTANCE hPrevInstance,
11:                      LPSTR     lpCmdLine,
12:                      int       nCmdShow)
13: {
14:     // Initialize the ATL module
15:     _Module.Init(NULL,hInstance);
16:
17:     // For a dialog-based application, simply
18:     // declare an instance of your ATL dialog
19:     // class and call its CDialogImpl::DoModal()
20:     // method.  The dialog window class contains
21:     // its own message loop, so none is required
22:     // here.  When the dialog box is dismissed,
23:     // just return from the WinMain() function.
24:     CMainDlg dlg;
25:     dlg.DoModal();
26:
27:     return 0;
28: }
```

ANALYSIS   The WinMain() function is simplicity itself, mostly because the dialog box implements its own message loop. All you really have to do is initialize the ATL module (line 15), create a modal dialog box, use it, and finally just return from the function (lines 24 and 25). The trick is the creation of the dialog box, because you'll need to write the entire file's content from scratch. In this case, I had to create the MainDlg.h file shown in Listing 13.11.

LISTING 13.11   MainDlg.h

```
1: // MainDlg.h : Declaration of the CMainDlg
2:
3: #ifndef __MAINDLG_H_
4: #define __MAINDLG_H_
5:
6: #include "resource.h"        // main symbols
7: #include <atlhost.h>
```

```
 8: #include <string.h>
 9:
10: extern CComModule _Module;
11:
12: //////////////////////////////////////////////////////////////////
13: // CMainDlg
14: class CMainDlg :
15:     public CDialogImpl<CMainDlg>
16: {
17: public:
18:     CMainDlg() :
19:         m_CNormalEdit(this),
20:         m_CSubEdit(NULL,this,1),
21:         m_hIcon(NULL)
22:     {
23:     }
24:
25:     ~CMainDlg()
26:     {
27:     }
28:
29:     enum { IDD = IDD_MAINDLG };
30:
31: BEGIN_MSG_MAP(CMainDlg)
32:     // Main message map
33:     MESSAGE_HANDLER(WM_INITDIALOG, OnInitDialog)
34:     MESSAGE_HANDLER(WM_SYSCOMMAND, OnSysCommand)
35:     COMMAND_ID_HANDLER(IDCANCEL, OnCancel)
36: ALT_MSG_MAP(1)
37:     // Alternate message map
38:     MESSAGE_HANDLER(WM_PASTE, OnPaste)
39: END_MSG_MAP()
40:
41: // Implementation
42:     LRESULT OnInitDialog(UINT uMsg, WPARAM wParam, LPARAM lParam,
        ➥BOOL& bHandled)
43:     {
44:         // Establish this dialog as the main application
45:         // window.  Start by adding the "About..." menu
46:         // item to system menu.
47:         //
48:         // IDM_ABOUTBOX must be in the system command range.
49:         ATLASSERT((IDM_ABOUTBOX & 0xFFF0) == IDM_ABOUTBOX);
50:         ATLASSERT(IDM_ABOUTBOX < 0xF000);
51:
52:         HMENU hSysMenu = GetSystemMenu(FALSE);
53:         if (hSysMenu != NULL) {
54:             TCHAR strAboutMenu[_MAX_PATH+1];
```

continues

13

LISTING **13.11**   continued

```
55:                    LoadString(_Module.GetResourceInstance(),
56:                              IDS_ABOUTBOX,
57:                              strAboutMenu,
58:                              _MAX_PATH);
59:                if ( lstrlen(strAboutMenu) > 0 ) {
60:                    AppendMenu(hSysMenu,MF_SEPARATOR,0,NULL);
61:                    AppendMenu(hSysMenu,MF_STRING,IDM_ABOUTBOX, strAboutMenu);
62:                } // if
63:            } // if
64:
65:        // Set the icon for this dialog
66:        m_hIcon = LoadIcon(_Module.GetResourceInstance(),
67:                          MAKEINTRESOURCE(IDR_MAINFRAME));
68:        if ( m_hIcon != NULL ) {
69:            SetIcon(m_hIcon,TRUE);  // Set big icon
70:            SetIcon(m_hIcon,FALSE); // Set small icon
71:        } // if
72:
73:        // Subclass the "sub" edit control
74:        m_CSubEdit.SubclassWindow(GetDlgItem(IDC_SUBEDIT));
75:
76:        // Attach the "norm" edit control
77:        m_CNormalEdit.Attach(GetDlgItem(IDC_NORMEDIT));
78:
79:        // Shove some text in the normal edit control, select
80:        // the text, then provide it the focus
81:        m_CNormalEdit.SetWindowText(_T("Copy me to the clipboard..."));
82:        m_CNormalEdit.SetSel(0,-1);
83:        m_CNormalEdit.SetFocus();
84:
85:        return 0;  // we set the focus, so return zero
86:    }
87:
88:    LRESULT OnSysCommand(UINT uMsg, WPARAM wParam, LPARAM lParam,
       ➥BOOL& bHandled)
89:    {
90:        if ((wParam & 0xFFF0) == IDM_ABOUTBOX) {
91:            CSimpleDialog<IDD_ABOUTBOX,TRUE> dlgAbout;
92:            dlgAbout.DoModal();
93:            return 0;
94:        } // if
95:
96:    return ::DefWindowProc(m_hWnd,uMsg,wParam,lParam);
97:    }
98:
99:    LRESULT OnCancel(WORD wNotifyCode, WORD wID, HWND hWndCtl,
       ➥BOOL& bHandled)
100:    {
101:        EndDialog(wID);
```

```
102:         return 0;
103:     }
104:
105:     LRESULT OnPaste(UINT uMsg, WPARAM wParam, LPARAM lParam,
         ➥BOOL& bHandled)
106:     {
107:         // Note the dialog is handling the WM_PASTE message
108:         // for the subclassed edit control.  Is there a more
109:         // object-oriented way to handle this?  (That will
110:         // be an exercise at the end of the day...)
111:         //
112:         // Check for the CF_TEXT format
113:         if ( !IsClipboardFormatAvailable(CF_TEXT) ) {
114:             // Text format is not supported
115:             return 0;
116:         } // if
117:
118:         // Pull the data from the clipboard
119:         if ( ::OpenClipboard(m_hWnd) ) {
120:             HANDLE hData = GetClipboardData(CF_TEXT);
121:             if ( hData != NULL ) {
122:                 // Assign the data to the edit control
123:                 LPTSTR pstrText =
124:                 reinterpret_cast<LPTSTR>(GlobalLock(hData));
125:                 if ( pstrText != NULL ) {
126:                     // Reverse the characters of the string
127:                     _strrev(pstrText);
128:
129 :                     // Assign text to the edit control (allow
130:                     // Undo)
131:                     m_CSubEdit.ReplaceSel(pstrText,TRUE);
132:
133:                     // Release the clipboard memory
134:                     GlobalUnlock(hData);
135:                 } // if
136:             } // if
137:
138:             // Close the clipboard
139:             CloseClipboard();
140:         } // if
141:
142:         return 0;
143:     }
144:
145: // Implementation
146: protected:
147:     HICON m_hIcon;
148:
```

13

continues

LISTING 13.11   continued

```
149:      CContainedWindowT<ATLControls::CEdit> m_CNormalEdit;
150:      CContainedWindowT<ATLControls::CEdit> m_CSubEdit;
151: };
152:
153: #endif //__MAINDLG_H_
```

ANALYSIS   Whew, there is a lot of code in Listing 13.11. The first thing to note is the definition of the class, starting with line 15:

```
class CMainDlg :
    public CDialogImpl<CMainDlg>
{
    (stuff)
};
```

Here you see CMainDlg inherits publicly from CDialogImpl (line 15).

If you look to the end of Listing 13.11 you'll see two CContainedWindowT attributes (lines 149 and 150):

```
CContainedWindowT<ATLControls::CEdit> m_CNormalEdit;
CContainedWindowT<ATLControls::CEdit> m_CSubEdit;
```

The dialog box itself will contain two edit controls, one of which will be subclassed. Note I used the templated version of CContainedWindow because I had a specific C++ class in mind to deal with the window itself (ATLControls::CEdit). The CMainDlg constructor constructs these variables (starting at line 18 of Listing 13.11):

```
CMainDlg() :
        m_CNormalEdit(this),
        m_CSubEdit(NULL,this,1),
        m_hIcon(NULL)
    {
    }
```

The "normal" edit control is constructed with a pointer to the dialog class (this provides the main message map), whereas the subclassed control is constructed with the parent class pointer, as well as a window class (NULL) and an alternate message map number (one in this case).

I then defined a public enumeration to present the dialog's template ID (line 29):

```
enum { IDD = IDD_MAINDLG };
```

The ID enumerator is followed by the message maps, starting with line 31. Note I have an alternate map that will be used to process messages for the subclassed edit control (line 36):

```
BEGIN_MSG_MAP(CMainDlg)
    // Main message map
    MESSAGE_HANDLER(WM_INITDIALOG, OnInitDialog)
    MESSAGE_HANDLER(WM_SYSCOMMAND, OnSysCommand)
    COMMAND_ID_HANDLER(IDCANCEL, OnCancel)
ALT_MSG_MAP(1)
    // Alternate message map
    MESSAGE_HANDLER(WM_PASTE, OnPaste)
END_MSG_MAP()
```

The message handlers follow the message map. In `OnInitDialog()`, I do a couple of things. For one, I modify the system menu to include an About dialog box. For another, I add an icon to the application. Normally, Windows would do this, but not in the case of a dialog box as the main application window. I admit that I took this idea from the MFC dialog-based application. The code of most interest to subclassing and containing windows is the following, starting with line 73:

```
// Subclass the "sub" edit control
m_CSubEdit.SubclassWindow(GetDlgItem(IDC_SUBEDIT));

// Attach the "norm" edit control
m_CNormalEdit.Attach(GetDlgItem(IDC_NORMEDIT));

// Shove some text in the normal edit control, select
// the text, then provide it the focus
m_CNormalEdit.SetWindowText(_T("Copy me to the clipboard..."));
m_CNormalEdit.SetSel(0,-1);
m_CNormalEdit.SetFocus();
```

It's here I actually subclass the one edit control and attach the other to a regular `AtlControls::CEdit` class. I place some initial text in the normal edit control, select it all, then set the focus to that control.

The `OnSysCommand()` handler is there merely to manage the About dialog. Here you see an example of using `CSimpleDialog`. If the system menu command isn't a request to view the About dialog, I pass the message off to the Windows default message handler. If it asks to see the About information, I create an instance of the About dialog and wait for the user to dismiss it.

Of course, because I'm using a dialog box, I must call `EndDialog()` to actually destroy the dialog box window and break out of the dialog's message loop. I manage this in `OnCancel()`.

The interesting subclassing work is performed in `OnPaste()`, but I'll save that for a moment and finish off the remainder of the tasks necessary to create the application. I've already referenced two dialog templates, a string for the About box menu, the application icon, and the RESOURCE.H file, so I need to create some resources.

13

Frankly, I resorted to the old-fashioned mechanism of code reuse. That is, I opened an existing MFC application and copied the resources from there into the ATLWindows3 sample project. You can see this if you look at the icon itself, for it implements the standard MFC icon. To reuse resources as I have, simply open the other project's resource file and drag and drop the items you're interested in using. I already had an MFC dialog-based application project open, so it coincided well. I took the main application's dialog, the About dialog, the version information, the string table, and the icon and dropped them into ATLWindows3 and made several minor edits (mostly to change the name to ATLWindows3). RESOURCE.H was automatically updated as I dragged the resources into my current project.

At this point, you should have everything you require to compile and test the application. If you try this yourself, you'll quickly appreciate the code the wizards provide for you. In any case, let's see what happens when you paste text into the subclassed edit control.

Edit Control Subclassed Behavior

The code is in place to actually perform the work and provide the benefit of subclassing the edit control in the first place. As you recall, I added an alternate message map to handle the edit control messages I want to tailor:

```
ALT_MSG_MAP(1)
    // Alternate message map
    MESSAGE_HANDLER(WM_PASTE, OnPaste)
```

In this case, I'm going to change the way pasting is handled by the control. I mapped in the WM_PASTE message and provided an OnPaste() handler:

```
LRESULT OnPaste(UINT uMsg, WPARAM wParam, LPARAM lParam, BOOL& bHandled)
{
    // Note the dialog is handling the WM_PASTE message
    // for the subclassed edit control.  Is there a more
    // object-oriented way to handle this?  (That will
    // be an exercise at the end of the hour...)
    //
    // Check for the CF_TEXT format
    if ( !IsClipboardFormatAvailable(CF_TEXT) ) {
        // Text format is not supported
        return 0;
    } // if

    // Pull the data from the clipboard
    if ( ::OpenClipboard(m_hWnd) ) {
        HANDLE hData = GetClipboardData(CF_TEXT);
        if ( hData != NULL ) {
            // Assign the data to the edit control
            LPTSTR pstrText =
```

```
                    reinterpret_cast<LPTSTR>(GlobalLock(hData));
        if ( pstrText != NULL ) {
            // Reverse the characters of the string
            _strrev(pstrText);

            // Assign text to the edit control (allow
            // Undo)
            m_CSubEdit.ReplaceSel(pstrText,TRUE);

            // Release the clipboard memory
            GlobalUnlock(hData);
        } // if
    } // if

    // Close the clipboard
    CloseClipboard();
} // if

return 0;
}
```

The majority of the code is basic clipboard work. If it looks like hieroglyphics, you can find a description of it in the online documentation (look under the Platform SDK, Windows Base Services, Interprocess Communication, Clipboard in the online manuals). The main line of code, however, is italicized:

```
strrev(pstrText);
```

This is where I reverse the string that would normally be pasted. This is clearly abnormal edit control behavior, so if the string you paste into the application's edit control is reversed, you know the subclassing code is working. In fact, you can see this in Figure 13.4, which shows you ATLWindows3 in action.

FIGURE 13.4

The results of using the subclassed edit control.

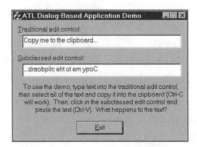

13

Just imagine the things you can do to a Windows control if you can do this to an edit control! I'll revisit subclassing in Day 15. That will lead you directly into custom ActiveX controls.

Summary

Even with as much as I packed into this lesson, I barely scratched the surface regarding the use of ATL to manage windows. ATL provides a lot of capability. You'll need a firm footing in basic Win32 application programming to fully exploit these possibilities, however.

I began the hour by discussing ATL's approach to windowing and by showing you the basic ATL windowing classes. I then gave a short example of a window managed by an ATL class, although it didn't do much. I followed that example with a more useful window example in which I used ATL's CWindowImpl class. I also showed you how to add message handlers to your window classes using the Message Handler wizard.

Then I went on to discuss ATL message mapping and how ATL's implementation compares with a more traditional approach. I described several types of ATL message maps, including the main map, alternate maps, chained maps, and reflected messages. The final topic I discussed was subclassing windows using CContainedWindow, although I also described in some detail how to create a dialog-based ATL application from scratch.

In Day 14, "ATL and Automation: Creating RoboObjects," I discuss automation and COM, which when combined with subclassing and custom control development, leads you to ActiveX and the capabilities you have there to enhance your applications using ATL.

Q&A

Q Is there a significant advantage to using ATL versus, say, MFC for application development?

A Yes and no. With ATL, you trade a more robust application framework for a smaller executable file that has no dependencies on external DLLs (unless you code it to be so). With MFC, you have a wonderfully robust application framework, but your executable images are much larger and will be tied to the MFC DLLs unless you link them statically (further increasing the size). As is usual for ATL, the windowing aspects are lean and mean, but quite effective.

Q Do I need this information if I'm just writing COM code?

A That's hard to answer specifically. In general, I'd say that you should have some exposure to the ATL windowing classes even if all you write is COM code. You might someday need to subclass a given control, for example, and the easiest way to do that is by using the ATL windowing classes. At least, these classes are tools you can fall back on should you someday require their support.

Workshop

The Workshop is designed to help you anticipate possible questions, review what you've learned, and get you thinking about how to put your knowledge into practice. The answers to the quiz are in Appendix A, "Answers."

Quiz

1. Which ATL window class is best for general-purpose window implementation? For child controls?

2. Why do you normally derive a class from the ATL windowing classes rather than use them directly?

3. What is an ATL message map and what ATL class provides for their implementation?

4. What are the four types of ATL message maps?

5. What is the purpose of window subclassing?

Exercises

1. Add a handler to the ATLWindows2 example to process mouse movement messages (WM_MOUSEMOVE) and print the mouse cursor position in the main window.

2. Create your own dialog-based ATL application (to get a feel for how it's done).

3. The alternate message map of the CMainDlg class in the ATLWindows3 example processes the subclassed messages for the child control. Can you suggest a more object-oriented approach? If so, how would you implement it?

13

WEEK 2

DAY 14

ATL and Automation: Creating RoboObjects

A main focus of COM in recent years is clearly automation. *Automation* refers to a wide variety of tasks, from the insertion of an object into a Word document to controlling an ActiveX control in an HTML document. When I refer to automation in this book, I'm specifically referring to a scripting capability, meaning that interpreted scripts (versus compiled code) can execute using COM objects available on the local system. The script itself glues the COM objects together, much as mortar connects bricks. The goal is to have the developer provide the reusable COM object (the brick) and allow the user to decide how to best employ the object. The user does this by writing a script (the mortar).

If you've ever written a Visual Studio or Microsoft Office macro, you've already written a script. Visual Studio, for example, exposes *scriptable objects* to expose functionality inherent in Visual Studio. Almost anything you can do with Visual Studio interactively, you can do with a script through the collection of Visual Studio scriptable objects. The objects together form the Visual Studio *object model*, which is how the script author views Visual Studio.

Today, you begin to see how COM implements automation and why COM implements the dual interface. For example, you'll see

- More about the dual interface and how ATL implements it
- What `IDispatch` provides that supports scripting
- How to invoke the `IDispatch` methods versus what the custom interface provides
- More about variants
- How a `safearray` is used in automation

The Dual Interface

If you refer to a classic COM programming text, such as Dale Rogerson's *Inside COM* (Microsoft Press, ISBN 1-57231-349-8), you will see references to the dual interface. The use of the dual interface is prevalent in COM. I've defined a *dual interface* as an interface that derives from `IDispatch` rather than from `IUnknown` directly. That definition is fine for the topics I presented earlier in the book.

Why is deriving from `IDispatch` more special than deriving from any other interface? Why the distinctive "dual interface" name? The answer lies with something known as the *dispinterface*.

Take a step back a moment and think about how you've used the COM objects you've developed so far. You create a C++ client application that uses a file (or files) output from MIDL. If you open those files and examine their contents, you find a lot of C and C++ definitions of the COM object you're about to use. When you compile your client code, the compiler opens the MIDL-generated files and extracts from them the definition of the COM interfaces you're using from your client. If there is a syntax error, such as a missing parameter, the compiler flags the error, and you correct your code. This is the classic way you use COM objects.

It's not, however, the only way you *can* use COM objects. In more formal terms, the classic way uses the COM object in question through *early binding*. The term *binding* itself refers to associating the COM object with your client. *Early binding* means you perform this association prior to the COM object's use, that is, at the time you compiled your client. If there is a way to bind a COM object early, there probably is a way to bind it later.

In fact, there is, and it's (not surprisingly) called *late binding*. *Late binding* means the COM object is associated with the client at runtime. If a script is missing an interface method's parameter, the scripting engine won't be aware of the error until that particular line of script is executed. The script and scripting engine have no foreknowledge of what the particular COM object exports until the script is run, and even then the scripting engine won't flag an error until the bad line in the script is executed.

But how did the script, or more precisely the scripting engine, know what interfaces and methods the COM object exposed? The answer is that the scripting engine read the COM object's type library, which contains most of the information contained within the original IDL file. The script identified the COM object by ProgID, and when the scripting engine executed the object instantiation (by ProgID), it converted the ProgID to a CLSID. It then loaded the COM object, rummaged through the type library, and stored some intermediate information away for later use. Perhaps the scripting engine will merely keep a pointer to the type library and look up every call as the script executes the object's methods. The engine might also create a memory-based image of interfaces and methods and query that when the script uses the COM object. These details are left to the script-engine designers, but the common thread here is the type library is consulted to determine the object's capability.

Another aspect of late binding is that the addresses of the object's methods aren't known beforehand, as they are when a compiled client uses the interface. In your C++ code, you use a *pointer* to a COM object to access its methods. A pointer is an address in memory, and this presupposes you can calculate the address in question. Scripts cannot do this, so they have to have some other mechanism for calling an interface's methods.

Scripts use something known as a *dispinterface*, or *dispatch interface*. In this case, all the object's methods are assigned a numerical identifier known as a DISPID, or *dispatch ID*. The script passes these DISPIDs to the dispinterface, which then executes the method on behalf of the script. In other words, the dispinterface provides a way to indirectly execute an object's methods without a pointer to the method in question. As you've probably guessed, IDispatch implements a dispinterface. When you use IDispatch as your object's base interface, you have not only your custom interface, but also a dispinterface—hence the name *dual* interface. Let's look at IDispatch a little more closely.

> **Note**
>
> IDispatch, as you'll see, is static by nature. Everything the interface supports is compiled into the type library. Modern, more dynamic scripting engines use the IDispatchEx interface, which I won't cover here. The basic concepts still apply, however.

14

IDispatch

IDispatch provides only four methods, although their implementation can be quite challenging:

- GetTypeInfoCount()
- GetTypeInfo()
- GetIDsOfNames()
- Invoke()

Based upon my previous description, you can probably guess what each of these methods does and why it's important. GetTypeInfoCount() retrieves the number of type interfaces the object supplies, either zero (none) or one (the object contains a type library). If the object does have a type library, GetTypeInfo() can be used to retrieve its ITypeInfo pointer to peruse the type library. Because methods are executed by DISPID, but are referenced by name in the script, GetIDsOfNames() converts the method name (string) to DISPID (integer). It also provides for parameter checking by actually accepting an array of strings, the first of which is the method name followed by any arguments. If the arguments don't correspond to the method, GetIDsOfNames() will return an error (DISP_E_UNKNOWNNAME). Finally, there is Invoke(), which is used to execute the method associated with the given DISPID. Where do DISPIDs come from?

Dispatch Identifiers

They come from you, the COM object's designer/implementer! Think back to Day 7, "The ATL Object Wizard: Customizing the Basic ATL Framework," where I discussed COM object properties. You might recall the IDL code that defined the IAddPropDemo interface (see Listing 14.1).

LISTING 14.1 IAddPropDemo Interface Definition

```
 1: [
 2:     object,
 3:     uuid(49E7910C-5431-11D3-896D-0000E8409B63),
 4:     dual,
 5:     helpstring("IAddPropDemo Interface"),
 6:     pointer_default(unique)
 7: ]
 8: interface IAddPropDemo : IDispatch
 9: {
10:     [id(1), helpstring("method SomeMethod")] HRESULT SomeMethod();
11:     [propget, id(2), helpstring("property SomeProperty")]
        ➥HRESULT SomeProperty([out, retval] short *pVal);
12:     [propput, id(2), helpstring("property SomeProperty")]
        ➥HRESULT SomeProperty([in] short newVal);
13:     [propget, id(3), helpstring("property SomeProperty2")]
        ➥HRESULT SomeProperty2([out, retval] Colors *pVal);
14:     [propput, id(3), helpstring("property SomeProperty2")]
        ➥HRESULT SomeProperty2([in] Colors newVal);
15: };
```

ANALYSIS Because the object is marked with the dual attribute (line 4) and derives from Idispatch (line 8), each method has an id() attribute (lines 10–14). Even though some methods have the same ID attribute (these are the property methods, one is in and one is out), the IDs run in order, and every method has an ID. Although there is no requirement that the IDs start at one or be contiguous (the wizard does this for you), each method that is to be executed through Invoke() must have an id() attribute. This is the DISPID that client scripts will use to execute the given method.

Now that you've seen a bit more about IDispatch and how a script might execute methods through Invoke(), it's time to see how ATL implements IDispatch.

ATL and `IDispatch`

Referring back to Day 7, you can see ATL derived the sample COM server from the IDispatchImpl template:

```
class ATL_NO_VTABLE CMyThirdATLObj :
    public CComObjectRootEx<CComSingleThreadModel>,
    public IDispatchImpl<IAddPropDemo, &IID_IAddPropDemo,
➥&LIBID_DAY7SERVER2Lib>,
    public CComControl<CMyThirdATLObj>,
    (edited for brevity)
{
    (edited for brevity)
};
```

IDispatchImpl takes several parameters as input:

```
template< class T, const IID* piid, const GUID* plibid,
         WORD wMajor = 1, WORD wMinor = 0,
         class tihclass = CComTypeInfoHolder >
class IDispatchImpl : public T
```

The parameters IDispatchImpl accepts are shown in Table 14.1

Table 14.1 IDispatchImpl Input Parameters

Parameter	Purpose
T	The dual interface (the specialization parameter)
piid	A pointer to T's IID
plibid	A pointer to T's LIBID
wMajor	The major version of the type library
wMinor	The minor version of the type library
tihclass	The class used to manage the type information for T

14

Most of the parameters make sense, given what you know about IDispatch. Clearly, ATL wants the interface pointer, the IID, and the library ID. The major and minor values are used if you go with the default tihclass value of CComTypeInfoHolder.

The secret to ATL's implementation of IDispatch is in CComTypeInfoHolder. It defines several public attributes (see Listing 14.2).

LISTING 14.2   CComTypeInfoHolder Public Attributes

```
 1: const GUID* m_pguid;
 2: const GUID* m_plibid;
 3: WORD m_wMajor;
 4: WORD m_wMinor;
 5:
 6: ITypeInfo* m_pInfo;
 7: long m_dwRef;
 8: struct stringdispid
 9: {
10:     CComBSTR bstr;
11:     int nLen;
12:     DISPID id;
13: };
14: stringdispid* m_pMap;
15: int m_nCount;
```

ANALYSIS m_pInfo, line 6, clearly saves the type library ITypeInfo pointer, but to speed things up, CComTypeInfoHolder keeps an array of method strings and their corresponding DISPIDs. This is the purpose of the stringdispid structure definition in lines 8–13. Whenever GetIDsOfNames() is called, CComTypeInfoHolder caches the string and its DISPID for later lookup (through m_pMap, line 14), thus speeding things up a bit for subsequent DISPID conversions.

ATL and IDispatchImpl take this one step further, as IDispatchImpl declares a static attribute _tih through which all the DISPIDs are executed (from ATLCOM.H):

static _tihclass _tih;

IDispatchImpl makes IDispatch::Invoke() calls through _tih (this is from IDispatchImpl in ATLCOM.H), as shown in Listing 14.3.

LISTING 14.3   IDispatchImpl Invoke() Implementation

```
1: STDMETHOD(Invoke)(DISPID dispidMember, REFIID riid,
2:     LCID lcid, WORD wFlags, DISPPARAMS* pdispparams,
       ➥VARIANT* pvarResult, EXCEPINFO* pexcepinfo, UINT* puArgErr)
```

LISTING 14.3   continued

```
3: {
4:     return _tih.Invoke((IDispatch*)this, dispidMember, riid, lcid,
5:                         wFlags, pdispparams, pvarResult, pexcepinfo,
6:                         puArgErr);
7: }
```

ANALYSIS As you can see, IDispatchImpl calls the _tih::Invoke() method in line 4, which (by default) maps to CComTypeInfoHolder::Invoke().

The fact that _tih is static supports a system-wide limitation in the use of IDispatch. There can be only a single dispinterface for a given COM object. Actually, you can implement as many IDispatch-based interfaces as you want in your COM object. It's just that the scripting clients will only use the interface marked as default in the type library definition of the IDL file. ATL supports this limitation by creating the single, static _tih. There are ways to get around this. If you find this limitation to be a problem for your architecture, I recommend you look to Richard Grimes' *Professional ATL Programming* from Wrox Press, ISBN 1-861001-4-01, for solutions to this limitation.

Invoking Methods

Now that you have some IDispatch background information, you can probably see how IDispatch is used. The client has two options for calling the interface's methods—it calls the method directly using the custom interface, or it negotiates the DISPID with the IDispatch interface and use what it finds with IDispatch::Invoke(). I'll briefly review both cases.

Invoke()

Although it might sound simple on the surface, it takes quite a bit of code to support using Invoke() from a client. After all, the client is probably using late binding, so before it can call Invoke(), or even GetIDsOfNames(), the client has to determine if there is a type library available by using GetTypeInfoCount(). If there is one, the client has to rummage though the type library, after calling GetTypeInfo() to obtain the base ITypeInfo pointer.

Only after all the type library work has been completed can the client determine what methods are available. Even then, the client will have to convert the textual representation of the method (which was coded into the script or other source location) to a DISPID prior to actually invoking the method.

14

My point is that, if you're concerned about performance, given a choice, you probably don't want to use the dispinterface side of your dual interface. Sometimes you don't have a choice, such as when you are using a script or after you have dropped an ActiveX control into your project using the *Components and Controls Gallery*. In this case, the file that Visual Studio generates uses IDispatch::Invoke() through MFC's CWnd::InvokeHelper() method, although you are using early binding, which does save some time. In most cases, however, when using a dual interface from C++, you have the option to use the custom interface.

Custom Interface Access

If you look back to Day 9, "Creating C++ Test Clients: You Can't Test What You Can't Execute," the examples I created used an ActiveX control. Three of the four examples used the custom interface, IDemoMFCClient, versus the dispinterface. Although this might have seemed an odd thing to do with an ActiveX control, it was a perfectly valid way to use the COM object to process the string data. True, you lost the user interface that the ActiveX control offered, but you were still able to use the object to successfully process string information. In fact, the grandfather of IDispatch, Visual Basic itself, provides you with a mechanism to bypass the dispinterface to directly access the custom interface.

Note

To use your object's custom interface, even though it is a dual interface, you create an instance of your object using the IID of the custom interface as the riid parameter to CoCreateInstance(), as you have done throughout this book.

Clearly, if you design an interface free of the requirements of the dual interface, you can pass parameters to and from the COM object in any manner you please. The dual interface, however, imposes the requirement that the parameters you pass must be variant compatible. That is, the parameters must come from the list of supported variant data types. Let's see what this is all about.

Variant Data Types

In Day 8, "ATL Object Methods: Adding Functionality to Your Interface," I described the variant as a discriminated union and discussed how ATL provides a class to help you manage variant data. I didn't really tell you *why* the variant exists in the first place. I saved that for this section.

Actually, you probably have already guessed why the variant data types exist. Scripting languages must limit the number of accepted parameter data types, and most scripting languages are by nature weakly typed (unlike C++, which is strongly typed). Most scripting languages are rather limited in their use of parameters. They don't have the rich mechanisms C and C++ provide, such as those for user-defined data types and variable argument lists. Scripting languages are limited to the predefined set of data types that the variant accepts. As a result, the Universal Marshaler was written to manage the variant data marshaling (even though no scripting engine I'm aware of can use the MTA, including Visual Basic).

The caveat here is that arrays of the variant data types can be passed into and out of variant-compatible interfaces. To do this, Microsoft created the safe array, SAFEARRAY. I'll first list the standard variant-compatible data types, and then I'll discuss the SAFEARRAY.

 Note

> Technically, clients can pass a variable number of parameters into a method, if the parameters are marked with the vararg IDL attribute and the final parameter is a SAFEARRAY.

Simple Data Types

The simple variant data types fall into two groups. There are, on the one hand, the data types themselves, and, on the other hand, there is the pointer *to* one of the data types. Table 14.1 lists the basic variant data types, their meaning, and their C++ equivalent data type. Table 14.2 shows you which data types can be passed as pointer values.

Table 14.2 Variant Data Types

Data Type	Meaning	C++ Data Type
VT_EMPTY	empty VARIANT	
VT_NULL	SQL-style NULL	
VT_I1	CHAR	char
VT_UI1	BYTE	unsigned char
VT_I2	SHORT	short

14

continues

Table 14.2 continued

Data Type	Meaning	C++ Data Type
VT_UI2	USHORT	unsigned short
VT_INT	INT	integer
VT_UINT	UINT	unsigned integer
VT_I4	LONG	long
VT_UI4	ULONG	unsigned long
VT_R4	FLOAT	float
VT_R8	DOUBLE	double
VT_DATE	DATE	DATE
VT_BSTR	BSTR	BSTR
VT_BOOL	VARIANT_BOOL	VARIANT_BOOL
VT_ERROR	SCODE	HRESULT
VT_CY	CY	CY
VT_UNKNOWN	IUnknown*	IUnknown*
VT_DISPATCH	IDispatch*	IDispatch*
VT_ARRAY	SAFE ARRAY	SAFEARRAY

Most of the data types should be familiar, although you might wonder about the CY and DATE data types. I'll leave their precise definitions to the online documentation, but essentially *CY* represents currency and a *DATE* represents a date. The DATE data type is really an 8-byte value (`double`), whereas the CY type is a structure.

As I mentioned, Table 14.2 shows you the variant data types you can pass as references by a pointer. There is an additional data type introduced here, the DECIMAL. The DECIMAL data type is used to pass large decimal values (mantissa, exponent, and sign) and is itself a structure. Note you can also pass a simple `void*`. Table 14.3 shows you which variants can be passed as pointer data types.

Table 14.3 Variant Pointer Data Types

Data Type	Meaning	C++ Data Type
VT_BYREF|VT_I1	CHAR*	char*
VT_BYREF|VT_UI1	BYTE*	unsigned char*
VT_BYREF|VT_I2	SHORT*	short*
VT_BYREF|VT_UI2	USHORT*	unsigned short*
VT_BYREF|VT_INT	INT*	integer*

Data Type	Meaning	C++ Data Type
VT_BYREF|VT_UINT	UINT*	unsigned integer*
VT_BYREF|VT_I4	LONG*	long*
VT_BYREF|VT_UI4	ULONG*	unsigned long*
VT_BYREF|VT_R4	FLOAT*	float*
VT_BYREF|VT_R8	DOUBLE*	double*
VT_BYREF|VT_DATE	DATE*	DATE*
VT_BYREF|VT_BSTR	BSTR*	BSTR*
VT_BYREF|VT_BOOL	VARIANT_BOOL*	VARIANT_BOOL*
VT_BYREF|VT_ERROR	SCODE*	HRESULT*
VT_BYREF|VT_CY	CY*	CY*
VT_BYREF|VT_UNKNOWN	IUnknown**	IUnknown**
VT_BYREF|VT_DISPATCH	IDispatch**	IDispatch**
VT_BYREF|VT_ARRAY	SAFE ARRAY*	SAFEARRAY*
VT_BYREF|VT_VARIANT	VARIANT*	VARIANT*
VT_BYREF|VT_DECIMAL	DECIMAL*	DECIMAL*
VT_BYREF	VOID*	void*

Another useful property of variants is that some of them can be *coerced*. That means they can be transformed from one data type to another. COM provides the conversion routines. They all follow the form

```
VarT1FromT2()
```

T1 is the desired variant data type, and *T2* is the original variant data type. For example, to convert a long value to a string (BSTR), you use the VarBstrFromI4() function. All the values shown in Table 14.4 can be coerced from one to another, with the exception of the *Disp* (IDispatch) value.

Table 14.4 Variant Coerced Data Types

Data Type	T1/T2 Identifier
char	I1
unsigned char	UI1
short	I2
unsigned short	UI2
long	I4

14

continues

Table 14.4 continued

Data Type	T1/T2 Identifier
unsigned long	UI4
float	R4
double	R8
DATE	Date
CY	Cy
BSTR	Bstr
BOOL	Bool
DECIMAL	Dec
IDispatch*	Disp

In the case of IDispatch, the coercion routine calls Invoke() to get the default value for the dispinterface (DISPID_VALUE) and coerces that.

Most of the coercion routines are pretty straightforward. Converting an integer to a float, for example, is fairly easy to do. Converting some of the other values can be more difficult, but the coercion routine makes intelligent decisions regarding the conversion. Coercion of a date or currency value to a string value, for example, uses the local formatting rules for each data type because the coercion can require internationalization.

You can also coerce the variant by using VariantChangeType() or CComVariant::ChangeType(). Each of these might return various failure codes, depending upon the outcome of the coercion.

Tip

If you simply want access to the variant, you can use the variant access macros you'll find in OLEAUTO.H (they're defined at the end of the file). For example, to extract the 4-byte integer value from the variant, you would use this macro:

```
V_I4(X)
```

X is the variant in question. An example use of this macro would be

```
// Assuming var is a variant representing a long value...
long i = V_I4(var);
```

Safe Arrays

A *safe array*, by COM automation definition, is an array that contains information about its size and data content. Actually, it isn't an array in the normal C++ understanding of the term. Instead, the safe array is a structure (SAFEARRAY). The base type of the array is indicated by VT_ *tag* | VT_ARRAY, which tells you the SAFEARRAY must contain variant data. In fact, the data is from a limited subset of variant data types as shown in Table 14.5.

Table 14.5 Legal SAFEARRAY Variant Data Types

Data Type	Data Type	Data Type
VT_I1	VT_UI1	VT_I2
VT_UI2	VT_INT	VT_UINT
VT_I4	VT_R4	VT_R8
VT_CY	VT_DATE	VT_BSTR
VT_DISPATCH	VT_ERROR	VT_BOOL
VT_VARIANT	VT_UNKNOWN	VT_DECIMAL
VT_RECORD		

The data referenced by an array descriptor is stored in *column-major order*, which is the same ordering scheme used by Visual Basic and FORTRAN (note, this is different than for C/C++, which is *row-major*). *Column-major* order is when the left-most dimension (as specified in the individual programming language syntax) changes within the inner-most loop. For example, consider the C/C++ code in Listing 14.4.

LISTING 14.4 C++ Row-Major Array Data Access

```
1: byte array[5][10] = {0};
2: for ( int i = 0; i < 5; i++ ) {
3:     for ( int j = 0; j < 10; j++ ) {
4:         // Assign the array value
5:         array[i][j] = i * j;
6:     } // for
7: } // for
```

In this case, each element in a given row (referenced by j) is modified before moving to the next row (referenced by i). In column-major ordering, you store the same data in the rows and columns, but the loops look like those in Listing 14.5 (still shown in C++ syntax).

14

LISTING 14.5   C++ Column-Major Data Access

```
1: byte array[10][5] = {0}; // columns first!
2: for ( int j = 0; j < 10; j++ ) {
3:     for ( int i = 0; i < 5; i++ ) {
4:         // Assign the array value
5:         array[j][i] = i * j;
6:     } // for
7: } // for
```

One access method is not necessarily better than the other. Simply put, there are two ways to do it, and the SAFEARRAY uses the other way (that is, other than the way C/C++ programmers are used to). You need to be aware of this when you access and/or modify the data contained within the SAFEARRAY using C++, or you will overrun the array bounds.

Unfortunately, there is no ATL wrapper for the SAFEARRAY, so you're forced to deal with the safe array API directly. I've included the more common safe-array API calls in Table 14.6.

> **Tip**
>
> I have seen other authors provide wrappers. Because I didn't write them, I didn't include them here. You'll find one such wrapper class on the MSDN CDs. Look for the article entitled "Article 5. The Safe OLE Way of Handling Arrays," by Bruce McKinney, April 1996. You'll find it under *Technical Articles, Visual Tools, Visual Basic, Extending Visual Basic with C++ DLLs*. You'll find a link to the source code (the CPP4VB sample) in the first article, "Extending Visual Basic with C++ DLLs."

Table 14.6   Commonly Used Safe Array API Calls

API Call	Purpose
SafeArrayCreate()	Creates a new SAFEARRAY
SafeArrayDestroy()	Destroys a SAFEARRAY
SafeArrayAccessData()	Allows direct access to the SAFEARRAY data
SafeArrayUnaccessData()	Terminates direct access to the SAFEARRAY data
SafeArrayCopy()	Creates a duplicate of an existing SAFEARRAY
SafeArrayCopyData()	Similar to SafeArrayCopy(), but copies data only (assumes the target array is properly set up)
SafeArrayGetDim()	Returns the dimensions of the SAFEARRAY
SafeArrayGetElement()	Retrieves a single element from the SAFEARRAY
SafeArrayGetElemsize()	Returns the size of the array elements (in bytes)
SafeArrayGetLBound()	Returns the lower bound for any dimension in the SAFEARRAY

API Call	Purpose
SafeArrayGetUBound()	Returns the upper bound for any dimension in the SAFEARRAY
SafeArrayLock()	Increments the lock count of the array, and places a pointer to the array data in pvData of the array descriptor
SafeArrayUnlock()	Decrements the lock count of the array so it can be destroyed or resized

There are a few more safe array API calls, and I encourage you to examine the online documentation for more information.

Using the same example as before (two-dimensional array, 10 rows, 5 columns), Listing 14.6 shows you how you would fill a safe array with data. The code itself comes from today's SADemo.cpp file.

LISTING 14.6 SADemo.cpp File Contents

```
 1: // SADemo.cpp : Defines the entry point for the console application.
 2: //
 3:
 4: #include "stdafx.h"
 5:
 6: int main(int argc, char* argv[])
 7: {
 8:     // Create the safe array
 9:     SAFEARRAY* pSA = NULL;
10:     SAFEARRAYBOUND saBound[2] = {{10, 0}, {5, 0}};
11:     pSA = SafeArrayCreate(VT_INT,2,saBound);
12:     if ( pSA == NULL ) {
13:         // Could not create the safe array
14:         cout << "***Error: could not create the safe array" << endl;
15:         return -1;
16:     } // else
17:
18:     // The safe array was created, so fill it with data
19:     cout << "Filling safe array" << endl;
20:     cout << "\tRow0\tRow1\tRow2\tRow3\tRow4" << endl;
21:     long iDims[2] = {0, 0};
22:     int iData = 0;
23:     HRESULT hr = E_FAIL;
24:     for ( iDims[0] = 0; iDims[0] < 10; iDims[0]++ ) {
25:         cout << "Col" << iDims[0] << "\t";
26:         for ( iDims[1] = 0; iDims[1] < 5; iDims[1]++ ) {
27:             // Assign the array value
28:             iData = iDims[0] * iDims[1];
29:             hr = SafeArrayPutElement(pSA,iDims,(LPVOID)&iData);
```

14

continues

LISTING 14.6 continued

```
30:                    if ( FAILED(hr) ) {
31:                        // Invalid element
32:                        cout << "xx\t";
33:                    } // if
34:                    else {
35:                        // Good element
36:                        cout << iData << "\t";
37:                    } // else
38:                } // for
39:            cout << endl;
40:        } // for
41:
42:        // Do something with the array...
43:        cout << "Retrieving safe array data" << endl;
44:        cout << "\tRow0\tRow1\tRow2\tRow3\tRow4" << endl;
45:        for ( iDims[0] = 0; iDims[0] < 10; iDims[0]++ ) {
46:            cout << "Col" << iDims[0] << "\t";
47:            for ( iDims[1] = 0; iDims[1] < 5; iDims[1]++ ) {
48:                // Assign the array value
49:                hr = SafeArrayGetElement(pSA,iDims,(LPVOID)&iData);
50:                if ( FAILED(hr) ) {
51:                    // Invalid element
52:                    cout << "xx\t";
53:                } // if
54:                else {
55:                    // Good element
56:                    cout << iData << "\t";
57:                } // else
58:            } // for
59:            cout << endl;
60:        } // for
61:
62:        // Destroy the array
63:        SafeArrayDestroy(pSA);
64:
65:        return 0;
66: }
```

ANALYSIS As you can see, there is a lot more code here than in the simple C++ array I presented earlier. Of course, some of the extra code is related to displaying the safe
array data after the array is filled.

The safe array is created in lines 8–16 using SafeArrayCreate(). I pass into the array
the variant type the array will contain (VT_INT), the dimensions of the array (2), and an
array containing the boundaries for each dimension (each stored in a SAFEARRAYBOUND
structure).

```
// Create the safe array
   SAFEARRAY* pSA = NULL;
   SAFEARRAYBOUND saBound[2] = {{10, 0}, {5, 0}};
   pSA = SafeArrayCreate(VT_INT,2,saBound);
   if ( pSA == NULL ) {
       // Could not create the safe array
       cout << "***Error: could not create the safe array" << endl;
       return -1;
   } // else
```

The SAFEARRAY is really a structure (see Listing 14.7).

LISTING 14.7   SAFEARRAY Structure Definition

```
 1: typedef struct FARSTRUCT tagSAFEARRAY {
 2:     unsigned short cDims; // Count of dimensions in this array.
 3:     unsigned short fFeatures; // Flags used by the SafeArray
 4:                               // routines.
 5: #if defined(WIN32)
 6:     unsigned long cbElements; // Size of an element of the array.
 7:                               // Does not include size of
 8:                               // pointed-to data.
 9:     unsigned long cLocks; // Number of times the array has been
10:                           // locked without corresponding unlock.
11: #else
12:     unsigned short cbElements;
13:     unsigned short cLocks;
14:     unsigned long handle; // Unused but kept for compatibility.
15: #endif
16:     void HUGEP* pvData; // Pointer to the data.
17:     SAFEARRAYBOUND rgsabound[1]; // One bound for each dimension.
18: } SAFEARRAY;
```

ANALYSIS   The members of the structure make sense, if you consider the safe array can be locked. For instance, the cDims member (line 2) keeps the number of dimensions, and fFeatures (line 3) contains flags used by the safe array API (one such flag is the contained data type). cbElements, lines 6 or 12, tells you how many bytes a given element will require for storage. cLocks, lines 9 or 13, keeps track of the number of outstanding locks the safe array has against it. There has to be a pointer to the data, which is kept in pvData, line 16. Finally, the array bounds are kept in rgsabound, line 17. Because a safe array with zero dimensions makes no sense, rgsabound is initially an array of one element, the single dimension. However, if you size the safe array with multiple dimensions, the API calls will handle growing the rgsabound array to contain the extra dimension information.

14

The SAFEARRAYBOUND is also a structure, and it looks like this:

```
typedef struct tagSAFEARRAYBOUND {
    unsigned long cElements;
    long lLbound;
} SAFEARRAYBOUND;
```

You specify the dimension's lowest element index value (lLbound), and then you specify how many elements are in that dimension (cElements). The lower index value need not be zero—it can be anything. (That's why the SafeArrayGetLBound() and SafeArrayGetUBound() safe array API calls exist.)

Referring back to Listing 14.6, I accessed individual array elements using SafeArrayGetElement() (line 49) and SafeArrayPutElement() (line 29). However, for speed, you can use SafeArrayLock() and SafeArrayUnlock() to lock the array and return a pointer to the actual array data in the safe array's pvData member. You can then access the data directly rather than ask an API call to manage it for you. The risky aspect of this approach is that no protection exists to keep you from overrunning the bounds of the array. Be careful. If performance isn't the top concern, the API calls will protect you against inadvertent array-bound overruns.

Of course, any time you allocate memory (create the array), you must release the memory. For the safe array, that means calling SafeArrayDestroy(), which I call on line 63. SafeArrayDestroy() releases the array data, and then it destroys the array structure itself.

 Note

> Even though safe arrays are supported by COM automation, any property or method that deals with a safe array as a parameter to the method must pass it into or out of the method as a variant (VT_ARRAY) in order to be OLE automation compliant. MIDL will flag an IDL compile error if you try to pass the safe array itself.

Summary

Today, I provided some background information about COM automation, or to be more precise, about IDispatch and the data IDispatch can handle. I began by describing the dual interface and how it is created from a custom interface and a dispinterface. I then went on to describe the methods IDispatch supports, the DISPID value that is associated with each interface method, and how ATL implements IDispatch.

I also described how IDispatch::Invoke() is used to call dispinterface methods and how you instantiate the dispinterface versus the custom interface. Because no script can possibly manage all conceivable data types, I talked about the variant and why it exists (the set of data COM will support implicitly). I quickly went over variant data coercion, which is how variants can be converted from type to type. Finally, I went over the safe array, including some of the API calls and how you use the safe array in practice.

You'll use this information, especially ActiveX implementation, in the remainder of this book. Day 15 provides more background for custom control development, which is also related to developing ActiveX controls.

Q&A

Q **You've mentioned ActiveX with dual interfaces a lot. Can an object have a dual interface, yet not be an ActiveX control?**

A Absolutely. The dual interface indicates the object is available for use by scripted languages. ActiveX builds on the dual interface by mandating the interface support other interfaces designed to do many other things, such as persist data values and negotiate screen real estate for user interface work. The dual interface is a requirement for ActiveX, but not the other way around.

Q **I see that the dual interface has a dispinterface and a custom interface. But how are they related?**

A Well, the DISPID, given to each of the custom interface methods is used by the dispinterface to identify the code that will be eventually executed by Invoke(). The custom interface is, therefore, required because its code is what Invoke() is going to execute. You can imagine Invoke() acting as a pseudo-vtable. When given a DISPID, it jumps to the correct place in memory and executes what it finds there. In fact, many implementations of Invoke() create vtable structures to do just that.

Workshop

The Workshop is designed to help you anticipate possible questions, review what you've learned, and get you thinking about how to put your knowledge into practice. The answers to the quiz are in Appendix A, "Answers."

Quiz

1. What is a dual interface?
2. What methods does IDispatch support and what are their respective purposes?
3. What is the purpose of the variant?
4. What is the purpose of the safe array?

14

Exercise

1. Modify the *SADemo* example to directly access the variant data contained within the safe array. (Hint: Wrap the access with two safe array API calls and keep track of your indices.) This is not a simple exercise, but it is illuminating.

WEEK 2

In Review

In this past week, you began to see more intermediate COM and ATL programming concepts and techniques. It's these concepts and techniques you'll need to move to the more advanced work in the upcoming (final) week. As this week began, you were introduced to some ATL helper classes and functions that ease your COM programming burden, as well as provide debugging support. You also saw a bit more about writing MFC-based test applications and how (and why) to handle runtime exceptions, as well as general error handling. You then moved to some heavy-duty programming when you studied multithreading concepts and how COM deals with multithreaded objects. To lighten things up a bit, you switched gears and saw how ATL supports traditional Win32 programming, although the classes you saw here also are used in the more advanced work you'll soon be studying. Finally, the week wrapped up with a look at COM automation and scripting support using the dual interface.

Day 8 laid the groundwork for all the ATL support classes and functions you'll use when working with COM and COM automation, as well as ATL's debugging support classes. Because reference counting is so critical, you saw ATL's `CComPtr` and the related `CComQIPtr` smart pointer classes that are designed to manage an object's reference count for you. You also saw how ATL wraps the BSTR, the variant, and Registry access. Finally, you looked at ATL's debugging support, such as `ATLASSERT()` and `ATLTRACE()`.

Day 9 left ATL for the moment and reviewed some basic MFC programming concepts and skills you'll need to create MFC-based test applications. You saw how to create a basic MFC application and add ATL support (such as for smart pointers). You then added your COM object, as well as other Windows controls, to create a test application that you can use to exercise your object.

Day 10 turned to general COM and C++ error management when you learned how to create custom HRESULTs and deal with C++ exceptions. You saw how to code your IDL file to transmit the custom HRESULT information to client applications. You also saw how to catch various C++ exceptions, as well as how to create your own custom error classes. Finally, you looked at rich error handling and IErrorInfo.

Day 11 introduced some basic multithreading programming concepts, especially the notion of data integrity. You saw how to create multiple threads in a Windows environment, as well as how to synchronize data access when multiple threads want to modify the same piece of data. The data synchronization mechanisms you looked at included critical sections, mutexes, events, and semaphores.

I find COM's threading models confuse many programmers, so Day 12 targets COM's threading models and tries to demystify the jargon. I described the COM apartment as the union of COM, a Win32 thread, and a given COM object. I also described the single-threaded and multithreaded apartments and how COM creates each when needed.

Day 13 introduced some of the ATL windowing support classes you'll use to write Win32 applications (and more advanced COM components). You saw, in some detail, how ATL supports windowing, Windows messages, and the important concept of window subclassing. You created a few Windows applications by hand, which probably helped you to appreciate the work the Visual Studio wizards do for you when they create ATL COM objects.

The week wrapped up with Day 14 where you learned more about the dual interface and how it supports COM-based scripting. You took a good look at the dispinterface and IDispatch, and you saw how variants help scripting engines by limiting their set of default data types. Finally, you worked a bit with the safe array.

Preview

Most of the information you learned this week is critically important to move to the more advanced topics that you'll meet next week. The week will begin with a study of the Windows GDI, basic animation techniques, and an introduction to a set of GDI wrapper classes that make GDI coding in ATL much easier. You'll also revisit window subclassing and learn how controls communicate with their parent window via control notification messages. With that information, you look at writing ActiveX controls and how they differ from traditional custom controls. For example, ActiveX controls implement connection points for container notifications rather than send Windows messages, as traditional controls do. Following that, you'll examine ATL's support for the class factory, with special emphasis on licensing issues and IClassFactory2 (used by some ActiveX controls). The final three days look at implementing ATL objects that support other advanced Microsoft technologies. This includes distributed objects using DCOM, database access using OLE DB, and transactional objects using MTS. I'll wrap things up with a brief look at COM+ under Windows 2000.

WEEK 3

At a Glance

This final week is geared toward using ATL to implement objects supporting more advanced Microsoft technologies, such as ActiveX, DCOM, OLE DB, and MTS. The week begins with a discussion of basic custom control creation, including the Windows GDI, window subclassing, basic animation techniques, and an introduction to basic control notification messaging. You'll then move to writing ActiveX true controls and learn to test your ActiveX controls using the Visual Studio ActiveX control Test Container. You'll be able to compare traditional control notification techniques with ActiveX notifications when you learn to implement connection points. The final three days will provide you with details for implementing ATL objects in three very different settings—distributed objects using DCOM, database objects using OLE DB, and transactional objects using MTS.

- Day 15: Look at the Windows GDI from a control programming perspective, discuss control notification messages, and revisit window subclassing.

- Day 16: Learn to write ATL-based ActiveX controls.

- Day 17: Add container notification support to your ActiveX control using connection points.

- Day 18: Examine the COM class factory in more detail, as well as study ATL's implementations, especially where licensing is concerned.

- Day 19: See how you can distribute your objects using DCOM.

- Day 20: Learn how OLE DB simplifies accessing databases and how ATL incorporates OLE DB.

- Day 21: Study transactional processing concepts and how to write objects for use within MTS, leading to COM+ object implementations.

DAY **15**

Custom Controls: Basic Control Development Techniques

In Day 14, "ATL and Automation: Creating RoboObjects," you examined the dual interface more closely and discovered what data types COM automation implicitly supports. During Day 16, "ATL and ActiveX: Modern Control Packaging," you'll take a look at the nuts and bolts of creating ActiveX controls using ATL. There is an intermediate step, however, and that's what is covered today. The intermediate step is the creation of basic custom controls. Many ActiveX controls subclass an existing Windows control or create entirely new user interface gizmos. In the former case, the subclassed control is likely to receive new painting behavior, whether it's a new font or color arrangement. In the latter case, all the painting work must be provided because the control is completely new.

Today, you will concentrate on some Windows programming basics that you need to understand and master in order to create world-class custom controls.

After I discuss some of these topics, you'll build both a subclassed and a custom control. Then, in Day 16, you'll take the custom control and wrap it in the ActiveX framework to make it a full-fledged ActiveX control.

Time to get started. The basics I'll cover today include

- Windows GDI concepts, such as the device context, bitmaps, drawing and painting, and flicker-free screen updates
- More about subclassing an existing control
- Building a completely new control from scratch

GDI Concepts

The Windows *Graphical Device Interface*, or *GDI*, is the primary operations center for any painting and rendering work you want to perform in your control. The GDI is one of the major components of Windows itself, and you can probably see why. After all, Windows provides for a graphical user interface—versus the character-based interface so common on the old DOS applications.

Most of the GDI API is implemented in the GDI32.DLL file, and if you write code against this DLL, you'll link GDI32.LIB when you compile your application. Of course, Visual Studio handles this for you, in most cases, so you need not worry about speci-fying the library yourself. At times, however, you might create a project from dust, and you will need to remember to adjust your link list to include this file.

It's the GDI that is responsible for marrying your computer's hardware to the standard API code you write. That means you'll draw a line on the screen using the single API call `LineTo()`, regardless of which computer is executing your code. Windows itself manages the video memory and *rasterization* (conversion of bits in memory to an image on the screen) for you, no matter what video hardware is being used. In general, this insulation is well done, and you don't need to concern yourself with the specific hard-ware in use.

The GDI is static, however. That means there is no inherent support for animation. (*Animation* in this sense means visual control changes and not, necessarily, the rapidly changing sequence of individual scenes that is normally referred to as animation.) If you want to animate your control, you'll have to do the work yourself. I'll show you some techniques for managing this in the upcoming "Flicker-Free Drawing" section. If you're interested in really high-powered control animation, be sure to check out either OpenGL or Microsoft's DirectX graphics libraries.

Almost everything you see when you're working with Windows is provided by GDI operations. It's probably not surprising, then, that there are hundreds of GDI API calls! You have calls for painting pixels, drawing lines and shapes, text output, font rasterization, coordinating mapping modes, and tons of system management calls. The GDI itself is broken into the main subsystems you see in Table 15.1.

Table 15.1   GDI Main Subsystems

Subsystem	Purpose
Device context lifetime management	Functions to create and destroy GDI device contexts
Device context attribute management	Functions to get and set device context attributes
Device context information	Functions to obtain general device context information
Drawing primitives	Functions that draw something, such as lines, rectangles, and text
GDI object management	Functions that deal with GDI objects, such as pens, brushes, and regions

As you see, most of the subsystems revolve around a device context, which I'll discuss in detail in the next section.

The Device Context

Whenever you see the word *context*, you should think *state*. You've already seen that *thread context* refers to the thread-state information that is typically stored in the TLS associated with each thread. The same concept applies to a *device context*. This is actually a structure the GDI maintains to indicate what device settings are in effect for the current rendering operation. The device context, or *DC*, stores the state information that the GDI requires to draw things to the screen or printer. These include the line width, the pen color, the coordinate-mapping mode in effect, and what font is to be used for text. The GDI stores this information and returns a handle to you. You deal with the DC via this handle. Note that no two device contexts are the same because each is set up with vastly different drawing requirements (font, color, and so forth).

The GDI will map a given device context structure to a particular device. What that really means is the GDI will make whatever adjustments are necessary to render a given image on a particular device. If color must be mapped to grayscale, the GDI will do the mapping for you. If a 1-pixel-wide pen is to be used for drawing a line, the GDI will make sure the actual line width is 1 pixel (at least to a close approximation).

The nice part about all this is that the same code you write to draw a rectangle to the screen can be used to print the rectangle on paper or plot the rectangle on a plotter. You simply use the GDI to draw a rectangle using the given DC, and Windows does the rest for you.

Device Context Primitives

The device context stores settings Windows uses when rendering the image. Table 15.2 shows you these primitives and their basic operations.

Table 15.2 Device Context Primitives

Primitive	Purpose
Lines, shapes, and curves	Draw lines, shapes, and curves with specified attributes (color, pen, end cap, and so forth)
Filled regions	Fill specified regions with a color or pattern
Bitmap	An array of bits corresponding to display pixels that will contain the output of the drawing function (each DC has one and only one)
Text	Font mapping

The GDI, through the DC, also provides for coordinate mapping modes, metafiles, paths, regions, clipping bounds, palettes, and special printing functions. If these terms are not familiar to you, or even if they are, I highly recommend Charles Petzold's *Programming Windows* (Microsoft Press, ISBN: 1-57231-995-X). He provides many, many detailed examples of each GDI subsystem and DC primitive, and his book is an excellent resource for Windows programming questions in general.

As I mentioned, you access the GDI via the DC's handle. Handles, as you recall, are somewhat like pointers in that they tell Windows which specific object to access (a DC in this case). Just as threads have handles, so do DCs. Let's see how you obtain a DC handle.

Device Context Handles

Although a handle is a handle is a handle, precisely *which* DC handle you request is important. For example, you might obtain a very different handle if you are painting your window's client area than if you want the DC handle for the entire screen. Most functions I describe will also require a handle to your window (another handle!).

When you are responding to a WM_PAINT message, you request the device context you need to update your window by calling BeginPaint(). After you've updated your window's appearance, you release the DC by calling EndPaint().

If you need a general-purpose DC, you use either GetDC() or GetWindowDC(), depending upon your painting requirements. GetDC() obtains the DC for the window's client area, whereas GetWindowDC() retrieves the DC for the entire window, including the nonclient areas (caption, border, and so on). After using the DC to perform your painting work, you release the DC resources to the system by calling ReleaseDC(). By the way, if you want the DC used by the entire desktop (screen), you use GetDC() with a window handle of NULL (commonly required by screen savers, for example).

The most general way to create a DC is by using CreateDC(). With this function, you provide the driver you want to use, the device you want to use, and other ancillary information, and the GDI will create a new DC. After you've used the DC, you must delete it using DeleteDC().

The final method of obtaining a DC is to create a copy of an existing DC using CreateCompatibleDC(). I'll use this function when I discuss flicker-free drawing techniques because I want copies of the device context and bitmap for the control. I draw on the copy, and then I transfer the final results to the control's DC and bitmap (which updates the screen in one move). As with CreateDC(), you delete this DC by using DeleteDC().

You must always take care to release or destroy any DC you create or obtain. Although Windows NT is a bit more forgiving, Windows 95 and 98 have a limited pool of resource memory. If your code leaks resources long enough, eventually it will crash the entire system. Just as you'll probably take great care to plan when to create or obtain a DC, also plan when you will destroy or release it.

I've mentioned that bitmaps are an array of bits that map to display pixels. I've told you the DC contains one and only one bitmap. They are important, so let's examine bitmaps from a DC perspective a little more closely.

Bitmaps

The bitmap is the workhorse of the rasterization code contained within the GDI. Any image you draw using the GDI will store its results in a bitmap. *How* those results appear when rendered is controlled by the DC. Therefore, every DC must be associated with a bitmap, although not every bitmap must have a DC. If you create a DC from scratch, using CreateDC() for example, it will (by default) reference a 1-pixel × 1-pixel monochrome bitmap that Windows will create on the DC's behalf.

Bitmaps are a resource, like the DC, and the same resource-usage caveat applies. If you create bitmaps, be sure you destroy them.

Contemporary Windows implementations provide for two types of bitmaps—device dependent and device independent. Device-dependent bitmaps are closely tied to a given output device (screen or printer) and are typically optimized for use with that device only. Device-independent bitmaps, on the other hand, can be shared among display devices and can be stored on disk (in a separate file or as a resource to your executable or DLL). Most DC work you'll perform deals with the device-dependent variety of bitmap, because its format and structure are usually closely tied (and optimized) for the given display hardware. If you want to save the control's image, or something along those lines, you need to convert the bitmap to a device-independent bitmap (which I won't cover today). There are examples included with the online documentation that show you how this is done.

To create a bitmap from scratch, you use either `CreateBitmap()` or `CreateCompatibleBitmap()`. The former is optimized for monochrome bitmaps, whereas the latter is better for color bitmaps. In each case, you'll pass in the rectangular size of the bitmap, as well as information about color plane and color bits per pixel. Typically, you obtain this by using the `GetDeviceCaps()` GDI function, using either `PLANES` or `BITSPIXEL` as the index parameter. When you're through with the bitmap, you destroy it by providing its handle to `DeleteObject()`.

Drawing and Painting

Given a DC and a bitmap, you're now ready to paint something. The usual process you will follow is this:

- Obtain a DC and create additional bitmaps, if required.
- Establish the DC settings to draw the output you desire.
- Render your output.
- Release any GDI resources you created to prevent resource leakage.

I've discussed the first item on the list, as well as the last. The remaining items are the establishment of DC settings and the actual painting operations.

In general, you set up your DC by calling a specific attribute's function or by selecting into your DC a GDI object. An example of an attribute function is `SetTextColor()`, which tells the DC (and the GDI) what colors to use to draw future text output. There are many, many attribute functions. Instead of trying to remember them all, I often use the online documentation to find the function I need. You'll easily recall the basic ones, however, as you become more familiar with the GDI.

Selecting a GDI object means that the DC is set up to use a given pen, brush, region, and so on. The default (or current) object might not be to your liking, and you're free to create a new object and have the DC use that for subsequent painting operations. Providing the DC with a GDI object is referred to as *selecting the object into the DC*

15

because you use the SelectObject() function to do so. (The poor grammar is historical and not my own misuse of the language!)

For example, you want to draw a red line 3-pixels wide. Drawing the line is easy. You simply use MoveToEx() to place the pen (X,Y coordinate) and LineTo() to draw the line. The trick is the red pen. To obtain this, you use CreatePen() or CreatePenIndirect(). If either of these functions is successful, the resulting pen handle is provided to the DC by calling SelectObject(). Now when you draw the lines, they'll be three pixels wide and red. After you're done with the pen, you select another object into the DC and destroy the pen object using DeleteObject(). I'll provide an example shortly.

To draw circles and rectangles, you create both a pen and a brush, and then you call Ellipse() or Rectangle(). The brush will be used to fill the circle or rectangle with a color or pattern, and the pen will be used to draw the border. To create an arbitrary shape, you can use either Polygon() or PolyPolygon() with the appropriate fill mode set, Get/SetPolyFillMode(). Polygon() renders a single polygon, whereas PolyPolygon() renders multiple, closed polygons. The fill mode is either ALTERNATE or WINDING depending upon the mode you desire (see the online references). When filled, the polygon(s) will be rendered using the current brush and pen.

The GDI provide for more exotic drawing capabilities, such as for rendering arcs and splines. Arc(), for example, draws an arc using the specified bounding rectangle and radial line endpoints. PolyBezier() draws the cubic *B-Spline* (Bézier curve) using the array of control points you provide as input. Both render the curves using the current DC pen object.

All the GDI drawing and painting functions will render to a DC, but the question quickly becomes *which* DC? If you draw your scene to the client DC you're given using BeginPaint(), for example, you'll quickly note the screen flickers whenever the scene is redrawn. Let's now look at this phenomenon and see how you might be able to cure it.

Flicker-Free Drawing

The problem is the DC you're given by BeginPaint() is a *screen DC*. That is, it is tied to the video output circuitry. Any time you make a change to the underlying bitmap, that information is immediately rendered onto the screen. If you clear the bitmap to white (or some other color) and then begin drawing, you'll see the screen flash to white for an instant and flicker as your painting code renders its output.

The secret to eliminating this is to always draw to a *memory DC*. A memory DC is a device context that sits in memory and is not tied to the video output circuitry. It's simply a copy of the DC that will be used to update the screen. The idea is to *buffer* your drawing operations by drawing to the memory DC first, then copying the completed image to the screen after you're done with your rendering. This operation is often referred to as *double-buffering* because you're using two independent bitmaps for your drawing.

You create a double buffer in three easy steps. First, you must create another DC. For this, you use the `CreateCompatibleDC()` GDI API call. `CreateCompatibleDC()` takes an existing device context as input and creates a copy based in memory. This new device context, however, accesses the standard 1-pixel × 1-pixel monochrome bitmap I mentioned earlier, so the second step is to create a compatible bitmap. For this, you use `CreateCompatibleBitmap()`, providing the size of the bitmap and the color information (usually accessed using `GetDeviceCaps()`, as I also mentioned previously). After you have both the DC and the DC's bitmap, you perform the third step, which is to select the bitmap into the DC using `SelectObject()`.

There is one thing to note, however. You release the DC back to the system at some point, which means you need to keep the original monochrome bitmap's handle available. You should select the monochrome bitmap *back* into the DC before you destroy it. Then you destroy the compatible bitmap you created.

An Example with GDI C++ Support Classes

All the GDI API calls I've mentioned cry out to be wrapped in C++ classes. For example, most API calls require a device context handle, which could be a class attribute. Also, there is usually a creation and a destruction API call, so why not let the class destructor manage the release of the resource?

Rather than writing code, which takes a lot of time and is prone to bugs, I reasoned I could use the MFC GDI classes. After all, MFC wraps the GDI for me, and I know the classes are very thin. That is, they don't add much overhead because GDI calls, in general, are performance minded. I also know MFC ships with the source code, as does ATL, so it is a simple matter of cutting and pasting the MFC GDI classes to a new set of files, removing the MFC-specific details, and adding the appropriate ATL details. Although it took me an hour and a half to do all this, I spent far less time than I would have if I created it all from scratch. One nice aspect of this is that you can use the MFC online documentation for information about these classes.

Note

If you already intend to ship the MFC DLL(s) with your control, by all means select the Supports MFC option from the ATL AppWizard when you create your initial project. If you do so, you won't need the GDI wrappers I present here. However, I believe that most people will be more interested in forgoing the MFC DLLs for simple custom control development. While the GDI wrappers will increase the size of your control's code slightly, the size growth is nothing compared to the size of the MFC DLLs (approaching 800KB). This also relieves you of the burden of shipping and installing the MFC DLLs.

The classes I reused from MFC include

- `CSize`, `CPoint`, and `CRect` helper classes
- `CGdiObject`, from which are derived `CPen`, `CBrush`, `CFont`, `CPalette`, `CBitmap`, and `CRgn`
- `CDC`, from which are derived `CPaintDC`, `CClientDC`, and `CWindowDC`

I used the resulting source files, MFCGDI.H (and the implementation in MFCGDI.INL) and MFCGDI.CPP to create the *BasicGDI* example application.

For fun, I created an ATL-based Win32 application, an image of which you see in Figure 15.1. Actually, it makes sense to do this in ATL. If you do so, the control painting code you write can be directly ported to the ATL ActiveX framework rather than translated from MFC or something else. In any case, the application animates floating blue bubbles. You right-click in the application's client area to get a context menu from which you can turn double buffering on or off and see the results. The goal of the example is to show you how flickering will be perceived as you draw your own custom control.

FIGURE 15.1

The BasicGDI example application user interface.

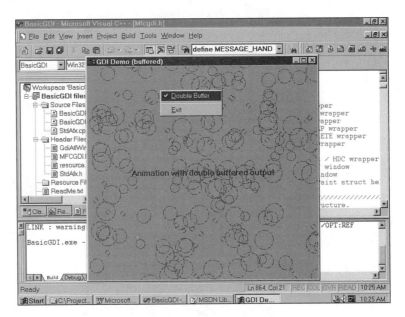

The application begins by creating a Windows timer. Every 100 milliseconds, the timer fires and I invalidate the client area. As I do, Windows generates a `WM_PAINT` message that I handle as you see in Listing 15.1.

LISTING 15.1   BasicGDI's `OnPaint()` Handler

```
 1: LRESULT OnPaint(UINT uMsg, WPARAM wParam, LPARAM lParam,
 2: ➥BOOL& bHandled)
 3: {
 4:     // Set up for painting
 5:     CPaintDC dcPaint(m_hWnd);
 6:
 7:     // Determine client area
 8:     CRect rcClient;
 9:     GetClientRect(&rcClient);
10:
11:     // Create a solid brush
12:     CBrush brBlue(RGB(0,128,255));
13:
14:     // Determine which DC to use
15:     CDC dcBuffer;
16:     CDC* pDC = NULL;
17:     CBitmap bmColor;
18:     CBitmap* pbmMono = NULL;
19:     if ( m_bDoBuffering ) {
20:         // Create the double buffer
21:         dcBuffer.CreateCompatibleDC(&dcPaint);
22:
23:         // Create a compatible bitmap
24:         bmColor.CreateCompatibleBitmap(&dcPaint,
25:                                      rcClient.Width(),
26:                                      rcClient.Height());
27:
28:         // Select in the color bitmap
29:         pbmMono = (CBitmap*)dcBuffer.SelectObject(&bmColor);
30:
31:         // Draw with this DC
32:         pDC = &dcBuffer;
33:     } // if
34:     else {
35:         // Draw with this DC
36:         pDC = &dcPaint;
37:     } // else
38:
39:     // Load the window's message
40:     TCHAR strMsg[_MAX_PATH+1] = {0};
41:     LoadString(_Module.GetResourceInstance(),
42:               m_bDoBuffering ? IDS_MSGBUFF : IDS_MSGFLICK,
43:               strMsg,
44:               _MAX_PATH);
45:
46:     // Fill the client area
47:     pDC->FillRect(&rcClient,&brBlue);
48:
49:     // Draw the objects
```

```
50:        DrawObjects(pDC,rcClient);
51:
52:        // Draw a message
53:        pDC->SetBkMode(TRANSPARENT);
54:        pDC->SetTextColor(RGB(0,0,0)); // black
55:        pDC->DrawText(strMsg,-1,&rcClient,
56:                        DT_SINGLELINE | DT_CENTER | DT_VCENTER);
57:
58:        // Copy then release double buffer
59:        if ( m_bDoBuffering ) {
60:            // Bitblt the buffer to the main DC
61:            dcPaint.BitBlt(rcClient.left,
62:                            rcClient.top,
63:                            rcClient.Width(),
64:                            rcClient.Height(),
65:                            &dcBuffer,0,0,SRCCOPY);
66:
67:            // Select in the monochrome bitmap
68:            dcBuffer.SelectObject(pbmMono);
69:
70:            // Destroy the color bitmap
71:            bmColor.DeleteObject();
72:        } // if
73:
74:        return 0;
75: }
```

ANALYSIS   Rather than deal with `BeginPaint()` and `EndPaint()` directly, I let the `CPaintDC` class manage those details. I create the painting DC using this code (lines 4 and 5):

```
// Set up for painting
CPaintDC dcPaint(m_hWnd);
```

With the painting DC, which is a screen DC, I can begin my painting work. After determining the client area's rectangular region, I create a blue brush (lines 11 and 12):

```
// Create a solid brush
CBrush brBlue(RGB(0,128,255));
```

Because you're free to choose which DC to use while the application is executing, I wrap the creation of the double-buffer DC in an `if` statement. If indeed you want to use the double buffer, I create and initialize it like this (lines 21–29):

```
dcBuffer.CreateCompatibleDC(&dcPaint);

// Create a compatible bitmap
```

```
bmColor.CreateCompatibleBitmap(&dcPaint,
                               rcClient.Width(),
                               rcClient.Height());

// Select in the color bitmap
pbmMono = (CBitmap*)dcBuffer.SelectObject(&bmColor);
```

As you can see, I create the double buffer as a compatible DC (line 21), and then I create a compatible (color) bitmap (line 24) and select it into the buffer DC (line 29). Note that I also save the original buffer DC's monochrome bitmap, which I'll later replace.

So that I can use the same basic painting code, I assign a temporary CDC pointer variable (pDC) to point to the screen (paint) DC or to the buffer DC that I just created (line 32 or line 36). After loading a textual message, which will be displayed within the client area, I begin the actual painting work (lines 46 through 56):

```
// Fill the client area
pDC->FillRect(&rcClient,&brBlue);

// Draw the objects
DrawObjects(pDC,rcClient);

// Draw a message
pDC->SetBkMode(TRANSPARENT);
pDC->SetTextColor(RGB(0,0,0)); // black
pDC->DrawText(strMsg,-1,&rcClient,
              DT_SINGLELINE | DT_CENTER | DT_VCENTER);
```

I first fill the entire client area using the blue brush I created (line 47). After the background is all blue, I draw the animated objects using the DrawObjects() method (called from line 50). This method merely examines and updates an array of structures that contain information about each bubble. It then renders the individual bubble given the DC. Finally, I render the message I previously loaded (line 55). Note the DC API calls to set the text background mode (TRANSPARENT) and color (black), which you see on lines 53 and 54, respectively.

The last thing I do is to transfer and clean up the double buffer, if one was used. Because I'm dealing with two DCs in the buffered case, I'll have to copy the buffer DC to the screen DC. This is the purpose of BitBlt() (short for *bit block transfer*), which you see on line 61. BitBlt() copies the bitmap from the buffer DC to the screen DC, and the image you see is now updated. I then need to return the original monochrome bitmap to the buffer DC and destroy the color bitmap I created. Here is the code (starting from line 60):

```
// Bitblt the buffer to the main DC
dcPaint.BitBlt(rcClient.left,
               rcClient.top,
               rcClient.Width(),
```

```
                    rcClient.Height(),
                    &dcBuffer,0,0,SRCCOPY);

// Select in the monochrome bitmap
dcBuffer.SelectObject(pbmMono);

// Destroy the color bitmap
bmColor.DeleteObject();
```

If you don't use the double buffer, the changes to the underlying bitmap are tied directly to the screen output, and no bitmap copy is required. The screen DC is already updated.

This painting code is greatly simplified, at least at this level, by the GDI classes I ported. I'll use these classes throughout the remainder of the book. But custom control creation involves more than just painting details. You also need to be concerned with the underlying messages the control reacts to and sends off. For that, I'll revisit subclassing in the next section.

Control Subclassing

As you saw in Day 13, "Creating ATL Applications: Where ATL Meets Win32," you can easily subclass standard Windows controls. The usefulness of subclassing is that you can intercept and process Windows messages normally destined for that control. This enables you to change the overall behavior of the control. Any Windows message is fair game, and I pulled a trick with the WM_PASTE message in Day 13. As I've mentioned, you'll normally want to change the painting behavior. I'll discuss how to do that shortly.

When handling control notifications, be aware that Windows controls typically notify the parent window when interesting events happen, such as a mouse click or keyboard keypress. This enables the parent window to take action based upon the user's input. Windows control notifications come in two flavors, one based upon WM_COMMAND (the old style), and one based upon WM_NOTIFY (the new style). In general, the implicit Windows controls, such as buttons and edit controls, pass notifications to their parent using WM_COMMAND. Newer Windows controls, such as those you'll find in the Common Controls library (list control, tree control, and so forth) use the newer style of notification based on WM_NOTIFY. Controls you write should follow the newer format, unless you're replacing older control notification logic and want to preserve your client code.

When you subclass a control, you might be interested in managing the existing control notifications, or you might even want to enhance the control by adding new notifications. This requires some understanding of how the WM_COMMAND and WM_NOTIFY messages are packaged and sent to the parent. I'll cover this now.

Note

As you'll see in Day 16, "ATL and ActiveX: Modern Control Packaging," and in Day 17, "ATL and Connection Points: Supporting COMs Event Model," ActiveX controls can use a different mechanism altogether to notify the container (parent window).

Control Command Messages

Sending a WM_COMMAND message to the parent window is easily accomplished by using CWindow::SendMessage(). WM_COMMAND requires that the LPARAM and WPARAM values are properly established before you ship the message off.

The WPARAM value is a combination of the notification code and the control ID. For example, imagine that you have a button with some control ID (you obtain this using GetDlgCtrlID() so you don't hard code it) and that this button is clicked with the mouse. The WPARAM value for the resulting WM_COMMAND message is

```
WPARAM wParam = (WPARAM)MAKELONG(GetDlgCtrlID(),BN_CLICKED);
```

Assuming the window handle for the button is stored in m_hWnd, the LPARAM value is simply assigned to m_hWnd:

```
LPARAM lParam = (LPARAM)m_hWnd;
```

With these two values established, you normally send the WM_COMMAND message to the parent window, the handle to which is in m_hParentWnd:

```
if ( SendMessage(m_hParentWnd,WM_COMMAND,wParam,lParam) ) {
    // Parent returned non-zero, so message was not handled
    ...
} // if
```

The parent returns zero from SendMesage(), indicating the parent received the command message and processed it. If not, a nonzero return value will throw you into the code that you provide in the case the command is not handled. You can also choose to ignore the return value, if you have no interest in the outcome of the command.

Control Notifications

Newer controls don't use the WM_COMMAND message for parent notifications. Handshaking was becoming too cumbersome as new controls and notifications were added. Because Microsoft knew more flexibility was needed when dealing with control notifications, the WM_NOTIFY message and notification protocol were invented.

In general, you need to create a notification structure and pass that along with the WM_NOTIFY message to the parent window. The basic structure is defined as the NMHDR (notification message header) structure:

```
typedef struct tagNMHDR {
    HWND hwndFrom;
    UINT idFrom;
    UINT code;
} NMHDR;
```

The hwndFrom member is your control's window handle, whereas the idFrom is the control's ID you can obtain using GetDlgCtrlID(). The code member is a control-specific notification code that indicates what type of event the notification represents.

The NMHDR structure itself is pretty limited, as you can see. Perhaps the simple notification stating that an event took place is enough, but often you'll want to provide the parent window a little more detail. To do that, you create your own structure, into which you incorporate the NMHDR structure:

```
typedef struct tagMyEventHeader
{
    NMHDR hdr;
    (additional notification data)
} NMMYEVENTHDR, FAR* LPNMMYEVENTHDR;
```

The additional notification data can be anything you want, but note it is common practice to place the NMHDR structure within your customized structure first and call it hdr.

Given the notification structure, customized or otherwise, you notify the parent window using code such as that in Listing 15.2.

LISTING 15.2   Example Parent Event Notification Using WM_NOTIFY

```
 1: // Get parent handle
 2: HWND hwndParent = GetParent(); // from CWindow...
 3: if ( hwndParent != NULL ) {
 4:     // Obtain control ID
 5:     int nID = GetDlgCtrlID();
 6:
 7:     // Create notification message
 8:     NMHDR msg;
 9:     msg.hwndFrom = m_hWnd;
10:     msg.idFrom = nID;
11:     msg.code = MY_NOTIFY_CODE; // insert particular code here
12:
13:     // Send it
14:     SendMessage(hwndParent,WM_NOTIFY,(WPARAM)nID,(LPARAM)&msg);
15: } // if
```

continues

LISTING 15.2 continued

```
16: else {
17:     // No parent?
18:     ATLASSERT(FALSE);
19: } // else
```

ANALYSIS As with the WM_COMMAND message, you can check the results of the
SendMessage() call (line 14), and if nonzero, you can process the result as you
wish. A nonzero return value doesn't necessarily indicate an error, because this behavior
is dictated by the control. Most controls ignore the return value entirely.

Control Paint Behavior

In general, when you are handling the painting behavior of an existing control, you either
take full control (and responsibility) for the visual aspects of the control, or you allow
the control to paint itself entirely. You then, somehow, repaint selected portions (*how* you
do that is control dependent!). In either case, you'll want to handle the WM_PAINT message, and possibly the WM_ERASEBKGND and WM_CTLCOLORXXXX messages, if the control you
are subclassing supports custom control colors.

I created a sample application that overrides the progress bar's normal painting behavior
to create a thermometer control, as you see in Figure 15.2.

FIGURE 15.2

The ThermoBar *sample
application user inter-
face.*

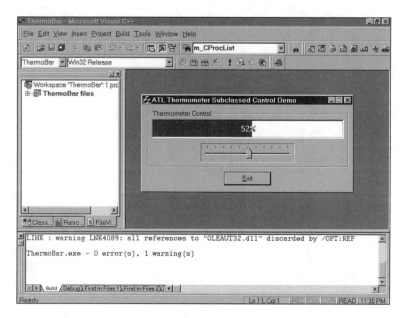

15

I won't go over the painting code in detail, but it's relatively straightforward. You'll note that I added all the methods of the `ATLControls::CProgressBarCtrl` to make using the thermometer control as easy as using the progress control. The control is truly subclassed, however, as the methods I added merely call the base ATLControls class. That class sends the information directly to the progress control.

The code in ThermoCtl.h and MainDlg.h shows you how I subclassed the progress bar common control. The progress bar itself is subclassed using `CContainedWindow::SubclassWindow()`, but you must be cognizant of the control's possible use in a dialog box situation. In that case, the control will likely be stuffed into another `CContainedWindow`. Calling `SubclassWindow()` on the dialog's instance of `CContainedWindow` won't actually subclass the progress bar itself (it subclasses `CThermoCtl`) because the bar is managed by a different instance of `CContainedWindow` (nested *within* `CThermoCtl`). Therefore, the `CThermoCtl::SubclassWindow()` and `UnsubclassWindow()` methods manage the subclassing of the progress bar for you.

In the case of a dialog box, however, the application's dialog code instead uses the `CThermoCtl::Attach()` method to actually subclass the thermometer control, which manages the subclassing of the progress bar for you automatically. This is more like the operation of the other controls you find in ATLCONTROLS.H, which you might remember from Day 13. The corresponding `Detach()` will be made for you in the control's destructor if you don't explicitly detach it yourself.

Now that you've seen how to subclass a control, send event notifications to your control's parent window, and paint an existing control differently, it's time to create a totally new control.

Building Something New

I'm going to develop a new control, and although it probably won't spark a user interface revolution, it should be a great platform for describing how to build a basic control. The goal will be to take the code from this control and insert it into the ActiveX framework I'll cover in Day 16. The control I'll build is a simple indicator, the LED.

If you're into electronics, you know about LEDs, but if not, the term stands for Light Emitting Diodes. *LEDs* are usually used to provide user feedback confirming that some state has been achieved or some activity is progressing. The LED I'll build is little more than a circle containing two sub arcs to simulate a three-dimensional appearance.

The control will manage three states, which will be indicated by color. The LED can be green, yellow, or red, and the parent window will dictate the state. When the state changes, the control will automatically update its appearance to reflect the new state.

It will also provide for four event notifications. It will notify the parent window if the user clicked or double-clicked within its client area using either the left or right mouse button. The notifications will be managed using the WM_NOTIFY Windows message, and I'll create four new notification structures to go with each event. Because the events are very similar, I can use a single structure and insert the specific event code, but I elect to create several structures to further demonstrate the technique.

I'll create the control using ATL classes (including the GDI classes I ported), and the parent window will be an ATL dialog-based application to provide you with additional sample ATL windowing code. I could have easily used MFC instead, but this enables me to demonstrate ATL WM_NOTIFY event handling. I'll start by creating the control, and then I'll describe how it's used in an application.

The Control

The control's source code is in the *BasicLED* sample project, in the Led.h file. The control itself is implemented in the CLED class, which derives from CWindowImpl. I used CWindowImpl rather than CComControl or AxWindowImpl (because those classes are targeted for ActiveX). I wanted a simple window-based control. Rather than spit out a huge listing and try to walk you through it, I'll take the major parts of the control piece by piece and describe their functions. If you're able to review this while running the project from within Visual Studio, you might find that helpful.

The CLED class is defined as shown in Listing 15.3.

LISTING 15.3   CLED's Basic Class Definition (Edited)

```
 1: ////////////////////////////////////////////////////////////////////////////
 2: // CLED
 3: class CLED :
 4:     public CWindowImpl< CLED, CWindow, CControlWinTraits >
 5: {
 6: public:
 7:     // Construction/destruction
 8:     CLED() :
 9:         m_iState(LED_GREEN)
10:     {
11:     }
12:
13:     ~CLED()
14:     {
15:     }
16:
17:     // LED state methods
18:     (edited for brevity)
```

```
19:
20: ....// Static control registration/location methods
21:     (edited for brevity)
22:
23:     // Message map
24:     (edited for brevity)
25:
26:     // Message handlers
27:     (edited for brevity)
28:
29: // Implementation
30: protected:
31:     // Maintain GDI resources
32:     CBrush m_brRed;
33:     CBrush m_brGreen;
34:     CBrush m_brYellow;
35:     CBrush m_brBackGnd;
36:     CPen m_pnBackGnd;
37:     CPen m_pnLtGray;
38:     CPen m_pnDkGray;
39:
40:     // Compatible DC variables (double buffer)
41:     CBitmap* m_pbmMono;
42:     CDC m_dcBuffer;
43:     CBitmap m_bmColor;
44:
45:     // State data
46:     CRect m_rcWndRect;
47:     int m_iState;
48:
49:     // Static creation data
50:     static BOOL m_bRegistered;
51:     static CLED* m_pThis;
52:
53: };
54:
55: // Static declarations
56: BOOL CLED::m_bRegistered = CLED::Register();
57: CLED* CLED::m_pThis = NULL;
```

ANALYSIS   As you can see, the CLED class derives from CWindowImpl using the CControlWinTraits window styles (line 4), which include WS_CHILD, WS_VISIBLE, WS_CLIPCHILDREN, and WS_CLIPSIBLINGS. The only odd style is the WS_CLIPSIBLINGS, which simply tells Windows that any windows encroaching on this control should be clipped. (They get what they deserve!)

The class has several attributes, most of which are GDI related, such as brushes and pens. You see these in lines 31 through 51. I also keep the double buffer around rather than create it each time I handle a WM_PAINT request (line 42). This adds a little bookkeeping overhead, but I gain performance while actually painting (I don't have to take time to create all the GDI stuff required). I maintain the control's client area rectangle, line 46, as well as its LED state (green, yellow, or red), line 47. There are two interesting static members, m_bRegistered (line 50) and m_pThis (line 51), that deserve some attention.

This control will be used from within a Windows dialog box. Windows itself will manage the creation of the control for me, so I have little input into the process. This is normally not a problem when dealing with intrinsic controls. But, if the control is a "one-time good deal," as this control is, the fact that *I* don't create the control (Windows does it for me) causes problems.

For one thing, for me to process Windows messages, I have to register my window's class. The window class must be registered *before* Windows tries to create an instance of the LED control. If it isn't, Windows terminates the application. You won't get an error, but you also won't see your application. Note this differs from the ThermoBar example because the PROGRESS_CLASS window class already existed when the dialog was created.

To sidestep this, I use the kind of trick that an old MFC hack would try. I created a CLED static registration method and attribute. If you're a C++ whiz, you'll undoubtedly remember that static data is initialized before the application's main routine is executed. If you're like me, you had to look that fact up. But trust me, it's true.

So, I created a static registration method that registers my control's window class and assigns the result of that to the static attribute m_bRegistered. The registration method is shown in Listing 15.4.

LISTING 15.4 CLED's Registration Method

```
 1: static BOOL Register()
 2: {
 3:     // Register the window class of the control
 4:     WNDCLASS wc;
 5:     wc.style = CS_GLOBALCLASS | CS_DBLCLKS;
 6:     wc.lpfnWndProc = WindowProc;
 7:     wc.cbClsExtra = 0;
 8:     wc.cbWndExtra = 0;
 9:     wc.hInstance = NULL;
10:     wc.hIcon = NULL;
11:     wc.hCursor = ::LoadCursor(NULL, IDC_ARROW);
12:     wc.hbrBackground = (HBRUSH)(COLOR_WINDOW+1);
13:     wc.lpszMenuName = NULL;
```

```
14:     wc.lpszClassName = "Led";
15:
16:     if (!::RegisterClass(&wc)) {
17:         ATLASSERT(FALSE);
18:         return FALSE;
19:     }
20:     return TRUE;
21: }
```

Another fine detail here is the area I've highlighted in Listing 15.4, which is the pointer to the window class's window procedure on line 6. You must provide a window procedure, yet CWindowImpl has its own. Actually, this isn't that much of a problem because CWindowImpl's window procedure is virtual. I create one of my own for CLED and use that. You can see this in Listing 15.5. It, also, is a static CLED method.

LISTING 15.5   CLED's Window Procedure

```
1: static LRESULT CALLBACK WindowProc( HWND hWnd, UINT uMsg,
2: ►WPARAM wParam, LPARAM lParam )
3: {
4:     switch (uMsg) {
5:         case WM_NCCREATE:
6:             { // scope
7:                 // Create a C++ object to handle the messages
8:                 m_pThis = new CLED;
9:                 ATLASSERT(m_pThis);
10:
11:                 // Attach the window handle to the new object
12:                 BOOL b = m_pThis->SubclassWindow(hWnd);
13:                 ATLASSERT(b);
14:                 return b;
15:             } // scope
16:             break;
17:
18:         default:
19:             return ::DefWindowProc(hWnd,uMsg,wParam,lParam);
20:     } // switch
21: }
```

ANALYSIS CLED's window procedure might seem quite odd at first. After all, it handles a single message: WM_NCCREATE (line 5). It works because of the CWindowImpl::SubclassWindow() call. As soon as that happens, this window procedure is bypassed in favor of CWindowImpl's. WM_NCCREATE is all this window procedure ever needs to handle.

The catch is that an instance of CLED must be created, which is what the highlighted code in Listing 15.4 manages in lines 8 and 9. A new instance of CLED is created (line 8), a pointer to which is stored in the static member CLED::m_pThis. When the dialog box wants to access the LED control, CLED's this pointer (stored in m_pThis) is returned using the static method CLED::LocateLED():

```
static CLED* LocateLED()
{
    // Return this pointer
    return m_pThis;
}
```

Of course, when you create things, you must also destroy them. I delete this instance of CLED by overriding CWindowImpl::OnFinalMessage():

```
virtual void OnFinalMessage(HWND hWnd)
{
    // Delete this
    ATLASSERT(m_pThis != NULL);
    If ( m_pThis != NULL ) {
        delete m_pThis;
        m_pThis = NULL;
    } // if

}
```

If this seems odd to you, good! It is odd. For one thing, this sort of hocus pocus is what ActiveX solves for you. For another, this technique works tremendously well in MFC because MFC's CWnd::GetDlgItem() returns, not an HWND, but a pointer to another CWnd item. MFC stores instances of CWnd items in a map. When you pass an HWND into the map, you get the associated CWnd back out. If I create a new CWnd item in my control's window procedure, that item is automatically placed into this map. The dialog box then simply retrieves it using CWnd::GetDlgItem(). ATL has no such map, and CWindow::GetDlgItem() returns a simple HWND. The pointer to the new CLED instance is lost.

If you're tempted to use CContainedWindowT to contain the LED's HWND, as you saw in Day 13, "Creating ATL Applications: Where ATL Meets Win32," everything works just fine except there will be *two* instances of CLED, and the one you're using isn't the one dealing with the control! CLED's window procedure creates a copy, and then CContainedWindowT creates a copy. It gets worse, and I know because I tried everything I could think of. I tried CContainedWindowT::Attach() and CContainedWindow::SubclassWindow(). I tried to register a new class in CLED using DECLARE_WND_CLASS_EX (which I did not cover in Day 13, but which is found in the online documentation) and forgo CLED's custom registration code.

15

Nothing worked. Finally, I just stuffed the true CLED pointer into a static member and created a static method to retrieve it. This limits me to a single instance of the control per dialog box, but my point here isn't to dazzle everyone with fancy control creation. It is, instead, to get to the meat of the control, which is its painting and event behavior. It also proves that not every old MFC hack will work in ATL! If you grant that the code I've shown will, in fact, create an instance of the LED control, I'll improve upon this control when I wrap it in the ActiveX framework.

Everything I've described gets you to the point at which the control is created and ready to render its user interface and process events. Before any painting takes place, Windows issues a WM_CREATE and a WM_SIZE message. I take advantage of this and use the WM_CREATE handler to create the GDI objects that I'll require. I use the WM_SIZE handler to create the double buffer. After all, when the control is sized, I know how big the underlying bitmap should be. If the control is somehow later resized, the buffer will automatically accommodate the change in size. CLED's OnCreate() handler is shown in Listing 15.6, and its OnSize() handler is shown in Listing 15.7.

LISTING 15.6   CLED's OnCreate() Handler

```
 1: LRESULT OnCreate(UINT uMsg, WPARAM wParam, LPARAM lParam,
    ➥BOOL& bHandled)
 2: {
 3:     // Create the GDI resources
 4:     m_brRed.CreateSolidBrush(RGB(255,0,0));
 5:     m_brGreen.CreateSolidBrush(RGB(20,255,20));
 6:     m_brYellow.CreateSolidBrush(RGB(255,255,0));
 7:     m_brBackGnd.CreateSolidBrush(GetSysColor(COLOR_BTNFACE));
 8:     m_pnBackGnd.CreatePen(PS_SOLID,1,GetSysColor(COLOR_BTNFACE));
 9:     m_pnLtGray.CreatePen(PS_SOLID,1,GetSysColor(COLOR_3DHILIGHT));
10:     m_pnDkGray.CreatePen(PS_SOLID,1,GetSysColor(COLOR_3DSHADOW));
11:     return 0;
12: }
```

LISTING 15.7   CLED's OnSize() Handler

```
 1: LRESULT OnSize(UINT uMsg, WPARAM wParam, LPARAM lParam,
    ➥BOOL& bHandled)
 2: {
 3:     // Store window rectangle coordinates and size
 4:     int cx = LOWORD(lParam);  // width of client area
 5:     int cy = HIWORD(lParam); // height of client area
 6:     m_rcWndRect.SetRectEmpty();
 7:     m_rcWndRect.right = cx;
```

continues

LISTING 15.7   continued

```
 8:        m_rcWndRect.bottom = cy;
 9:
10:        // Build a compatible memory DC
11:        if ( m_dcBuffer.m_hDC != NULL ) {
12:            // I've been resized, so delete any existing double buffer
13:            // and create a new one.
14:            m_dcBuffer.SelectObject(m_pbmMono); // select in old bitmap
15:            m_bmColor.DeleteObject(); // delete GDI object
16:            m_dcBuffer.DeleteDC(); // delete memory DC
17:        } // if
18:
19:        // Now, build the new double buffer
20:        CDC dcParent;
21:        dcParent.Attach(::GetDC(GetParent()));
22:        m_dcBuffer.CreateCompatibleDC(&dcParent);
23:        m_bmColor.CreateCompatibleBitmap(&dcParent,
24:                                         m_sWndRect.Width(),
25:                                         m_sWndRect.Height());
26:        m_pbmMono = (CBitmap*)m_dcBuffer.SelectObject(m_bmColor);
27:        ::ReleaseDC(GetParent(),dcParent.Detach());
28:        return 0;
29: }
```

ANALYSIS   CLED::OnCreate() (in Listing 15.6) is pretty basic GDI stuff—I'm just creating brushes and pens, as you can see from lines 3 through 10. Also, CLED::OnSize() in Listing 15.7 also isn't too different from the double-buffer creation code you saw in "Flicker-Free Drawing." I use the parent window's DC when I create the buffer because I don't have any other DC against which to model it. (The parent's DC makes the most sense anyway, because I want to snuggle my control into the parent's environment.)

After Windows creates and sizes the window, Windows issues a WM_ERASEBKGND and a WM_PAINT message. Because I'll always paint the entire control's area in WM_PAINT, the WM_ERASEBKGND message is superfluous. CLED's handler for that, CLED::OnEraseBkgnd(), simply returns one (1) to tell Windows it handled the background erasure. When it does that, Windows won't erase the background for me and I save some time (and possible flickering). The handler for the WM_PAINT message, shown in Listing 15.8, is more interesting.

LISTING 15.8   CLED's OnPaint() Handler

```
1: LRESULT OnPaint(UINT uMsg, WPARAM wParam, LPARAM lParam,
2: ➥BOOL& bHandled)
3: {
4:     // Set up for painting
```

```
 5:     CPaintDC dcPaint(m_hWnd);
 6:
 7:     // Clear the client area
 8:     CBrush* pOldBrush =
 9: ➡(CBrush*)m_dcBuffer.SelectObject(&m_brBackGnd);
10:     CPen* pOldPen = (CPen*)m_dcBuffer.SelectObject(&m_pnBackGnd);
11:     m_dcBuffer.FillRect(&m_rcWndRect,&m_brBackGnd);
12:
13:     // Create a control drawing rectangle
14:     CRect rcClient(m_rcWndRect);
15:
16:     // Square the drawing rectangle to produce a circular
17:     // control
18:     SquareDrawRect(rcClient);
19:
20:     // Draw color circle with gray border
21:     m_dcBuffer.SelectObject(&m_pnDkGray);
22:     switch ( m_iState ) {
23:         case LED_GREEN:
24:             m_dcBuffer.SelectObject(&m_brGreen);
25:             break;
26:
27:         case LED_YELLOW:
28:             m_dcBuffer.SelectObject(&m_brYellow);
29:             break;
30:
31:         case LED_RED:
32:         default: // Red
33:             m_dcBuffer.SelectObject(&m_brRed);
34:             break;
35:
36:     } // switch
37:     m_dcBuffer.Ellipse(&rcClient);
38:
39:     // Create a rectangle for 3D effect
40:     CRect rcLines(m_rcWndRect);
41:     rcLines.DeflateRect(3,3);
42:
43:     // Draw ornamental lines (add 3D appearance)
44:     //
45:     // Upper arc
46:     m_dcBuffer.SelectObject(&m_pnLtGray);
47:     CPoint ptStart((m_rcWndRect.Width()/2),0);
48:     CPoint ptEnd(0,(m_rcWndRect.Height()/2));
49:     m_dcBuffer.SetArcDirection(AD_COUNTERCLOCKWISE);
50:     m_dcBuffer.Arc(rcLines,ptStart,ptEnd);
51:
```

continues

LISTING 15.8 continued

```
52:      // Lower arc
53:      m_dcBuffer.SelectObject(&m_pnDkGray);
54:      ptStart.x = m_rcWndRect.Width()/2;
55:      ptStart.y = m_rcWndRect.Height();
56:      ptEnd.x = m_rcWndRect.Width();
57:      ptEnd.y = m_rcWndRect.Height()/2;
58:      m_dcBuffer.Arc(rcLines,ptStart,ptEnd);
59:
60:      // Transfer image to screen
61:      dcPaint.BitBlt(m_rcWndRect.left,m_rcWndRect.top,
62:                     m_rcWndRect.Width(),m_rcWndRect.Height(),
63:                     &m_dcBuffer,0,0,SRCCOPY);
64:
65:      // Clean up
66:      m_dcBuffer.SelectObject(pOldBrush);
67:      m_dcBuffer.SelectObject(pOldPen);
68:
69:      return 0;
70: }
```

ANALYSIS The painting code is pretty straightforward, although I did add a helper function `SquareDrawRect()`, which I call from line 18. This converts any arbitrary rectangular region to a square region so that the control will draw perfectly circular LEDs.

Whenever the parent forces the control to paint, it uses the current LED state to determine the color of the LED, as you can see from line 22. However, you can force the control to repaint if you change the state:

```
enum State {LED_GREEN = 0, LED_YELLOW, LED_RED};

void SetState( int iState )
{
    // Check range and accept if valid
    ATLASSERT((iState >= LED_GREEN) && (iState <= LED_RED));
    if ((iState >= LED_GREEN) && (iState <= LED_RED)) {
        // Accept the state and redraw
        m_iState = iState;
        InvalidateRect(NULL);
    } // if
}
```

This simply checks the input value's bounds and redraws the control if the value is valid.

The last area of the control I'll discuss is the parent-window event notification. You can pick any number of event triggers, but I choose to implement mouse clicks for this sample. If the user clicks or double-clicks within the LED's control rectangle, the control will issue a WM_NOTIFY message to the parent window. The notification structure for each event closely follows the left-button click's structure:

```
#define LEDCTRL_NOTIFY_LCLICK 412350
typedef struct tagClick {
    // Click notification message
    NMHDR hdr;        // WM_NOTIFY message header
    POINT pt;         // location of click
    long fwKeys;      // keyboard state
} NMLCLICK, FAR* LPNMLCLICK;
```

I provide the usual NMHDR information, as well as the location of the click and any keyboard modifiers. I get this information directly from the particular mouse message, which in this case is WM_LBUTTONUP. After the left mouse button is released, I handle the resulting WM_LBUTTONUP message as you see in Listing 15.9.

LISTING 15.9   CLED's OnLButtonUp() Handler

```
 1: LRESULT OnLButtonUP(UINT uMsg, WPARAM wParam, LPARAM lParam,
 2: ➥BOOL& bHandled)
 3: {
 4:     // Get parent handle
 5:     HWND hwndParent = GetParent();
 6:     if ( hwndParent != NULL ) {
 7:         // Obtain control ID
 8:         int nID = GetDlgCtrlID();
 9:
10:         // Create notification message
11:         NMLCLICK msg;
12:         msg.hdr.hwndFrom = m_hWnd;
13:         msg.hdr.idFrom = nID;
14:         msg.hdr.code = LEDCTRL_NOTIFY_LCLICK;
15:         msg.pt.x = LOWORD(lParam);
16:         msg.pt.y = HIWORD(lParam);
17:         msg.fwKeys = wParam;
18:
19:         // Send it
20:         SendMessage(hwndParent,WM_NOTIFY,(WPARAM)nID,(LPARAM)&msg);
21:     } // if
22:     else {
23:         // No parent?
24:         ATLASSERT(FALSE);
25:     } // else
26:
27:     return 0;
28: }
```

The remaining three events are handled in a similar manner. With the control code itself complete, it's time to turn to the application that will use the control.

The Application

I created another ATL dialog-based application to use as a test container for the LED control. It actually isn't too difficult, given the code I had from Day 13. I edited all of the files, changed some names, and out popped the new application. The majority of the code from Day 13 remained intact, and I won't belabor every detail. Maybe someday I'll write a custom AppWizard to handle the details for me.

In any case, I did have to modify the files for the application to deal with the new control and handle the events. The basic user interface I designed is shown in Figure 15.3.

FIGURE 15.3

The BasicLED sample application user interface.

The LED control is shown in the upper-left corner, and you can change its state using the radio buttons. If the control notifies the application of an event, I handle the WM_NOTIFY message and display a string in the LED Notifications text control. I did get somewhat fancy and start a timer after an LED event—after the timer fires I clear the event window. This just prevents old notifications from remaining onscreen overlong.

Summary

Today, you took another step towards building a true ActiveX control. I placed this lesson between the discussion of dual interfaces and the true ActiveX controls so I would be sure everyone has been introduced to the Windows GDI and has seen some basic custom control design and implementation work. Although it's true the majority of the LED code won't be necessary when it's housed in an ActiveX control, I believe the exercise to create a standard Windows control is useful. You don't want to deal with basic GDI issues when you're trying to understand ActiveX wrapper code!

To make sure everyone is up to speed, I began today by discussing the Windows GDI in general, and the device context and bitmap specifically. The bitmap stores what will be drawn, whereas the DC tailors how it will be drawn (among other things). I then went on to describe animation flickering and to show why all controls you create should render themselves to a double buffer. A quick execution of BasicGDI should convince you, if I haven't already done so.

I described the standard Windows mechanisms for notifying a parent window of an interesting event. I mentioned you can use either WM_COMMAND or WM_NOTIFY, although all contemporary controls use WM_NOTIFY. I then briefly discussed an example where I subclassed the progress meter custom control to render it as a thermometer control.

Finally, I created a brand new control, the LED. I showed you how to register the control, change its LED state, and paint the resulting control. I discussed how to send the event notification to the parent application when the user clicks the mouse within the window rectangle. I then briefly described the test application I devised to test the control.

As I mentioned, this leads to incorporating the basic control logic into an ActiveX control, which you'll see in Day 16. I'll reserve the event notifications for the lesson after that (Day 17). If you're having as much fun as I am, read on!

Q&A

Q Why did you reuse the MFC GDI wrappers and do they impose a performance penalty?

A I knew MFC faithfully wrapped the GDI API, and I firmly believe the API cries out to be wrapped. Because I had access to the MFC source code, it made sense to pull it from MFC and make it ATL. I had to make changes, but those changes didn't seriously impair the operation of the GDI classes. I also know the MFC developers worked diligently to keep the GDI wrappers as simple and as light as possible. This is thoroughly in keeping with the goals of the ATL development team. There will be some minor performance penalty for using the classes, but no more so than using any C++ class over equivalent C code. I have not as yet tested the classes to determine how much larger the resulting compiled object will be, but my intuition tells me it won't add significantly to the size. (Much within the classes is declared inline, which helps to reduce the size and increase the speed.) Frankly, it's just easier to write GDI code using the MFC wrappers!

Q You spent some time discussing the control's registration code. Is this useful anywhere else?

A I believe it is. I've seen development teams come up with their own Windows controls, and in some cases, they had good reason for not turning them into COM-based controls. For example, ActiveX requires you to upgrade early versions of Windows 95. If you're shipping shrink-wrapped software, you know why this can be problematic. It means you have to get the upgrade from Microsoft and distribute it, which makes *you* responsible for the upgrade. Your customer-service crew could be in for a workout. If you have no compelling reason to convert your control to ActiveX, you can use the technique I presented to simplify your installation and reduce the overall application's footprint. (You don't need the overhead of shipping the ActiveX container code either.) Whether you roll your own custom control or wrap it in ActiveX is completely situational. At least, you have another weapon in your arsenal.

Workshop

The Workshop is designed to help you anticipate possible questions, review what you've learned, and get you thinking about how to put your knowledge into practice. The answers to the quiz are in Appendix A, "Answers."

Quiz

1. Can you name three GDI API calls used to obtain a device context?
2. Why should you always destroy GDI resources when you're through with them?
3. What causes animation flickering and how do you reduce its effects? Is the technique you suggest 100 percent effective?
4. What are the two standard control notification protocols and, in general, how do they differ?
5. Why would the LED control create its double buffer in the WM_SIZE handler instead of when the control is created (WM_CREATE)?

Exercises

1. Change the behavior of the bubbles in BasicGDI (go sideways, or down).
2. Add painting code to display the LED control in a disabled state (HINT: IsWindowEnabled() returns FALSE).
3. Add an event to the LED control, for example, when the focus shifts to and away from the control.

WEEK 3

DAY 16

ATL and ActiveX: Modern Control Packaging

If there is one topic I have been looking forward to covering it is ATL and ActiveX. I've always liked coding little widgets and doodads, and ActiveX allows me to insert my little doodads into a tremendous variety of applications. ATL manages the ActiveX framework quite well, and it does so with very little fat (compare ATL to MFC, for example).

ActiveX is a big topic, however, which is why I broke some of the related issues into separate days. For example, during the Day 15, "Custom Controls: Basic Control Development Techniques," I described using the GDI to create a custom control, and the focus there was on the control behavior and how to implement that behavior. It will require *two* lessons to take that simple LED control and put it into an ActiveX setting:

- Today I will provide you with the background you need to understand ActiveX.
- During Day 17, "ATL and Connection Points: Supporting COMs Event Model," I will show you how to notify the parent window (called the container in ActiveX parlance) of an event.

It might seem odd to require two lessons to discuss how ATL simplifies the custom control you created during Day 15, "Custom Controls: Basic Control Development Techniques," but it's important you understand the nuts and bolts.

Today I'll concentrate on the ActiveX paradigm and framework, and you'll take some of the LED code from Day 15 and roll it into an ActiveX control. For example, you'll see

- Many of the basic ActiveX concepts you'll need to understand to master ActiveX programming
- How ATL supports ActiveX
- How ATL provides for property persistence
- How to incorporate custom control behavior in an ActiveX setting

ActiveX Concepts

You might think of ActiveX as a glitz blitz from Microsoft, but it's actually a technology built upon the COM foundation. The name is glitzy, I agree. ActiveX technology originated with 16-bit Windows and Visual Basic when some enterprising developers realized they could build custom controls and have Visual Basic automatically incorporate these controls into their applications. These controls were known as *VBX* controls (for *Visual Basic Extension* controls) or OLE controls.

There was at least one major problem with VBXs, however. Visual Basic hadn't exposed a standardized, well-documented interface to implement them. As often happens, some controls were better implemented than others were, so the market was full of well-written controls and cheap knock-offs.

Microsoft, being the marketing giant it is, realized the controls market was significant and decided to standardize the way controls hooked into Visual Basic. Microsoft wisely expanded its scope, however, and provided a standard any application could follow to incorporate these new controls. The standard was completed in 1996 and is referred to as the *OCX 96 Specification*. This specification introduced many things, but one of the major features was the reduction in the number of interfaces the control had to support to meet the specification. This simplified the developer's job.

You've probably read a lot about ActiveX. I find many people get confused because ActiveX seems to find its way into so many technologies. Is it for Visual Basic? Is it for the Web? Actually, ActiveX represents a number of technologies rather than just one. Each of the ActiveX technologies defines the interfaces between the objects to implement the given technology. The major ActiveX technologies include

- *Active Documents*, which enable the Internet Explorer browser to support nonHTML documents (such as a Word 97 document)
- *Active Scripting*, which enables applications to support standardized scripting logic for Visual Basic for Applications and JScript
- *ActiveX Controls*, which is a packaging technology for reusing controls across platforms and development environments (the focus of this lesson)
- *Active Server Components*, which enable the Web server (IIS) to interface to server-scripted components (such as ASP scripts)

16

I'm interested in discussing the ActiveX control today, primarily because of ATL's superior support for this technology. ATL also supports ActiveX Server Components, and through some code you provide, ActiveX Scripting. You can read more about ActiveX Scripting in Sam's Publishing *MFC with Visual C++ 6 Unleashed*, ISBN 0-672-31557-2, where scripting capability is added to an MFC application.

I'll now focus on the ActiveX control itself.

Properties and Methods

From Day 7, "The ATL Object Wizard: Customizing the Basic ATL Framework," I'm sure you recall how properties and methods differ—yet are the same. I won't reiterate that topic here. You've seen the mechanics. Instead, I want to focus on how your control's user perceives your control and how you can design better ActiveX controls.

With the exception of the C++ application programmer, all your control's users will see your control as exposing its functionality through properties and methods (C++ programmers see only methods). A property, such as a color or caption, is an attribute of the control. Even though *you* know it requires two methods to manage the property, your user simply sees the control with some color and a caption. The methods your control provides, on the other hand, implement the user's perception of what your control does.

Sometimes the difference between the property and the method is blurry, although in other cases there is a clear difference. The trick when designing controls is to think like a user and try to see your control from his perspective. Although you could implement a method such as ActivateAlertColor(color) for some type of indicator control, perhaps it makes more sense to implement a property, AlertColor, and a method, Alert(). It might mean a bit more work on your part, but the object model that your control presents to the user will be more intuitive.

Another aspect to the ActiveX property is that there are actually three types of properties: ambient, stock, and custom. You're familiar with the *custom* properties, because those are the properties you implement. They're properties specific to your control implementation. ATL provides support for a large number of typical properties, and collectively these properties are known as the *stock* properties. These properties are common to a wide variety of controls, such as background and foreground color, caption, and font. The third set of properties is called *ambient* properties because the container provides your control with this information to help the control better blend visually into the container's user interface. They provide your control with some insight as to how the control is being used within the container. For example, the container will tell you if the control is currently in a design mode or a runtime mode. ATL provides support for all these property types. I'll describe them in more detail as I discuss building the control itself in "ActiveX Interfaces and ATL."

Property Pages

Ultimately your control will actually have two users. The obvious user is the soul who paid for a bundle of software that happened to include your ActiveX control or who downloaded it from a Web site. The other user, however, is the developer who is reusing your control in her code. You, as the control developer, must address both users. I'll leave the end user's satisfaction to your creative genius and clearly superior coding skills (you obviously have good taste in reference material!). The developer user, however, merits some more discussion.

The developer user will incorporate your control into her code and wire up the methods and properties of interest into her application. Your control will have two very different environments in which it must work. First, it must operate at design time. And second, it must execute at runtime when the container itself is executed.

At design time, the developer is free to establish specific properties, such as an initial color or caption. The development environment should take these properties and persist them so that when the control is in its runtime environment, it is initialized with the correct settings. The developer user establishes these settings by accessing property pages your control or ATL provides (ATL provides several property pages to address the stock properties).

How many property pages you create and what they contain is control-specific. The truly interesting thing about these property pages is they are themselves COM objects! A COM object implements each property page you insert into your control. That's why you have the option of adding a property page object to your ATL framework using the ATL Object Wizard.

The property pages give the developer user easy access to the properties your control exposes. The property page as a COM object will interact with your ActiveX control to persist the property settings that the developer user selected. The actual property persistence is specific to the development environment (Visual C++ stores the control property information in the .RC file as text-encoded hex values).

Invisible and Windowless Controls

I tend to think of ActiveX controls as a user interface tool. That is, if I want to build a better button, I can do it with ActiveX. This isn't always the case, however. Visual Basic, for example, has no built-in mechanism to deal with the Windows timer or to access the Registry. It gains access to the timer and Registry via ActiveX controls, but clearly these controls have no user interface implications. Instead, these controls are *invisible* ActiveX controls. They follow the ActiveX specification, but they don't provide a user interface. You decide if your control is to be invisible when you add the ActiveX object to your ATL framework.

A *windowless* ActiveX control isn't the same as an invisible ActiveX control. The primary purpose of the windowless control is to allow for nonrectangular painting regions and transparency. It also gains a performance boost.

Window creation is an expensive process. It takes time and resources to create and manage a window. Windowless controls, on the other hand, don't create a new window themselves if the container supports windowless control operation (the control will create a window for itself, if not, for backward compatibility). Instead, they rely upon the host container for normal window operations. For example, the container manages obtaining a device context, captures the mouse, or queries for the keyboard focus for you.

Component Categories and `IObjectSafety`

Component categories are not specific to ActiveX, although many contemporary ActiveX controls implement certain component categories. The component category is really related to OLE, another COM-based technology. In the OLE sense, embeddable objects align themselves with specific categories, such as Safe for Scripting or Document Object.

The available component categories are stored in the Registry under `HKEY_CLASSES_ROOT/Component Categories`, and if you open the Registry and look there, you see a collection of GUIDs. Each GUID represents a component category, and each one should have a readable category name. For example, the GUID {7DD95801-9882-11CF-9FA9-00AA006C42C4} represents the Safe for Scripting category.

Any COM object that feels it is safely scriptable records this very GUID under its CLSID when it registers (under the `Implemented Categories` key). If it meets the criteria for other categories, those are added as well.

Containers looking for objects that are safe for scripting can zip through the Registry and locate all objects that contained this GUID in their Implemented Categories key. Of course, the same is true for any other category.

You are certainly free to implement your own category GUIDs, known as *category IDs*, or *CATIDs*, and a quick look at my Registry tells me other people have done so. In general, though, you'll want to use the categories Microsoft has implemented. The difficulty you'll face is determining what those categories are and what criteria you have to meet to claim your control fits that category. This is not a well-documented area of COM development. For example, what makes an object safely scriptable? In general terms, if your control claims it fits into this category, you are telling the world your control won't "do anything bad" to the system when it is used in a scripting environment. Precisely what "do anything bad" means is left up to you. Hmm.

Frequently, COM objects will belong to several categories. If you open the COMCAT.H file that ships with Visual C++, you should find a number of standard CATIDs, and the Safe for Scripting CATID is in OBJSAFE.H. You'll find other CATIDs in ACTIVSCP.H, EFFECT.H, MSDATSRC.H, and SHLGUID.H. Your control might belong to any of the categories you find in these files or even in categories you create yourself. As I mentioned, how you determine whether your control fits a given category is, unfortunately, not often documented and left up to you.

There is a Component Category Manager, however, and the manager will handle the registration details for you. The manager is also a COM object (CLSID_StdComponentCategoriesMgr), and it exposes two interfaces: IID_ICatRegister and IID_ICatInformation. You can use these two interfaces to either register your control as belonging to a standard category or determine which objects registered on the given system implement which categories.

I mention this because some containers will refuse to instantiate your control if your control doesn't indicate it belongs to certain categories. An example is that Internet Explorer will not bring up your control if it isn't Safe for Scripting. I'll add component categories to the LED control in the upcoming "Adding Component Categories" section to show you how to implement them.

The IObjectSafety interface was developed to provide a mechanism for the container to dynamically set and retrieve your control's safety level (initialization and scripting). Frequently, ActiveX controls that support Component Categories also support this interface. Luckily, ATL provides an implementation for you. I'll also address this interface later in the "Adding Component Categories" section.

ActiveX Interfaces and ATL

You've actually already created two ActiveX controls so far in this book, but I didn't present them specifically as implementations of ActiveX. I merely wanted to create a COM object I could easily load into Visual Basic or one I could #import into Visual C++. Now, it's time to revisit ActiveX from an ATL standpoint.

For this section, I'll create a new ActiveX control that I'll later use to implement the LED control. If you bring up Visual Studio and create a new ATL project, call it Day16Server and accept the default DLL implementation. After the project is created, add an ActiveX (full control) ATL object. I set the names as you see in Figure 16.1, but I accepted the default for the rest of the property pages with these exceptions: check the ISupportErrorInfo and IConnectionPoint options under Attributes and select the Enabled stock property. I'll reuse this control during Day 17, when I discuss connection points (hence that selection here).

16

FIGURE 16.1

The Day16Server ActiveX control's Names Property Page.

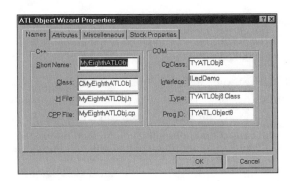

Control Interfaces

Visual Studio will grind for a moment and spit out your ActiveX control. Before you make any modifications, take a look at all the base classes for this control. Wow! This object supports a lot of interfaces, as you can see in Listing 16.1.

LISTING 16.1 CMyEighthATLObj's Base Classes

```
1: class ATL_NO_VTABLE CMyEighthATLObj :
2:     public CComObjectRootEx<CComSingleThreadModel>,
3:     public CStockPropImpl<CMyEighthATLObj, ILedDemo,
4: ➥&IID_ILedDemo, &LIBID_DAY16SERVERLib>,
5:     public CComControl<CMyEighthATLObj>,
6:     public IPersistStreamInitImpl<CMyEighthATLObj>,
7:     public IOleControlImpl<CMyEighthATLObj>,
8:     public IOleObjectImpl<CMyEighthATLObj>,
```

continues

LISTING 16.1 continued

```
 9:     public IOleInPlaceActiveObjectImpl<CMyEighthATLObj>,
10:     public IViewObjectExImpl<CMyEighthATLObj>,
11:     public IOleInPlaceObjectWindowlessImpl<CMyEighthATLObj>,
12:     public ISupportErrorInfo,
13:     public IConnectionPointContainerImpl<CMyEighthATLObj>,
14:     public IPersistStorageImpl<CMyEighthATLObj>,
15:     public ISpecifyPropertyPagesImpl<CMyEighthATLObj>,
16:     public IQuickActivateImpl<CMyEighthATLObj>,
17:     public IDataObjectImpl<CMyEighthATLObj>,
18:     public IProvideClassInfo2Impl<&CLSID_TYATLObj8,
19: ➥&DIID__ILedDemoEvents, &LIBID_DAY16SERVERLib>,
20:     public IPropertyNotifySinkCP<CMyEighthATLObj>,
21:     public CComCoClass<CMyEighthATLObj, &CLSID_TYATLObj8>
22: {
23:     (edited for brevity)
24: };
```

ANALYSIS You saw a few of the base classes when you looked at the ATL architecture in
Day 5, "ATL Architecture: How ATL Implements COM." For example, you see
CComObjectRootEx and CComCoClass, lines 2 and 21, respectively.

The basic ATL ActiveX support comes from the CComControl base class, line 5, which
has CWindowImpl as one of its base classes (the other is CComControlBase which handles
some initialization chores). Because I had you add the Enabled stock property, your control is based upon CStockPropImpl (line 3). This class manages the stock properties ATL
understands so you don't have to do any extra work to persist their values. If you look to
the very bottom of the class definition, you'll find this member (not shown in Listing 16.1):

```
BOOL m_bEnabled;
```

Had you selected other stock properties, there would be additional members representing
them inserted here also.

The majority of the other base classes are either there to directly control the
ActiveX nature of the control or are helpers. An example of a helper interface is
ISupportErrorInfo, which you see in line 12 of Listing 16.1. The major control inter-
faces are shown in Table 16.1

TABLE 16.1 CMyEighthATLObj-Supported ActiveX Interfaces

Interface	Purpose
IOleControl	Supports keyboard mnemonics, ambient properties, and events
IOleObject	Supports control/container communication

Interface	Purpose
IOleInPlaceActiveObject	Supports message translation, window frame state (activated or deactivated), and document window state (activated or deactivated)
IViewObjectEx	Supports flicker-free drawing, transparency, hit-testing, and control sizing
IOleInPlaceObjectWindowless	Supports control message processing and participation in drag-and-drop operations
ISpecifyPropertyPages	Supports control property pages
IQuickActivate	Supports high-performance initialization and loading handshaking between the control and the container
IDataObject	Supports data transfer and data change notifications (especially for binding)
IPropertyNotifySink	Supports container notification of property changes (especially for binding)

You'll also note a few other interfaces. Some are for supporting connection points, which I'll cover during Day 17. These include IConnectionPointContainer and IProvideClassInfo2 (lines 13 and 18). Others are persistence interfaces that I'll cover in the next section.

Persistence Interfaces

Because much of the functionality your ActiveX control exposes is through properties, it makes sense to be able to store those properties somewhere for later recall. That is, you want them to *persist*, which means the properties should be reconstituted when the control is again instantiated. ATL provides quite a bit of support for property persistence, and you'll examine this more closely, beginning with the "ATL ActiveX Property Map" section.

There are a couple of COM interfaces you'll require to actually store any data. I've listed these in Table 16.2.

TABLE 16.2 CMyEighthATLObj Supported Persistence Interfaces

Interface	Purpose
IPersistStreamInit	Supports initialized stream-based persistence
IPersistStorage	Supports container-based data storage

In a nutshell, IPersistStreamInit allows your control to store data to a stream, but unlike IPersistStream, the control can be initialized to a certain state by using the IPersistStreamInit::InitNew() method. IPersistStorage allows for the container to pass into your control a storage into which you stuff or retrieve your persisted properties. Both interfaces support OLE compound documents, although there is no requirement that the container store your properties in such a fashion (Visual C++ doesn't, for example).

The properties your control stores are managed by ATL using another map. In this case, it's the property map I mentioned during Day 7.

ATL ActiveX Property Map

The ATL property map is another mapping construct that allows ATL to rummage through your object's properties and persist those you indicate should be stored for recall. The ActiveX control I've been describing, implemented by the *CMyEighthATLObj* C++ class, has the property map shown in Listing 16.2 as a starting point.

LISTING 16.2 CMyEighthATLObj's Property Map Implementation

```
1: BEGIN_PROP_MAP(CMyEighthATLObj)
2:     PROP_DATA_ENTRY("_cx", m_sizeExtent.cx, VT_UI4)
3:     PROP_DATA_ENTRY("_cy", m_sizeExtent.cy, VT_UI4)
4:     PROP_ENTRY("Enabled", DISPID_ENABLED, CLSID_NULL)
5:     // Example entries
6:     // PROP_ENTRY("Property Description", dispid, clsid)
7:     // PROP_PAGE(CLSID_StockColorPage)
8: END_PROP_MAP()
```

As is usual, ATL wraps individual map entries within a pair of beginning and ending macros. The BEGIN_PROP_MAP(theClass) macro expands to the code shown in Listing 16.3.

LISTING 16.3 ATL's BEGIN_PROP_MAP() Macro Definition

```
1: #define BEGIN_PROP_MAP(theClass) \
2:     typedef _ATL_PROP_NOTIFY_EVENT_CLASS __ATL_PROP_NOTIFY_EVENT_CLASS; \
3:     typedef theClass _PropMapClass; \
4:     static ATL_PROPMAP_ENTRY* GetPropertyMap()\
5:     {\
6:         static ATL_PROPMAP_ENTRY pPropMap[] = \
7:         {
```

This listing defines a static method `GetPropertyMap()` (line 4) that returns a pointer to the map the macro also declares (the `pPropMap[]` array, line 6). The `GetPropertyMap()` method is significant as the ATL implementations of the persistence interfaces use this method to determine what properties to persist.

Jumping to the end of the map, ATL closes the map with a `NULL` entry and provides the implementation for `GetPropertyMap()`, shown in Listing 16.4.

LISTING 16.4 ATL's `END_PROP_MAP()` Macro Definition

```
1: #define END_PROP_MAP() \
2:             {NULL, 0, NULL, &IID_NULL, 0, 0, 0} \
3:         }; \
4:       return pPropMap; \
5:     }
```

In between the beginning and ending macros lie the properties themselves. Of course, there are several ATL macros available to help you build this map. I've listed them all in Table 16.3.

TABLE 16.3 ATL Property Map Property Storage Macros

Interface	Purpose
PROP_ENTRY()	Standard property persistence
PROP_ENTRY_EX()	Standard property persistence from multiple IDispatch interfaces
PROP_PAGE()	Property persistence via a property page
PROP_DATA_ENTRY()	Persists C++ class members

`PROP_ENTRY()` accepts three parameters: a descriptive string, a DISPID that represents the property, and the CLSID of a property page that can be used to modify the property (if there is none, you pass in `CLSID_NULL`). `PROP_ENTRY_EX()` is nearly the same as `PROP_ENTRY()`, with the exception of a fourth parameter, an `IDispatch` interface pointer, that will be used to obtain the property value. If you happen to have multiple `IDispatch` interfaces contained within your object, you use this macro to persist all their properties. `PROP_PAGE()` is relatively simple. You provide the CLSID of a property page and ATL stores its data for you. The final macro, `PROP_DATA_ENTRY()`, is also relatively simple. It stores one of your C++ class's attributes.

The sample control already has three properties persisted: the `Extents` and its `Enabled` state. An ActiveX control's `Extent` value is a measure of the control's maximum drawing area. You cannot paint outside of this area. If you do, you'll overpaint part of the container. The Enabled value represents the state of the control when it is initialized, as in it is enabled or disabled (in an IsWindowEnabled() sense). If the control is disabled, it should be drawn to appear disabled and not respond to user inputs.

This is probably enough background to understand what ATL has provided as a starting point. Let's squeeze that LED control from Day 15 into the ActiveX framework.

ActiveX and Custom Controls

It's time to put the LED control into your ATL ActiveX project. This will actually involve several steps, but none of them are too difficult. After all, you've already done the hard part, which is to specify what the control will do and implement its basic behavior (especially painting and user input).

The first step is to modify what the wizards gave you. Often the code is fine as is, but in this case it can use some touching-up. Then, you should add the LED-specific behavioral code. Normally, after the behavioral code is inserted, you handle the control's event notifications, but I'll reserve that for Day 17. Finally, you test your control in a variety of containers to see that things are working as they should in each case. I'll start with the basic modifications and work my way through the rest of the steps.

Initial Code Modifications

The first thing I will change is the implementation of ISupportErrorInfo. The code the wizard provided is wonderful if you intend to expose two or more interfaces, even though only one is currently listed. Rather than have the wizard's code in the control, I would rather use ISupportErrorInfoImpl to manage the single interface I intend to expose.

This change is a simple one to make. You might recall this line of code from Listing 16.1:

```
public ISupportErrorInfo,
```

This should be changed to

```
public ISupportErrorInfoImpl<&IID_ILedDemo>,
```

At this time, the implementation the wizard provided can be removed (you'll find it in MyEighthATLObj.h), shown in Listing 16.5.

LISTING 16.5   Typical ATL `ISupportErrorInfo` Implementation

```
 1: // ISupportsErrorInfo
 2: STDMETHOD(InterfaceSupportsErrorInfo)(REFIID riid)
 3: {
 4:     static const IID* arr[] =
 5:     {
 6:         &IID_ILedDemo,
 7:     };
 8:     for (int i=0; i<sizeof(arr)/sizeof(arr[0]); i++)
 9:     {
10:         if (InlineIsEqualGUID(*arr[i], riid))
11:             return S_OK;
12:     }
13:     return S_FALSE;
14: }
```

Adding a Property Page

The next change I will make is to add a property page. As you recall, the LED control had a single property, State. I'll add a property page that allows the developer user to set the LED's initial state, which will then be persisted with the control's other property stream data.

To add a property page, I invoke the ATL Object Wizard just as I did to create the ActiveX control. Under the Controls category, I select the Property Page list item and click Next.

This brings up the familiar Names property page, which I completed as you see in Figure 16.2. Some of the text is clipped, so here is the text I inserted:

- Short Name: *MyEighthATLObjPPage1*
- CoClass: *TYATLObj8PPage1*
- Type: *TYATLObj8PPage1 Class*
- ProgID: *TYATL.Object8PPage1*

I let the filenames default based upon the short name.

I left the Attributes page alone. The default values there were fine. I did change the settings on the Strings property page, however. You can see how I set their values in Figure 16.3.

FIGURE **16.2**

The Day16Server ActiveX control's Property Sheet's Names Property Page.

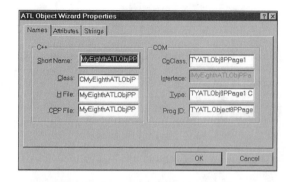

FIGURE **16.3**

The Day16Server ActiveX control's Property Sheet's Strings Property Page.

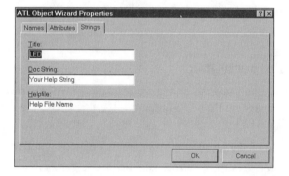

After I clicked OK, Visual Studio ground out some code for me and created a dialog template for the property page, which I modified as you see in Figure 16.4.

FIGURE **16.4**

The LED ActiveX control's LED Property Page.

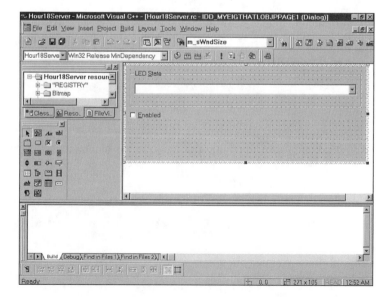

The first thing to do is to include the ATLControls.h file so you can retrieve the data from the property page controls. I added the file to STDAFX.H to incorporate it into the precompiled header file.

With the ATLControls.h file included, you can use the `CComboBox` and `CButton` (for the check box) classes. I added these lines to the end of the property page definition:

```
// Implementation
protected:
    CContainedWindowT<ATLControls::CComboBox> m_CState;
    CContainedWindowT<ATLControls::CButton> m_CEnabled;
```

I also had to modify the constructor to initialize the contained window classes (shown highlighted):

```
CMyEighthATLObjPPage1() :
    m_CState(this),
    m_CEnabled(this)
{
    m_dwTitleID = IDS_TITLEMyEighthATLObjPPage1;
    m_dwHelpFileID = IDS_HELPFILEMyEighthATLObjPPage1;
    m_dwDocStringID = IDS_DOCSTRINGMyEighthATLObjPPage1;
}
```

It might be silly, but I didn't care for the string identifiers the wizard created for me. While I was working with the constructor, I modified their values to trim the length a bit. I changed IDS_TITLEMyEighthATLObjPPage1 to IDS_TITLEPP1, IDS_HELPFILEMyEighthATLObjPPage1 to IDS_HELPFILEPP1, and IDS_DOCSTRINGMyEighthATLObjPPage1 to IDS_DOCSTRINGPP1. Note I had to change them here, in the string table, and in the RESOURCE.H file. I can also move these initializations into the constructor's initialization list rather than leave them where the wizard inserted them. In this case, however, I leave them in place.

I now have the contained window members and the controls on the dialog box, but I haven't married the two. To do this, I had to add a handler for WM_INITDIALOG using the usual method of invoking the wizard through the ClassView tab of the Workspace window.

My final WM_INITDIALOG handler is shown in Listing 16.6. As you can see, I not only married the ATL CContainedWindow class to the ATLControls class, but I also pulled the current property settings from the LED control and placed them in the property page controls. Note that because I'm accessing the LED control's properties here, I have to be sure to add them to the source code for the control before I compile the code. If I don't, it will fail (the interface methods aren't there yet!).

LISTING 16.6 CMyEighthATLObjPPage1's OnInitDialog() Handler

```
 1: LRESULT OnInitDialog(UINT uMsg, WPARAM wParam, LPARAM lParam,
 2: ➥BOOL& bHandled)
 3: {
 4:     // Array of string IDs corresponding to the
 5:     // states.
 6:     static const UINT arr[] =
 7:     {
 8:         IDS_STATEGREEN,
 9:         IDS_STATEYELLOW,
10:         IDS_STATERED
11:     };
12:
13:     // Hook up the contained window members to the
14:     // controls themselves
15:     m_CState.Attach(GetDlgItem(IDC_STATE));
16:     m_CEnabled.Attach(GetDlgItem(IDC_ENABLED));
17:
18:     // Loop through the string ID array and fill the
19:     // combo box.
20:     TCHAR strItem[16] = {0};
21:     for (int i = 0; i < sizeof(arr) / sizeof(arr[0]); i++) {
22:         // Retrieve the string
23:         LoadString(_Module.GetResourceInstance(),arr[i],strItem,16);
24:
25:         // Stuff it into the combo box
26:         m_CState.InsertString(i,strItem);
27:     } // for
28:
29:     // Retrieve properties
30:     CComPtr<ILedDemo> spILedDemo;
31:     HRESULT hr = m_ppUnk[0]->QueryInterface(IID_ILedDemo,
32: ➥(void**)&spILedDemo);
33:     short iState = 0, iEnabled = 0;
34:     if ( FAILED(hr) ) {
35:         // Use bogus values
36:         iState = iEnabled = 0;
37:     } // if
38:     else {
39:         // Pull the properties from the control
40:         spILedDemo->get_State((States*)&iState);
41:         spILedDemo->get_Enabled(&iEnabled);
42:     } // else
43:
44:     // Set the controls
45:     m_CState.SetCurSel(iState);
46:     m_CEnabled.SetCheck(!iEnabled ? BST_UNCHECKED : BST_CHECKED);
47:
48:     // Clear the dirty bit
49:     SetDirty(FALSE);
```

```
50:
51:     return 0;
52: }
```

This brings the data into the property page, so there must be a way to get it back out again. That's what the Apply() method is for. Here is the default implementation (see Listing 16.7).

LISTING 16.7 CMyEighthATLObjPPage1's Original Apply() Handler

```
 1: STDMETHOD(Apply)(void)
 2: {
 3:     ATLTRACE(_T("CMyEighthATLObjPPage1::Apply\n"));
 4:     for (UINT i = 0; i < m_nObjects; i++)
 5:     {
 6:         // Do something interesting here
 7:         // ICircCtl* pCirc;
 8:         // m_ppUnk[i]->QueryInterface(IID_ICircCtl, (void**)&pCirc);
 9:         // pCirc->put_Caption(CComBSTR("something special"));
10:         // pCirc->Release();
11:     }
12:     m_bDirty = FALSE;
13:     return S_OK;
14: }
```

ANALYSIS The Apply() method comes from the property page's IPropertyPageImpl base class, and the member m_nObjects (line 4) refers to the number of interfaces tied to this property page.

Because I'll only have a single interface using this property page (ILedDemo), I removed the for loop and added the code to actually process the resulting properties. You can see this in Listing 16.8.

LISTING 16.8 CMyEighthATLObjPPage1's Revised Apply() Method

```
1: STDMETHOD(Apply)(void)
2: {
3:     ATLTRACE(_T("CMyEighthATLObjPPage1::Apply\n"));
4:
5:     // Set the properties
6:     HRESULT hr = S_OK;
7:     try {
8:         // Obtain the control's pointer
```

continues

LISTING **16.8** continued

```
 9:          CComPtr<ILedDemo> spILedDemo;
10:          hr = m_ppUnk[0]->QueryInterface(IID_ILedDemo, (void**)&spILedDemo);
11:          if ( FAILED(hr) ) throw hr;
12:
13:          // Put the state information
14:          hr = spILedDemo->put_State((States)m_CState.GetCurSel());
15:          if ( FAILED(hr) ) throw hr;
16:
17:          // Put the enabled information
18:          hr = spILedDemo->put_Enabled(!m_CEnabled.GetCheck() ? FALSE : TRUE);
19:          if ( FAILED(hr) ) throw hr;
20:      } // try
21:      catch(HRESULT hrErr) {
22:          // Some error...
23:          hr = hrErr;
24:      } // catch
25:      catch(...) {
26:          // Unexpected error
27:          hr = E_UNEXPECTED;
28:      } // catch
29:
30:      // Clear the dirty bit
31:      m_bDirty = FALSE;
32:
33:      return hr;
34: }
```

ANALYSIS If the Apply button is activated and clicked, I first obtain a pointer to the LED control object, as I show in line 10. All the objects that this property page are attached to are kept in an array, m_ppUnk, which is an attribute of the property page's parent class, IpropertyPageImpl (from ATLCTL.H). Because there is only a single control this page supports, I can safely use the first array element. Assuming I did obtain a pointer to the LED control object, I establish the new State and Enabled property information—lines 14 and 18, respectively.

As with any property sheet, the Apply button won't be activated until a page's dirty bit is set. The bit should be set whenever a property changes, so I added two command handlers: one for the State combo box's CBN_SELCHANGE notification and one for the Enabled button's BN_CLICKED notification. I added these handlers in the usual way (invoking the message handler wizard from the ClassView tab of the Workspace window). The handler implementations are shown in Listing 16.9.

LISTING 16.9 CMyEighthATLObjPPage1's Command Handlers

```
 1: LRESULT OnClickedEnabled(WORD wNotifyCode, WORD wID, HWND hWndCtl,
 2: ➥BOOL& bHandled)
 3: {
 4:      // Set the dirty bit
 5:      SetDirty(TRUE);
 6:
 7:      return 0;
 8: }
 9: LRESULT OnSelchangeState(WORD wNotifyCode, WORD wID, HWND hWndCtl,
10: ➥BOOL& bHandled)
11: {
12:      // Set the dirty bit
13:      SetDirty(TRUE);
14:
15:      return 0;
16: }
```

ANALYSIS As you can see, setting the dirty bit is an easy task because I can use `IPropertyPageImpl::SetDirty()` (lines 5 and 13). This completes my addition of the property page itself. Now it's time to add the page to the LED control. The first change to make is to modify the property map for the Enabled property. Because I put a check box on my property page for Enabled, it makes sense to use the page to set the value. Therefore, this property map value

```
PROP_ENTRY("Enabled", DISPID_ENABLED, CLSID_NULL)
```

changes to this

```
PROP_ENTRY("Enabled", DISPID_ENABLED, CLSID_TYATLObj8PPage1)
```

While I was there, I added the State property using the property wizard you saw during Day 7. I called the Property State and made it a short type with no additional parameters. After I did this, I examined the IDL file to determine what DISPID had been assigned to the State property (it should be 1, but I checked anyway). Knowing this, I added this property map macro:

```
PROP_ENTRY("State", 1, CLSID_TYATLObj8PPage1)
```

I'll discuss the actual implementation of the State property shortly, when I address porting the LED code itself into the ActiveX control framework.

Adding Component Categories

Adding supported Component Categories is a breeze with ATL because it kindly provides you with another map called the *category map*. As is usual for ATL, there is a

16

BEGIN_CATEGORY_MAP() macro, and END_CATEGORY_MAP() macro, and it provides for two category insertion macros, IMPLEMENTED_CATEGORY() and REQUIRED_CATEGORY(). I won't iterate through the BEGIN_CATEGORY_MAP() and END_CATEGORY_MAP() macros because they're similar to the other mapping macros you've seen. The IMPLEMENTED_CATEGORY() and REQUIRED_CATEGORY() macros, however, indicate that the control either implements the category or requires that the container understand the given category.

You add the category map by hand, because there is no wizard to help. However, it's not difficult, as long as you know where to find the appropriate CATIDs (I mentioned the relevant header files earlier in the "Component Categories and IObjectSafety" section). As for the LED control, several categories apply:

- CATID_Insertable
- CATID_Control
- CATID_Programmable
- CATID_PersistsToStorage
- CATID_PersistsToStreamInit

The ATL Object Wizard added the first three of these to your .RGS file under the Registry location that supported categories used to occupy (under your object's CLSID entry). This grew to be too cumbersome, so the Component Manager was created, and contemporary categories fall under the Implemented Categories key of your object's CLSID key. Even though the categories exist in the .RGS file, you should still place them in the category map. CMyEighthATLObj's category map appears as you see in Listing 16.10.

LISTING 16.10 CMyEighthATLObj's Category Map

```
1: BEGIN_CATEGORY_MAP(CMyEighthATLObj)
2:     IMPLEMENTED_CATEGORY(CATID_Insertable)
3:     IMPLEMENTED_CATEGORY(CATID_Control)
4:     IMPLEMENTED_CATEGORY(CATID_Programmable)
5:     IMPLEMENTED_CATEGORY(CATID_PersistsToStorage)
6:     IMPLEMENTED_CATEGORY(CATID_PersistsToStreamInit)
7: END_CATEGORY_MAP()
```

When you recompile and reregister your control, these component categories are automatically registered for you.

Adding `IObjectSafety` Support

ATL also provides an easy solution to implementing `IObjectSafety` using the
`IObjectSafetyImpl` template. If you add this template to the list of base classes
for your control, you inherit the `IObjectSafety` interface functionality:

```
public IObjectSafetyImpl<CMyEighthATLObj,
➥INTERFACESAFE_FOR_UNTRUSTED_CALLER ¦
➥INTERFACESAFE_FOR_UNTRUSTED_DATA>
```

Of course, you also need to add the `IObjectSafety` interface to your COM map:

```
COM_INTERFACE_ENTRY(IObjectSafety)
```

In this case, I claim the LED control is safe for untrusted callers and data. Because
the control is benign and adequately checks incoming parameter boundaries, I feel it is
safe in both cases, and so I added the `INTERFACESAFE_FOR_UNTRUSTED_CALLER` and
`INTERFACESAFE_FOR_UNTRUSTED_DATA` settings to the `IObjectSafety` implementation.
This might not always be the case, however, and you should make that judgement on an
individual control basis.

Note

> If you are porting code from VC5 to VC6 and you used `IObjectSafetyImpl`,
> note the implementation has changed. If you don't also change your code
> to match the new implementation (as I've shown), you'll receive compiler
> errors.

LED Control Code Modifications

Having all the preliminaries out of the way, it's time to paste in some of the LED behavioral code you created during Day 15. The majority of the basic code will remain intact,
but you'll need to make several changes and enhancements to comply with the ActiveX
framework. There are really only two areas that apply, the basic painting code and a bit
of the State property code. I'll start with the simpler of the two—State.

LED State Property

So that you could add the LED's property page, I mentioned already adding the basic
property handlers for the LED control (so I could compile the property page code). In this
section, I'll fill in the implementations of the handlers and add some other details, such
as the State enumeration (to the IDL file) and the C++ data member that will actually
store the state.

The first change to make is to add the `State` enumeration to *Day16Server*'s IDL file:

```
typedef enum States
{
    [helpstring("Normal state (green)")] LED_GREEN = 0,
    [helpstring("Caution state (yellow)")] LED_YELLOW = 1,
    [helpstring("Alert state (red)")] LED_RED = 2
} States;
```

This is placed before the first object declaration. Then, you should change the `State` property methods to incorporate the enumerated values versus the `short` values the wizard inserted:

```
HRESULT State([out, retval] States *pVal);
HRESULT State([in] States newVal);
```

Because you changed the IDL file, you also change the method implementations in CMyEighthATLObj. First, you change the class definition (in MyEighthATLObj.h):

```
STDMETHOD(get_State)(/*[out, retval]*/ States *pVal);
STDMETHOD(put_State)(/*[in]*/ States newVal);
```

You'll also change their implementations in MyEighthATLObj.cpp, but you'll be adding code there anyway to actually implement the property. Before you edit the MyEighthATLObj.cpp file, however, add this member to the bottom of the *CMyEighthATLObj* class definition (just past `m_bEnabled`):

```
States m_iState;
```

Also modify the class constructor to initialize the property to a good value:

```
CMyEighthATLObj() :
    m_iState(LED_GREEN)
{
}
```

With the class definition complete, add the implementation code you see in Listing 16.11 to MyEighthATLObj.cpp.

LISTING 16.11   CMyEighthATLObj's State Property Implementation

```
1: STDMETHODIMP CMyEighthATLObj::get_State(States *pVal)
2: {
3:     if ( pVal == NULL ) {
4:         // NULL pointer, so return an error code
5:         return E_POINTER;
6:     } // if
7:
8:     HRESULT hr = S_OK;
9:     try {
```

```
10:        // Simply return the value
11:        *pVal = m_iState;
12:      } // try
13:      catch(...) {
14:        // Some error
15:        hr = E_UNEXPECTED;
16:      } // catch
17:
18:      return hr;
19: }
20:
21: STDMETHODIMP CMyEighthATLObj::put_State(States newVal)
22: {
23:      HRESULT hr = S_OK;
24:      try {
25:        // Check the value
26:        if ((newVal >= LED_GREEN) && (newVal <= LED_RED)) {
27:            // In range...
28:            m_iState = newVal;
29:
30:            // Redraw...
31:            FireViewChange();
32:        } // if
33:        else {
34:            // Bad parameter
35:            hr = E_INVALIDARG;
36:        } // else
37:      } // try
38:      catch(...) {
39:        // Some error
40:        hr = E_UNEXPECTED;
41:      } // catch
42:
43:      return hr;
44: }
```

ANALYSIS The implementation is pretty straightforward. Note I did change the parameter data type from short to States. It is interesting that I force the control to redraw when the State property changes by using CComControl::FireViewChange() (line 31). Although you might be tempted to use CWindow::InvalidateRect(), you'll quickly find that your control will blow up if you do. FireViewChange() is the correct function to call to force the control to redraw itself.

Because you've already added the State property to the property map, you're done with the LED control's properties. Let's turn now to the painting behavior.

LED Drawing Code

Although the basic drawing code that produced the LED during Day 15 remains intact, the implementation of the drawing code will look quite different to you when it's packaged in an ActiveX control. Part of the reason is that you obtain your device context in a slightly different manner. Another oddity is that some containers render the control as a metafile, so you have to take that into account. You can't double buffer metafile output. You also have to deal with the various custom, stock, and ambient properties that didn't exist when the control stood alone. So the code has grown a bit, but it also does more.

Before I get to the actual painting code, I'll show you what changes I made to the basic CMyEighthATLObj.cpp file. First, I added the pens and brushes from Day 15 as class members (using my MFC GDI wrappers), but I skipped adding the double buffer members. I'll create the double buffer on the fly here because the control doesn't receive WM_SIZE messages. During Day 17, I'll show you how to receive property change notifications, such as when the control's extent values change. I added the pens and brushes towards the end of the class definition (see Listing 16.12)

LISTING 16.12   CMyEigthATLObj's GDI Resource Attributes

```
1: // Maintain GDI resources
2: CBrush m_brRed;
3: CBrush m_brGreen;
4: CBrush m_brYellow;
5: CPen m_pnLtGray;
6: CPen m_pnDkGray;
```

Of course, I had to initialize the pens and brushes, so I added this code to the CComObjectRootEx::FinalConstruct() method, which I show you in Listing 16.13.

LISTING 16.13   CMyEigthATLObj's FinalConstruct() Method Implementation

```
1: HRESULT FinalConstruct()
2: {
3:     // Create the GDI resources
4:     m_brRed.CreateSolidBrush(RGB(255,0,0));
5:     m_brGreen.CreateSolidBrush(RGB(20,255,20));
6:     m_brYellow.CreateSolidBrush(RGB(255,255,0));
7:     m_pnLtGray.CreatePen(PS_SOLID,1,GetSysColor(COLOR_3DHILIGHT));
8:     m_pnDkGray.CreatePen(PS_SOLID,1,GetSysColor(COLOR_3DSHADOW));
9:
10:     return S_OK;
11: }
```

ANALYSIS As you see from lines 4–8, I create the brushes and pens using the GDI wrapper methods. When I need a brush or a pen to paint the LED, I'll simply use the attribute for the given brush or pen.

Because LEDs are supposed to be circular, I copied over the `SquareDrawRect()` method from Day 15's code and added it to CMyEighthATLObj. As before, I use that function to turn the drawing rectangle into a square so that the `CDC::Ellipse()` method draws a true circle.

Now for the drawing code. Rather than choke up the rest of the day with a huge listing, I'll break it down piece by piece to give you a better idea as to what is happening.

The `CMyEighthATLObj::OnDraw()` method implements the painting behavior of the control. It begins like this:

```
HRESULT OnDraw(ATL_DRAWINFO& di)
```

Note the ATL_DRAWINFO structure you're passed. This structure isn't well documented but is terribly important to your drawing code. From it, you will retrieve your device context for drawing. You will also check to see if you're rendering to a metafile, drawing in a zoomed mode, or drawing to an icon or thumbnail version of your control. The structure, from ATLCTL.H, is defined as you see in Listing 16.14.

LISTING 16.14 ATL_DRAWINFO Structure Definition

```
 1: struct ATL_DRAWINFO
 2: {
 3:     UINT cbSize;
 4:     DWORD dwDrawAspect;
 5:     LONG lindex;
 6:     DVTARGETDEVICE* ptd;
 7:     HDC hicTargetDev;
 8:     HDC hdcDraw;
 9:     LPCRECTL prcBounds; //Rectangle in which to draw
10:     PCRECTL prcWBounds; //WindowOrg and Ext if metafile
11:     BOOL bOptimize;
12:     BOOL bZoomed;
13:     BOOL bRectInHimetric;
14:     SIZEL ZoomNum;       //ZoomX = ZoomNum.cx/ZoomNum.cy
15:     SIZEL ZoomDen;
16: };
```

To save space for the remaining drawing code, I won't go over each line of code. The members you'll use later, though, are hdcDraw (the DC to draw to), prcBounds (drawing rectangle), and dwDrawAspect (normal drawing or icon/thumbnail). For more detail,

I recommend Richard Grimes' *Professional ATL COM Programming* from Wrox Press (ISBN 1-861001-4-01).

The first thing to do is to check to see if you're drawing normally or to some special condition, such as an iconified format or to a thumbnail. The LED control's drawing code begins with the code in Listing 16.15.

LISTING 16.15 LED Control's Special Drawing Condition Implementation

```
1: // If an icon or thumbnail, don't paint
2: if ( di.dwDrawAspect != DVASPECT_CONTENT ) {
3:     // Iconified or thumbnailed
4:     return S_OK;
5: } // if
```

You can certainly add the code to draw in these special formats. I didn't here for brevity.

Because I now know I'm rendering a normal version of the control, I extract my drawing rectangle as shown in Listing 16.16.

LISTING 16.16 LED Control's Drawing Rectangle Normalization

```
1: // Pull window rectangle
2: CRect rcBounds(*(RECT*)di.prcBounds);
3:
4: // Create a normalized drawing rectangle with
5: // (left,top) coordinates of (0,0)
6: CRect rcClient(rcBounds);
7: rcClient.NormalizeRect();
8: rcClient.OffsetRect(-rcClient.left,-rcClient.top);
```

I first create a CRect object, representing the drawing rectangle I can revisit throughout the painting process. I then create a second rectangle for drawing the circular LED, just as you saw in Day 15.

The next thing I do is pull the drawing device context and stuff it into one of my MFC GDI classes:

```
// Pull painting DC
CDC dcPaint;
dcPaint.Attach(di.hdcDraw);
```

Later, I'll detach the DC prior to exiting the drawing code. What I need to know now is what kind of DC is it I have? Am I drawing to a metafile? If so, I can't create a compatible bitmap and device context for double buffering, so I need to create a flag that will allow me to skip the nonmetafile code:

```
// If a metafile, don't create the double buffer
BOOL bIsMetaFile = dcPaint.GetDeviceCaps(TECHNOLOGY) ==
➥DT_METAFILE ? TRUE : FALSE;
```

With my painting DC in place, I declare the double buffer variables and create them if required (see Listing 16.17).

LISTING 16.17 LED Control's Double Buffer Creation Implementation

```
 1: // Compatible DC variables (double buffer)
 2: CBitmap* pbmMono;
 3: CDC dcBuffer;
 4: CBitmap bmColor;
 5:
 6: // Build a compatible memory DC if not a metafile
 7: CDC* pDC = &dcPaint;
 8: if ( !bIsMetaFile ) {
 9:     dcBuffer.CreateCompatibleDC(dcPaint);
10:     bmColor.CreateCompatibleBitmap(&dcPaint,
11:                                 rcBounds.Width(),
12:                                 rcBounds.Height());
13:     pbmMono = (CBitmap*)dcBuffer.SelectObject(&bmColor);
14:     pDC = &dcBuffer;
15: } // if
```

I now have the appropriate device context selected into pDC, so I begin my generic painting. First, I select the brushes and pens I require, then I clear the background (see Listing 16.18).

LISTING 16.18 LED Control's Drawing Initialization

```
 1: // Create background color brush and pen
 2: COLORREF clrBackGnd;
 3: OLE_COLOR oclrBackGnd;
 4: GetAmbientBackColor(oclrBackGnd);
 5: OleTranslateColor(oclrBackGnd,NULL,&clrBackGnd);
 6: CBrush brBackGnd(clrBackGnd);
 7: CPen pnBackGnd(PS_SOLID,1,clrBackGnd);
 8: CBrush* pOldBrush = (CBrush*)pDC->SelectObject(&brBackGnd);
 9: CPen* pOldPen = (CPen*)pDC->SelectObject(&pnBackGnd);
10:
11: // Clear the client area
12: pDC->FillRect(&rcClient,&brBackGnd);
```

ANALYSIS Because the container might use any color as the background color, I determine what that color might be by using CComControl:: GetAmbientBackColor() (line 4). This is one of those ambient properties I mentioned earlier. The color itself comes back to me as an OLE_COLOR, which is *not* a COLORREF value. To convert the color, I call OleTranslateColor() and use the results from that, as you see in line 5.

After I have cleared the background of the control (line 12), I paint the control itself. I first make sure the control will be drawn in a square region to produce a perfect circle, and then I select the color of the LED, based upon its state. Because I elected to handle the stock property Enabled, I also check for that. If the control is disabled, I paint it with the background color (already selected into the DC) rather than a control state color (green, yellow, or red), as shown in Listing 16.19.

LISTING 16.19 LED Control's Basic Drawing Implementation

```
 1: // Square the drawing rectangle to produce a circular
 2: // control
 3: SquareDrawRect(rcClient);
 4:
 5: // Draw color circle with gray border
 6: pDC->SelectObject(&m_pnDkGray);
 7: if ( m_bEnabled ) {
 8:     switch ( m_iState ) {
 9:         case LED_GREEN:
10:             pDC->SelectObject(&m_brGreen);
11:             break;
12:
13:         case LED_YELLOW:
14:             pDC->SelectObject(&m_brYellow);
15:             break;
16:
17:         case LED_RED:
18:             default: // Red
19:             pDC->SelectObject(&m_brRed);
20:             break;
21:
22:     } // switch
23: } // if
24: pDC->Ellipse(&rcClient);
```

With the basic LED circle drawn, I draw the ornamental lines as you saw during Day 15 (see Listing 16.20).

LISTING 16.20 LED Control's Ornamental Line Drawing Implementation

```
 1: // Create a rectangle for 3D effect
 2: CRect rcLines(rcClient);
 3: rcLines.DeflateRect(3,3);
 4:
 5: // Draw ornamental lines (add 3D appearance)
 6: if ( m_bEnabled ) {
 7:     // Draw using hilighted color
 8:     pDC->SelectObject(&m_pnLtGray);
 9: } // if
10: else {
11:     // Not enabled...
12:     pDC->SelectObject(&m_pnDkGray);
13: } // else
14:
15: // Upper arc
16: CPoint ptStart((rcBounds.Width()/2),0);
17: CPoint ptEnd(0,(rcBounds.Height()/2));
18: pDC->SetArcDirection(AD_COUNTERCLOCKWISE);
19: pDC->Arc(rcLines,ptStart,ptEnd);
20:
21: // Lower arc
22: pDC->SelectObject(&m_pnDkGray);
23: ptStart.x = rcBounds.Width()/2;
24: ptStart.y = rcBounds.Height();
25: ptEnd.x = rcBounds.Width();
26: ptEnd.y = rcBounds.Height()/2;
27: pDC->Arc(rcLines,ptStart,ptEnd);
```

Note I did check for the Enabled state, and if the control is disabled, I draw it using standard Windows colors to create a disabled appearance.

The next thing I do is check to see if the control is in design mode. If the control is in design mode, I paint its name in the upper left-hand corner of the control window. This involves two more ambient properties: UserMode and DisplayName (see Listing 16.21).

LISTING 16.21 LED Control's Design Mode Identification Implementation

```
 1: // If in design mode, place some text over the
 2: // control
 3: BOOL bRunMode = FALSE;
 4: GetAmbientUserMode(bRunMode);
 5: if ( !bRunMode ) {
 6:     // In design mode...pull container's ambient
 7:     // display name and show that.
 8:     TCHAR strName[32] = {0};
```

continues

16

LISTING 16.21   continued

```
 9:     CComBSTR bstrName;
10:     GetAmbientDisplayName(bstrName.m_str);
11:     USES_CONVERSION;
12:     LPTSTR strAmbientName = OLE2T(bstrName);
13:
14:     // If there is no ambient display name, use
15:     // the project name.
16:     if ( !_tcslen(strAmbientName) ) {
17:         // No ambient display name
18:         TCHAR strProjName[32]  = {0};
19:         LoadString(_Module.GetResourceInstance(),IDS_PROJNAME,
                     ➥strProjName,32);
20:         _tcscpy(strName,strProjName);
21:     } // if
22:     else {
23:         // Use the ambient name
24:         _tcsncpy(strName,strAmbientName,32);
25:     } // else
26:
27:     // Use default font/color, place in
28:     // upper-left corner
29:     pDC->SetBkMode(TRANSPARENT);
30:     pDC->TextOut(0,0,strName,_tcslen(strName));
31: } // if
```

Because the container might not have set the DisplayName property, I check the length of the returned string. If it's empty, I use the project's name (which I set to be LED).

This completes the basic painting effort, but there remains the disposition of the double buffer (see Listing 16.22).

LISTING 16.22   LED Control's Drawing Cleanup Implementation

```
 1: // Transfer image to screen, if double buffered
 2: if ( !bIsMetaFile ) {
 3:         dcPaint.BitBlt(rcBounds.left,rcBounds.top,
 4:                         rcBounds.Width(),rcBounds.Height(),
 5:                         &dcBuffer,0,0,SRCCOPY);
 6:
 7:     // Clean up the double buffer
 8:     dcBuffer.SelectObject(pOldBrush);
 9:     dcBuffer.SelectObject(pOldPen);
10:     dcBuffer.SelectObject(pbmMono);
11:     bmColor.DeleteObject();
12: } // if
13:
```

```
14: // Detach the painting DC
15: dcPaint.Detach();
16:
17: return S_OK;
```

If the control is not being rendered to a metafile, the actual image is copied from the double buffer to the screen DC, and then the double buffer is destroyed. In either case, the screen DC is detached from the GDI class, and the OnDraw() routine terminates.

Test the Control with the ActiveX Test Container

With the drawing code, the control is now fully functional. The remaining action is to test the control. You can create a quickie MFC or Visual Basic test application, as you've done throughout the book. You can also create an ATL test application, but that involves a bit too much work. The ATL Object Wizard creates a simple HTML file you can use with Internet Explorer simply to invoke your control, and it would be a simple matter to add to that file. But an excellent choice, in this particular case, is to use the Visual Studio Test Container (the source code for which is shipped with Visual Studio, if you're interested).

The Test Container makes sense for an ActiveX control because it gives you total control over almost every aspect of the control's environment. For example, you can change the ambient properties, such as background color and the control's display name, to see how the control reacts to different settings. You can easily persist properties, and bring the control to life from a totally persisted state (as an application would do). You can even test the control's methods and properties individually and invoke the control's property pages to test the communication between the property page and the control. A simple right-click on the control will manage most of this for you.

I find myself using the Test Container most often with debug builds of my controls. That way, if my code does trip an assertion, I'm already in the debugger. Of course, you can also set breakpoints. If you run the debugger from Visual Studio with your control's project loaded (and with no other test application assigned to your control), you should see the dialog box shown in Figure 16.5.

You can select the Test Container from the menu on the right. Select it, then click OK, and the container will execute (after the usual dialog box indicating the container has no debugging information available).

16

Figure 16.5

*Visual Studio's
Executable for Debug
Session dialog box.*

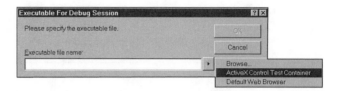

After the container is running, you load the LED control by selecting the Edit, Load New
Control menu item and choosing the TYATLObj8 Class item from the list control the
container presents. Click the control's class and OK, and the container will load the control.

If you right click the control, you should see the context menu shown in Figure 16.6.
Selecting the Properties item will bring up your control's property pages (as well the last
menu item, TYATLObj8 Class Object). If the control had additional methods, you can
exercise those using the Invoke Methods item.

Figure 16.6

*The LED control within
the Test Container.*

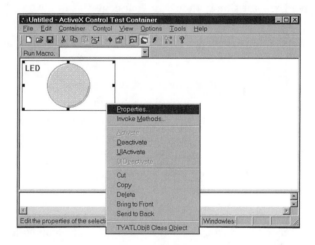

You can access other container and control features through their respective menus,
Container and Control. For example, you can adjust the ambient settings through the
Container, Ambient Properties menu item, or you can draw a metafile using the Control,
Draw Metafile menu item.

Feel free to play with the various menu items to get a feel for what you can do with an
ActiveX control. Be sure to test the interaction with the control's property pages, especially the Apply button!

Summary

It's surprisingly hard to pack this much ActiveX information into a single chapter! But, I hope, there is enough meat here to get you started. If you pick up other references, you should be able to at least understand their lingo and follow their examples.

I began my discussion of ActiveX by introducing some basic ActiveX concepts, such as the types of ActiveX servers, ActiveX properties (custom, stock, and ambient), ActiveX property pages, invisible and windowless controls, and Component Categories and IObjectSafety.

I then briefly discussed ATL and how it implements ActiveX. You looked at the control interfaces ATL provides implementations for, such as for IOleControl and IOleObject, as well as some handy ATL base classes for controls like CComControl. I also talked about the persistence interfaces you'll be interested in for ActiveX, such as IPersistStorage and IPersistStreamInit. Speaking of persistence, I also showed you how the ATL property map helps you store your control's properties between instances.

Finally, I incorporated the LED control from Day 15 into the ActiveX framework that ATL provides. This was a somewhat involved process, but not a terribly difficult one. I began by modifying the basic framework code to add ISupportErrorInfoImpl, but I quickly moved on to add a custom property page, Component Category support, and support for IObjectSafety. Then I shifted my focus to add the actual LED code, such as the State property and the custom-drawing code.

During Day 17, you'll see this control again. I'll add more capability then, especially for events.

Q&A

Q **The basic premise that you proposed for the custom control (Day 15) was that I could implement a quick knock-off control that was also private to my application. It appears a lot of the work here is similar to the work you did during Day 15. Is there an advantage to using ActiveX to host a custom control, yet still keep the control private to a given application?**

A I see the primary advantage to ActiveX in this case is object reuse. (I, personally, always wrap things in ActiveX, if it makes sense from an application design perspective.) For example, imagine you create a thick-client application that uses some custom ActiveX controls. Later, if you decide to use a thin-client instead (such as a browser), you can easily reuse your ActiveX components. In other words, you have a wider range of containers from which to choose.

If you're interested in keeping your control private to your application, you'll want to check into Day 18, "ATL, Class Factories, and Licensed Objects: Creating Objects and Protecting Your Investment," where I discuss `IClassFactory2` and control licensing. You can implement things so that no valid license exists except in the applications you write. Others won't be able to use your control at all. I have seen many applications, however, that obviously created custom controls for a single use. The technique I presented during Day 15 would fit that model, although I'd modify it to allow more than a single instance of the control (such as an array of control pointers or something like that).

Q   You've provided the overview, but is there more I need to know to implement and distribute ActiveX controls?

A   There is always more to learn! This was a brief introduction, but there is much more to learn if you want to implement professional quality ActiveX controls. Space here didn't permit me to touch on a great number of issues revolving around ActiveX. That said, however, what you read here should be enough to get you started implementing high-quality controls quickly. I provide some additional references in Appendix E, "ATL Information Resources."

Workshop

The Workshop is designed to help you anticipate possible questions, review what you've learned, and get you thinking about how to put your knowledge into practice. The answers to the quiz are in Appendix A, "Answers."

Quiz

1. What specification currently governs ActiveX?
2. What are the three types of ActiveX properties and how do they differ?
3. What is the difference between an invisible control versus a windowless control?
4. Why are there component categories? `IObjectSafety`?
5. What is the main ATL class that implements ActiveX control functionality?
6. What is initialized stream-based persistence?
7. What is the ATL property map used for?
8. How do you add property sheets to you control?
9. What is the `ATL_DRAWINFO` structure used for?

Exercise

1. Change the `State` property from color based to state based (such as `LED_NORMAL`, `LED_WARNING`, and `LED_ALERT` for green, yellow, and red, respectively). Then add three other custom properties for the color associated with each state. HINT: Use `OleTranslateColor()` to convert the color you receive to a `COLORREF` value you can use. Also, there is a stock-color property page, `CLSID_StockColorPage`, that you can use instead of defining your own (use it with the `PROP_PAGE()` property map macro). This is a fairly meaty exercise!

16

WEEK 3

DAY 17

ATL and Connection Points: Supporting COM's Event Model

Today you'll look at the connection point. A *connection point* is a mechanism COM uses to provide notifications in lieu of the Windows messages (WM_COMMAND and WM_NOTIFY). You saw the messages in Day 15, "Custom Controls: Basic Control Development Techniques." During Day 15, your control issued a Windows message to the parent window and waited for the response (because SendMessage() blocks). The connection point, however, provides you with two interfaces. One you use to notify the container of an event, while the container uses the other to send notifications or results back to your object. Actually, the protocol is more like *sender* and *receiver* because the interfaces aren't tied to a specific object or function.

Connection points, as you'll see, are useful for more than notifying the container of an event. The container also uses connection points to authorize your control's request to change a property, as well as to send the notification that your control's property has now changed. The protocol works in many different situations.

Let's see how to add connection points to your project. In this lesson, you will study

- The basics of using connection points
- The protocol of connection points
- Property change notification sinks
- How to add event notifications to your control
- How to add property-modification request notifications to your control

Connection Point Basics

Connection points are a mechanism Microsoft provides to implement bidirectional communication between the client and the server, or in this case, the container and the ActiveX control. They're not just used with ActiveX, but they are quite useful to establish communication regarding control notifications and container property changes.

Kraig Brockschmidt, in his classic *Inside OLE* (Microsoft Press, ISBN 1-55615-843-2), has probably written the best description of connection points when he talks about *connectable objects*. He points out that, for the most part, COM objects *listen*. That is, the interfaces you've implemented so far in this book have all been available to the client to use at any time. They lie around and wait for the client to ask them to do something.

There are times, however, when an object has something interesting to say to the client. Kraig mentions events, notifications, and requests. You'll see examples of all three things during this day.

- An *event* is something dynamic. The control responds to it and also desires to inform the container of its occurrence. The LED control fires mouse events.
- A *notification* is the control's statement that something has now completed or a certain agreed-upon state has been achieved. As you'll see shortly, the LED control informs the container whenever a property changes.
- A *request* can be sent from the control to the server to obtain permission to perform an action. In the case of the LED control, it asks permission before applying any changes to its properties (you'll also see this shortly).

For the object to actively initiate communication with the client, the object has to be given an *outgoing* interface (versus the *incoming*, or *listening* interface that the object traditionally exposes). When the object and client meet (the client invokes the COM object), the client passes the object an interface pointer that the object will use to talk to the client. Figure 17.1 shows you this graphically.

Client uses `ConnectionPoint: :Advise()` to pass sink pointers to the object.

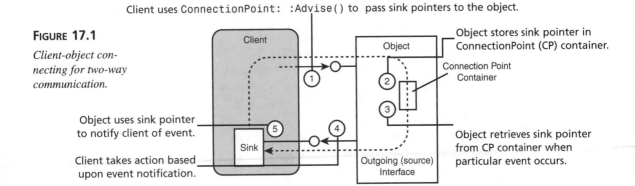

FIGURE 17.1

Client-object connecting for two-way communication.

Object stores sink pointer in ConnectionPoint (CP) container.

Object uses sink pointer to notify client of event.

Client takes action based upon event notification.

Object retrieves sink pointer from CP container when particular event occurs.

17

The object (container or control) that initiates the communication is called the *source*. The object receiving the communication is called the *sink*. If the client merely calls an object's interface method, it is communicating unidirectionally. However, if the client passes the object a *sink* pointer, the client and COM object can establish bidirectional communications. This is the standard mechanism that Visual Basic and scripting clients use.

If a single object talks to another single object, you can simply pass interface pointers between the objects and leave it at that. They can call each other's methods and establish some sort of custom communication protocol. The situation becomes more complicated, however, when you have a single source that needs to direct several sink objects or if you have a sink object that is listening to multiple sources (as shown in Figure 17.2). In that case, you need some sort of connection mapping, which is precisely what the connection point protocol provides you.

FIGURE 17.2

Multiple objects, sources, and sinks.

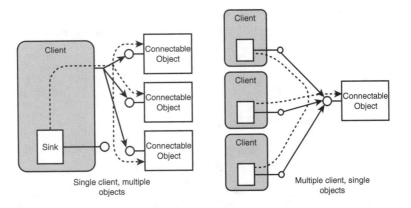

Single client, multiple objects

Multiple client, single objects

At this point, you might become quite confused about clients and servers versus sources and sinks. Before things get muddled, let me try to clear this up. When it comes to connection points, at least for the sake of this discussion, ignore the usual COM definition of client and server. Instead, think of the object that initiated the conversation as the server. The object that receives this communication is the client.

Here is the strange part. Connection point servers, when they generate an event, call the sink interface of the client. The client implements the sink interface, not the server. The server knows of the interface (passed to it by the client) and simply calls it. If you refer back to Figure 17.1, this might become clearer. The COM object could not have implemented the sink interface within the client application. No matter who implemented the object (you, me, or Microsoft), the client expects the COM object to be able to use the client's sink interface to send the client events. If the client never offers its sink interface, the object never calls it.

The *source* interface, which is the connection point itself, must be either a custom interface or a dispinterface. Clients will implement a corresponding sink interface. Although Visual Basic can handle custom connection point interfaces, scripting clients cannot. So for maximum use, you should always implement sink interfaces as dispinterfaces. In fact, if you check Support Connection Points from the Attributes page of the Object Wizard when you insert a new object, the wizard will insert a connection point interface into your IDL file for you. It will be marked with the IDL attribute source in the type library and will be a dispinterface. ATL will provide the source code you need to back the IDL definition.

ATL helps you implement connection points by creating for you a connection point map in a *connection point container*. Perhaps the container is holding a single sink interface pointer, or maybe it has several sinks interested in some particular piece of information. The connection point container manages these situations by implementing the IConnectionPointContainer interface, which has two methods: EnumConnectionPoints() and FindConnectionPoint(). Happily, their uses are self-evident. You can rummage through the sink map for all available sink interfaces (EnumConnectionPoints()), or you can target a specific one (FindConnectionPoint()).

Let's take a closer look at this protocol. Understanding it is helpful when you're adding connection point support to your ActiveX control a bit later in the day.

Connection Protocol

I mentioned the client passes its sink pointer to the server, but that description doesn't do the protocol justice. Here is a bit more detail.

When your control is nestled into a container, your control will (likely) implement an interface that supports IConnectionPointContainer (you'll see which interface shortly). The container will QueryInterface() your control for this interface, and then query that interface for the IConnectionPointContainer interface.

Given the connection point container, the application then uses `FindConnectionPoint()` to get an `IConnectionPoint` interface pointer. `IConnectionPoint` has five methods, only two of which I'll mention here: `Advise()` and `Unadvise()`.

`Advise()` is what the container uses to pass in its sink pointer:

```
HRESULT Advise(IUnknown *pUnk,      // Pointer to the client's advise sink
               DWORD *pdwCookie);  // Pointer to the connection point
                                   // identifier used by Unadvise
```

Your control's container, then, calls `Advise()` to provide you with an interface pointer your control will use to notify the container of some specific event along with a *cookie*. Your control will use this pointer, as conditions warrant, until the container tells your control to turn off the events by using the `Unadvise()` method:

```
HRESULT Unadvise(DWORD dwCookie);   // Connection token
```

The cookie is nothing more than a 32-bit value that the sink provides you. It identifies, to the sink, which particular connection point will be deactivated using `Unadvise()`. It might have no particular meaning to you, but it most likely will mean something to the sink. You should save the cookie `Advise()` provides you for the corresponding call to `Unadvise()`. By definition, the cookie will be nonzero if the `Advise()` method was successful.

ATL provides two handy helper functions you can use to easily manage your connection points—`AtlAdvise()` and `AtlUnadvise()`. `AtlAdvise()` is defined as you see in Listing 17.1 (from ATLBASE.H).

LISTING 17.1   ATL's `AtlAdvise()` Definition

```
1: HRESULT AtlAdvise(IUnknown* pUnkCP, // IUnknown of object to connect with
2:                   IUnknown* pUnk,   // Client's IUnknown
3:                   const IID& iid,   // Connection point GUID
4:                   LPDWORD pdw );    // Pointer to cookie
```

ANALYSIS   Although there are more parameters to `AtlAdvise()` than there would be to a given connection point's `Advise()` method, it still represents a significant code savings to you. `AtlAdvise()` searches the connection point map for the `IID` parameter value (line 3) implemented by the `pUnkCP` object (line 1). You pass in your object's `IUnknown` pointer and a pointer to a cookie variable (a `DWORD`), and `AtlAdvise()` sets up the connection point for you. The `IID` parameter is typically the `IID` for the particular connection interface to which you are trying to establish a connection.

`AtlUnadvise()` is defined as you see in Listing 17.2.

LISTING 17.2 ATL's AtlUnadvise() Definition

```
1: HRESULT AtlUnadvise(IUnknown* pUnkCP,  // IUnknown of object connected with
2:                     const IID& iid,    // Connection point GUID
3:                     DWORD dw );        // Cookie
```

ANALYSIS Here, you once again pass in the IUnknown of the object that you've established a connection with (line 1), the connection GUID (line 2), and the cookie passed to you by AtlAdvise() (line 3). The first two parameters are the same as those you passed into AtlAdvise().

I tend to use connection points—as I'll show you in the upcoming section, "Creating an Event Connection Point." However, there may be times when you will want to use connection points in their most basic form (using AtlAdvise()/AtlUnadvise() or the connection point interface equivalent). Perhaps you want to allow connections intermittently, for example. To help you with this, there are two sample applications you can examine for additional information. The first sample, *Connect*, ships with VC6 and can easily be installed in the usual manner from your VC6 CDs. The other, *AtlSink*, is referenced by Knowledge Base article Q181277 and can be downloaded from Microsoft from a URL shown in the article.

Your control will use the connection point container to find each relevant sink interface pointer, and then it will call the appropriate method, which that interface exposes, to signal the container of the event.

IPropertyNotifySink

The main connection point container interface is IPropertyNotifySink. ActiveX uses other historical interfaces that provide similar bidirectional communication (such as IOleControlSite and IOleClientSite), but they aren't derived from IConnectionPointContainer. IPropertyNotifySink *is* derived from IConnectionPointContainer, and it is the primary way your control negotiates property changes with the container.

For example, if your control supports properties marked with the bindable and requestedit attributes (database values, perhaps), your control is required to call the methods of IPropertyNotifySink. When you change a bindable property, you are required to call IPropertyNotifySink::OnChanged(). When you're about to change a requestedit property, you first call IPropertyNotifySink::OnRequestEdit() to obtain the container's permission before changing the property. You should abide by the action the container specified upon return from this call. You'll see this later in the day, when I plug in these request events to the LED control.

Making It Happen: Adding Events to the LED Control

To make connection points a bit more concrete, I copied the LED ActiveX control from the last lesson and renamed everything to match this day (that is, "16" went to "17", and so on). I also created a new custom interface, ILedDemo2, to implement the exercise I suggested at the end of Day 16. That is, I allow the user to change the colors associated with the LED states, which I also renamed (to LED_NORMAL, LED_WARNING, and LED_ALERT). If you examine the IDL file, you'll see I recreated the ILedDemo interface, and I incorporated it into the ILedDemo2 interface. (You cannot inherit an interface that itself inherits IDispatch because that confuses the dual interface issue. Which one is now the true custom interface?)

When I originally created the ActiveX control's object, I checked the Supports Connection Points option. This created a dispinterface called _ILedDemoEvents, which I duplicated for this day (calling it _ILedDemo2Events). I did nothing with _ILedDemoEvents in the last day, but I'll work a great deal with _ILedDemo2Events today.

Because I have the basic definition of my connection point event interface (via the Object Wizard), let's see how to add some code to support connection point notification.

Creating an Event Connection Point

I already took the first step toward creating an event connection point when I created the object, which in this case was the ActiveX control. The wizard put the definition of the _ILedDemo2Events dispinterface into my IDL file. That interface has no methods, which is a situation I'll correct now.

If you display the *Day17Server*'s project in the ClassView tab of the Workspace window, you should see the _ILedDemo2Events interface as one of the tree nodes (see Figure 17.3). In the usual way, right click on this tree node and select the Add Method menu item. In the wizard's dialog, create a new method called LClick that returns an HRESULT and has this parameter list:

```
[in] long x, [in] long y, [in] long fwKeys
```

Do this three more times, once each for the LDblClick() method, the RClick() method, and the RDblClick() method. With these four methods in place, you can generate your *connection point proxy*. This proxy actually implements IConnectionPoint for you.

To generate the connection point proxy, go back to the ClassView tab of the Workspace window and right click on the C++ implementation for your interface (CMyNinthATLObj in this case), which implements ILedDemo2. There should be a menu item called

17

Implement Connection Point shown on the context menu. Click that menu item. This should bring up the Implement Connection Point dialog you see in Figure 17.4.

The Visual Studio ClassView Workspace window tab.

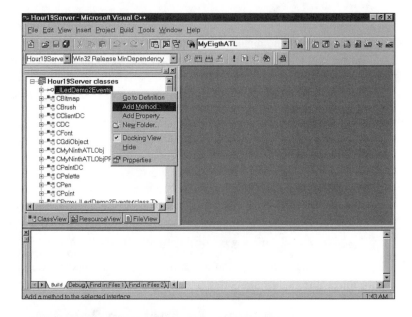

The Implement Connection Point dialog.

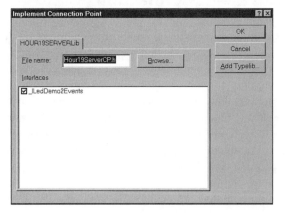

Note

The wizard uses the project's type library to create the connection point proxy, so be sure you have inserted all the event methods and recompiled the IDL file before invoking the wizard. You can always add more event methods and recreate the proxy, however.

The dialog is asking which dispinterface to use when adding the connection point, and in this case you should check _ILedDemo2Events. You also have the option of changing the implementation file name, but the default name of Day17ServerCP.h will suffice in this case. After you click OK, Visual Studio will create for you a new C++ class called CProxy_ILedDemo2Events, which is implemented in the Day17ServerCP.h file. The wizard will also modify the interface's implementation file (MyNinthATLObj.h) to include the proxy's header file and add the proxy's IID to the ATL connection point map. (This is another ATL map used to lay out the connection points that the interface supports.)

> **Note**
>
> There is a bug in this wizard. The wizard adds the leading underscore to the event dispinterface, which tells type library browsers they may ignore this private event interface. The wizard does not always take into consideration that this is an event dispinterface, however, when it adds the event interface's IID to the connection point map. The wizard sometimes blindly adds IID_ to the event interface's name. This produces the string IID__ISomeInterfaceEvents. The compiler will not find this IID value, producing the compiler error, error C2065, as well as a few others. You must edit the source code yourself to add a leading D (to produce the value DIID__ISomeInterfaceEvents). Your code will now compile correctly.

17

If you examine the Day17ServerCP.h file the wizard created, you should see four methods: Fire_LClick(), Fire_LDblClick(), Fire_RClick(), and Fire_RDblClick(). These correspond to the four methods you added to _ILedDemo2Events and are the methods you call to fire the event notification to the container. I've shown the first, Fire_LClick(), in Listing 17.3.

LISTING 17.3 CProxy_ILedDemo2Events::Fire_LClick() Method Implementation

```
 1: HRESULT Fire_LClick(LONG x, LONG y, LONG fwKeys)
 2: {
 3:     CComVariant varResult;
 4:     T* pT = static_cast<T*>(this);
 5:     int nConnectionIndex;
 6:     CComVariant* pvars = new CComVariant[3];
 7:     int nConnections = m_vec.GetSize();
 8:
 9:     for (nConnectionIndex = 0; nConnectionIndex < nConnections;
        ➥nConnectionIndex++)
10:     {
11:         pT->Lock();
12:         CComPtr<IUnknown> sp = m_vec.GetAt(nConnectionIndex);
```

continues

LISTING 17.3   continued

```
13:            pT->Unlock();
14:            IDispatch* pDispatch = reinterpret_cast<IDispatch*>(sp.p);
15:            if (pDispatch != NULL)
16:            {
17:                VariantClear(&varResult);
18:                pvars[2] = x;
19:                pvars[1] = y;
20:                pvars[0] = fwKeys;
21:                DISPPARAMS disp = { pvars, NULL, 3, 0 };
22:                pDispatch->Invoke(0x1, IID_NULL, LOCALE_USER_DEFAULT,
                      ➥DISPATCH_METHOD, &disp, &varResult, NULL, NULL);
23:            }
24:        }
25:    delete[] pvars;
26:    return varResult.scode;
27:
28: }
```

ANALYSIS I won't go through Listing 17.3 in gory detail, but it does show you a little about how ATL implements connection points. The `m_vec` variable, used in line 7, is defined in `IConnectionPointImpl` to be `CComDynamicUnkArray`, and the array it represents is used to contain all the clients of this connection point. The `for` loop, beginning on line 9, retrieves each client, packages the parameter data (X, Y location of the click and the keyboard state, lines 18 through 20), and then ships it off (as a variant) to the client (line 22).

With the event methods in place, you can now add the message handlers for the mouse clicks to CMyNinthATLObj. Do this in the usual way (as you did in Day 15), then insert the code you see in Listing 17.4. I just show the handler for WM_LBUTTONUP, but the code is similar for the other handlers.

LISTING 17.4   CMyNinthATLObj::On_LButtonUp() **Method Implementation**

```
1: LRESULT OnLButtonUp(UINT uMsg, WPARAM wParam, LPARAM lParam,
                      ➥BOOL& bHandled)
2: {
3:     // Check to see if events are frozen
4:     if ( !m_nFreezeEvents ) {
5:         // Events are not frozen, so notify
6:         // the container of the event
7:         try {
8:             // Fire the event
9:
Fire_LClick((long)LOWORD(lParam),(long)HIWORD(lParam),(long)wParam);
```

```
10:            } // try
11:            catch(...) {
12:                    // Unexpected error...just return...
13:                    /* nothing */;
14:            } // catch
15:       } // if
16:
17:       // Allow ATL to handle the message too.
18:       bHandled = FALSE;
19:
20:       return 0;
21: }
```

ANALYSIS In this case, the code is actually simple to implement, although it looks more complex due to the C++ exception handler and frozen events (to be discussed shortly). Really all that happens is that I extract from the Windows message the information I need to report (X,Y coordinate of the mouse click and the keyboard state) and call Fire_LClick(), which you see on line 9. To give ATL a crack at the message, I set bHandled to FALSE in line 18. If I don't do this, other mouse actions will cease to work, such as the context menu (right click) in the Test Container. (Yes, I learned this the hard way.)

Speaking of the Test Container, if you use it to test your control at this point, you'll see the event notifications shown in the lower-split window, as you see in Figure 17.5.

FIGURE 17.5

The ActiveX Test Container with resulting LED event notifications.

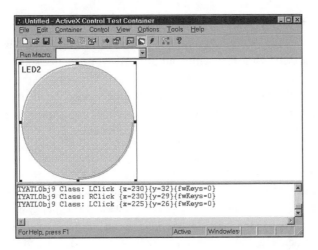

The LED ActiveX control now has the capability to notify the container that an event has occurred. The container, however, might not want to receive event notifications. In that case, you should honor the container's request, as you'll see in the next section.

Frozen Events

The container might call your control's IOleControl::FreezeEvents() method, at which time the container tells your control *not* to fire events. You can easily access event freeze state by examining your CComControl::m_nFreezeEvents member. This short value represents a count of the number of times the container has frozen your control's events without a subsequent unfreeze.

For example, if you wanted to fire some generic event, your method begins something like this:

```
// Check to see if events are frozen
if ( m_nFreezeEvents ) {
    // Events are frozen
    bHandled = FALSE;
    return 0;
} // if
```

Precisely how you handle this situation will vary depending upon where you check and how you want to handle the result. Listing 17.4 showed you how I handled it for the left mouse button click event in the LED control. I also provided some handy helper functions for the LED control that I'll show you in the next section. You should always check m_nFreezeEvents to be sure the container desires events; and if it does not, you shouldn't fire them.

Requesting Edits and Notifying Change

The container also works with your control when setting properties. If you use the requestedit IDL attribute with your property, your control should first request permission from the container to modify that property. After you set the property, assuming the property is marked as bindable in the IDL file, you fire another event telling the container the property is now modified. The container uses these two events when binding your control to another data source, such as a database.

To request permission to change a property value, you fire a *request edit* notification event. After you change the property, you fire a *changed* notification event. These events are managed through the IPropertyNotifySink interface, as you saw earlier, which ATL implements in its IPropertyNotifySinkCP class. If IPropertyNotifySinkCP is included in your control's list of base classes, ATL uses a special class, CFirePropNotifyEvent, that implements two static methods: FireOnRequestEdit() and FireOnChanged(). (Conversely, if your control doesn't include IPropertyNotifySinkCP, these two methods are implemented by CComControl and essentially do nothing.)

Now your property logic is a bit more complicated, but not overly so. You first fire FireOnRequestEdit(), you modify the property, and then you fire FireOnChanged().

If FireOnRequestEdit() returns S_FALSE, the container denied the request to edit the property, so you simply exit the property mutator method.

Rather than sprinkle the check for frozen events all through the LED control code, I wrote three helper functions that make this check and then fire the actual event. Two of the methods wrap the events I just discussed, whereas the third wraps the FireViewChange() event I mentioned in the last day. (It tells the container the control needs to be redrawn.) The helper functions are shown in Listing 17.5

LISTING 17.5 CMyNinthATLObj Event Helper Method Implementations

```
1: // Event helpers
2: HRESULT FireViewChange()
3: {
4:     // Check to see if events are frozen
5:     if ( m_nFreezeEvents ) {
6:         // Events are frozen
7:         return S_FALSE;
8:     } // if
9:
10:     // Fire the event
11:     return CComControlBase::FireViewChange();
12: }
13:
14: HRESULT FireOnRequestEdit(DISPID dispID)
15: {
16:     // Check to see if events are frozen
17:     if ( m_nFreezeEvents ) {
18:         // Events are frozen
19:         return S_FALSE;
20:     } // if
21:
22:     // Fire the event
23: return CFirePropNotifyEvent::FireOnRequestEdit(GetUnknown(),
24: ➥dispID);
25: }
26:
27: HRESULT FireOnChanged(DISPID dispID)
28: {
29:     // Check to see if events are frozen
30:     if ( m_nFreezeEvents ) {
31:         // Events are frozen
32:         return S_FALSE;
33:     } // if
34:
35:     // Fire the event
36:     return CFirePropNotifyEvent::FireOnChanged(GetUnknown(),dispID);
37: }
```

17

To best see this in action, take a look at Listing 17.6, which shows you the State2 property mutator method.

LISTING 17.6   CMyNinthATLObj's put_State2() Method Implementation

```
 1: STDMETHODIMP CMyNinthATLObj::put_State2(States2 newVal)
 2: {
 3:     HRESULT hr = S_OK;
 4:     try {
 5:         // Request the edit
 6:         hr = FireOnRequestEdit(DISPID_STATE2);
 7:         if ( hr != S_OK ) throw hr;
 8:
 9:         // Check the value
10:         if ((newVal >= LED_NORMAL) && (newVal <= LED_ALERT)) {
11:             // In range...
12:             m_iState = (States2)newVal;
13:
14:             // Redraw...
15:             FireViewChange();
16:
17:             // Fire changed notification
18:             FireOnChanged(DISPID_STATE2);
19:         } // if
20:         else {
21:             // Bad parameter
22:             hr = E_INVALIDARG;
23:         } // else
24:     } // try
25:     catch(HRESULT hrErr) {
26:         // RequestEdit denied
27:         hr = hrErr;
28:     } // catch
29:     catch(...) {
30:         // Some error
31:         hr = E_UNEXPECTED;
32:     } // catch
33:
34:     return hr;
35: }
```

ANALYSIS   Looking at the code in Listing 17.6 shows you why the helper functions are so handy (I've italicized them in the listing). The actual event is fired within the FireOnChanged() helper function, called from line 18, which checks m_nFreezeEvents to see if the event can actually be fired. If not, it doesn't fire the event. The code to check this, however, isn't smattered throughout the various property methods. This cleans things up a bit. It doesn't impede the actual property modification, unless the container denies the request to edit the property.

Summary

When two objects require two-way communication, connection points are a good way to implement that communication. The object receiving the communication implements a sink interface, whereas the object initiating the communication implements the connection point. The receiving object passes its sink interface to the sending object, which stores it in its connection point container. When the sender needs to notify the receiver, it iterates through its connection points and calls the particular sink interface.

ATL helps with this process by creating a connection point proxy based upon the interface's event interface. The event interface is a dispinterface stored in the type library that clients can easily access. You fire the events by calling the methods implemented in the connection point proxy. Your control's container can then respond to the events as appropriate.

ATL also implements IPropertyNotifySink, which is used to fire the request edit and changed notifications. The container uses these when the property is tied to a data source, perhaps a database. If the container returns S_FALSE when you fire the request edit notification, you should not change the property.

And there you have it! Your ActiveX control is fully functional. If you plan to give it away, you're done! On the other hand, if you want to sell the control and make a little cash, you'll want to license the control. I'll talk about that in Day 18, "ATL, Class Factories, and Licensed Objects: Creating Objects and Protecting Your Investment," when I revisit the class object.

Q&A

Q Is there an advantage to implementing properties with the requestedit and bindable attributes?

A At first, you might not think so, given you now have to ask permission, of all things, before you change a property. But it's actually a grand idea to support these attributes. These events tie your control to an external data source, and that's an advantage in every case. It provides another reuse avenue for your control that, I hope, increases its customer appeal. The overhead for doing this is minimal, at least at the code level. There are some issues with connection points and remote objects (the enumeration through the container is very expensive). In general, however, the runtime overhead isn't that ridiculous either. Not much implementation pain for possibly a lot of market gain.

Q How does the connection point proxy fit into the scheme of connection points in general?

A The literature I've read regarding pure connection points makes no mention of the proxy, so I assume it's tied more closely to ATL. I hadn't heard of it prior to ATL, but that isn't to say the term didn't previously exist. In any case, the proxy is code that Visual Studio will generate for you, by means of a wizard. The proxy wizard, if you could call it that, reads your control's type library and creates C++ code to reach into the connection point container and send the notice to each sink interface it finds. The *proxy* part probably refers to the fact the code generated is in addition to the code already in place for `IConnectionPointImpl`, which the proxy uses as a base class.

Workshop

The Workshop is designed to help you anticipate possible questions, review what you've learned, and get you thinking about how to put your knowledge into practice. The answers to the quiz are in Appendix A, "Answers."

Quiz

1. What is a connection point? A connection point container?
2. What `IConnectionPoint` methods does the client use to activate and deactivate a particular sink?
3. What functionality does `IPropertyNotifySink` provide for?
4. What IDL property attributes allow for requesting property changes and binding?

Exercise

1. Add an event to the LED control, such as when the focus shifts to and away from the control.

DAY 18

ATL, Class Factories, and Licensed Objects: Creating Objects and Protecting Your Investment

Now that you've come this far, it might seem like a step back to look at the class factory again. But in reality, your object's class factory plays a critical role in your object's lifetime: It creates the object! It makes sense to give this important piece of the COM puzzle a little airtime. A nice segue is that ATL provides terrific class factory support, so this isn't just another dry theory chapter.

There are two basic COM class factory interfaces that I'm aware of: IClassFactory and IClassFactory2. You might recall I introduced these interfaces all the way back in Day 2, "Exploring COM: The Technology ATL Supports." I'll revisit these interfaces again in this lesson (briefly), and then I'll move on to some interesting ATL implementations of these two interfaces.

So let's get started. Here's what is in store for you in this day:

- Another visit with IClassFactory and IClassFactory2
- A look at the standard ATL implementations of IClassFactory and IClassFactory2 and how you select them
- An examination of some more exotic ATL class factory implementations
- A survey of methods and implementations of object licensing
- An examination of remote licensing over the Internet

Class Factories Revisited

Every COM object that has a CLSID and can be created using CoCreateInstance() has a class object, more commonly called the object's class factory. The class factory is responsible for actually instantiating the object itself. The object's client, in reality, requests that a new object be instantiated by the class factory, and if the class factory can do so, it will.

Unless Microsoft has internal class factory interfaces of which I'm not aware, there are only two class factory interfaces: IClassFactory and IClassFactory2. As you remember, IClassFactory is the bare-bones, object-creation interface, whereas IClassFactory2 provides for runtime licensing.

In this section, I'll briefly discuss each interface and its methods. You won't often find yourself implementing a new class factory, because ATL provides terrific support in this area. It's important, however, to know what is going on under the covers.

IClassFactory

Table 18.1 shows the IClassFactory interface methods (beyond the usual IUnknown methods).

TABLE 18.1 IClassFactory Interface Methods

Method	Purpose
CreateInstance()	Creates a new (uninitialized) object
LockServer()	Locks the object's server in memory

CreateInstance() is the workhorse creation method. You pass in a controlling IUnknown (for aggregation, or NULL if the object is not to be aggregated), a reference IID, and the address of an output variable that will contain a pointer to the new object. If you receive anything from this method but S_OK, it means the object wasn't created for some reason. The two most common reasons that the object is not created are that the interface you requested doesn't exist for this object (E_NOINTERFACE) or you were trying to aggregate an object that doesn't want to be aggregated (CLASS_E_NOAGGREGATION). Of course, there is always the possibility the system ran out of memory (E_OUTOFMEMORY). If there is an error, the class factory should place NULL in the output object pointer variable, although you should not depend on this (some implementations simply return an error HRE-SULT).

If you intend to create many objects supported by a given class factory, you might want to call LockServer(TRUE) for performance reasons. This locks the class factory into memory, decreasing the time it will take to create the second and subsequent copies of the object. The class factory will remain in memory until you decrement the lock count by calling LockServer(FALSE).

IClassFactory2

IClassFactory is, by far, the more commonly used for creating COM objects. In addition, the class factory is the perfect place to make intelligent decisions about how and when your object is to be created. If you reach the decision not to create an object from within your class factory, for whatever reason, you can patently deny clients access to your object. One clear use of this encompassing power is to force clients to provide a license to use the object, although I'm sure you can imagine other uses as well. If you're interested in licensing your object, you'll want to use IClassFactory2.

IClassFactory2 provides the same interface methods as IClassFactory, so I won't reiterate those. Table 18.2, however, shows you the additional methods IClassFactory2 supports.

TABLE 18.2 IClassFactory2 Interface Methods

Method	Purpose
GetLicInfo()	Fills a LICINFO structure with information on the licensing capabilities of this class factory
RequestLicKey()	Creates and returns a license key that the caller can save and use later when calling CreateInstanceLic()
CreateInstanceLic()	Creates an instance of the licensed object given a license key obtained from RequestLicKey()

I introduced this briefly in Day 2. Remember the overall goal is to enable your object to be created and, ultimately, used on either a licensed or an unlicensed machine. You can require that the machine your object is to run on has a license (the first case), or you might require that only the application using your object contain a license key. This key will allow the application to execute on otherwise unlicensed machines.

The first situation, where the machine is licensed, is referred to as a *full machine license* in the online documentation. The second scenario allows the application to embed a copy of the license within its code that the licensed object will use for creation, allowing only this single application instance the right to instantiate the object. Essentially, these two scenarios break down to global machine permission or single instance permission (via the license key) to use the given object.

Global machine permission has been in use for some time, and it is relatively simple to implement. For example, when the object is installed, it can be installed with an encrypted license file. If the class factory finds and properly decodes the license file, it will create an instance of the object.

The second situation is called *runtime licensing* and is a bit more difficult to implement because ultimately the object is to run in an unlicensed environment. In this case, the application using the licensed object must carry with it the license key. When it tries to create an instance of the object, it passes the license key to the class factory for validation. If the key passes validation, the class factory creates the object. Typically, the license key is a simple textual message, and the validation is nothing more than a simple string comparison. Although simple, this scheme is actually quite effective.

Both scenarios revolve around the LICINFO structure (from OCIDL.H):

```
typedef struct  tagLICINFO
    {
    LONG cbLicInfo;
    BOOL fRuntimeKeyAvail;
    BOOL fLicVerified;
    } LICINFO;
```

You obtain a copy of the given object's LICINFO information through its GetLicInfo() method. The cbLicInfo member is simply the structure size, in bytes. The fLicVerified member indicates the presence of a global license. If this value is FALSE, the IClassFactory(1 or 2)::CreateInstance() method will fail with the error CLASS_E_NOTLICENSED. You then have to turn to runtime licensing.

For this, you check the fRuntimeKeyAvail member. If this member is FALSE, the object doesn't support runtime licensing and you'll require a global license to use the object. On the other hand, if this is TRUE, a call to RequestLicKey() should succeed. (If both fLicVerified and fRuntimeKeyAvail are FALSE, you won't get an object!)

Your application should then call RequestLicKey() to obtain a copy of the runtime license key, which will be returned as a BSTR. This is the key your application must take with it to other unlicensed machines to instantiate copies of the licensed object. The BSTR itself can contain almost anything (it need not be textual) and can very well be encrypted. As I mentioned, however, it's usually just a string.

When the application containing the runtime key is executed on an unlicensed machine, a call to CreateInstance() should fail outright (with the error CLASS_E_NOTLICENSED). In that case, the application should pass the runtime license key to the CreateInstanceLic() method, at which time the class factory will validate the license key and create an object if the key is indeed valid. If the key isn't valid, you again get the CLASS_E_NOTLICENSED error.

I'll discuss some implementations of this later in the day. The standard Microsoft implementation is rather simplistic, but there are other clever things you can do as well. With this understanding of IClassFactory and IClassFactory2, let's see how ATL implements the class factory behavior.

ATL ClassFactory Implementations

ATL implements for you three variations of IClassFactory and a single variation of IClassFactory2. If you create an ATL project, you get, by default, the standard IClassFactory implementation. If, however, you're interested in IClassFactory2, the other two implementations of IClassFactory, or you want to create your own class factory, you edit your object's header file and add one of the macros you see in Table 18.3.

TABLE 18.3 ATL Class Factory Selection Macros

Macro	Purpose
DECLARE_CLASSFACTORY()	Uses the default ATL class factory implementation (macro not required if you want standard IClassFactory behavior)
DECLARE_CLASSFACTORY_EX()	Creates and uses your own class factory implementation (you supply the code)
DECLARE_CLASSFACTORY2()	Uses ATL's implementation of IClassFactory2 (you supply license code)
DECLARE_CLASSFACTORY_AUTO_THREAD()	Uses the ATL class factory that implements an object thread pool
DECLARE_CLASSFACTORY_SINGLETON()	Uses the ATL class factory that provides a single object for all instantiation requests

18

Although I won't discuss creating your own class factory in this book, I will describe each of the other standard ATL class factories and provide an example for each. Later in the day, I'll revisit IClassFactory2 and licensing issues, in general, because this topic warrants further discussion. I'll begin with the standard implementation of IClassFactory.

CComClassFactory

The ATL class that implements IClassFactory is CComClassFactory. If you create an ATL project and don't add any of the macros you see in Table 18.3, this is the class factory ATL uses by default. Although it isn't incorrect to specify this with the DECLARE_CLASSFACTORY() macro, you aren't required to do so.

Actually, you're already familiar with this class factory, because it's the only one you've used throughout the book so far. Because this implementation is pretty straightforward, I'll move on to the more interesting ATL classes.

CComClassFactory2

The other standard ATL class factory implementation comes from CComClassFactory2, and you use this class by inserting the DECLARE_CLASSFACTORY2() macro into your object's C++ class definition (typically in the *<object>*.h file).

LISTING 18.1 CMyTenthATLObj's Class Definition (Edited)

```
 1: #include "LicenseImpl.h"
 2:
 3: ////////////////////////////////////////////////////////////////////////
 4: // CMyTenthATLObj
 5: class ATL_NO_VTABLE CMyTenthATLObj :
 6:     public CComObjectRootEx<CComSingleThreadModel>,
 7:     public CComCoClass<CMyTenthATLObj, &CLSID_TYATLObj10>,
 8:     public ILicenseDemo
 9: {
10: public:
11:     CMyTenthATLObj()
12:     {
13:     }
14:
15: DECLARE_CLASSFACTORY2(CLicenseImpl)
16:     ...
17: (edited for brevity)
18: };
```

ANALYSIS   CComClassFactory2 provides most of the code you need to fully implement
IClassFactory2, except for the actual licensing implementation. This omission
is for flexibility. You provide the license code and, in the preceding example, I implemented it in the LicenseImpl.h file (the CLicenseImpl class), which I included on line 1.
(You'll see this file in detail later in the day, when I discuss licensing methods and
implementations.) I then told ATL which license class to use when I declared my intention to use IClassFactory2 on line 15.

Your license implementation must provide the three static methods described in Table 18.4.

TABLE 18.4   Required CComClassFactory2 Static License Methods

Method	Purpose
VerifyLicenseKey()	Compares the (provided) runtime license key against the actual key and returns results of the comparison
GetLicenseKey()	Returns the runtime license key for embedding into the application
IsLicenseValid()	Checks for a global machine license and return results of that check

VerifyLicenseKey() accepts a BSTR that represents the embedded license key. The
application using your object calls this method and passes in the key it originally
obtained from GetLicenseKey(). Note GetLicenseKey() calls IsLicenseValid() prior
to issuing the license key to prevent inadvertent compromise of the key! Your job in
VerifyLicenseKey() is to verify the two license values are the same. If they are, return
TRUE. If not, return FALSE, and the class factory will reject the instantiation request.

The IsLicenseValid() method is used to check for a machine license, and the results of
this are used to complete the fLicVerified member of the LICINFO structure. You
simply return TRUE or FALSE, depending upon the outcome of your verification efforts.
Your implementation of the global machine license verification goes here.

Figure 18.1 shows you the *LicDemoClient* MFC example dialog-based application that
uses the licensed object, LicenseDemo. Had the object failed to instantiate because of a
missing or incorrect license file, the application would display CLASS_E_NOTLICENSED in
the result field.

18

FIGURE **18.1**

*The LicDemoClient
application user inter-
face.*

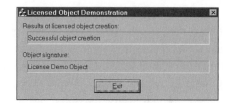

CComClassFactoryAutoThread

You've now seen the two standard ATL class factory implementations. ATL provides two
other implementations, the first of which I describe here. CComClassFactoryAutoThread
implements a class factory that draws from a thread pool when it creates objects. A
thread pool is a collection of available threads with which you instantiate COM objects.
The class factory selects a thread, using a *thread allocator*, and then it creates an object
and passes its pointer back to you. This type of behavior is commonly found on back-end
or enterprise servers, but those applications are not the only ones that benefit from this
class factory.

The AutoThrdDemo example on the CD uses the ATL CComClassFactoryAutoThread
class to create objects on one of four threads. As is common for this class
factory, AutoThrdDemo is a local server (EXE) rather than an in-process
server (DLL). You begin your implementation of this class factory by adding the
DECLARE_CLASSFACTORY_AUTO_THREAD() macro, as shown in Listing 18.2.

LISTING 18.2 CMyEleventhATLObj's Class Definition (Edited)

```
 1: ////////////////////////////////////////////////////////////////////////
 2: // CMyEleventhATLObj
 3: class ATL_NO_VTABLE CMyEleventhATLObj :
 4:     public CComObjectRootEx<CComSingleThreadModel>,
 5:     public CComCoClass<CMyEleventhATLObj, &CLSID_TYATLObj11>,
 6:     public IAutoThreadDemo
 7: {
 8: public:
 9:     CMyEleventhATLObj()
10:     {
11:     }
12:
13: DECLARE_CLASSFACTORY_AUTO_THREAD()
14:     ...
15: (Edited for brevity)
16: };
```

However, to use the thread-pooled class factory, you also must modify the basic definition of CExeModule. CExeModule, defined in STDAFX.H, normally uses CComModule as its base class. Instead, you use CComAutoThreadModule as the base class and provide a thread allocation class (typically CComSimpleThreadAllocator):

```
class CExeModule : public CComAutoThreadModule
➡<CComSimpleThreadAllocator>
{
(Edited for brevity)
};
```

As you recall from Day 5, "ATL Architecture: How ATL Implements COM," the standard ATL thread allocator, CComSimpleThreadAllocator, provides CComAutoThreadModule with a pool of four threads, allocated and used in a simple round-robin fashion. If you'd like to be more exotic, feel free to create a new allocator. CComAutoThreadModule will call its GetThread() method to obtain a thread when required.

To prove this class factory works as I've advertised, I created the AutoThrdClient application to go with the AutoThrdDemo object. The user interface is similar to the LicDemoClient you saw in Figure 18.1. I ran eight instances of AutoThrdClient, which I show in Figure 18.2. They filled my screen! But you can clearly see the four thread IDs indicated, with each used twice.

18

FIGURE 18.2

The AutoThrdClient application instances.

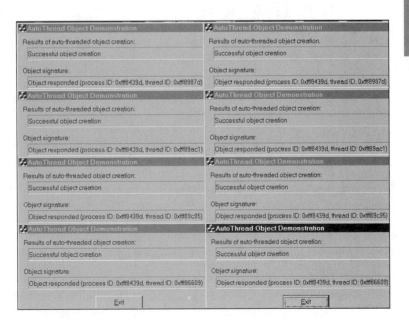

AutoThrdDemo was created as a local server, which is an executable file. Whenever a new instance of this is created, it uses the original object's process with a thread obtained by the class factory's thread allocator. Had this been a traditional IClassFactory implementation, you would see four different process IDs, as well as four different thread IDs.

CComClassFactorySingleton

The antithesis of CComClassFactoryAutoThread is CComClassFactorySingleton, which creates a single object for all object instantiation requests. This one object serves all interface method calls—one process, one thread, and all requests. I've seen this class factory used for several local-server (EXE) tasks, such as global-event logging and server-job scheduling. I've used this class factory in the SingletonDemo example you'll find on the CD.

If you open the MyTwelfthATLObj.h file and examine its contents, you should see something like Listing 18.3.

LISTING 18.3 CMyTwelfthATLObj's Class Definition (Edited)

```
 1: ////////////////////////////////////////////////////////////////////
 2: // CMyTwelfthATLObj
 3: class ATL_NO_VTABLE CMyTwelfthATLObj :
 4:     public CComObjectRootEx<CComSingleThreadModel>,
 5:     public CComCoClass<CMyTwelfthATLObj, &CLSID_TYATLObj12>,
 6:     public ISingletonDemo
 7: {
 8: public:
 9:     CMyTwelfthATLObj()
10:     {
11:     }
12:
13: DECLARE_CLASSFACTORY_SINGLETON(CMyTwelfthATLObj)
14:     ...
15: (Edited for brevity)
16: };
```

This is where I declare the use of CComClassFactorySingleton using the DECLARE_CLASSFACTORY_SINGLETON() macro. That's all there is to it! Any time a client requests this object, he will receive an interface pointer to a single instance of this object.

To prove this, I created the SingletonClient application to go along with the SingletonDemo object. Just as in the AutoThrdClient you just saw, I ran two instances of the application to see what process and thread ID popped up. I show you the results in Figure 18.3.

FIGURE 18.3

The SingletonClient application instances.

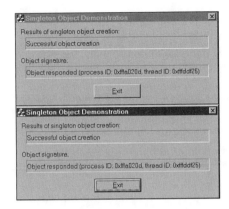

You've now seen examples of using each class factory ATL implements. All but `IClassFactory2` require very little effort on your part. `IClassFactory2`, however, does require a little work because you must implement the basic licensing scheme. I'll discuss that next.

Implementing Licensing

18

Frankly, if you're interested in making your living writing and marketing software, especially COM objects or applications derived from COM objects, you're probably interested in licensing. After all, piracy is a problem today. Even basically honest people sometimes copy files they shouldn't. Licensing solves many issues related to piracy, but its use is more along the lines of "keeping honest people honest." Ardent hackers will probably always find a way to steal your code. You can, at least, make it hard on them and impossible for the average user.

How complicated your licensing scheme becomes is up to you. Microsoft provides a file-based scheme with MFC ActiveX controls, which I re-implemented in ATL. I'll show you this shortly. I'm sure you can imagine more creative schemes. For example, you might write a value to the Registry and check for that. You could, alternatively, write a secret and/or hidden file to some directory on the local hard drive.

I discuss the file-based approach in the next section. I'll leave implementing more devious methods to your creative genius.

File-Based Licensing Method and Implementation

The file-based method is a common and relatively effective method of licensing software. The algorithm is simple. You create a file with a specific string located in a specific place within the file. You then embed the same string in your object's source code. When it's time to create the file, ATL will call your object's static `IsLicenseValid()` method, which opens the file, extracts the string (from where it thinks the string should be), and finally returns the results of the comparison between the stored string and the string pulled from the file.

Because I have implemented licensed MFC-based ActiveX controls, I knew MFC provided an implementation of this file-based approach. I did some rummaging though the MFC source code, found the implementation, and based the `IsLicenseValid()` code in Listing 18.4 on the MFC scheme I found. The code you see in Listing 18.4 actually fully implements the static functions you're required to provide to satisfy `CComClassFactory2`.

LISTING 18.4 LicenseImpl.h

```
 1: // LicenseImpl.h : Declaration of the CLicenseImpl class
 2:
 3: #ifndef __LICENSEIMPL_H_
 4: #define __LICENSEIMPL_H_
 5:
 6: extern CComModule _Module;
 7:
 8: /////////////////////////////////////////////////////////////////////////
 9: // License string implementations
10: static const TCHAR _szLicFileName[] = _T("LicenseDemo.lic");
11: static const WCHAR _szLicString[] = L"Copyright (c) 1999 My Company";
12:
13: /////////////////////////////////////////////////////////////////////////
14: // CLicenseImpl
15: class CLicenseImpl
16: {
17: // Construction
18: public:
19:     CLicenseImpl()
20:     {
21:     }
22:
23:     ~CLicenseImpl()
24:     {
25:     }
26:
27: // CComClassFactory2 License Implementation
28:     static BOOL VerifyLicenseKey(BSTR bstr)
29:     {
30:         // Compare what is provided against what is expected
31:         return !wcscmp(bstr,_szLicString);
32:     }
33:
```

```
34:     static BOOL GetLicenseKey(DWORD dwReserved, BSTR* pBstr)
35:     {
36:         // Check their pointer
37:         if ( pBstr == NULL ) {
38:             // NULL pointer...
39:             return FALSE;
40:         } // if
41:
42:         // Create a BSTR representation of the license key
43:         *pBstr = SysAllocString(_szLicString);
44:         return (*pBstr != NULL);
45:     }
46:
47:     static BOOL IsLicenseValid()
48:     {
49:         // Assume invalid
50:         BOOL bVerified = FALSE;
51:
52:         // Look for license file in same directory as this DLL.
53:         TCHAR strPathName[_MAX_PATH+1];
54:         ::GetModuleFileName(_Module.GetModuleInstance(),
55:                             strPathName,_MAX_PATH);
56:         LPTSTR pszFileName = _tcsrchr(strPathName, '\\') + 1;
57:         _tcscpy(pszFileName,_szLicFileName);
58:
59:         // Open the file and compare the contents to the stored
60:         // key value.
61:         HANDLE hLicFile = NULL;
62:         try {
63:             // Open file, read content and compare.
64:             hLicFile = CreateFile(strPathName,
65:                                   GENERIC_READ,
66:                                   FILE_SHARE_READ,
67:                                   NULL,
68:                                   OPEN_EXISTING,
69:                                   FILE_ATTRIBUTE_NORMAL,
70:                                   NULL);
71:             if ( hLicFile == NULL ) {
72:                 // Error creating file...let the catch block clean up
73:                 throw -1;
74:             } // if
75:
76:             // Determine how long the key should be
77: #ifdef _UNICODE
78:             DWORD iExpectedKeyLen = lstrlen(_szLicString);
79: #else
80:             USES_CONVERSION;
81:             LPTSTR pszKey = OLE2T(_szLicString);
```

continues

18

LISTING **18.4**   continued

```
 82:             DWORD iExpectedKeyLen = _tcslen(pszKey);
 83: #endif // _UNICODE
 84:
 85:             // Pull file contents, if there is a license string
 86:             if (iExpectedKeyLen != 0) {
 87: #ifdef _UNICODE
 88:                 // Add two for leading bytes in Unicode text file
 89:                 iExpectedKeyLen += 2;
 90: #endif // _UNICODE
 91:
 92:                 // Allocate the buffer for file data (on stack)
 93:                 LPBYTE pbContent = (BYTE*)_alloca(iExpectedKeyLen);
 94:
 95:                 // Read the file and extract the expected key
 96:                 DWORD dwBytesRead = 0;
 97:                 if ( !ReadFile(hLicFile,pbContent,iExpectedKeyLen,
     ➥&dwBytesRead,NULL) ) {
 98:                     // Error reading file...let the catch block
 99:                     // clean up
100:                     throw -1;
101:                 } // if
102:
103:                 // Check bytes read versus bytes expected
104:                 if ( dwBytesRead != iExpectedKeyLen ) {
105:                     // Error reading file or invalid file...
106:                     // let the catch block clean up
107:                     throw -1;
108:                 } // if
109:
110: #ifdef _UNICODE
111:                 // Note license file must also be in Unicode...
112:                 // It will have two leading bytes, which must
113:                 // be skipped for comparison here.
114:                 LPBYTE pbContent2 = pbContent + 2;
115:                 if ( !memcmp(_szLicString,pbContent2,
     ➥(size_t)iExpectedKeyLen-2) ) {
116: #else // !_UNICODE
117:                 if ( !memcmp(pszKey,pbContent,
     ➥(size_t)iExpectedKeyLen) ) {
118: #endif // _UNICODE
119:                     // License is valid
120:                     bVerified = TRUE;
121:                 } // if
122:             } // if
123:         } // try
124:         catch(...) {
125:             // Unexpected error...
126:             /* nothing */;
127:         } // catch
```

```
128:
129:            // Close the file handle
130:            if ( hLicFile != NULL ) {
131:                CloseHandle(hLicFile);
132:            } // if
133:
134:            return bVerified;
135:        }
136: };
137:
138: #endif // __LICENSEIMPL_H_
```

ANALYSIS　　IsLicenseValid()begins by assuming the license verification will fail, line 50:

```
BOOL bVerified = FALSE;
```

It then looks to the object's directory for the license file, the name of which is stored in _szLicFileName (lines 52–57):

```
// Look for license file in same directory as this DLL.
TCHAR strPathName[_MAX_PATH+1];
::GetModuleFileName(_Module.GetModuleInstance(),
                    strPathName,_MAX_PATH);
LPTSTR pszFileName = _tcsrchr(strPathName, '\\') + 1;
_tcscpy(pszFileName,_szLicFileName);
```

After the complete file path has been generated, it opens the license file for reading, from lines 64–74:

```
hLicFile = CreateFile(strPathName,
                      GENERIC_READ,
                      FILE_SHARE_READ,
                      NULL,
                      OPEN_EXISTING,
                      FILE_ATTRIBUTE_NORMAL,
                      NULL);
if ( hLicFile == NULL ) {
    // Error creating file...let the catch block clean up
    throw -1;
} // if
```

If the file can be read, it plays some games to obtain the license key string and length (lines 76–83). This is the first area where you'll see a difference between Unicode systems and ANSI systems:

```
// Determine how long the key should be
#ifdef _UNICODE
```

18

```
    DWORD iExpectedKeyLen = lstrlen(_szLicString);
#else
    USES_CONVERSION;
    LPTSTR pszKey = OLE2T(_szLicString);
    DWORD iExpectedKeyLen = lstrlen(pszKey);
#endif // _UNICODE
```

The length of the license key will be stored in iExpectedKeyLen (line 78 for
Unicode or line 82 for ANSI), whereas a pointer to the converted key string content
(for ANSI builds) will be obtained by OLE2T() with the converted string indicated by
pszKey (line 81).

After you know the length of the license string, you can read that many bytes from the
file. Before you do that, though, remember to add two bytes to the length if you're
building a Unicode version (lines 87–90). The license file, if in Unicode, contains a two-
byte header that you must skip when you later compare the license values or you'll *never*
verify the license:

```
#ifdef _UNICODE
    // Add two for leading bytes in Unicode text file
    iExpectedKeyLen += 2;
#endif // _UNICODE
```

Note

This implementation assumes the license file is a text file, and if the object is
built with the Unicode libraries, the text file was also stored as Unicode. I
provide both versions of the license file with this example.

Now you can read the file, after you allocate some memory for the file contents using
line 93:

```
// Allocate the buffer for file data (on stack)
LPBYTE pbContent = (BYTE*)_alloca(iExpectedKeyLen);
```

This allocates iExpectedKeyLen bytes on the stack, so you won't have to worry about
deleting the memory. I next read the file and verify the read was successful (lines 95–108):

```
// Read the file and extract the expected key
DWORD dwBytesRead = 0;
if ( !ReadFile(hLicFile,pbContent,iExpectedKeyLen,
➥&dwBytesRead,NULL) ) {
    // Error reading file...let the catch block
    // clean up
    throw -1;
} // if
```

```
// Check bytes read versus bytes expected
if ( dwBytesRead != iExpectedKeyLen ) {
    // Error reading file or invalid file...
    // let the catch block clean up
    throw -1;
} // if
```

At this point, you can see that the license string should be at the beginning of the license file, not somewhere in the middle or at the end. If you want your string to be somewhere else in the file, you'll have to move the file pointer there (SetFilePointer()) before you read the contents.

With the contents of the file secured, IsLicenseValid() checks the license key values using lines 110–121:

```
#ifdef _UNICODE
    // Note license file must also be in Unicode...
    // It will have two leading bytes, which must
    // be skipped for comparison here.
    LPBYTE pbContent2 = pbContent + 2;
    if ( !memcmp(_szLicString,pbContent2,
➥(size_t)iExpectedKeyLen-2) ) {
#else // !_UNICODE
    if ( !memcmp(pszKey,pbContent,(size_t)iExpectedKeyLen) ) {
#endif // _UNICODE
        // License is valid
        bVerified = TRUE;
    } // if
```

It compares the key values using a simple memory comparison, although I've highlighted a trick in the Unicode version to skip the leading two file-header bytes of the Unicode file (line 115). Note I also have to subtract two from the comparison length before I execute memcmp() with the Unicode strings (line 114). This removes the two bytes of the header from the length.

If the comparison is successful, bVerified is set to TRUE and later returned after closing the license file (lines 129 through 134):

```
// Close the file handle
if ( hLicFile != NULL ) {
    CloseHandle(hLicFile);
} // if

return bVerified;
```

If you elect to implement a fancier algorithm than this, IsLicenseValid() is where you implement it. If you determine there is a global machine license, return TRUE. If not, return FALSE and expect the application to provide a runtime license key that you'll later validate using VerifyLicenseKey().

18

To copy the license file (.LIC) from the source directory to the directory with the compiled object as the project builds, follow these steps:

- Create the .LIC file (ANSI or Unicode).
- Add the file to your project (place it under the Resource Files tree node in the
  FileView of the Workspace window).
- Right click on the .LIC file, after you have inserted it into the project, and select
  the Settings menu item.
- Select the list item All Configurations from the Settings For: Drop List control.
- Click on the Custom Build tab and insert the text you see in Figure 18.4.
- Click OK.

FIGURE 18.4

*The Custom Build tab
for the .LIC file post-
build copy.*

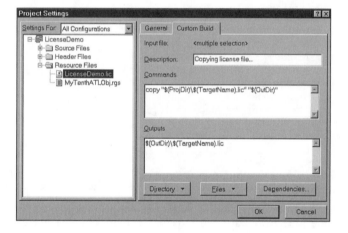

This scheme works for compiled applications. Remote licensing of objects, the type a
user needs when loading a licensed ActiveX control from over the Internet, adds a new
dimension.

Remote Licensing

ActiveX controls that implement IClassFactory2 are licensed globally at design time, as
you know. Any valid purchaser/licensee may use the ActiveX control without limitation
on his local machine as he is building his application(s). When your application is compiled, the ActiveX control will embed a copy of the license into your application program. When a user executes your application, the program passes the ActiveX control the
license string. At that time, the control compares that string to its correct license string. If
they match, the control will load and execute. If they don't, the ActiveX control does not
load and execute, and the user gets an error message from your application.

But what about HTML? You don't compile a control into a user's browser, and you certainly don't compile HTML (or any derivations, such as Dynamic HTML), so how is a license string embedded into an HTML document? The answer is: It isn't. You must provide a license file for the license manager to use to verify the control's license. The license file, typically named *<ctrlname>*.lpk, should be found in the same Web server directory as the control. The license manager is another ActiveX control that executes on the user's machine. You must insert this HTML <object> tag exactly as shown to invoke the license manager (which must appear before any other objects to preclude license errors):

```
<object
classid="clsid:5220cb21-c88d-11cf-b347-00aa00a28331"
align="baseline" border="0" width="50" height="50"><param
name="LPKPath" value="<ctrlname>.lpk">
</object>
```

The value of the <param> tag (LPKPath) is a path to the license file, which must be present on your server. As shown, the file resides in the same directory as the HTML page with this <object> tag. This tag must be the first <object> in your document HTML stream for the controls to operate correctly. After the license manager control's HTML code has been inserted, you can insert the remaining ActiveX controls on your page, licensed or unlicensed.

The trick is to create the license file. For that, you use a tool that Microsoft provides (which I included on the CD with this day's code) called *LPK_Tool*. LPK_Tool implements a common user interface paradigm—a dual list of controls that indicate membership in the collection of all ActiveX controls (licensed and unlicensed) and those you wish to include in the license file. I show LPK_Tool in action in Figure 18.5.

18

FIGURE 18.5

The Microsoft LPK_Tool user interface.

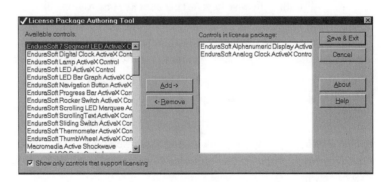

Using the tool is simplicity itself. Simply choose the ActiveX controls you want to insert into the license file and shift them to the right list control. After you have all the controls you want stuffed into the license file inclusion list, click the Save&Exit button, name the file, and copy the file to your Web server.

Note The issue of remote licensing is completely separate from that of digital signatures. Digital signatures tell your users the file came from a trusted source (you) and is unmolested. Using *LPK_Tool* merely helps you license your object. If you want to apply a digital signature, as well as a license, you'll need to follow additional steps beyond the scope of this book. If you are interested in learning more about digital signatures, a good article to begin with is "Signing and Marking ActiveX Controls," by Paul Johns, available from the MSDN library.

Summary

Your object's class factory is a critical component because it is responsible for creating instances of your object. It's also the perfect place to play games with how or if objects are created.

IClassFactory is the standard COM interface for object creation, although if you want to license your objects, you should use IClassFactory2. ATL provides four class factory implementations, three of which are based upon IClassFactory, leaving one for the licensed case. CComClassFactory is the basic ATL class factory implementation. CComClassFactoryAutoThread implements IClassFactory but, given a thread allocation object, creates objects on a new thread. CComClassFactorySingleton creates a single instance of your object, no matter how many clients request a copy. Finally, CComClassFactory2 implements IClassFactory2.

The only ATL implementation that requires you to write code for its implementation is IClassFactory2, which has you implement three static functions. VerifyLicenseKey() verifies a runtime license key. GetLicenseKey() provides that key during application development (GetLicenseKey() uses IsLicenseValid() to verify a global license exists before passing out the license string). IsLicenseValid() actually implements your logic to determine if a valid global machine license exists on the current machine.

Finally, I discussed implementing licensing and provided a file-based solution you can insert into your own objects. I then discussed how licensed ActiveX controls are used over the Internet and introduced the License Manager object and the LPK_Tool utility.

Day 19 should prove very interesting, because you'll leave the confines of your computer to reach out and instantiate remote objects using Distributed COM, or DCOM. Your network awaits!

Q&A

Q **If I wanted to implement my own class factory, where would I start?**

A I'd first make sure that my own class factory is required. The implementations ATL provides do quite a bit for you and are well debugged. That said, however, I have seen other situations where new class factories were implemented to solve certain problems, especially with back-end servers. If I determined my own class factory was necessary, the very first place I'd start is with the ATL source code. You'll find all the ATL class factories implemented in the ATLCOM.H file. If you do implement a custom class factory, remember you can use the DECLARE_CLASSFACTORY_EX() macro to incorporate it into your object.

Q **I have a licensed ActiveX control that will be used over the Internet. Will the License Manager work on the remote computer if the license is stored in the Registry on the developer's computer?**

A Oh sure. The LPK_Tool and the License Manager act as an *application surrogate*, if I can coin the phrase. That is, no matter how the license is implemented on the development machine, the LPK_Tool accesses the license key through IClassFactory2::RequestLicKey() just as any application would. It then creates a file, *<filename>*.lpk, which contains an encrypted version of the runtime license key. (This is an educated guess. I've not ripped apart a .LPK file to find out, but it makes sense.)

The purpose of the License Manager is to retrieve the .LPK file you created and decrypt the runtime key (or keys if there are multiple licensed objects within the same HTML document). How the original license was stored on the development machine has no effect upon the final outcome because the key is encrypted in the .LPK file that is sent to the remote user.

Workshop

The Workshop is designed to help you anticipate possible questions, review what you've learned, and get you thinking about how to put your knowledge into practice. The answers to the quiz are in Appendix A, "Answers."

Quiz

1. What is a class factory? A class object?

2. What is the purpose of the additional methods IClassFactory2 exposes?

3. What are the ATL class factory implementation classes and which class factory do they implement?

4. How do you use a class factory other than the default? What is the default class factory?

5. How do you use a larger thread pool when using `CComClassFactoryAutoThread`?

6. What methods must you provide when using `CComClassFactory2` and what is each method's purpose?

7. How is licensing handled remotely over the Internet?

Exercises

1. Implement a standard local server object much like the ones I created, only base it on `IClassFactory`. Then create a client application much like those I provide. See what process and thread IDs pop up when you execute four instances of the application.

2. Add licensing to the LED ActiveX control from the last day. For extra credit, create a .LPK file for the control.

3. Implement a Registry-based licensing scheme versus the file-based scheme I presented.

DAY 19

Distributed ATL: DCOM Around the Net

I can't tell you why, but I've always liked writing code for networking. Drivers, protocols, applications—it doesn't matter. If one computer sends data to another, I want to get in on it. That's probably why I find this topic so interesting. DCOM, or Distributed COM, is not a new form of COM. Rather, it allows COM to extend the boundaries of referential locality to include any machine connected on the network, so long as the security arrangements permit such connections.

DCOM, although not brand new, is relatively new to the COM programming world. Classic COM has been around for some time, but it took time for the networking end of things to germinate in Redmond (it would have been great to have been a part of *that*!). In this day, you'll look at DCOM or, in other words, how to write COM code that can happily exist on a local or on a remote machine. Although it's not totally plug-and-play, it also isn't difficult.

Although I haven't the space to write the definitive work on DCOM in this chapter, I can concentrate on the nuts and bolts of implementing a real-world distributed application. The example for this day should support my claim because it's pretty meaty by demo code standards.

So, to begin, in this day, you'll see

- Some DCOM basic concepts
- What it takes to create distributed objects, and what effect latency and data transfer have on your application
- Briefly how DCOM works
- DCOM client code to invoke both local and remote objects, as well as the associated server code
- A brief discussion of security

DCOM Basic Concepts

Probably the best aspect of DCOM is that it is, after all, COM. You'll need to do very little to create applications that use DCOM versus traditional (local) COM objects. (In fact, I created this day's example as a standard COM object, and then I added the code to distribute it.) DCOM is based upon an open standard, the Distributed Computing Environment, or DCE. More specifically, DCOM uses the services of the Remote Procedure Calls (RPC) API, which the DCE provides.

The trouble with RPC is that it is procedurally based, not object-based, so it took a great deal of work for Microsoft to shove COM on the Net. Worse, if you're trying to integrate systems, Microsoft's implementation of RPC is nonstandard, so until the Open Software Foundation completes its work to implement DCOM, you'll be sharing objects primarily with Windows systems.

DCOM is, understandably, security conscious. You don't want strangers walking into your house at night. Opening up the valuable data on your computer to just anyone amounts to the same thing. Because of DCOM's security awareness, you'll see different behavior on Windows 95 and 98 systems versus Windows NT and 2000.

Windows NT was built from the ground up with security in mind. Windows 2000 strengthens an already formidable security model. But Windows 95 and 98 were not created with such security-mindedness. To you, this means although you can automatically launch a distributed object if it's housed on an NT or 2000 system (and you have the authority to do so), you can't launch the same COM object on a Windows 95 or 98 system. You'll need to start the COM server on the Windows 95 and 98 system first. After that, remote systems can access the object.

Note Windows 95 and 98 will also terminate the server after the remote client has finished with it, so if you want it to remain available, you'll need to keep an outstanding reference to the object. After its reference count dips to zero, it's gone and can't be remotely activated. Most developers create a simple application that invokes the object locally and remains active until the system shuts down.

While I'm discussing Windows 95 and 98, and NT for that matter, you'll find updates to DCOM available from Microsoft's Internet site. If you have a network and want to try DCOM, you should make sure you have the latest operating system enhancements. If you're not a member of MSDN, you can download the upgrades from the Microsoft Internet site. I've provided the specific URLs in Table 19.1.

Table 19.1   Microsoft DCOM Upgrade URLs

Operating System	DCOM Upgrade URL
Windows 95	`http://www.microsoft.com/Com/` `DCOM/Dcom95/download.asp`
Windows 98	`http://www.microsoft.com/Com/` `DCOM/Dcom98/download.asp`

Windows NT 4.0 SP4	`http://support.microsoft.com/`
	`support/NTServer/`
	`Content/ServicePacks/`
	`SP4_Central_40.asp`

19

Although DCOM has these limitations, its benefits outweigh its limitations. Let's look a bit at some of the other issues you should be aware of when you write distributed code.

Distributing Objects

In a sense, DCOM isn't that different from traditional COM, at least as far as using the objects is concerned. But if you intend to distribute an object, you'll probably design things a bit differently than you would for an in-process server (or a local server, for that matter).

The first thing to be aware of is the type of data and format you pass between the local and remote systems. You should be as efficient and frugal as possible. For example, imagine you're using a COM object that provides you with some sort of enumeration interface. This is very common in traditional COM programming. You enumerate by calling the enumeration interface over and over again, until you are told there is no more to enumerate. This involves repeated communication between the client and the COM object, once for each enumeration call.

This makes for a poor distributed design, however. If the enumeration method is actually supported by a remote object, you have to take the time to package up the call, ship it to the remote system, allow time for the remote object to interpret the method call, perform the enumeration, and package up the result to be returned to you. Although this might not sound like much, given today's high-speed networks, all these little bits of time add up.

A distributed object performs the enumeration for you, and then it ships the entire result set back to you in one big lump of data. This increases your client-side work because you must unpack the data and make sense of it all, but the processing time is far less than you'll typically sustain by enumerating remotely.

In general, network-savvy developers try to pack as much as possible into a single remote call and make as few calls as possible to achieve their objectives. Of course, you must balance this design constraint with any other you have in your system. If you need to make more remote calls because of some other factor, by all means, do so. Be aware of the possible delays associated with using your remote object and design accordingly.

Also, DCOM is currently designed for nongraphical interfaces. That means that passing a window handle to a remote object has no meaning other than establishing the fact that that window has a handle. The remote object cannot process the handle in any meaningful fashion. For this reason, interfaces that expect handles to windows, device contexts, or other graphical objects should be marked in the IDL file as `local`. This tells MIDL the interface is not remotable.

Latency

I mentioned network delays earlier, but what I really should have said was *latency*. Latency means delay, which translates to *waiting*. Using remote objects adds to the latency you already sustain by using COM in the first place. The latency involved with using an in-process COM object in the main STA is minimal—it's not much more than a DLL. Even if the object is in a secondary STA, COM has optimized the communication (marshaling) channel to minimize latency.

If your COM object is in another process, however, things begin to slow down a bit. If you make rapid-fire calls to the out-of-process server, you'll notice the performance degradation versus the in-process server, even to perform the same actions. The latency involved with the network is hundreds of times worse, maybe even worse than that in some situations! Actual numbers are nondeterministic, so write your code and take some measurements to see how things are doing in your particular case. Sometimes the latency doesn't affect you, or you're willing to sustain the latency in return for access to the remote system.

The bottom line is that accessing remote objects is expensive in terms of time, so be frugal with your remote object calls. Use the remote object when you need to, but don't make unnecessary calls if you can find a way to avoid it.

After reading all this, you might get the impression using remote objects is either difficult or unwise. Actually, neither is the case. DCOM makes using remote objects a breeze, and no computer is an island in today's networked world. I mentioned these issues to make you aware of their impact on your designs so that you factor in these problems. Let's move on to some DCOM-specific topics to see how DCOM works.

Surrogates and Servers

When you use DCOM, you'll notice differences between Windows NT and Windows 95 and 98. For example, I mentioned the security aspects earlier in the day. Because Windows 95 and 98 don't implement a robust security model, you can't remotely launch an object. By that, I mean you must first start the COM server on the remote machine and *then* access it from another computer.

There is also another issue with respect to Windows NT versus Windows 95 and 98, and it has to do with *surrogate processes*. Reflect for a moment on the types of COM objects. Well, you have DLLs (in-process servers) and EXEs (local servers). Imagine the remote COM object is a DLL. How do you execute a singular DLL on a remote system? Does your client code travel across the network to execute the DLL? After all, no DLL can stand on its own, even when using DCOM.

The solution is that a surrogate process is started on your client application's behalf. That is, the remote system executes a generic application that does nothing more than house your remote COM server DLL. But this *only* takes place on remote systems using Windows NT. Windows 95 and 98 *must* use EXE-based COM servers if the server is to be remotable. That doesn't mean you should exclude DLL-based remote COM servers. It does mean, however, that you need to know something about the system to which you are connecting.

The surrogate application that Windows NT starts for you is named DLLHOST.EXE, which you'll find in the C:\WINNT\System32 directory. If you'd rather create your own surrogate application, you can do that, too. I'll tell you a little more about this in the next section when I address the Registry changes that DCOM introduces.

Changes to the Registry

Because traditional COM predates DCOM, Microsoft couldn't change the layout of the Registry wholesale. Instead, they tweaked it a bit and added a new Registry requirement for remote objects. This method is in keeping with the COM spirit. Existing clients, who

19

know nothing about remote objects, will still execute, even if the object is, in fact, a new version remotely activated.

I'm not going to address how the process I just described works because ATL supports remote objects from the beginning. If you're interested in the whole story, I'd recommend Richard Grimes' excellent book *Professional DCOM Programming* from Wrox Press, ISBN 1-861000-60-X. I'll leave you with the thought that you can make applications believe they're using local objects when the object is actually remote. Richard discusses this in his book.

Instead, because you're using ATL (and reading my book to learn how to do so), it stands to reason you're not dealing with legacy components. You'll create a remotable object from the start. To help you with that task you can use the ATL AppWizard.

Yes, it's true. From the very beginning your ATL project is remotable, if it's an EXE-based COM server. Even if you created a DLL-based object, you can copy the necessary information to your project from a dummy EXE-based project.

If you look way back to Day 2, "Exploring COM: The Technology ATL Supports," I told you about the CLSID branch of the HKEY_CLASSES_ROOT Registry hive, where all the known (registered) COM objects store their persistent COM-related information. What I didn't tell you then is that there is an AppID branch there also. It's this AppID branch you need for DCOM. (The AppID branch is also replicated in HKEY_LOCAL_MACHINE).

The ATL AppWizard creates not one but two .RGS (ATL Registry script) files for you when you create a local server project. If you open this Day's project, *Day19Server*, you'll find the two .RGS files named MyThirteenthATObj.rgs and Day19Server.rgs. The first file, as shown in Listing 19.1, contains this script code.

LISTING 19.1   MyThirteenthATObj.rgs File Contents

```
 1: HKCR
 2: {
 3:     TYATL.Object13.1 = s 'TYATLObj13 Class'
 4:     {
 5:         CLSID = s '{6C6E5088-8555-11D3-B286-0000E8409B63}'
 6:     }
 7:     TYATL.Object13 = s 'TYATLObj13 Class'
 8:     {
 9:         CLSID = s '{6C6E5088-8555-11D3-B286-0000E8409B63}'
10:         CurVer = s 'TYATL.Object13.1'
11:     }
12:     NoRemove CLSID
13:     {
14:         ForceRemove {6C6E5088-8555-11D3-B286-0000E8409B63} =
                                      ➥ s 'TYATLObj13 Class'
```

```
15:          {
16:                  ProgID = s 'TYATL.Object13.1'
17:                  VersionIndependentProgID = s 'TYATL.Object13'
18:                  LocalServer32 = s '%MODULE%'
19:                  val AppID = s '{6C6E507C-8555-11D3-B286-0000E8409B63}'
20:                  'TypeLib' = s '{6C6E507B-8555-11D3-B286-0000E8409B63}'
21:          }
22:      }
23: }
```

ANALYSIS Notice the italicized portion:

```
val AppID = s '{6C6E507C-8555-11D3-B286-0000E8409B63}'
```

If this key/value pair exists in the Registry when COM comes snooping for your object's CLSID, COM knows the object can be remotable. What the AppID means to COM depends upon whether the object is on the local or the remote system. You'll find the fine details in *Professional DCOM Programming*.

The corresponding AppID value is written to the Registry by the Day19Server.rgs script (see Listing 19.2).

LISTING 19.2 Day19Server.rgs File Contents

```
1: HKCR
2: {
3:      NoRemove AppID
4:      {
5:              {6C6E507C-8555-11D3-B286-0000E8409B63} = s 'Day19Server'
6:              'Day19Server.EXE'
7:              {
8:                      val AppID = s {6C6E507C-8555-11D3-B286-0000E8409B63}
9:              }
10:      }
11: }
```

ANALYSIS You can, if you want, add some information to the {6C6E507C-8555-11D3-B286-0000E8409B63} AppID key that provides COM with specific remote activation information. You would do this after line 8. However, I will skip past most of the specifics of the AppID key because, for the most part, you won't need to modify it by hand. Instead, you'll probably use a special program that Microsoft supplies with every DCOM-configured system. It is called DCOMCnfg.exe, and I'll discuss it in a moment.

19

Note
You can find references to AppID in the online documentation that makes reference to the shell and application launching. That's because there are two kinds of AppIDs. The other kind of AppID really means application ID and is used to associate a given application with an icon or shell invocation verb, such as printing or opening the specific document type. The AppID to which I refer here is *not* that AppID.

There One specific detail I will mention is that the `AppID` key is used to tell the system either the network name of the remote COM object server(`RemoteServerName`), or if the system *is* the remote object's computer, what surrogate should be used if the object is in-process (`DllSurrogate`). If the `DllSurrogate` key is missing, DLLHOST.EXE will be used. To use another surrogate, you add its path to this named value. I'll revisit this later in the day when I discuss security issues and why you might want to provide a surrogate yourself.

The AppID is used by COM to locate the object, if remote, or to locate the surrogate, if the object is being activated remotely is in-process. COM knows to do this. If you use `CLSCTX_REMOTE_SERVER` for the activation context, you pass `CoCreateInstance()` (or `CoGetClassObject()`).

Note
This is contrasted by `CoCreateInstanceEx()`, which has the server name passed to it in the `COSERVERINFO` structure. In that case, COM uses what you pass it, and the `AppID` key is not accessed if the `COSERVERINFO` parameter is nonNULL.

As you recall, both `CoCreateInstance()` and `CoCreateInstanceEx()` call `CoGetClassObject()`. `CoCreateInstance()` has no `COSERVERINFO` structure parameter, so `CoGetClassObject()` is passed `NULL` for that field. COM then looks to the AppID for the server information if the context was `CLSCTX_REMOTE_SERVER`. This topic will pop up again when I discuss DCOM and security later in the day. Both the `AppID` key and the `COSERVERINFO` structure allow you to configure the remote activation security arrangements.

Configuring DCOM with DCOMCnfg.exe

Security is a huge topic, and greatly undercovered in the literature. Perhaps this is because Windows 95 has no security, and most developers became used to ignoring the issue. DCOM forces you to examine certain security issues, but it also forces you to deal with security at a very low level. There are two alternatives to this.

Your first alternative is to use the Microsoft Transaction Server to distribute your objects. The last two days of the book are devoted to MTS and issues revolving around transactions and COM's involvement in an MTS environment. The second alternative to specifying every detail yourself is to use the DCOM Configuration program, DCOMCnfg.exe.

DCOMCnfg.exe differs slightly between Windows NT or Windows 95 and 98. As you might expect, the differences are related to the remote activation settings for objects on the system.

When you run DCOMCnfg.exe, you're presented with the application you see in Figure 19.1. I'll address the Windows 95 version because that's what I have on my system. I'll describe the Windows NT differences as they crop up.

FIGURE 19.1

*Windows 95
DCOMCnfg.exe's
Applications tab.*

You have three major tabs to work with, Applications, Default Properties, and Default Security. The first tab, Applications, enables you to tailor the specific details for a given application. The second and third tabs allow you to specify default settings for *all* remote COM objects on your system. The defaults will be applied to remotely activated objects if their individual AppID keys are missing the specific information.

To modify an individual application's settings, select the application from the list and click the Properties button. This will bring up another set of tabs, three for Windows 95 and 98, and four for Windows NT. The three common tabs are General, Location, and Security. Windows NT adds a fourth tab, Identity. The General tab simply provides information, such as where on disk the object's file resides. The Location tab enables you to specify where the object should run, both remotely and locally. This is where you can specify the remote computer name, for example, if you want to execute the object remotely. The Security tab differs from Windows NT to Windows 95 and 98. Essentially, you can decide who can access the object. Windows NT takes that a step further and allows you to tailor who can remotely launch the object. The fourth tab that Windows NT provides, Identity, allows you to set the user account under which the object should be executed.

If you customize a specific application, DCOMCnfg.exe will record the new information in the object's AppID Registry key. Just make your changes to the application and click OK twice. You can elect to set the system defaults for remote activation. You use the other two main DCOMCnfg.exe tabs for that.

Default Properties, (see Figure 19.2), enables you to activate and deactivate DCOM for the given computer system. You can shut and lock the door, if you want. You also can specify the default *authentication* and *impersonation* levels. The authentication level determines when the remote user is validated for use. It represents a range of authentication levels—from nothing to severe. For example, you can never validate, or you can ask remote users to validate themselves with each packet they send your computer. The impersonation level puts a reverse twist on things. Normally, you don't trust remote users. The impersonation level specifies your trust in remote *servers*. If you trust the server, you allow it so use your client account on your behalf when executing the remote object. If you don't trust the remote server, you select a lower level of trust, all the way down to its treating you as an anonymous user (on Windows NT).

FIGURE 19.2

Windows 95 DCOMCnfg.exe's Default Properties tab.

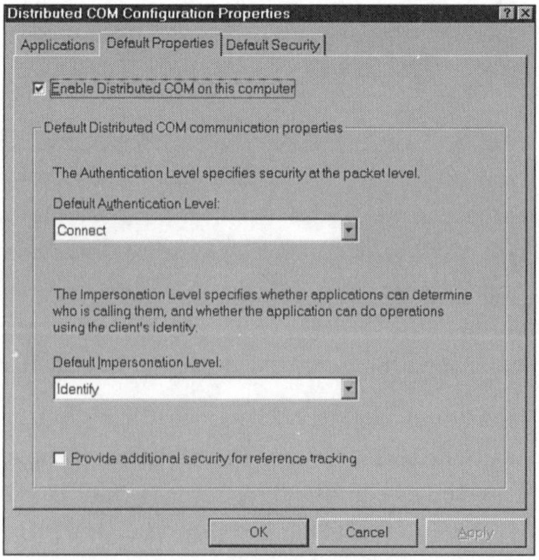

The Default Security tab, shown in Figure 19.3, allows you to specify who can access remote objects and change their properties from a system perspective (versus an application perspective). Windows NT also allows you to set permissions for the launching user. In all cases, you're establishing who is authorized to access and rummage through your system.

FIGURE 19.3

Windows 95 DCOMCnfg.exe's Default Security tab.

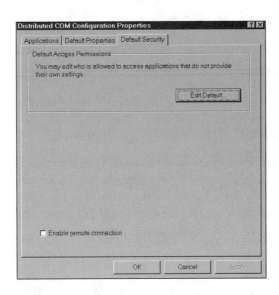

Before you can execute remote objects, assuming you have access to a network as you try this day's sample application, you'll need to establish the appropriate settings on your remote system. DCOMCnfg.exe is the easiest way to do this—outside of MTS.

With this introduction to DCOM under your belt, let's look at how DCOM works. It's far more complicated than I describe here, but at least, you'll gain an understanding of how DCOM transmits data and provides for object lifetime management.

How DCOM Works

I mentioned DCOM rides on top of DCE RPC. DCE RPC rides on top of your network, which is specific to your location. Although the majority of Windows users are connected using Ethernet and TCP/IP, there are alternative network configurations you can use. DCOM provides you with the option of using any protocol Microsoft's RPC will allow. DCOM uses the network protocol to wrap its own protocol.

Although much of the DCOM protocol revolves around implementing COM via network packets (packet data layout, and so forth), DCOM must also be concerned with the remote object's lifetime. For example, the remote computer might crash, severing the connection between the COM object and client. Conversely, the client computer might crash, or the client might forget to release the COM object, in which case the server computer must identify the problem and take action. Let's first look at some protocol issues, and then examine the object lifetime situation.

Protocols

The term *protocol* has several meanings when you're talking about network-related issues. In one sense, you're talking about the underlying network language. Two or more computers can agree to speak the same language. TCP/IP (*Transport Control Protocol/ Internet Protocol*), for example, is the language of the Internet and is probably the most widely used network protocol in use today. NetBEUI, or the *NetBIOS Extended User Interface* protocol, is another protocol Windows uses from time to time.

In these cases, the computers agree on how the bytes are arranged in a network packet, which is no more than a data buffer. For Ethernet, the packet size can range from 64 to about 1500 bytes, although newer Ethernet cards allow for smaller packets. The protocols also decide what to do in the case the originating data buffer is larger than a single network packet, and what to do when multiple packets arrive out of order (which happens a lot over the Internet).

DCOM lets the network operating system deal with these issues, instead implementing its own protocol given the network packet. DCOM also specifies how to arrange bytes in the packet to most efficiently transmit COM information from one computer to another. Most of the data is marshaled interface method parameter data, although some space is assigned to identify the packet as a DCOM packet and to provide for other overhead (such as security and thread identification).

The term *protocol* also indicates a formal means of conversation, however. Network protocols, and DCOM for that matter, not only specify how to arrange bytes in a network packet, but they also specify the handshaking required to both send and receive data. For example, the TCP/IP UDP (*Universal Datagram Packet*) packet implements a connectionless protocol. The sender completes the packet and fires it to the receiver with no regard to the eventual outcome. The packet might get lost on the way, and the sender would never know (except in the specific case of RPC, which does provide a mechanism for making sure a datagram reached its destination).

The TCP/IP TCP packet, on the other hand, implements a connection-based protocol. Both sender and receiver acknowledge the transmission and receipt of the packet. Therefore, if a given packet is lost for some reason, the sender will retransmit the data so that the receiver can faithfully reconstruct it. The cost for this is greatly increased network traffic, but given your application it may be worth the cost, such as when copying a file over a network.

DCOM also implements its own handshaking protocol, mostly related to COM details. For example, DCOM sends the remote computer its authentication information, which the remote computer can refute. Assuming the security checks pass, the object must be located on the remote computer and its security details established. Eventually, the two computers agree that you can instantiate the remote object and begin that process. Of course, you have to terminate the connection and shut the remote COM server down. All this involves a fairly intricate handshaking protocol that, luckily, DCOM implements for you.

If the details of this interest you, definitely read *Professional DCOM Programming*. Dr. Grimes examines the DCOM protocol in some detail, as well as other interesting DCOM issues in more depth than I can visit in this lesson. Happily for the general DCOM-consuming public, the details are hidden in the bowels of DCOM. You don't need to know the details just to *use* DCOM, only to better optimize your use *of* DCOM.

Networks are notoriously unreliable, believe it or not. That is one of the major reasons such intricate protocols are invented—to overcome the unreliable transmission medium, the network. What happens if your officemate yanks your network cable from the wall just as you're using a remote object on their computer? That sort of issue comes up next.

Object Lifetime

If your officemate performs such a dastardly deed, I'd remind him that he might have used DCOMCnfg.exe to block DCOM traffic instead of resorting to such an offensive act. Then I'd have him fix the cable.

Joking aside, networks *do* break. It happens all the time, in fact. Sometimes it severely affects you, whereas at other times you might never know there was a problem (thanks to Cisco and the Internet router). Although I hope office workers aren't ripping cords from walls, DCOM still has to be concerned with the details when a network breaks and connections are lost.

You can look at this problem from two perspectives. On the one hand, you might be the client using the remote object. If your network connection is lost, so is your COM object. Your application should be robust enough to handle this situation. On the other hand, you might be the COM object that loses its client. In this case, you run forever because your reference count was never decremented via IUnknown::Release(). Note a lost connection in this case is no different from the case where a client misaligns AddRef() and Release() calls. In both cases, the COM object gains immortality.

The client application knows immediately if DCOM has determined that the network died. You'll get an error HRESULT back from COM (actually the object's proxy DLL), usually RPC_E_UNKNOWN_IF (0x800706b5, the interface is unknown).

The second situation is a bit more complex. After all, unless connection points are involved (yes, you can DCOM connection points), the server won't know the client is unavailable. It just sits in memory waiting for another client method invocation. If the client never calls back, it waits forever, as I mentioned.

The only real solution to this lies with the DCOM protocol itself, which provides for a *ping*. The word *ping* comes from *Packet Internet Groper*, which is an application that network administrators often use to see if a remote computer is responding. If the ping returns successfully, you know the remote computer is up and running. If not, the remote computer is inaccessible for some reason. Whatever the reason, you won't be getting anything from the remote computer, including DCOM information.

DCOM implements a form of ping that is more efficient. After all, there might be many objects active, resulting in a lot of overhead network traffic just to see if two computers are still connected. Anyway, DCOM pings the client computer from time to time. It's a bit more complicated than this, but essentially if DCOM gets no response from the client computer after a given number of pings, DCOM takes action and ferociously terminates the COM object (no immortal COM objects in this case).

That's enough light theory. Let's write some DCOM code!

Coding for DCOM

Well actually, writing DCOM code is the same as writing traditional COM code. That's actually good news. For one thing, all that you've learned so far still applies. For another, it means a COM object's location can still be relatively transparent, which was an original COM goal.

A Sample DCOM Server

I'll start with the COM object itself. If you open this day's example, *Day19Server*, you'll find it is an EXE-based COM server with a single COM object that exposes the IPropAppDemo interface. Rather than continue writing COM objects that perform trivial mathematical calculations, I wanted to write an object that proved it was running on another machine. I can ask for the time, or for unused disk space (both excellent examples), but instead I thought of something a bit more challenging. I decided to write a COM object that would enumerate both the active applications and processes on the target computer. This should prove, unquestionably, that the object is running on a remote system if the application and process lists are different from those running locally. This also gives me a chance to show you how to pass an array of data between COM objects and servers.

IPropAddDemo exposes two methods: GetProcessInfo() and GetApplicationInfo(). Because I used the evil word *enumerate* in the same breath as *remote object*, and I did that on purpose, I knew I had to design the methods to be efficient. Here are their IDL definitions (see Listing 19.3).

LISTING **19.3** IProcAppDemo IDL Interface Definition

```
 1: [
 2:     object,
 3:     uuid(6C6E5087-8555-11D3-B286-0000E8409B63),
 4:
 5:     helpstring("IProcAppDemo Interface"),
 6:     pointer_default(unique)
 7: ]
 8: interface IProcAppDemo : IUnknown
 9: {
10:     [helpstring("method GetProcessInfo")]
        ➥HRESULT GetProcessInfo([out] long * piNumElements,
        ➥[out, size_is(1,*piNumElements)] PROCAPPDATA ** ppwArray);
11:     [helpstring("method GetApplicationInfo")]
        ➥HRESULT GetApplicationInfo([out] long * piNumElements,
        ➥[out, size_is(1,*piNumElements)] PROCAPPDATA ** ppwArray);
12: };
```

ANALYSIS You may recognize the parameter list for each method, lines 10 and 11, as using implementations of the *conformant array* I discussed briefly in Day 8, "ATL Object Methods and Properties: Adding Functionality to Your Interface." The methods here will enumerate the data and stuff the results into an array composed of PROCAPPDATA elements, which is also defined in the IDL file:

```
typedef struct tagPROCAPPDATA
{
    long iData;
    BSTR bstrData;
} PROCAPPDATA;
```

Of course, GetProcessInfo() will return the process information for the given system, whereas GetApplicationInfo() will return active application task information. If you've seen the Windows NT *Task Manager*, this COM object provides the data for the first two tabs, *Applications* and *Processes*, although I don't go to the extent Windows NT does for process information.

19

Enumerating Active Applications

Enumerating the current applications involves a combination of EnumWindows() and
SendMessageTimeout(). GetApplicationInfo() executes EnumWindows(), and for each
window handle the system returns, it checks to see if the window has a caption and is
visible (user-level applications usually have captions and are visible windows, even if
minimized). After all the active, visible windows are known, GetApplicationInfo()
sends each of them a WM_NULL message with a timeout. If the application doesn't respond
in time, it is assumed hung and reported to be so.

Listing 19.4 shows you the EnumWindows() callback function, whereas Listing 19.5
shows you the GetApplicationInfo() method itself.

LISTING 19.4   CMyThirteenthATLObj's EnumWnd32() Callback Function

```
1: BOOL WINAPI CMyThirteenthATLObj::EnumWnd32(HWND hwnd, LPARAM lParam)
2: {
3:     // Pull out the map
4:     std::map<long,char*>* pMap =
5:                 reinterpret_cast<std::map<long,char*>*>(lParam);
6:
7:     // Pull the caption
8:     TCHAR strCaption[_MAX_PATH+1] = {0};
9:     ::GetWindowText(hwnd,strCaption,_MAX_PATH);
10:
11:    // Check for a caption
12:    if ( lstrlen(strCaption) ) {
13:        // Check for visibility
14:        if ( ::IsWindowVisible(hwnd) ) {
15:            // Insert into map. Note the map will handle the
16:            // destruction of the string.
17:            TCHAR* szText = new TCHAR[(lstrlen(strCaption+1))];
18:            lstrcpy(szText,strCaption);
19:            pMap->insert(std::pair<long,char*>((long)hwnd,szText));
20:        } // if
21:    } // if
22:
23:    return TRUE;
24: }
```

LISTING 19.5   CMyThirteenthATLObj's GetApplicationInfo() Method

```
1: STDMETHODIMP CMyThirteenthATLObj::GetApplicationInfo
   ➥(long *piNumElements, PROCAPPDATA **ppwArray)
2: {
3:     HRESULT hr = S_OK;
```

```
 4:    try {
 5:        // Check their pointers
 6:        CHECKPTR(piNumElements)
 7:        CHECKPTR(ppwArray)
 8:
 9:        // Clear the map and iterator
10:        m_map.clear();
11:
12:        // Enumerate the windows
13:        if ( !EnumWnds(EnumWnd32,(LPARAM)&m_map) ) {
14:            // Error enumerating
15:            throw E_UNEXPECTED;
16:        } // if
17:
18:        // The map now contains all of the windows,
19:        // so allocate the return array based upon the
20:        // number of windows. Note the use of
21:        // CoTaskMemAlloc(), as the data will be deleted
22:        // by the client.
23:        int iNumWnds = m_map.size();
24:        PROCAPPDATA* ppwd =
➡(PROCAPPDATA*)CoTaskMemAlloc(sizeof(PROCAPPDATA)*iNumWnds);
25:
26:        // Assign the data
27:        std::map<long,char*>::iterator itr = m_map.begin();
28:        int iCount = 0;
29:        while ( itr != m_map.end() ) {
30:            // Assign the status. If the window times out,
31:            // the application is considered hung.
32:            DWORD dwResult = 0;
33:            BOOL bResponding = ::SendMessageTimeout((HWND)itr->first,
34:                                 WM_NULL,
35:                                 0, 0,
36:                                 SMTO_BLOCK | SMTO_ABORTIFHUNG,
37:                                 5000, // 5 seconds
38:                                 &dwResult);
39:            ppwd[iCount].iData = (long)bResponding;
40:
41:            // Assign the filename
42:            CComBSTR bstrData(itr->second);
43:            ppwd[iCount++].bstrData = bstrData.Copy();
44:
45:            // Get the next mapping
46:            itr++;
47:        } // while
48:
49:        // Return the data
50:        *piNumElements = iNumWnds;
```

19

continues

LISTING **19.5** continued

```
51:          *ppwArray = ppwd;
52:     } // try
53:     catch(HRESULT hrErr) {
54:          // Pointer error
55:          hr = hrErr;
56:     } // catch
57:     catch(...) {
58:          // Some other error
59:          hr = E_UNEXPECTED;
60:     } // catch
61:
62:     return hr;
63: }
```

The other interesting thing about EnumWnd32() is that I use the Standard Template Library's map class to store the window handles and their associated captions. Because I don't know beforehand how many active windows exist on the given system, I need a flexible container that can grow dynamically as I find them. I also have to associate a window handle with its caption. I'll need the window handle for the SendMessageTimeout() call you see in GetApplicationInfo(). The STL map class is a perfect solution in this case. I use the HWND value as the map's key, which references the caption string. Later, I can iterate the map and extract all the HWNDs and associated captions.

If the window doesn't respond to the SendMessageTimeout() call, I presume it's hung. Otherwise, it's running. I create a new PROCAPPDATA item and stuff the window caption and the result of SendMessageTimeout() inside it. It's important to note the following detail, however. I didn't use the C++ new operator to allocate the memory for the structure. Instead, I used CoTaskMemAlloc(). The responsibility for the memory will transfer from server to client when GetApplicationInfo() finishes processing. The memory might be in the same address space, at least in the case of an in-process COM server. In this case it can't be. (This is, at the very least, a local server; and my intent is to have it be remotable, too). CoTaskMemAlloc() takes this into account, and when combined with CoTaskMemFree() on the other end, COM will correctly manage the memory allocation and deallocation for me. I should also point out the STL map class manages the destruction of the window's caption string for you, so you needn't do that yourself, either.

GetApplicationInfo() loops through all the items in the map, and for each item places the data in a new PROCAPPDATA structure. The entire array of PROCAPPDATA structures is then returned to the client, along with the number of applications found.

I'm also again using the simple CHECKPTR() macro I introduced in Day 7, "The ATL Object Wizard: Customizing the Basic ATL Framework." CHECKPTR(), as you may remember, checks the COM pointer for NULL, and if it's NULL, throws an exception. If the pointer is nonNULL, it sets the return value to NULL. If the client fails to check the HRESULT, the pointer value he'll try to use is NULL versus a random value if for some reason a given method should fail.

Enumerating Active Processes

Writing EnumWindows() code is easy. Writing code to enumerate the active process list isn't so easy. For that, I turned to the Microsoft Knowledge Base article Q175030. The reason it's so difficult is that Windows NT and Windows 95 and 98 are very different under the desktop shell. I'll leave a detailed description of the enumeration code to the article. I literally cut and pasted its code into two source files, changed a few things to satisfy the C++ compiler, and tried it.

The KB article's code provides for an enumeration callback function much like EnumWindows() does. I wrapped my object's functionality in the EnumProc32() callback function you see in Listing 19.6.

LISTING 19.6 CMyThirteenthATLObj's EnumProc32() Callback Function

```
 1: BOOL WINAPI CMyThirteenthATLObj::EnumProc32( DWORD dwProcessID,
    ➥WORD w16, LPTSTR pszFilename, LPARAM lParam )
 2: {
 3:     // Pull out the map
 4:     std::map<long,char*>* pMap =
 5:                 reinterpret_cast<std::map<long,char*>*>(lParam);
 6:
 7:     // Allocate the filename. Note the map will
 8:     // handle destruction of the string.
 9:     if ( _tcslen(pszFilename) ) {
10:         TCHAR* szFile = new char[_tcslen(pszFilename)];
11:         ATLASSERT(szFile != NULL);
12:
13:         // Copy it
14:         _tcscpy(szFile,pszFilename);
15:
16:         // Assign the PID
17:         long iPID = (long)dwProcessID;
19:         if ( w16 ) {
18:             // 16-bit process under WinNT...
19:             iPID = (long)w16;
20:         } // if
21:
22:         // Insert into map
```

continues

19

LISTING 19.6   continued

```
23:            pMap->insert(std::pair<long,char*>(iPID,szFile));
24:      } // if
25:
26:      return TRUE;
27: }
```

I can show the code for GetProcessInfo(), but it's very similar to GetApplicationInfo() and probably not worth repeating here. You'll find the enumeration code in Listings 19.1 and 19.3 in EnumProc.cpp and the GetApplicationInfo() and GetProcessInfo() code in MyThirteenthATLObj.cpp.

After I inserted all the COM server code, debugged it, and tested it, it was time to turn to the client side of the coin.

An Example DCOM Client

You might be surprised to find more changes are required to COM clients than to COM servers when DCOM is involved. The client will usually specify the server information, unless it is embedded in the remote object's locally-held AppID value. Even so, the client can play dumb and invoke the object as usual. You can configure the remote object's AppID key information using DCOMCnfg.exe. If you do this, there are also no client application code changes.

That won't do for this example, however. In this case, I want an application that prompts for a server; and if the user provides one, it accesses the object on that computer and pulls the active application and process lists when called upon.

I settled on the user interface you see in Figures 19.4 and 19.5, which is much like Windows NT's Task Manager application. Figure 19.4 shows a local invocation, whereas 19.5 shows a remote location (to the computer named Snoopy).

FIGURE 19.4

Day19Client's user interface, local invocation.

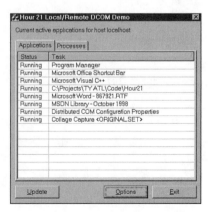

FIGURE 19.5

Day19Client's user interface, remote invocation.

I returned to MFC, versus ATL, for the client implementation. In this case, the dialog-based application uses the tab control with two tabs, one for the application list and one for the process list. I also added an Update button, to manually tickle the COM object for updated information, and an Options button to enable you to set the timer to automatically update the displayed list.

The Tab Control

Because this isn't a book on MFC control customization, I'll only briefly describe the user interface code. The tab control implements tabs that notify you when the tab selection changes. After you receive that notification, you can elect to display different visual information in the tab control's client area.

In this case, I created two dialog boxes to which I assigned MFC property page C++ classes. There is one for the Applications tab and one for the Processes tab. When the dialogs are added to the tab control, which I customized using MFC to allow for this behavior, they size themselves to snuggle into the tab control's entire client area. After a given tab is clicked, I determine which tab is the active tab and make that dialog box (faking it as a property sheet) visible. The other, I make invisible.

The Property Pages and List Controls

The property pages themselves are fairly simple. They contain a single control, a Common Controls list control. I chose this control because it's what Windows NT uses, and I like the associated header controls. The property pages derive from a custom property page class (which I wrote) that does little more than store the pointer to the COM object that will provide the data for the list control.

What I don't like about the list control is that the report view is a little sparse. Although the online documentation tells me I can activate gridlines and full row selection, I've never been able to actually make that happen. (They're extended window styles that the control accepts but does not act upon.) So, I implemented this behavior myself in ListCtrlEx.cpp. Yes, I subclassed it! As with any control, if you don't like it, change it.

19

The normal control behavior is to only allow item (row) selection from the first (left-most) column. Because this looks odd for this application, I decided to allow full row item selection even though, for this example, I don't do anything with the selected row. Because I also wanted gridlines, while I was at it I added some custom painting logic to manage painting gridlines as I painted the highlighted row. It turned out so well, I'm sure I'll reuse this subclassed control tomorrow, "ATL and OLE DB: Storing More," when I access database information.

How the columns are actually filled is specified by the list control itself, not by my custom code. Many developers feel the control is difficult to work with. It really isn't, and I'd recommend you review the online documentation regarding the list control from the common controls library if the code is unclear to you. (Be sure to look up the list control, not the listbox control, which is the simple, intrinsic Windows control). In any case, the Application tab's list is filled by the code you see in Listing 19.7.

LISTING 19.7 CApplicationPPage's FillListControl() Method

```
 1: void CApplicationPPage::FillListControl()
 2:     (Edited for brevity)
 3:     ....
 4:     // Request enumeration
 5:     long iNumElements = 0;
 6:     PROCAPPDATA* ppad = NULL;
 7:     HRESULT hr = m_pIProcAppDemo->
           ➥GetApplicationInfo(&iNumElements,&ppad);
 8:     if ( FAILED(hr) ) {
 9:         // Some error...
10:         (Edited for brevity)
11:         ....
12:     } // if
13:     ....
14:     // Insert list data
15:     LVITEM lvItem;
16:     int iItem = 0;
17:     BOOL bAppHung = FALSE;
18:     while ( iItem < iNumElements ) {
19:         // I'm not using a (auto) sorted list, so the item
20:         // number we hand the control should not change.  However...
21:         int iActualItem = 0;
22:         for ( int iSubItem = 0;
23:               iSubItem < APPCOLUMNCOUNT;
24:               iSubItem++) {
25:             // Complete basic item information
26:             lvItem.mask = LVIF_TEXT;
27:             lvItem.iItem = iActualItem; // bogus for first column...
28:             lvItem.iSubItem = iSubItem;
```

```
29:
30:                    // Testing only...
31:                    switch ( iSubItem ) {
32:                        case 0: // record number
33:                            { // scope
34:                                CString strStatus;
35:                                if ( !ppad[iItem].iData ) {
36:                                    // App is hung
37:                                    strStatus.LoadString(IDS_APPHUNG);
38:                                    bAppHung = TRUE;
39:                                } // if
40:                                else {
41:                                    // App is running
42:                                    strStatus.LoadString(IDS_APPOK);
43:                                } // else
44:                                lvItem.pszText = strStatus.GetBuffer(0);
45:
46:                                // Insert at desired location
47:                                lvItem.iItem = iItem;
48:                                iActualItem = m_CAppList.InsertItem(&lvItem);
49:                            } // scope
50:                        break;
51:
52:                        case 1:
53:                            { // scope
54:                                CString strItem;
55:                                CComBSTR bstrData; // will SysFreeString...
56:                                bstrData.Attach(ppad[iItem].bstrData);
57:                                strItem = bstrData.m_str;
58:                                lvItem.pszText = strItem.GetBuffer(0);
59:
60:                                // Determine text width
61:                                pDC->DrawText(strItem,rcText,DT_CALCRECT);
62:                                if ( rcText.Size().cx > sWidest.cx ) {
63:                                    sWidest.cx = rcText.Size().cx;
64:                                } // if
65:
66:                                // Update this column
67:                                m_CAppList.SetItem(&lvItem);
68:                            } // scope
69:                    } // switch
70:                } // for
71:
72:            // Next item
73:            ++iItem;
74:        } // while
75:
76:        // Release the array memory
```

continues

LISTING **19.7**   continued

```
77:     CoTaskMemFree(ppad);
78:
79:     (Edited for brevity)
80:     ....
81: }
```

ANALYSIS   The important logic in FillListControl(), in pseudocode, goes like this:

```
array = GetApplicationInfo()
while (array items to process)
    for ( column 0 to column 1 )
        switch (column)
            case column 0:
                fill column 0 from array item
            case column 1:
                fill column 1 from array item
        end switch
    end for
    get next array item
end while
```

The remaining code is there to make things look nice on the screen, and it is of lessor importance.

The Client DCOM Code

After all the underlying user interface code is complete, I turn to adding the network-specific code. For this, I have to add some mechanism to request the server from the user, and I use that information when invoking the COM object that ultimately fills the list controls. I decide to request the remote computer's name as the application initializes.

The server request dialog is relatively simple, as you see from Figure 19.6.

FIGURE **19.6**

Day19Client's Host Connection dialog.

If you type in "localhost" (or leave it blank), or if you use the special IP address 127.0.0.1, I execute the COM object on the local machine. Any other value, I'll assume, represents a remote computer's name or server IP address. The server name can be UNC

(//MYCOMPUTER), IP domain name (MYCOMPUTER.MYNET.COM), or a DNS-resolvable name (MYCOMPUTER). The IP address is in the standard dotted notation (111.222.333.444). This flexibility should make my application's users happy, but in reality the host name interpretation functionality is actually provided by DCOM rather than by my own code.

After I have the computer's name (or address), whether remote or local, I invoke the main application dialog. The DCOM-specific code is shown in Listing 19.8, which comes from the dialog's OnInitDialog() handler.

LISTING 19.8   CDay19ClientDlg's OnInitDialog() handler

```
 1: BOOL CDay19ClientDlg::OnInitDialog()
 2: {
 3:     CDialog::OnInitDialog();
 4:
 5:     (Edited for brevity)
 6:     ....
 7:
 8:     // Massage the server name
 9:     if ( m_strHost.IsEmpty() ) {
10:         // No server name given, so assume "localhost"
11:         m_strHost = _T("localhost");
12:     } // if
13:
14:     // Create the COSERVERINFO structure
15:     COSERVERINFO csi = {0};
16:     COSERVERINFO* pcsi = &csi; // assume a remote host
17:     if ( _tcsicmp(m_strHost,_T("localhost")) &&
18:          _tcscmp(m_strHost,_T("127.0.0.1"))) {
19:         // Remote host
20:         csi.dwReserved1 = 0;
21:         csi.dwReserved2 = 0;
22:         csi.pwszName = m_strHost.AllocSysString();
23:         csi.pAuthInfo = NULL;
24:     } // if
25:     else {
26:         // localhost
27:         pcsi = NULL;
28:     } // else
29:
30:     // Create the MULTI_QI structure
31:     MULTI_QI mqi = {&IID_IProcAppDemo, NULL, 0};
32:
33:     // Open the process query object
34:     HRESULT hr = CoCreateInstanceEx(CLSID_TYATLObj13,
35:                                     NULL,
36:                                     CLSCTX_LOCAL_SERVER,
```

19

continues

LISTING 19.8 continued

```
37:                                          pcsi,
38:                                          1,
39:                                          &mqi);
40:     ::SysFreeString(csi.pwszName); // no longer required
41:     if ((FAILED(hr)) || (FAILED(mqi.hr))) {
42:         // Couldn't create the object...
43:         AfxMessageBox(IDS_E_NOCREATE,MB_OK | MB_ICONERROR);
44:         EndDialog(IDCANCEL);
45:         return TRUE;
46:     } // if
47:
48:     // Pull the interface pointer
49:     m_pIProcAppDemo = (IProcAppDemo*)mqi.pItf;
50:
51:     // Add the property sheets to the tab control
52:     m_CTabSheet.AddTab(&m_dlgApplications,_T("Applications"),
53:                         m_pIProcAppDemo.p);
54:     m_CTabSheet.AddTab(&m_dlgProcesses,_T("Processes"),
55:                         m_pIProcAppDemo.p);
56:
57:     // Set the infobar text
58:     CString strFormat;
59:     strFormat.LoadString(IDS_APPTAB);
60:     m_strInfoBar.Format(strFormat,m_strHost);
61:     UpdateData(FALSE);
62:
63:     (Edited for brevity)
64:     ....
65: }
```

ANALYSIS   If the host name string is empty, I set it to "localhost" in lines 9–12. Later, I check for this value (and 127.0.0.1). If the value isn't the local computer, I complete the COSERVERINFO structure (lines 15 and 16, and lines 20–24):

```
COSERVERINFO csi = {0};
COSERVERINFO* pcsi = &csi; // assume a remote host
....
csi.dwReserved1 = 0;
csi.dwReserved2 = 0;
csi.pwszName = m_strHost.AllocSysString();
csi.pAuthInfo = NULL;
```

I can provide additional security information through csi.pAuthInfo, but I'll rely upon DCOMCnfg.exe to manage that for me on the remote computer.

If the local computer is to be used, I use NULL for the COSERVERINFO field in
CoCreateInstanceEx() (line 27):

```
pcsi = NULL;
```

With the COSERVERINFO structure complete, I next turn to the MULTI_QI structure.
MULTI_QI is used to specify multiple interfaces to create. This is more efficient than creating them one at a time remotely. In my case, I'm only going to create a single object
exposing a single interface, IProcAppDemo, as you can see from lines 30 and 31:

```
// Create the MULTI_QI structure
MULTI_QI mqi = {&IID_IProcAppDemo, NULL, 0};
```

At this time, the remote computer is specified in COSERVERINFO, and the particular interface to which I want a reference is identified in MULTI_QI. I now have enough information to call CoCreateInstanceEx() (lines 34–49)

```
HRESULT hr = CoCreateInstanceEx(CLSID_TYATLObj13,
                                NULL,
                                CLSCTX_LOCAL_SERVER,
                                pcsi,
                                1,
                                &mqi);
::SysFreeString(csi.pwszName); // no longer required
if ((FAILED(hr)) || (FAILED(mqi.hr))) {
    // Couldn't create the object...
    AfxMessageBox(IDS_E_NOCREATE,MB_OK | MB_ICONERROR);
    EndDialog(IDCANCEL);
    return TRUE;
} // if

// Pull the interface pointer
m_pIProcAppDemo = (IProcAppDemo*)mqi.pItf;
```

I pass several things into CoCreateInstanceEx():

- The CLSID of the object I'm interested in.

- The context (CLSCTX_LOCAL_SERVER).

- A pointer to the COSERVERINFO structure (which is NULL if I'm referencing the local
  computer).

- The number of interfaces contained in the MULTI_QI structure (one).

- A pointer to the MULTI_QI structure itself.

- If I want more than one interface, I pass in an array of MULTI_QI structures and
  adjust the number of MULTI_QI elements I sent to CoCreateInstanceEx(),
  accordingly.

19

You might find it odd I use a creation context of CLSCTX_LOCAL_SERVER. However, COM knows I'm trying to access a remote system by the information I supplied in the COSERVERINFO structure. In this case, the context indicates the type of COM server I want instantiated on the remote end (EXE). This also works when I'm dealing with the local system.

If CoCreateInstanceEx() itself is successful, I check the returned HRESULT field in the MULTI_QI structure for each interface I requested (in this case one). If all those MULTI_QI structures indicate the interface creation was also successful, I extract each interface from the MULTI_QI structure (lines 48 and 49 of Listing 19.8):

```
// Pull the interface pointer
m_pIProcAppDemo = (IProcAppDemo*)mqi.pItf;
```

After I have my remote interface, I have what I need to fill the application and process lists. To start the list processing, I first add each property sheet to the tab control, and then I adjust the information text message to tell the user he is looking at the active applications on the particular computer he selected earlier (lines 51–61 from Listing 19.8):

```
// Add the property sheets to the tab control
m_CTabSheet.AddTab(&m_dlgApplications,_T("Applications"),
                   m_pIProcAppDemo.p);
m_CTabSheet.AddTab(&m_dlgProcesses,_T("Processes"),
                   m_pIProcAppDemo.p);

// Set the infobar text
CString strFormat;
strFormat.LoadString(IDS_APPTAB);
m_strInfoBar.Format(strFormat,m_strHost);
UpdateData(FALSE);
```

The last thing to do—and this is important—is to define the preprocessor value _WIN32_DCOM. This value tells the compiler to pick up the DCOM-specific information in the system header files. Without it, your application won't compile because it won't find the DCOM-related structures and the new CoCreateInstanceEx() COM API call.

Running the Application Remotely

After you compile the COM server and the client application, you're ready to run the server remotely. Before you do, though, you'll need to do a couple of things.

First, change the COM object's project to have it compile its proxy/stub DLL (as I show you in Appendix B, "Proxies, Stubs, and Their Compilation and Maintenance"). You must also ship the proxy/stub DLL with the COM server and register both on the remote computer. This goes for *both* DLL-based and EXE-based COM servers. If you forget the proxy/stub DLL, `CoCreateInstanceEx()` will fail with the `HRESULT E_NOINTERFACE` (0x80004002).

The second action you must take is to enable DCOM on the remote system and set the security permissions so that you can access the object remotely. Use DCOMCnfg.exe for this. The settings you use are dictated by your particular needs, but if you have no preference, I'd recommend these settings you see in Table 19.2. Don't forget to reset the security settings when you're through with the example to close the security hole these settings open.

TABLE **19.2** DCOMCnfg.exe Settings

Tab	Setting
Default Properties	Check the Enable Distributed COM on this computer check box
Default Properties	Set the Default Authentication Level to None
Default Properties	Set the Default Impersonation Level to Anonymous (NT) or Identify (95/98)
Default Security	Add Everyone with Full Access to Default Access Permissions(NT), or simply add World (95/98)
Default Security	Check the Enable Remote Connection check box (95/98 only)
Default Security	Add *Everyone* with Allow Launch to Default Launch Permissions (NT only)

You can alternatively establish the settings for the sample application itself using DCOMCnfg's Applications tab. This reduces the security risk if that is of concern.

Security Issues

Clearly, you must protect your data in today's interconnected world. Viruses are bad enough, but there are individuals out there who take great pleasure in destroying your data remotely. DCOM, although a wonderful addition to COM for entrusted users, can be used as a weapon against you. Here are some things to consider.

First, many network administrators lock the enterprise firewall to DCOM access. If they're Microsoft certified, they'll know how this is done, so I won't list the details here. This is already common practice for ftp enterprise access.

Second, security is generally considered to consist of authorization and authentication. *Authorization* refers to selecting *who* can perform certain actions, whereas *authentication* provides the *how* and *when* the authorized users are validated. If there is no enterprise

19

guideline for establishing authorization and authentication, one should be considered. Also, you generally won't allow the permissions I recommended previously when executing DCOM applications. I recommended these settings merely to allow you to easily configure DCOM for testing and experimentation. Real-world DCOM use should be much more restrictive.

Third, use Windows NT or Windows 2000 as your enterprise computing standard (no, Microsoft didn't pay me to plug their products). Windows NT was designed to meet the United States Government's C2 security model, which although not as secure as technically possible, is as about as secure as a public operating system can be. Windows NT has security built into its very core, and Windows 2000 strengthens the model by adding Kerberos. Windows 95 and 98 have no such protection and are relatively simple to hack.

Finally, if you are running Windows NT or 2000, you might consider writing your own surrogate process. Your surrogate can monitor sensitive data and flag (or log) access to that data by DLLs under remote control. You can also implement special interfaces to access sensitive data, and if the client does not use those interfaces, deny access—even if the user passes authentication. I'm sure there are many more ideas than these few, but these are presented to let you see there are things you can do to allow DCOM access, yet make it more secure.

The bottom line is that enterprises are becoming increasingly interconnected, which opens new worlds to hackers. If you connect your computer to a network, someone, somewhere, can gain access and cause damage. To minimize the potential damage, consider security issues when you're designing your systems.

Beyond DCOM

As wonderful as DCOM is, it has inherent scalability limitations. Why? They result from the pinging that takes place between the client and server. If you have a server farm consisting of a handful of computers, or even dozens of computers, the ping traffic is negligible. However, imagine trying to establish a DCOM session with remote users over the Internet. If that thought made you laugh, perhaps you see my point. DCOM cannot scale well.

So, perhaps you research this and find you can deactivate the pinging. That's good thinking, but what have you really done? You've deactivated DCOM's capability to find orphan objects and their clients, so you'll leak objects. As with any system that implicitly supports memory leaks, the system won't scale at all—because sooner or later you'll run out of memory.

There is also the additional concern of firewall limitations. A network system administrator will rarely open the enterprise firewall to external DCOM access. That invites intruders into the trusted enterprise network. So what do you do if you want to access remote objects, but you now see why you can't use DCOM for Internet-level object distribution?

The answer is SOAP, or the Standard Object Activation Protocol now being developed cooperatively by Microsoft and DevelopMentor. This fascinating technology is beyond the scope of this day, but you can read more about it at `http://www.develop.com/soap/`.

In a nutshell, however, SOAP specifies an XML-formatted document that implements specific tags that represent information required to access remote objects. The XML information is then transported over the Internet using the standard HTTP protocol.

To use SOAP, for example, you include the object's CLSID and interface's IID in specific XML tags when instantiating the object remotely. Then when you execute a remote method, you pass in formatted representations of the parameters that the remote host will format, on your behalf, into a standard COM object method invocation. The remote SOAP server then formats any returned information into another XML document and ships it back to you, again using the HTTP protocol. Several SOAP server implementations are currently in development and should be available by the time you read this.

Because SOAP is based upon XML, it's quite flexible. Because SOAP rides atop HTTP, it tunnels through firewalls in the same manner Web page information does. If you're very much interested in remote object activation and use, you'll be hearing a lot more about this exciting new technology in the near future.

19

Summary

This day gave a brief introduction to Distributed COM. Because DCOM is truly COM, very few changes are required to your code to use the Distributed COM capabilities. In fact, you can configure the Registry so that no client application changes are required.

I began the day by discussing some of the basics of DCOM. I mentioned DCOM is based upon DCE RPC and can use any network protocol Microsoft's RPC implementation supports. I talked about some design issues you'll face when creating distributed objects versus objects you intend to use locally. For example, you'll want to examine how you pass data to and from the object. Also, you can't process graphical information given GDI handles remotely. I discussed latency and how it affects your overall processing timelines. I talked about process surrogates for Windows NT distributed objects.

Finally, I briefly addressed changes to the Registry to support DCOM. To help you with the Registry, I introduced DCOMCnfg.exe.

I went on to talk about how DCOM works. I discussed protocols in general and, specifically, the fact that DCOM implements its own protocol. I also mentioned DCOM must manage the remote object's lifetime, especially when the connection between client and server is severed.

The last part of the day was spent examining this day's sample application. Although it contained only a handful of code lines that dealt with DCOM-specific issues, I designed the COM object itself with distribution in mind. I passed data between the object and its client using a conformant array, which I allocated using `CoTaskMemAlloc()`, to be freed on the client side using `CoTaskMemFree()`. I also mentioned a new technology that replaces DCOM in the Internet world, SOAP.

Day 20 addresses another interesting Microsoft COM technology: OLE DB. If you are interested in accessing databases, the next day is for you.

Q&A

Q I'm interested in writing and shipping a shrink-wrapped application to end users that use DCOM. Can I install the DCOM upgrades you mentioned through an installation script or application?

A Yes, you can. Windows NT 4.0 came with DCOM, though Service Pack 2 did make some changes. You won't need to install DCOM from scratch there. Windows 98 also came with DCOM, although an upgrade is available. Unfortunately, the DCOM upgrade is not redistributable according to the legal verbiage included with the file (DCOM98.EXE). Windows 95 was originally shipped without DCOM support, although Service Release 2 did have the necessary files. You'll need to install DCOM95.EXE, which you can download from the Microsoft Internet site (see Table 19.1). DCOM for Windows 95 is redistributable, and the installation program can be executed in a silent mode. It will require an additional reboot, though, so take that into consideration.

Q I'm interested (or concerned, or worried) about the security issues you brought up. Is there some way to simplify my security configuration requirements, especially on a per-object basis?

A From a pure DCOM perspective, you're limited to using DCOMCnfg.exe or managing the Registry changes yourself. Worse, you'll probably have to deal with the raw Security API at some time. You do have the option of installing MTS on your enterprise server computers and using MTS to distribute your objects and adjust the security settings for you, however. I'll discuss this in more detail in the last two days when I address role-based security and MTS packages.

Workshop

The Workshop is designed to help you anticipate possible questions, review what you've learned, and get you thinking about how to put your knowledge into practice. The answers to the quiz are in Appendix A, "Answers."

Quiz

1. Do DCOM objects differ from traditional COM objects?
2. Can you launch a DCOM object remotely?
3. What are some issues to consider when designing distributed objects?
4. What is an AppID as related to DCOM?
5. What is DCOMCnfg.exe used for?
6. How does DCOM know the network connection between client and COM object has been broken?

Exercise

1. Devise an experiment that will show the latency associated with the network when using a remote COM object.

19

DAY 20

ATL and OLE DB: Storing More

If you're not performing computations, you're probably accessing data. These days, especially with IIS and Web components, you're most likely talking to a database to store intermediate results or look up tabular information. Managing data is something computers do very well, and accessing data stored in a database is something most developers have to do sometime during their careers.

In this case, I'm going to talk about how to access a database using COM, or to be more specific, using OLE DB, which is Microsoft's COM database access technology. As it happens, ATL has wonderful support for accessing databases using OLE DB. After you have the database designed, you simply use the wizard to create the code that you require to access the data it contains.

So let's take a look at this fascinating technology to see how it can be used from your ATL components. In this lesson, I'll discuss

- OLE DB as a technology
- OLE DB architecture and object model

- How ATL supports OLE DB
- How to write a basic OLE DB consumer
- An OLE DB sample application

An Overview of OLE DB

Computers are useful for many things, but certainly one area in which they excel is data storage and management. The database or, more correctly, the *DBMS* (*Database Management System*) is a collection of data, as well as a system that functions to manage the data.

As in many areas of computing, however, things didn't start so well. There was a definite early lack of standardization, so data stored in one vendor's DBMS was inaccessible to code written according to another vendor's specifications. Along the way, standards did evolve. The most notable improvement was *Open Database Connectivity (ODBC)*, which is a suite of API calls you can use to manage your DBMS programmatically. ODBC remains a standard today and is commonly used, although some vendor-specific DBMS access technologies are also in wide use for performance reasons.

ODBC is a monolithic set of API calls, however, and clearly there had to be a COM solution for DBMS access. Microsoft introduced OLE DB to fill this niche. You can elect to have OLE DB ride on top of ODBC, or you can use the Microsoft-specific Jet DBMS interface (good with Access and SQL Server).

Because OLE DB provides COM access to the DBMS, it makes sense ATL should support OLE DB (which comes with its own set of templates that both you and ATL will use). In this section, you'll read a little about OLE DB itself, and then you'll look at how ATL supports OLE DB. Later in the day, I'll give you a sample application that uses OLE DB as you work with a small parts database.

OLE DB

Figure 20.1 shows you how OLE DB fits into Microsoft's scheme of *Universal Data Access (UDA)*. As you can see, OLE DB accesses a data source through a *provider*, which can be ODBC or some DBMS-specific access technology. OLE DB grabs data from the provider and packages it for shipment to the *consumer* (the application). If the consumer is *script-based* (relies upon a dual interface), the consumer can use Active Data Objects (ADO) to interface to OLE DB, which is better suited to direct interface use.

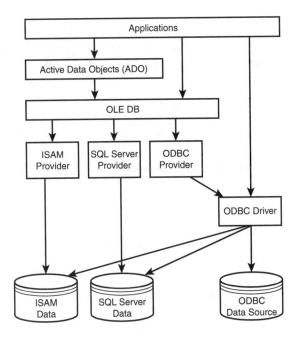

FIGURE 20.1

The Microsoft UDA model.

OLE DB clearly is at the heart of the UDA model.

Therefore, OLE DB was designed with several goals in mind: flexibility, performance, and reliability. For example, ODBC doesn't handle hierarchical data; but given the right provider, OLE DB can. OLE DB is flexible. OLE DB provides common services among providers, such as shared queries and cursors. OLE DB performs. OLE DB is highly integrated with the operating system, especially where networking is concerned, because OLE DB provides for remote DBMS access. Because OLE DB works so well with the operating system, OLE DB is reliable (or as reliable as the operating system!).

OLE DB Services

OLE DB itself connects consumers to providers through *services*. Some services include query processing, cursor processing, data synchronization, and hierarchical data management (through ADO and the SHAPE language) and others.

Each OLE DB service is actually a COM object, so the services can easily be shared between providers. If you're implementing a provider, therefore, you needn't implement the basic functionality OLE DB provides. This decreases your development workload and testing requirements.

20

OLE DB Objects

You can think of OLE DB in terms of services, but it also makes sense to think of OLE DB in terms of objects and the OLE DB Object Model. OLE DB provides four main objects in its object model:

- Data Source
- Sessions
- Commands
- Rowsets

The objects are hierarchically arranged, as I show in Figure 20.2.

FIGURE 20.2

The OLE DB object model.

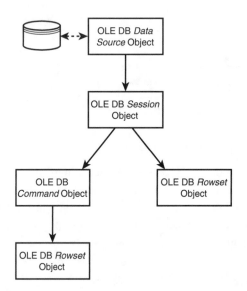

The *data source* object provides OLE DB with the capability to gain access to a DBMS and begin manipulating data. Through the data source object, you log into the DBMS (with the appropriate permissions) and create sessions. The *session* object provides for the data interaction with the DBMS. That is, the session object supplies a query and retrieves the data. When you execute a session query, either using the *command* object or directly from the session, the data is returned in a *rowset* object. Command objects support the language of the given DBMS, usually SQL (both the Data Manipulation Language and the Data Definition Language), although any other language can be supported. The rowset object allows you scroll through the data and perform a number of operations, the exact nature of which depend somewhat upon the capabilities of the DBMS itself.

There are other OLE DB objects, although they're not usually thought of in terms of the OLE DB object model. These objects include:

- Error
- Transaction
- Enumerator

The *error object* supports extended error information, such as for SQL errors. The *transaction object* provides transactional capabilities that are especially useful when you're dealing with nested transactions. Finally, the *enumerator object* helps you search for available data sources or for other enumerators.

That's OLE DB in a nutshell. It implements nearly 60 interfaces, and it is very much more complicated than I can fully describe in this lesson (or even this book). Because my goal is to show you how ATL manages OLE DB, I'll leave further OLE DB research to you. If you're interested in reading more about OLE DB and DBMS access in general, check out *Sams Teach Yourself Database Programming with Visual C++ 6 in 21 Days* (Sam's Net, ISBN 0-672-31350-2), or *Visual C++ 6 Database Programming Tutorial* (Wrox Press, ISBN 1-861002-41-6).

ATL and OLE DB

ATL supports OLE DB, both providers and consumers, through the ATL Object Wizard (see Figure 20.3). Unlike the other Object Wizard objects, the OLE DB code that the wizard inserts is not a self-supporting COM object. Instead, the wizard adds OLE DB classes you use to access your data source (which you also provide). I'll write more on this shortly.

FIGURE 20.3

The ATL Object Wizard.

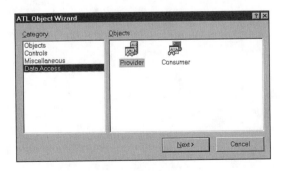

If you select the OLE DB provider object, the wizard will display the property page you see in Figure 20.4. This property page asks you for some basic COM information, such as CoClass and ProgID (similar to the Attributes property page you're familiar with), as well as names for the OLE DB provider COM objects.

FIGURE 20.4

The ATL Object Wizard's OLEDB Provider property page.

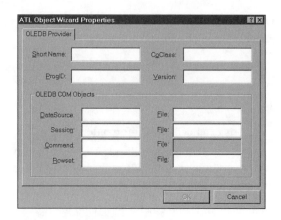

The code the wizard provides helps you implement the 16 basic provider interfaces, which I won't list here because of space limitations. The online documentation does a good job of listing these and describing their functionality (look in the online documentation under *Visual C++ Documentation, Reference, Microsoft Foundation Class Library and Templates, OLE DB Templates*). Clearly, implementing an OLE DB provider is nontrivial, even though the task is simplified because of the OLE DB intrinsic services. Therefore, I'll not address the provider further in this lesson. Besides, far more people use databases than implement access to databases, so it makes sense to concentrate on the consumer anyway.

If you select the consumer object from the Object Wizard's object list, Visual Studio will display the property page you see in Figure 20.5.

FIGURE 20.5

The ATL Object Wizard's OLE DB Name property page.

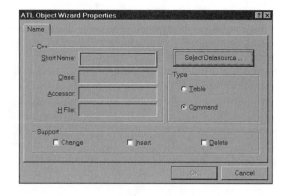

Here you connect to your database by clicking the Select Datasource button. Ultimately, Visual Studio will open your data source and extract information from that source which will be turned into ATL source code for you.

Tip

> Visual Studio provides you with a tremendous productivity gain here. Before you select your data source, try to design its table structure completely. If you later change the composition of the data source, you can re-insert the OLE DB consumer code, but you'll lose any source code you have inserted into the code that Visual Studio previously provided.

After you click the Select Datasource button, Visual Studio will present you with the Data Link Properties property sheet, which you'll use to specify your data source and connection information. You can see the first page in Figure 20.6.

FIGURE 20.6

The Data Link Properties Provider property page.

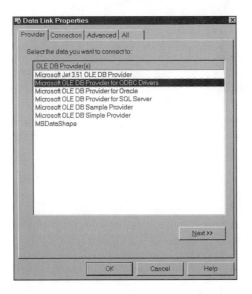

Here you see all the OLE DB providers currently registered on my computer, with the ODBC provider highlighted. After you select a provider and click the Next button, you'll move to the Connection property page (Figure 20.7).

You have the option of connecting to your data source by either using a data source name (DSN) or by building a connection string manually. (I'll show an example of using a DSN shortly.) If the data source is protected, you can enter the access information. You can also change the catalog (essentially, the directory where the database is located). After you've provided all the information, you can test your connection using the Test Connection button. If the connection is valid, Visual Studio will whir a moment, ask you for the table you want to access, and finally return you to the ATL Object Wizard's Name property page.

20

FIGURE 20.7

*The Data Link
Properties Connection
property page.*

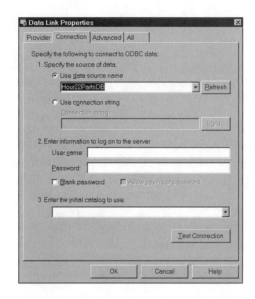

This time, however, the property page will have valid data source information. What is displayed will depend upon the data source and table you selected; but, in all cases, the information will be used to build implementations of the ATL consumer classes:

- CDataSource
- CSession
- CTable
- CCommand
- CAccessor
- CRowset

This is tremendously helpful because the wizard links ATL classes and members to the corresponding table columns in your data source. After having done it a few times myself, I can tell you that using the wizard sure beats doing it by hand! I'll go over the code that the wizard inserts when I discuss the Parts example in the next section.

The classes are used as base classes. The name of the derived class will be based upon your data source. The class functions are fairly self-explanatory. For example, CDataSource encapsulates the connection to your data source through the provider you selected. The CSession class manages a single access session to your data source. The CTable class enables you to access a simple rowset, which is one with no parameters. (You get this if you select the Table type option in the Name property page, shown in Figure 20.5.) The CCommand class allows you to access a rowset using a parameterized operation (select the Command type option, as in Figure 20.5). CAccessor statically binds a record to the data source and actually represents one of several accessor classes. The other classes include `CDynamicAccessor`, `CDynamicParameterAccessor`, and `CManualAccessor`. Which you use will depend upon several factors, so be sure to check the online documentation for details. The most commonly-used class is `CAccessor`, and this is what the wizard provides you with. The last class is the `CRowset` class, which is the object OLE DB and ATL use to both set and retrieve data from your data source.

With that brief introduction to the ATL consumer template classes, it's time to see them in action in an example.

Writing a Consumer Application

To demonstrate ATL and OLE DB, I elected to create a parts inventory database using Microsoft Access. The layout of the database is shown in Figure 20.8.

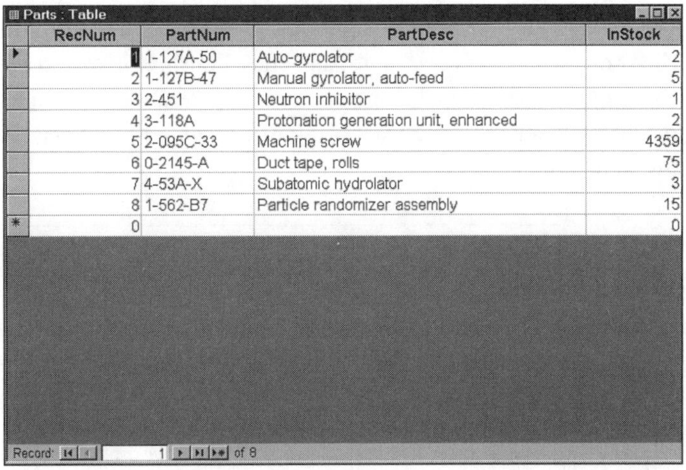

Parts : Table

RecNum	PartNum	PartDesc	InStock
1	1-127A-50	Auto-gyrolator	2
2	1-127B-47	Manual gyrolator, auto-feed	5
3	2-451	Neutron inhibitor	1
4	3-118A	Protonation generation unit, enhanced	2
5	2-095C-33	Machine screw	4359
6	0-2145-A	Duct tape, rolls	75
7	4-53A-X	Subatomic hydrolator	3
8	1-562-B7	Particle randomizer assembly	15
0			0

Record: 1 of 8

FIGURE 20.8

The Parts sample database.

I have no idea what these parts do! It's just an example. In any case, the primary key is the record number, followed by the part number, the part description, and the quantity in stock.

Creating the DSN

Before you try to use the database, you probably want to create a data source name. To do this, open the Control Panel and select the ODBC Applet. Click the System DSN tab. You should see something similar to what appears in Figure 20.9.

FIGURE 20.9

*The ODBC System
DSN property page.*

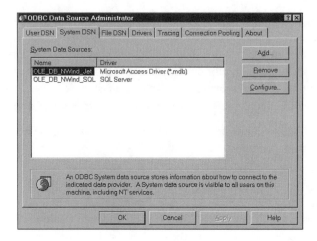

If you don't see your data source listed in the System Data Sources list control, click the
Add button to bring up the dialog box you see in Figure 20.10. In this case, select the
Microsoft Access Driver (*.mdb) and click Finish. This will bring up the ODBC
Microsoft Access Setup dialog you see in Figure 20.11. I complete the information on
this dialog by clicking the Select button, searching for the Day 20 database, and clicking
OK after I find it.

Note

There are three types of DSNs you can use. The User DSN ties the database
connection to a specific user. The File DSN uses a text file you create to provide ODBC with the connection information rather than storing this information in the Registry. Finally, the System DSN ties the database connection
to a given system, allowing all users to access the database.

For this sample, using the System DSN makes the most sense to me, so that's
what I suggest you use in this case. If you have reasons to use the other DSN
types, by all means use what makes the most sense to you. If you're interested in learning more about the DSNs themselves, see Knowledge Base
article Q159557, "XL97: Using System, User, and File Data Sources," or one
of the books I mentioned previously.

After I click OK, I see that the database is added to the list of system DSNs, Figure
20.12. The database can now be easily accessed by my application when I simply provide the DSN, which in this case is Day20PartsDB.

FIGURE 20.10

The ODBC Create New Data Source Wizard.

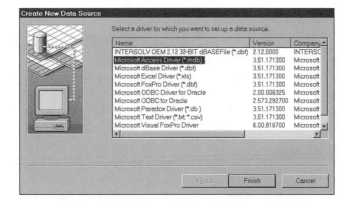

FIGURE 20.11

The ODBC Microsoft Access 97 Setup dialog box.

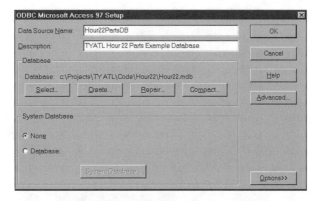

FIGURE 20.12

The ODBC System DSN property page, revisited.

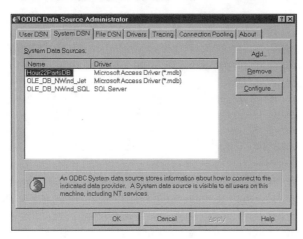

20

Creating the COM Object

With the DSN created, I turned to creating the COM object. Although the ATL Object
Wizard can add ATL code directly to an MFC application, I thought it more interesting
to shield the database access within a COM object that I create. My object's client, then,
doesn't need to worry about requesting the next rowset. Rather, the client asks for the
next part in the parts inventory. This provides a better abstraction from the client's point
of view.

I begin by creating a new ATL project named Day20Server, and to that I add a simple
COM object, named as you see in Figure 20.13. I then select the attribute options I've
shown in Figure 20.14.

FIGURE 20.13

*The ATL Object
Wizard's Names
property page.*

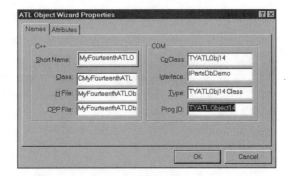

FIGURE 20.14

*The ATL Object
Wizard's Attributes
property page.*

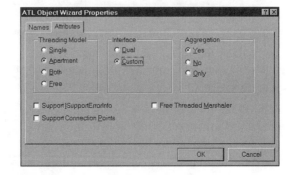

After Visual Studio finishes creating my new object, I add a number of methods, such as
`FirstPart()`, `LastPart()`, `NextPart()`, and `PrevPart()`. I also elect to allow the user to
delete and insert parts using `DeletePart()` and `InsertPart()`, respectively. Because the
user might want to update his view, I add `Refresh()`. `Refresh()` is especially useful with
Microsoft Access because Access introduces some delay when updating its records. After
you make a change, you might have to wait a moment and then refresh the view to see
your changes.

Now it is time to add the OLE DB source code. I invoke the ATL Object Wizard again and select the OLE DB consumer object. This gives me the Data Link Properties property sheet that I mentioned earlier. In this case, I selected the Day20PartsDB DSN from the Use Data Source Name drop-down list control. Because the database is not protected, I don't add anything to the User Name or Password controls. Because I am using a DSN, I ignore the initial catalog control.

After I click OK, Visual Studio asks me which table to use, as you see in Figure 20.15. Because there is only one table, I click OK (the table was preselected for me).

FIGURE 20.15

The ATL Object Wizard's Select Database Table dialog box.

The wizard then populates the various edit controls on the Name property sheet. I check the Insert check box to have the wizard add the corresponding property that will allow me to insert new parts into the Parts database. I then click OK, and the wizard adds the OLE DB code to my Day20Server project, found in the Parts.H file shown in Listing 20.1.

 Note Experienced database developers would most likely use a stored procedure rather than send the SQL command to the database each time that the command is to be executed (as I've shown in Listing 20.1). Microsoft Access doesn't provide stored procedures, so I didn't use one in this case. OLE DB does allow for this, however. So if you're using a database that will execute stored procedures, you can use OLE DB to execute them. See the online documentation for more details.

20

LISTING 20.1 Parts.H file Contents

```
1: // Parts.H : Declaration of the CParts class
2:
3: #ifndef __PARTS_H_
4: #define __PARTS_H_
5:
6: class CPartsAccessor
```

continues

LISTING 20.1   continued

```
 7: {
 8: public:
 9:     LONG m_RecNum; // Record number
10:     TCHAR m_PartNum[33]; // Part number
11:     TCHAR m_PartDesc[129]; // Part description
12:     LONG m_InStock; // Part Availability
13:
14: BEGIN_COLUMN_MAP(CPartsAccessor)
15:     COLUMN_ENTRY(1, m_RecNum)
16:     COLUMN_ENTRY(2, m_PartNum)
17:     COLUMN_ENTRY(3, m_PartDesc)
18:     COLUMN_ENTRY(4, m_InStock)
19: END_COLUMN_MAP()
20:
21: DEFINE_COMMAND(CPartsAccessor, _T(" \
22:     SELECT \
23:         RecNum, \
24:         PartNum, \
25:         PartDesc, \
26:         InStock \
27:     FROM Parts"))
28:
29:     // You may wish to call this function if you are inserting a
30:     // record and wish to initialize all the fields, if you are
31:     // not going to explicitly set all of them.
32:     void ClearRecord()
33:     {
34:         memset(this, 0, sizeof(*this));
35:     }
36: };
37:
38: class CParts : public CCommand<CAccessor<CPartsAccessor> >
39: {
40: public:
41:     HRESULT Open()
42:     {
43:         HRESULT hr;
44:
45:         hr = OpenDataSource();
46:         if (FAILED(hr))
47:             return hr;
48:
49:         return OpenRowset();
50:     }
51:     HRESULT OpenDataSource()
52:     {
53:         HRESULT hr;
54:         CDataSource db;
```

```
55:            CDBPropSet dbinit(DBPROPSET_DBINIT);
56:
57:            dbinit.AddProperty(DBPROP_AUTH_PERSIST_SENSITIVE_AUTHINFO,
58:                              false);
59:            dbinit.AddProperty(DBPROP_INIT_DATASOURCE,
60:                              OLESTR("Day20PartsDB"));
61:            dbinit.AddProperty(DBPROP_INIT_PROMPT, (short)4);
62:            dbinit.AddProperty(DBPROP_INIT_LCID, (long)1033);
63:            hr = db.Open(_T("MSDASQL"), &dbinit);
64:            if (FAILED(hr))
65:                return hr;
66:
67:        m_session.Close(); // close and load props anew
68:
69:        return m_session.Open(db);
70:    }
71:    HRESULT OpenRowset()
72:    {
73:        // Set properties for open
74:        CDBPropSet propset(DBPROPSET_ROWSET);
75:        propset.AddProperty(DBPROP_IRowsetChange, true);
76:        propset.AddProperty(DBPROP_UPDATABILITY,
77:                            DBPROPVAL_UP_INSERT);
78:        propset.AddProperty(DBPROP_CANSCROLLBACKWARDS, true);
79:        propset.AddProperty(DBPROP_IMMOBILEROWS, true);
80:
81:        return CCommand<CAccessor<CPartsAccessor> >::Open(m_session,
82:                                                          NULL,
83:                                                          &propset);
84:    }
85:    CSession m_session;
86: };
87:
88: #endif // __PARTS_H_
```

ANALYSIS   Most of what you see in Listing 20.1 is wizard-generated, but you can see a few modifications. First, to be sure the properties I set will be in place each time the rowset is opened, I add line 67 to CParts::OpenDataSource():

```
m_session.Close(); // close and load props anew
```

I then add two properties to the rowset, lines 78 and 79. Because Microsoft Access supports backward scrolling, I add the DBPROP_CANSCROLLBACKWARDS property. I also want new parts added to the end of the parts list, so I add the DBPROP_IMMOBILEROWS property:

```
propset.AddProperty(DBPROP_CANSCROLLBACKWARDS, true);
propset.AddProperty(DBPROP_IMMOBILEROWS, true);
```

20

The one thing I didn't yet add to the CParts class is the capability to update the database or delete parts records. For that, I create a second accessor using the same technique that I used to create the first. I name this accessor CPartsFinder because I want to modify the SQL command to locate a specific record for updating or deletion.

 Note
OLE DB has a known bug. If you receive the error HRESULT DB_E_ERRORSOC-CURRED (0x80040E21), you probably have an automatically updated primary key in your database table. Knowledge Base article Q235332, "FIX: SQLOLEDB: IRowset::SetData() Returns DB_E_ERRORSOCCURRED with Identity Column," discusses the bug in more detail.

CPartsFinder begins life the same as CParts, but to support the parameterized query, I add some code and change some things the wizard provides. As CPartsFinder is very similar to Listing 20.1, I'll italicize the changes I make to the basic file.

The first change is to add a *parameter map*, which will be used to insert the specific record number to be retrieved into the SQL command that I'll define in a moment. In this case, I add this code just before the DEFINE_COMMAND() macro:

```
BEGIN_PARAM_MAP(CPartsFinderAccessor)
    COLUMN_ENTRY(1, m_RecNum)
END_PARAM_MAP()
```

I then modify the SQL command to retrieve a specific record using the SQL WHERE clause:

```
DEFINE_COMMAND(CPartsFinderAccessor, _T(" \
    SELECT \
        RecNum, \
        PartNum, \
        PartDesc, \
        InStock \
    FROM Parts \
    WHERE RecNum=?"))
```

To locate a specific part record, you first set m_RecNum to the appropriate record number and then open a new database connection using this accessor. After you locate the record and make your changes, you close the database connection. I do this in CMyFourteenthATLObj::UpdatePart() and DeletePart(), for example. DeletePart() is shown in Listing 20.2.

LISTING 20.2 CMyFourteenthATLObj::DeletePart() Implementation

```
 1: STDMETHODIMP CMyFourteenthATLObj::DeletePart(long iRecNum)
 2: {
 3:     HRESULT hr = S_OK;
 4:     try {
 5:         // Delete the record
 6:         m_CPartsFinder.m_RecNum = iRecNum;
 7:
 8:         // Locate parts record
 9:         hr = m_CPartsFinder.Open();
10:         if ( hr == S_OK ) {
11:             // Database connection open
12:             hr = m_CPartsFinder.MoveNext();
13:             if ( FAILED(hr) ) {
14:                 // Record not found!
15:                 m_CPartsFinder.Close();
16:                 throw hr;
17:             } // if
18:
19:             hr = m_CPartsFinder.Delete();
20:             if ( FAILED(hr) ) {
21:                 // Record not deleted!
22:                 m_CPartsFinder.Close();
23:                 throw hr;
24:             } // if
25:
26:             // Close database connection
27:             m_CPartsFinder.Close();
28:     } // try
29:     catch(HRESULT hrErr) {
30:         // Pointer error
31:         hr = hrErr;
32:         OnSQLError();
33:     } // catch
34:     catch(...) {
35:         // Some other error
36:         hr = E_UNEXPECTED;
37:     } // catch
38:
39:     return hr;
40: }
```

20

ANALYSIS With the basic database support in place, you can now use the methods CRowset provides, such as MoveFirst() and MoveNext(), as I do in Line 12 of Listing 20.2. These are just what I required for implementing my parts data manipulation methods, which thinly wrap the rowset mechanization. You'll find my implementations in MyFourteenthATLObj.h and MyFourteenthATLObj.cpp, although I did include

CMyFourteenthATLObj::FirstPart() in Listing 20.3. The others are very similar, differing, for the most part, only in which rowset method they call.

LISTING 20.3 CMyFourteenthATLObj::FirstPart() Implementation

```
 1: STDMETHODIMP CMyFourteenthATLObj::FirstPart(long *piRecNum,
    ⮞BSTR *pbstrPartNum, BSTR *pbstrPartDesc, long *piInStock)
 2: {
 3:     HRESULT hr = S_OK;
 4:     try {
 5:         // Check their pointers
 6:         CHECKPTR(piRecNum)
 7:         CHECKPTR(pbstrPartNum)
 8:         CHECKPTR(pbstrPartDesc)
 9:         CHECKPTR(piInStock)
10:
11:         // Return first row's data
12:         hr = m_CParts.MoveFirst();
13:         if ( FAILED(hr) ) throw hr;
14:
15:         // Fill return parameters
16:         FillVars(piRecNum,pbstrPartNum,pbstrPartDesc,piInStock);
17:     } // try
18:     catch(HRESULT hrErr) {
19:         // Pointer error
20:         hr = hrErr;
21:         OnSQLError();
22:     } // catch
23:     catch(...) {
24:         // Some other error
25:         hr = E_UNEXPECTED;
26:     } // catch
27:
28:     return hr;
29: }
```

ANALYSIS FirstPart() uses a couple of helper functions and the macro I wrote in Day 8, "ATL Object Methods: Adding Functionality to Your Interface," to check the COM pointer for NULL. The FillVars() helper function simply stuffs the data into the return parameters:

```
void FillVars(long *piRecNum, BSTR *pbstrPartNum,
⮞BSTR *pbstrPartDesc, long *piInStock)
{
    // Record number
    *piRecNum = m_CParts.m_RecNum;

    // Part number
```

```
    CComBSTR bstrData(m_CParts.m_PartNum);
    *pbstrPartNum = bstrData.Copy();
    bstrData.Empty();

    // Part description
    bstrData = m_CParts.m_PartDesc;
    *pbstrPartDesc = bstrData.Copy();
    bstrData.Empty();

    // Number in stock
    *piInStock = m_CParts.m_InStock;
}
```

The OnSQLError() helper, line 21, checks to see if the OLE DB provider recorded an error record when any OLE DB error HRESULT came back from the DBMS. The idea here is to provide a bit more feedback about why there is an error condition, especially if the error comes from deep within OLE DB (see Listing 20.4).

LISTING 20.4   OnSQLError() Helper Method Implementation

```
 1: HRESULT OnSQLError(BOOL bDisplay = TRUE, BSTR * pbstrSrc = NULL,
    ➥BSTR * pbstrDesc = NULL)
 2: {
 3:     // Get OLE DB SQL error and provider strings
 4:     CComPtr<IErrorInfo> pErrorInfo;
 5:     HRESULT hr = GetErrorInfo(0,&pErrorInfo);
 6:     if ( FAILED(hr) ) return hr;
 7:
 8:     if ( pErrorInfo.p != NULL) {
 9:         // Check for multiple error records
10:         CComQIPtr<IErrorRecords,&IID_IErrorRecords>
            ➥pErrorRecords(pErrorInfo);
11:         ATLASSERT(pErrorRecords.p != NULL);
12:         if ( pErrorRecords.p == NULL ) return E_POINTER;
13:
14:         // Pull the number of error records
15:         ULONG iRecs = 0;
16:         hr = pErrorRecords->GetRecordCount(&iRecs);
17:         if ( FAILED(hr) ) return hr;
18:
19:         if ( iRecs > 0 ) {
20:             CComPtr<IErrorInfo> pErrorInfoRecord;
21:             hr = pErrorRecords->GetErrorInfo((iRecs-1),0x00000409,
22:                                               &pErrorInfoRecord);
23:             if ( FAILED(hr) ) return hr;
24:
25:             CComBSTR bstrSource;
26:             hr = pErrorInfoRecord->GetSource(&bstrSource);
27:             ATLASSERT(SUCCEEDED(hr));
```

continues

20

LISTING 20.4 continued

```
28:              if ( pbstrSrc != NULL ) *pbstrSrc = bstrSource.Copy();
29:
30:              CComBSTR bstrDescription;
31:              hr = pErrorInfoRecord->GetDescription(&bstrDescription);
32:              ATLASSERT(SUCCEEDED(hr));
33:              if ( pbstrDesc != NULL ) *pbstrDesc =
                     ➥bstrDescription.Copy();
34:
35:              if ( bDisplay ) {
36:                  // Display the error in a message box
37:                  USES_CONVERSION;
38:                  TCHAR* pstrSrc = OLE2T(bstrSource);
39:                  TCHAR* pstrDesc = OLE2T(bstrDescription);
40:                  ::MessageBox(NULL,pstrDesc,pstrSrc,MB_OK¦MB_ICONERROR);
41:              } // if
42:          } // if
43:      } // if
44:
45:      return hr;
46: }
```

> **Note**
>
> There is an OLE DB interface for locating SQL errors called ISQLErrorInfo. You might find this interface handy. I use my own SQL error helper because it gives me the provider string, as well as the error string. ISQLErrorInfo ::GetSQLInfo() returns the SQLSTATE information, which is a five-character SQL state string defined by the ANSI SQL standard. It also gives a numerical provider-specific error number. I don't find this information as useful as what I extract from the IErrorInfo record, but feel free to choose whichever you prefer.

ANALYSIS The helper function displays a message box containing the driver name and the error (line 40), and you can extract that information as parameters if you wish. The one thing to note is that I took the same approach as ATL, hard coding my *locale ID* (line 21),. which tells COM (and Windows) how to display textual information, time, currency, and so forth. I used (DWORD)0x0409, which is American English. (ATL did the same thing in Parts.H, where it set the LCID to 1033L which is 0x0409.) Had this been a real application, you would probably retrieve the default locale ID in use on the system and use that—instead of hard-coding American English (GetSystemDefaultLCID()).

The last thing I'll touch before moving to the client application is opening and closing the database. I used FinalConstruct() and FinalRelease() for these tasks (see Listing 20.5).

LISTING 20.5 CMyFourteenthATLObj::FinalConstruct() and FinalRelease()
Implementations

```
 1: HRESULT FinalConstruct()
 2: {
 3:     // Open database connection
 4:     return Refresh();
 5: }
 6:
 7: void FinalRelease()
 8: {
 9:     // Close database connection
10:     m_CParts.Close();
11: }
```

In FinalConstruct(), I call the Refresh() method (line 4)to open the database (the crux of which is Listing 20.6).

LISTING 20.6 CMyFourteenthATLObj::Refresh() Implementation

```
 1: // Close and reopen the session to
 2: // refresh the rowset.
 3: m_CParts.Close();
 4: hr = m_CParts.Open();
 5: if ( hr == S_OK ) {
 6:     // Database connection open
 7:     hr = m_CParts.MoveNext();
 8:     if ( FAILED(hr) ) {
 9:         // No items in the database!
10:         m_bDbEmpty = TRUE;
11:     } // if
12:     else {
13:         // Database contains items
14:         m_bDbEmpty = FALSE;
15:
16:         // Force S_OK
17:         hr = S_OK;
18:     } // else
19: } // if
20: else {
21:     OnSQLError();
22: } // else
```

20

ANALYSIS If I can open the database on line 4, I move to the first element using MoveNext() (line 7). If there is no element, I know the database is empty, and I record that fact. I also force the HRESULT to S_OK in line 17 if the database does open correctly.

Returning anything else from `FinalConstruct()`, even another success code, terminates the COM object. OLE DB can, and does, return other success codes, so I eliminate the possibility. `FinalRelease()` simply closes the database connection (line 10 of Listing 20.5).

After I completely implement all the COM object's methods, I turn to the client application. Let's look at its implementation now.

Creating the Client Application

As far as ATL and OLE DB are concerned, my job is done. But I still have no way to actually interact with the parts database. For that, I create a client application that uses the Day20Server parts database wrapper object.

I decided to get a bit more fancy with this client. An obvious client application would provide a couple of Next and Previous buttons and allow you to scroll through the rowset. Rather than revert to that, I read the parts data and place each row in the list common control, as you see in Figure 20.16.

FIGURE 20.16

The Day20Client user interface.

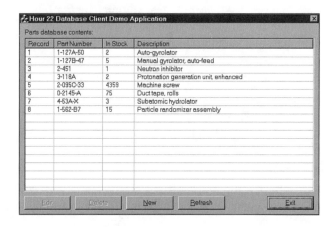

The application is a beefed-up dialog-based MFC application with the list control and a few buttons. You can add new parts, delete existing parts, and edit the part data (I have a separate dialog box for editing and insertion). Of course, you can also refresh the parts view (the view can potentially update faster than Access can change the database). The most complicated part of this example client application is the list control.

After establishing the column titles and widths, I fill the list control with parts data using the parts database COM object I just created. I created a helper function called `CDay20ClientDlg::FillListControl()` that loops through the parts records and fills each column of the list control (columns are called *subitems* in list control terms). You see this in Listing 20.7.

LISTING 20.7 `CDay20ClientDlg::FillListControl()` Implementation

```
 1: void CDay20ClientDlg::FillListControl()
 2: {
 3:     // Bring up hourglass
 4:     CWaitCursor wc;
 5:
 6:     // Don't update at this time...
 7:     m_CPartsList.SetRedraw(FALSE);
 8:
 9:     // Clear the list control
10:     m_CPartsList.DeleteAllItems();
11:
12:     // Grab the first part
13:     long iRecNum, iInStock;
14:     CComBSTR bstrNum, bstrDesc;
15:     HRESULT hr = m_pIPartsDbDemo->FirstPart(&iRecNum,&bstrNum,
16:                                        &bstrDesc,&iInStock);
17:     if ( FAILED(hr) ) return;
18:
19:     // Insert list data
20:     LVITEM lvItem;
21:     int iItem = 0;
22:     while ( hr != DB_S_ENDOFROWSET ) {
23:         // We're not using a (auto) sorted list, so the item
24:         // number we hand the control should not change.  However...
25:         int iActualItem = 0;
26:         for ( int iSubItem = 0; iSubItem < PARTCOLUMNCOUNT;
                    ➥iSubItem++) {
27:             // Complete basic item information
28:             lvItem.mask = LVIF_TEXT;
29:             lvItem.iItem = iActualItem; // bogus first column...
30:                                         // Will auto-correct after insert
31:             lvItem.iSubItem = iSubItem;
32:
33:             // Insert data into the list column by column
34:             switch ( iSubItem ) {
35:                 case 0: // record number
36:                     { // scope
37:                         // Convert integer
38:                         TCHAR strRecNum[16] = {0};
39:                         itoa(iRecNum,strRecNum,10);
40:                         lvItem.pszText = strRecNum;
41:
42:                         // Insert at desired location
43:                         lvItem.iItem = iItem++;
44:                         iActualItem =
                            ➥m_CPartsList.InsertItem(&lvItem);
45:                     } // scope
46:                     break;
```

continues

20

LISTING 20.7 continued

```
47:
48:                 case 1: // Part number
49:                     { // scope
50:                         // Convert text
51:                         USES_CONVERSION;
52:                         lvItem.pszText = OLE2T(bstrNum);
53:
54:                         // Update this column
55:                         m_CPartsList.SetItem(&lvItem);
56:                     } // scope
57:                     break;
58:
59:                 case 2: // Number in stock
60:                     { // scope
61:                         // Convert integer
62:                         TCHAR strNumStk[16] = {0};
63:                         itoa(iInStock,strNumStk,10);
64:                         lvItem.pszText = strNumStk;
65:
66:                         // Update this column
67:                         m_CPartsList.SetItem(&lvItem);
68:                     } // scope
60:                     break;
70:
71:                 case 3: // Part description
72:                     { // scope
73:                         // Convert text
74:                         USES_CONVERSION;
75:                         lvItem.pszText = OLE2T(bstrDesc);
76:
77:                         // Update this column
78:                         m_CPartsList.SetItem(&lvItem);
79:                     } // scope
80:                     break;
81:             } // switch
82:         } // for
83:
84:         // Get the next part
85:         hr = m_pIPartsDbDemo->NextPart(&iRecNum,&bstrNum,
86:                                         &bstrDesc,&iInStock);
87:     } // while
88:
89:     // Now we can update the list...
90:     m_CPartsList.SetRedraw(TRUE);
91:
92:     // Disable the edit and delete buttons
93:     EnableControls(FALSE);
94: }
```

The important logic in `FillListControl()` follows this pseudocode:

```
part = FirstPart()
while (part is valid)
    for ( column 0 to column 3 )
        switch (column)
            case column 0:
                fill column 0 from part
            case column 1:
                fill column 1 from part
            case column 2:
                fill column 2 from part
            case column 3:
                fill column 3 from part
        end switch
    end for
    part = NextPart()
end while
```

This logic is similar to what you saw in Day 19 "Distributed ATL: DCOM Around the Net," when I populated the application and process lists.

With the client application accessing the COM object that in turn accesses the DBMS, an end user now has the capability of reading and modifying the Parts database.

Note

> Creating a COM object to access the parts database satisfies my object-oriented design tendencies. However, you could just as easily add the ATL OLE DB support directly to the MFC application and skip the COM object altogether. See the online documentation article "How Do I Add OLE DB Consumer Support To an MFC Application Without Using the Wizard?" for details.

Summary

In this day you studied Microsoft's COM-based DBMS access technology, OLE DB. I began by describing OLE DB, both from an architectural standpoint and from an object model standpoint. I told you how OLE DB provides services through nearly 60 interfaces that simplify your DBMS programming tasks.

To further simplify matters, ATL provides tremendous support for OLE DB, even to the point of reading your database and creating ATL source code tailored to your needs. You looked at the ATL Object Wizard again, and learned how the wizard collects the information it needs to generate your source code. I then briefly described the ATL OLE DB classes, including `CDataSource`, `CSession`, and `CRowset`.

20

With that background, I described how I created the parts inventory example. I talked about creating a System DSN so that OLE DB could work through ODBC to access the Parts database. I then created a COM object designed to wrap the database access, although I could have incorporated this capability directly into the MFC client application. I discussed the code the wizard creates for me, based upon the Parts database I created. I then went on to talk about some of the modifications I made to the wizard-generated code and why I made those modifications. After that, I briefly described two of the parts access methods that I implemented. These were designed to wrap the database access from the client application. I also talked about a few helper functions I use to enhance the COM object, such as OnSQLError().

The last topic I discussed was the creation of the client application itself. I specifically described the code that fills the list control because that is the main application logic for dealing with the database COM wrapper object. That code also deals with the Windows list common control, which many developers find confusing.

With OLE DB under your belt, it's time to move on. The final day, "ATL and MTS: Coding with a Better COM," will discuss MTS- and ATL-based COM objects operating in an MTS environment. You're almost done!

Q&A

Q Is it possible to have more than one session with the database, so that I can create multiple commands and select the command I want to execute?

A Yes, and you add more commands by adding more OLE DB objects using the ATL Object Wizard. I did this with the Parts database example. You'll need to edit your CAccessor class, specifically the DEFINE_COMMAND() macro, to insert the new command (usually SQL). The resulting rowset will also likely be different than the generic rowset the wizard created, so you might have to adjust your column mappings. This is where an error function, such as OnSQLError(), is so helpful. You can more easily identify SQL command errors using this function than you can if all that OLE DB returns to you is a failed HRESULT.

Q Will OLE DB work with other databases than Access? Specifically, can I use a remote database implemented in SQL Server?

A Yes, and if OLE DB doesn't provide support for the database in question, you can also write your own provider, although this is quite an undertaking. Nearly all the major Windows-platform database vendors provide OLE DB support.

Workshop

The Workshop is designed to help you anticipate possible questions, review what you've learned, and get you thinking about how to put your knowledge into practice. The answers to the quiz are in Appendix A, "Answers."

Quiz

1. What is OLE DB?
2. What are OLE DB Services?
3. What objects will you find in the OLE DB object model?
4. How does ATL support OLE DB?
5. Do you have to access your data source using ODBC and a System DSN?

Exercise

1. Add a new SQL command to look for all parts with zero in stock. Then set some of the parts counts to zero and test using the basic client application, modified to look for all parts or just empty parts bins. (Hint: Add a check box to the main dialog and then look at its state to determine which search criteria you should use.)

20

DAY 21

ATL and MTS: Coding with a Better COM

Have you ever created an application that wrote some information to a file, then failed during processing? What if the file was then corrupted or otherwise lost data? This experience, although it's more than a minor annoyance, is one I am generally able to recover from (even when the data I was writing is gone forever). Imagine that same situation, however, in a doctor's office where information is being sent to a patient's records at the local hospital. What happens if the application fails in this case? This situation is quite a bit more serious than just losing some log file data, especially if the patient's condition is critical.

The loss of critical data is precisely the impetus for transactional processing. Transactional processing, to me anyway, always conjured images of bank transactions. But there are many other examples where transactional processing makes good sense, including the doctor's office scenario I just described.

If you aren't already aware of this fact, COM itself is moving towards a transactional basis with the advent of COM+ and Windows 2000. Many of the internals of the Microsoft Transaction Server will find their way into the COM runtime environment, so it makes sense to take a good look at MTS to see why it is so attractive to the COM+ development team.

Before I dive into actually coding for MTS, I will discuss some of the basic concepts related to transactional processing, in general, and then move on to MTS architecture. After you understand some of the basic concepts, I'll implement a transactional object and use it from a simple MFC test application. I'll wrap up this lesson with an overview of COM+ as it is related to MTS and COM. In this last day I'll cover

- Basic transactional concepts
- The primary MTS components
- Possible transactional participants
- Some of the benefits of using MTS in a COM setting
- How to create an MTS transactional object
- How to create a client to use the transactional object
- How to incorporate your object into MTS using the MTS Explorer
- What to expect from MTS 3.0 and COM+ in Windows 2000

Transaction Concepts

When you think of a *transaction*, think of an operation that is all or nothing. That is, if the entire transaction requires eight steps, a failure in any one step forces the entire operation to fail. More than that, if the transaction fails, the entire system reverts to the state it was in prior to the transaction. It is as if the transaction was never attempted at all.

Consider this idea for a moment. It is as if the transaction was never attempted at all. One implication of this is the patient whose records were botched has a clean slate. The error won't corrupt the hospital's records. After the patient's records are successfully updated, the doctor knows that the records are correct. If the transaction fails, it doesn't adversely affect the overall system (unless time is an issue). If the transaction is successful, you can be sure everything went as planned.

From a computing standpoint, this is an incredible challenge. It's hard enough to recover from system errors even in relatively simple applications. To recover the initial state and make the entire system believe that nothing happened is a huge undertaking. It involves many specialty components, which-md]acting together—can record every system move and roll the moves back to an earlier point. To complicate matters, the rollback must be synchronized among all the components so that they all roll back to the same point in time.

For such a system to exist, there has to be a set of ground rules. A transaction, if it is to be managed *as* a transaction in the formal sense, must exhibit certain properties and meet other processing requirements. Let's take a look at some of them.

ACID Properties

For the transaction paradigm to work correctly, transactional processes usually must be *ACID*, meaning atomic, consistent, isolated, and durable. If your transaction fails to meet one of these criteria, it fails to be a true transaction (although you still might wish to run it within the MTS environment). Here is what each term means to your process.

Atomic

An *atomic* process is one that executes completely or not at all. The process should be considered a single unit of work, and if any subset of the effort fails, the entire task is considered a failure and re-executed. The single patient record update is atomic, whereas updating a batch of records is probably not atomic. If a single record fails to update correctly, the application can simply try to update the remote database again. In the case of the batch processing, however, the failure of a single record's attempt to update doesn't necessarily mean the entire batch is a failure.

Consistent

Consistency is related to the state of your system both before and after the transaction. That is, before the transaction begins, everything should be operating normally as specified by your nominal business logic. After the transaction has executed, the system remains in a stable, known state. In the doctor's office, this criteria means the patient record database is not corrupted before or after the patient's record is updated.

Isolated

If your particular transaction is unaware of any other concurrently executing transaction, it is said to be *isolated*. Your transaction can depend upon the outcome of a previous transaction, but it can't depend upon the outcome of a concurrent transaction. Concurrent transactions might fail, leaving your transactional outcome in question. The record update of the patient that I mentioned earlier should not be tied to another record update that happens at the same time. If there is a dependency, the transactions must be serialized.

Durable

Durability isn't so much a requirement of the transaction as it is a requirement of the participants in the transaction. The transactional participants must be capable of rolling the system back to a consistent state if a given transaction fails. How they do this is up to

21

them, but it's a stringent requirement and difficult to implement. It means the particular transactional participant must be prepared to handle all situations, including a complete system failure, while processing transactions. When the system is reinitialized, the transactional participant must be able to begin processing precisely where it left off. Using the same patient record example, the hospital database that is to be updated must be durable. Many databases implement durability using a tagged log file. This enables them to read tags and determine at what point their previous processing terminated. They also can roll back any or all transactions based upon the log entries.

Commit and Abort

The transactional environment (MTS in this case) will ask participants in a transaction whether their individual parts of the transaction were successful. This involves a two-step process known as *two-phase commit*. MTS first asks each participant to prepare to commit the change in system state (get ready to write the record updates into the hospital database). Then, after all participants are ready, MTS asks each to actually commit the change in state (write the record updates and close the hospital database).

As each participant prepares to commit the changes, the system's state is *locked*. That is, no other changes can take place because the system is in an inconsistent state (violates the consistency rule above). The system just has to wait for all the participants to prepare to commit their respective changes and then actually vote on the final outcome. After the voting is complete, the system will be returned to a consistent state, either by completing the current transaction or by rolling the system back to a previously consistent state. At this time, the system locks are removed, and other transactions can progress.

When the participant votes on the outcome of the transaction, they can either vote to *commit* the transaction or to *abort* it. If all participants vote to commit the system change, MTS will allow the transaction to complete, and the new system's state will take effect. If any participant votes to abort the transaction, all participants are told, by MTS, to abort the transaction and roll the system's state back to a previously consistent state.

Distributed Transactions

Nothing I've mentioned so far precludes any participant from acting upon the transaction just because they're remotely located. In fact, remote participants are common in today's enterprise. One server computer executes the transactions, while a second server computer manages the database against which the transactions are applied.

In this case, a copy of the transactional environment must exist on each machine. Some component within the local transaction processing mechanism coordinates transactions on the remote computers. This process can be a challenge to implement, as you can imagine. Not only must you worry about the outcome of the transaction (and broadcast that outcome to the remote computers), but you must also be prepared if the network is severed, and you can't communicate with the remote computers.

Microsoft solved these transactional and distribution issues, as well as many other sticky situations, when they implemented the Microsoft Transaction Server. Let's look now at MTS to see what components are available and what actions they perform.

MTS Components

As you might imagine, MTS is not a simple piece of software. It's quite complex, in fact. This stems, in part, from the transactional processing requirements levied upon the transactional environment I just described. But part of the complexity revolves around locating and activating COM objects, which I haven't really addressed yet today. That issue will come up in the next section.

There are all sorts of components within MTS! Some component has to operate at the lowest level of the transaction to provide a participant with commit and abort capability. Because all your MTS objects must be in-process servers, there must be a surrogate process to load and execute them (similar to what was used for DCOM in Day 19, "Distributed ATL: DCOM Around the Net"). Something needs to coordinate the transactions, both locally and remotely. You'll need a way to administer the system. Clearly, some mechanism must be in place to package the transactional components and distribute them, as well as to manage the security aspects of distributed processing. I'll begin with the lowest-level MTS component and move around the MTS architecture from component to component.

Context Object

The low-level MTS objects I mentioned include the *context object* and the associated *context wrapper object*. If you write COM objects for use within the MTS environment, MTS will manage your object's lifetime for the client application. MTS does this to allow for object pooling, which keeps currently unused objects in memory for quicker activation. The context objects together also keep other runtime information handy, such as the results of expensive security checks.

When a client application instantiated your COM object within the MTS environment, MTS creates a wrapper object that represents your true COM object. You see this in Figure 21.1. The client makes method calls through the wrapper object, which passes the calls to your true COM object for processing. At some point, the client will release your object's last interface, which in normal COM processing causes your object to be

21

removed from memory. However, the wrapper object references your true COM object, and MTS can now place your COM object on inactive reserve, so to speak. The next client to request your object will get an interface pointer to the pooled object rather than a brand new object, thus providing the client with an interface pointer more quickly.

FIGURE 21.1

The context wrapper and context object relating with the true COM object.

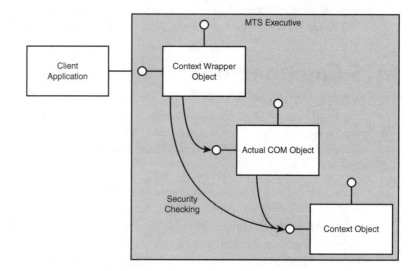

This has a number of implications. First, as a client, you no longer actually control the lifetime of the COM object. MTS does. Second, you don't deal with the COM object yourself. MTS does. Third, because MTS can provide clients with interface pointers from pooled objects, MTS can implement a stateless processing architecture and require both your COM objects and clients to adhere to that architecture. It's the last implication that affects you the most.

It affects you because MTS can now provide *any* of your pooled objects to process *any* client method call. This leads to better response time, which leads to better scalability. The true goal of MTS is to provide an architecture that increases scalability. If a client application requests an object interface pointer, calls an interface method, then releases its hold on the object, MTS can pump through more object method calls than would otherwise be possible. That also means that MTS takes responsibility for pooling the objects. Therefore, you must write thread-safe code, because even if your COM object is marked as Apartment (single) threaded, MTS will treat it as free threaded (that is, you can't maintain information within your object from one method call to another).

Consider how MTS can create a wrapper object that impersonates your object. How can MTS know beforehand what interfaces your object exposes and what parameters are required? It is amazing, if not a bit frightening, that MTS can do this at all. The best description of this capability is certainly Richard Grimes' latest effort, *Professional Visual C++ MTS Programming* (Wrox Press, ISBN 1-861002-39-4). He explains how this is done and why. The technique is known as *interception*, and it is quite advanced.

In any case, because any pooled object can handle any client's method call, there must be some way to associate a given client with a given MTS object and provide information for future client method calls. This is the job of the context object itself (as you see in Figure 21.1). The context object maintains information about the original client application that created the true COM object and about the security aspects of using the true COM object. The context object also provides for the transactional needs of the true COM object if it is participating in a transaction.

One of the biggest differences between using COM traditionally and using COM from within MTS is that within MTS you use the context object to create instances of other COM objects from within your COM object. You can't simply use the COM CoCreateInstance() API call. Creating objects through the context object allows MTS to know which objects your COM object created and enables them to participate in the transaction.

Table 21.1 lists the interface methods IObjectContext provides.

TABLE 21.1 IObjectContext Methods

Method	Description
CreateInstance()	Creates an object within an MTS activity
EnableCommit()	Indicates the object's internal state is consistent
DisableCommit()	Indicates the object's internal state is inconsistent
IsInTransaction()	Indicates the object is currently participating in a transaction
SetAbort()	Indicates the current transaction should be aborted
SetComplete()	Indicates the current transaction should be committed
IsSecurityEnabled()	Indicates security is enabled
IsCallerInRole()	Indicates whether client application is specified in the given role

I'll discuss activities and roles (mentioned in Table 21.1) in the upcoming "Transaction Packages and Activities" section. The context object (and MTS) works with your COM object through the IObjectControl interface, which your object should support. Its methods are shown in Table 21.2.

21

TABLE 21.2 IObjectControl Methods

Method	Description
Activate()	Called when your object is to be activated or reactivated
Deactivate()	Called when your object is to be deactivated
CanBePooled()	Called when your object is deactivated to determine if it can be placed into an object pool

Your object can take appropriate measures when being activated and deactivated, such as acquiring or releasing database connections. MTS will execute CanBePooled() just prior to Deactivate() to see if you'll allow MTS to store your object for later use. MTS 2.0 (Windows NT 4.0) can't pool objects, so if you're working in that environment, you should always return FALSE. On the other hand, MTS 3.0 (Windows 2000) can support object pooling, so return TRUE or FALSE depending upon your object's capabilities.

The context object and wrapper are probably the biggest additions MTS provides to COM, and you'll see them heavily used in COM+ on Windows 2000 where MTS is now a part of the operating system. Even if your object is not participating in a transaction, I'm sure you can see the scalability benefits of pooled objects and quick activation.

The MTS Surrogate

MTS specifies all transaction objects (those you write) must be in-process COM servers. If that's the case, MTS must have a mechanism to bring the COM DLLs into memory and execute their methods. To do this, MTS provides a surrogate process in a manner similar to DCOM. The surrogate is a different application (MTX.EXE, for MTS 2.0 under Windows NT 4.0), but the concept is the same.

To use the surrogate, however, MTS will adjust your object's Registry settings when you add your object to a package (I'll discuss packages a bit later). When you add your object to a package, your object's threading model is changed to free, and a LocalServer32 key is added. The LocalServer32 key provides the path to the MTS surrogate and also provides it with the package ID on the command line.

That's a frightening concept, too. MTS changes your object's Registry settings! Worse, it apparently changes your object's threading model from Apartment to free. Actually, the threading model refers to the surrogate and not to your object. Still, it's chilling the first time you see it happen!

MTS Executive

The larger square area in Figure 21.1 represents the MTS Executive. The *Executive* is the main MTS process that provides the glue and the magic necessary to carry out the transactional processing and object reuse. For example, it's the Executive that intercepts your COM object's creation and creates the context objects MTS will associate with your object.

Distributed Transaction Coordinator

The Distributed Transaction Coordinator, or DTC, is the component responsible for managing transactions that span single or multiple computers. More specifically, it has these responsibilities:

- Enables transactional processing using multiple differing data sources over potentially remote connections
- Implements the transaction protocol (such as the two-phase commit)
- Provides for the transactional outcome voting by transaction participants, coordinates the commit/abort functionality, and notifies each participant that they can roll back

The DTC is also responsible for creating the *transaction object*, which is a COM object that represents the transaction as a whole. The transaction object implements the ITransaction interface. The methods of ITransaction are shown Table 21.3

TABLE 21.3 ITransaction Methods

Method	Description
Commit()	Commits the transaction
Abort()	Aborts the transaction
GetTransactionInfo()	Returns certain information about the transaction

The transaction object also implements a second interface, IGetDispenser, which I'll discuss in the "Your Transactional Objects" section. The primary purpose of the transaction object is to represent the transaction and to provide a conduit for enlisting resources. You'll see more about resource enlistment shortly when I discuss transactional participants.

MTS Explorer

Given the complexity and power of MTS, there must be some way to administer and manage it. In Day 6, "The ATL App Wizard: Back to Basics," I mentioned the Microsoft Management Console (MMC). ATL supports MMC snap-in object creation. As it happens, an MMC snap-in object administers MTS via the MMC. As you can see from

21

Figure 21.2, the snap in provides you with the capability to access remote computers and to create and administer MTS packages.

FIGURE 21.2

The MTS Explorer user interface.

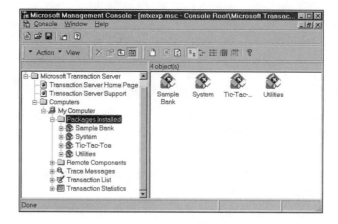

Transaction Packages and Activities

An MTS *package* is a grouping of objects that will work together in a given application. A package is really no more than a collection of objects that are grouped together for convenience. Perhaps it is convenient to distribute them in this way, or perhaps they're easier to manage when lumped together. You decide which object resides in which package.

One aspect of managing a package is the specification of its security information. MTS enables you to view the Windows NT security model in a more abstracted view. Rather than deal with security at the lowest levels, as you did with DCOM, you can view security as *role-based*. That is, users who can identify themselves as belonging to a particular role, such as Administrators or Developers (the choice of role and name is yours), can access the MTS objects and institute transactions. This greatly eases security administration, because MTS and the MTS Explorer handle the lower-level details for you. You simply establish the roles the package supports and ship the package.

Packages are easily distributed to other computers within the enterprise. If you include the objects and their proxy/stub DLLs, MTS will push the package to a user's computer and register the contained objects for you. When that happens, MTS already knows which computers have which packages, so you no longer have to deal with DCOM and the COSERVERINFO structure (or the object's AppID Registry settings). This simplifies object distribution and use.

Some or all the objects in a given package might work together in a given *activity*, which represents a set of transactions (one or more) that act as a single thread, even across remote machine boundaries. The activity is how MTS manages the consistency of the transactions, as well as their isolation at the distributed-object level. MTS must be aware of all transactional objects, especially remote objects, because some other object concurrently executing during a transaction might attempt to corrupt the system's integrity. You can imagine an activity as a way to apply an imaginary single-thread to all your objects. MTS will honor that imaginary single thread and not allow other objects to interfere. When you assemble your package, you also can decide what objects participate in which activities if you so choose.

You've now seen the major components of MTS. You have the context wrapper and context object, your true COM object, and the MTS executive. The DTC coordinates the transaction. You use the MTS Explorer to manage MTS and to create packages containing your COM objects for distribution and administration. Within the packages themselves, you group the objects together into activities, which MTS uses to assign objects to single, logical processes. It's time now to look at the objects that actually perform the work in a transaction.

Transaction Participants

So far you've examined the MTS architecture, but you haven't really seen who does the real work. MTS provides services, but you or other vendors provide the objects that perform the task at hand. Let's see some of these.

Resource Managers

Aside from the custom objects that implement the business logic of the transaction, *resource managers* are probably the most important object participating in a transaction. The resource manager, or RM, provides the transactional implementation for a given data source, such as a database. It is the RM that provides the durability and enforces the consistency within a given transaction. RMs, along with the resource dispenser, also provide for scalability by pooling resources.

Resource Dispensers

Resource dispensers are related to resource managers in that they manage the non-durable aspects of the transaction, such as a database connection. (The data stored in the database is made durable, but the connection to the database is not.) You might consider the resource dispenser as the participant that provides you with transient resources that are used only for a single transaction.

Resource dispensers typically work within transactions, but this need not be so. You can request resources from a dispenser without creating a transaction. In fact, some resource dispensers don't have an associated resource manager. An example is the Shared Property Manager, or SPM, which you'll see in the next section.

21

It is true, however, that resource dispensers are typically singleton objects, just like the ATL-based objects you saw in Day 18, "ATL, Class Factories, and Licensed Objects: Creating Objects and Protecting Your Investment." This singleton nature provides for consistency and shared resources within a given transaction, even though the resource dispenser itself doesn't maintain state between transactions.

Shared Property Manager

It is certainly possible you might have several objects participating in a given transaction and that those objects require the same resources. Yet your objects should be stateless. That is, they don't carry state from transaction to transaction. (Instead, they store results in a durable resource, such as a database.) In fact, MTS could destroy and recreate your objects between transactions. Therefore, keeping state data within your object is of little benefit. Given this, how do you share state data between objects participating in the same transaction?

The answer is you use the *Shared Property Manager* (usually pronounced spam). The SPM shares state data between objects using named property groups. The MTS objects accessing a shared property must all belong to the same package. Note that you can initialize a property with data from a durable resource and manage it within a transaction, such as a counter. The SPM can hold the initialized counter while the transaction objects perform their tasks to determine the new counter value. Then, when the transaction is to be committed, the new counter value can be read from the SPM and stored in a durable resource for later use in another transaction.

Your Transactional Objects

The objects you write that participate in transactions use the resources provided by managers and dispensers. They also vote on the outcome of the transaction. Your object's vote comes when the method completes. It is indicated by the last call you make to IObjectContext, as I show in Table 21.4.

TABLE 21.4 Transaction Management Settings

Method	Done?	Consistent?
DisableCommit()	No	No
EnableCommit()	No	Yes
SetAbort()	Yes	No
SetComplete()	Yes	Yes

The customary practice is to call SetAbort() as the first action in your method. Then later, you change your mind as you progress through your transaction. If your method throws an exception or has some other disaster befall it, the transaction will be automatically aborted. If you call DisableCommit() or EnableCommit(), what you're really asking is that MTS continue to poll your object to see if your part of the transaction is complete. After you have completed your part, you should call SetComplete() if things progressed well, or just exit the method if not (assuming you called SetAbort() early in the method). If you do abort a transaction, your method returns an error HRESULT to prevent the client application from attempting further processing that will have to be rolled back.

Benefits of Using MTS

I've actually already mentioned many benefits of using MTS, but I'd like to discuss several in a slightly different context (no pun intended). I've discussed MTS and its components in terms of transactional processing alone. But MTS provides something far more exciting than transactions for COM developers. In addition to being a transaction-processing environment, MTS is also an *Object Resource Broker*, or *ORB*.

In Day 19 when I discussed DCOM, remember that somehow I had to explicitly tell COM which remote computer to use. Perhaps I stored that information in the Registry, or I provided it directly using the COSERVERINFO structure I passed to CoCreateInstanceEx(). Sometimes this isn't a problem, but a cleaner implementation somehow informs COM where things are placed. If this is done, I don't need to be concerned with a given object's location myself. I leave that detail to COM.

Another worry is security. In Day 19, I blew past the security issues by completely opening the computer to external DCOM access. In real enterprise situations, however, doing this is completely unacceptable, even on trusted networks (accidents do happen). Because there is so much detail involved with the Security API, and because few developers are truly knowledgeable when it comes to programming with the Security API, it would be nice to see a higher-level approach to security. In the best of all worlds, I can change the security aspects of my distributed objects without having to reprogram them.

MTS solves both of these issues and more, and COM+ offers many more features and benefits than plain MTS. Let's look at the two benefits I mentioned.

Distribution

MTS provides you with a packaging and distribution mechanism you access through the MTS Explorer. Through the Explorer, you can create a new package, add components (DLLs only), set some package attributes and properties, and then push the package out to other computers. MTS records which computers have the package, and because MTS knows what objects are included in the package, it can locate all the remote computers that have a particular object. Now, you don't need to know where an object is located. MTS handles the location for you.

MTS stores this information in its *Catalog*, which will grow in importance with COM+. The Catalog also resides in the Registry, at least for now, and is used to associate objects and packages. Gone are the standalone installation applications and registration scripts. In their place is a simple, easy-to-use process that provides the added benefit of location persistence.

Declarative Security

As you create your package, you can also set the security aspects of the package. As it's pushed to the remote computer(s), it maintains the security aspects you preset. This security information is an additional object property that is applied at runtime with the object's own internal properties. In effect, it is metadata.

The nice aspect of metadata is that it's easily changed without recompiling the objects themselves. For this reason, such attributes are known as declarative attributes, or in the specific case of security, as *declarative security*. MTS takes responsibility for managing the lower-level aspects of the Security API for you, enabling you to set (or change) security settings at a higher level of abstraction.

This higher level of abstraction is called the *role*. You might also see this referred to as *role-based security*. That is, you allow access to your computers and objects based upon a given user's inclusion in a specific role authorized for such access. You're free to pick the roles and who is grouped within a particular role, but MTS enforces the role when it comes time to instantiate and use a given object. The best news is that absolutely no coding is required to support this. You manage it all through the MTS Explorer.

These two benefits alone form the underpinnings of COM+, although COM+ brings much more to you than this. You'll look briefly at some of the additional features of COM+ in the section, "MTS and COM+." These benefits are also why MTS is commonly referred to as "a better COM." Knowing what you now know about Distributed COM, perhaps you'll agree.

Coding for MTS

With the introduction to MTS you received so far today, you're now ready to create an object designed to be used within MTS. As is normally the case, there is a little more to the story than the theory reveals. It's one thing to understand MTS, but it's another to actually write code that uses it.

During the remainder of today, you'll create a transactional component that uses the Shared Property Manager to store then retrieve a string. Along the way you'll create a client to use the transactional object and create an MTS package from within the MTS Explorer that establishes the transactional parameters for your object.

S2000

Designing COM objects for use in the MTS environment requires a slightly different approach than designing traditional COM objects. The major reason is that you can't maintain state information within a transactional object. For one thing, holding state data reduces the scalability of your object. For another, the state data isn't durable, and it will likely interfere with other transactions (breaking the isolation property). If something awful were to happen to your object, it's also conceivable that the loss of the state data could impact your system's consistency, leaving things in some indeterminate state.

Another design realization is that you no longer control the creation and lifetime of your object—MTS and the context objects do that. When a client application instantiates your transactional object, they really receive a pointer to the context wrapper. MTS can elect to store your object in an object pool in a deactivated state (MTS 2.0 under Windows NT 4.0 won't do this, but MTS 3.0 under Windows 2000 can). This implies a secondary design requirement—you shouldn't perform any object initialization from within the constructor of your COM object's C++ class or perform cleanup in the destructor. The object might not be constructed and destroyed each time it is used.

There are other minor details I'll get to as I describe today's sample COM object, *Day21Server*. Let's start with the object and then move to the client.

Your Transactional Object

Initially, creating a transactional object isn't that different from creating any other object, although you'll need to remember some extra steps. The object begins life by using the ATL AppWizard.

Help from the Wizard

If you fire up Visual Studio and create an ATL project using the ATL AppWizard, remember two things. First, all MTS objects are in-process servers. DLLs. MTS can't work with local servers (EXEs). Second, don't forget to check the Support MTS check box before you click Finish. As you recall from Day 6, "The ATL App Wizard: Back to Basics," clicking this button causes the AppWizard to add several files to your project's link list and provides a reminder notice to reregister the object with MTS after compilation.

21

Changes to Basic ATL Files

At this point, your object looks very much like any other ATL object. Now you'll start to tailor your object to work within the MTS environment. The first step is to add the additional MTS header files required to identify the MTS components you'll be dealing with.

Additional Header Files

The major header file you'll require is MTX.H, which identifies general MTS components and interfaces such as IObjectContext and IObjectControl. Almost anything you'll do with MTS requires this header file, so you might either include it within STDAFX.H (to add it to your precompiled headers) or include it with each object's class definition header file. (I tend to use the latter approach to affirm the given object is destined for MTS.)

Other MTS header files include the files shown in Table 21.5. I use MTXSPM.H with today's sample object because I need to create an instance of the Shared Property Manager.

TABLE 21.5 MTS Header Files

File	Description
MTSEVENTS.H	Defines MTS event interfaces
MTSGRP.H	Defines MTS interfaces for enumerating running packages
MTXADMIN.H	Defines MTS administrative utility interfaces, such as those for working with the Catalog or remote components
MTXATTR.H	Defines MTS transactional attributes, such as TRANSACTION_REQUIRES_NEW
MTXDM.H	Defines MTS interfaces for creating resource dispensers and managers
MTXSPM.H	Defines MTS interfaces for working with the Shared Property Manager resource dispenser

You might require none or several of these header files, depending upon your application. If you use an interface that later won't compile (as undefined), you might rummage through these files to see which you need to include in your project.

Supporting IObjectControl

For the Day21Server example, I created a simple COM object with a dual interface, much like the objects I've created throughout the book. It has a CoClass value of TYATLObj15 and provides a single custom interface IMTSDemo. I saved the code in MyFifteenthATLObj.h and MyFifteenthATLObj.cpp.

With MTX.H defined in my object's header file, the first major code change that I made to support MTS was to add IObjectControl to my object's list of base classes. The code in Listing 21.1 comes from MyFifteenthATLObj.h.

LISTING 21.1 MyFifteenthATLObj.h Contents (Abbreviated)

```
1: // MyFifteenthATLObj.h : Declaration of the CMyFifteenthATLObj
2:
3: #ifndef __MYFIFTEENTHATLOBJ_H_
4: #define __MYFIFTEENTHATLOBJ_H_
5:
6: #include "resource.h"        // main symbols
7: #include "mtx.h"             // MTS support
8:
9: #define CHECKPTR(p) if ( p == NULL ) { hr = E_POINTER; throw hr; } \
10:                    else { *p = NULL; }
11:
12: ////////////////////////////////////////////////////////////////////
13: // CMyFifteenthATLObj
14: class ATL_NO_VTABLE CMyFifteenthATLObj :
15:     public CComObjectRootEx<CComSingleThreadModel>,
16:     public CComCoClass<CMyFifteenthATLObj, &CLSID_TYATLObj15>,
17:     public IDispatchImpl<IMTSDemo, &IID_IMTSDemo,
18: ➥&LIBID_DAY21SERVERLib>,
19:     public IObjectControl
20: {
21:     (Edited for brevity.)
22:     ...
23: };
```

ANALYSIS Here you see I included MTX.H (line 7), which defines the IObjectControl interface. Because MTS will expect to control my object through this interface, I must add it to the list of base classes for my ATL C++ object.

Because I added IObjectControl as a new base interface, I also had to add it to the COM map:

```
BEGIN_COM_MAP(CMyFifteenthATLObj)
    COM_INTERFACE_ENTRY(IMTSDemo)
    COM_INTERFACE_ENTRY(IDispatch)
    COM_INTERFACE_ENTRY(IObjectControl)
END_COM_MAP()
```

This leaves the implementations, which I also kept in MyFifteenthATLObj.h (see Listing 21.2).

21

LISTING 21.2 IObjectControl Implementation

```
 1: // IObjectControl
 2: STDMETHOD(Activate)()
 3: {
 4:     HRESULT hr = GetObjectContext(&m_spIObjectContext);
 5:     return hr;
 6: }
 7:
 8: STDMETHOD_(BOOL,CanBePooled)()
 9: {
10: #if(_WIN32_WINNT >= 0x0500)
11:     return TRUE;
12: #else
13:     return FALSE;
14: #endif // !(_WIN32_WINNT >= 0x0500)
15: }
16:
17: STDMETHOD_(void,Deactivate)()
18: {
19:     m_spIObjectContext = NULL;
20: }
```

ANALYSIS Note that I change the implementation of CanBePooled() depending upon the operating system where I will use the object I'm compiling. Because MTS 2.0 (Windows NT 4.0) doesn't support object pooling, I return FALSE (line 13). However, if I'm compiling for Windows 2000, I return TRUE (line 11). There is no reason this object can't be pooled, so I allow for this.

I implemented these methods by hand because they're quite simple to implement, and given the frequency with which they'll be called, defining them inline makes sense. However, I could have easily had the ATL Object Wizard insert the IObjectControl implementations for me when I inserted my object. To do t his, I would check the IObjectControl check box on the MTS tab of the MTS object properties dialog (Figure 6.10).

I also do nothing within the class constructor, and the class destructor isn't even redefined (it uses the C++ default). Instead, I initialize a pointer to the object's associated context object in Activate() (line 4), which I later invalidate in Deactivate() (line 19). MTS will execute these methods when my object is called into action and later released, so I know the initialization and release of the context object will be handled properly.

Note As I mentioned earlier in the section "Coding for MTS," don't perform any initialization or cleanup actions in the ATL class's constructor or destructor when coding for MTS. Initializing or destroying things in the constructor or destructor will preclude the object from being properly initialized when pooled.

After the IObjectControl is implemented, I turn to implementing the basic object functionality.

SetComplete() and SetAbort()

I invoke the ATL Add Method wizard from the ClassView tab of the Workspace window so I can add a method to IMTSDemo. The object is fairly simple-minded. It creates an instance of the Shared Property Manager and places a provided string value in a property group. It then reads the string back from the property group and returns it in an [out] BSTR parameter. I add the TestTx() method with these parameters:

[in] BSTR bstrInString, [out] BSTR * pbstrOutString

I complete the implementation with the code you see in Listing 21.3 (from MyFifteenthATLObj.cpp).

LISTING 21.3 CMyFifteenthATLObj's TestTx() Method

```
 1: STDMETHODIMP CMyFifteenthATLObj::TestTx(BSTR bstrInString,
 2: ➥BSTR *pbstrOutString)
 3: {
 4:     HRESULT hr = S_OK;
 5:     try {
 6:         // Check their pointer
 7:         CHECKPTR(pbstrOutString)
 8:
 9:         // Check for context object
10:         if ( m_spIObjectContext.p == NULL ) throw E_NOTX;
11:
12:         // Presume the transaction will fail
13:         m_spIObjectContext->SetAbort();
14:
15:         // Create the Shared Property Group Manager
16:         CComPtr<ISharedPropertyGroupManager> spISPGM;
17:         hr =
18: ➥m_spIObjectContext->CreateInstance(CLSID_SharedPropertyGroupManager,
19:                                   IID_ISharedPropertyGroupManager,
20:                                   (LPVOID*)&spISPGM);
21:         if ( FAILED(hr) ) throw hr;
22:
```

21

continues

LISTING 21.3   continued

```
23:        // Get the Shared Property Group
24:        CComPtr<ISharedPropertyGroup> spISPG;
25:        CComBSTR bstrSPGName(_T("TxDemoGroup"));
26:        long lIsoMode = LockSetGet;
27:        long lRelMode = Process;
28:        VARIANT_BOOL bExists = VARIANT_FALSE;
29:        hr = spISPGM->CreatePropertyGroup(bstrSPGName,
30:                                          &lIsoMode,
31:                                          &lRelMode,
32:                                          &bExists,
33:                                          &spISPG);
34:        if ( FAILED(hr) ) throw hr;
35:
36:        // Create a shared property
37:        CComPtr<ISharedProperty> spISP;
38:        hr = spISPG->CreatePropertyByPosition(0,&bExists,&spISP);
39:        if ( FAILED(hr) ) throw hr;
40:
41:        // Create a variant and assign it the incoming BSTR
42:        CComVariant varIn(bstrInString);
43:
44:        // Put the BSTR into the shared property
45:        hr = spISP->put_Value(varIn);
46:        if ( FAILED(hr) ) throw hr;
47:
48:        // Create an empty BSTR variant
49:        CComVariant varOut;
50:        varOut.ChangeType(VT_BSTR);
51:
52:        // Retrieve the BSTR shared property
53:        hr = spISP->get_Value(&varOut);
54:        if ( FAILED(hr) ) throw hr;
55:
56:        // Extract the BSTR and pass back
57:        CComBSTR bstrOut;
58:        bstrOut.Attach(varOut.bstrVal);
59:        *pbstrOutString = bstrOut.Copy();
60:
61:        // Complete the transaction
62:        m_spIObjectContext->SetComplete();
63:    } // try
64:    catch(HRESULT hrErr) {
65:        // MTS or pointer error
66:        hr = hrErr;
67:
68:        // Fail the transaction
69:        if ( m_spIObjectContext.p != NULL ) {
70:            m_spIObjectContext->SetAbort();
71:        } // if
```

```
72:     } // catch
73:     catch(...) {
74:         // Some other error
75:         hr = E_UNEXPECTED;
76:
77:         // Fail the transaction
78:         if ( m_spIObjectContext.p != NULL ) {
79:             m_spIObjectContext->SetAbort();
80:         } // if
81:     } // catch
82:
83:     return hr;
84: }
```

This method uses a custom HRESULT, which I defined in the object's IDL file:

```
// Custom HRESULTs
cpp_quote("// Custom HRESULTs")
cpp_quote("#define E_NOTX MAKE_HRESULT(SEVERITY_ERROR,FACILITY_ITF,
➦(unsigned long)0x01);")
```

This is thrown if I determine there is no context object (that means you can't use this object outside of MTS):

```
if ( m_spIObjectContext.p == NULL ) throw E_NOTX;
```

I next assume the transaction will fail by calling IObjectContext::SetAbort():

```
m_spIObjectContext->SetAbort();
```

If for some reason the object fails (power outage, exception, and so forth), the transaction won't inadvertently commit potentially inconsistent results. With the preliminaries out of the way, I can get down to business.

This object creates an instance of the Shared Property Manager, although at this point you would normally implement your own (more realistic) business logic. The process begins by creating the Shared Property Group Manager, as shown in Listing 21.4.

LISTING 21.4   Instantiating the Shared Property Group Manager

```
1: // Create the Shared Property Group Manager
2: CComPtr<ISharedPropertyGroupManager> spISPGM;
3: hr =
4: m_spIObjectContext->CreateInstance(CLSID_SharedPropertyGroupManager,
5:                                    IID_ISharedPropertyGroupManager,
6:                                    (LPVOID*)&spISPGM);
7: if ( FAILED(hr) ) throw hr;
```

21

ANALYSIS The Shared Property Group Manager object (line 2) is used to create new shared property groups or to obtain access to existing groups. As I mentioned previously, it is a resource dispenser that you use to share state among multiple objects within a given transactional process. Because of the concurrency, scalability, and state issues I've mentioned along the way, you can't use global variables in a distributed, transactional environment. You instead store such information in shared property groups. They protect your data by implementing locks and semaphores, thus preventing lost updates and properties left in unpredictable states. My goal for using a shared property group here is to enlist a resource dispenser from a transaction to demonstrate that my object actually participated in a transaction.

My use of the word *enlist* in the previous paragraph wasn't accidental. When you process transactions, you'll likely need resources, such as databases, ODBC connections, and possibly other custom resources. If your object is working within a transaction, it obtains resources by enlistment. At times, the enlistment is automatic, such as when you use a database. As your object tries to open the ODBC connection, assuming you're using ODBC, you enlist the ODBC connection resource dispenser. After you obtain the open ODBC connection and begin to use the database, you enlist the database resource manager. These two resources are enlisted automatically by MTS on your behalf. That also means they participate in your transaction and can vote to abort the transaction if there is a failure on their part.

Other resources, though, must be enlisted manually, as I've done with the SPM. I didn't just instantiate the SPM using `CoCreateInstance()`, as I would a normal COM object. Instead, I requested an instance of the SPM through the context object using `IObjectContext::CreateInstance()` (line 4). If you want to access objects from a transaction that don't participate in the transaction, use `CoCreateInstance()`. However, if you want to instantiate transactional objects from within a given transaction, create them through the context object.

In any case, I now have the Shared Property Group Manager active and can create a new property group, as shown in Listing 21.5.

LISTING 21.5   Instantiating a Shared Property Group

```
1: // Get the Shared Property Group
2: CComPtr<ISharedPropertyGroup> spISPG;
3: CComBSTR bstrSPGName(_T("TxDemoGroup"));
4: long lIsoMode = LockSetGet;
5: long lRelMode = Process;
6: VARIANT_BOOL bExists = VARIANT_FALSE;
7: hr = spISPGM->CreatePropertyGroup(bstrSPGName,
```

```
 8:                                    &lIsoMode,
 9:                                    &lRelMode,
10:                                    &bExists,
11:                                    &spISPG);
12: if ( FAILED(hr) ) throw hr;
```

ANALYSIS   I create the group using a name, TxDemoGroup, which can be used by other (concurrent) transactional objects that want access to the same property group (line 3). In this case, I know that no group currently exists, so I create one. If you know the group name and that the group already exists, you use the `ISharedPropertyGroupManager::get_Group()` method. Alternatively, you can enumerate the known groups using the `get__NewEnum()` method (two underscores).

With the new property group in hand, I create a shared property:

```
// Create a shared property
CComPtr<ISharedProperty> spISP;
hr = spISPG->CreatePropertyByPosition(0,&bExists,&spISP);
if ( FAILED(hr) ) throw hr;
```

You can create properties by position or by name. After you create a property using either method, however, you must always use the related methods to pull the property information back out. That is, if you created a named property, you can't later retrieve it by position. Positional properties are more efficient.

At this time, I have a shared property group in which I've created a shared property. This new shared property is available for storing any variant data I desire, although it begins life as an integer variant. This will change automatically as I add variant data that differs in type, as I'm about to do with a BSTR variant:

```
// Create a variant and assign it the incoming BSTR
CComVariant varIn(bstrInString);

// Put the BSTR into the shared property
hr = spISP->put_Value(varIn);
if ( FAILED(hr) ) throw hr;
```

The string passed to my object is now stored in the shared property. Although other objects can now access the string, I'm going to turn right around and extract the string to return to the client:

```
// Create an empty BSTR variant
CComVariant varOut;
varOut.ChangeType(VT_BSTR);
```

21

```
// Retrieve the BSTR shared property
hr = spISP->get_Value(&varOut);
if ( FAILED(hr) ) throw hr;
```

Here, I create a new variant and change it from VT_EMPTY to VT_BSTR. I then pass the variant to the shared property interface and pull the BSTR from storage. The BSTR is now copied into my variant, so I need to extract it from there to return to the client:

```
// Extract the BSTR and pass back
CComBSTR bstrOut;
bstrOut.Attach(varOut.bstrVal);
*pbstrOutString = bstrOut.Copy();
```

CComBSTR will manage the BSTR destruction for me, after a copy is passed back to the client (who must destroy that copy). If all this happens without error, I'm satisfied that the transaction is complete. I then tell MTS I'm happy with the current system state and will vote to allow the transaction to commit (after this method returns):

```
// Complete the transaction
m_spIObjectContext->SetComplete();
```

Only after I call SetComplete() will the transaction commit, at least as far as this object is concerned. Other enlisted resources can still abort the transaction.

Although I will still need to register this object with MTS, I'll defer that discussion until after I briefly describe the client application's development.

The Client Application

To test the transaction object, I create an MFC dialog-based test application that requested a string from the user and had a static text control to display the results (you can see the application in action in Figure 21.10). The only notable difference between using this transactional object and any other object you've seen throughout the book is that the object is created, used, and destroyed within the scope of a single button's handler. Previous test clients all created the object in OnInitDialog() and held the reference to the object for the duration of the client application's execution.

Because this object is transactional, holding an object reference for more than a single transaction makes little sense (at least to me). Doing so is not incorrect. As it happens, though, the context wrapper will either destroy the object itself after the method call ends, or it will stuff the object into the object pool. In either case, the client is holding a pointer to the context wrapper object, which remains valid between transactions. The next time the client application calls the transactional object, it will be dealing with (most likely) a different transactional object—even if the client held a reference to the same context wrapper. I prefer to release the wrapper object and keep things clean.

The code I used to create the transactional object is shown in Listing 21.6. As you can see, there isn't any special consideration regarding the transactional nature of the object. I simply create it, use it, and destroy it, just as I would any other COM object.

LISTING 21.6   CDay21ClientDlg's `OnDoTx()` Method

```
 1: void CDay21ClientDlg::OnDoTX()
 2: {
 3:     // See if there is a string to hand to MTS
 4:     UpdateData(TRUE);
 5:     if ( m_strMTSText.IsEmpty() ) {
 6:         // No string!
 7:         AfxMessageBox(IDS_E_NOSTRING,MB_OK | MB_ICONERROR);
 8:         return;
 9:     } // if
10:
11:     // MTS COM object
12:     CComPtr<IMTSDemo> spIMTSDemo;
13:
14:     // Open the transactional object
15:     HRESULT hr = spIMTSDemo.CoCreateInstance(CLSID_TYATLObj15,
16:                                              NULL,
17:                                              CLSCTX_SERVER);
18:     if ( FAILED(hr) ) {
19:         // Couldn't create the object...
20:         AfxMessageBox(IDS_E_NOCREATE,MB_OK | MB_ICONERROR);
21:         m_strResult.Empty();
22:     } // if
23:     else {
24:         // Call method
25:         CComBSTR bstrIn(m_strMTSText), bstrOut;
26:         hr = spIMTSDemo->TestTx(bstrIn,&bstrOut);
27:         if ( FAILED(hr) ) {
28:             // Couldn't create the object...
29:             AfxMessageBox(IDS_E_NOCREATE,MB_OK | MB_ICONERROR);
30:             m_strResult.Empty();
31:         } // if
32:         else {
33:             // Display resulting string
34:             m_strResult = bstrOut.m_str;
35:         } // else
36:     } // else
37:
38:     // Update the control
39:     UpdateData(FALSE);
40: }
```

21

ANALYSIS After checking for an input string (lines 5 through 9), I create an instance of the transactional object (line 15). I create a BSTR representation of the user's string (line 25) and pass it to the transactional object (line 26). If everything works as it should, the string is returned, and I display it for visual comparison (lines 34 and 39). The interesting thing to note here is that I create and use this (transactional) object the same as than any other (nontransactional) COM object.

So how does the transactional object become transactional if the client does nothing special to create it within MTS? Clearly, the object itself didn't make a call to join a transaction, although it did link with MTS libraries. I didn't modify the object's registration script, so if the client tries to invoke the object at this point, the object is created outside of MTS (which precludes any transactional activity). What step is missing?

The MTS Explorer and Package Creation

The missing link is registration of the object with MTS by creating a package through the MTS Explorer (or the Component Services Explorer, if you're using Windows 2000). Let's see how this is done.

To fire up the MTS Explorer under Windows NT 4.0, select it from the Start menu by selecting Programs, Windows NT 4.0 Option Pack, Microsoft Transaction Server, Transaction Server Explorer. If you're using Windows 2000, bring up the Component Services Explorer by selecting Administrative Tools from the Control Panel. I'll only work with the Windows NT 4.0 Explorer for this discussion. The Windows 2000 Explorer is very similar, although it uses different icons and has a slightly different visual tree representation.

After you select the MTS Explorer menu item, the management console should activate and present you with its basic user interface, as you saw in Figure 21.2. I expanded the tree control to show you the packages currently installed on my computer, which are the default packages you get when you install MTS. The steps I'll take you through will add a new package to this list.

The first step is to invoke the Package Wizard by right clicking the expanded Packages Installed node under My Computer. This brings up a context menu, from which you select New, Package. After you select this menu item, you see the initial wizard dialog that I show in Figure 21.3.

FIGURE 21.3

The MTS Explorer Package Wizard (initial) dialog.

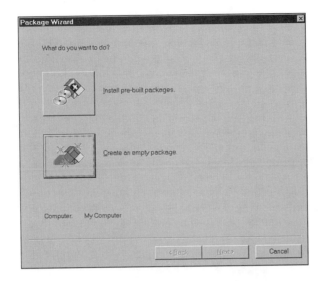

In this case, because you need to create a new package to house the new transactional object, click the *Create an Empty Package* button to view the second wizard page that you see in Figure 21.4

FIGURE 21.4

The MTS Explorer Package Wizard Create Empty Package dialog.

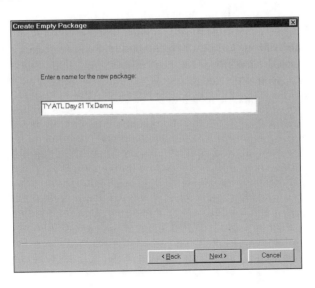

This wizard dialog enables you to name the new package. Enter the name you see in Figure 21.4 and click the *Next* button.

This brings up the wizard's *Set Package Identity* dialog shown in Figure 21.5. Here you establish which user can execute the package. I elect to use the interactive user, but you can specify an individual if you wish. I then click Next.

21

FIGURE 21.5

The MTS Explorer Package Wizard Set Package Identity dialog.

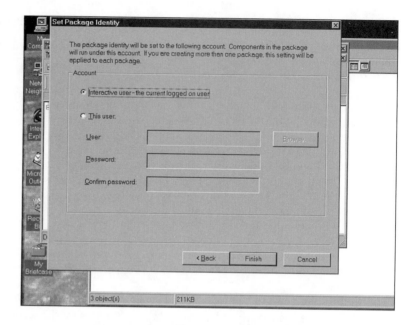

At this point, the wizard creates the new package and inserts it into the Installed Packages node under My Computer in the MTS Explorer. I now have a package, but it has no objects. To add objects, I expand my new package's node and select the Components node underneath. Because there are no components, the right-hand MTS Explorer pane is blank. However, I use this pane to add my transactional object. I simply bring up a copy of Windows Explorer, find the transactional object (Day21Server.dll), then drag and drop its file icon into the component pane. After I do, MTS Explorer appears as you see Figure 21.6.

FIGURE 21.6

The MTS Explorer with the new package and transactional object inserted.

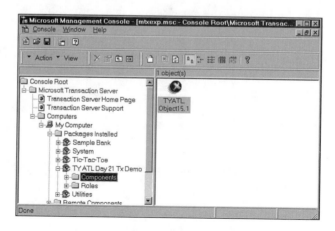

The package is now complete, although real world packages almost certainly include more objects. You add them in the same way as I added the first object. It's now time to customize the package a bit. I need to establish some specific settings for the object itself and then change some properties of the entire package.

Starting with the object, I right-click the object's icon in the right-hand Components pane, as you see in Figure 21.7. This brings up the *Properties* property sheet. I select the *Transaction* page that you see in Figure 21.8.

FIGURE 21.7

The MTS Explorer transactional object context menu.

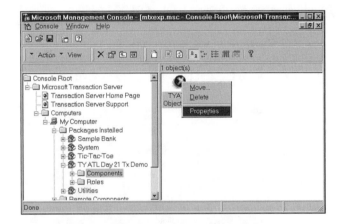

FIGURE 21.8

The MTS Explorer transactional object Properties Transactions property page.

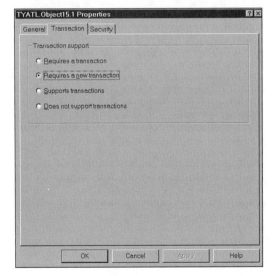

21

Here I tell MTS that the object is transactional in nature. Also, by selecting the Requires a New Transaction radio button, I tell MTS to create a brand new transaction each time the object is invoked. I then click OK and turn my attention to the package as a whole.

There are two types of MTS packages, *Server* and *Library*. Server packages are executed in a dedicated server process, primarily to protect other server processes from damage if this particular package has a problem. Library packages, on the other hand, run in the caller's process.

The default package type is Server, but because I want a Library package (I'm not requiring the additional protection), I access the package's properties and change the setting. To activate the package's Properties property sheet, I right-click the package's node within MTS Explorer and select the Properties menu item. After the property sheet is activated, I select the Activation tab, as you see in Figure 21.9.

FIGURE 21.9

The MTS Explorer package Properties dialog's Activation property page.

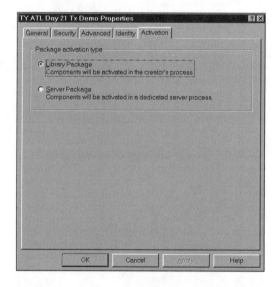

Here I change the package style. I first click the Library Package radio button and then OK to apply the change and dismiss the Properties dialog.

The package is now complete, and my object is known to MTS. At this time I run my test client application, the results of which are shown in Figure 21.10. If there is an error, I would see an error message here.

FIGURE 21.10

The transactional object's test client application user interface.

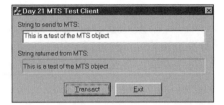

At this point I now have a fully functional MTS transactional object. There is one more thing you should know, however, and it's important. If you later change the source code for the object and recompile, Visual Studio will reregister the object. This will wipe out certain Registry changes that the MTS Explorer made when the object was inserted into the MTS package. Although this isn't a problem, you can't use the object from MTS until you refresh the MTS Registry settings.

One way to do this is to run the MTS Explorer again and expand the tree control until you find the package that contains the object in question. Expand the package's node to reveal the Components node. If you right-click the Components node (in the left-hand MTX Explorer pane) and bring up the associated context menu, you'll find a Refresh menu item available. Just click that menu item, and MTS will refresh the Registry settings for all components contained within the package.

If the menu doesn't have a Refresh menu item, click the Components node with the left mouse button to select it. Then try right-clicking again. You should now see the Refresh menu item.

MTS and COM+

Before I end today's lesson and the book as a whole, I want to mention COM+ and Windows 2000. By the time you read this, Windows 2000 will have moved from a release candidate (I have RC2) to a released operating system. After that happens, the very nature of COM changes. In this book, I discussed what will, undoubtedly, be known as the traditional COM approach. That is, you create COM objects with a given threading model and ship them to clients for their use. COM+ changes things a bit.

Your basic developmental approach will change little—you'll write code and ship it. But the environment your COM objects will find themselves within will be very different from that find of the older Windows operating systems.

COM+ is effectively a marriage between MTS, COM, and the operating system—not for transaction processing, but for the ORB capabilities MTS provides and the concept of the context object and object pooling. MTS greatly simplifies both the security aspects and the distribution aspects of using remote COM objects. MTS also paved the way for quick

21

object activation, via object pooling and the context object. COM+ will reuse these technologies, as well as add a few twists of its own. One way to illustrate COM+ is shown in Figure 21.11.

FIGURE **21.11**

COM+, MTS, and COM/DCOM relationship in Windows 2000.

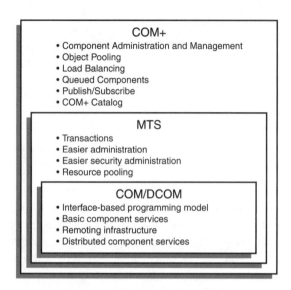

COM+
- Component Administration and Management
- Object Pooling
- Load Balancing
- Queued Components
- Publish/Subscribe
- COM+ Catalog

MTS
- Transactions
- Easier administration
- Easier security administration
- Resource pooling

COM/DCOM
- Interface-based programming model
- Basic component services
- Remoting infrastructure
- Distributed component services

Although I haven't the space to fully discuss COM+, there are two technologies COM+ will provide that are of particular interest, and one that, sadly, didn't make it to the final release.

New COM+ Event Model

COM+ brings a new event model, and although all that you learned on Day 17, "ATL and Connection Points: Supporting COM's Event Model," can still be used, you have a new alternative event model known as *Publish and Subscribe*.

The problems with connection points are many, although I didn't present them as a flawed architectural mechanism in Day 17. Actually, for simple control events, they work just fine. However, when you distribute connection points, you begin to run into trouble. Enumerating the connection point container, for example, is problematic. Furthermore, if you have a complex system, you have no (built-in) mechanism to multiplex or prioritize events. Also, there is no support for automatic object activation upon receipt of an event. The COM object must be up and running and have called `IConnectionPoint::Advise()` to receive events. There are other problems with the basic connection point architecture, but I'm sure you get my point.

The COM+ event model follows a different approach. An object that wishes to fire an event under COM+ will now publish the event to an intermediate object called the *event class*. The event class, in turn, submits the event to any number of subscribers, any of which might need activation to handle the event (remote or not). The event class manages the list of known subscribers, and mechanisms in place within COM+ make you known as either a publisher or a subscriber. This architecture is far more scalable and flexible than mere connection points.

New COM+ Queued Components

COM, as it is used today, couples the temporal relationship between creation of an object and its use. That is, you create a COM object, use its interface methods (synchronously), and then release the object. Any information transferred between the COM object and its client is via [out] parameters.

Distributed systems, however, offer an alternative mechanism through messages and message queues. Instead of immediately creating a COM object, an application can create an object for later use and place it in a queue. When the object is removed from the queue, it can begin processing and return any information through a queue or as a publish/subscribe event (which can awaken the originator if action is required). In this case, the temporal coupling between object creation and use is broken, increasing scalability and server availability.

COM+ offers such queued components through the use of *Microsoft Message Queue* (*MSMQ*). COM+, when asked to create a queued component, will first create a proxy object known as the *recorder*. As the client makes interface calls to the recorder, the recorder serializes the calls and places them as messages into MSMQ. After the client commits (yes, *commits*) the interface calls, COM+ will later retrieve the messages from the queue and create a *player* object and the actual COM object for which the messages were intended. The COM object then deals with the player as if the player is the original client application and responds to the player's method calls accordingly. Errors and data can be passed back to the true client as queued messages or events, as I mentioned earlier.

COM+ In-Memory Database

One truly useful feature that is dropped from the initial release of COM+ is the *In-Memory Database* (*IMDB*). As you know, transaction processing is stateless. Any information that must persist between transactions (method calls) must be stored with a durable resource. With COM and MTS, durable resources usually mean external databases. But databases involve connections and overhead, which eats away at the scalability of your system. For example, there are only so many ODBC connections available.

21

But imagine taking that same database and placing it in memory so you can access it in the same way you accessed the Shared Property Manager in the *Day21Server* sample. Now persisting state is much more scalable, especially if the state information isn't long-term. An example of this is a Web user's session information, which might span many transactions, but which is relevant only as long as the user remains active with the Web server.

Sadly, as I was writing this section, I found this feature was dropped from COM+! (A list server that I subscribe to notified me via email.) Although this is a sad loss for COM+, I hope the IMDB will eventually be released in a Windows 2000 Service Pack. It's simply too useful to drop.

With this brief discussion of Windows 2000 and COM+ completed, it's time to wrap up this last summary and close the book.

Summary

Today, you examined some of the basic concepts behind transactional processing in general, and specifically, those behind MTS. I mentioned that a transaction is an all-or-nothing proposition. If any single transaction participant votes to abort the transaction, the entire transaction is aborted.

I talked about the properties associated with transaction processing, such as atomicity, consistency, isolation, and durability. I also mentioned the transactional two-phase commit process in which the transactional environment tells the participants to prepare to commit and then to actually commit the change. Finally, I discussed some of the issues involved with distributed transactions.

I went on to describe some of the major components in MTS itself. For example, I described the context and context wrapper objects that sandwich the actual COM object, and I explained why these additional objects are necessary. I discussed the MTS surrogate, the MTS Executive, the Distributed Transaction Coordinator, the MTS Explorer, and MTS packages, and their activities.

MTS provides the transactional environment, but there must be a suite of objects that participate in the transaction. I described resource managers and resource dispensers, and I discussed the Shared Property Manager, specifically. I finally described how the IContextObject transaction methods can be used from your transactional objects to properly vote on the outcome of the transaction when your object's method finishes.

I covered the benefits of using MTS, especially from an object perspective. I told you MTS acts as an Object Resource Broker that coordinates the distribution and security management aspects of remote objects. I briefly mentioned that you can use the MTS Explorer to administer the security and distribution aspects of your MTS packages without having to recompile your objects to change settings.

I next moved from the theoretical to the practical and described how you create a transactional object. I started by telling you to design your objects to be stateless, which will increase scalability and reduce the chance the system can be left in an inconsistent state. I also mentioned MTS now controls your object's lifetime because it can elect to pool your object for later reuse. This implies you can't do anything in your ATL C++ class constructor or destructor. Instead, you should implement IObjectControl, and when MTS activates and deactivates your object, you perform your initialization and cleanup.

I went on to create a transactional object. I started with the ATL AppWizard, where I selected an in-process server and MTS support. I then added MTX.H to my object's header file and added IObjectControl (from MTX.H) to my object's base class list. Because I required the Shared Property Manager, I also included MTXSPM.H. After I completed the transactional object, I created an MFC dialog-based application to test the object.

Before I could execute the object transactionally, however, I had to register the object with MTS by including it in a package. To do that I invoked the MTS Explorer, created a new package, added the object I just created, and set some properties for both the object and the package. For the object properties, I elected to force MTS to create a new transaction each time the object executes. Regarding the package, I decided to make it run as a library package rather than a server package.

Finally, I ended the lesson with a brief introduction to COM+ in Windows 2000, which integrates COM, MTS, and the operating system to form a new and different COM runtime environment. I then briefly described two new features COM+ brings to the table, the publish and subscribe event model and queued objects.

To close the book with a few words, I would leave you with this thought: ATL is a very powerful tool that will dramatically increase your productivity. It is also very versatile, as I'm sure you've noticed as you implemented the MTS components, ActiveX dialog boxes, and all manner of simple COM objects just within the pages of this book. I've been able to provide you with the briefest of introductions to ATL. I certainly enjoyed presenting the material, and my hope is you found it interesting and useful. Don't stop here, though. Much more information is out there. Practice building COM objects, even if, eventually, you discard the objects themselves. Take with you the experience and knowledge you've gained. I wish you the best of luck!

21

Q&A

Q Can I run MTS from Windows 95 or 98, or do I have to use Windows NT or 2000?

A Although you can run MTS from Windows 95 and 98, it isn't of tremendous benefit to do so. Those operating systems aren't very robust with respect to security and process isolation, and to be honest, some resource managers won't run on those platforms either (SQL Server comes to mind here). Your best bet is to run MTS from Windows NT today and Windows 2000 tomorrow. Then, you see the full capability and benefit MTS can provide your enterprise.

Q Working within the MTS environment appears to be a new programming paradigm. Is it?

A Yes, it is. Although your COM objects are not required to actually deal with transactions (although they could), MTS allows for easy object distribution and administration through its ORB personality. To gain these benefits, you have to code things in a slightly different way. The major difference is that you now must create stateless objects. If your object wants to maintain some form of state between method calls, it must write the intermediate state to a durable resource, such as a database or queue. This is a definite paradigm shift for many developers. If you realize your object will be completely destroyed between method invocations, you'll probably code your object accordingly (and correctly)!

Q What sorts of things should I avoid doing if I want to program to a stateless model?

A You'll certainly avoid global variables of any kind, but also you will not code any class attributes that might be used to store information from one method call to another (or one transaction to another). Everything must be contained within a single interface method call. Although I didn't do it for my simple example, you would be wise to use critical sections when tromping through sensitive code. Your object can be used in a free-threaded scenario, even if you didn't mark it to do that when you created it.

Q It appears as if some of the authority I had as the objects developer has been lifted and given to an administrator capable of running the MTS Explorer. That is, they can rearrange package contents using my object at will. Is this true?

A It does not *appear*—it's a fact. Although it might seem you've lost the authority to dictate how your object is used, what's really happened is that others have gained the freedom to reuse your objects in new and different ways that you might not have foreseen. I believe that if you look at it this way, everyone wins.

Workshop

The Workshop is designed to help you anticipate possible questions, review what you've learned, and get you thinking about how to put your knowledge into practice. The answers to the quiz are in Appendix A, "Answers."

Quiz

1. What are the four basic properties of a transaction?
2. What is a two-phase commit?
3. How many transaction participants does it take to commit a transaction? To abort one?
4. What purpose does the context wrapper object serve? The context object?
5. What purpose does the DTC serve?
6. How do you administer MTS?
7. What is the basic difference between a resource manager and a resource dispenser?
8. When would you use the SPM?
9. What are the two major benefits of using COM through MTS?
10. What is a stateless object and why does MTS expect your objects to be stateless?
11. How is your object's lifetime controlled within the MTS environment?
12. Why should you not perform initialization or cleanup actions in your C++ class's constructor or destructor?
13. What methods does IObjectControl specify and what is each method's purpose?
14. Why should you call IObjectContext::SetAbort() early in your transactional object's processing?
15. What is the Shared Property Manager and why is it useful?
16. What are some of the new features COM+ provides?

Exercises

1. Examine the online documentation for additional information regarding the use of and programming for MTS.
2. Force the Day21Server object to recompile, or simply reregister the object, and then run the Day21Client test client application. What response do you see? Then, refresh the object using the MTS Explorer and try again. What happens? Where did the initial error originate?

21

WEEK 3

In Review

In this, the final week, you saw how ATL can be used to implement other advanced Microsoft technologies. The week began with a discussion of general Windows control programming issues, such as animation techniques, the Windows GDI, control notification messages, and window subclassing. Then you took that information and learned how to create true ActiveX controls using ATL. In order for your controls to notify their container, you implemented connection points. Because some ActiveX controls are licensed, you moved on to study ATL and COM's class factory interfaces, especially IClassFactory2 and licensing. To better create distributed objects, you looked at DCOM and issues surrounding the design of remote objects. So that your objects can more easily access stored information, you looked at OLE DB and how to implement OLE DB templates from within your ATL project. Finally, you looked at transactional processing concepts and some practical issues you face when writing components designed to work within MTS. This led to a brief introduction to COM+ and the way it incorporates MTS and transactional processing into the COM runtime infrastructure.

Day 15 discussed several concepts that are important to control programmers, including painting issues, the Windows GDI, animation techniques, and parent-window notification of interesting events. I also introduced revised MFC classes to assist you with GDI programming.

19

Day 16 took the information from the previous day and wrapped the custom control you created within ATL's ActiveX control framework. Here you looked at some of the base interfaces that support ActiveX and at some of the changes you must make to your control code to have it work from within an ActiveX setting (especially painting). You also used a new container to test your control, the Visual Studio ActiveX Test Container.

Day 17 looked at connection points and their implementation. Connection points are the means by which ActiveX controls notify their containers of custom events. You saw how to add connection points, as well as how Visual Studio can create a connection-point proxy automatically through a wizard.

Although, on the surface, Day 18 might have appeared out of order with respect to advanced ATL programming, in reality I placed this information here to address licensed ActiveX controls. The day covered general ATL class factory implementations, to including the IClassFactory, IClassFactory2, the autothreaded object, and the singleton object. Because licensing is growing in importance, I also addressed implementing licensing from within ATL and provided two practical solutions (one in the text and one as an example's solution).

Day 19 addressed a favorite topic of mine—distributing objects and DCOM, in particular. You saw that although Distributed COM is just COM over the network, you should consider the design constraints that the network imposes when you create objects intended for distributed use. You saw how to use DCOMCnfg.exe to configure DCOM on a given system, and you learned what changes should be made to client applications that intend to use distributed objects.

Day20 talked about OLE DB and the OLE DB support that Visual Studio (through the ATL Object Wizard and ATL) provides for you. You saw how to access a DBMS from Visual Studio and automatically create OLE DB templates to work with the DBMS from within your COM object. You also saw how to create multiple and different SQL calls by modifying the basic wizard-generated code.

Finally, Day 21 introduced MTS and general transactional processing concepts. It also discussed practical programming issues you face when working from within a transactional environment. You saw how the context wrapper object intercepts your actual COM object to fool your client application into working with the wrapper instead of your object. MTS (instead of the client application) can now control your object's lifetime. This supports object pooling. You also saw how you work with the context object to commit or abort transactions. You implemented IObjectControl, which MTS uses to activate and deactivate your object. Along the way, you used the Shared Property Manager, a built-in resource dispenser, to store intermediate transaction results. Finally, you saw some of the features and benefits of using COM+ in Windows 2000 and how COM+ differs from the traditional COM runtime environment you've been using throughout the book.

Appendix A

Answers

Answers for Day 1

Quiz

1. Why rely so heavily on the wizards to generate code?

   Why not? They generate a ton of code automatically—that's code *you* didn't have to write. A few mouse clicks and edit controls later, you have a very heavy-duty starting point. Use the tools at hand, and you can dramatically improve your productivity.

2. Can you add additional objects to the ATL project (as you added the first)?

   You sure can. Simply use the same procedure. Note, however, that the objects will be unrelated except for the fact they're compiled into the same physical DLL.

3. I see you can add methods and properties to your object—what are properties?

   I'll begin to cover this question in depth in Day 3, but C++ methods and properties are the same—they're simply methods. However, to some clients, such as Visual Basic, they appear as attribute values. Visual Basic hides the fact that the property is, in reality, a method from the Visual Basic programmer. It provides the Visual Basic programmer a more simplified view of the object.

Exercise Solutions for Day 1

1. Modify the ATL source code to return a different message.

   See *Day1ServerEx12* for a solution to this and the second exercise. Note that I created a new interface (and project), and the integer value I return is the length of the message.

2. Add a second method to the IHelloWorld interface to return an integer value instead of a string.

   See *Day1ServerEx12* for a solution to this and the first exercise.

3. Create a Visual Basic test client for your ATL COM object.

   See *Day1ClientVB* for a solution to this exercise. The major Visual Basic code is shown here:

```
Private Sub Form_Load()
    'Declare object (late binding)
    Dim strMsg As String
    Dim iLen As Long
    Dim objEx12 As TYATLObj1Ex12
    Set objEx12 = New TYATLObj1Ex12

    'Fill text controls
    objEx12.SayHello strMsg
    txtMsg = strMsg
    objEx12.MsgLength iLen
    txtMsgLen = iLen
End Sub
```

In this case, there are two text controls—one for the message and one for the length. Normally, in Visual Basic you would see this arrangement:

```
strMsg = objEx12.SayHello
```

However, this must be specified in the Interface Definition Language (IDL) file by using the retval method attribute (which you'll read more about in Day 8, "ATL Object Methods: Adding Functionality to Your Interface"). I didn't specify the attribute because I haven't yet introduced it.

This exercise is a bit challenging because the object uses a custom interface instead of a dual interface (which you'll study starting tomorrow). To be able to use the object, you'll need to add it to the Visual Basic project references, which you access from Project, References. From the checkable list, select *Day1ServerEx12 1.0 Type Library*. You should then be able to create instances of the object.

Answers for Day 2

Quiz Answers

1. How do you instantiate a COM object?

   You can use one of two methods: use `CoCreateInstance()` or `CoGetClassObject()`. Note that if you use `CoGetClassObject()`, you pass in the CLSID of the object in question but use `IID_IClassFactory` (or `IID_IClassFactory2`) as the reference IID. Given a pointer to the object's class factory interface, you call its `CreateInstance()` method to actually instantiate copies of your COM object.

2. Why are interface definitions immutable after they are publicly published?

   If you change an interface, after it is published, client applications will likely break either due to the syntactic or semantic differences you introduced.

3. What is a dual interface?

   It is an interface that inherits from `IDispatch` rather than from `IUnknown` directly.

4. How do you invoke the COM runtime?

   You call `CoInitialize()` or `CoInitializeEx()`.

5. What interface does the COM runtime call to create an instance of a COM object?

   That depends upon whether the COM object is licensed or not. If it's unlicensed, COM calls `IClassFactory`. If it's licensed, COM calls `IClassFactory2`.

6. What is the essential difference between the STA and the MTA?

   When using the STA, COM provides multithreaded data synchronization through the use of a Windows message queue. Your COM object is free to implement non-thread—safe code. This is not the case with the MTA, for which you must implement thread-safe code using classic multithreaded data synchronization techniques.

7. How is data transmitted from address space to address space?

   Through a proxy/stub DLL that implements marshaling.

8. What macros do you use to test for the success or failure of a COM method call?

   `SUCCEEDED()` and `FAILED()`.

Exercise Solutions for Day 2

1. Review the code you created for Day 1 to see if you can find references to CLSIDs, IIDs, and ProgIDs. Do you see any reference to `IUnknown`?

You'll find these items referenced in the server's .RGS and .IDL source files. They're also spelled out further in the *<project>*_i.c and *<project>*.h files (post-compilation) that you'll use with your Visual C++ client application. Regarding IUnknown, you should find this line in the project's .IDL file:

```
interface IHelloWorld : IUnknown
```

This tells COM your interface is based upon IUnknown in much the same way the list of base classes is used when defining a C++ (derived) class. IDL is *not* C++, although it is very C++-like. You'll read more about IDL starting tomorrow, "The COM Interface: COM's Foundation."

2. After you have compiled and registered the object from Day 1, open the Registry Editor (regedit.exe) and search for the value 58EC7AED, which represents the first eight characters of the object's CLSID. Is the information you find similar to what you see in Figure 2.3?

It should be very like what you see in Figure 2.3, because I used Day 1's object as the model for the figure. You will likely see only a single difference, that being the directory in which the COM object's file resides.

Answers for Day 3

Quiz Answers

1. How do you create a GUID?

The honest truth is you do not, the COM runtime does. You shouldn't create GUIDs by hand because you won't be guaranteed the GUID is unique. That said, you would call the COM API CoCreateGUID().

2. How would you create a GUID as text to be pasted into your source code?

Use GuidGen to create the GUID and copy it to the clipboard. Then simply paste the resulting text into your source file.

3. What two server source files should be included in your client's source code? Do you have to have both?

You'll need the .h and "_i.c" file created by MIDL. You only require the .h file if you used the features of the MIDL_INTERFACE() macro.

4. What is a vtable?

A vtable is a table of pointers to an interface's methods.

5. Can a single COM server (DLL or EXE) support more than one COM object?

Sure, not a problem.

6. Can several COM objects support the same interface (IID)?

   A trick question. Not only can they, they must. All COM interfaces must support IUnknown. But if you look to the general case, the answer is also yes. You're always free to reimplement other interfaces if you desire, even if third-party COM objects implement them.

7. How do you cast COM pointers?

   You don't cast pointers in the C++ sense, even if you know the interfaces are related via inheritance. This is dangerous for two reasons. First, you might be dealing with a proxy instead of the true object, in which case the cast would be meaningless. Second, you could goof up marshaling. Instead you use QueryInterface() to request a new interface pointer to a specific interface in the inheritance chain.

8. What is the general layout of an IDL file?

   The standard COM IDL information is imported, objects are defined, and (finally) the type library is defined. If you added structures and enumerations yourself, you should place them prior to their first use, typically between the COM IDL importation and the first defined object.

9. What are the required attributes for a COM object in IDL?

   object and uuid(). object tells MIDL to create a COM interface versus a DCE RPC interface, and uuid() provides the COM object with its GUID. Although the helpstring() and pointer_default() attributes aren't required, it is a good idea to specify them also.

10. How are a COM object's properties and methods different?

    In the truest sense, they're not different. Both are really interface methods. Some programming environments enable the programmer to perceive them differently, however. Those environments hide the fact that the properties of an object are really accessor and mutator methods and display the properties as if they were simple object variables.

11. Do you have to implement a type library?

    No, but realize that, if you don't, you can't use Universal Marshaling and your object won't be automation-compatible. If you want to eliminate the type library, simply delete the code from the IDL file and the type library won't be created. You can, if you want, create the type library but ship it as a separate file. In either case, you'll need to remove the reference to the type library from your resource (.rc) file. To do that, click View, Resource Includes in Visual Studio and remove the type library's compile-time directive.

Exercise Solutions for Day 3

1. MIDL creates files in addition to the .h and the _i.c files I mentioned. Can you spot which ones?

   If you have a project named *<project>*, here is the complete list of files MIDL will create if used normally:

   - *<project>*.h
   - *<project>*_i.c
   - *<project>*.tlb
   - *<project>*_p.c
   - DLLDATA.C

   MIDL can create other files given certain command line inputs, but you'll not use these often when working with ATL. The ATL AppWizard establishes the appropriate MIDL settings for you when it creates your project.

   Note that for you to get the _p.c and DLLDATA.C files, you must have at least one interface defined in your .IDL file. (You'll need these files to create the proxy/stub DLL, or when merging the proxy/stub DLL into your in-process server.)

2. Read the MSDN article "Designing COM Interfaces" by Charlie Kindel (included with the MSDN CDs or online at

   `http://msdn.microsoft.com/library/techart/msdn_design.htm`).

   Charlie provides a nice set of guidelines, with explanation, for designing and implementing your own COM interfaces. He breaks the article into four parts: general rules; elements of good design; good design patterns; and a tutorial using MIDL. It's an excellent next step in learning to design effective COM interfaces now that you understand the basics.

Answers for Day 4

Quiz Answers

1. Why are templates beneficial?

   They capture algorithms for reuse without regard to the actual specialization parameter. You can reuse the template for a variety of specialization classes instead of defining a specific class or function to handle a particular data type.

2. What is a specialization parameter?

   It's simply the class the compiler will use to create an instance of the template. You decide what classes the template will use when you write your code, and these become the specializations when the compiler expands the template.

3. Can a generic class be derived from other classes?

   From other templates? Yes, and yes.

4. Do the template and the implementation have to be in the same source file?

   Not at all. Though this is common, you can separate them, especially if you're concerned about recompilation. If the header file is used by many source files, even a minor change can force a major recompilation, which can be time consuming.

5. Can a generic function reside in a class?

   In a generic class? Absolutely, in both cases.

Exercise Solutions for Day 4

1. Modify the generic stack to become a generic queue.

   You'll find the solution to this exercise in the QueueTemplate project.

2. Modify the generic stack to use a linked list rather than an array.

   You'll find the solution to this exercise in the ListTemplate project. Note, an advantage to this implementation is your stack size is limited to available memory and not to an arbitrary array size.

Answers for Day 5

Quiz Answers

1. What is the overriding goal of ATL?

   To produce the fastest, tightest code possible. If you need more support, such as the C runtime library, you'll have to take actions to introduce it into your project.

2. What ATL classes and templates are used to implement IUnknown?

   CComObjectRoot, CComOjbectRootEx<>, and CComObject<>. Note also the definitions for the IUnknown methods are contained in the END_COM_MAP() macro.

3. How does C++ multiple inheritance (versus nested classes) better support the COM object model?

   This presumes a comparison with the alternative, which is a nested class implementation. Multiple inheritance provides for an *is-a* relationship rather than a *has-a* relationship, which is the model a nested interface class would provide. After all, an IDispatch interface *is-a* IUnknown interface—it isn't a *has-a* relationship.

4. What is the purpose of the ATL COM map and object maps?

   They provide an efficient mechanism for ATL to search for implemented COM objects and their interfaces.

5. How does ATL support self-registration and why must I use it judiciously?

   ATL uses the ATL `Registrar`, which is a COM object itself. The `Registrar` accepts registry scripts which provide the data that will be written to or removed from the Registry. You must be careful when writing scripts by hand, because the `Registrar` will happily remove keys that would be better left intact, such as `HKEY_CLASSES_ROOT\CLSID`, which is where all of the (legacy) COM registration information resides.

Exercise Solutions for Day 5

1. Open atlbase.h and atlcom.h and peruse the source code you find there. (You'll find most of the mysterious macros ATL uses defined in these two files.)

   This is just an exercise designed to acquaint you with the ATL source files. At times, you'll find it helpful to look at ATL's source code to see how a given feature is implemented. You need not look at anything specific here, but realize you can look at the source code, and that the source code is the best authority regarding how things work and what is available for your use.

2. Modify the registry script from Day 1 to write a value to `HKEY_LOCAL_MACHINE\Software\TYATL`. Does this value disappear when you deregister the COM server? (You can de-register the COM server by running regsvr32.exe from the command line with the `switch /u`.) Please heed my warnings!

   See *Day5ServerEx3* for a solution to this exercise.

Answers for Day 6

Quiz Answers

1. In general, what are the three most interesting files the wizard creates for you, at least at this time?

   STDAFX.H, *<project>*.IDL, and *<project>*.CPP, where *<project>* is the project name you used when you created the project using the ATL AppWizard. STDAFX.H defines your ATL module and brings in the basic ATL header files. *<project>*.IDL is fairly minimal, but it does define your project's type library. *<project>*.CPP contains the code required to implement the basic server functionality whatever the additional COM object supports.

2. To which server type are the three additional ATL AppWizard options directed (integrating the proxy/stub code, MFC support, and MTS support)?

   Strictly in-process (DLL) servers.

3. What ATL object supports server locking and registration, and what is its C++ base class?

   The ATL Module, supported by the `CComModule` base class.

4. What mechanism does the ATL local server use to manage its lifetime?

   It creates a separate thread that monitors an event. When all outstanding COM objects have been released, the event is signaled and the monitor thread issues a `WM_QUIT` message to the server's message pump, thus terminating the server's process.

5. What is one benefit of using a service-based server instead of a local server?

   The service-based server remains active in memory, even if there are no outstanding COM objects. When a request for a supported COM object is issued, the server is resident in memory and ready to create the object. This saves the time required to create a new process and execute the local server's initialization code.

6. How do you access the ATL Object Wizard?

   You can access it via the Visual Studio Insert menu or the Workspace window by right-clicking on the project (root) tree node. You should see a menu item in the resulting context menu that enables you to add a new ATL object.

7. If I provide information in the Names property page I later regret, can I correct the values?

   Sure, but it'll involve a little work on your part. If you're just unhappy with the filenames you're using, you can simply rename the files and reinsert them into your project and recompile. It's more often the case that you wish you'd selected a different CLSID, IID, or ProgID value. For the most part, you'll find this information in the IDL and RGS files. However, references to any and all these values can be sprinkled throughout your source files. I'd recommend you perform a text search through all your source files for the offending value and change every occurrence you find. You should find several for each of these settings. Remember, though, that the wizard merely inserts code tailored to your specifications. Code is code, and everything can be changed. The trick is to find everything, everywhere, and make the changes you require.

8. If I accidentally add an in-process only object to my local server code, will that adversely affect my project?

No, your code should compile and execute just fine, with the following exception: You won't be able to instantiate DLL-only objects if they're implemented in an EXE-based server.

9. I just what to create a common COM object. Which object should I insert into my ATL project?

Use the Simple object from the Objects list. The other objects and controls you can insert all implement additional interfaces required to perform specific tasks. If you don't need to manage such tasks, don't implement the additional interfaces.

10. Are the objects I see as provided by the Object Wizard all I can insert?

Sorry, this is a trick question! The answer is Yes, if you stick with what Microsoft has provided you with Visual Studio. However, the answer I would provide is No, because you can write your own additions to the Object Wizard, just as you can create your own AppWizards. If you do this, you can insert your own objects as easily as you insert those coming from Microsoft.

Exercise Solutions for Day 6

1. Modify the local server source code to bring up a user interface. Do you still require the monitor thread?

You'll find the solution to this exercise in the *Day6ServerEx1* project. You will require the monitor thread if the executable is brought up as a COM server only. You know this if the command line contains the Embedding switch. If you see this command line option, you start the monitor thread. If you don't see this option, you can let the user close the application through the user interface.

2. Create an in-process server and request that the proxy/stub code be incorporated into the server. How do the DLL exported functions differ?

You'll find the solution to this exercise in the *Day6ServerEx2* project. The DLL exported functions now share implementation between the proxy/stub DLL and the actual COM server. You'll notice the addition of the preprocessor value _MERGE_PROXYSTUB. If you define this value, which you must do yourself (and recompile), you'll find the proxy/stub functions merged with the COM DLL functions (DllCanUnloadNow(), DllGetClassObject(), and so on). Detailed instructions are available at the beginning of the *<project>*.cpp file.

3. Create a service-based server and examine the source code the wizard provides. Does it make sense, or is it magic?

This is just an example to get you to look at the server code I skipped during the day. The code will definitely look like gibberish if you've never programmed an NT service! But it isn't magic. I'll leave it to you to create the service-based project and examine the code.

4. Add a second, or even a third object to your server. What files change?

Aside from the addition of the new files that support the new objects, your project file (.DSP) changes to add the new files to the compilation, the .IDL file changes to add the new interfaces, and the *<project>*.cpp file changes to add the object to the object map.

5. Create two ATL in-process projects, inserting a simple object into one and an ActiveX (client) control into the other. What differences in the various source files do you see?

With the exception of the actual object implementation files, which will differ significantly, there are very few changes to the supporting project files. The ActiveX object will implement a dual interface, which your simple object might or might not implement (depending upon the settings you choose with the Attributes property page). In this case, the IDL file will differ slightly as the base interface is declared. Other than that, there will be no significant differences.

6. Rummage through the online documentation to see if you can find further descriptive references to the types of ATL objects you can insert using the Object Wizard.

This was just an exercise to acquaint you with some of the online documentation. For this specific exercise, you might refer to *Visual C++ Documentation, Reference, Active Template Library, Articles, Creating an ATL Project* for more information.

Answers for Day 7

Quiz Answers

1. How do I invoke the ATL method wizard?

With your ATL project open for editing, you first activate Visual Studio's Workspace window. Then you must expose the interface to which you will add the method (by expanding the tree control, if necessary). When the interface's tree node is visible, you right-click on the node to bring up a context menu. If you select Add Method from the menu, you will activate the wizard.

2. What source files does the wizard modify?

The project's IDL file, and the interface's implementation files (.CPP and .H). The remaining project files are untouched.

3. What do the [in], [out], and [in, out] attributes do for me?

Actually, it isn't so much what they do for you and I as much as it is what they do for the marshaling process. They're hints to MIDL that allow for certain optimizations. [in] causes the parameter's value to be passed between client and server, with no requirement to pass data back the other way. [out] signifies the data will be returned to the client, but the client must allocate the memory and pass to the method a pointer to this memory. The resulting value is returned to the client in this memory. [in, out] tells MIDL both situations will be in effect for a given parameter. MIDL will make sure the value of the parameter is sent to the server, but the server is free to modify the value and return it in the same chunk of memory.

4. How do I add a new interface based upon an existing one?

By hand. No wizard is available to help with this. First, design the interface using IDL. Remember to create a new IID for the interface and inherit the old interface so you don't have to re-implement that functionality. After the IDL is complete, edit the header file of the former interface and change the inheritance chain to use the new versus the old interface. Add the new interface to the COM map (usually near the beginning of the map for efficiency). Then, add the new method(s) to the C++ class definition. After the header file is complete, add the implementation of the methods to the class's implementation (.CPP) file.

5. With respect to IDL, what is the difference between using the string attribute versus passing in an array of chars and using size_is()?

At some level there is very little difference. In both cases the array is correctly marshaled, assuming you pass in a good value to size_is() that accurately reflects the true size of the array. But size_is() requires an extra parameter to indicate the array size, whereas string is able to correctly marshal string data without the added parameter. Therefore, string is more efficient when dealing with parameters, although the marshaling code will need to examine the string to determine its length.

6. How do COM object methods and properties differ?

In the truest sense, they do not differ at all. Some development environments, however, make the property accessor and mutator methods appear as if the property were an attribute rather than two methods. This is a simplification for that environment's programmer.

7. Why did this day use an ActiveX control to demonstrate properties rather than a simple COM object?

   There are two reasons. First, properties are usually associated with ActiveX controls or scriptable COM objects—traditional COM objects don't require this paradigm because they're not typically used in the same way ActiveX controls are (in more simplistic development environments). Second, I wanted to demonstrate the property in use from within Visual Basic, and that's easiest to do using an ActiveX control because you can load it using the Components dialog (no specific Visual Basic coding knowledge is required).

8. What IDL attributes signify a method as a property accessor or mutator method?

   Property accessor methods use the `propget` method attribute, whereas mutator methods use either `propput` or `propputref`. If the method has neither of these attributes, it won't be treated as a property.

9. How do you create a read-only property?

   You can uncheck the Put Function check box when you create the property using the ATL property wizard, or later, you can simply remove the mutator method from your source code by hand. (Remember to remove it from both the IDL file and the C++ implementation files.)

10. Can a given property be tied to a data source (such as a database)?

    Oh yes. In fact, that's one of the more powerful features of ActiveX properties, in my opinion. I'll cover this in more detail in Day 16, but for now realize you would use the `bindable` attribute, perhaps in combination with the `defaultbind`, `displaybind`, and `requestedit` attributes.

11. What is the ATL property map used for?

    Although I didn't discuss how you use the ATL property map in this day (that's for Day 16), I did mention it's used to persist the property(ies) you implement. The development environment, for example, will persist the property settings you provide when you insert the ActiveX control. Visual C++, by the way, persists the property settings in the .RC file so that when the control is activated at runtime, the property(ies) are then re-established from the client application's resources.

12. Why would I use an enumerated property?

    I would enumerate all the properties available to provide a further value-added service to my control's clients. It also is quite useful to help limit the values a client can apply to the property—you don't have to do because much error checking as COM will do that for you. COM will know what values are appropriate for the given interface property method and will flag values out of tolerance as an error (a failed `HRESULT`).

Exercise Solutions for Day 7

1. Add a method to IAddMethodDemo that halves the incoming value. Is any special error checking necessary?

   See the *Day7ServerEx1* project for a solution to this example. Because you are returning an [out] value, you check the pointer for NULL, but you shouldn't require any special mathematical checking—unless you want to limit the bounds of the incoming value. (Note, you're dividing by two, so you don't need to check the denominator for zero.) I added a new interface, IAddMethodDemo3, to support this method—as well as the method for Exercise 3.

2. Modify the example MFC client application to incorporate the method you created in Exercise 1.

   See the *Day7ClientEx2* project for a solution to this example. This solution incorporates the IAddMethodDemo3 interface for the next exercise.

3. Add a third interface to the object, called IAddMethodDemo3, which has a new method that doubles the incoming value. Should this new interface derive from IAddMethodDemo or IAddMethodDemo2?

   See the *Day7ServerEx1* project for a solution to this example. It should derive from IAddMethodDemo2 to support both IAddMethodDemo2 and IAddMethodDemo.

4. The MFC test application used an earlier version of the ActiveX control (without SomeProperty2). Modify the MFC test application to incorporate the new version and test SomeProperty2. What happens when you try to reload the control using the Components and Controls Gallery? (Hint: you might need to delete some files and other things before you reload the ActiveX control.)

   See *Day7ClientEx4* for a solution to this exercise. To reinsert the same ActiveX control, you must delete the files Visual Studio created previously from both your project and the disk (in this case, delete addpropdemo.cpp and .h). You should also remove the control from your dialog template before reinserting.

   Remember, when running my solution, you still must click the Change button to actually submit the property changes to the control (and have them reflected in the application's user interface). A slightly better design would foist the property value on the control when the application's information changes, but I'll leave that slight modification to you.

5. Add a third property to the ActiveX control and test it using Visual Basic. For extra credit, use an enumeration.

See *Day7ServerEx5* and *Day7VBClientEx5* for a solution to this exercise. I did get a bit fancy and changed the ActiveX control's painting code to reflect the text color and border setting. (I elected to implement the third property as a border setting, which I enumerated in the IDL file.) When you execute the VB client application and change the color or border values, the control reflects the change automatically.

A

Answers for Day 8

Quiz Answers

1. What are the two ATL smart COM interface pointer classes and how do they differ?

   CComPtr and CComQIPtr. The difference is CComQIPtr will assign the member attribute p as a result of a QueryInterface(). If the QueryInterface() fails, the pointer p is set to NULL. If it succeeds, the pointer p references the new interface. CComPtr simply manages the pointer you assign.

2. What is a BSTR and why manage it with CComBSTR?

   A BSTR is a length-prefixed, wide-character string used in COM automation. The CComBSTR class abstracts the BSTR and wraps the BSTR manipulation API for you.

3. What is a variant and why manage it with CComVariant?

   The variant data type was developed to reduce the set of data types that Visual Basic and scripted components would be required to support. The variant is actually a discriminated union that contains all the data types that the automation infrastructure supports. You use CComVariant for the same reason that you would use CComBSTR to manage BSTR data: You can work at a higher level of abstraction, thus increasing your productivity and reducing potential code defects.

4. How are the category and level used to control debug stream message output?

   Which ATL debugging macro uses these? The category and level are used by ATLTRACE2() to control debug stream message flow. The category allows you to select specific types of messages to display, whereas the level enables you to specify the severity of the messages to display. Messages from the wrong category or of lesser importance will not be sent to the debug stream.

5. What is an assertion and why do you use it?

   When you are speaking to another person and you make an assertion, you are stating a fact (presumably a true one!). Debugging assertions are the same—you are stating that the expression passed to the ATLASSERT() macro is TRUE. If your assumption is incorrect, ATL will notify you and allow you to correct your logic. This is useful to correct logical defects well before the code goes to the testing crew.

Exercise Solutions for Day 8

1. Add debugging support to the IHelloWorld interface you developed in Day 1. Where would you most likely place an ATLASSERT() and why?

   I would modify the code to include two debugging entries (shown highlighted):

```
STDMETHODIMP CMyFirstATLObj::SayHello(BSTR *pbstrMessage)
{
    // Check their pointer
    ATLASSERT(pbstrMessage != NULL);
    if ( pbstrMessage == NULL ) {
        // NULL pointer, so return an error code
        return E_POINTER;
    } // if

    // Their return pointer was good, so create a BSTR
    // using their pointer.  We allocate the memory for
    // the string here.  The client application is
    // responsible for freeing the memory.
    ATLTRACE("CMyFirstATLObj: String sent to client\n");
    *pbstrMessage = ::SysAllocString(L"Hello, ATL!");

    return S_OK;
}
```

   I'd place the assertion prior to the pointer check to indicate the pointer the client provided is nonNULL. If you created a string dynamically, you can also place its textual value in the debugging output stream to be reflected in the debugger's window. In this case the string was hard-coded to be "Hello, ATL!", so I didn't bother writing it to the output stream.

Answers for Day 9

Quiz Answers

1. How do I create an MFC application?

   You use the MFC AppWizard, which you invoke using the Visual Studio File menu and selecting New. Make sure the Project tab is active. From there, select the directory into which the project will be created and provide a project name. From there, follow the wizard!

2. Which two MFC classes will your main application classes derive from?

   If you're building a dialog-based application, you'll require classes derived from CWinApp and CDialog.

3. What MFC API function do I use to invoke the COM runtime?

AfxOleInit(). You're also wise to check the return value. If AfxOleInit() returns TRUE, everything is fine and your application can continue processing.

4. How do I add an event handler to my application (a button click, for example)?

Unless you're very familiar with MFC, you should use the ClassWizard. Using the Message Map tab, select the control ID of the control in question, then the event type you'd like to handle (BN_CLICKED, in this case). Click Add Function, name it, then edit the code.

5. How do I add a C++ variable to manage the Windows control information? How is the information transferred?

You should again use the ClassWizard. This time, use the Member Variables tab to select the control ID. With that selected, click Add Variable, then name it and give it a data type. You later transfer data between the variable and the associated Windows control using MFC's DDX, which you invoke using UpdateData(). UpdateData(TRUE) transfers data from the Windows control to your variable, whereas UpdateData(FALSE) transfers data from your variable to the Windows control.

6. What three mechanisms can I use to integrate my COM object into my application?

You can include the MIDL-generated files to define and declare the GUIDs associated with your object, then create pointers based upon those GUIDs. You can also use the Components and Controls Gallery to add an ActiveX control you can place on your dialog. And finally, you can use the Visual C++ built-in COM support using the #import directive.

Exercise Solutions for Day 9

1. Create a Visual Basic test application that mimics the behavior of the MFC applications I've shown you here. Which was easier for you to create? How would you change the Visual Basic code if the object under test did not have a dual interface?

See *Day9VBClientEx1* for a solution to this exercise. If the object does not have a dual interface, you should follow the steps I outlined for Exercise 1.3, which is to add the object's type library to the project's references. You can then Dim an instance of the object, which you bind early using New in the Set.

Answers for Day 10

Quiz Answers

1. What are the three main components (bit fields) of an HRESULT?

   The severity (*severity*), the facility code (*facility*), and the error code (*code*).

2. Which facility code is the only code you can use for custom HRESULT implementation?

   FACILITY_ITF.

3. What C++ keywords facilitate C++ exception handling, and does ATL support this automatically?

   try, catch, and throw.

   No, you must specifically enable C++ exception handling via your project's settings.

4. What data types can be thrown?

   Any valid C++ data type, including a C++ class.

5. What is the sequence of events for completing the rich error object?

   After making sure your interface implements ISupportErrorInfo, you create an instance of ICreateErrorInfo using CreateErrorInfo(). You call the ICreateErrorInfo methods to fill the object's data fields. You then query for IErrorInfo and provide that interface pointer to SetErrorInfo(). You can also use AtlReportError().

Exercise Solutions for Day 10

1. Add a new method to IDemoError that incorporates the forced exception code from *ExceptDemo*, except omit the try/catch blocks to allow the exception to trickle to the client. What happens when the client receives the exception?

   See *Day10ServerEx1* for a solution to this exercise (I reused the code from *Day10Client*, slightly modified to access this object rather than the original *Day10Server* object, so I didn't include that code with this solution—the changes were minor). The situation is most dramatic when you use release-build components (debug-build components will throw you into the debugger). The client application simply dies with a generic abnormal termination error message. Note that my solution forcibly throws the particular exception, but in reality *any* exception would provide the same client application reaction.

2. I fibbed. I am a purist. Modify the `OnVerify()` handler in `CDay10ClientDlg` to implement the full rich error protocol.

   See *Day10ClientEx2* for a solution to this exercise.

Answers for Day 11

Quiz Answers

1. What is a critical section? What is a mutex? How do they differ?

   A critical section is both a concept and a Windows construct. Conceptually, it's a limited code path that only a single thread can access at any one time. Windows implements the critical section with the `CRITICAL_SECTION` data type. The mutex is a kernel object that acts like a critical section. It can be used between processes, however, not just between threads in a single process (as with the critical section).

2. Why is `PulseEvent()` not useful given an auto-reset event object?

   `PulseEvent()` sets and then resets the event. The auto-reset event will reset itself after it is set. However, it is not an error to use `PulseEvent()`.

3. How does a semaphore differ from the other synchronization objects?

   The semaphore indicates the availability of a resource, whereas the other mechanisms simply limit threads from progressing through code.

4. What are the two thread creation functions you can use and which is better?

   `CreateThread()` and `_beginthreadex()`. As for which is better, that depends upon your application. If you're avoiding the C runtime library, use `CreateThread()`. Otherwise, you might as well use `_beginthreadex()`.

5. If in your process you create two additional child threads, how many threads are running in your process?

   Clearly the answer can't be two! The answer is three. There are the two child threads you created, as well as your main process thread.

6. What are some testing techniques you can use to help better test your multithreaded applications?

   Test early and often, insert many assertions, test using both debug and release configurations, and test using a variety of platforms (operating systems and numbers and types of processors).

Exercise Solutions for Chapter 11

1. Modify the CanDemo4 example to set the event whenever a single can is released—instead of when all 12 cans have been released.

   See CanDemo4Ex1 for a solution to this exercise.

Answers for Day 12

Quiz Answers

1. What are the four types of COM process models and how do they differ?

   Single-threaded process (only one STA), apartment-model process (two or more STAs), free-threaded process (the MTA only), and mixed-model process (the MTA and one or more STAs).

2. What requirement does COM impose on a thread that creates an STA and why?

   It must implement a Window message loop to be used to synchronize access to the COM object.

3. Why are single-threaded objects avoided in favor of apartment-threaded objects, which are also single threaded?

   Single-threaded objects always exist in the main process thread's STA, whereas apartment-threaded objects can exist in any STA. Objects instantiated in the main process thread's STA degrade the performance of that thread.

4. When would you select the free-threading model over the both-threading model?

   Generally, you will select the free model over the both model when your COM object creates child threads of its own. The child thread access to the parent COM object is better in the MTA than it is in the STA.

5. How does ATL support your choice of threading model?

   It registers your object appropriately, it uses synchronized base classes if required, and it implements support for the Win32 `CRITICAL_SECTION`.

Exercise Solutions for Day 12

1. Find the *Day12Server*'s proxy/stub DLL (Day12Serverps.dll) and right click on its filename (you should be able to de-register the COM server at the corresponding context menu). Now try the *Day12Client* application again using mixed mode. What happens now?

The client will fail to create either COM object in the MTA because COM can't find the proxy/stub DLL required to marshal the parameter data from the MTA to the main STA (the client).

2. Change `MySeventhATLObj`'s threading model from *Free* to *Both* and recompile. After de-registering the Day12Serverps.dll server (as in the previous example), run the *Day12Client* application. Which object's signature appears when you select a mixed mode environment?

   The client will fail to create the Apartment-threaded COM object in the MTA for the same reason as in the last exercise. You will be able to create the `Both` threaded object, however, with either the STA or the MTA mode selected. COM will actually create the object in the main STA, even though you might have requested the MTA, so no proxy/stub DLL is required. Hence, no error occurs.

Answers for Day 13

Quiz Answers

1. Which ATL window class is best for general-purpose window implementation? For child controls?

   I'd use `CWindowImpl` for general-purpose window containment and `CContainedWindow` for child controls.

2. Why do you normally derive a class from the ATL windowing classes rather than use them directly?

   Because you typically want to add functionality to your window beyond that which ATL provides. Anything specific to your window must be added to a derived class you implement.

3. What is an ATL message map and what ATL class provides for their implementation?

   ATL message maps implement the code necessary to intercept specific Windows messages and provide handlers for the customized behavior. The virtual base class `CMessageMap` defines the basic message mapping capability, although the message mapping macros actually implement it.

4. What are the four types of ATL message maps?

   Main, alternate, chained, and reflected.

5. What is the purpose of window subclassing?

The purpose of subclassing is to tailor the behavior of an existing window by intercepting its Windows messages and reacting to the specific messages necessary to tailor the behavior. This is most commonly done for painting customizations, but this need not be the only reason.

Exercise Solutions for Day 13

1. Add a handler to the ATLWindows2 example to process mouse movement messages (WM_MOUSEMOVE) and print the mouse cursor position in the main window.

   See ATLWindows2Ex1 for a solution to this exercise.

2. Create your own dialog-based ATL application (to get a feel for how it's done).

   Because I've created several, I'll leave this exercise to you. Use any of the example applications I've provided as guides.

3. The alternate message map of the CMainDlg class (in the ATLWindows3 example) processes the subclassed messages for the child control. Can you suggest a more object-oriented approach? If so, how would you implement it?

   In this case, the parent is handling the message for the child, which breaks encapsulation when the parent interferes with the normal text pasting operation (the text is internal data to the edit control). A better approach is to create a new C++ class to manage (and subclass) the edit control. You'll read more about how to do this in Day 15.

Answers for Day 14

Quiz Answers

1. What is a dual interface?

   A dual interface is the conglomeration of a dispinterface and a custom interface. It is implemented by the custom interface deriving from IDispatch.

2. What methods does IDispatch support and what are their respective purposes?

   GetTypeInfoCount() confirms the presence of type information. If the information is present, GetTypeInfo() retrieves the ITypeInfo pointer the client will use to peruse the type library. GetIDsOfNames() associates a DISPID with the method's textual (string) representation. The DISPID is eventually passed to Invoke(), which actually executes the method on behalf of the client.

3. What is the purpose of the variant?

It dictates the standard data types that scripting languages can depend upon the COM infrastructure to correctly marshal on their behalf.

4. What is the purpose of the safe array?

The safe array is a type safe (variant) array structure that is used by scripting languages to pass array information between objects. It allows for dynamic array growth, although the dimensions themselves are permanently fixed after the array is created.

Exercise Solutions for Day 14

1. Modify the *SADemo* example to directly access the variant data contained within the safe array. (Hint: wrap the access with two safe array API calls and keep track of your indices.)

This is not a simple exercise, but it is illuminating. See SADemoEx1 for a solution to this exercise.

Answers for Day 15

Quiz Answers

1. Can you name three GDI API calls used to obtain a device context?

`BeginPaint()` coupled with `PAINTSTRUCT`, `GetDC()`, and `CreateDC()`. You can also use `CreateCompatibleDC()`.

2. Why should you always destroy GDI resources when you're through with them?

There is limited resource memory available on Windows 95 and 98. If you consume all the resource memory, the system can become unstable.

3. What causes animation flickering and how do you reduce its effects? It the technique you suggest 100% effective?

The animation will flicker as you update it while viewing it. You can reduce the flicker effects by double buffering your rendering. You draw to an off-screen bitmap, and then you copy it to the screen in one move. This is most effective for small areas. As your bitmap grows larger, it takes more time to perform the `BitBlt()`, and you might see some minor flickering. However, the effect will greatly reduce the flickering that appears when the screen is updated directly.

4. What are the two standard control notification protocols and, in general, how do they differ?

   The control issues either a `WM_COMMAND` or a `WM_NOTIFY` message. `WM_COMMAND` packs everything into a single message and its parameters, whereas the `WM_NOTIFY` incorporates the concept of an event structure into which you can place almost any pertinent data.

5. Why would the LED control create its double buffer in the `WM_SIZE` handler instead of when the control is created (`WM_CREATE`)?

   This allows for dynamic double buffer creation. If the control is resized, you have to destroy the original double buffer anyway (the bitmap is the incorrect size). Creating the double buffer when the control is created (as in `WM_CREATE`) creates a static double buffer you would otherwise have to resize when handling `WM_SIZE` anyway.

Exercise Solutions for Day 15

1. Change the behavior of the bubbles in *BasicGDI* (go sideways, or down).

   See BasicGDIEx1 for a solution to this exercise (I made them go down...).

2. Add painting code to display the Thermometer control in a disabled state (as when `IsWindowEnabled()` returns `FALSE`).

   See ThermoBarEx2 for a solution to this exercise.

3. Add an event to the `LED` control, such as when the focus shifts to and away from the control.

   See BasicLEDEx3 for a solution to this exercise. Note to see the event in the event window you should tab to the `LED` control instead of clicking it with the mouse.

Answers for Day 16

Quiz Answers

1. What specification currently governs ActiveX?

   The *OCX 96 Specification*.

2. What are the three types of ActiveX properties and how do they differ?

   Custom, stock, and ambient. Custom properties are those you implement that are specific to your control. Stock properties are properties common to many ActiveX controls ATL implements for you. Ambient properties are properties the container

A

provides at runtime to enable your control to better integrate into the container's environment.

3. What is the difference between an invisible control versus a windowless control?

Invisible controls don't provide a user interface, whereas windowless controls rely upon their parent container for windowing activities, such as keyboard input, mouse capture, and painting. A benefit of a windowless control is you can paint to nonrectangular regions.

4. Why are there component categories? IObjectSafety?

Component categories enable containers to select the COM objects they want to use, especially when they are presenting the user with a choice of object. IObjectSafety allows the container to query for and set the object's safety level when dealing with untrusted users and data.

5. What is the main ATL class that implements ActiveX control functionality?

CComControl.

6. What is initialized stream-based persistence?

Stream persistence enables you to store control information (properties) to a stream (as in compound document storages and streams). Initialized stream-based persistence allows your control be automatically initialized from persisted data contained within the stream.

7. What is the ATL property map used for?

ATL combines its implementations of the ActiveX persistence interfaces and the property map to identify which control properties you want persisted.

8. How do you add property sheets to you control?

You first add the basic code using the ATL Object Wizard, and then you wire up the properties on the property page with those contained within the control.

9. What is the ATL_DRAWINFO structure used for?

It provides you with drawing information you'll require to paint your control, such as the device context, the drawing mode (normal, icon, or thumbnail view), whether your control is zoomed or not (draw a subset of the entire control), and whether your control is being rendered to a metafile (don't double buffer your drawing).

Exercise Solutions for Day 16

1. Change the *State* property from color-based to state-based (such as LED_NORMAL, LED_WARNING, and LED_ALERT for green, yellow, and red, respectively). Then add three other custom properties for the color associated with each state. HINT: Use OleTranslateColor() to convert the color you receive to a COLORREF value you can use. Also, there is a stock color property page, CLSID_StockColorPage, you can use instead of defining your own (use it with the PROP_PAGE() property map macro).

   This is a fairly meaty exercise! I implemented this in the sample application for Day 17. See *Day17Server* for my solution to this exercise.

Answers for Day 17

Quiz Answers

1. What is a connection point?

   A connection point is an object that provides for two-way communication between COM objects. A connection point container stores, for later retrieval, the connection points associated with client sink interfaces (there might be more than one).

2. What IConnectionPoint methods does the client use to activate and deactivate a particular sink?

   To activate a connection point, the client passes its sink interface pointer to the server's connection point interface using IConnectionPoint::Advise(). To break off communications, the client calls the Unadvise() method.

3. What functionality does IPropertyNotifySink provide for?

   It allows the container to deny changes to properties and receive notifications when the properties do change.

4. What IDL property attributes allow for requesting property changes and binding?

   You specify the property should request change permission using the IDL attribute requestedit. If the interface is bindable, you notify the container when the change is made so the container can process any changes on its end.

Exercise Solutions for Day 17

1. Add an event to the LED control, such as when the focus shifts to and away from the control.

See *Day17ServerEx1* for a solution to this exercise. Note to see the focus events, the control must not be created windowless, so be sure to uncheck the Allow Windowless Activation from Container Options.

Answers for Day 18

Quiz Answers

1. What is a class factory? A class object?

   A class factory creates instances of a given COM object. *Class object* is just another name for *class factory*.

2. What is the purpose of the additional methods IClassFactory2 exposes?

   To provide for global and runtime object licensing.

3. What are the ATL class factory implementation classes and which class factory do they implement?

   CComClassFactory (IClassFactory), CComClassFactory2 (IClassFactory2), CComClassFactoryAutoThread (IClassFactory), and CComClassFactorySingleton (IClassFactory).

4. How do you use a class factory other than the default? What is the default class factory?

   You insert the DECLARE_CLASSFACTORY_XXXX() macro that corresponds to the class factory you wish to use. The default is to use CComClassFactory (macro DECLARE_CLASSFACTORY(), although the macro is not required).

5. How do you use a larger thread pool when using CComClassFactoryAutoThread?

   You provide a thread allocation class to CComAutoThreadModule other than CComSimpleThreadAllocator.

6. What methods must you provide when using CComClassFactory2 and what is each method's purpose?

   VerifyLicenseKey(), GetLicenseKey(), and IsLicenseValid().
   VerifyLicenseKey() compares the provided key with the object's stored key and returns the result of that comparison. GetLicenseKey() returns the runtime license key, after the validity of the calling application has been established (it must be made from a fully licensed machine and pass IsLicenseValid()). IsLicenseValid() implements the global licensing algorithm and is used to determine if the object is being instantiated on a fully licensed machine.

7. How is licensing handled remotely over the Internet?

You create a .LPK file on a fully licensed machine and place the file on your Web server. Then, you instantiate the License Manager for each Web page you display. The License Manager retrieves the .LPK file and provides the runtime licensing functions for you.

Exercise Solutions for Day 18

1. Implement a standard local server object much like the ones I created, only base it on IClassFactory. Then create a client application much like those I provide and see what process and thread IDs pop up when you execute four instances of the application.

See *Day18ServerEx1* and *Day18ClientEx1* for a solution to this exercise.

2. Add licensing to the LED ActiveX control from the previous day. For extra credit, create a .LPK file for the control.

See *Day18ServerEx2* for a solution to this exercise.

3. Implement a Registry-based licensing scheme in place of the file-based scheme I presented.

This is also implemented in *Day18ServerEx2* (the licensing is implemented in LicenseImpl2.h). I included a Registry script file, LicenseEx2.reg, that you can use to install the license. Note, you probably don't want to implement the license in such an obvious place using such an obvious key name and value. Also, you should consider encrypting the license when stored in the Registry, if you store it as textual information.

Answers for Day 19

Quiz Answers

1. Do DCOM objects differ from traditional COM objects?

Not necessarily, though you can optimize things for the network rather than for normal COM use, such as when using enumeration interfaces.

2. Can you launch a DCOM object remotely?

Yes, if you're using Windows NT or 2000. For Windows 95 and 98, the server must already be active.

3. What are some issues to consider when designing distributed objects?

The issues include how you set up the interface methods to package and transmit data, the effects of latency upon the overall system you're designing, what happens to your system if the network and/or server go down, and possible security risks.

4. What is an AppID as related to DCOM?

It is a GUID used as a Registry key under which is stored information regarding the distributed aspects of the object.

5. What is DCOMCnfg.exe used for?

DCOMCnfg.exe is an application program that makes configuring an individual COM object (application) or an entire system much easier than if you had to edit the Registry by hand. Through DCOMCnfg.exe you can manage both the authorization and authentication aspects of using the object remotely.

6. How does DCOM know the network connection between client and COM object has been broken?

The client will know the connection is broken the next time it makes an interface method call. The object will be unavailable, so the proxy will return an error HRESULT. On the other side of the network, the COM object will know the connection has been broken when it tries to ping the client and repeatedly fails.

Exercise Solutions for Day 19

1. Devise an experiment that will show the latency associated with the network when using a remote COM object.

See *Day19ClientEx1* for a solution to this exercise. There are several approaches you might take. I elected to wrap the execution of the object's method with QueryPerformanceCounter() calls, which give me the total milliseconds elapsed from just prior to just after the method call. *Day19ClientEx1* gives you the option of running locally or remotely.

If you run my solution to this exercise, you can probably tell I had fun writing the application. If you like MFC programming, as well as ATL programming, there are a few good MFC nuggets in this application as well (but that's a topic for another book).

Answers for Day 20

Quiz Answers

1. What is OLE DB?

   OLE DB is Microsoft's COM-based DBMS access technology, although it is flexible enough to deal with any sort of data source (not just databases).

2. What are OLE DB Services?

   You can think of OLE DB Services as the *glue* that OLE DB provides to marry providers and consumers. The OLE DB Services also lighten your development load by making shared components available to perform commonly implemented provider tasks, such as query processing.

3. What objects will you find in the OLE DB object model?

   Data Source, Sessions, Commands, and Rowsets.

4. How does ATL support OLE DB?

   The obvious answer is ATL provides OLE DB classes and templates to provide a lot of the standard code you'll need to work with OLE DB. But I also like the Visual Studio support for creating instances of the ATL OLE DB classes themselves. The ATL Object Wizard does a terrific job of helping create the source code by reading your data source and creating customized code.

5. Do you have to access your data source using ODBC and a System DSN?

   No! I used ODBC because it is commonly installed on end-user systems, and the System DSN is a simple way to configure ODBC to make my database widely available on the given system. But as you see from Figure 20.1, ODBC underlies only part of OLE DB. Some data sources implement OLE DB interfaces directly, such as SQL Server. To use these, you'll likely need to download the latest version of MDAC, the Microsoft Data Access Components platform SDK, which you'll find at http://www.microsoft.com/data/download.htm.

Exercise Solutions for Day 20

1. Add a new SQL command to look for all parts with zero in stock. Then set some of the parts counts to zero and test using the basic client application, modified to look for all parts or just empty parts bins. (Hint: add a checkbox to the main dialog, then look at its state to determine which search criteria you should use.)

See *Day20ServerEx1* and *Day20ClientEx1* for a solution to this exercise. There are a number of ways you could tackle this situation, the simplest of which is to just filter the available parts number in the CDay20Client::FillListControl() method. If you're displaying empty parts bins, you add records to the list control only if the available parts count is greater than (or equal to zero) depending upon some user input (I suggested a check box, but any mechanism would work).

I took a different approach to play with OLE DB a bit. I added another SQL query to CParts. To facilitate the user's query selection, I created the IPartsDbDemo2 interface and added methods to set the mode (show all parts or just empty bins). When the user makes a selection (empty or all) on the user interface, he sets the mode, which closes the current database connection and opens a new one with the appropriate query (but only if he changed the mode!).

Answers for Day 21

Quiz Answers

1. What are the four basic properties of a transaction?

   ACID. Atomicity (all or nothing), consistency (data in good shape before and after), isolation (transactions protected from concurrent transactions), and durability (resource managers can roll back system state no matter the situation).

2. What is a two-phase commit?

   The transactional environment first notifies the transaction participants they should prepare to commit, then, finally, tells them to actually commit the transacted change.

3. How many transaction participants does it take to commit a transaction? To abort one?

   All participants must agree to commit the transaction. If a single participant votes to abort, the entire transaction aborts.

4. What purpose does the context wrapper object serve? The context object?

   The context wrapper object appears as the true COM object to the client application. The context object stores additional metadata regarding the true COM object MTS will require through the life of the transaction (such as security data).

5. What purpose does the DTC serve?

   It enables transactions using differing data resources over potentially remote connections, it implements the transactional protocol (such as the two-phase commit), and it provides for transactional outcome voting (commit/abort).

6. How do you administer MTS?

   Through the MTS explorer, which is a MMC application.

7. What is the basic difference between a resource manager and a resource dispenser?

   Resource managers implement durable resources, whereas resource dispensers implement transient resources only meant to remain consistent for the duration of the transaction.

8. When would you use the SPM?

   Use it when you have state data you want to share among several transaction participant objects.

9. What are the two major benefits of using COM through MTS?

   Package distribution and declarative security.

10. What is a stateless object, and why does MTS expect your objects to be stateless?

    It means you don't store any information within the object between method calls or transactions. MTS mandates stateless objects to increase scalability and to help enforce isolation and consistency.

11. How is your object's lifetime controlled within the MTS environment?

    MTS controls your object's lifetime by wrapping your object in a context wrapper that isolates your object from the client application. In that way, MTS can actually keep your object in memory (pooled) for quicker activation later. MTS then controls your object through `IObjectControl`.

12. Why should you not perform initialization or cleanup actions in your C++ class's constructor or destructor?

    This is related to the answer for Question 2. MTS can pool your object, in which case neither the constructor nor the destructor will execute. The first time your object is activated, the initialization in the constructor will execute, but not in subsequent activations.

13. What methods does `IObjectControl` specify, and what is each method's purpose?

    `Activate()`, `Deactivate()`, and `CanBePooled()`. MTS calls `Activate()` and `Deactivate()` when your object is initially instantiated and released, and each time it is used, thereafter, if it is pooled. These methods are where you place your initialization and cleanup code. MTS calls `CanBePooled()` prior to `Deactivate()` to determine whether your object can, in fact, be shuffled off to an object pool rather than completely destroyed.

14. Why should you call `IObjectContext::SetAbort()` early in your transactional object's processing?

A

This forces the transaction to abort if your object fails to complete its processing, for whatever reason (computer went down, exception, and so forth). This assures you that you'll have another attempt at completing the transaction rather than possibly leaving the system in an inconsistent state.

15. What is the Shared Property Manager, and why is it useful?

The SPM is a resource dispenser MTS provides to allow for inter-object data sharing within a single transaction. It's useful for storing data that other transactional objects require to complete their own transactional processing (if they also are participating in the same transaction as your object).

16. What are some of the new features COM+ provides?

I mentioned the new COM+ event model (publish/subscribe) and queued objects specifically, but other features include those you find on Figure 21.12. These include load balancing, the COM+ catalog (that replaces the current COM object registration mechanism), object pooling, enhanced administration, and object management capabilities.

Exercise Solutions for Day 21

1. Examine the online documentation for additional information regarding the use of and programming for MTS.

There are a number of articles and informative documents related to MTS programming, especially if you subscribe to MSDN (or access MSDN from the Web, msdn.microsoft.com). Here are some examples:

- General MTS information: *Platform SDK*, *COM and ActiveX Object Services*, and *Microsoft Transaction Server 2.0 Service Pack 1* (All subdocuments)
- MTS code samples: *Technical Articles*, *Enterprise Development*, *Banking Samples*, and *HelpDesk*
- Designing for MTS: *Backgrounders*, *Enterprise Computing*, *Building Successful Client/Server Applications*, and *Integrate the Enterprise*

2. Force the *Day21Server* object to recompile, or simply re-register the object, then run the *Day21Client* test client application. What response do you see? Then, refresh the object using the MTS Explorer and try again. What happens? From where did the initial error come?

When you reregister the object, you overwrite the Registry information the MTS Explorer placed there on behalf of your object. If you run the client application, it will activate the object, but this line of code I inserted will force an error:

```
if ( m_pIObjectContext.p == NULL ) throw E_NOTX;
```

The reason for this is the object is running, but it has no context object because the `ObjectControl::Activate()` method was not executed (by MTS as it activated your object). Because `Activate()` is not called, `m_pIObjectContext.p` is `NULL`, and the custom error `HRESULT` is thrown.

APPENDIX **B**

Proxies, Stubs, and Their Compilation and Maintenance

Unless you're using Universal Marshaling, or you've aggregated the Free Marshaler, you'll need to compile and ship not only your COM object but also its proxy/stub DLL. The basic code for the proxy/stub DLL is generated for you automatically by the MIDL compiler when it compiles your IDL file.

When you create a new ATL project using the ATL AppWizard, you should find these files, in addition to the files you usually modify to implement your object's functionality, in your project's directory:

- *<project>*ps.def
- *<project>*ps.mk

The first file, *<project>*ps.def serves as the typical DLL exported, method-definitions file you need when compiling a DLL. The second file, *<project>*ps.mk, is the proxy/ stub's makefile, to be used with Visual Studio's *nmake* command line compiler.

As you add objects and interfaces, Visual Studio will also create and maintain a third file, DLLDATA.C. This file contains settings and lists used to tailor the final proxy/stub DLL.

If you need the proxy/stub DLL, it can be a maintenance nightmare to keep everything properly lined up. A code change here or there might require a new proxy/stub DLL. How do you know? I find the best alternative is letting Visual Studio make that decision for me. Typically, I change the project settings to include the proxy/stub DLL compila-tion. This is actually very easy to do. Merely access the Project Setting dialog from the Project, Settings menu item, and complete the information shown in Figure B.1, by performing the following steps:

Note This project information came from the sample COM server in Day 19, "Distributed ATL: DCOM Around the Net."

1. Change the selected project build type to All Configurations.
2. In the Post-build Description edit control, type in `Building proxy/stub DLL....`
3. There are two lines you need to enter into the Post-build Commands list control. The first compiles the proxy/stub DLL:

   ```
   nmake -f "<project>.mk"
   ```

   The second command will be executed if the first succeeds. The second command registers the DLL on your development system:

   ```
   regsvr32 /c /s "<project>.dll"
   ```

   This command executes the *RegSvr32* utility to register the DLL. It uses the special Visual Studio command line option /c, as well as the silent mode, /s.
4. Click OK, save the project file, and recompile.

Now any time you make changes that might force a proxy/stub DLL rebuild, the compi-lation will take place automatically.

FIGURE B.1

The Visual Studio Project Setting dialog, Post-build tab.

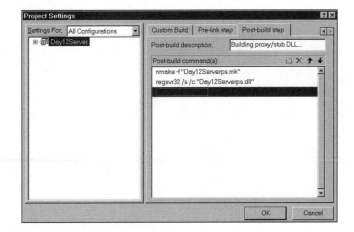

B

APPENDIX C

ATL Quick Reference

I've arranged the majority of the (documented) ATL templates (and classes) into the following ten groups:

- ATL Windowing Support (see Figure C.1)
- ATL Class Factory Support (see Figure C.2)
- ATL Module Support (see Figure C.3)
- ATL Control Support (see Figure C.4)
- ATL Persistence and Property Page Support (see Figure C.5)
- ATL Connection Point Support (see Figure C.6)
- ATL General Interface Support (see Figure C.7)
- ATL Helper Classes (see Figure C.8)
- ATL Database and Data Transfer Support (see Figure C.9)
- ATL MMC Support (see Figure C.10)

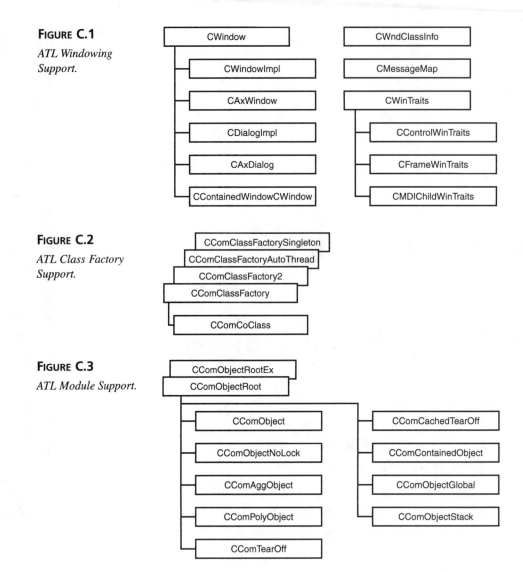

FIGURE C.1

ATL Windowing Support.

FIGURE C.2

ATL Class Factory Support.

FIGURE C.3

ATL Module Support.

FIGURE C.4
ATL Control Support.

FIGURE C.5
ATL Persistence and Property Page Support.

FIGURE C.6
ATL Connection Point Support.

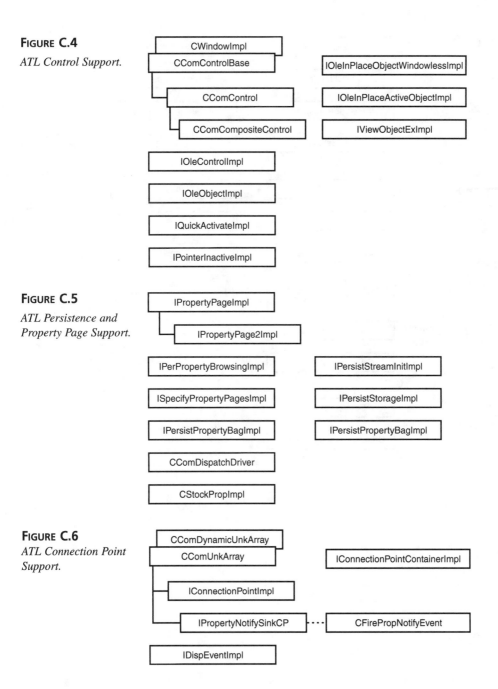

C

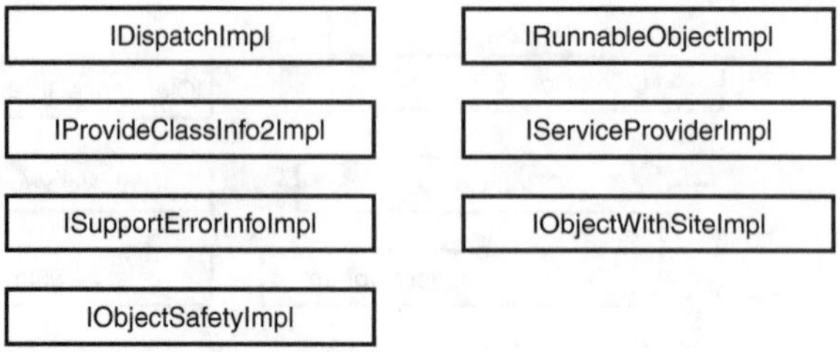

FIGURE C.7

ATL General Interface Support.

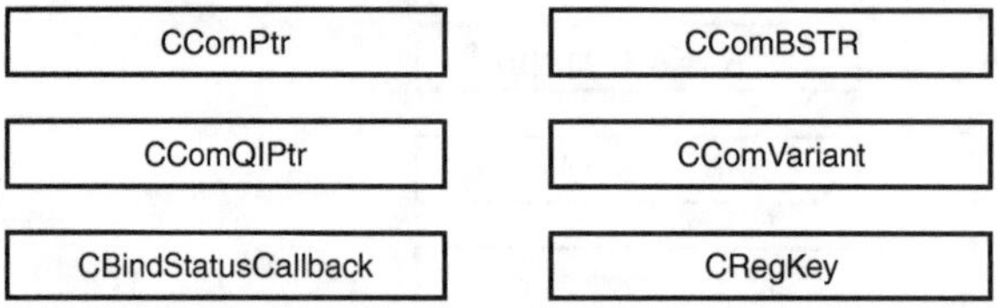

IDispatchImpl

IRunnableObjectImpl

IProvideClassInfo2Impl

IServiceProviderImpl

ISupportErrorInfoImpl

IObjectWithSiteImpl

IObjectSafetyImpl

FIGURE C.8

ATL Helper Classes.

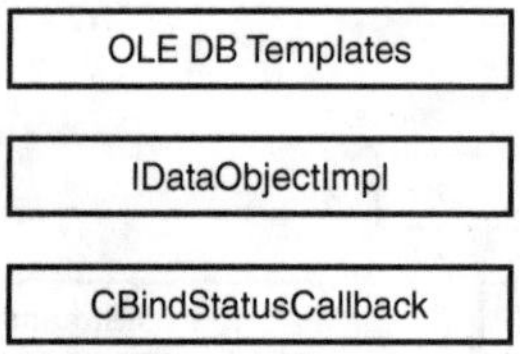

CComPtr

CComBSTR

CComQIPtr

CComVariant

CBindStatusCallback

CRegKey

FIGURE C.9

ATL Database and Data Transfer Support.

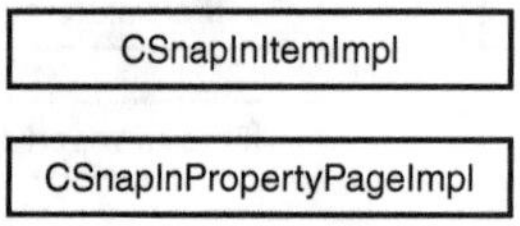

OLE DB Templates

IDataObjectImpl

CBindStatusCallback

FIGURE C.10

ATL MMC Support.

CSnapInItemImpl

CSnapInPropertyPageImpl

APPENDIX D

ATL String Conversion Macros

In parts of the book, I've used the ATL string conversion macros. ATL provides macros to convert from nearly any string type to almost any other string type. They follow this basic pattern:

```
(converted string *) = MACRONAME(original string *)
```

The macro itself is named according to this convention:

```
{from type}2{to type}
```

Given this convention, converting from an OLECHAR (or a BSTR) string to a TCHAR string would require the OLE2T macro:

```
USES_CONVERSION; // only required once per scope
OLECHAR wstrString] = _L"My wide-character string.";
TCHAR* strString = OLE2T(wstrString);
```

The USES_CONVERSION macro defines a private function that performs some of the conversions. It is used to allocate memory on the stack for the conversion, so it should be used within the scope of the conversion itself. You don't need to be concerned about releasing the memory associated with the converted string, because that will be automatically released when the variable goes out of scope.

The conversion macros take their direction from the current compiler settings. That is, if both of the From and To types are the same, no conversion is required (a value is simply returned). Table D.1 shows how the T and OLE types are converted based upon the current (project) compiler settings.

TABLE D.1 Conversion Macro Compiler Type Assignments

Compiler Directive	T Becomes	OLE Becomes
None	ANSI	WIDE
OLE2ANSI	ANSI	ANSI
_UNICODE	WIDE	WIDE
OLE2ANSI and _UNICODE	WIDE	ANSI

You use the macros by selecting the starting type, the ending type, and deciding if the ending type is const (in which case you add a *C* to the macro name, such as A2COLE for converting an ANSI string to a const OLESTR). The compiler directives that are in place will resolve the correct starting and ending types for you. Table D.2 provides you with the complete set of conversion macros. Here A indicates ANSI (or a standard char*-based string), T indicates a TCHAR-based string, W is a wide-character string, OLE is an OLESTR-based string, and BSTR is self-explanatory.

TABLE D.2 ATL Conversion Macros

Macro	Conversion
A2BSTR	LPSTR to BSTR
OLE2A	LPOLESTR to LPSTR
T2A	LPSTR/LPOLESTR to LPSTR
W2A	LPWSTR to LPSTR
A2COLE	LPSTR to LPCOLESTR
OLE2BSTR	LPOLESTR to BSTR
T2BSTR	LPSTR/LPOLESTR to BSTR
W2BSTR	LPWSTR to BSTR
A2CT	LPSTR to LPCTSTR/LPCOLESTR
OLE2CA	LPOLESTR to LPCSTR
T2CA	LPSTR/LPOLESTR to LPCSTR

Macro	Conversion
W2CA	LPWSTR to LPCSTR
A2CW	LPSTR to LPCWSTR
OLE2CT	LPOLESTR to LPCSTR/LPCOLESTR
T2COLE	LPSTR/LPOLESTR to LPCOLESTR
W2COLE	LPWSTR to LPCOLESTR
A2OLE	LPSTR to LPOLESTR
OLE2CW	LPOLESTR to LPCWSTR
T2CW	LPSTR/LPOLESTR to LPCWSTR
W2CT	LPWSTR to LPCSTR/LPCOLESTR
A2T	LPSTR to LPSTR/LPOLESTR
OLE2T	LPOLESTR to LPSTR/LPOLESTR
T2OLE	LPSTR/LPOLESTR to LPOLESTR
W2OLE	LPWSTR to LPOLESTR
A2W	LPSTR to LPWSTR
OLE2W	LPOLESTR to LPWSTR
T2W	LPSTR/LPOLESTR to LPWSTR
W2T	LPWSTR to LPSTR/LPOLESTR

D

The ATL string conversion macros are especially useful when dealing with internationalization issues or general COM Unicode character transformation. If you want to use these macros in another environment, such as MFC, simply include the ATLCONV.H file in your source code.

APPENDIX E

ATL Information Resources

No single book can hope to cover every conceivable aspect of something as complex as COM programming and ATL. To help you address other references to fill your informational needs, I've compiled the following list.

> **Note**
>
> There is no order of preference within a given section. I consider all of the references to be of the highest quality.

The books I reference are books I personally use, reviewed, or co-wrote that have received at least four-star ratings at www.amazon.com, which is where readers, rather than editors and paid reviewers, voice their opinions. The single exception is *Professional MFC with Visual C++ 6*, which received three stars, but is well worth purchasing (most of the online reviews didn't like the fact this book, unlike the previous version, shipped without an associated CD).

The periodicals are ones that target COM programming and ATL specifically. I did not list general-purpose Windows programming periodicals.

The Internet sites are hard-core ATL programming sites with high-quality, informational content. Most have downloadable samples with complete source code, as well as Frequently Asked Question (FAQ) sections you might find helpful.

Books on COM and ATL

Box, Don. *Essential COM*. Addison-Wesley Pub. Co.(0-201634-46-5), 1998

Box, Don, et al. *Effective COM*. Addison-Wesley Pub. Co.(0-201379-68-6), 1998

Grimes, Richard. *Professional ATL COM Programming*. Wrox Press Inc. (1-861001-40-1), 1998

Grimes, Richard. *Professional DCOM Programming*. Wrox Press Inc. (1-861000-60-X), 1997

Grimes, Richard, et al. *Beginning ATL 3 COM Programming*. Wrox Press Inc. (1-861001-20-7), 1999

Major, Al. *COM IDL & Interface Design*. Wrox Press Inc. (1-861002-25-4), 1999

Rector, Brent, et al. *ATL Internals*. Addison-Wesley Pub. Co. (0-201695-89-8), 1999

Rogerson, Dale. *Inside COM*. Microsoft Press (1-572313-49-8), 1997

Books on MFC

Blaszczak, Mike. *Professional MFC with Visual C++ 6*. Wrox Press Inc. (1-861000-15-4), 1999

White, David, Kenn Scribner, and Eugene Olafsen. *MFC Programming with Visual C++ 6 Unleashed*. Sams Publishing (0-672-31350-2), 1999

Books on Related Topics

Josuttis, Nicolai M. *The C++ Standard Library: A Tutorial and Reference*. Addison-Wesley Pub. Co. (0-201379-26-0), 1999

Miller, Kevin. *Professional NT Services*. Wrox Press Inc. (1-861001-30-4), 1998

Petzold, Charles. *Programming Windows, Fifth Edition*. Microsoft Press. (1-572319-95-X), 1998

Robison, Lyn. *Sams Teach Yourself Database Programming with Visual C++ 6.0*. Sams Publishing (0-672-31350-2), 1998

Schildt, Herbert. *The Complete Reference: C++*. Osborne McGraw-Hill (0-078824-76-1), 1998

Periodicals

Microsoft Internet Developer, www.microsoft.com/mind

Microsoft System's Journal, www.microsoft.com/msj

Visual C++ Developer's Journal, www.vcdj.com

Internet: Microsoft-Related Sites

Microsoft COM. www.microsoft.com/com/

MSDN (Microsoft Developer Network) Online. msdn.microsoft.com/

Microsoft Visual C++. msdn.microsoft.com/visualc/

Internet: General ATL Sites

Chris's Developer Tools (Chris Sells). www.sellsbrothers.com/tools/

EnduraSoft (my home page). www.endurasoft.com

Stingray ATL FAQ. www.stingray.com/atl_faq/

Tom Armstrong's ATL FAQ. www.widgetware.com/faqatl.htm

Wrox Press (home page). www.wrox.com

Wrox COMdeveloper. www.comdeveloper.com

E

Index

W-Z

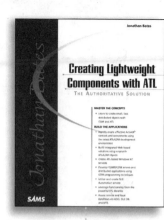

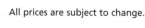